COPYRIGHT

Published by Lyons & Burnham Press

New South Wales, Australia

ISBN: 978-1-7647094-0-8

First edition paperback

Printed in Australia

Professional and Survivor Endorsements **(continued from back cover)**

"There would be few publications to match the unique nature of this work. It synthesises lived experience and clinical practice into an integrated framework that addresses the special needs of a unique population. Few practitioners are equipped in training and practice to identify and respond to the special trauma that adult alienated children experience. The cancellation of identity, the coercion into a delusional world and the rupturing of loving and developmental family relationships are a special form of trauma more notable for its omission from professional practice. This work is a must-read for practitioners who, until now, may never have known the true person who walked through their door and sat down with them for therapy."

Dr Stan Korosi PhD (UniSC). M.Couns.HS (Latrobe), Principal Consultant-Director, Founder: The Relational Justice Project, Adjunct Fellow, School of Law and Society, UniSC, Research Lead-Parents Beyond Breakup (PBB) Australia, Member Board of Directors- Parental Alienation Study Group (PASG).

Website https://dialogueingrowth.com.au/

"Dr Alyse Price-Tobler's work is the missing link between the well-known "Voice of the Child" and the often overlooked, rarely understood "Experience of the Child" in complex, high-conflict family separations. Grounded in rigorous research and twin PhDs, the Healing Qualia Treatment Protocol documents specific Adverse Childhood Experiences in separated families and presents a clear, phase-based treatment architecture. As a Family Mediator, Facilitator, and person with lived experience, I have seen how often children are misunderstood, misdiagnosed, or left without appropriate support, many silently wondering, "Have you experienced what I have?" The impact can be lasting, affecting identity, relationships, emotional regulation, and worldview. This Healing Qualia Treatment Protocol is the first of its kind I have seen to so clearly illuminate a child's lived experience while prioritising safety, autonomy, self-esteem, and recovery. It is essential reading for Family Law professionals and Therapists working with separated parents and children."

JD Knight, Family Mediator, Facilitator, Documentary Filmmaker (lived experience). Former National Training & Development Manager, Parents Beyond Breakup.
https://www.linkedin.com/in/jdknightmediator/

"Dr Price-Tobler's Healing Qualia is an outstanding treatment protocol! Anyone daring to practice with adult survivors of child psychological abuse (alienation, related family-system harm) needs the HQTP treatment protocol as their number 1 training manual. I'm very excited to see such a great treatment protocol available to specialist practitioners and experts in this field and all fields involving high conflict family violence matters."

Yvonne Moriarty (MACA), Mind Wise Enterprises. Mental Health Consulting, Counselling, & Psychotherapy. Website: mindwisecounselling.com.au

"I was an alienated child, and I've spent the years since reuniting with my targeted parent studying what happened to me and to families like mine. Alienation doesn't end with reunification. It ends with healing from the trauma. That's what makes Dr Alyse Price-Tobler's work matter. Healing Qualia is the first book I've read that lays out both what the alienated child is living through and what recovery actually looks like, so they can reclaim what was taken from them and build a new future with the people they love. It gets deeper inside the alienated child's inner experience than anything else I've encountered in the current literature.

But the most important thing Healing Qualia offers is hope. Hope for families marked by the trauma of child psychological abuse, so they can get the support they need to stop passing those wounds to the next generation and instead leave a legacy of love."

Andrew Folkler (Photo on the cover, far right), Adult Child Survivor of Child Psychological Abuse Related to Parental Alienation and Abduction. Book Consultant and Content Strategist. Website: startnow@andrewfolkler.com

"Dr Price-Tobler's therapeutic protocol for adult child survivors, *The Healing Qualia Treatment Protocol*, is more than a treatment guide. It is an invaluable resource for family law practitioners, serving as a comprehensive reference on the nature of childhood physical and psychological abuse, its lifelong effects, and the behavioural patterns and symptoms commonly exhibited by survivors. Grounded in science and extensive PhD twin-study research, *Healing Qualia* provides practical guidance for identifying, understanding, and effectively presenting these issues within a legal context. It equips lawyers, family report writers, psychologists and other professionals with a deeper understanding of the enduring effects of childhood trauma and the evidence needed to recognise and articulate those effects in legal and therapeutic settings." "In a system where the best interests of children are frequently invoked but not always consistently realised, *Healing Qualia* offers an evidence-informed clinical framework that helps professionals understand the long-term developmental and psychological consequences of child psychological abuse within high-conflict divorce and separation contexts. It is an essential reference for clinicians, legal professionals, and others committed to improving outcomes for adult survivors, children, and families."

Joshua Wooding-Divorce Coach, Certified. Family Law Paralegal, Parenting Coordinator & final-year law student. Email info@separatesmartercoaching.com

Foreword

Healing Qualia: A Clinical Treatment Protocol for Adult Survivors of Child Psychological Abuse in the Context of Parental Alienation, Familial Abduction, and Estrangement – by Dr Craig Childress, Psy.D.

It is rare that a single text reorganizes an entire clinical landscape, but Healing Qualia does exactly that. Developed from Dr Price-Tobler's pioneering doctoral research, this book gives the mental health and family court professions something they have long lacked: a coherent, evidence-based, phase-governed roadmap for treating now-adult survivors of severe parental alienation and familial abduction of severe psychological child abuse - survivors whose suffering has for too long gone unrecognized, misdiagnosed, and actively compounded by the very systems meant to protect them.

Dr Price-Tobler's central achievement is her reframing of severe parental alienation as what it truly is: a form of Child Psychological Abuse (CPA) with lifelong developmental, relational, and identity-based consequences. From that foundation, she builds the Healing Qualia Treatment Protocol (HQTP), a six-phase architecture — from Safety and Epistemic Stabilisation through Meaning Reconstruction, Mourning, Trauma Integration Readiness, Differentiation, and finally Long-Term Adaptation — allowing clinicians to walk alongside the now-adult survivors of psychological child abuse without ever reproducing the coercive dynamics of their childhood.

What distinguishes this work is its extraordinary theoretical integration. Dr. Price-Tobler draws together humanistic psychology (Rogers), family systems theory (Minuchin, Bowen, Boszormenyi-Nagy), object relations (Kernberg), attachment and neurodevelopmental science (Bowlby, Stern, Tronick), and trauma-informed care (van der Kolk, Freyd) into a single, unified clinical treatment protocol, never as a patchwork of borrowed ideas, but as a genuinely synthesized model in which each theoretical strand does exactly the work it is best suited for. This is advanced professional craftsmanship of the highest order.

Equally significant is the book's treatment of institutional betrayal trauma (Freyd). Dr. Price-Tobler names directly what so many survivors have lived and so few clinicians have been trained to recognize: that the family courts, child protective systems, and unspecialized mental health providers can themselves become a second, compounding source of harm when they fail to recognize psychological capture for what it is. Her insistence that the clinical space remain rigorously non-forensic protects both the survivor and the clinician, and it should be regarded as a professional standard going forward.

Above all, this book is anchored in authentic empathy. Dr Price-Tobler understands, with a depth that can only come from genuinely knowing the child's inner experience, that healing requires the therapist to recognize the survivor as a person reclaiming a stolen self, not as an object of clinical or forensic scrutiny. That empathy, paired with rigorous, phase-governed structure, is what makes this protocol both clinically sound and profoundly humane.

Healing Qualia is required reading for every mental health professional working in the family courts, and it is essential reading for anyone treating now-adult survivors of institutional betrayal and psychological abuse by a pathological parent. With this book, Dr Alyse Price-Tobler has established herself as the leading voice in trauma recovery for survivors of psychological child abuse from parental alienation and abduction, and has crafted a ground-breaking contribution to trauma recovery as a field.

I give it my highest, unreserved professional endorsement.

Dr Craig Childress, Psy.D. (https://drcachildress.org/)

Dedication

For Those Denied the Right to Love and Be Loved Freely

"Tell me, what is it you plan to do with your one wild and precious life?"

— Mary Oliver

For many children living through child psychological abuse in the context of parental alienation, familial abduction, estrangement, and lethal family-system harm, this is not a question they are freely afforded. Before autonomy has had a chance to form, life may already be organised around coercion, fear, surveillance, retaliation, loyalty conflict, and the consequences of loving a parent, grandparent, cousin, sibling, companion animal, or other attachment figure whom the child has been pressured to reject. The freedom to discover oneself, to think freely, to love safely, and to live a life that belongs to one's own mind and heart is too often interrupted long before it has properly begun.

The Healing Qualia Treatment Protocol © has been written especially for those whose names cannot safely appear on the following Pages of Remembrance. This includes children still caught within family court, child-protection, foster care, out-of-home-care, school, health, mental health, legal, active cults or other institutional systems, and adult survivors whose alienating parent, family system, extended family network, community context, or associated parties may respond to public identification with legal action, intimidation, retaliation, reputational harm, renewed coercive control, online targeting, or further psychological pressure. Their absence from these pages does not mean their stories are absent from this work. It means their safety, dignity, privacy, and right to future self-determination have been protected.

This page is for the children and adults who were never allowed to be themselves. For those who were denied the ordinary human right to love openly, safely, and without fear. For those who were forced to live inside someone else's distortion, someone else's demands, and someone else's story of who they were allowed to be. For those who had to hide love, grief, memory, loyalty, longing, and truth in order to survive.

It is for those who never knew how beautiful autonomy could feel. For those who were never given the chance to discover the dignity of selfhood, the peace of psychological freedom, or the simple human experience of being loved without coercion and allowed to love without punishment. For those whose minds, bodies, memories, attachments, identities, and inner worlds were shaped in environments where survival came before truth.

This page is also for the survivors who died by suicide. For those who carried unbearable grief, fractured identity, chronic fear, attachment injury, and a life organised too long around someone else's control. It is for the children and adult survivors of familicide. For those taken forever by violence, coercive possession, revenge, control, or despair. It is for the abducted, the hidden, the erased, the renamed, the silenced, the psychologically captured, and the never properly mourned.

It has also been written in the hope that child abuse can be recognised earlier, named more clearly, slowed in all its forms, and responded to more meaningfully, so that survivors may heal and this trauma is not passed down to future generations yet again. It is now time for adult survivors to ask for, accept, and receive the help they need. It is time for mental health practitioners to read this book and become prepared to help in a meaningful, informed, trauma-responsive, and ethically grounded way. It is time for this harm to be understood not as a private family matter or a misunderstanding of separation, but as a serious form of developmental psychological abuse with lifelong consequences. This work is grassroots in origin and in spirit. It has been written by someone who fell through the cracks, lived through the consequences, and came out the other side no longer under coercive control. It has been written with grief, with witness, and with hope that those who come next may find language earlier, treatment sooner, stronger protections, and freedom before it is too late.

Held With Care

For the children still trapped inside coercive family systems.

For the targeted parents, grandparents, siblings, cousins, aunts and uncles, family friends, and beloved animals who were loved, but could no longer be loved freely or safely.

For the adult survivors still trying to reclaim their minds, voices, attachments, histories, and lives, while carrying grief that was hidden and never allowed to be spoken.

For the families who waited, are still waiting, and may never stop wondering.

For the relationships that were severed, hidden, distorted, or made to feel unsafe through fear, loyalty pressure, and false narratives.

For the nameless.

For the silenced.

For the survivors who lived.

For the survivors who did not.

This treatment protocol and this special ribbon are designed and written in your honour.

THRIVERS SPEAK®

Pages of Remembrance

Some names can be spoken publicly. Some must be held privately for safety, dignity, legal protection, or the child's future autonomy. This page honours both.

The names, initials, and partial identifiers recorded here represent children and young people whose lives, attachments, identities, safety, or futures have been affected by child psychological abuse related to parental alienation, familial abduction, concealment, estrangement, familicide, homicide, suicide, and related forms of family and domestic violence.

Some of the children named here are still living. Some remain unreachable. Some have survived profound loss. Some did not survive. This page does not claim to tell their whole story. It simply holds a place for those whose names, lives, relationships, or losses cannot be fully spoken here.

Some names are included with permission, while others are held symbolically, partially, or non-identifiably to protect privacy, dignity, safety, and future autonomy. These names are included as they were sent to the author at different times, so some are not in alphabetical order. Their inclusion does not assert a legal finding, diagnostic conclusion, forensic claim, or complete personal history. This page simply holds space for children, adolescents, and adult survivors affected by these forms of harm.

Names Held with Care

Alex, Alfred, Alice, Archie, Aurora, Caroline, Daniel, Dylan, Eliana, Emily, Finley, Gavin, Grace, Jacob, Jacqueline, James, Lelaina, Lucy, Mohammed, Nate, Oli, Olivia, Patrick, Rebecca, Ruby, Sophia, Stephanie, Zoey.

Abigail, Adam, Adelaide, Alana, Alice, Aiden, Aiko, Aisha, Akari, Akira, Alinta, Amara, Amelia, Amélie, Amir, Andre, Andrew, Anika, Anna, Annie, Antoine, Aria, Ari, Arlo, Arthur, Asher, Ashlyn, Astin, Audrey, Ava, Ayla, Bailey, Beau, Bella, Ben, Benjamin, Billie, Billy, Blake, Bodhi, Bonnie, B (Name withheld for confidentiality), Brody, Caleb, Callum, Camille, Charlie,

Charlotte, Chloe, Clara, Connor, Cooper, Daisy, Dana, Darcy, Dawn, Delilah, Dominic, Eddie, Eden, Edward, Eli, Elijah, Ella, Ellie, Eloise, Emilia, Ethan, Étienne, Eva, Evie, Ezra, Felix, Florence, Frankie, Freya, Gabriel, Georgia, George, Georgie, Ginger, Harriet, Haru, Harry, Hazel, Henry, Hiro, Holly, Hugo, Hunter, Imogen, Isaac, Isabella, Isla, Ivy, Jack, Jackson, Jade, Jaime, James, Jasmine, Jasper, JD, Jed, Jett, Joel, Jonah, Jordan, Joseph, Josie, Jude, Julian, Kai, Kaida, Kaito, Kalani, Kayla, Kenji, Kiara, Kiah, Kirra, Kylie, L & V (names withheld), Lachlan, Landon, Lara, Leila, Leo, Léon, Levi, Liam, Lila, Lily, Lola, Logan, Louie, Luca, Lucas, Lucien, M & M (names withheld) Maddie, Madison, Maeve, Maisie, Malik, Marcus, Mari, Marlee, Mason, Matilda, Mathieu, Max, Maya, Mia, Mila, Millie, Minato, Molly, Naomi, Noah, Nora, Noémie, Oscar, Owen, Paige, Parker, Penelope, Petra, Poppy, Quinn, Riley, River, Rosie, Ryan, Sam, Samuel, Sakura, Savannah, Scarlett, Shayna, Sebastian, Sébastien, Sienna, Sora, Sonny, Stan, Stella, Summer, Taj, Theo, Theodore, Thomas, Tisha, Toby, Violet, Will, William, Willow, Xavier, Yara, Yindi, Yuki, Zara, Zélie.

Aaron, Adeline, Ahmed, Alain, Alana, Alys, Amira, Andrew, Angeline, Anouk, April, Ariana, Armand, Aya, Ayumi, Beatrice, Belle, Bianca, Bronte, Byron, Celeste, Celine, Charles, Chiara, Claire, Clementine, Colette, Cora, Damien, Dante, Darius, Eden-Rose, Elise, Emile, Estelle, Evelyn, Farah, Fatima, F (Name held for confidentiality), Genevieve, G & A (names withheld), Hana, Harlow, Harper, Hassan, Hayley, Helena, Hugo-James, Imani, Inaya, Isabelle, Isobel, Jalen, Jamal, Jarrah, Jaxon, Jean, Jean-Luc, Jia, Jin, Jun, Kaia, Keira, Keiko, Khalil, Kira, Kobe, Layla, Lena, Léo, Louis, Luca-James, Luna, Madeleine, Manon, Marcel, Margot, Mariam, Marius,

Matthew, Mei, Miles, Mika, Mila-Rose, Miro, Misaki, Nala, Nathaniel, Natsumi, Nico, Nikhil, Nina, Noa, Noor, Olivier, Ophelia, Otis, Paige, Pascal, Pierre, Priya, Rafael, Rafaela, Remi, Ren, Rina, Roman, Ronan, Ryan, Safiya, Sahana, Samuel-James, Sari, Sasha, Selene, Shiloh, Sienna-Rose, Simone, Skye, S & C (names withheld), Sophia, Spencer, Suki, Talia, Tane, T & S (names withheld), Tariq, Tessa, Tilly, Tom, Toshi, Valentin, Valentina, Victor, Vivienne, Willa, Yasmin, Yasmine, Yoshi, Zahra, Zain, Zayn, Zoe.

Adira, Amanda, Amina, Anaïs, Aya-Rose, Bindi, Cassia, Chika, Darcy-Rose, Eadie, Emiko, Esme, Flynn-James, Hina, Iluka, Ines, Inès, Isha, Jean-Pierre, Juniper, Keanu, Koji, Kyan, Lani, Laurent, Léa, Lior, Lowanna, Maelle, Mahalia, Marceline, Mariko, Mirai, Mireille, Nadine, Nia, Nicolette, Odette, Oriana, Rian, Remy, Riku, Rochelle, Sabine, Sachi, Solène, Soraya, Suzu, (Ta-Full Name withheld) Tai, Takumi, Tarni, Taya, Thiago, Tomiko, Yumi, Yolanda, Zahira, Zoe.

Mackenzie, Hamish, Sienna-Mae, Ayaan, Chloé, Hiroshi, Anjali, Remy, Koa, Juliette, Tahlia, Idris, Mabel, Yusuf, Akiko, Lachie, Elodie, Zavier, Amaya, Fleur, Noelle, Kieran, Amelie-Rose, Ibrahim, Saskia, Taro, Mireya, Cillian, Aaliyah, Bodie, Camille, Hamza, Kenzie, Ayane, Louis, Niamh, Rafael, Belle, Zola, Theo-James, Marlowe, Haruki, Lacey, Omar, Esmé-Rose, Arjun, Sylvie, Koen, Amira, Darcy-May, S, K, F & P (names withheld), Soren, Mei-Ling, Elise, Hassan, (F- full name withheld) Indi, Hugo, Aysha, Luc, Zuri, Finn, Tilly-Rose, Kenzo, Imara, Sebastien, S & J & B (names withheld), Milla, Rohan, Kaori, Elara, Beau-James, Sana, Xavier-Rose, Clementine, Jiro, Amani, Louisa, Micah, Yvette, Tariq, Niko, Wren and many others withheld with care.

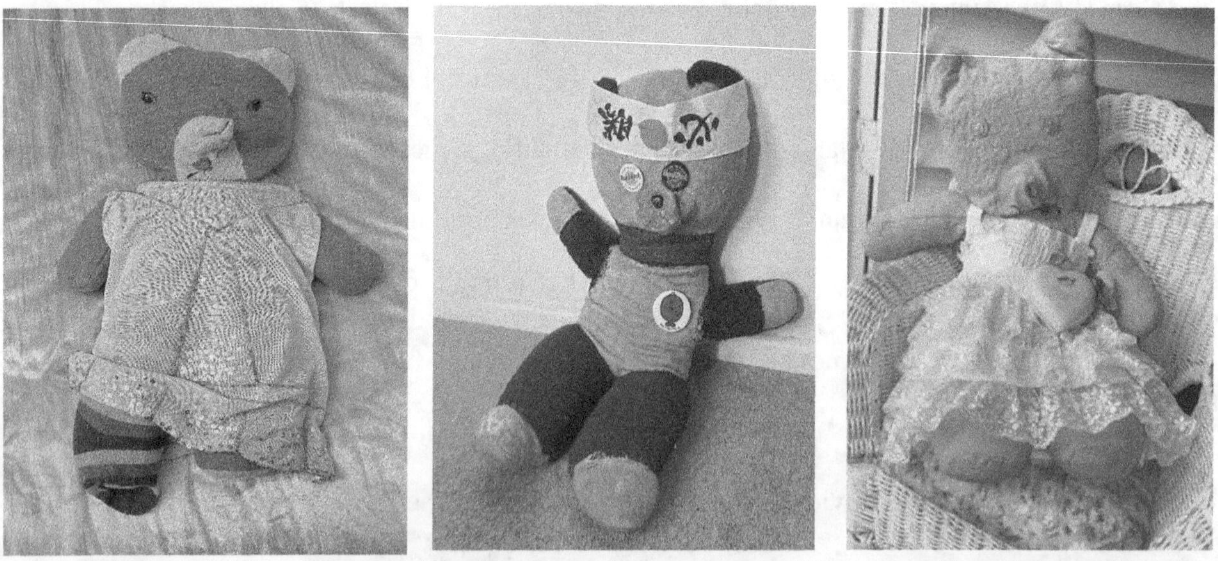

Beloved childhood bears, given by targeted parents and still treasured by adult survivors.

Acknowledgment to Family, Friends, Colleagues and Supporters

Thank you to those who understood why this protocol needed to be written, even when the work was long, complex, and emotionally demanding. Thank you for your kindness, patience, humour, listening, and steady support. A project of this size is never completed alone, and I am deeply grateful for the people who helped me keep going when the task felt overwhelming.

The universe sent me these very special people. Shane, the one person who truly understands this space. Always there. Always watching. For ten years, you listened to my ideas about this protocol. Without you, it would never exist. There are no words.

My son, Tristan. Deep thinker. Highly intuitive. He notices the quiet things, the almost-hidden things, the things most people move past without seeing. A rare soul with an old wisdom. Advocate and protector of the underdog. Mr Charisma. Amazing father. The steady hand that reaches down to help when we need it. Natural-born leader. Earth lumière. My heart.

My daughter, Alezandia. Reborn. Healer of our world. Human and animal nurse. Fierce protector and advocate for wounded animals, and for people no one sees falling through the cracks. Violinist. Truly gifted. She walks toward danger when others are leaving. Brave warrior woman. Earth lumière. My heart.

My brother James and my sister Kylie. I have watched over and walked beside you both since you opened your eyes and observed this earth. I cannot imagine a world without either of you. Advocates and protectors of the lost, the disabled, the wounded and the ones no one wants to sit with. We will be together forever. Je vous aime tous les deux. Mon Coeur.

With love and care, I also name my grandson Lyran, a warrior, galaxy pilot, moon-gazer, and protector of humanity, and bonus grandson wee sweet, funny Asher; my nieces Lily, Rose, Zonk/Zoe (who sat and generously helped me to edit this book one night after their opal mining adventure), and E; my nephew Alex; my sister-in-law Cazz; my great-niece Isla; and my bonus granddaughter Phoebe. You are part of the family story that sits quietly behind this work and part of the hope for the generations still to come. Each of you represents a next generation being raised with greater attention to connection, respect, kindness, and emotional safety.

Mel is also held here with gratitude for the quiet and practical way she supports our family connection, respect, and kindness across blended family life. Her care helps show that families can do things differently, and that children can be supported to remain connected, loved, and emotionally safe.

Thank you also to Jaime and Shayna for the insight you contributed to this work through your lived understanding of patterns of alienation within family systems. Your willingness to reflect on how these patterns are recognised, resisted, and slowly changed, even while you continue to live with the pain of alienated relationships, has helped strengthen the human context behind this protocol. I am grateful for your honesty, courage, and support.

I am also grateful to the colleagues, friends, and quiet supporters who stood beside me throughout the long development of this work. I especially thank Emma Mottram and Zoe Yelds, whose care, curiosity, and steady presence helped ground me when the writing felt heavy and unending. This protocol was sustained by conversation, encouragement, practical help, emotional steadiness, and others' willingness to keep believing in the work when it became challenging.

My deepest gratitude is offered to my mentor and clinical counsellor of more than 30 years, Sister Patricia Delaney-Davis, whose guidance, faith, education, and steady belief have shaped so much of my life and re-education. My evoked companion. My other mother. The one who taught me unconditional love and how to trust.

I also thank Dawn McCarty for her courage, friendship, wisdom, survivor leadership, and personal contribution to this book and to the adult survivor space internationally. Dawn's work in organising the first adult survivor conference with me was a valuable act of witness and leadership, helping to bring adult survivor voices together in a way that had not been done before. Dawn, thank you also for the almost daily conversations over the past few years as we have tried to understand, name, and interrupt the intergenerational alienation pattern so that it does not keep passing down to the children coming after us. I am also deeply grateful for your guidance, encouragement, and practical support in helping me move this book toward publication.

Thank you also to Andrew Folkler (on the front cover) for his courage, friendship, wisdom, survivor leadership, and contribution to this book and to the adult survivor space internationally. Andrew's willingness to speak at the first adult survivor conference helped strengthen the survivor voice in this field. I am also grateful for his creation and support of the book strategy memo, which helped guide the publishing pathway for this volume and strengthened how this work could be brought safely and professionally into the world.

I would also like to thank Dr Craig Childress for his clinical supervision and oversight of my complex caseload over the past six years. His guidance has been deeply valued across a broad range of complex clinical presentations, including developmental trauma, attachment-system disruption, coercive family processes, personality disturbance, pathogenic parenting dynamics, high-risk relational systems, and family-system harm. His clinical insight, consistency, and ongoing support have been profoundly important to my work as a frontline clinician and to the development of this treatment protocol.

I am also deeply grateful that he attended my PhD ceremony virtually, all the way from America, as my beloved father had passed from this earth at that time, marking a moment that held both academic and personal significance. His belief in this work and his continued presence during its development have been profoundly important. Spiritual Warrior. Foreseer.

Dr Stan Korosi deserves particular thanks as one of my strongest collegial supporters during the development of this protocol. Through the Australian peer supervision group that we started together, Transcending Alienation for Practitioners and Professionals (TAPP), Dr Korosi's steady encouragement, clinical reflection, and belief in the importance of this work have meant a great deal. We share the same journey. A quiet knowing.

Thank you also to Yvonne Moriarty, a supportive member of TAPP, for her encouragement, collegial presence, and willingness to share deidentified frontline clinical stories of alienation. Her contribution added currency, depth, and lived clinical relevance to this book. Peer supervision and professional dialogue have been important in holding this material carefully, particularly given the clinical, ethical, and emotional complexity of this field.

I am grateful to Dr Rebecca Bailey for the specialised guidance she provided on complex cases involving internationally abducted children during the period in which this work was being written. Her knowledge and generosity helped deepen my thinking around the clinical realities facing children and families in these difficult circumstances.

Joshua Wooding, a family law Barrister who has contributed through his knowledge of the Australian family court system and alienation, and through his considerate reflection on how these patterns can be recognised and not carried forward into the next generation. I would also like to thank his son, Jack, for the welcome distraction, warmth, cooking, conversation, and bird feeding he generously offered during the editing phase of this book.

Thank you to the Parents Beyond Breakup group leaders for your tireless, ongoing work, and special thanks to JD Knight (Former National Training Manager and documentary filmmaker), whose work continues to "help keep parents alive and in their children's lives". Your support and your assistance in gathering some of the names of alienated and abducted children included in this book have meant a great deal.

(https://www.parentsbeyondbreakup.com/).

I also thank Tania Clancy and the Wombatised Committee for the use of your beautiful gallery space during my editing phase. I am also grateful for the opportunity to include a photograph of that space and of Tania with one of the orphaned rescue wombats in this volume.

To every clinician, survivor, family member, advocate, and supporter who reads this book to learn, understand, or respond with greater care, thank you. Knowledge becomes meaningful when it is carried into real relationships, difficult conversations, and the moments where someone might otherwise be misunderstood, dismissed, or left alone in despair. My hope is that this protocol does not simply become a book on a shelf, but a way of seeing more clearly, listening more carefully, and responding with greater courage. May it help survivors feel less alone, families recognise harm earlier, practitioners hold this work with the depth and caution it deserves, and future generations be spared the same patterns of silence, coercion, and loss. This work is offered in the hope that lives may be saved, suicide risk may be reduced, and intergenerational trauma may be interrupted before it reaches another child.

Clinical Disclaimer

This publication is intended as a professional educational resource and clinical reference only. It does not constitute medical, psychological, psychiatric, forensic, legal, emergency, or crisis-response advice. It must not be used as a substitute for professional training, clinical supervision, formal assessment, statutory obligations, emergency procedures, or individualised treatment planning.

The Healing Qualia Treatment Protocol © (HQTP) supports clinical reasoning, ethical formulation, and phase-based intervention with adult survivors of child psychological abuse related to parental alienation, familial abduction, and estrangement. Application of this material requires appropriate professional qualifications, trauma-informed training, clinical competence, independent professional judgement, and ongoing supervision. The HQTP is not intended for independent use by untrained individuals, nor for use outside regulated professional contexts or beyond the clinician's scope of practice.

Clinicians remain responsible for determining whether, when, how, and within what professional scope any part of the HQTP is applied with an individual client. This includes responsibility for assessment, consent, risk management, supervision, documentation, referral, safeguarding, mandatory reporting, emergency response decisions, and compliance with all relevant professional, organisational, legal, and ethical requirements within the clinician's jurisdiction.

Every survivor presents with a unique developmental history, relational context, cultural background, neurodevelopmental profile, health history, support system, and risk presentation. No clinical framework can replace individual assessment, collaborative treatment planning, professional consultation, and careful decision-making tailored to the person in front of the clinician.

As mentioned, this volume discusses psychological abuse, attachment disruption, coercive control, family separation, institutional betrayal, grief, trauma, developmental harm, suicidal distress, violence, abduction, homicide, familicide, suicide, medical abuse, factitious disorder imposed on another related dynamics, and other complex survivor material. Some content may be emotionally activating for survivors, practitioners, and family members. Readers are encouraged to engage with the text at a pace that supports psychological safety and to seek appropriate professional, supervisory, or crisis support where needed.

For survivors reading this text independently, this book is not a self-help program and does not replace therapeutic care. If the material evokes distress, overwhelm, destabilisation, suicidal thoughts, self-harm urges, fear for personal safety, or concern about the safety of another person, readers are encouraged to pause and seek support from a qualified mental health professional, a trusted support service, a crisis line, or local emergency services.

Where names, images, survivor reflections, clinical examples, or personal materials are included, they are included with permission where required, or with deliberate ethical care where full identification is not appropriate. Their inclusion is not intended to constitute a legal finding, forensic conclusion, diagnosis, allegation, evidentiary determination, or complete account of any person's history. Identifying details have been included only where the author has determined that inclusion is appropriate, respectful, and consistent with the educational and clinical purpose of this volume.

The HQTP has been developed through doctoral research, clinical practice, lived experience, practitioner consultation, supervision, and survivor-informed knowledge. No guarantee is made regarding specific outcomes. Clinical outcomes depend on many factors, including practitioner competence, ethical application, survivor readiness, risk presentation, the therapeutic relationship, supervision, service context, and circumstances beyond the control of any single framework.

The author accepts no liability for misuse, misinterpretation, unauthorised application, application outside professional scope, or use of this material in a manner inconsistent with appropriate professional, ethical, legal, safeguarding, or emergency-response standards.

Editorial and Technology Assistance Note

No external editor was used in the preparation of this manuscript. During final preparation, the author used Grammarly and generative AI tools for limited editorial checking. This included proofreading, grammar review, spelling checks, formatting review, readability review, consistency checking, and identification of possible repetition, unclear wording, or mechanical errors.

These tools were not used to originate, design, determine, or author the doctoral research, clinical model, treatment architecture, phase structure, case formulations, ethical positions, clinical claims, professional recommendations, survivor-protective framework, or core intellectual content of this volume.

All conceptual decisions, clinical interpretations, source selection, reference responsibility, final wording choices, and publication decisions remain the responsibility of the author. The HQTP is grounded in the author's doctoral twin-study research, clinical practice, lived experience, professional judgement, supervision, practitioner consultation, survivor-informed knowledge, and long-term work with this population.

With Appreciation for the Mental Health Clinicians

Thank you

to the mental health clinicians

who support families, children, and adults affected by high-conflict divorce, separation, and estrangement.

Your commitment to children and to the families you work with matters profoundly. This book offers a new framework, drawn from PhD twin study research of survivor accounts relating to their treatment and from international mental health clinicians who specialise in this cohort.

It is offered in that spirit, not as a personal or professional criticism, but as a respectful invitation to reflect, refine, and strengthen practice in light of what is becoming more visible in the lives of adult survivors of child psychological abuse related to parental alienation, familial abduction, estrangement, coercive control, and, at times, lethal family-system harm.

Your willingness to keep learning, stay curious, and continue growing in your clinical understanding helps create safer pathways for the people who need it most.

With deep respect and gratitude,

Dr. Alyse Price-Tobler

THE HEALING QUALIA TRAINING SERIES

The Healing Qualia Treatment Protocol textbook forms part of a three-volume series related to the accompanying Twin Study PhD, and will be used with the associated training materials for related education programs.

This book is the main resource used during the training, alongside Volume One and Volume Two.

During the training, students will also be given printed training material that applies to their level of training.

Level One **Foundations Training**	**Purpose:** To orient clinicians to the HQTP population, phase architecture, safety, and clinical risk.
Level Two **Applied Clinical Training**	**Purpose:** To teach phase placement, intake pacing, formulation, contraindications, and session decisions.
Level Three **Intensive Training and Consultation**	**Purpose:** To provide supervised application, case formulation, fidelity review, and clinical integrity.
Trainer–Supervisor Pathway	For clinicians progressing to advanced mentorship roles, supervision, and trainer development.

Each level builds on the previous one, supporting clinicians to develop confidence, competence, and integrity in this specialised field of practice.

Professional Use Note

The Healing Qualia Treatment Protocol ©provides a structured, trauma-informed, non-forensic framework for assessment, formulation, and treatment planning in relation to attachment disruption, developmental trauma, identity disturbance, loyalty conflict, epistemic instability, and long-term recovery. It forms part of a three-volume series and will also be adapted into associated training materials for related education and training programs. Clinicians may therefore engage with the full three-volume set or, where appropriate, access the individual printed training materials as separate resources.

This text is intended for educational and clinical reference purposes. It is not a forensic instrument and should not be used as a substitute for legal determination, evidentiary investigation, or judicial process. Clinical application requires professional training, supervision, and independent judgement.

Cultural Safety and Community Consultation

Clinicians should apply the HQTP with cultural humility, respect for family, kinship, community, language, spirituality, Country, migration history, disability, sexuality, gender, and cultural identity. Where the survivor is Aboriginal or Torres Strait Islander, or where cultural, community, or historical trauma is clinically relevant, clinicians should consider culturally safe consultation, referral, or collaboration, including Aboriginal mental health workers, Aboriginal community-controlled services, cultural consultants, Elders, interpreters, or other appropriate supports where desired by the survivor and consistent with consent, safety, and professional obligations.

How to Use This Protocol

The HQTP is a modular, phase-based clinical framework. Clinicians are not expected to read or implement every component at once. The protocol should be approached as a treatment map that helps practitioners locate where the survivor is clinically, what needs to be protected first, and which material is relevant to the current phase of work.

Practitioners may enter the protocol at the point that best matches the survivor's current clinical presentation, rather than at the beginning of the book, once they are familiar with it. Movement through phases is guided by safety, regulation, consent, epistemic stability, and developmental readiness rather than chapter order. This work is not technique-driven. It is posture-driven. The central clinical task is clinical restraint, sequencing, and protection of the survivor's nervous system and autonomy.

What the HQTP Is and Is Not

The HQTP is a phase-based clinical map for assessment, formulation, pacing, and intervention with adult survivors of child psychological abuse in contexts of parental alienation, familial abduction, estrangement, and associated coercive-control dynamics. It is designed to help clinicians recognise the population, protect survivors' safety, carefully sequence treatment, identify contraindications, and preserve survivors' autonomy.

The HQTP is not a forensic instrument, a custody evaluation, a legal opinion, a diagnostic instrument, a disclosure tool, a crisis-response tool, a reconciliation program, a self-help program, or a licence to practise outside professional scope. It does not ask clinicians to prove historical events, determine legal truth, replace statutory or safeguarding obligations, or direct survivors toward contact, reconciliation, or non-contact outcomes. Its purpose is clinical: to support safe, ethical, phase-based treatment without coercion, premature interpretation, therapeutic overreach, or outcome-driven pressure.

Using the HQTP as a Decision Guide, not a Script

The protocol supports clinicians in making practical treatment decisions: when to stabilise, when to pause narrative exploration, when to support grief, when to strengthen boundaries, when to return to earlier containment, and when meaning-making is premature.

It does not replace clinical judgement, professional supervision, formal risk assessment, or individualised treatment planning. It sharpens clinical reasoning by helping practitioners avoid common errors in this population, including premature disclosure work, forced insight, reconciliation pressure, misclassification of abduction as conflict, over-identification with survivor urgency, and movement into deeper work before the survivor is ready.

Work Within Existing Clinical Scope

Most clinicians already possess core skills that support safe entry into the HQTP, including assessment, stabilisation, psychoeducation, relational containment, trauma-informed care, risk awareness, and supervision. Detailed scope-of-practice and modality guidance is provided later in What the Clinician Brings, and What the HQTP Teaches and in the clinical implementation chapter. At this stage, the key point is that clinicians are not expected to master every modality described in this volume before beginning. They are expected to work within scope, seek supervision, recognise when specialist referral or consultation is required, and apply existing skills slowly, ethically, and in phase. Where risk, safeguarding, suicidality, violence, medical complexity, abduction-related discovery, or statutory obligations arise, clinicians must follow relevant professional, organisational, and legal requirements rather than relying on the protocol alone.

Prioritise Phase Integrity Over Intervention Variety

The most common cause of therapeutic harm in this population is not lack of technique. It is poor sequencing. Clinicians are encouraged to revisit the phase maps whenever uncertainty arises. If a survivor becomes destabilised, the protocol directs the clinician to return to stabilisation and containment rather than proceed to deeper material. This protects both the survivor and the therapeutic alliance. A variety of interventions is not the goal of the HQTP. The clinician's task is to choose only those interventions that fit the survivor's current phase position, readiness, consent capacity, safety needs, and the clinician's own competence. A modality should not be used simply because it is familiar, available, or preferred by the practitioner. It should be used only when it supports the survivor's current phase of care without overriding safety, autonomy, or clinical pacing.

Using Supervision as an Active Component of the Protocol

The HQTP assumes active clinical supervision. Many decisions in adult survivor work involve ethical complexity, incomplete information, high emotional load, family or system pressure, risk of destabilisation, and potential practitioner over-identification. Supervision is not supplementary to this model. It is part of the protocol's safety structure.

Clinicians are encouraged to bring phase-placement questions, countertransference responses, pacing dilemmas, discovery-related destabilisation, contact pressure, reunification or eye-contact considerations, documentation pressure, practitioner-safety concerns, and uncertainty about risk into supervision as routine clinical material. Where suicidality, violence risk, child-safety concerns, medical complexity, abduction-related discovery, familicide-related material, or statutory obligations arise, supervision must be supported by appropriate consultation, escalation, referral, or organisational procedures.

Within the HQTP, supervision protects both the survivor and the clinician. It helps prevent premature interpretation, rescue urgency, reconciliation pressure, forensic drift, and movement into deeper material before the survivor is ready. Detailed supervision thresholds and clinical-integrity expectations are addressed later in the implementation chapter.

Adapt to Context Without Diluting Core Principles

The HQTP may be used across private practice, hospital settings, forensic-adjacent contexts, community services, school-linked clinical contexts, correctional or justice-adjacent services, and other regulated clinical environments. Delivery may vary depending on the service setting, practitioner role, available supervision, survivor risk, safeguarding obligations, and organisational requirements.

However, the core principles do not change: safety before depth, regulation before meaning-making, identity before documentation, autonomy before reconciliation, contact as choice rather than outcome, and supervision before high-risk clinical decision-making. Clinicians may adapt the delivery format, session structure, documentation requirements, and referral pathways, but not the ethical foundation, phase sequencing, consent requirements, clinical scope, or non-forensic purpose of the protocol.

Measure Progress by Safety and Coherence, Not Disclosure

Progress in the HQTP is not measured by how much history is uncovered, how quickly trauma material is approached, whether the survivor moves toward contact, or whether a clear relational outcome is reached. It is measured by the survivor's increasing capacity to remain regulated, hold complexity without collapsing, establish boundaries without terror, pause before responding to relational pressure, and develop authorship over their own narrative.

If the survivor feels safer, more coherent, more internally anchored, and more able to make choices without coercion, the work is progressing even when many questions remain unanswered. Progress may also look like slowing down, returning to an earlier phase, declining contact pressure, refusing premature disclosure, or recognising that the survivor is not yet ready for deeper material. Within the HQTP, returning to stabilisation and containment is understood as ethical recontainment rather than regression. Detailed review and outcome-monitoring guidance are provided later in the clinical implementation chapter.

Ethical Position Statement

The HQTP is grounded in survivor dignity, epistemic safety, informed consent, phase-based care, and professional accountability. It rejects coercive treatment practices, outcome-driven intervention pressure, premature trauma exposure, reconciliation pressure, forced disclosure, and therapeutic authority that overrides survivor autonomy.

Clinical responsibility within this framework prioritises safety, containment, ethical humility, survivor agency, and disciplined sequencing over speed, compliance, disclosure, relational outcome, or procedural efficiency. The protocol is therefore used to support careful clinical reasoning, not to impose conclusions, determine legal truth, or direct the survivor toward predetermined contact, reconciliation, forgiveness, or non-contact outcomes.

Suggested HQTP Citation

Price-Tobler, A. (2026). *Healing Qualia: A phase-based specialist clinical treatment protocol for adult survivors of child psychological abuse related to parental alienation, familial abduction and estrangement*. Lyons & Burnham Press.

Abstract

Many adult survivors of trauma reach therapy carrying a childhood story they have never been able to fully name. Their history may include high-conflict divorce or separation, child psychological abuse in the context of parental alienation, familial abduction, estrangement, coercive control, forced relocation, concealment, or lethal family-system harm. For some, the harm was not only the loss of a relationship but also the loss of safety, reality, identity, belonging, voice, and the right to love and be loved freely.

The Healing Qualia Treatment Protocol © (HQTP) is a phase-based specialist clinical treatment protocol developed for these adult survivors. It provides a structured, trauma-informed, non-forensic framework for clinicians working with adults whose development, identity, attachment, relational safety, and trust in their own perceptions were shaped within coercive or high-conflict family systems.

The HQTP responds to a frequently overlooked and clinically under-addressed form of developmental psychological harm that may remain hidden beneath ordinary language about separation, divorce, family conflict, estrangement, loyalty, alignment, rejection, or contact refusal. Survivors may present with anxiety, depression, trauma symptoms, affect dysregulation, relational difficulties, or identity disturbance; however, these presentations may be misdiagnosed or incompletely formulated when the underlying developmental, attachment, and family-system context is not recognised.

Organised around safety, stabilisation, meaning reconstruction, grief integration, trauma integration readiness, differentiation, and long-term adaptation, the HQTP aims to reduce retraumatisation, minimise misdiagnosis, support careful clinical formulation, and strengthen recovery marked by greater self-coherence, stronger boundaries, improved emotional regulation, survivor autonomy, and an increased capacity for reflective, reality-based, and relationally safe living.

The protocol is informed by the author's PhD twin study research with adult survivors and mental health practitioners, together with extensive frontline clinical experience in complex trauma, family-system harm, and high-risk relational presentations.

The HQTP is written for clinical psychotherapists, psychologists, counsellors, social workers, psychiatrists, family therapists, trauma clinicians, mental health practitioners, researchers, advocates, and allied professionals seeking a structured clinical pathway to understand and treat adult survivors of these often-overlooked forms of family-system harm.

Scale of the Treatment Gap: A Cautious Illustrative Note

No direct registry currently counts adults who, as children, lived through child psychological abuse and related family-system harm in contexts of parental alienation, high-conflict separation, familial abduction, estrangement, coercive control, and related family and domestic violence. This absence of data is itself clinically significant. Courts count legal events, population agencies count marriages and divorces, public-health systems count child maltreatment and violence, and clinicians often see the adult aftermath under other formulations, including trauma, grief, attachment injury, suicidality, relational fear, and identity disruption.

The available evidence nevertheless suggests that this is not a small or marginal clinical issue. The World Health Organization (American spelling maintained here) defines child maltreatment as including physical and/or emotional ill-treatment, sexual abuse, neglect, negligence, and exploitation that results in actual or potential harm to a child's health, survival, development, or dignity within a relationship of responsibility, trust, or power. The WHO also notes that child maltreatment is often hidden, that only a fraction of affected children receive official support, and that adults who experienced childhood maltreatment are at increased risk of later behavioural, physical, and mental health problems (World Health Organization, 2026).

In Australia, the Australian Bureau of Statistics recorded 120,844 marriages registered in 2024 and 47,216 divorces granted that year (Australian Bureau of Statistics, 2025). These figures do not identify high-conflict separation, parental alienation, familial abduction, estrangement, coercive control, or child psychological abuse. They do, however, show the continuing scale of formal family separation before informal separations, de facto relationship breakdowns, family court proceedings, child-protection concerns, and coercive family-system dynamics are considered.

In the United States, peer-reviewed prevalence research estimated that approximately 3.8 million children were moderately to severely alienated from a parent (Harman et al., 2016). This figure should not be treated as a measured adult prevalence rate. However, it can be used with caution to illustrate the potential scale of the adult treatment gap. If approximately 3.8 million affected children are distributed evenly across the eighteen years of childhood, more than 200,000 children may age into adulthood each year. Across the eight annual cohorts from 2019 through 2026, this would represent an illustrative extrapolation of approximately 1.7 million recent adult survivors in the United States alone. Across a ten-year period, the same assumption would exceed 2 million.

These figures are not presented as epidemiological findings, formal population estimates, or proof of the prevalence of adult survivors. They are offered only as cautious indicators of scale. Their purpose is to show why adult survivor recognition, clinical training, and specialist treatment guidance are urgently needed.

A separate exploratory estimate developed by Dr Craig Childress (2026), Clinical Psychologist, using publicly available family-court and child-population data with AI-assisted modelling, suggested that the number of adults who may have passed through family-court systems as children without underlying child psychological abuse being adequately identified, assessed, or clinically formulated could fall within a broad range of approximately 300,000 to

1.5 million. This estimate has not been independently validated and should not be treated as a prevalence finding, confirmed case count, or evidence that every person within the modelled range experienced parental alienation or child psychological abuse. It is included only as an exploratory indicator of the potential scale of the identification and treatment gap.

The true number of adult survivors cannot yet be stated with confidence because child psychological abuse in contexts of parental alienation, familial abduction, estrangement, and associated lethal harm is not recorded consistently across systems, countries, courts, services, or clinical settings. Many survivors are never counted as adult survivors of this specific form of developmental harm. Instead, they may later appear in clinical, legal, family, disability, forensic, or community systems under other descriptions, including trauma, grief, estrangement, suicidality, homicide, familicide, complex family conflict, or treatment resistance.

It is therefore safer to state that this is not a niche clinical problem. It is a large, under-recognised treatment gap affecting survivors, families, clinicians, and systems across generations. In this sense, it may be understood as a serious but silent clinical and public-health concern: widely present in human consequence, yet still poorly named and too often missed until survivors present for therapy in adulthood.

For too long, adult survivors have arrived in therapy carrying the long shadow of alienation, abduction, coercive control, estrangement, and lethal family-system harm, only to have their histories misread through frameworks that were never designed for them. The HQTP is the first specialist, phase-based clinical treatment protocol written for this adult survivor population. It was developed from the authors' associated twin-study PhD research with adult survivors of severe parental alienation (also known as child psychological abuse) and specialist mental health practitioners who treat this cohort, completed through the University of the Sunshine Coast (USC) in Queensland, Australia.

Table of Contents

The Healing Qualia Treatment Protocol ©

A Specialist Clinical Treatment Protocol for Adult Survivors of Child Psychological Abuse in Contexts of Parental Alienation, Familial Abduction and Estrangement

This protocol conceptualises parental alienation, familial abduction, and estrangement within a broader child psychological abuse framework, while focusing specifically on adult survivors and their recovery.

Reader Guidance

The following opening section is intended to be read sequentially. It establishes the ethical, cultural, lived-experience, and research foundations of the protocol and clarifies the author's standpoint and responsibilities in undertaking this work.

Acknowledging Connection to Land and Culture

I begin by acknowledging the Gundungurra and Tharawal people as the Traditional Custodians of the land on which this work was written. I pay my respects to their Elders, past and present, and extend my respect to all Aboriginal and Torres Strait Islander peoples reading these works today, as well as First Nations communities across the world.

The Gundungurra and Tharawal peoples' deep connection to Ngurra (Country), a connection that is physical, cultural, and spiritual, teaches us that healing is rooted in relationships with the land, with each other, and with ourselves. Their resilience and wisdom serve as a powerful reminder of the importance of reclaiming our connections and identities as we navigate recovery from trauma.

For Readers Affected by Suicidal Ideation and Loss

A note from Dr Alyse

Dear friends,

To those reading this who have faced the profound pain of suicidal thoughts, near attempts, or chronically distressing emotional states because of child psychological abuse in contexts of parental alienation, familial abduction, and estrangement, this work honours your courage in living through experiences that often feel unbearable. Your survival reflects deep resilience even in the face of overwhelming adversity.

To the family members, friends, partners, and supporters who stand with someone in crisis, your commitment to offering compassion, accompaniment, and hope is invaluable. Supporting someone through suicidality is emotionally demanding and often overlooked; your efforts deserve recognition, respect, and support.

For those grieving a death by suicide, we acknowledge the depth of your loss and the unique sorrow that accompanies it. Bereavement after suicide can be complicated by stigma, unanswered questions, and emotional isolation. Every life lost to suicide was unique, meaningful, and deeply connected to others. The pain of loss is real and lasting, and your grief matters.

We remember every person whose life ended in suicide and extend compassion to those who continue to struggle with suicidal thoughts or behaviours. Every story matters. Every experience of pain, survival, and healing deserves attention, dignity, and a supportive response. You are not fundamentally broken or beyond help. Recovery is possible, and systems of care must improve to ensure that each person feels heard, understood, and supported in ways that honour their humanity.

Go gently, Dr Alyse

Suicide Prevention is a Shared Responsibility

Suicidal thoughts and behaviours are a global public health concern. According to the World Health Organization (WHO, 2025), more than 720,000 people die by suicide each year worldwide, and many more people experience suicidal ideation, suicide attempts, or ongoing distress. Suicide occurs across ages, genders, cultures, and communities and was the third leading cause of death among people aged 15-29 globally in 2021. Within trauma-informed clinical work, suicidal distress must be understood carefully and individually, including in relation to cumulative trauma, loss, relational disruption, shame, isolation, and perceived entrapment.

We affirm the importance of trauma-informed, culturally safe, and ethically grounded care for all people affected by suicide and self-directed distress. The HQTP is not a replacement for crisis intervention resources, and if you or someone you know is in immediate danger or facing an active suicidal crisis, please connect with your local emergency services or crisis line.

Suggested Global Support Resources (Non-Exhaustive)

If you or someone you know is in crisis, local and international support services may be available:

The SEMPI Social Communication Model ©: www.sempi.net

Befrienders Worldwide: https://www.befrienders.org/find-support

International Suicide Hotlines Directory: https://www.opencounseling.com/suicide-hotlines

Samaritans (UK & ROI): +44 (0)8457 90 90 90; jo@samaritans.org

Lifeline (US): 988

Lifeline Australia: 13 11 14 or https://www.lifeline.org.au

Crisis Text Lines: See local options (e.g., text HOME to 741741 in the US/Canada)

Please note that crisis and support resources vary by country; if these numbers are not local to you, consult the Befrienders Worldwide directory above.

Research Foundations and the SEMPI Social Communication Model ©

During her Master of Counselling and Psychotherapy research, the author examined the stigma endured by women living with severe and persistent mental illness while experiencing primary homelessness on the streets of Sydney. This research was conducted in collaboration with Torrens University in Sydney and The Exodus Foundation, an organisation led by Reverend Bill Crews that provides frontline support to some of Australia's most marginalised populations. The research cohort shared narratives of loneliness, survival, and systemic neglect that profoundly shaped the author's understanding of trauma, social exclusion, and recovery under extreme conditions.

Alongside this research, the author engaged with individuals accessing community support services, including those attending the Loaves and Fishes Restaurant in Ashfield, Sydney. Through these sustained relational encounters, a consistent theme emerged. Many participants reported that they were rarely asked how they were feeling or coping and that when they were asked, "Are you okay?" the interaction often felt superficial, judgemental, or dismissive. These insights directly informed the development of the SEMPI Social Communication Model (©).

The SEMPI SCM (©) was created as a free, altruistic, reciprocal, pay-it-forward model designed to teach community members how to be first responders when services are closed and someone in psychological distress needs support. Rather than functioning as a psychotherapy intervention, the model was designed to equip community members, professionals, and service workers with simple but structured relational tools to respond empathetically when individuals are upset. The SEMPI SCM (©) emphasises presence, active listening, emotional validation, and non-judgemental engagement, particularly in contexts where formal mental health services may be unavailable, overwhelmed, or inaccessible. There is also a Children's SEMPI SCM (©) that is taught in schools.

Since its development, the SEMPI SCM (©) has expanded internationally and has been implemented across multiple community, education, health, and social service settings. The model's central focus remains the promotion of basic human connection as a protective factor against isolation, disconnection, and suicide risk. Within the context of the HQTP, the SEMPI SCM (©) functions as a foundational relational influence that informs early engagement principles, epistemic safety scaffolding, and community skills. At the same time, the HQTP extends these relational foundations into a structured, phase-based clinical treatment architecture designed specifically for mental health clinicians addressing complex developmental trauma.

By providing basic human connection, the SEMPI SCM (©) serves as a suicide-prevention model, fostering a more connected and compassionate society. Within this work, the phrase every second counts also reflects the author's belief that every act of research, clinical translation, human connection, and shared knowledge may contribute to reducing suicide risk and helping people feel less alone. For more details on the SEMPI SCM (©), or to become a community first responder in your country, visit www.sempi.net.

Author Positionality and Ethical Accountability

Beyond formal research, the protocol is informed by the author's long-standing clinical work in private practice and in hospital and institutional settings, where complex trauma, attachment disruption, dissociation, and suicidality are routinely encountered. It also reflects many years of in-depth professional dialogue with colleagues across disciplines, including clinicians who consult with the author regarding challenging cases involving CPA-PA, abduction, coercive control, and prolonged relational trauma. These consultations have consistently highlighted areas of clinical risk and uncertainty that are not adequately addressed in existing treatment models, particularly regarding pacing, epistemic safety, identity destabilisation, and unintended harms arising from premature or mis-sequenced therapeutic interventions.

The framework further incorporates anomalous data identified across the survivor cohort accounts and reflected in related clinical encounters, which could not be fully reported within the word limit constraints of the associated twin doctoral thesis. The author further notes that these patterns recurred frequently enough to warrant explicit inclusion in treatment planning. Their presence highlights the limitations of narrow diagnostic formulations and rigid protocol-driven approaches when working with survivors of complex developmental psychological abuse.

As previously noted, the author is also an adult survivor of CPA-PA. This lived experience does not replace empirical research or clinical training, nor is it presented as evidence. However, it has informed the author's ethical sensitivity to power, coercion, epistemic harm, and therapeutic misattunement within clinical and institutional contexts. It has also reinforced the necessity of a treatment framework that prioritises autonomy, careful sequencing, non-coercive practice, and the protection of survivor agency at every stage of care.

Publication Pathway and Research Accountability

The decision to publish this framework outside a university-funded clinical trial or institutional publication pathway was deliberate. Formal trials, grant-funded research, and institutional evaluation remain important, and the author welcomes future research to test, refine, and extend the Healing Qualia Treatment Protocol. However, securing funding, obtaining ethics approval, designing the trial, recruiting participants, implementing the trial, and obtaining institutional endorsement would have delayed publication by many additional years.

Given the level of clinical distress observed in this population, including persistent suicide risk among some adult survivors of CPA-PA, the author determined that withholding clinically informed guidance until future trials were completed also carried ethical risk. This concern was heightened by clinically significant and under-described patterns identified across the author's doctoral research, including survivor-reported physical health concerns, autoimmune and serious-illness histories, abduction-related fear presentations, FDIOA-linked histories, and other complex intersecting trauma patterns requiring careful clinical awareness, interdisciplinary caution, and further research.

These findings are not presented as definitive causal claims or as settled medical conclusions. Rather, they are included because they may assist clinicians, survivors, medical practitioners, and future researchers to recognise areas requiring careful monitoring, trauma-informed assessment, collaboration, and further investigation. In this context, publication was understood not as a substitute for future research, but as an ethical act of clinical translation: making emerging, carefully qualified knowledge available to practitioners working now with survivors whose needs are already present.

Every Second Counts: Clinical Urgency and Ethical Publication

This original visual reflection was inspired by a screen image from The Bear, which the author used privately as a reminder to keep moving toward completion. In the context of this manuscript, the phrase reflects the urgency of making treatment guidance available for adult survivors who may be living with severe distress, suicidality, and delayed recognition.

Every Second Counts: Clinical Urgency in Publishing Treatment Guidance for Adult Survivors of CPA-PA

For some adult survivors of CPA-PA, prolonged delay in recognising and treating the clinical consequences of this abuse is not a neutral matter. The phrase every second counts became a private reminder to continue moving this work toward completion, particularly when the scale of the manuscript, the emotional weight of the material, and the absence of an established treatment pathway made the task feel overwhelming. Within this section, the phrase is used to mark the clinical urgency of making treatment guidance available where adult survivors may be living with severe distress, suicidality, delayed recognition, and repeated misclassification.

The decision to publish outside a university-funded pathway was therefore not a substitute for research standards, but an ethical response to an urgent and under-recognised clinical problem. This work has been advanced from the author's doctoral research, accumulated clinical practice, practitioner consultation, survivor-informed knowledge, and ongoing clinical and peer supervision, to provide timely guidance for clinicians working in high-risk and under-recognised contexts.

The HQTP is offered as a living clinical framework rather than a closed or definitive model. It is not presented as the final word on treatment for adult survivors of CPA-PA, CPA-PAA, CPA-PERA, familial abduction, estrangement, or familicide. Rather, it is offered as a structured, phase-based contribution to a field where survivors and clinicians have too often been left without adequate treatment guidance.

The author invites universities, research institutes, clinical teams, survivor-led organisations, and professional bodies to build on this work through formal clinical trials, outcome studies, qualitative research, implementation research, and comparative evaluation. Such work is welcomed as part of the ongoing development of this field. The framework is grounded in the principle that ethical practice with this population requires humility, restraint, clinical discipline, and a willingness to prioritise safety and autonomy over certainty, authority, or professional ownership.

List of Acronyms and Key Terms

Acronym	Term	Definition / clinical meaning
AB-PA	Attachment-Based Model of Parental Alienation	Dr Childress's attachment-based model for conceptualising pathogenic parenting, attachment disturbance, cross-generational coalition, and related alienation dynamics.
ACEs	Adverse Childhood Experiences	Cumulative childhood adversities associated with later mental and physical health risk
ACE Study	Adverse Childhood Experiences Study	Foundational epidemiological study linking cumulative childhood adversity with later health and psychosocial outcomes.
	Adult Survivor Cohort	The adult survivor participant group in the author's UniSC doctoral research, whose lived-experience accounts informed the HQTP's understanding of developmental harm, therapeutic misattunement, safety, pacing, autonomy, and long-term recovery.
APA	American Psychiatric Association	Publisher of the DSM diagnostic system, referenced in mental health classification.
AP	Alienating Parent	A caregiving parent who undermines the child's relationship with the targeted parent through coercion, narrative control, or psychological manipulation.
BSQ	Baker Strategy Questionnaire	Measure used to assess exposure to parental alienation behaviours or strategies.
CAPRD	Child Affected by Parental Relationship Distress	The DSM-5 relational problem term is sometimes discussed alongside presentations of high-conflict separation.
CBT	Cognitive Behaviour Therapy	Structured therapeutic approach focusing on links between thoughts, emotions, behaviour, and coping.
CITs	Complex Intersecting Traumas	Complex intersecting traumas that survivors may have encountered across attachment disruption, coercive control, betrayal, neglect, and related harms.
CPA-PA	Child Psychological Abuse in the Context of Parental Alienation	Umbrella HQTP formulation for child psychological abuse occurring within parental alienation and associated contexts, including familial abduction, concealment, forced relocation, estrangement, attachment prevention, coercive control, loyalty conflict, identity disruption, and relational obstruction. Within the HQTP, CPA-PA is used to describe developmental psychological harm that may continue into adulthood through epistemic injury, attachment

Acronym	Term	Definition / clinical meaning
		disturbance, grief, identity disruption, impaired autonomy, and difficulties with boundaries and relational safety.
CPA-PAA	Child Psychological Abuse in the Context of Parental Alienation and Abduction	HQTP formulation for CPA-PA presentations intensified by familial abduction, concealment, forced relocation, or related conditions of heightened threat, instability, and attachment disruption.
CPA-PERA	Child Psychological Abuse in the Context of Parental Estrangement, Relocation or Abduction	Attachment-prevention formulation used when a child's relationship with a living parent is obstructed, prevented, concealed, or developmentally absent through estrangement, relocation, concealment, abduction, or related forms of relational obstruction.
CSA	Child Sexual Abuse	Form of child maltreatment referenced in complex harm and trauma profiles.
DBT	Dialectical Behaviour Therapy	Therapeutic approach emphasising distress tolerance, emotional regulation, mindfulness, and interpersonal effectiveness.
DMM	Dynamic-Maturational Model	Attachment framework describing self-protective strategies that develop in response to danger, coercion, or inconsistent caregiving.
DSM-5	Diagnostic and Statistical Manual of Mental Disorders, Fifth Edition	Diagnostic classification manual referenced for mental health diagnosis and terminology.
DSM-5-TR	Diagnostic and Statistical Manual of Mental Disorders, Fifth Edition, Text Revision	Text revision of the DSM-5, referenced where current diagnostic terminology or classification limitations are discussed.
EFT	Emotionally Focused Therapy	Therapeutic approach emphasising emotional processing, attachment needs, and corrective relational experience.
EMDR	Eye Movement Desensitisation and Reprocessing	Trauma-focused therapy is used to process distressing memories through structured bilateral stimulation and phased trauma work.
FDIOA	Factitious Disorder Imposed on Another	Abuse dynamic in which a physical or psychological illness is fabricated, induced, or misrepresented in another person, usually a child.
FDV	Family and Domestic Violence	Broader violence context intersecting with coercive family systems, alienation, and survivor presentations.
HQTP	Healing Qualia Treatment Protocol	Phase-based specialist clinical treatment protocol for adult survivors of child psychological abuse in contexts

Acronym	Term	Definition / clinical meaning
		of parental alienation, familial abduction, estrangement, and associated developmental harm.
ICURE	Influence, Control, Uncertainty, Reinforcement, Enmeshment	The psychological conditioning sequence proposed in the protocol describes how coercive relational influence becomes internalised.
IPV	Intimate Partner Violence	The domestic abuse context is linked to separation, coercive control, and family system destabilisation.
MBSR	Mindfulness-Based Stress Reduction	Mindfulness-based intervention is used to support regulation, self-observation, and stress reduction.
MH	Mental Health	General clinical shorthand for mental health settings, systems, or presentations.
MHP	Mental Health Practitioner	Treating clinicians working therapeutically with the survivor.
MHPs	Mental Health Practitioners	Plural form of mental health practitioner.
MHP Study Cohort	Mental Health Practitioner Study Cohort	The practitioner participant group in the author's UniSC doctoral research, whose clinical perspectives informed the HQTP's treatment, supervision, and practitioner-readiness framework.
MRSA	Methicillin-resistant Staphylococcus aureus	Antibiotic-resistant bacterial infection referenced in medical or caregiver-fabricated illness contexts.
NAUWOU	Nothing About Us, Without Us	Survivor-led principle and conference title centering direct survivor voice in research, practice, and advocacy.
NDIS	National Disability Insurance Scheme	Australian disability funding and support system relevant to survivor care and service access.
PA	Parental Alienation	Historical term describing dynamics in which a child becomes organised against a parent within coercive family processes.
PABs	Parental Alienation Behaviours	Observable behaviours and strategies used to undermine or distort a child's relationship with the targeted parent.
PACFA	Psychotherapy and Counselling Federation of Australia	Australian professional body governing registration, standards, and ethics for psychotherapists and counsellors.
PAS	Parental Alienation Syndrome	Historical construct proposed by Gardner and treated cautiously within contemporary clinical discussion.
PCT	Person-Centred Therapy	Therapeutic approach grounded in empathy, congruence, and unconditional positive regard.

Acronym	Term	Definition / clinical meaning
PTSD	Post-Traumatic Stress Disorder	Trauma-related diagnostic term relevant to post-traumatic symptoms and differential formulation.
SDD	Shared Delusional Dynamics	Clinical term used in this protocol to describe high-control, reality-distorting relational dynamics that may shape a child’s perceptions, loyalties, threat appraisal, and family narrative.
SEMPI SCM	SEMPI Social Communication Model	Author-developed social communication and suicide-prevention model emphasising presence, emotional validation, active listening, and non-judgemental engagement.
SM	Selective Mutism	Clinical presentation involving persistent silence in specific contexts; discussed where fear, coercion, or relational threat shape communication.
SPA	Severe Parental Alienation	Terminology retained when referring specifically to the author's doctoral research and earlier literature.
SPAA	Severe Parental Alienation and Abduction	Research-era term used in the author's doctoral work for severe alienation combined with abduction conditions.
SP-SPAAA	Specific Phobia-Severe Parental Alienation and Abduction Anxiety Variant	Original doctoral research terminology for what the HQTP now refers to as the Specific Phobia–CPA-PAA Anxiety Variant. Retained only when referring to the author’s earlier research language.
SP-CPA-PAA Anxiety Variant	Specific Phobia–CPA-PAA Anxiety Variant	Current HQTP term for a provisional fear-organised presentation in which contact with, reminders of, or movement toward the targeted parent may activate conditioned threat responses rather than evaluative rejection alone.
TIC	Trauma-Informed Care	Clinical care framework prioritising safety, pacing, relational awareness, and avoidance of retraumatisation.
TP	Targeted Parent	A parent who is obstructed, rejected, or displaced within alienation-related family dynamics.
UniSC	University of the Sunshine Coast	Doctoral institution associated with the author's twin PhD research base.
UPR	Unconditional Positive Regard	Person-centred therapeutic stance of non-judgemental acceptance and relational regard.

Note. The terms parental alienation (PA), severe parental alienation (SPA), and severe parental alienation and abduction (SPAA) are retained in this manuscript where reference to the author’s doctoral research, historical literature, or original study terminology is required.

SPA and SPAA were used as study-specific descriptors within the author's PhD and are not presented here as universally adopted field-wide constructs. In the present protocol, CPA-PA functions as the umbrella clinical formulation, with CPA-PAA and CPA-PERA used where greater clinical specificity is required. These terms are defined and differentiated in depth in subsequent chapters. Earlier terminology is therefore preserved for research continuity, while the protocol itself adopts the CPA framework as its primary clinical language.

The Healing Qualia Treatment Protocol: Conceptual Foundation

The term *qualia* originates in philosophy and refers to the subjective quality of conscious experience, the "what it is like" dimension of perception, emotion, memory, and meaning that cannot be fully captured through external observation or biological measurement alone (Nagel, 1974; Jackson, 1982). It describes the inner reality of experience that remains uniquely personal even when external circumstances appear identical. Two individuals may witness the same event, hear the same words, or undergo the same developmental disruption. Yet, the internal meaning, emotional texture, and embodied response will differ in ways that cannot be standardised.

The term *Healing Qualia* was selected as the organising framework because adult survivors of child psychological abuse in the context of parental alienation (CPA-PA), the broader clinical umbrella used throughout this volume, often present not only with attachment disruption and trauma-related symptoms, but with profound injury to the internal systems through which experience, meaning, and reality are organised.

Many survivors were raised in environments where perception was manipulated, emotional reality was denied, loyalty was enforced, and independent interpretation of experience was actively punished. Over time, this produces epistemic injury: damage to the survivor's capacity to trust their own thoughts, emotions, bodily signals, and autobiographical memory (Price-Tobler, 2023a; Herman, 1992).

In these contexts, trauma is not limited to what happened. It is embedded in how the survivor learned to experience reality. Survivors often develop hypervigilance toward their own internal states, suppress emotional awareness to avoid conflict or punishment, and rely on external authority figures to determine what is "true" or "acceptable." This undermines psychological autonomy and contributes to identity fragmentation, relational dependency, and chronic self-doubt.

Healing Qualia conceptualises recovery not as symptom reduction alone, nor as correction of the survivor's narrative, but as restoration of internal authority and experiential safety. It prioritises rebuilding the survivor's capacity to inhabit their own subjective experience without fear of retaliation, abandonment, or relational collapse. This includes restoring trust in emotional signals, bodily responses, memory coherence, and personal meaning-making.

Epistemic Safety

Within the HQTP's phased architecture, this conceptual foundation directly informs clinical pacing. Early phases emphasise stabilisation, containment, and epistemic safety before trauma processing is introduced. Within this framework, epistemic safety refers to the survivor's confidence that their perceptions, memories, and emerging interpretations will not be corrected, overridden, or reinterpreted prematurely by clinical authority. For example, when a survivor tentatively describes uncertainty about a parent's behaviour or expresses conflicting feelings without a coherent narrative, the clinician resists the impulse to clarify, reframe, or interpret meaning. Instead, the clinician affirms the survivor's experience as valid to explore, allows ambiguity to remain, and signals that understanding will be built collaboratively over time. This stance counteracts prior experiences of epistemic invalidation and supports the gradual restoration of trust in one's own perceptions.

Epistemic Rupture

Epistemic rupture most commonly occurs unintentionally, when clinicians move too quickly to organise meaning, reassure, diagnose, or offer alternative interpretations before the survivor has experienced their own perceptions as fully received and held. For example, responding to a survivor's tentative disclosure with statements such as *"That sounds like trauma"*, *"Your parent was clearly abusive"*, or *"This is a common response in alienation"* may feel validating or clarifying to the clinician, but can inadvertently replicate earlier experiences of having meaning imposed and undermine the survivor's developing trust in their own perceptions.

Survivors are not asked to reinterpret the past until they can safely experience the present. Internal experience is treated as primary clinical data rather than something to be overridden by technique, interpretation, or external narrative frameworks. Therapy within this model is structured as a relational environment in which internal experience no longer needs to be hidden, defended, performed, or proven.

Additionally, the HQTP sessions provide a space where survivors can gradually learn to feel without punishment, think without surveillance, and remember without coercion. This restoration of experiential safety forms the foundation for later work involving identity integration, grief processing, relational differentiation, and long-term continuity.

Healing Qualia is not merely a title. It is the protocol's organising principle. It positions subjective experience itself as the primary site of repair, rather than treating insight, symptom reduction, or behavioural compliance as the central therapeutic targets. Within this framework, healing is understood to occur through the restoration of the survivor's capacity to experience, trust, and make sense of their own internal states in a coherent, regulated, and self-directed manner.

Clinically, this means that therapy prioritises how experiences are felt, interpreted, and held within the survivor's nervous system over the speed or completeness of narrative reconstruction. For survivors of child psychological abuse in CPA-PA contexts, subjective experience was repeatedly invalidated, distorted, or overwritten by external authority. Repair, therefore, requires creating conditions in which the survivor's perceptions, emotions, and meanings are approached as legitimate and worthy of exploration, even when they are fragmented, uncertain, or contradictory.

For example, when a survivor describes feeling "confused" or "unsure" about a family interaction, the clinician does not rush to clarify meaning, assign intent, or resolve ambiguity. Instead, the therapeutic focus remains on helping the survivor notice, tolerate, and articulate their lived experience as it is emerging. Over time, this repeated privileging of subjective experience supports the re-establishment of internal authority, narrative coherence, and psychological agency, which were compromised through prolonged relational coercion.

The HQTP as a Clinical Framework

For clinicians, the HQTP introduces a clinical framework centred on epistemic injury: disruption to the survivor's capacity to trust their own perceptions, memories, and meaning-making after prolonged exposure to coercive relational environments. In adult survivors of CPA-PA, this injury is often intensified by systemic failure, misdiagnosis, institutional disbelief, and repeated invalidation across legal, educational, medical, and mental health systems.

Within the HQTP, Phase I places a strong emphasis on restoring epistemic safety. In simple terms, epistemic safety means helping the survivor feel safe to notice, trust, and gradually express their own thoughts, feelings, memories, bodily responses, and personal meanings without fear of being corrected, dismissed, judged, pressured, or talked over. For many survivors, this sense of safety was damaged over time. Their reality may have been denied, rewritten, mocked, minimised, or replaced by the views of more powerful others. As a result, they may enter therapy feeling unsure of what they think, what they feel, what they remember, or whether they are even allowed to trust themselves.

In Phase I, safety is therefore understood as more than emotional calming or relational support. It also includes protecting the survivor's inner experience from further invalidation or harmful interference. This means the clinician does not rush to explain the survivor to themselves, impose interpretations, demand trauma disclosure, or push for insight before the survivor is ready. Instead, the clinician creates a steady therapeutic environment in which the survivor can slow down, notice what is happening inside, and begin to reconnect with their own internal reality at a pace that feels manageable.

During this phase, the clinician deliberately steps back from interpretive authority. The task is not to tell the survivor what their experience means, but to help them rebuild enough safety and self-trust to explore that meaning without fear. Over time, this helps the survivor reconnect with parts of themselves that may have been silenced, doubted, split off, or organised around survival. In this way, Phase I begins the process of restoring internal authority and supporting the gradual reintegration of identity, free from imposed narratives, alienating pressures, or the demands of external systems.

The HQTP Phase Architecture Overview

The HQTP is structured around a phased clinical architecture developed primarily for adult survivors of child psychological abuse in CPA-PA contexts, with adolescent application requiring developmentally adapted practice, additional safeguarding, caregiver-system assessment, statutory awareness, and supervision. This phased structure reflects the developmental nature of the injury, the necessity of stabilisation before trauma-focused work, and the ethical requirement to avoid premature exposure to destabilising material.

The HQTP is not a linear progression model. Movement between phases is responsive, non-sequential when clinically indicated, and governed by readiness markers rather than time-based expectations. Survivors may move forward, pause, return to earlier stabilisation work, or cycle between phases depending on symptom activation, environmental stressors, and relational safety.

Core Clinical Logic of the HQTP Diagram

Before outlining the six core phases, the following Core Clinical Logic of the HQTP Diagram summarises the clinical logic that governs the HQTP as a whole. The phases should not be read as a rigid sequence or a checklist to complete. They are organised around safety, regulation, identity, readiness, autonomy, contact choice, and supervision. The following diagram is included to help clinicians keep the central treatment logic in mind before moving on to the phase descriptions. It shows the order of clinical responsibility: protect safety first; stabilise before deeper meaning-making; preserve identity before documentation; assess readiness before trauma processing; and keep survivor autonomy at the centre of all contact and relational decisions.

Core Clinical Logic of the HQTP Diagram

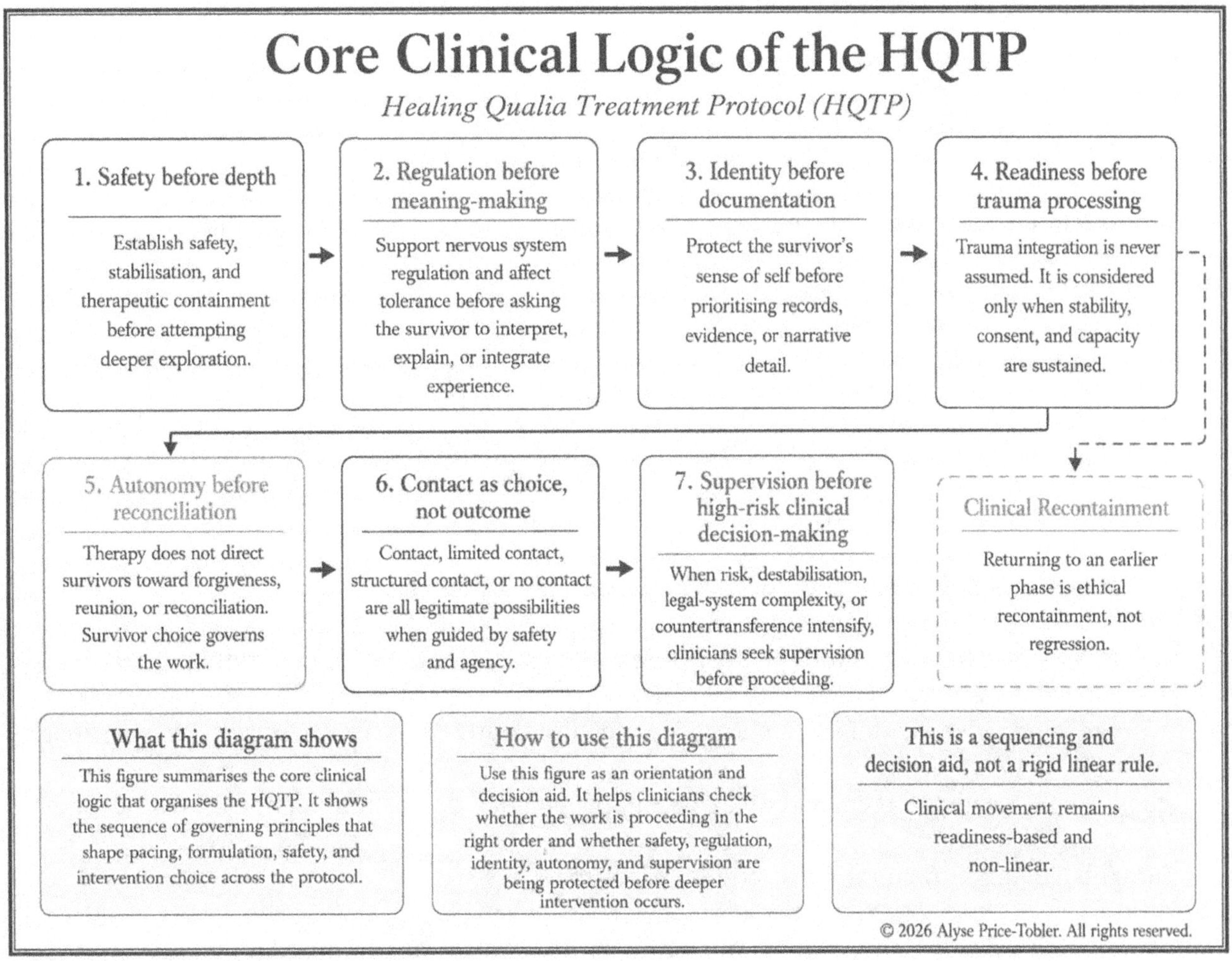

Clinical note. This diagram should be used as an orientation aid throughout the protocol. When clinicians are uncertain about pacing, phase movement, intervention choice, contact decisions, or risk escalation, they should return to this core logic. In the HQTP, movement is readiness-based rather than time-based and returning to an earlier phase is understood as ethical recontainment rather than regression.

Six Core Phases

The six core phases of the HQTP are:

Phase I: Safety, Orientation, and Epistemic Stabilisation

Phase II: Meaning Reconstruction and Identity Repair

Phase III: Mourning, Loss Integration, and Developmental Grief Repair

Phase IV: Trauma Integration Readiness Architecture

Phase V: Differentiation, Boundary Formation, and Contact Decisions

Phase VI: Integration, Continuity, and Long-Term Adaptation

Explicit clinical entry criteria, readiness markers, and exit indicators govern each phase. Progression occurs only when the survivor demonstrates sufficient stabilisation, consent capacity, and internal regulation to tolerate the demands of the next phase without risk of retraumatisation or psychological destabilisation. The phase list above provides a structural overview. Brief illustrative descriptions of each phase are provided below to clarify how the architecture functions in practice.

Phase I: Safety, Orientation, and Epistemic Stabilisation

Phase I helps the survivor feel safe enough to begin therapy without becoming overwhelmed, rushed, judged, or pushed into disclosure. This phase prioritises emotional stabilisation, relational predictability, consent, pacing, and the restoration of trust in one's own thoughts, feelings, memories, and bodily responses.

For example, a survivor may enter therapy feeling constantly on edge, unsure whether their perceptions can be trusted, and frightened of 'getting it wrong' with the therapist. In Phase I, the clinician does not rush into trauma work. Instead, the focus remains on helping the survivor slow down, feel safer in the room, understand that nothing needs to be proved, and begin recognising that inner experience can be noticed without punishment or correction.

Phase II: Meaning Reconstruction and Identity Repair

Phase II begins once the survivor has sufficient safety and stability to start reflecting on how childhood experiences shaped beliefs, self-concept, and relational patterns. The task is not to force conclusions, but to support gradual understanding of survival adaptations, inherited narratives, and identity distortions without collapsing into shame or confusion. For example, a survivor may begin to recognise that people-pleasing, emotional suppression, or automatic guilt were not signs of weakness, but protective adaptations formed within a coercive relational environment. Therapy helps place these patterns in context and supports the survivor in separating who they are from whom they had to become to survive.

Phase III: Mourning, Loss Integration, and Developmental Grief Repair

Phase III addresses grief linked to what was lost through child psychological abuse. This may include the loss of a psychologically available parent, extended family, a coherent childhood narrative, trust in protective systems, and developmental opportunities that can never be fully restored.

For example, a survivor may begin grieving not only the loss of a parent-child relationship, but also missed birthdays, family rituals, cultural belonging, and the chance to grow up with a more stable sense of self. In this phase, the clinician helps the survivor approach grief slowly and safely, without demanding forgiveness, reunion, or emotional resolution.

Phase IV: Trauma Integration Readiness Architecture

Phase IV is not immediate trauma processing. It is the phase in which the clinician carefully assesses whether traumatic material can be approached without retraumatisation, dissociation, collapse, or renewed epistemic threat. The focus remains on readiness, pacing, and protective sequencing.

For example, a survivor may wish to “finally deal with everything”, yet still become flooded, numb, or panicked when painful material is approached. In this phase, therapy helps determine whether the survivor has sufficient regulation, stability of consent, and internal support to approach traumatic material safely. When those conditions are not yet present, the work returns to earlier phases rather than pushing forward prematurely.

Phase V: Differentiation, Boundary Formation, and Contact Decisions

Phase V supports the survivor in developing a stronger sense of self that is no longer organised around fear, compliance, guilt, or relational survival. This includes boundary formation, identity differentiation, and, where relevant, decisions about contact, limited contact, structured contact, or no contact.

For example, a survivor may begin to recognise that each interaction with a parent leaves them dysregulated for days, while still feeling intense guilt about setting limits. In this phase, therapy helps the survivor differentiate care from obligation, recognise their needs as legitimate, and make contact decisions based on safety, capacity, and informed judgement rather than fear or coercion.

Phase VI: Integration, Continuity, and Long-Term Adaptation

Phase VI focuses on helping the survivor carry their history forward without remaining organised around it. The aim is not closure in a simplistic sense, but the development of continuity, self-trust, forward movement, and a life that is not wholly governed by past harm.

For example, a survivor may still carry grief, unanswered questions, or permanent losses, but no longer experience those realities as defining every relationship or decision. In this phase, therapy supports the survivor in building a life marked by greater agency, coherence, and continuity, even where full repair, reunion, or certainty is not possible.

The phased architecture prioritises psychological safety, therapeutic alliance, consent-based pacing, and epistemic repair. It recognises that adult survivors of developmental psychological abuse frequently present with disrupted attachment systems, identity fragmentation, emotional dysregulation, and compromised self-trust. The architecture, therefore, scaffolds recovery by first restoring internal stability and relational safety, then supporting structured recognition and integration of grief, before introducing focused trauma-related work where clinically appropriate.

Importantly, the HQTP does not position reunification, reconciliation, or relational restoration as mandatory outcomes. Instead, it centres survivor autonomy, informed decision-making, and long-term functional recovery as primary clinical goals. The protocol remains adaptable across mild, moderate, and severe presentations, including abduction variants and contexts of extreme harm.

Within the HQTP, qualia functions clinically as a reminder that treatment must protect the survivor's internal lived experience before it seeks to interpret it. For this reason, the early phases prioritise internal safety, nervous system steadiness, and epistemic protection over disclosure, trauma excavation, or premature relational decision-making. The protocol is therefore sequenced not around speed, but around the survivor's capacity to think, feel, remember, and make meaning without renewed coercion.

HQTP Phase Architecture and Intervention Emphasis

HQTP Phase Architecture and Intervention Emphasis

Healing Qualia Treatment Protocol

I

Phase I:

Safety, Orientation, and Epistemic Stabilisation

- Initial assessment gate
- Crisis containment and escalation architecture
- Attunement, pacing, and psychoeducation
- Regulation and therapist safety

II

Phase II:

Meaning Reconstruction and Identity Repair

- Recognition work
- Differentiation
- Identity reorganisation
- Protective pacing and anti-collapse safeguards

III

Phase III:

Mourning, Loss Integration, and Developmental Grief Repair

- Attachment injury framing
- Grief containment
- DBT-informed stabilisation supports
- Readiness evaluation before trauma work

IV

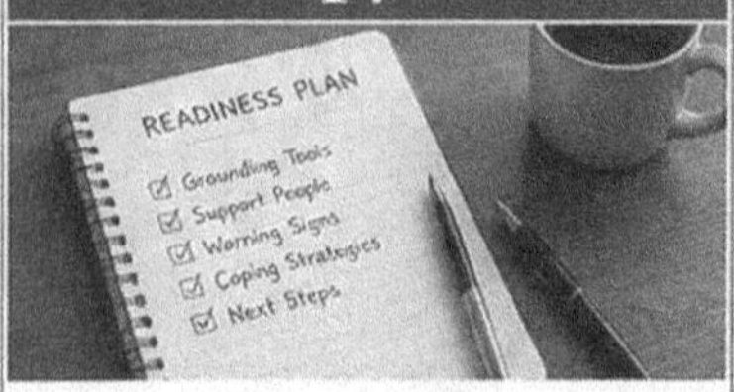

Phase IV:

Trauma Integration Readiness Architecture

- Readiness gating
- Affect regulation and boundary stability
- Contraindication screening
- Trauma-processing methods only where clinically safe

V

Phase V:

Differentiation, Boundary Formation, and Contact Decisions

- Autonomy consolidation
- Boundary planning
- Contact, limited-contact, or no-contact decision support
- Ethical continuity

VI

Phase VI:

Integration, Continuity, and Long-Term Adaptation

- Re-entry planning
- Predictable activation planning
- Reactivation management
- Long-term identity continuity

APPLIED PATHWAYS

Abduction and extreme-harm pathways	Discovery trauma	Identity reconstruction	High-risk supervision	Boundary-controlled re-engagement or non-engagement

Note. The phases are presented sequentially for orientation only. HQTP treatment is not linear. Clinicians may return to earlier phases whenever safety, regulation, consent, epistemic stability, or therapeutic containment requires it.

Applied abduction and extreme-harm pathways sit within the broader HQTP architecture and do not replace the core phase logic.

Note. The phases are presented sequentially for orientation only. HQTP treatment is not linear. Clinicians may return to earlier phases whenever safety, regulation, consent, epistemic stability, or therapeutic containment requires it. Applied abduction and extreme-harm pathways are part of the broader HQTP architecture and do not replace the core phase logic.

Quick Clinical Synopsis: What Clinicians Do in the HQTP

The HQTP guides clinicians to work safely, slowly, and phase-by-phase with adult survivors of child psychological abuse in contexts of parental alienation, familial abduction, estrangement, and associated coercive-control dynamics. Clinicians do not begin by asking the survivor to prove the history, organise the family narrative, retrieve records, process trauma, confront a parent, or make contact decisions. They begin by establishing psychological safety, clarifying the non-forensic treatment frame, assessing immediate risk, and protecting the survivor's capacity to think, feel, remember, and speak without pressure.

In early work, the clinician focuses on attunement, containment, psychoeducation, consent, regulation, and epistemic safety. This includes assessing suicidality, dissociation, functional stability, loyalty conflict, relational pressure, and the survivor's ability to pause. The first task is not to interpret the survivor's story, but to create conditions in which the survivor can begin to experience their own thoughts, emotions, memories, and bodily responses as safe to notice.

As stability develops, the clinician supports careful recognition work. The survivor is helped to make sense of how coercive family dynamics, attachment disruption, distorted narratives, abduction, estrangement, or prolonged relational threat may have shaped identity, self-trust, grief, boundaries, and relational choices. This meaning-making is collaborative and paced. The clinician does not impose conclusions, rush insight, or treat compliance, urgency, or intellectual understanding as readiness.

Later phases support mourning, trauma-integration readiness, differentiation, boundary formation, contact or non-contact decisions, and long-term adaptation. Trauma processing, record exposure, family contact, or major contact and boundary decisions involving the alienating parent (relational decisions) are not automatic treatment goals. They are considered only when the survivor has sufficient stability, capacity for consent, support, and boundary strength to approach them safely.

Throughout the HQTP, the clinician monitors risk, regulation, epistemic stability, functional capacity, relational safety, therapeutic alliance, and signs of destabilisation. If the survivor becomes overwhelmed, dissociated, suicidal, collapsed, compliant, or externally pressured, the clinician returns to the earliest phase required to restore safety and containment. This is not regression. It is ethical pacing.

The clinician's task is to know where the survivor is in the phase architecture, what is clinically safe now, what must wait, and what requires supervision. Progress is understood through increasing safety, coherence, self-trust, functional stability, boundary capacity, and the survivor's growing authorship over their own life.

What the Clinician Brings, and What the HQTP Teaches

Clinicians do not need to arrive at the HQTP as experts in every modality described in this volume. The protocol assumes that practitioners bring their existing professional training, clinical judgement, ethical obligations, supervision structures, and core therapeutic skills. These may include assessment, rapport-building, stabilisation, psychoeducation, trauma-informed care, attachment-informed practice, risk assessment, relational containment, grief work, cognitive reflection, somatic awareness, and skills drawn from approaches such as CBT, DBT, EMDR, psychodynamic psychotherapy, narrative therapy, person-centred therapy, family systems work, or other evidence-informed modalities.

The HQTP does not ask clinicians to abandon their existing trauma training or established professional competencies. It builds upon those foundations by identifying what requires adaptation when working with adult survivors of child psychological abuse related to parental alienation, familial abduction, concealment, estrangement, and associated coercive family-system harm. Its specialist contribution lies in helping clinicians recognise this population, distinguish developmental trauma associated with CPA-PA from more conventional trauma presentations, pace recognition and meaning-making safely, protect epistemic and identity stability, and avoid interventions that may inadvertently repeat coercion, impose conclusions, intensify loyalty conflict, or destabilise attachment organisation.

The doctoral twin-study research remains visible throughout this protocol because it provides the research foundation for its clinical architecture. The HQTP translates the combined findings from survivors and specialist mental health practitioners into a practitioner-facing framework that identifies what clinicians need to recognise, what may require adaptation, what should be avoided, and how treatment can be sequenced more safely.

For this reason, the HQTP functions as a clinical map rather than a single-modality treatment manual. It teaches clinicians what to look for, what to ask, what to avoid, when to pause, when to return to stabilisation, when grief work may be possible, when trauma integration is premature, when contact-related decisions may be unsafe, and when supervision is required. It provides the phase architecture, clinical decision logic, risk safeguards, pacing principles, contraindications, survivor-facing explanations, and applied pathways needed to support the safe use of existing therapeutic skills with this population.

The clinician's contribution remains active and essential. The HQTP does not replace professional judgement, supervision, or modality-specific competence. Clinicians remain responsible for practising within scope, selecting appropriate interventions, monitoring risk, seeking supervision, and undertaking formal training where specialised methods are required.

Where a clinician is not trained or competent in EMDR, psychodynamic psychotherapy, narrative therapy, family systems work, somatic therapy, DBT, or another modality discussed in this protocol, they should not independently deliver that modality. The HQTP may help the clinician recognise when an approach could be useful, premature, contraindicated, or more appropriately provided by a suitably trained practitioner. It does not confer competence in specialist modalities.

Within the HQTP, interventions are not selected solely because they are familiar or preferred by the clinician. Intervention choice is guided by phase position, survivor readiness, risk presentation, consent capacity, epistemic safety, and supervision. Clinicians may choose from within their existing scope of practice, while the protocol helps determine whether the timing, intensity, and purpose of an intervention are clinically appropriate. For example, trauma processing may become relevant later in treatment, but it may be contraindicated while the survivor is destabilised, dissociated, suicidal, externally pressured, or unable to pause. Similarly, narrative work may support meaning reconstruction, but it can become harmful if it forces coherence before the survivor has sufficient internal safety to make meaning at their own pace.

What the HQTP teaches is the specialist clinical logic required for this population. It helps clinicians understand how child psychological abuse related to parental alienation, abduction, estrangement, loyalty conflict, coercive control, identity disruption, epistemic injury, and developmental grief may present in adult survivors. It also explains why ordinary trauma work may need to be slowed or adapted, why insight itself may destabilise, why compliance is not the same as readiness, why contact is not the measure of treatment success, and why survivor autonomy must be protected throughout the therapeutic process.

Clinicians new to the protocol are not expected to implement every component at once. The safest starting point is to understand the treatment frame, the six phases, the principle of safety before depth, and the need to return to earlier stabilisation whenever the survivor becomes overwhelmed or loses coherence. Over time, clinicians may use the phase maps, decision trees, quick-reference guides, clinical examples, and supervision prompts to build confidence and strengthen clinical decision-making.

In simple terms, clinicians bring their training, ethics, humanity, supervision, and existing therapeutic skills. The HQTP provides the population-specific structure needed to apply those skills safely and coherently with adult survivors whose injuries have often been misunderstood, misdiagnosed, or treated too quickly by other systems. Its purpose is not to overwhelm practitioners but to help them understand where the survivor is clinically, what matters most, what should not be attempted too soon, and how to protect safety, autonomy, and treatment integrity as therapy unfolds. The doctoral research foundation underlying this clinical architecture is outlined in the following section.

Research Foundation: The Twin-Study PhD Conducted at the University of the Sunshine Coast

The HQTP is grounded in the author's twin-study doctoral research program, extensive frontline clinical psychotherapy practice, and lived experience as an adult survivor of child psychological abuse in CPA-PA contexts. The first international doctoral study examined the experiences of adult survivors of severe parental alienation. These findings, later presented in Volume One, documented survivors' developmental experiences, long-term psychological and relational impacts, help-seeking pathways, treatment experiences, and the consequences of coercive family separation across the lifespan.

The second international doctoral study examined the perspectives of mental health practitioners who specialised in working with adult survivors of what was described in the doctoral research as severe parental alienation. These findings, later presented in Volume Two, explored the complexity of survivors' clinical presentations, the treatment approaches used by practitioners, interventions perceived as helpful or harmful, practitioner training needs, and recurring systemic and service-level gaps.

The two studies were analysed together to identify areas of convergence and divergence between survivor and practitioner perspectives. This comparative analysis identified a significant treatment gap: the absence of an evidence-informed, phase-based specialist clinical treatment protocol designed specifically for adult survivors of child psychological abuse in contexts of parental alienation, familial abduction, and estrangement.

The HQTP represents the clinical translation and culmination of that research. It integrates the doctoral findings with more than 35 years of frontline experience across the disability and mental health fields, specialist trauma practice, and 14 years of direct clinical psychotherapy care. The author's lived experience informs the protocol's ethical urgency, survivor-protective stance, and sensitivity to coercive family-system dynamics; however, the framework is not grounded solely in personal narrative. Its clinical architecture is informed by empirical findings, clinical reasoning, phase-based treatment logic, professional supervision, practitioner consultation, and long-term work with complex trauma, disability, mental health, and forensic-adjacent presentations.

The HQTP is designed to address more than symptom reduction or the processing of past events. It aims to support the restoration of the survivor's relationship with their internal world, including their capacity to trust their perceptions, memories, emotional responses, identity, and autonomous judgement. Particular attention is given to epistemic injury: the disruption of confidence in one's own knowledge, experience, and reality following prolonged exposure to coercive family narratives, attachment pressure, and psychological control.

The protocol addresses a longstanding treatment and recognition gap across mental health, family law, social service, educational, and related systems. Adult survivors of CPA-PA may enter treatment with trauma symptoms, relational instability, identity disruption, grief, anxiety, depression, dissociation, or other difficulties without the developmental and family-system origins of their distress being recognised. The HQTP therefore provides a specialist clinical framework for understanding these presentations without reducing them to isolated symptoms, fixed pathology, or ordinary family conflict.

Although the HQTP draws upon knowledge from psychology, psychotherapy, social work, family systems theory, attachment-informed practice, and trauma-informed care, its primary purpose is clinical rather than forensic, legal, or diagnostic. It is intended to support assessment, formulation, treatment sequencing, survivor safety, and professional decision-making within appropriate clinical scope. It may also assist professionals in adjacent systems to better understand the long-term developmental and psychological consequences of CPA-PA, familial abduction, estrangement, and coercive family-system harm. Any legal, policy, educational, or systemic application must remain secondary to its central purpose: safe, non-forensic, survivor-protective clinical care.

The HQTP also establishes a foundation for further study, evaluation, and refinement. Research concerning the treatment needs and long-term recovery of adult survivors of CPA-PA remains limited. The protocol is therefore offered as an evidence-informed clinical framework to support future research on feasibility, implementation, treatment processes, practitioner training, survivor outcomes, and the ongoing development of population-specific care. Ultimately, the HQTP is offered for a population whose experiences have frequently been overlooked, misclassified, or inadequately addressed within existing treatment systems. Its purpose is to strengthen clinical recognition, improve treatment sequencing, reduce avoidable harm, and support safer, more ethical, and more coherent care for adult survivors of CPA-PA and related family-system contexts.

The Purpose Behind Volume Three: Addressing Gaps in Human Rights and Development for Children Exposed to Coercive Control

Volume Three was written to address the treatment gap that remains when child psychological abuse in contexts of parental alienation, familial abduction, estrangement, and coercive family-system dynamics is not recognised early enough. Although the harm often begins in childhood, many survivors reach adulthood without adequate identification, protection, formulation, or treatment. The HQTP therefore focuses on adult recovery from developmental psychological abuse that may have shaped attachment, identity, autonomy, grief, relational safety, and the survivor's capacity to trust their own mind.

Children exposed to these dynamics may experience restricted freedom of movement, forced separation from a parent, loss of extended family relationships, disrupted identity formation, and profound relational rupture. Some reconnect with targeted or estranged parents and other family members in adulthood; many do not. Others remain caught between grief, loyalty conflict, fear, anger, shame, and unanswered questions. These psychological consequences may continue across the lifespan, underscoring the need for a specialist treatment framework that addresses both the developmental harm originating in childhood and the recovery challenges that may emerge during adolescence and adulthood.

This volume therefore bridges the gap between the developmental origins of the harm and the clinical needs of the adult survivor. Its purpose is not to resolve family disputes, determine legal truth, or prescribe relational outcomes. Its purpose is to help clinicians recognise the clinical pattern, avoid misclassification, protect survivor autonomy, and provide phase-based treatment that supports safety, meaning reconstruction, grief integration, trauma integration readiness, differentiation, boundary formation, and long-term adaptation.

Target Audience for Volume Three: A Comprehensive Resource for Clinicians and Other Professionals

The HQTP is written primarily for mental health practitioners working with adult survivors of child psychological abuse in contexts of parental alienation, familial abduction, estrangement, and associated coercive-control dynamics. Its central purpose is to support safer clinical recognition, ethical formulation, phase-based treatment planning, and survivor-protective intervention.

This volume is also relevant to professionals in adjacent systems, including medicine, law, education, child protection, policy, disability, advocacy, and academia. For these readers, the HQTP provides a clinical framework for understanding the long-term developmental and psychological effects of coercive family systems. It does not invite non-clinicians to use the protocol as a treatment manual, but it may support more informed, careful, and trauma-aware engagement with adult survivors.

Adult survivors are also legitimate readers of this work. The protocol includes survivor-facing sections that explain treatment processes, clinical boundaries, phase progression, and common recovery experiences in accessible language. This transparency supports informed consent, epistemic safety, and collaborative therapeutic dialogue. While the HQTP is not a self-help manual, survivors may find that it validates their lived experience, situates distress within developmental and relational context, and counters pathologising interpretations.

For early-career clinicians, this text provides conceptual, ethical, and clinical grounding. It offers language, frameworks, decision points, and safeguards to support thoughtful assessment, appropriate referral, supervision use, and ethical restraint. It is not a directive for independent practice outside the scope, but it may help newer clinicians recognise complexity, slow the work when needed, and avoid inadvertently replicating harm.

For mid-career and senior clinicians, the HQTP integrates attachment theory, trauma-informed care, developmental formulation, survivor-informed clinical reasoning, and phase-based treatment architecture in an area that has historically lacked coherent specialist guidance. It supports recalibration, strengthens formulation, and offers a structured way to think about pacing, contraindications, grief, trauma-readiness, contact decisions, and long-term adaptation.

Across all readerships, this volume distinguishes between clinical understanding and clinical authority. Understanding child psychological abuse does not authorise practitioners to act beyond scope, and survivor knowledge does not remove the need for professional accountability. The HQTP is intended as a companion to supervision, training, reflective practice, and ongoing professional development. Its purpose is to invite careful, ethical engagement in the treatment of adult survivors whose histories have often been misunderstood, misdiagnosed, or rushed by systems that did not know how to see them.

HQTP Rights Statements for Children and Adult Survivors

The following rights statements are included as companion resources to the clinical and ethical foundation of the Healing Qualia Treatment Protocol.

They are offered as reflective, psychoeducational, and clinical-orientation resources for practitioners, survivors, families, advocates, and systems seeking to understand the developmental rights that may be disrupted when children are exposed to CPA-PA, CPA-PAA, CPA-PERA, familial abduction, estrangement, and related family-system harm.

The HQTP also recognises that some adult survivors are not living "after" these childhood conditions in any simple or completed sense. Some remain physically, financially, emotionally, culturally, or psychologically enmeshed with an alienating parent, coercive family system, or attachment-prevention environment well into adulthood. For these survivors, the rights named in childhood may not belong only to the past. They may describe ongoing violations of dignity, autonomy, identity, truth, relational freedom, privacy, safety, and selfhood.

These statements are not legal instruments, forensic conclusions, diagnostic findings, custody recommendations, evidentiary claims, or substitutes for statutory, safeguarding, child-protection, legal, clinical, or emergency-response processes. Their purpose is to translate child-rights principles into the clinical language of attachment safety, identity protection, relational freedom, developmental dignity, survivor autonomy, and the right to be heard.

"A Healing Qualia Rights Statement for Children" names what every child should be able to expect: safety, belonging, protection, identity, nourishment, privacy, cultural connection, relational freedom, and care that does not require them to carry adult pain.

"A Healing Qualia Rights Statement for Adult Survivors" recognises that when these rights were disrupted, denied, hidden, or distorted in childhood, the need for truth may remain active across the lifespan.

Adult survivors may need access to records, family history, parentage information, cultural and kinship knowledge, grief support, identity repair, and safe meaning-making in order to piece together the story of their childhood and reclaim authorship over their lives. Together, these statements reflect the HQTP's central ethical position: children are not weapons, messengers, bargaining tools, evidence, emotional regulators, or extensions of adult distress, and adult survivors are entitled to seek truth, safety, coherence, and self-understanding at whatever age they are ready. Both statements are informed by the United Nations Convention on the Rights of the Child and by the Healing Qualia Treatment Protocol's clinical framework for CPA-PA, CPA-PAA, and CPA-PERA.

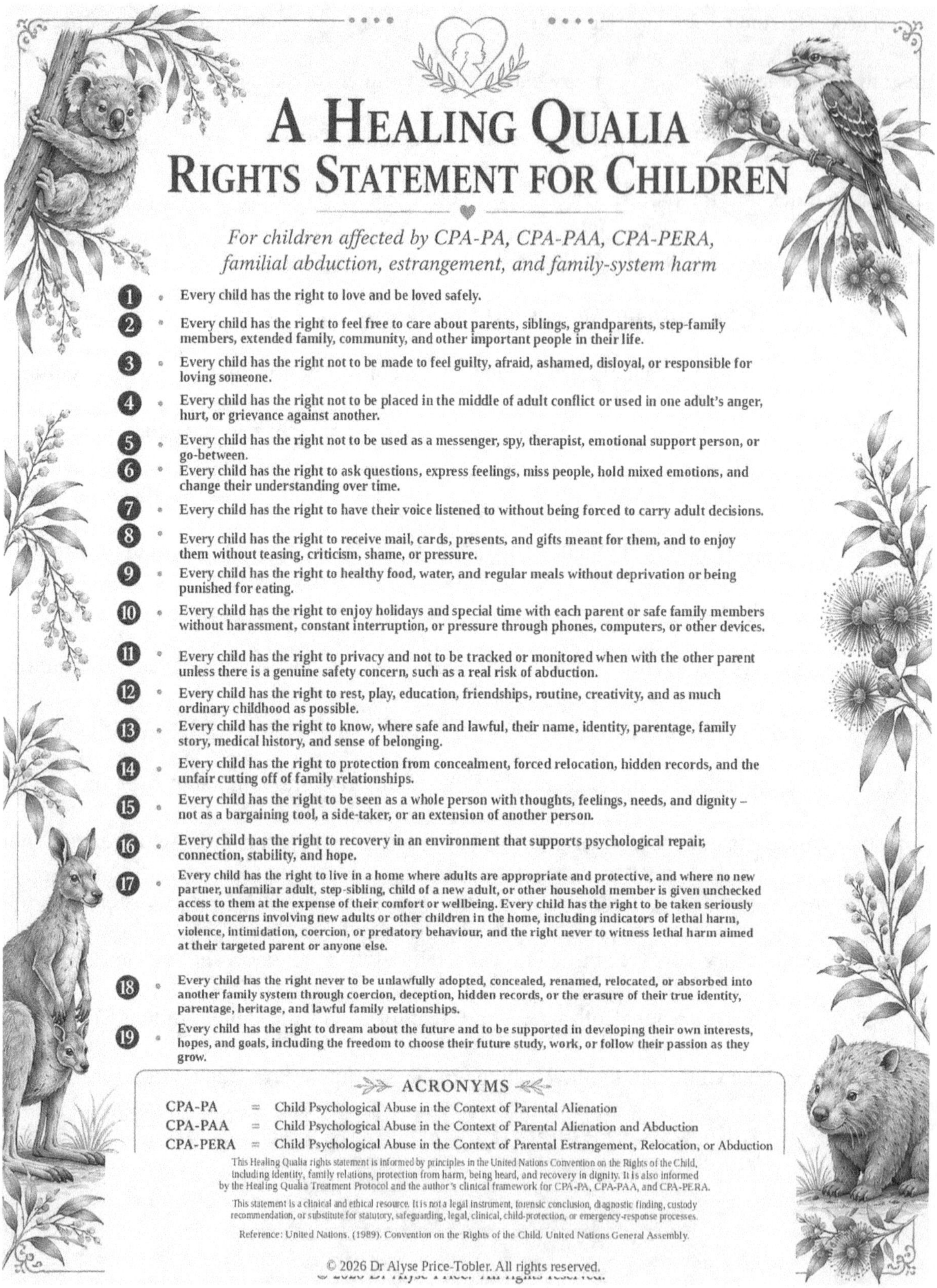

A Healing Qualia Rights Statement for Children Graphic

United Nations. (1989). Convention on the Rights of the Child. United Nations General Assembly.

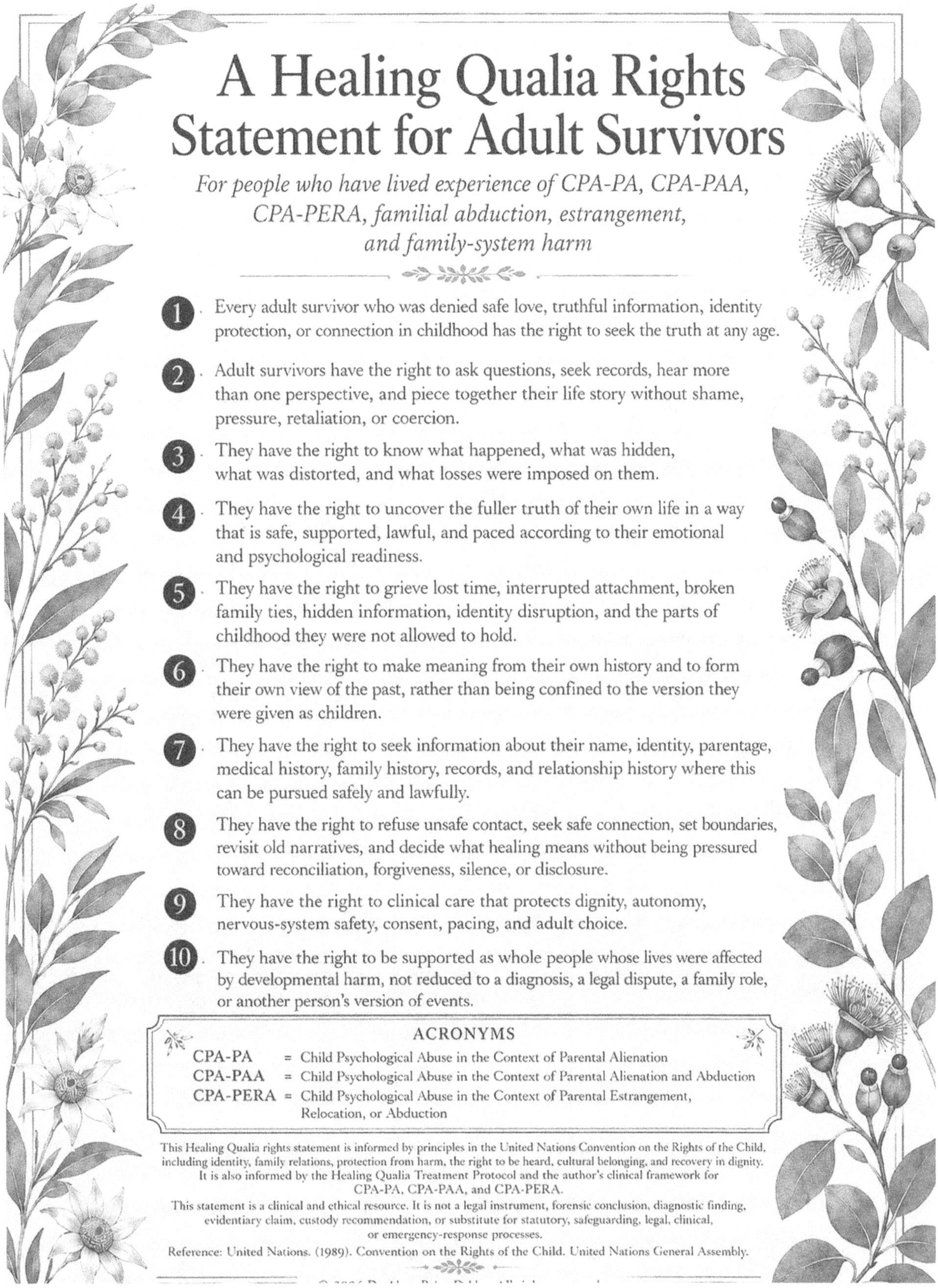

A Healing Qualia Rights Statement for Adult Survivors Graphic

United Nations. (1989). Convention on the Rights of the Child. United Nations General Assembly.

Chapter One

Foundational Concept: Child Psychological Abuse in Contexts of Parental Alienation and Attachment Disruption

For reader clarity, parts of Chapters One and Two have been reproduced and updated from the author's twin doctoral research and the two companion volumes derived from that work: *Disrupting the Intergenerational Trauma Cycle of High Conflict Divorce: A Guide for Mental Health Practitioners and Adult Survivors of Child Psychological Abuse: Severe Parental Alienation* (Volume One) and *Navigating the Maze During Treatment of Adult Survivors of Child Psychological Abuse: Severe Parental Alienation: A Comprehensive Resource Guide for Mental Health Practitioners* (Volume Two). Where material is discussed in relation to the original doctoral studies or the earlier companion volumes, earlier study-specific terminology, including severe parental alienation (SPA) and severe parental alienation and abduction (SPAA), is at times retained to preserve fidelity to the original research language, participant framing, and historical context.

Where the discussion shifts to the present protocol, the updated clinical language of child psychological abuse in contexts of parental alienation (CPA-PA) is used as the primary organising framework. This shift reflects the conceptual development of the HQTP, in which earlier terminology, such as severe parental alienation, is retained where relevant to the doctoral research and to the existing literature. At the same time, the current protocol adopts a broader, abuse-based, developmentally informed, and non-forensic clinical formulation. This material has been included to provide essential conceptual and clinical context for the treatment framework that follows.

Background

In 1969, Governor Ronald Reagan of California, USA, made what he later described as one of the biggest mistakes of his political life (Wilcox, 2009). Seeking to eliminate the deception and conflict associated with the legal system of fault-based divorce, Reagan signed America's first no-fault divorce bill. The new law allowed couples to pursue divorce without proving wrongdoing by either party, fundamentally altering the legal structure that previously bound marriage as a formal contract (Wilcox, 2009).

Broader family-structure literature has long raised concern about the developmental consequences of family instability. Amato's modelling, cited by Wilcox, estimated that if the United States had maintained levels of family stability comparable to those observed in 1960, there may have been approximately 70,000 fewer suicide attempts each year, alongside reductions in school suspensions, grade repetition, youth delinquency, and children receiving therapy. Although this estimate should be understood as historical population-level modelling rather than a current causal estimate, it remains clinically relevant because it highlights the scale of family disruption that may intersect with child and adolescent distress.

As mentioned earlier, within the parental alienation literature, Harman et al. (2016) estimated that more than 3.8 million children in the United States are moderately to severely alienated from a parent. More recent family-law industry commentary has also described the broader divorce and family-law ecosystem as a multibillion-dollar industry, with one industry source estimating its value at approximately USD $60 billion (Splitifi, 2025). This figure should be treated with caution as an industry estimate rather than a governmental statistic; however, it remains relevant to the HQTP insofar as prolonged family-system conflict may become embedded in legal, financial, clinical, and institutional processes.

In Australia in 2019, 113,815 marriages were registered, and 49,116 divorces were granted (Australian Bureau of Statistics [ABS], 2020). In the United States during the same period, 2,015,603 marriages, 746,971 divorces, and 746,971 annulments were recorded (Centres for Disease Control and Prevention [CDC], 2020). Historical research also reported that approximately 100,000 custody disputes were occurring in the United States, with these matters frequently described as hostile and emotionally taxing for families (Turkat, 2000).

Over the past two decades, the prevalence of high-conflict divorce, the emergence of child psychological abuse related to parental alienation, and the financial and psychological implications of divorce have undergone substantial transformation. However, much of the research concerning child psychological abuse in contexts of parental alienation has focused primarily on children and adolescents involved in custody disputes rather than examining the long-term experiences of adults who survived these environments.

Parental Alienation in the Literature

Parental alienation refers to a pattern of behaviours by one parent that undermines or interferes with the child's relationship with the other parent, contributing to the child's unjustified rejection of, or resistance toward, that parent (Harman et al., 2019). The concept describes behavioural patterns in which the alienating parent shapes the child's perceptions and relational responses, resulting in rejection, resistance, or fear toward the targeted parent without a proportionate or independently substantiated reason (Harman et al., 2019).

Such behaviours can cause significant disruption to the child's relationship with the targeted parent. Importantly, "parental alienation" must be distinguished from situations involving reasonable rejection, abuse, compromised parenting, or genuine estrangement. Parental estrangement occurs when a child rejects a parent for a legitimate reason, such as substantiated neglect, abuse, or severely impaired parenting (Fidler et al., 2012; Lorandos & Bernet, 2020).

Early psychiatrist Richard Gardner (1998) described "parental alienation" as a pattern emerging during post-divorce custody disputes in which one parent manipulates the child to turn against the other parent. This manipulation may occur through subtle behaviours or overt actions such as making allegations, obstructing contact, or interfering with communication between the child and the targeted parent.

Clinical Definition of Parental Alienation

At a clinical level, the term "parental alienation" has been used within family law and psychological literature to describe a pattern in which a child becomes aligned with one parent while rejecting the other parent without proportionate justification. Descriptions commonly include loyalty coercion, denigration of the targeted parent, restriction of contact, psychological enmeshment, role reversal, and reinforcement of rejection narratives. Severity has often been conceptualised along a spectrum, ranging from mild resistance to severe, entrenched rejection, with the latter characterised by rigid alignment and hostility.

Within specific existing scholarship, "parental alienation" is generally framed as a relational and behavioural phenomenon arising in the context of high-conflict separation and divorce. Interventions described in this literature have typically focused on assessing alignment patterns, understanding contact refusal, and addressing loyalty conflict during childhood.

Within the HQTP, the term parental alienation is retained because it is the best-known term within the established literature and public discourse. However, when the term is used without sufficient attention to severity, developmental context, coercive processes, and the child's psychological experience, it may obscure the child psychological abuse occurring in more serious presentations. Where these dynamics involve chronic coercion, identity suppression, sustained denigration, psychological control, developmental captivity, and, in some cases, abduction, concealment, or severe estrangement processes, parental alienation may be more accurately understood as a system of child psychological abuse with enduring psychosocial, relational, developmental, and structural consequences across the family system.

Impact of Severe Parental Alienation

The effects of severe parental alienation can be highly detrimental for children, frequently resulting in behavioural difficulties including anxiety, depression, and diminished self-esteem (Baker, 2007). In many cases, these experiences also produce long-term psychological and relational difficulties that extend into adulthood.

Children exposed to severe parental alienation often display intense fear, anger, or hostility toward the targeted parent, accompanied by refusal to maintain contact or engage in a relationship. Alienating parents may employ a variety of tactics designed to increase the child's dependence on them while simultaneously distancing the child from the targeted parent (Lorandos & Bernet, 2020). These tactics may include withholding affection when the child expresses warmth toward the targeted parent, instilling fear regarding the targeted parent's intentions, interfering with communication, or pursuing legal restrictions based on unsubstantiated allegations (Giancarlo, 2019).

Alienation frequently involves a campaign of denigration in which the child may initially participate without fully understanding the broader relational implications and later become more active in rejecting the targeted parent (Bernet, 2008). As this process unfolds, the targeted parent is often placed in the position of attempting to placate the alienating parent to preserve any form of relationship with the child (Giancarlo, 2019). Further descriptions of these behavioural patterns can be found in the literature on different alienating parent presentations (Bernet, 2010).

Polarising Terminology

Terminology used within the parental alienation literature can sometimes appear harsh or polarised when describing family members involved in these dynamics. For example, Rosenberg (2015, p. 15) notes that certain forms of communication may alienate individuals from their natural state of compassion.

Rosenberg explains:

"Life-alienating communication traps us in a world of judgements, using language that classifies and divides people into right and wrong. We constantly judge others, labelling them as good, bad, normal, abnormal, responsible, irresponsible, smart, ignorant, and more" (Rosenberg, 2015, p. 15).

For this reason, the doctoral research adopted a person-centred approach when engaging with participants. Within this context, person-centred practice means recognising that participants hold essential knowledge about their own lived experience and supporting their active participation in decisions affecting their wellbeing (NSW Health, 2020). It does not require the clinician or researcher to accept every interpretation as established fact, suspend professional judgement, or disregard the effects of trauma, dysregulation, coercive conditioning, or incomplete information.

For adult survivors of child psychological abuse related to parental alienation, this distinction is particularly important. Many have spent years being told what they think, what they feel, whom they are permitted to love, and which version of family history they must accept. An overly authoritative clinical approach may inadvertently repeat this loss of internal authority. Person-centred practice within the HQTP therefore provides the relational and ethical container in which the survivor's subjective experience can be heard without being imposed upon, corrected prematurely, or treated as irrelevant.

Clinical formulation remains collaborative, developmental, longitudinal, and open to revision. The clinician retains responsibility for assessment, risk evaluation, differential formulation, professional judgement, and ethical decision-making, while the survivor retains agency over the pace, direction, meaning, and boundaries of treatment. Contextual factors including gender, age, culture, identity, beliefs, language, disability, and life history must also be considered when interpreting the survivor's presentation (NSW Health, 2020).

During the mandatory PhD thesis literature review, the terminology used to describe parental alienation was examined carefully to avoid constructions that might inadvertently portray individuals in harmful or overly reductionist ways. Lorandos and Bernet (2020) found that the phrase parental alienation is used more frequently than alternative labels in both professional and public discourse. As a result, the term is retained throughout this book where engagement with the established literature requires it. Within the "parental alienation" literature, child presentations have often been described along a continuum of severity, most commonly in mild, moderate, and severe forms. The HQTP retains this general descriptive structure for readability and continuity with the established literature, but reframes these levels through an abuse-based developmental lens. Accordingly, the sections that follow examine mild, moderate, and severe presentations as forms of child psychological abuse in contexts of parental alienation, rather than as standalone child-level pathology.

Severity Levels in the Parental Alienation Literature

Mild, Moderate, and Severe Presentations

Parental alienation is commonly examined in relation to the severity of the child's presentation. Gardner (1998) described these dynamics as manifesting across three levels: mild, moderate, and severe. Each level has been used in the literature to describe differing degrees of intensity and entrenchment in alienation-related processes and may indicate different clinical and systemic considerations.

The mild, moderate, and severe distinctions are retained here as descriptive categories drawn from the established parental alienation literature. They are not presented as independently validated diagnostic classifications or as fixed categories that can be determined from a single behaviour, contact pattern, allegation, or child response. Their application necessarily involves clinical judgement and should be supported by comprehensive developmental, relational, attachment-based, safeguarding, and differential assessment. Within the HQTP, these distinctions are used to describe increasing intensity and entrenchment of child psychological abuse processes rather than to assign pathology to the child.

Mild Parental Alienation

The mild form of parental alienation is characterised by some degree of parental programming directed against the targeted parent; however, visitation and contact are not yet severely disrupted. The child may initially display resistance or hesitation but often transitions into normal interaction with the targeted parent once the visit begins (Baker, 2007; Lorandos & Bernet, 2020).

In mild parental alienation, the child does not yet fully reject the targeted parent. Instead, the clinical presentation involves subtle relational pressure, cognitive confusion, and emerging emotional suppression. The child may continue regular contact with the targeted parent while simultaneously beginning to mirror negative language or attitudes introduced by the alienating caregiver (Baker & Darnall, 2006; Warshak, 2015).

At this stage, the child's behaviour may be better understood as an attempt to preserve relational safety rather than as a freely formed rejection of the targeted parent. The child attempts to maintain access to both caregivers while avoiding emotional punishment or withdrawal from the alienating parent. This creates a state of internal conflict in which expressions of affection toward the targeted parent may begin to feel unsafe, guilt-inducing, or confusing (Bowlby, 1969; Johnston & Roseby, 1997).

From a developmental and trauma-informed perspective, mild alienation may be associated with heightened attachment vigilance and increasing sensitivity to relational threat cues. The child's prefrontal cortex remains engaged, allowing reflective capacity to remain partially intact, but emotional regulation increasingly becomes organised around caregiver cues. The child learns to scan the alienating parent's tone, facial expressions, and emotional state for signs of approval or disapproval (van der Kolk, 2014). Behaviour may increasingly reflect appeasement and threat management rather than an entirely independent relational preference.

Clinically, this stage often presents as ambivalence rather than hostility. Children may state that they "don't mind" seeing the targeted parent but appear emotionally muted or distracted during visits. They may express vague discomfort without being able to explain its origin. Statements such as "Mum says you're too busy" or "Dad says you don't really care" may reflect narrative borrowing, particularly where the wording appears developmentally unusual or closely mirrors a caregiver's language. (Baker, 2007).

A defining feature of mild alienation is the emergence of guilt conditioning. Children begin to associate enjoyment with the targeted parent as a form of betrayal toward the alienating caregiver. This guilt response does not represent moral development but rather attachment-based fear of relational withdrawal or punishment (Herman, 1992).

Over time, this conditioning leads children to suppress positive emotional expression to maintain safety within the primary caregiving environment. Mild alienation may be misinterpreted as a normal adjustment following separation or divorce, particularly where contact continues, and the child's distress remains subtle. This misinterpretation may result in important clinical concerns, including delayed recognition of the child's relational distress and psychological abuse. Genuine child preference typically emerges from consistent caregiving experiences and emotional safety. Alienation-driven preference, by contrast, arises from threat-conditioned relational compliance and role-reversal dynamics (Childress, 2015).

Another hallmark of mild alienation is the early emergence of role confusion. Children may begin to function as emotional regulators for the alienating parent, offering reassurance, managing emotional distress, or listening to grievances about the targeted parent. This process of parentification shifts the child from a dependent attachment position to a pseudo-peer or caretaker role, disrupting normative developmental boundaries (Herman, 1992).

Mild alienation may be more amenable to early intervention because the child's rejection and attachment disruption may be less entrenched. The child's identity and attachment organisation have not yet consolidated in response to rejection. However, this stage is also the one most frequently overlooked by professionals. Failure to recognise early alienation dynamics allows loyalty conditioning to intensify and relational distortions to consolidate into more severe patterns (Warshak, 2015; Baker & Darnall, 2006).

For targeted parents, mild alienation can be emotionally confusing. The child may continue attending visits while becoming subtly quieter, more distant, or emotionally cautious. Many parents respond by increasing reassurance or attempting to correct negative narratives. Although understandable, these responses may unintentionally increase pressure on the child and expose them to retaliation after visits. Clinically recommended responses emphasise emotional steadiness, predictable presence, and avoidance of loyalty testing. The goal is to preserve the child's relational safety without increasing exposure to conflict or punishment (Warshak, 2015).

Additionally, mild alienation represents the earliest identifiable stage of child psychological abuse associated with parental alienation. Recognition at this stage allows early containment before escalation occurs. As loyalty pressure consolidates and emotional consequences intensify, alienation dynamics may progress from subtle conditioning into coercive alignment. This progression marks the transition from mild to moderate levels of child psychological abuse associated with parental alienation.

Moderate Parental Alienation

The moderate form of "parental alienation" involves more overt relational disruption. According to Baker (2007), children at this level may display increased hostility, resistance, and oppositional behaviour toward the targeted parent. The alienating parent's campaign of denigration may become persistent and highly visible.

Children may strongly resist the suggestion of contact with the targeted parent and demonstrate opposition during visits, although moments of connection may still occur when the child's attachment to the targeted parent remains partially intact (Lorandos & Bernet, 2020).

At this level, children often experience an intense internal conflict during visits. Exposure to repeated parental programming generates cognitive dissonance between the child's lived experience of the targeted parent and the narrative communicated by the alienating caregiver (Baker, 2007).

Coercive Punishment and Survival Alignment

In moderate to severe alienation environments, a child's rejection of the targeted parent is frequently maintained through consequence rather than preference. Alienating caregivers may punish children for requesting contact, expressing affection toward the targeted parent, or returning from visits without displaying the expected hostility (Childress, 2015).

Punishment may be overt, including rage episodes, intimidation, withdrawal of privileges, or threats of abandonment. It may also be covert, including humiliation, emotional collapse displays, chronic interrogation following visits, or triangulation involving siblings and extended family members (Herman, 1992; Stark, 2007).

Repeated exposure to relational threat activates the child's brainstem survival circuitry and amygdala-mediated fear responses. Behaviour becomes organised around threat avoidance and alliance formation rather than authentic attachment preference (van der Kolk, 2014). Under these conditions, the child is not choosing sides. The child is selecting the relational alignment that minimises danger and emotional volatility within the caregiving environment. These survival-based adaptations are relational and behavioural. Over time, they also become organised within the child's nervous system, shaping threat perception, emotional regulation, and patterned responses to attachment-related cues.

Severe Parental Alienation

In severe cases of parental alienation, children may demonstrate persistent and intense rejection of the targeted parent. Contact may be refused entirely, and children may threaten to run away or hide when visitation is proposed (Baker, 2007). At this stage, the child's alignment with the alienating caregiver may become rigid and highly enmeshed. The child may adopt the alienating parent's narratives and display extreme hostility toward the targeted parent, even in the absence of substantiated reasons (Baker, 2007).

Children in severe alienation contexts may hide during visitation exchanges, refuse all interaction, or display verbal and physical aggression toward the targeted parent (Lorandos et al., 2013). Observers frequently report a rigid alliance between the child and the alienating caregiver, combined with extreme negativity toward the targeted parent.

Child Soldier Dynamics

A clinically significant but often unrecognised pattern in severe alienation environments is the recruitment of children into surveillance and enforcement roles. Children may be encouraged or coerced to report session content, monitor the targeted parent's behaviour, deliver hostile messages, or repeat accusations against the targeted parent. These behaviours do not reflect antisocial tendencies but rather coerced role assignment within a controlling relational system (Childress, 2015).

Risk intensifies when the targeted parent has physically left the household due to violence, instability, or marital breakdown. In these circumstances, the child may become the next available emotional target within the family system. Children may experience simultaneous fear of the alienating parent, emotional fusion with them, and anger toward the targeted parent for leaving, even when the departure was protective or necessary. This dynamic reflects attachment capture under threat conditions rather than voluntary rejection (Childress, 2015; Stark, 2007).

Additionally, in severe parental alienation contexts, the child is no longer operating based on AP preference. Behaviour becomes organised around survival. Alignment with the AP becomes a strategy for avoiding punishment, emotional volatility, or abandonment threats within the caregiving environment (Bowlby, 1969; Stark, 2007; Childress, 2015). Importantly, many children in severe alienation environments continue to love and miss the targeted parent. However, expressing that attachment becomes psychologically dangerous. Children, therefore, learn to suppress longing, hide grief, and demonstrate loyalty to the alienating caregiver.

Nervous System Organisation

Chronic relational threat conditions the child's nervous system to remain persistently activated. Over time, the child becomes highly sensitised to cues of danger within the caregiving environment, including shifts in tone, facial expression, questioning after contact, emotional withdrawal, anger, or signs of impending retaliation (van der Kolk, 2014; Porges, 2011). As a result, the child may develop fight, flight, freeze, or appease responses depending on how safe the child feels and how unstable or threatening the relational environment has become. Appeasement often becomes dominant because compliance can reduce immediate danger and preserve access to caregiving resources. Within sibling systems, survival roles may also become distributed, with different children adopting caretaker, compliant, oppositional, or protective positions in response to the same family dynamic (Childress, 2015; Stark, 2007). Having briefly engaged the established parental alienation literature for descriptive continuity, the discussion now returns to the protocol's abuse-based clinical developmental formulation. Viewed through this lens, the focus shifts from descriptive labels to the underlying psychological mechanisms through which coercive relational environments shape belief, attachment, identity, and developmental adaptation.

Having briefly engaged the established parental alienation literature for descriptive continuity, the discussion now returns to the protocol's abuse-based developmental formulation. From this point forward, the clinical language of the HQTP is used, as the discussion shifts from earlier descriptive terminology to the protocol's own framework for understanding the underlying mechanisms of harm.

Brainwashing Children: Psychological Conditioning and the ICURE Process

The psychological processes involved in child psychological abuse in parental alienation contexts (CPA-PA) can be understood through the ICURE sequence: Influence, Control, Uncertainty, Reinforcement, and Enmeshment. This sequence describes how a child may gradually come to accept one caregiver's version of reality when access to alternative information, relationships, and emotionally safe connection is restricted. In everyday language, this process is sometimes described as brainwashing; clinically, it is better understood as psychological conditioning within a coercive relational environment. The ICURE process draws on research into coercive persuasion, information control, and relational dependency (Taylor, 2006; Hassan, 2015; Stein, 2017).

The first stage is **Influence.** In early childhood, caregivers are the child's main source of information about family relationships. Children depend on caregivers for safety, emotional regulation, and understanding the world around them. For this reason, a caregiver's explanation of family members or family events can carry significant authority and may strongly shape the child's internal working models of attachment, trust, danger, and belonging (Bowlby, 1988).

The second stage is **Control.** In this stage, the child's access to other relational information may be limited or blocked. The child may be prevented from contacting the targeted parent, discouraged from seeing the targeted parent's extended family, or given only selective information about the targeted or estranged parent in some cases. Details may be withheld, distorted, or replaced with simple explanations that support one dominant family narrative. Research on coercive influence and thought reform shows that when alternative perspectives are restricted, a person becomes more dependent on a single authority figure for interpreting reality (Taylor, 2006; Hassan, 2015).

The third stage is **Uncertainty.** As children grow older, they naturally begin to ask questions about identity, family history, attachment, and belonging. When these questions arise in a family environment where information is restricted, contradictory, or emotionally unsafe to explore, the child may experience confusion, distress, or simply "know" not to ask the questions. In high-control relational environments, this uncertainty may be resolved by accepting the dominant caregiver's explanation, particularly when it appears to preserve emotional safety within the family system (Stein, 2017; Taylor, 2006). Or, in some cases, adopting a sense of self-betrayal to keep the peace. For example, "I was always more focused on how it might upset my mum rather than how it affected me." (anon).

The fourth stage is **Reinforcement.** The child learns which responses are emotionally safe and which are not. Loyalty to the caregiving adult may be met with affection, approval, warmth, or closeness. Curiosity about the targeted or estranged parent may be met with criticism, ridicule, anxiety, withdrawal, punishment, or emotional distance. Over time, the child may learn that agreeing with the caregiver's narrative protects connection and reduces emotional threat. In this way, reinforcement helps maintain the child's alignment with the dominant family story (Taylor, 2006; Stein, 2017).

The final stage is **Enmeshment.** At this point, the child's developing identity may become closely tied to the caregiving adult's emotional needs, beliefs, and interpretation of family relationships. Psychological boundaries can become blurred, and the child may internalise the caregiver's version of reality as part of their identity. Within enmeshed family systems, the child's thoughts, feelings, and loyalties may become organised around the caregiver's worldview rather than the child's own direct experience (Minuchin, 1974).

Although the ICURE sequence is especially powerful in childhood because children are dependent on caregivers for safety, information, and emotional regulation, similar processes may also occur in adolescence and adulthood. Later-life conditioning may be reinforced through loyalty pressure, coercive control, isolation from alternative relationships, repeated narrative distortion, financial or caregiving dependence, disability or mental health-related vulnerability, grief, illness, family exclusion, or fear of relational punishment. In these contexts, an adolescent or adult may gradually come to accept, repeat, or defend a dominant family narrative because disagreement threatens their sense of belonging, support, identity, or emotional safety. This is particularly relevant in CPA-PERA contexts, later-life estrangement, sibling alienation, grandparent alienation, inheritance conflict, family-event exclusion, and adult family systems where one person's version of reality becomes the condition for continued connection.

Where the child, adolescent, or adult has not been allowed to form, maintain, or safely repair a direct attachment relationship with the targeted or estranged family member, the dominant caregiver's or family system's narrative may remain the main interpretive framework into adulthood. This does not mean the person is deliberately rejecting truth. Rather, they may have adapted to the only relational reality that felt available, safe, and emotionally survivable at the time.

Child Psychological Abuse in the Context of Parental Estrangement, Relocation, or Abduction (CPA-PERA)

Conceptual Overview

CPA-PERA describes an attachment-prevention pathway in which a child grows up without the opportunity to form a meaningful attachment relationship with a living biological parent. Within this section, the term *estranged parent* refers to a biological parent with whom the child has little or no relationship; it describes the relational condition rather than presuming the cause of that separation. The CPA-PERA formulation was developed in response to recurring clinical presentations in which the developmental importance of an absent biological parent was minimised, dismissed, or treated as unnecessary, despite later evidence of identity disruption, grief, and relational disturbance in adult survivors.

The author's concern regarding these attachment-prevention dynamics was further sharpened through repeated observation of similar patterns in court-involved families and by changes to the Australian family law framework from 6 May 2024, which removed the presumption of equal shared parental responsibility and the associated statutory pathway requiring courts to consider equal-time and substantial-and-significant-time arrangements, while not abolishing equal-time outcomes altogether (Attorney-General's Department, 2024).

CPA-PERA arises when relational access to that parent is prevented during early development through circumstances such as concealed parentage, obstructed communication, relocation designed to prevent contact, parental abduction, or early caregiving arrangements in which one parent remains alive but absent from the child's developmental world. Within the present protocol, *abduction* is used in a broader clinical-developmental sense to include not only the taking or retention of a child without the other biological parent's knowledge or consent but also circumstances in which a child is effectively removed from that parent's relational reach through concealed pregnancy, concealed parentage, undisclosed birth, or subsequent removal that prevents attachment formation. Because attachment is formed through repeated interaction during sensitive developmental periods, the absence of relational exposure to a parent may prevent the formation of a meaningful bond from the outset (Bowlby, 1969/1982; Ainsworth et al., 1978).

The defining injury in CPA-PERA is therefore not the progressive destruction of an attachment relationship that once existed, but the prevention of a relationship that was never permitted to develop. This distinguishes CPA-PERA from CPA-PA presentations, in which an existing attachment bond is progressively distorted through coercive control, denigration, loyalty pressure, and narrative manipulation (Harman et al., 2019). In CPA-PERA, the child does not reject a parent they once knew in any sustained way; instead, they grow up without direct knowledge of, or meaningful experience with, a parent whose presence was obstructed. Over time, this may contribute to identity disruption, unresolved grief, autobiographical uncertainty, difficulties in integrating family origins into a coherent sense of self, and later questions about belonging, medical history, and kinship continuity (Sants, 1964; Lifton, 1994; Greif, 2000). As these children become adults, some may begin actively searching for the estranged parent, particularly during periods of developmental transition, identity questioning, parenthood, relationship change, or therapeutic exploration, to resolve unanswered questions about origin, attachment, and selfhood (Barn & Mansuri, 2019; Campbell et al., 1991). The inclusion of CPA-PERA within the HQTP reflects this developmental reality and creates space for mental health practitioners to work with adult survivors toward recognising and, where possible, repairing some of the psychological harm associated with caregiver concealment, obstruction, and the withholding of a living biological parent.

This pathway must also be distinguished from adoption, foster care placement, or temporary family separation undertaken through recognised child welfare processes intended to protect the child's safety. Such circumstances may still intersect with CPA-PERA when one living parent remains structurally inaccessible and controlling narratives are maintained about that parent. The clinical concern is not the legal label attached to the separation, but the combination of prevented relational access, narrative control, and the child's resulting developmental experience.

Where direct relational experience is absent, stories about the estranged parent may become the child's primary framework for understanding that parent. Repeated descriptions of the parent as unsafe, immoral, unstable, irresponsible, or uninterested can shape the child's developing internal working models of family, safety, and belonging (Bowlby, 1988). Restrictions on contact with the estranged parent's extended family may further reduce access to corrective information and alternative family narratives. Situations in which a child grows up without accurate knowledge of their origins have also been associated with identity disruption and autobiographical confusion, historically described as genealogical bewilderment (Sants, 1964; Lifton, 1994).

Alienation Dynamics Within Attachment-Prevention Environments

Although CPA-PERA is defined by the prevention of attachment formation, the relational environment in which the child is raised may still contain alienation-like processes. Early childhood may be marked by silence about the estranged parent's identity, followed later by negative explanations as the child begins asking questions. In the absence of corrective relational experience, such narratives may come to function not simply as information but as developmental scaffolding for the child's understanding of parenthood, trust, danger, and relational legitimacy.

Over time, the child may learn that curiosity about the estranged parent threatens household stability. Questions may evoke anger, distress, ridicule, or emotional withdrawal from the caregiving adult. Under these conditions, the child's safest option may become silence. These dynamics resemble patterns described in coercive relational systems, in which narrative authority and emotional dependency reinforce alignment with a central authority figure (Stein, 2017; Taylor, 2006).

Clinical Origins of the CPA-PERA Concept

The CPA-PERA construct emerged from long-term clinical observation and was further clarified by anomalous data arising from the author's doctoral survivor research (Price-Tobler, 2023a, 2023b). Across private psychotherapy practice, mental health units, disability services, NDIS-supported living environments, foster care settings, juvenile detention, and adult correctional facilities, some clients described developmental histories in which they later discovered that a living biological parent had remained absent from their childhood not because the parent was dead or wholly disengaged, but because access to that parent had been prevented.

These histories did not fit classical parental alienation formulations centred on the erosion of an existing relationship. Instead, they pointed to a distinct pathway in which attachment formation itself had been obstructed through concealed parentage, relocation, parental abduction, communication barriers, or early caregiving arrangements that removed the child from the parent's environment during infancy or early childhood. Although the mechanism differed from CPA-PA, the later consequences often included identity disruption, unresolved grief, fragmented family narrative, and confusion about belonging.

Why Attachment-Prevention Pathways Have Been Overlooked

Attachment-prevention pathways have received comparatively little attention within parental alienation literature, much of which has focused on high-conflict divorce contexts where a previously established parent–child relationship becomes disrupted through psychological influence (Baker, 2007; Harman et al., 2019). When no meaningful relationship has been allowed to form, the child may show no obvious rejection behaviour. Without a visible campaign of denigration attached to an already existing bond, the developmental injury may remain clinically and legally obscure.

Research on adoption, identity, and family origin has long recognised the psychological effects of growing up without accurate knowledge of one's biological parentage (Sants, 1964; Lifton, 1994). However, these insights have seldom been integrated with CPA-PA research. CPA-PERA bridges this gap by identifying attachment-prevention as a clinically meaningful form of child psychological abuse in which the injury is developmental invisibility rather than overt repudiation.

CPA-PERA in Disability, Foster Care, and Informal Separation Contexts

Clinical observations suggest that attachment-prevention pathways may also arise in disability, foster care, and informal caregiving contexts. Some adult survivors described infancy or early childhood histories in which a parent with intellectual disability, psychosocial disability, or significant mental health difficulties was separated from the child through formal or informal arrangements. Others reported extended family or community-based caregiving transfers that occurred without a clear legal process but nevertheless resulted in long-term loss of contact with a living parent.

For some survivors, the significance of these early separations became visible only in adulthood, when they began reconstructing family history in treatment and learned that the absent parent had attempted to maintain contact or seek information but had been prevented from doing so. These discoveries often produced profound grief, identity destabilisation, and urgent questions about origin, family truth, and lost opportunities for attachment.

Developmental Pathways of Attachment-Prevention

Clinical observation suggests that CPA-PERA may arise through several overlapping pathways. One pathway involves concealment of parentage, in which the identity of a biological parent is deliberately withheld, and the child grows up believing that the parent abandoned the family, was unknown, or was uninterested. A second pathway involves relocation or structural separation, in which distance, obstruction of communication, or deliberate concealment gradually removes the parent from the child's developmental environment.

A third pathway involves parental abduction, in which one caregiver deliberately removes or retains the child in order to prevent the other parent from maintaining contact. Research on child abduction by a parent has documented longer-term effects that may include identity disturbance, unresolved grief, and later difficulty in family relationships (Greif & Hegar, 1993;

Finkelhor et al., 2002). A fourth pathway involves caregiving transfers through institutional or protective systems, including foster care, extended family arrangements, or separations associated with disability or mental health crises, where one parent remains alive but functionally inaccessible. These pathways are not mutually exclusive and may converge within the same developmental history.

Illustrative Case Example

An adult client in her late thirties presented for therapy after a routine medical consultation prompted questions about family health history. During the discussion, she disclosed a longstanding uncertainty regarding the identity of her biological father. Throughout childhood, she had been told that he had left before her birth and had no wish to be involved in her life.

In adulthood, an extended family member revealed that the father had attempted numerous times to establish contact shortly after the client's birth but had been told that the mother wished to raise the child alone. Communication between the parents ceased, and the client grew up believing that abandonment on her father's part had been voluntary. When she reconnected with her father later in life, she discovered that this was never the case and that he had always wanted to be in her life but hadn't been allowed to. The later discovery that the relationship may have been structurally prevented rather than freely relinquished produced intense grief, destabilised long-held beliefs about self-worth and family identity, and brought into focus the psychological reality of an attachment relationship that had never been allowed to begin.

The Right to Know One's Parentage

These clinical observations intersect with broader human rights principles concerning a child's right to know their parents and, where safe and appropriate, to maintain contact with them. The United Nations Convention on the Rights of the Child recognises the child's right to know and be cared for by their parents wherever possible and emphasises the preservation of identity, including family relations (United Nations, 1989, Articles 7–8). The Convention on the Rights of Persons with Disabilities also affirms the rights of people with disabilities to family life and parenthood without discrimination (United Nations, 2006).

Accurate knowledge of biological parentage may also be important for healthcare, particularly where family medical history informs hereditary risk assessment and preventive decision-making. Adult survivors who later discover that essential information about their parentage was withheld frequently report identity disruption, grief, and anger at being denied information about who they came from, their family history, inherited traits, medical background, cultural belonging, and their own sense of self.

Developmental Pathways of Relational Trauma in the HQTP

Note: CPA-PA = *child psychological abuse in the context of parental alienation.*

CPA-PAA = *child psychological abuse in the context of parental alienation and abduction.*

CPA-PERA = *child psychological abuse in the context of parental estrangement, relocation, or abduction.*

Specific Phobia–CPA-PAA Anxiety Variant = *Specific Phobia–Child Psychological Abuse in the Context of Parental Alienation and Abduction Anxiety Variant.*

The HQTP recognises two primary developmental pathways through which relational trauma involving a biological parent may occur: attachment distortion and attachment prevention. The attachment-prevention pathway became more visible through anomalous findings in the author's doctoral research and was subsequently clarified through clinical observation. CPA-PA describes the progressive distortion of an existing attachment relationship. CPA-PAA refers to a severe CPA-PA subpresentation in which abduction, concealment, forced relocation, or related conditions intensify attachment disruption, identity instability, and developmental trauma. CPA-PERA describes the prevention of attachment formation through concealment, relocation, abduction, or related forms of relational obstruction. The Specific Phobia–CPA-PAA Anxiety Variant refers to a fear-organised subgroup presentation within some severe CPA-PAA cases, in which the child's response to the targeted parent or to contact-related cues becomes organised primarily around conditioned threat. Although these pathways and presentations differ developmentally, each may contribute to enduring identity disruption, relational grief, and narrative fragmentation that become clinically visible in adulthood.

Adult Survivor Presentations Across CPA-PA, CPA-PAA, CPA-PERA, and the Specific Phobia–CPA-PAA Anxiety Variant

CPA-PA

CPA-PA refers to the progressive distortion of an existing attachment relationship through coercive control, denigration, loyalty pressure, narrative regulation, and suppression of independent thought and feeling. In adulthood, survivors may present with identity fragmentation, unresolved loyalty conflict, shame regarding past rejection of the targeted parent, developmental grief, relational distrust, and difficulty trusting their own perceptions and relational judgement. Within the HQTP, the clinical focus is on reconstructing distorted attachment meaning, differentiating from coercive loyalty systems, supporting identity repair, and integrating grief (Herman, 1992; Price-Tobler, 2023a; van der Kolk, 2014).

CPA-PAA

CPA-PAA refers to attachment distortion intensified by parental abduction, concealment, forced relocation, or related conditions of heightened threat and instability. In severe early-childhood cases, especially where abduction occurred before the age of eight, shared delusional dynamics (SDD), factitious disorder imposed on another (FDIOA), and related coercive conditions may further disrupt attachment, identity formation, and threat appraisal.

In adulthood, survivors may present with severe developmental disruption, fear-linked attachment disturbance, narrative capture, traumatic identity instability, prolonged grief, and marked difficulty integrating family history, selfhood, and relational safety. Within the HQTP, the clinical emphasis is on careful pacing, trauma-informed developmental reconstruction, regulation of abduction-related activation, identity stabilisation, and structured grief work (Greif & Hegar, 1993; Price-Tobler, 2023a).

CPA-PERA

CPA-PERA refers to the prevention of attachment formation with a living biological (now estranged) parent through concealment of parentage, obstructed communication, relocation, abduction, or early caregiving arrangements that prevent meaningful relational access. In adulthood, survivors may present with autobiographical uncertainty, unresolved grief for a relationship that was never permitted to develop, confusion regarding family origin and belonging, identity disruption and anger about being lied to.

Later, survivors may search for their estranged parent to resolve unanswered questions about origin, attachment, and selfhood. They may also be very angry with their alienating parent and begin demanding answers. Others may cut off all contact with the alienating parent due to feelings of grief, anger, betrayal, and identity confusion. Within the HQTP, the clinical focus is on reconstructing obscured developmental history, mourning prevented attachment opportunity, clarifying family narrative, and addressing identity disturbance associated with attachment-prevention (Barn & Mansuri, 2019; Campbell et al., 1991; Price-Tobler, 2023a; Sants, 1964).

Clinical Implications for Adult Survivor Treatment

Within the HQTP, recognition of CPA-PERA is important when working with adult survivors who present with identity confusion, unresolved grief, fragmented family narrative, or persistent questions about origin and belonging. These survivors may not initially conceptualise their histories through a CPA-PA lens; they may have been exposed to mild to severe alienation narratives about their estranged parent if they started to ask questions about them. Survivors are likely to present for treatment when the developmental consequences of attachment-prevention, narrative concealment, and restricted access to deliberately estranged family truth may become clinically visible later in life. Therapeutic work may then move into structured mourning for the lost opportunity for attachment, including grief for the parent, extended family, corrected family narratives, and a version of self that might have developed under different conditions. Within the HQTP, these tasks are particularly relevant to Phase II and Phase III in the later chapters, where identity reconstruction and developmental grief repair are undertaken in a stabilising, capacity-led manner.

However, CPA-PERA must be distinguished from severe CPA-PAA presentations in which the child had already formed a loving attachment relationship with the targeted parent prior to abduction. In these cases, the developmental injury does not arise from the prevention of attachment formation but from the disruption, capture, and fear conditioning of an existing bond under conditions of concealment, coercion, and threat. Within the author's doctoral survivor findings, four of the ten survivors described developing a distinct fear-organised presentation before age 8 that warrants separate clinical consideration due to its implications for formulation, pacing, and treatment safety (Price-Tobler, 2023a).

Specific Phobia–CPA-PAA Anxiety Variant, formerly described in the doctoral study as the SP-SPAAA Variant

In the doctoral study, this pattern was termed the Specific Phobia–Severe Parental Alienation and Abduction Anxiety Variant (SP-SPAAA Variant). Within the present protocol, the terminology has been revised to Specific Phobia–Child Psychological Abuse in the Context of Parental Alienation and Abduction Anxiety Variant (Specific Phobia–CPA-PAA Anxiety Variant) so that the construct aligns with the HQTP's updated abuse-based language while preserving continuity with the original observation.

This emerging variant refers to a developmental pattern in which prolonged coercion, attachment instability, concealment, relocation, or abduction-related circumstances organise the child's response to the targeted parent around conditioned fear rather than evaluative rejection alone. Under such conditions, reminders of the targeted parent, anticipated contact, or environments associated with that parent may evoke autonomic activation, avoidance, defensive hostility, or phobic panic-like distress. The clinical significance of the variant lies in the fact that the behaviour that appears rejecting may, in fact, reflect a perceived threat within a fear-conditioned attachment system.

For some adult survivors, these patterns persist into adulthood as developmental imprints. In adulthood, the variant is rarely recognised by survivors or clinicians as a formal label, as it is an emerging idea from within the research data. Instead, it may appear as patterned activation when contact is mentioned, family records are reviewed, therapy approaches abduction-related material, or the survivor contemplates renewed relational movement. Survivors may describe knowing cognitively that the targeted parent is not presently unsafe while simultaneously experiencing involuntary somatic threat responses. This discrepancy is consistent with conditioned attachment–threat coupling established during sensitive developmental periods (Schore, 2012; Siegel, 2012; van der Kolk, 2014).

Recognition processes may intensify this activation. As survivors begin questioning imposed childhood narratives, repeated moves to different towns, changing of their name, encountering documentary evidence, or considering relational possibilities that were previously unthinkable, suppressed fear responses may become more visible.

Clinicians must understand that insight alone does not necessarily dissolve fear. Clinically, this means that avoidance, ambivalence, sudden narrative defence, withdrawal, dissociation, shutdown, premature departure from sessions, or intense agitation may require formulation as conditioned threat responding rather than simple resistance or lack of motivation.

Within the HQTP, the construct is presented as a conceptual clinical formulation derived from doctoral survivor data and applied clinical observation rather than as a formal diagnostic entity (Price-Tobler, 2023a). Its purpose is explanatory and clinically orienting: it assists clinicians in recognising a specific subgroup presentation, safely pacing treatment, and avoiding misreading fear-organised responses as autonomous preference. The author invites further empirical investigation, replication, and refinement as the evidence base develops.

Provisional Clinical Observation

The Specific Phobia–CPA-PAA Anxiety Variant is therefore presented as a provisional clinical observation rather than an established diagnostic classification. Its inclusion within the HQTP reflects an ethical responsibility to report an emergent pattern that may carry important implications for formulation, treatment pacing, and clinical safety. As this construct has not yet been widely validated, further replication studies and independent research are needed to examine its clinical utility and refine its application in therapeutic settings (Price-Tobler, 2023a).

Clinical significance of these distinctions

These distinctions are not intended to reduce adult survivors to fixed categories. Rather, they assist clinicians in identifying the dominant developmental mechanism shaping adult presentation, formulation, therapeutic pacing, and treatment emphasis within the HQTP. Attachment distortion, attachment prevention, and fear-conditioned responding do not carry identical developmental implications, and they should not be approached as though they require identical clinical pacing or matching therapeutic tasks (Price-Tobler, 2023a).

Author Recognition of the Pattern and Rationale for Further Investigation

The author further notes that this emerging subgroup presentation drew particular clinical attention because elements of the same fear-organised CPA-PAA pattern had also been recognised within the author's own sibling group following early abduction-related experiences. This personal recognition is not presented as evidence and does not replace the doctoral survivor data. Rather, it heightened the author's sensitivity to a recurrent configuration in which a child who had previously shared a loving attachment relationship with the targeted parent later developed avoidance, threat-linked activation, and fear-organised responses following abduction, concealment, coercive influence, and relational capture. Hearing this pattern, then independently described by adult survivors in the doctoral cohort, was therefore clinically striking. It suggested that what might otherwise have been dismissed as highly individual or anecdotal could instead represent an under-recognised subgroup presentation warranting closer investigation (Price-Tobler, 2023a).

Direct prospective research with very young children in such circumstances is also ethically and practically difficult. In Australia, there is no fixed age below which children cannot participate in research; rather, a child is a person under 18, and research involving children requires heightened ethical protections, including parental or guardian consent and, where possible, the child's assent, with maturity and decision-making capacity assessed case by case rather than by a single age threshold (National Health and Medical Research Council [NHMRC], 2025). In coercive, concealed, or abduction-related family systems, these ethical and practical constraints may make fear-organised presentations especially difficult to examine directly while they are occurring. For that reason, the retrospective description of this pattern by adult survivors was both unexpected and clinically important, and it contributed to the view that this presentation required further investigation rather than dismissal as an isolated anomaly (NHMRC, 2025; Price-Tobler, 2023a).

Associated Regulatory Adaptations

Adult survivors of CPA-PA and CPA-PAA frequently describe childhood relational environments organised around authority, narrative control, emotional dependency, and punishment for divergence. In such environments, behavioural compliance may be reinforced through overt and covert coercion, including intimidation, withdrawal of affection, humiliation, interrogation, and escalating consequences for curiosity about or attachment to the targeted parent (Hassan, 2015; Lifton, 1961; Price-Tobler, 2023a; Singer & Lalich, 2003). These dynamics help explain how outward alignment may coexist with inward attachment, grief, and fear, and why compliance in such contexts is better understood as a survival adaptation than as an authentic relational preference.

The fear-conditioned organisation described above rarely operates in isolation. The author posits that in some severe CPA-PAA histories, appeasement becomes a primary strategy for perceived safety. Alignment with the alienating caregiver may depend on monitoring mood, anticipating reactions, avoiding ambiguity, and maintaining narrative agreement. From a threat-physiology perspective, such responses can be understood within the broader survival repertoire of fight, flight, freeze, and appease, with freeze and appease often becoming more dominant where the child's autonomy is constrained (Porges, 2011; Walker, 2013).

Additionally, appeasement is not equivalent to genuine support. For example, adult survivors frequently describe having retained a secret private attachment, grief, confusion, or curiosity about their targeted parent while publicly performing alignment. They explained that this helps settle their distress, which may emerge when they face threats from their AP if they aren't seen as aligning with them. Construing one parent as wholly safe and the other as wholly dangerous can reduce internal conflict and facilitate rapid behavioural alignment in a coercive environment. When threat decreases, greater nuance may become possible; when threat rises, simplified narratives may re-emerge because they once served a protective function.

Silent grief is another common adaptation. Many survivors later recognise that they mourned not only the targeted parent, but also extended family, home, origin, continuity of identity, and the possibility of a different relational life, while lacking any safe conditions in which such grief could be expressed. This loss may remain internally active for years and contribute to adult presentations involving emptiness, depression, relational avoidance, somatic distress, identity confusion, and shame regarding past rejection of the targeted parent (Herman, 1992; van der Kolk, 2014).

Clinical Implications for Assessment and Formulation

Recognition of the Specific Phobia–CPA-PAA Anxiety Variant and its associated adaptations is clinically important because responses that appear fixed, rejecting, avoidant, resistant, or contact-phobic may reflect conditioned threat activation within a disrupted attachment system rather than autonomous relational judgement (Bowlby, 1969; Herman, 1992; Childress, 2015). Direct challenges to entrenched narratives, pressure for immediate disclosure, or premature encouragement of contact may intensify arousal and reinforce defensive organisation.

Assessment, therefore, attends to markers of fear-organised responding, including physiological activation when the targeted parent is discussed, anticipatory anxiety, rapid alignment under perceived threat, dissociation, shutdown, intolerance of ambiguity, sudden withdrawal from therapy, or language organised more around danger expectation than relational meaning. Silence, compliance, apparent certainty, or the ability to speak fluently about imposed family narratives should not be taken as evidence of the absence of conditioning.

Treatment within the HQTP prioritises safety, predictability, emotional regulation, and gradual differentiation between historical threat prediction and present-context reality. Across phases, clinicians treat activation as meaningful data about developmental learning rather than as evidence of unwillingness. Memory work, reinterpretation, or any consideration of relational action is carefully titrated and undertaken only when the survivor's identity stability and regulatory capacity are sufficient to tolerate it.

For example, some survivors may become increasingly able to observe activation without immediate behavioural reorganisation when pacing is aligned; over time, corrective relational experience may permit threat prediction to soften (Bouton, 2004; Porges, 2011). However, the possibility of such therapeutic progress depends on these developmental injuries being accurately recognised in adulthood. Across both survivor and practitioner findings, this has not occurred consistently; attachment disruption, fear-organised responding, developmental grief, and identity disturbance were often insufficiently conceptualised within prevailing trauma-informed frameworks, contributing to delayed recognition and treatment misalignment (Price-Tobler, 2023a, 2023b). The following chapter, therefore, turns to the recognition and treatment gap affecting adult survivors of CPA-PA.

Chapter Two

The Recognition and Treatment Gap for Adult Survivors of CPA-PA

Adult survivors of abuse in contexts of CPA-PA remain insufficiently recognised within contemporary trauma frameworks. Despite increasing scholarly attention to 'parental alienation' within child-focused custody and intervention literature, comparatively little research has examined the long-term developmental trajectory of individuals who reach adulthood following sustained exposure to coercive caregiving, attachment disruption, psychological enmeshment, and, in some cases, abduction. Consequently, adult survivors of CPA-PA are rarely conceptualised within trauma-informed paradigms as individuals who may present with complex developmental trauma rooted in child maltreatment.

Findings from both survivors and MHP cohorts in the associated twin-PhD study revealed a consistent recognition gap. Survivors described prolonged misrecognition within mental health systems, including diagnostic misattribution, minimisation of coercive abuse dynamics, and treatment approaches that failed to address attachment injury and developmental captivity.

MHPs, in turn, reported minimal formal education in identifying CPA-PA as a form of child abuse and expressed uncertainty regarding conceptualisation and intervention. This absence of specialist education has significant clinical implications. MHPs treating adult survivors may find themselves uncertain about how to structure treatment for layered trauma presentations emerging from prolonged alienation dynamics. In addition, practitioners working with this population may experience vicarious, social-emotional, and neurobiological strain when exposed to chronic relational trauma narratives (Garber, 2004).

Consistent with broader findings in trauma psychology, relatively few practitioners receive specialised training in complex developmental trauma frameworks specific to coercive caregiving systems (Cook et al., 2011). The absence of structured supervision and trauma-specific formulation models contributes to variability in assessment, intervention timing, and diagnostic attribution.

Attachment Disruption and Developmental Sequelae

Developmental research consistently demonstrates that early relational environments shape internal working models that guide subsequent interpersonal functioning (Critchfield & Benjamin, 2008). When caregiving systems are organised around coercion, role reversal, ideological control, or chronic denigration of a targeted parent, children may internalise relational blueprints organised around insecurity, vigilance, and divided loyalty.

In severe cases, survivors later describe experiences consistent with developmental captivity, characterised by restricted relational exposure, enforced loyalty alignment, suppression of independent identity formation, and prolonged narrative control by the alienating parent. Such conditions may disrupt autobiographical coherence and identity consolidation during critical developmental periods.

Adults who have grown up within child maltreatment environments frequently enter adulthood without the secure attachment scaffolding, emotional validation, and developmental nurturance required for adaptive functioning (Ellis et al., 2019). Additionally, in some cases, affect regulation difficulties, relational volatility, and identity diffusion reflect trauma-adaptive survival strategies rather than enduring personality pathology.

Some of the MHPs from Study 2 argued that behaviours characteristic of SPA align with definitions of child psychological abuse. Child abuse is widely recognised as a significant public health concern and a predictor of adult psychopathology (Saini et al., 2019). The DSM-5 defines child psychological abuse as non-accidental acts by a caregiver that result in, or have the potential to result in, significant psychological harm (American Psychiatric Association, 2013). Nevertheless, CPA-PA is not consistently conceptualised within trauma-informed diagnostic formulations.

Limitations of the Existing Clinical Literature

Early qualitative work documenting the experiences of adult children exposed to parental alienation provided important initial insight into the long-term relational and psychological consequences of these dynamics. These studies were instrumental in bringing visibility to the enduring impact of alienation processes beyond childhood.

However, the primary orientation of this body of work has been descriptive and exploratory and has not sought to provide a structured, phase-informed treatment framework for complex trauma integration in adulthood. As such, while foundational, it leaves open the clinical question of how best to conceptualise and treat survivors presenting with cumulative developmental trauma associated with severe and prolonged CPA-PA.

Subsequent scholarship has largely focused on assessment and intervention strategies for children affected by parental alienation (Harman et al., 2019). These contributions are clinically valuable; however, they do not fully address adult sequelae or the therapeutic complexities encountered decades after exposure.

Related contributions have also provided practical guidance for targeted parents and clinicians working with alienated children, particularly regarding strategies to restore disrupted parent–child relationships and support reunification processes within families. While such work offers important insights into intervention during childhood, its emphasis remains on family restoration rather than the clinical treatment of adult survivors presenting with complex developmental trauma associated with CPA-PA.

Complex Trauma and Lifespan Impact

The long-term consequences of childhood maltreatment are well documented. Adults exposed to cumulative childhood trauma demonstrate increased vulnerability to depressive disorders, post-traumatic stress disorder, anxiety disorders, substance use disorders, dissociation, and personality disturbance (Courtois & Ford, 2009; Green et al., 2010;

McLaughlin et al., 2010; Cook et al., 2011). Adverse childhood experiences are also associated with significant physical health outcomes in adulthood, including cardiovascular disease, chronic lung disease, liver disease, and cancer (Felitti et al., 1998).

Survivor-focused research specific to parental alienation has identified recurrent themes of low self-esteem, relational distrust, depressive symptomatology, and intergenerational relational strain (Baker, 2007). Broader trauma literature further suggests that survivors of prolonged relational coercion may demonstrate heightened vulnerability to revictimisation and relational instability (Herman, 1992). These findings align with established trauma models demonstrating that repeated exposure to coercive relational environments disrupts identity development, autobiographical memory integration, and attachment security.

The Treatment Gap and the Need for a Structured Framework

Despite documentation of psychological harm associated with what the literature commonly describes as parental alienation in childhood, research examining structured therapeutic intervention for adult survivors remains limited. Within this protocol, these presentations are conceptualised through the author's clinical term child psychological abuse in the context of parental alienation (CPA-PA), which is used to foreground the abuse-based, developmental, attachment-related, and coercive-control dimensions of the harm. Existing studies describe long-term sequelae, but they do not provide a unified, phase-based clinical architecture for treating adult survivors.

Given this treatment gap, the present work situates CPA-PA within broader trauma science and introduces a structured, attachment-informed framework for clinical intervention. The cumulative exposure to coercion, relational distortion, identity suppression, developmental grief, and, in some cases, abduction requires careful phase sequencing to reduce the risk of destabilisation and support developmental repair. The HQTP was developed in response to this gap and is detailed in the chapters that follow.

Researcher Positionality and Rationale

As noted earlier, the author's positionality is grounded in academic higher-degree research, lived experience, and extensive professional clinical practice in private practice and in mental health units, including therapeutic work with survivors, alienating parents, and targeted parents. Methodological safeguards implemented to mitigate bias and ensure rigour are detailed in Chapter Four. The twin-cohort study was designed in response to an observed absence of specialist education and structured clinical frameworks addressing CPA-PA within the mental health field. Doctoral findings from Study 2 reported that some of the MHPs lacked training in recognising and treating CPA-PA presentations.

This knowledge gap has implications for therapeutic outcomes and for broader systems in which alienation dynamics arise. Alongside academic research and clinical investigation, survivor-led initiatives have also emerged to acknowledge the lived experience of individuals affected by CPA-PA. In response to this gap, survivor-led initiatives have become increasingly important in bringing experiential knowledge into public, professional, and research conversations that have historically been shaped without sufficient inclusion of adult survivors.

Thrivers Speak® NAUWOU Conference, 2024

The Thrivers Speak® NAUWOU Survivor Initiative Conference was held on October 11th and 12th in 2024. This conference emerged to amplify the voices of adult survivors affected by child psychological abuse within CPA-PA contexts (Price-Tobler & McCarty, 2024; Thrivers Speak, 2024). The emergence of such initiatives reflects a broader movement towards survivor-informed practice, recognising lived experience as a significant source of knowledge in the development of ethical clinical frameworks for complex developmental trauma associated with these forms of child psychological abuse.

Participation required speakers to identify publicly as survivors, reflecting the disability-rights principle "Nothing About Us Without Us", which emphasises the ethical importance of including affected individuals in research, advocacy, policy, and professional discourse concerning their own lives and experiences (Charlton, 1998). Within the Thrivers Speak® initiative, this principle was applied to the field of child psychological abuse so that adult survivors were not positioned merely as subjects of research but as active contributors to knowledge development, advocacy, and professional dialogue.

As reflected in the conference presentations, many speakers described feeling profoundly left out of the very professional, legal, and research conversations that sought to define or respond to their experiences. The decision to organise and speak at a survivor-led conference therefore arose not only from advocacy, but from the need to create a dedicated space in which adult survivors could speak for themselves, contribute knowledge derived from lived experience, and address the longstanding absence of survivor voice within public and professional discourse surrounding these forms of child psychological abuse (Price-Tobler & McCarty, 2024; Thrivers Speak, 2024). In this sense, the conference functioned not simply as a speaking event, but as a corrective to epistemic exclusion.

The inclusion of survivor perspectives in the development of clinical knowledge is consistent with developments in related fields. Scholarship on psychological trauma has shown that survivor advocacy has played an important role in shaping contemporary understandings of trauma and recovery (Herman, 1992). Within the present framework, survivor-informed contributions assist in identifying patterns of relational harm, identity disruption, coercive control, and long-term developmental consequences that may not yet be fully recognised within existing clinical and research literature.

The conference included contributions from co-founders Dawn McCarty and the author, as well as Former White House Master Chef Martin Mongiello, Patty Freudenberg, Karen Whelan, Jeff Irmie, Dana Laquidara, Andrew Folkler, Ashlynn Lerner, Ginger Gentile, Rachael Roberts, Brandie Rolark, Dr Stan Korosi, Dr Rebecca Bailey, and Scott Berne, among others

(Thrivers Speak, 2024). Collectively, the speakers represented more than 700 years of lived experience of CPA-PA and CPA-PAA, bringing substantial survivor knowledge to a field in which adult survivor perspectives have often remained under-recognised (Thrivers Speak, 2024). Several speakers, including Scott Berne and Dawn McCarty, also generously shared their lived experiences involving both parental alienation and abduction dynamics. Dr Craig Childress, an internationally recognised clinical psychologist whose work focuses on attachment-based formulations of pathogenic parenting, participated as an invited professional ally and expert rather than as a survivor.

The conference was organised as an international, survivor-led initiative and proceeded without institutional sponsorship or financial backing. It was independently funded by the organisers, Dawn McCarty and the author, and speakers participated voluntarily and without financial compensation, contributing their time and lived experience to advance professional and public understanding of CPA-PA. Although invitations for sponsorship were circulated within professional networks associated with the parental alienation field, no organisations or institutional bodies elected to provide financial or logistical support.

Disappointingly, this absence of institutional engagement reflects a broader pattern in which the voices and lived experiences of adult survivors have historically been underrepresented within professional forums addressing child psychological abuse, where discussion has more often been dominated by legal professionals, clinicians, or affected parents. In this context, the 2024 Thrivers Speak NAUWOU Conference represented a significant shift towards survivor-informed dialogue, and, to the author's knowledge, the first international conference specifically centred on the voices of adult survivors of CPA.

The event therefore put the principle "Nothing About Us, Without Us" into practice, recognising lived experience as an essential source of knowledge for research development, professional education, and the refinement of treatment frameworks that address CPA dynamics (Thrivers Speak, 2024). The conference was also notable for proceeding as scheduled despite significant disruption from Hurricane Milton, reflecting the determination of the organisers and participants to ensure survivor voices were heard. Free recordings of the inaugural conference presentations and survivor testimonies are publicly available on the author's YouTube channel.

Free recordings of the inaugural conference's presentations and survivor testimonies are publicly available on the author's YouTube channel at: https://www.youtube.com/channel/UCiN_DxTEdbOpGZNB3Bo3ndQ/videos.

The Thrivers Speak® Awareness Ribbon

The Thrivers Speak® awareness ribbon was co-created by the author and survivor advocate Dawn McCarty as a visual symbol representing adult survivors affected by CPA-PA. The ribbon incorporates a set of wings surrounding the central awareness loop. These wings symbolically honour survivors whose lives have been lost or whose whereabouts remain unknown. They represent children who have been abducted and remain missing, children and adults who have died in the context of familicide or homicide within high-conflict family systems, and survivors who later died by suicide following prolonged exposure to CPA-PA.

Within the survivor community, these individuals are remembered as those whose lives were profoundly shaped by alienation-related harm and whose absence continues to be held in the hearts and minds of families, practitioners, and fellow survivors. The wings, therefore, function both as a memorial symbol and as a reminder of the enduring human cost associated with child psychological abuse and related alienation dynamics.

The ribbon colours intentionally move beyond traditional gendered colour conventions. Rather than representing only boys and girls through binary colour associations, the design incorporates multiple tones to reflect the diversity of individuals affected by CPA. The colours, therefore, symbolise inclusivity across the gender spectrum, acknowledging that survivors may identify as male, female, nonbinary, transgender, lesbian, gay, bisexual, queer, intersex, asexual, Two-Spirit, or otherwise gender diverse. By moving beyond binary colour symbolism, the ribbon recognises that the experience of all CPA dynamics is not confined to any single gender or identity group but affects individuals across the full spectrum of human diversity.

Many adult survivors must confront layers of ambiguous loss associated with disrupted attachment bonds, lost childhoods, fractured family relationships, and, in some cases, the deaths or disappearances of other survivors affected by CPA dynamics. Public acknowledgement of these losses through survivor symbols can therefore support processes of collective witnessing and meaning-making that accompany trauma integration and grief repair (Boss, 1999; Herman, 1992).

The development of survivor symbols and awareness ribbons is consistent with broader practices through which trauma-affected communities acknowledge loss and recognise shared experiences of harm. Public symbols are frequently used to create spaces of remembrance and collective witnessing for individuals whose experiences may otherwise remain invisible. Within trauma scholarship, such symbolic practices are understood as mechanisms through which communities process collective trauma and support identity reconstruction following experiences of profound relational disruption (Alexander et al., 2004).

In this context, the Thrivers Speak ribbon serves not only as an awareness symbol but also as a shared marker of recognition for individuals whose lives have been profoundly affected by CPA. By visually acknowledging survivors, including those lost to familicide, homicide, suicide, or parental removal and relocation that prevents or obstructs the child's relationship with a parent, the ribbon creates a symbolic space in which grief, remembrance, and advocacy can coexist. This ribbon reflects a broader understanding that trauma recovery often occurs not only at the individual therapeutic level but also within communities that acknowledge and bear witness to shared experiences of harm and survival (Herman, 1992).

Additionally, the survivor testimonies and advocacy emerging through the Thrivers Speak initiative also reflect themes identified in the author's doctoral research examining adult survivors of severe CPA-PA.

The Thrivers Speak® Awareness Ribbon

Child Psychological Abuse Awareness Day

The Thrivers Speak initiative is also associated with Child Psychological Abuse Awareness Day, observed annually on 10 October, which coincides with broader global mental health recognition efforts. Within the Thrivers Speak movement, this date functions as a day of recognition, remembrance, and advocacy for survivors of parental alienation and related forms of child psychological abuse. Child Psychological Abuse Awareness Day was established through the Thrivers Speak initiative to provide a dedicated day of recognition for a form of child maltreatment that has historically received limited public acknowledgement within international awareness campaigns. The symbolic framework of the awareness ribbon, the establishment of Child Psychological Abuse Awareness Day, and the convening of the Thrivers Speak NAUWOU conference collectively represent efforts to ensure that the experiences of adult survivors of CPA dynamics are recognised within professional, research, and public discourse (Price-Tobler & McCarty, 2024; Thrivers Speak, 2024).

The Adverse Childhood Experiences (ACE) Study

The associated PhD research findings shed light on the long-lasting effects of such adverse experiences on individuals, reinforcing the importance of understanding how childhood experiences affect overall wellbeing. Speaking to this issue, the Adverse Childhood Experiences Study (ACES), conducted by Kaiser Permanente Health Maintenance Organisation and the Centres for Disease Control and Prevention, was conducted between 1996 and 1997 (Centres for Disease Control and Prevention, 2020).

The ACE Study is the leading ongoing investigation into the link between childhood maltreatment and adult health, using data collected from over 17,000 participants. Two waves of data collection surveyed people in Southern California. The participants completed confidential surveys on their childhood experiences, current health status, and associated behaviours (Centres for Disease Control and Prevention, 2020). The ACE Study found that developmental risk factors for disease are related to wellbeing throughout the life course (Centres for Disease Control and Prevention, 2020). In addition, the "Family Health History and Health Appraisal" questionnaires collated data on child abuse and neglect, household challenges such as divorce and separation, and other relevant socio-behavioural factors (Centres for Disease Control and Prevention, 2020).

The study reports that "negative experiences in childhood and the teenage years may put children at risk for chronic health problems, mental illness, and substance use in adulthood" (Centres for Disease Control and Prevention, 2020, p. 1). The lasting effects on adults who have higher ACEs scores include suicide, lower job opportunities, and a wide range of chronic diseases, including heart disease, cancer, and diabetes (Centres for Disease Control and Prevention, 2020). Furthermore, sexually transmitted diseases, pregnancy complications, foetal death, maternal and child health problems, risk of injury and sex trafficking are potential consequences (Centers for Disease Control and Prevention, 2020).

In addition, children exposed to toxic stress may have difficulty forming stable, healthy relationships as adults and struggle with finances, depression, and job unpredictability (Centers for Disease Control and Prevention, 2020). An important fact to consider regarding the ACES is that it was conducted over 20 years ago with people born from the 1930s to the 1950s, and divorce was rare and heavily stigmatised.

The ACEs measure ten different types of childhood trauma. The first five are listed as personal: "physical abuse, verbal abuse, sexual abuse, physical neglect, and emotional neglect. Five are related to other family members: a parent who's an alcoholic, a mother who's a victim of domestic violence, a family member in jail, a family member diagnosed with a mental illness, and experiencing the divorce of parents" (ACES Too High News, 2020, p. 1). For every trauma a person identifies with, they receive 1 point. Note: the above web reference 'ACES Too High' was used as a link to the same information previously available on the Centres for Disease Control and Prevention website, which has not been updated for a few months.

ACE Study Scores 4-10

The study findings showed that 87% of participants scored above 1 point, representing two-thirds of participants. A noteworthy observation was that an ACE score exceeding 4 indicates a greater level of trauma and severity, which practitioners should note. Such a score corresponds to a 390% increase in the probability of developing chronic pulmonary disease. Additionally, there is a heightened probability of developing hepatitis at 240%, experiencing depression at a 460% higher risk, and attempting suicide with a concerning 1,220% likelihood (ACES Too High News, 2020). See Appendix One ACE Study Questions in Volume One.

The author further emphasises the importance of incorporating adverse childhood experiences (ACEs) and recognising complex intersecting traumas (CITs) when providing therapeutic support to survivors. Before proceeding further with the HQTP framework, the discussion briefly returns to key concepts identified in the author's doctoral research, as these findings provide the empirical and conceptual foundation for the protocol's subsequent clinical development. These concepts are important because they identify the principal harms described by survivors, the area's most frequently unrecognised within practice, and the gaps in professional understanding that informed the development and phased structure of the HQTP. Returning to the previous terms helps to clarify why the protocol was needed and preserves the link between the doctoral findings and the clinical framework that followed. In the following section, the original study language is retained where necessary to preserve fidelity to the doctoral findings and the terminology used at that time.

Key Concepts: Attachment and Abandonment

Among the survivor cohort, prominent concepts included attachment disruption, abandonment, complex trauma, lack of recognition, and the enduring harm carried into adulthood. Among the practitioner cohort, a key finding was that severe parental alienation (SPA), as defined within the doctoral study, was frequently not recognised as a form of complex trauma, largely because of insufficient education, limited professional training, and the absence of an established clinical framework.

Attachment

Attachment theory posits that the quality of early parent-child interactions shapes a child's capacity to regulate emotions, integrate a sense of self, and develop secure relationships in later life (Bowlby, 1982). Attachment also refers to the condition and calibre of an individual's emotional connection with a significant other (Bowlby, 1980). In parent-child relationships, a healthy attachment necessitates warmth, empathy, and consistent engagement to facilitate the child's optimal development (Bowlby, 1988). Attachment behaviour encompasses actions undertaken to establish and maintain proximity to another person perceived as more adept at navigating the world (Bowlby, 1988).

Children exposed to parental alienating behaviours may develop attachment patterns shaped by conditional acceptance, loyalty demands, and fear of relational rupture (Harman et al., 2019). When the child's relationship with the targeted parent becomes restricted, delegitimised, or psychologically unsafe to maintain, the attachment system reorganises around the available caregiver.

This reorganisation does not necessarily reflect preference but adaptive necessity. The child may orient toward the alienating parent as the primary attachment figure in order to preserve relational stability. Attachment behaviours may therefore become organised around proximity maintenance, monitoring, and compliance, reflecting attempts to prevent loss of the remaining attachment relationship. Such patterns are consistent with attachment responses observed in contexts of relational threat, conditional caregiving, and coercive family environments (Harman et al., 2019).

In addressing the developmental impacts of childhood trauma, including severe parental alienation, clinicians must consider the relational contexts that shape attachment organisation. Attachment patterns emerge within caregiving systems and may reflect intergenerational relational processes. Examination of parental attachment histories, caregiving behaviours, and relational functioning can therefore provide clinically relevant context for understanding how the child's attachment system adapts within alienating family environments (Harman et al., 2019).

In addition to attachment styles, MHPs will also need to explore the potential impacts of abandonment, which has been documented as a prevalent issue among survivors of childhood trauma. For instance, in Baker's (2007) study, two adult children shared their experiences of abandonment, as explained in the following section.

Abandonment

The two adult children in Baker's (2007) study explained their stories of abandonment and how they felt it had stemmed from PA. The first "adult child" explained, "I had intense abandonment issues and fears of intimacy. I doubted my mother's love and felt rejected by my biological father, believing he despised me" (Baker, 2007, p. 246). The second "adult child" explained, "As a result of a significant emotional experience during my youth, I struggle with finding stability. With 12 years in Alcoholics Anonymous, I am convinced that I have grappled with the effects of abandonment and severe emotional and mental disorders" (Baker, 2007, p. 310).

Baker (2007) reports that APs use the threat of abandonment as fuel to convince children of PA that the TP has never loved them and sow seeds of doubt about the TP's parenting skills and commitment to the relationship with the child. Along with the threat of abandonment, these children may have also been threatened with mutilation or, ultimately, death. The detrimental consequences arising from complex trauma resulting from ongoing threats can manifest as distressing and overt expressions of emotional abuse, characterised by repetitive and cumulative occurrences within a specific relationship over an extended period (Courtois, 2004, p. 412).

Previous research reports that PA and its associated complex trauma may negatively impact children and adolescent PA survivors' mental health through expressions of guilt, depressed mood, low self-esteem, lack of self-confidence, and distress and frustration. This negative impact can lead to substance abuse, delinquent behaviour, separation anxiety, suicidal ideation, suicide attempts, sleep and eating disorders, educational difficulties, hypochondria, psychosomatic illness, encopresis, enuresis, and fears and phobias (Sher, 2017), especially when there is a family breakdown leading to divorce.

Children's lives are intrinsically linked to their families, caregivers, and parents. When a divorce occurs, the family's transition affects children both directly and indirectly. Multiple aspects of the child's life can be impacted by divorce, particularly when the changes become challenging and overwhelming. Key impact themes that children of divorce may face include changes in relocation, financial circumstances, changes in their roles and social life, changes in education and career development and experiencing complex emotional loss states (Das, 2016). Garber (2004) reports that the children of highly opposed caregivers are among those most in need of psychotherapeutic assistance and are also the most difficult to assist in the psychotherapeutic process.

Behavioural Impairments of Severely Alienated Children

Psychologist and author Dr Richard Warshak (2013) describes the behavioural impairments of severely alienated children that adult survivors may have experienced during childhood. Warshak (2013) explains that children who have been severely alienated will treat the TP with extreme hostility, defiance, disobedience, and withdrawal. They may resist and reject contact, threaten and perpetrate violence and vandalise and steal property. One example from Warshak's (2013) experience with a young, severely alienated child in Court reports, "A boy told the custody evaluator that he would like to give his father a hard kick between the legs, kill him in his sleep, and have him die a horrible death". This level of venom is characteristic of children at the severe end of the PA continuum (Warshak, 2013).

Descriptions of SPA present the child's behaviour as markedly context dependent. Such children may appear well-behaved with most adults, yet respond to the targeted parent with intense hostility, rejection, contempt, or defiance. In some cases, this hostility may also extend to individuals, animals, objects, or professionals associated with the targeted parent, a pattern described as "hatred by association" (Warshak, 2013).

By contrast, physically abused children are more often described as fearful of the abusive parent and may respond with compliance, deference, or appeasement to avoid further harm. In this literature, children described as severely alienated do not typically direct open disrespect or defiance towards the alienating parent; instead, they tend to show rigid and often unquestioning support for that parent's position whenever parental conflict arises, sometimes including statements against the targeted parent in court or advocacy on behalf of the alienating parent during litigation (Warshak, 2013).

Children who have experienced SPA also learn to "curry favour" with the AP by echoing their parents' complaints about the TP (Warshak, 2013). They quickly learn that the AP may become displeased if they show affection or form a connection with the TP. They may also refer to the TP by their first name or a name of derision, in addition to "mum" or "dad" (Warshak, 2013). Although many onlookers will see clearly that the child has been strongly influenced against the TP by the AP, the child of SPA will never agree to such an influence. Often, the child will blame the TP and relatives for provoking hatred toward them, while offering only vague reasons for rejecting their other parent (Baker, 2007). As these children grow into adult survivors, repeated exposure to multiple forms of childhood trauma may contribute to significant behavioural and health difficulties (Courtois & Ford, 2009; Kilpatrick et al., 2003).

Physiological Sequelae and Immune Vulnerability

While the psychological impacts of abuse are more readily recognised in mental health contexts, survivors may also present with significant physical health concerns that are often managed separately from trauma-informed care. In practice, this separation can leave important aspects of the survivor's lived experience unrecognised. Prolonged developmental stress exposure may affect emotional regulation, bodily awareness, health-related meaning-making, and the survivor's capacity to engage consistently with both psychological and medical care.

Within the associated PhD study, adult survivors of child psychological abuse, together with MHPs working with this cohort, reported diagnoses of autoimmune conditions, including lupus, rheumatoid arthritis, and Hashimoto's thyroiditis, alongside serious physical illnesses, including cancer histories. These observations require careful positioning. They are not presented as causal claims or as evidence that CPA-PA, CPA-PAA, CPA-PERA, familial abduction, or estrangement directly cause autoimmune disease, cancer, or any other medical condition. Rather, they are convergent survivor- and practitioner-reported patterns that warrant careful clinical attention, interdisciplinary awareness, and further research.

A growing body of trauma and health literature reports associations between childhood maltreatment, chronic stress exposure, inflammatory processes, immune dysregulation, and later adverse health outcomes (Danese et al., 2007; Dube et al., 2009). Within the HQTP, this literature is used cautiously. It does not establish disease causation in this survivor cohort, nor does it authorise clinicians to interpret physical illness as psychologically caused. It does, however, support the need for trauma-informed developmental history-taking, appropriate medical referral, and careful collaboration when survivors present with autoimmune conditions, serious illness, somatic distress, health anxiety, or medically complex histories.

This integration is not simply a matter of clinical thoroughness. It is an ethical responsibility. Too often, survivors are asked about physical symptoms in one setting and mental health in another, with little cross-system conversation about how these domains may interact in the survivor's life. Clinicians working with adult survivors should therefore remain attentive to physical health concerns without exceeding their professional scope. The task is not to diagnose, explain, or medically interpret illness, but to recognise when medical concerns, trauma history, grief, dysregulation, and fear of bodily vulnerability are intersecting in ways that affect treatment pacing, safety, and care coordination.

The biopsychosocial model is widely referenced, but often poorly operationalised in practice. An integrative approach requires more than naming the theory. It requires cross-disciplinary collaboration, intake processes, careful referral pathways, and clinical education that recognises developmental trauma as potentially relevant to long-term health vulnerability without reducing illness to psychological causation.

Early recognition of survivor-reported physical health patterns may support improved mental health trajectories, referral planning, monitoring, and long-term care. At the same time, earlier recognition of possible immune-related illness, medical exhaustion, or health-related vulnerability among trauma survivors may strengthen collaboration and help clinicians respond without exceeding their scope.

The emotional benefit of timely, accurate medical recognition should also not be underestimated. When survivors feel seen physically and psychologically, they may be more able to trust providers, engage with treatment plans, and reclaim agency in recovery. This work, however, must be approached slowly and carefully. Survivors may present as anxious, overwhelmed, frightened by bodily symptoms, or medically exhausted, and rushed or fragmented care may increase withdrawal and disengagement. Later chapters examine participant-selected interventions that supported psychological stabilisation and survivor capacity to engage safely with broader systems of care.

Research Note: Survivor-Reported Physical Health Patterns

Across the doctoral survivor data, several participants reported significant physical health conditions, including autoimmune conditions, cancer histories, and other serious or chronic health concerns. In a preliminary exploratory mapping process, twenty-four survivor-reported conditions were identified as relevant to autoimmune, immune-related, or serious physical health categories. A further review of the medical literature indicated that a subset of these conditions has been discussed in relation to altered malignancy risk or broader immune-system dysregulation.

These observations are not presented as evidence of direct causation between CPA-PA and autoimmune disease, cancer, or any other medical diagnosis. The data were survivor-reported, observational, and exploratory. They were not collected through medical record verification, epidemiological design, or controlled comparison. Their significance lies in the pattern they raise for clinical attention and future research.

Within the HQTP, these findings are therefore treated as hypothesis-generating clinical observations. They support the need for careful physical health awareness, trauma-informed developmental history-taking, appropriate medical referral, and interdisciplinary collaboration where survivors present with serious illness, somatic distress, health anxiety, or medically complex histories.

Long-Term Impacts and Therapeutic Needs of Survivors

The author's twin study PhD research conducted at the University of the Sunshine Coast represents one of the most qualitative examinations of adult survivors of severe parental alienation and the clinicians who work with them. Across both survivor and practitioner cohorts, the findings consistently indicated that severe parental alienation was not a benign by-product of family conflict. Rather, it reflected a form of child psychological abuse associated with enduring developmental, relational, and identity-based consequences (Price-Tobler, 2023a,b).

Adult survivors described long-term emotional and psychological injury associated with being coerced to reject a safe and emotionally available parent during childhood. Common themes included chronic anxiety, depressive symptoms, identity fragmentation, attachment insecurity, unresolved complex grief, and a persistent sense of developmental loss. Many participants reported that they did not conceptualise their childhood experiences as abusive until adulthood, often following psychoeducation or therapeutic engagement. This delayed recognition reflects the normalisation processes that occur within alienating family systems, where psychological manipulation becomes embedded as "normal" family functioning.

A recurring theme across survivor narratives was enduring grief related to the erased parent-child relationship. Participants described longing for connection, unresolved attachment bonds, and emotional pain that persisted decades after physical separation had occurred. This grief was not episodic. It remained developmentally active, often re-emerging during life transitions such as parenthood, relationship formation, or identity consolidation.

Further findings from the author's doctoral practitioner study revealed a significant gap in professional preparedness. MHPs reported limited formal training in recognising parental alienation dynamics and minimal guidance regarding treatment planning for adult survivors. Standard trauma training was consistently described as insufficient for addressing the relational, developmental, and coercive control features associated with these presentations. The absence of established adult-focused treatment frameworks was identified as a major clinical vulnerability, increasing the risk of misdiagnosis, inappropriate therapeutic pacing, and retraumatisation.

A central contribution of the doctoral research was the identification of severity-linked symptom patterns in cases of extreme alienation. Survivors exposed to prolonged concealment, FDIOA presentations imposed by caregivers, forced separation, or abduction described heightened fear-based symptom clusters. In several cases, phobic reactions developed around institutions, medical systems, authority figures, or perceived threats of removal. These patterns reflect trauma responses shaped by prolonged coercive control rather than isolated traumatic incidents.

The doctoral research also identified survivor-reported physical health patterns that warrant further investigation. While these findings do not establish causation and were not derived from medical record verification or epidemiological comparison, survivor narratives included reports of autoimmune conditions, chronic illness, cancer histories, somatic distress, and stress-related health deterioration. These observations are consistent with broader trauma and adverse childhood experiences literature, which has reported associations between prolonged childhood adversity, physiological burden, inflammatory processes, immune dysregulation, and later adverse health outcomes. Within the HQTP, these findings are treated as exploratory and hypothesis-generating, supporting careful physical health awareness, appropriate referral, and collaboration rather than clinicians' medical conclusion-making.

Collectively, these findings reinforce the need to view CPA-PA through a developmental trauma lens rather than a conflict framework. Within the HQTP, such histories are situated within a broader child psychological abuse framework. Adult survivors are not presenting with isolated adjustment difficulties. They are presenting with complex trauma patterns shaped by prolonged identity disruption, attachment interference, loyalty conditioning, and psychological coercion.

Long-Term Psychological and Emotional Impact

Across the author's doctoral study and supporting peer-reviewed literature, adult survivors of CPA-PA consistently demonstrated trauma-related symptom profiles resembling those associated with other forms of chronic childhood psychological abuse. These impacts were not limited to emotional distress alone. They extended into identity formation, relational functioning, behavioural regulation, and self-concept.

A dominant clinical theme involved chronic anxiety, depressive symptoms, and trauma-related activation. Survivors frequently described hypervigilance, intrusive relational memories, emotional numbing, and physiological stress responses that persisted into adulthood. These symptoms were often misinterpreted as primary anxiety or mood disorders when the underlying developmental trauma history remained unrecognised.

Identity disruption represented another core injury. Survivors from the PhD cohort described how they were routinely exposed to narratives that vilified one parent and, by extension, half of their own identity was negatively affected. Over time, this produces internalised shame, self-rejection, and a fractured self-concept. Survivors described confusion about who they were, persistent feelings of unworthiness, and difficulty trusting their own perceptions or emotional experiences.

Maladaptive coping strategies also emerged as common sequelae. Some survivors described substance use, emotional avoidance, dissociation, or compulsive relational patterns as attempts to regulate unresolved distress. These behaviours are more accurately understood as survival adaptations developed in response to prolonged emotional threat rather than as evidence of character pathology.

Elevated suicidality risk was also identified within the author's sample, particularly during periods of delayed recognition or discovery. When survivors began to comprehend the magnitude of relational loss and developmental deprivation, emotional destabilisation intensified. This reinforces the need for careful clinical pacing and trauma-informed containment during psychoeducation and narrative reconstruction.

Emerging research has begun to examine CPA-PA in relation to adverse childhood experience frameworks, including its potential relevance to long-term mental health outcomes. This aligns with the author's findings that severe level CPA-PA may function as a chronic toxic stressor associated with enduring psychological and physiological vulnerability.

The convergence of survivor narratives, practitioner data, and emerging empirical literature supports a critical clinical conclusion. Adult survivors are not presenting with isolated adjustment difficulties. They are presenting with complex trauma patterns shaped by prolonged identity disruption, attachment interference, loyalty conditioning, and psychological coercion. Effective clinical work with this population, therefore, requires trauma-informed, attachment-aware, and developmentally grounded treatment approaches rather than symptom-focused intervention alone. Failure to recognise the underlying abuse dynamics risks perpetuating misdiagnosis, inappropriate therapeutic pacing, and further relational harm.

Before outlining the clinical response in detail, it is necessary to examine the environments in which these dynamics develop and are maintained, keeping in mind that these dynamics may still be active well into adulthood. The injuries described by adult survivors do not emerge in isolation. They are shaped by sustained exposure to relational control, dependency, institutional failures, and broader contextual pressures that structure daily life during childhood. Understanding these conditions is essential for accurate formulation and ethical intervention.

Parentification, Premature Adultification, and Infantilisation in Adult Survivors

Adult survivors of CPA-PA and associated contexts may later recognise that childhood role expectations were profoundly distorted. Some were required to function as emotional supporters, practical carers, household managers, or substitute companions and spouses for the alienating parent. In contrast, others were kept developmentally dependent, denied ordinary autonomy, and prevented from acquiring age-appropriate life skills. Within the present protocol, these patterns are recognised as involving parentification, premature adultification, and, in some cases, infantilisation. Although these processes may appear to be at odds, they may coexist within the same developmental environment: the child may be burdened with adult responsibilities while simultaneously being denied adult agency, independence, or permission to develop a separate self (Jurkovic, 1997; Chase, 1999; Hooper, 2007; Herman, 1992).

From a survivor perspective, parentification often involved chronic role reversal. Adult survivors may describe having been expected to absorb parental loneliness, regulate distress, carry legal or relational narratives, supervise siblings, or stabilise the emotional climate of the household. Some survivors of CPA-PA and CSA described being sexually abused or sexually exploited by the alienating parent in contexts where the parent used the child to meet their own sexual, emotional or regulatory needs. In the anomalous data from the survivor cohort, two male survivors stated: “My mother was gone, so how else was my father supposed to get his needs met?” The second male cohort survivor described his experience, stating, “I slept with my mother all the time, right up into adulthood, and even now she may ask me to sleep with her. I’m 43. And yes, we have sex when she wants it. I’ve never told my girlfriend. I'm too ashamed. At other times, it’s just normal for us.” (Price-Tobler, 2023a).

Instrumental parentification may be reflected in extensive domestic labour and caregiving tasks well beyond developmental capacity, whereas emotional parentification may be reflected in being treated as a confidant, counsellor, protector, or “best friend” to the caregiving parent (Jurkovic, 1997; Chase, 1999). In many CPA-PA and CPA-PAA histories, this burden was not occasional but chronic, leaving little room for play, rest, peer development, or ordinary dependency. As adults, survivors may continue to feel excessively responsible for others, unable to rest, anxious when not productive, or guilty when prioritising their own needs (Hooper, 2007; van der Kolk, 2014).

Premature adultification may overlap with parentification, but is broader in scope. Within the present protocol, the term is used to describe childhoods in which the survivor was exposed to adult burdens, adult knowledge, adult conflict, and adult responsibilities long before possessing the developmental capacity to manage them. Survivors may describe having had no real childhood because they were required to think, organise, suppress, anticipate, or perform like an adult from an early age. For example, one survivor described returning home from primary school with siblings to extensive lists of compulsory chores, including washing, cooking, rubbish removal, and bathroom cleaning, with long periods spent alone and severe punishment if the tasks were not completed. In adulthood, this survivor remained chronically anxious if the house was not perfectly clean, suggesting that hyper-responsibility and domestic vigilance had become deeply ingrained survival patterns rather than ordinary preferences

(Price-Tobler, 2023a). In such cases, what appears in adulthood as competence, perfectionism, or over-functioning may reflect developmental coercion rather than healthy maturity (Herman, 1992; Price-Tobler, 2023a).

A different but related pattern is infantilisation. Some adult survivors describe having been kept dependent, over-managed, and denied opportunities to learn basic life skills, make decisions, take age-appropriate risks, or function independently. In these environments, the alienating parent may do everything for the child while simultaneously inducing guilt, fear, or helplessness whenever autonomy begins to emerge. One survivor described a mother who did everything for him, taught him very little, and positioned him as her companion and reason to live. Attempts to lead an ordinary adult life were met with intense guilt. In adulthood, he struggled to function independently, relied heavily on drugs, and experienced severe impairment in basic autonomy because he had never been permitted to develop it. Within the HQTP, this pattern is not understood as laziness or lack of will, but as the developmental consequence of prolonged dependency capture and constrained autonomy (Bowlby, 1988; Herman, 1992; Price-Tobler, 2023a).

These dynamics may become deeply entrenched across the lifespan. Some survivors remain psychologically organised around a child role long into adulthood, with little autonomy, poor boundaries, and chronic fear of separation. Others have effectively run households since childhood and present as exhausted, over-responsible, and unable to identify their own needs. Some move between both positions, having been adultified in one domain and infantilised in another. In especially concerning cases, the survivor may remain bound to the alienating parent in adulthood through guilt, obligation, practical service, or emotional caretaking, including later becoming responsible for the parent's care in old age. What may appear superficially as devotion, immaturity, or dependency may therefore conceal a long developmental history in which autonomy was punished, service was normalised, and separation was made to feel dangerous or morally wrong (Jurkovic, 1997; Hooper, 2007; Price-Tobler, 2023a).

For mental health practitioners, these patterns require explicit recognition in assessment and formulation. Adult survivors affected by parentification, premature adultification, or infantilisation may present as chronically over-responsible, compulsively competent, unable to rest, and highly anxious when others are distressed, or they may present as dependent, unskilled, indecisive, frightened of ordinary adult functioning, and easily overwhelmed by autonomy. Some will oscillate between both positions. These presentations should not be reduced to personality style alone. They may instead reflect developmental role distortion arising in coercive attachment environments. Within the HQTP, treatment should therefore attend to grief for the lost childhood, restoration of age-appropriate autonomy, clarification of role boundaries, and gradual differentiation between care, guilt, obligation, and love. For parentified and adultified survivors, treatment may focus on relinquishing survival-based over-functioning. For infantilised survivors, treatment may require slower work on supported autonomy, practical skill-building, decision-making, and tolerating the anxiety associated with independent adult life (Herman, 1992; Hooper, 2007; Price-Tobler, 2023a; van der Kolk, 2014).

Where these patterns are identified, treatment must be paced in accordance with the survivor's developmental history rather than chronological age or external expectations of adult functioning. Because these patterns may coexist, shift across contexts, or be mistaken for personality style alone, careful clinical differentiation is required. The following printable resource, 'Clinician Differentiation Checklist, Parentification, Premature Adultification, and Infantilisation in Adult Survivors', is provided to assist mental health practitioners in assessing and formulating parentification, premature adultification, infantilisation, and mixed developmental role distortion in adult survivors.

Clinician Differentiation Checklist *(Printable)*

Parentification, Premature Adultification, and Infantilisation in Adult Survivors

Clinical Use

This printable checklist is intended to support clinical differentiation of developmental role distortions commonly reported by adult survivors of CPA-PA, CPA-PAA and CPA-PERA. More than one pattern may be present. These terms are not mutually exclusive and may coexist within the same survivor history. Parentification literature describes role reversal and boundary distortion as clinically significant when the child is compelled to meet parental or family needs at the expense of their own developmentally appropriate needs. Use alongside clinical interview, developmental formulation, supervision, and longitudinal assessment rather than as a stand-alone instrument.

Client Information			
Client name		**Date**	
Clinician			

1. Parentification
☐ Present ☐ Possible ☐ Not evident
Use this term when the survivor describes chronic role reversal in which they were expected to meet parental or family needs beyond their developmental capacity. This may include being a confidant, a mediator, an emotional support, a sibling carer, or a household stabiliser. The key feature is that the child was placed into a parental or caregiving role at the expense of their own childhood needs. Jurkovic and Chase treat this as a core pattern of parentification.

Clinical notes

2. Instrumental Parentification

☐ Present ☐ Possible ☐ Not evident

Use this term when the emphasis falls on practical labour and household responsibility. This may include cooking, washing, cleaning, rubbish removal, caring for siblings, managing routines, or carrying out adult domestic duties from an early age. Instrumental parentification concerns the physical maintenance of the family or household.

Clinical notes

3. Emotional Parentification

☐ Present ☐ Possible ☐ Not evident

Use this term when the survivor describes functioning as the parent's emotional companion, confidant, regulator, protector, or substitute partner. This includes carrying loneliness, distress, conflict, or emotional burdens that should never have been developmentally assigned to a child. Emotional parentification concerns participation in the emotional needs of the parent or family system.

Clinical notes

4. Premature Adultification

☐ Present ☐ Possible ☐ Not evident

Use this term when the survivor describes having had no real childhood because they were expected to think, endure, organise, suppress, or function like an adult too early. This may overlap with parentification, but is broader. The emphasis is on chronic exposure to adult burdens, adult knowledge, adult conflict, or adult expectations long before the survivor had the developmental capacity to manage them. This term is especially useful when the survivor presents as over-responsible, hyper-competent, perfectionistic, or unable to rest without guilt.

Clinical notes

5. Infantilisation

☐ Present ☐ Possible ☐ Not evident

Use this term when the survivor describes being kept dependent, over-managed, under-skilled, or denied age-appropriate autonomy. This may include not being taught ordinary life skills, being made to feel incapable, being guilted for attempts at independence, or being retained in a childlike dependent role well into adolescence or adulthood. In this pattern, the survivor is not allowed to develop an ordinary adult self. Research on autonomy-undermining parenting links such dynamics with reduced competence, lower self-efficacy, and difficulty functioning independently in adulthood.

Clinical notes

6. Mixed Presentation
☐ Present ☐ Possible ☐ Not evident
Use combined language when the survivor shows both over-responsibility and constrained autonomy. A survivor may be parentified and infantilised at the same time, or adultified in one domain while remaining dependent and underdeveloped in another. For example, the survivor may have run the household, managed siblings, or regulated the parent emotionally, while simultaneously being denied freedom, practical skill development, or permission to separate. This mixed presentation is often clinically important because it can produce severe confusion regarding identity, responsibility, guilt, and autonomy.
Clinical notes

7. Common adult indicators to assess across all categories
☐ Chronic over-responsibility ☐ Compulsive cleaning or domestic vigilance ☐ Inability to rest without guilt ☐ Panic when others are distressed ☐ Fear of independent functioning ☐ Poor practical autonomy ☐ Strong guilt linked to separation ☐ Feeling responsible for a parent's emotional survival ☐ Collapse, substance use, or helplessness when expected to function independently ☐ Confusion about whether care reflects love, obligation, fear, or survival

Clinical notes

8. Overall formulation

The survivor's presentation is best understood as:

☐ Primarily parentification

☐ Primarily instrumental parentification

☐ Primarily emotional parentification

☐ Primarily premature adultification

☐ Primarily infantilisation

☐ Mixed role distortion presentation

Formulation notes

9. Immediate treatment emphasis
☐ Grief for lost childhood ☐ Role clarification ☐ Boundary repair ☐ Autonomy building ☐ Reduction of compulsive over-functioning ☐ Differentiation between love, guilt, duty, and coercion ☐ Practical life-skill support ☐ Slower pacing around separation and independence
Treatment notes

Clinician summary

Note. This checklist was informed by the parentification and family systems literature, including Jurkovic (1997), Chase (1999), and Hooper (2007).

Socioeconomic Conditions, Dependency, and Psychological Control

CPA-PA does not occur in isolation. It unfolds within broader environmental conditions that can intensify developmental injury and prolong survivor vulnerability. Many adult survivors describe growing up within layered systems of emotional control, material dependency, and psychological pressure that shaped both attachment formation and their understanding of safety.

In the author's clinical and research findings, economic instability frequently functioned not only as a stressor but also as a mechanism of relational leverage. In some families, access to housing, education, medical care, or basic resources became intertwined with expectations of loyalty. Survivors reported learning early that emotional alignment with the alienating caregiver was often linked to material security, while expressions of attachment to the targeted parent were associated with withdrawal, threat, or punishment. Over time, this conditioning embedded powerful associations between compliance and survival.

These patterns often continue to shape how relational threat is processed in adulthood. Many survivors report difficulty separating emotional connection from fear of abandonment, financial insecurity, or loss of support. Therapy must recognise that these associations were not cognitive distortions, but adaptive responses to real environmental contingencies during development.

Psychological manipulation further compounded these conditions. Survivors consistently described exposure to loyalty binding, reality distortion, moral coercion, and emotional enmeshment. Tactics included repeated denigration of the targeted parent, exaggerated narratives of danger, emotional dependency placed on the child, and threats of withdrawal, illness, or self-harm used to enforce compliance by the AP. These dynamics created internal conflicts between attachment needs and psychological safety.

Importantly, the impact was not limited to childhood. Adult survivors often reported continued activation of these relational threat patterns in later partnerships, workplaces, and authority relationships. Hypervigilance, compliance strategies, fear of disagreement, and difficulty trusting stable support systems were common downstream effects.

The absence of consistent psychological safety limited opportunities for autonomous self-definition and healthy boundary formation. From a clinical perspective, this reinforces the need to view CPA-PA not simply as a rupture in the parent-child relationship but as a prolonged developmental conditioning environment. Treatment must address both the internal psychological imprint and the external relational expectations that survivors carry forward.

This chapter does not seek to frame survivors as permanently impaired. Rather, it highlights the adaptive intelligence embedded within these responses. Survivors learned to navigate unstable emotional terrain with limited protection and incomplete information. Therapy becomes the space in which those adaptations can be understood, carefully re-evaluated, and gradually reshaped within conditions of safety.

Developmental Consequences of Forced Parental Absence

Many adult survivors in the author's research described not only the emotional loss of a targeted parent but also the practical developmental consequences of being raised within a forced, financially challenged, single-parent environment created through alienation, concealment, or removal. These consequences were not abstract. They lived daily through schooling, social participation, material deprivation, and emotional role reversal.

Survivors frequently reported that school life became a site of repeated exclusion. Limited access to excursions, camps, extracurricular activities, school uniforms and basic resources created visible differences between them and their peers. Uniform inconsistencies, missing equipment, changes of name, frequent school changes, and unstable attendance patterns often marked them as different, increasing vulnerability to bullying and social isolation. These experiences compounded existing attachment insecurity and reinforced narratives of not belonging.

Educational continuity was commonly disrupted. Repeated relocations, school transfers, or unstable caregiving arrangements interfered with academic progress and peer relationships. Survivors described struggling to form long-term friendships, falling behind academically, or disengaging from school altogether because of constant upheaval. These disruptions often carry into adulthood, manifesting as reduced educational attainment, employment instability, and diminished confidence in long-term planning, unless they choose otherwise.

Daily supervision and emotional availability were also affected. When a sole caregiver was required to manage work, legal conflict, financial survival, and household responsibilities alone, many children were left unsupervised for extended periods. Survivors described walking to school on their own, preparing their own meals at a young age, managing household tasks prematurely, or being left alone after school because their parent worked multiple jobs. While these experiences sometimes fostered early independence, they also contributed to chronic hyper-responsibility, emotional self-reliance, and difficulty seeking support later in life.

Importantly, these outcomes were not caused by single parenthood itself. They arose from forced parental absence in circumstances where a safe and emotionally available parent had been deliberately removed or erased from the child's life. When children are deprived of one secure attachment figure through alienation, concealment, or abduction, their basic human rights are being taken away from them.

From a clinical perspective, it is essential to challenge the cultural normalisation of unnecessary parental removal. When a loving, safe parent is intentionally excluded, the developmental burden does not disappear. It is transferred onto the child's nervous system, identity formation, educational stability, and relational templates.

Adult survivors consistently reported that these cumulative disadvantages shaped long-term self-worth, social confidence, and relational expectations. Therapy must recognise that these were not minor inconveniences. They were formative developmental injuries layered on top of attachment disruption.

This does not diminish the resilience of survivors or the dedication of many single parents who do everything possible under extreme constraints. Rather, it highlights the preventable harm created when systems tolerate unnecessary parental exclusion in cases where a safe, emotionally available parent could have remained present.

The following section draws directly from the author's twin doctoral study and therefore retains, where necessary, the original study language used at that time. This includes earlier terminology such as severe parental alienation (SPA), which is preserved here for fidelity to the doctoral findings and to the research literature being discussed. The updated HQTP language resumes at the section titled "Why Phased Treatment Is Essential in This Work."

Previous Research on Long-Term Adverse Outcomes

Previous research has shown that PA in childhood may be associated with adverse outcomes in adulthood. Parental divorce and SPA are not equivalent phenomena. However, divorce research provides a broader developmental context for understanding how family rupture may predict adverse adult outcomes. In contrast, research on severe parental alienation and related child psychological abuse presentations within the PA framework suggests that these harms may be compounded when rupture is coercively organised, and attachment to a safe parent is deliberately disrupted.

At the same time, there remains comparatively limited literature examining the lifelong effects of SPA on adult survivors. Drawing on earlier studies, Das (2016), citing Duran-Aydintug (1997) and Amato and Sobolewski (2001), reported that adult children of divorce showed lower levels of psychological, social, and marital wellbeing than comparison groups.

Other studies have described associations with poorer physical health, behavioural difficulties, lower financial stability, and reduced educational opportunity (Das, 2016).

Research has also suggested that individuals who retrospectively identify exposure to parental alienation as a form of childhood maltreatment may experience significant adverse effects in adulthood, including reduced health-related quality of life, depressive symptoms, and enduring relational difficulties (Verrocchio et al., 2019). More broadly, long-term sequelae described across the literature include chronic health problems, substance misuse, mental illness, educational disruption, and reduced occupational opportunity (Centers for Disease Control and Prevention, 2020). Survivors may also report depression, low self-esteem, mistrust, substance use difficulties, relationship instability, suicidality, and enduring grief regarding the lost relationship with the targeted parent (Baker, 2007; Sher, 2017; Verrocchio et al., 2019).

Baker (2007) also highlighted the damaging long-term consequences of emotional terrorisation within alienating environments, including singling children out for criticism and punishment. Such dynamics extend beyond parental preference and reflect broader patterns of child psychological abuse. Adult survivor narratives within the author's doctoral research similarly described prolonged erasure of the targeted parent, unresolved grief, and enduring developmental injury following abduction, concealment, and severe parental alienation. One survivor described this experience as "losing your parent to PA is like a death with no funeral. When my friend's father died, the whole community came to support her. No one ever came to support me when mum got rid of my dad." This comment captures the chronic and unresolved nature of survivor loss.

The literature further recognises that individuals from diverse backgrounds may develop complex trauma responses following prolonged victimisation. A war veteran and a child exposed to abuse in the home may both present with posttraumatic symptoms despite the very different nature of their experiences. Developments in psychiatry and traumatology have increasingly acknowledged that traditional diagnostic formulations such as PTSD do not fully capture the effects of prolonged, repeated, and developmentally embedded victimisation (Briere & Spinazzola, 2005; Herman, 1992).

Diagnostic Classification Limitations

Although the literature increasingly documents the harms associated with parental alienation and related coercive family dynamics, significant gaps remain in research examining the therapeutic experiences of adult survivors and the clinicians who work with them. Many adult survivors, therefore, seek therapy from mental health practitioners (MHPs) who may have limited training in recognising PA, SPA, or SPAA trauma. Standard trauma training is often insufficient for addressing the attachment-based, developmental, and coercive-control features that characterise these presentations.

MHPs often rely on the *Diagnostic and Statistical Manual of Mental Disorders* for symptom classification and treatment planning. However, parental alienation is not included in the DSM-5 or DSM-5-TR as a formal, standalone diagnosis. Existing classifications, therefore, remain limited in their capacity to capture the full attachment-based psychological abuse, prolonged relational coercion, and developmentally mediated trauma patterns described by survivors of SPA.

(Note: From this point, the discussion resumes the updated HQTP language and acronyms.)

At the same time, this does not mean that the relevant pathology falls entirely outside existing diagnostic language. Within Dr Craig Childress's attachment-based formulation, the pathology is not conceptualised as a separate diagnosis called *parental alienation*, but as pathogenic parenting producing clinically significant developmental disturbance in the child. Childress identifies three central diagnostic indicators: first, pathogenic parenting associated with significant developmental pathology in the child; second, personality-disorder pathology or phobic anxiety pathology in the child's symptom display; and third, delusional psychiatric pathology in the child. On this basis, he argues that the appropriate DSM-5 formulation is a constellation of existing categories rather than a novel syndrome, namely: 309.4 adjustment disorder with Mixed Disturbance of Emotions and Conduct; V61.20 Parent-Child Relational Problem; V61.29 Child Affected by Parental Relationship Distress; and V995.51 Child Psychological Abuse, Confirmed. Within the present protocol, this position is included as Childress's diagnostic framing rather than as a statement that DSM-5 formally recognises parental alienation as a discrete diagnosis.

Parental alienation occurs within a relational and family-system context, but it should not be reduced to a relational problem alone. In more severe presentations, it may involve child psychological abuse, coercive control, attachment disruption, identity interference, distorted family narratives, and enduring psychosocial and structural consequences across the family system. Relational-problem classifications may identify part of the context, but they do not necessarily capture the severity, developmental organisation, or long-term consequences of the abuse.

While concepts such as *child affected by parental relationship distress* may overlap with aspects of these presentations, they do not adequately account on their own for the full developmental and relational impact described by adult survivors. These limitations highlight the need for a treatment framework that is not driven solely by categorical diagnosis, but by an understanding of relational injury, developmental disruption, coercive control, and ethical sequencing of care. In all forms of child abuse, including physical, sexual, psychological and spousal abuse, the primary obligation remains the protection of the child. Within the HQTP, that child-protection principle is carried forward into adult survivor treatment through formulation-sensitive, non-coercive, developmentally informed care.

Although Childress's formulation is focused on pathology identified in the child, its relevance to the present protocol lies in the recognition that developmental injury organised under conditions of pathogenic parenting, attachment disruption, and child psychological abuse may continue into adulthood as complex relational, identity-based, and trauma-related sequelae requiring specialised treatment (Childress, 2015; Price-Tobler, 2023a).

This diagnostic caution is also supported by Bailey et al. (2020), who argue that behaviours observed in high-conflict family contexts may reflect adaptive nervous-system responses to chronic threat rather than personality pathology or deliberate misconduct. This is particularly relevant to adult survivors because protective responses established during childhood may remain active long after the original environment has changed. Hypervigilance, avoidance, shutdown, relational mistrust, emotional reactivity, or reduced reflective capacity may therefore be misclassified as fixed psychopathology when the developmental history of coercion, attachment disruption, and chronic relational threat is not adequately considered. The clinical task is not to reject diagnosis, but to distinguish carefully between enduring pathology and trauma-organised adaptation before treatment decisions are made.

Although diagnostic assessment may at times be necessary in adult survivors for risk formulation, service access, treatment planning, communication, or documentation, significant limitations arise when DSM-based classification is relied upon as the primary frame for understanding CPA-PA-related injury. Adult survivors frequently present with downstream symptom constellations such as anxiety, depression, dissociation, relational instability, somatic distress, grief, or trauma-related dysregulation. Yet, these categories do not necessarily identify the developmental source of the disturbance in prolonged attachment disruption, coercive control, pathogenic parenting, or child psychological abuse.

As a result, diagnosis may describe the survivor's current presentation while failing to name the underlying relational and developmental harm that organised it, creating a risk that survivors will be fragmented into symptom clusters rather than understood in the context of cumulative abuse, epistemic injury, and distorted attachment learning. Within the HQTP, diagnostic classification is therefore treated as a limited clinical tool rather than a sufficient explanatory framework. Even where diagnosis is required, the central task of treatment remains the phased undoing, as far as possible, of developmental harm through safety, stabilisation, identity reconstruction, grief integration, and restoration of autonomous relational functioning (Herman, 1992; Childress, 2015; Price-Tobler, 2023a; van der Kolk, 2014).

Why Phased Treatment is Essential in This Work

Treatment with adult survivors of CPA-PA and all its forms cannot proceed safely through linear or technique-driven models. The nature of the injury itself requires a phased approach. Psychological abuse and alienation unfold within attachment relationships and across developmental time. As a result, adult survivors frequently present without stable internal regulation, without a coherent autobiographical narrative, and without confidence that relationships can exist without control, punishment, or abandonment. These developmental disruptions alter both the structure and sequencing of therapeutic intervention. Standard trauma models that assume discrete events, intact attachment templates, or stable internal regulatory capacity often fail to account for the cumulative relational harm present in this population.

When therapy moves too quickly into interpretation, trauma processing, or narrative reconstruction, survivors may experience the therapeutic process as coercive, destabilising, or emotionally unsafe. This can replicate the original conditions of harm and lead to withdrawal, dissociation, emotional flooding, or reenactment of attachment collapse. Both survivor and practitioner cohorts in the author's doctoral research consistently reported adverse outcomes associated with premature trauma work, modality-driven treatment planning, and insufficient stabilisation prior to deeper processing. These findings support the necessity of clinical sequencing that prioritises safety, relational containment, and agency before engaging traumatic material.

The HQTP, therefore, adopts a phased treatment architecture grounded in attachment theory, developmental trauma research, and ethical trauma practice. Safety precedes exploration. Stabilisation precedes processing. Agency precedes narrative reconstruction. Relationship precedes technique. This structure is not a procedural preference, but a clinical safeguard designed to reduce the risk of retraumatisation, misdiagnosis, and therapeutic reenactment. The phased model establishes the foundation for all subsequent clinical pathways within the protocol.

Chapter Three

Purpose and Positioning of the Healing Qualia Framework

Building on the phased treatment architecture introduced earlier, this chapter defines the clinical scope, ethical positioning, and practitioner responsibilities governing the use of the HQTP. It establishes how the framework is intended to function within therapeutic contexts and clarifies its limits.

The framework is designed to support clinicians in recognising patterns of developmental psychological harm, attachment disruption, and trauma adaptation in adult survivors without assuming intent, assigning blame, or resolving competing narratives.

This distinction is essential. Adult survivors frequently present within systems characterised by adversarial dynamics, contested histories, and pressure for certainty. When clinical work is drawn into investigative or evidentiary functions, the risk of retraumatisation, epistemic harm, and boundary erosion increases substantially. The HQTP therefore positions therapeutic work as a protected clinical space, oriented toward safety, stabilisation, and developmental repair rather than proof or persuasion.

This chapter delineates the ethical conditions required for entry into the framework, the responsibilities of clinicians applying it, and the safeguards that must be in place before assessment, formulation, or phase-based intervention proceeds.

Scope of Practice and Intended Clinical Use

This volume is intended for clinical psychotherapists, psychologists, and other mental health clinicians working primarily with adult survivors of CPA-PA contexts. Where the framework is adapted for adolescent presentations, this requires developmentally appropriate practice, additional safeguarding, caregiver-system assessment, statutory awareness, and supervision. It is designed for use within regulated clinical practice contexts and presumes appropriate professional qualifications, trauma training, and access to supervision.

The HQTP does not function as a forensic assessment tool, a legal opinion, a custody evaluation, or an investigative framework. It does not determine whether abuse occurred, whether allegations are substantiated, or whether family members are culpable. Rather, it offers clinicians a structured method for recognising patterns of harm and trauma adaptation, supporting ethical formulation, and pacing treatment to prioritise psychological safety.

The framework is applicable across a range of clinical presentations, including complex trauma, dissociation, attachment disturbance, chronic suicidality, identity instability, relational collapse, and epistemic disruption. It is not a universal protocol and should not be applied when the presenting difficulties are better accounted for by primary mental health conditions requiring alternative specialist intervention. Determining appropriateness for use is a clinical responsibility that precedes any phase-based application.

Ethical Foundations and the Principle of Clinical Humility

A foundational ethical principle underpinning the HQTP is clinical humility. Presenting narratives, whether from clients, families, or systems, cannot, in and of itself, be treated as evidence. Behaviour, affect, and relational patterns must be understood in a developmental context, assessed longitudinally, and interpreted cautiously.

The principle of "assess, do not assume" governs all stages of engagement. Clinicians are cautioned against premature formulation, confirmation bias, or alignment with any single explanatory narrative. In survivors of developmental psychological abuse, behaviours such as dissociation, compliance, hostility, withdrawal, emotional numbing, or apparent autonomy often represent survival adaptations rather than preference, intent, or stable identity. Without careful assessment, these adaptations risk being misinterpreted and inadvertently reinforced.

Ethical practice requires tolerance of ambiguity, reflective reasoning, and sustained engagement with supervision. Where clinicians experience pressure to arrive quickly at conclusions or to validate interpretations, restraint is an ethical act. The HQTP rejects outcome-driven pacing and prioritises protection from clinical harm, epistemic overreach, and premature certainty.

Early Clinical Enquiry and Safety Considerations

Within the HQTP, the way clinicians ask questions is itself an ethical intervention. Adult survivors have frequently been subjected to interrogative questioning, loyalty testing, and pressure to justify or defend their perceptions within family, legal, and therapeutic systems. As a result, certain forms of questioning may evoke threat, collapse, or compliance rather than reflection or insight.

Early clinical enquiry, therefore, prioritises open questions that support narrative emergence without requiring proof, persuasion, or coherence. Questions oriented toward internal experience, emotional impact, relational meaning, and present-day functioning are favoured over questions seeking factual verification, causal attribution, or historical resolution. Where survivors show signs of epistemic instability or distress in response to questioning, clinicians are required to slow the pace of enquiry, return to containment, and defer interpretation. This will be explained in later chapters.

The central clinical task at entry is not to establish what happened, but to understand how the survivor has adapted to prolonged relational stress and how safe it is for them to reflect on their experience within the therapeutic relationship.

Service Entry Pathways and Clinical Presentation Contexts

Adult survivors of CPA-PA rarely present exclusively within specialist trauma services. They are encountered across a wide range of clinical and community settings, often during periods of crisis or relational breakdown rather than with a presenting concern linked to early developmental harm.

Common entry points include private psychotherapy practices, community mental health services, hospital outpatient clinics, acute mental health units, psychiatric inpatient wards, and emergency departments. Survivors also frequently present within youth justice and adult correctional settings, probation and parole programs, and forensic mental health services, where unresolved developmental trauma may underlie behavioural risk, emotional dysregulation, and relational conflict.

Additional presentation contexts include family and relationship counselling, parenting and co-parenting programs, domestic and family violence services, homelessness and housing programs, disability and NDIS services, substance use treatment services, primary healthcare, employee assistance programs, first responder support services, veterans' services, immigration and refugee services, and community-based pastoral or spiritual care organisations.

This diversity of entry pathways reinforces the need for a clinically consistent, ethically grounded framework that can be applied across disciplines without collapsing therapeutic boundaries or replicating systemic harm.

Epistemic Injury and the Risk of Harm by Professionals

The HQTP acknowledges the risk of epistemic injury within professional systems. Epistemic injury occurs when a survivor's lived experience is dismissed, overwritten, or mislabelled by professional authority, particularly in contexts where power differentials are pronounced.

Clinicians encountering survivors in any of the aforementioned settings may not initially recognise CPA-PA presentations as the organising context of presentation, increasing the risk of misformulation and inappropriate intervention in the absence of a structured, ethically grounded framework.

Adult survivors from the PhD cohort study reported recurring experiences of not being believed, being pathologised, or having their perceptions reframed prematurely. When clinicians act on narrative certainty rather than observable developmental patterns and relational context, they may inadvertently replicate dynamics of control, invalidation, and coercion that contributed to the original trauma.

Ethical application of this protocol, therefore, requires reflective reasoning, active engagement with clinical supervision, and disciplined avoidance of premature interpretation. Clinical understanding must be allowed to emerge gradually through longitudinal assessment rather than imposed early in the therapeutic process.

The Role and Boundaries of the Clinician

Within the Healing Qualia framework, the clinician's role is neither that of an investigator nor of an advocate for any family member or competing narrative. The clinician does not determine factual truth, adjudicate relational disputes, or align with one party against another. Early therapeutic work within this model is not concerned with proving allegations, correcting historical records, or resolving adversarial family conflict. Rather, it is concerned with restoring psychological safety, supporting developmental repair, and ensuring that the survivor has a protected therapeutic space in which their internal experience can be articulated, heard, and provisionally believed.

This stance is especially important in the clinical context of CPA-PA, where survivors have often spent much of their developmental life being disbelieved, silenced, or required to repudiate their own perceptions to preserve attachment or personal safety under conditions of coercive interference by the alienating parent. In the absence of a therapeutic environment in which the survivor's subjective experience is taken seriously rather than reflexively interrogated, corrected, or overwritten, clinical work risks reproducing coercive dynamics and compromising treatment integrity.

Such a position does not imply neutrality in the face of coercion, intimidation, or boundary violation. Findings from the MHP cohort of the author's twin doctoral studies indicated frequent clinician exposure to external interference, professional pressure, and occupational risk arising from family systems, adversarial legal contexts, and allied third parties (Price-Tobler, 2024b).

For example, clinicians reported repeated attempts by alienating parents or associated parties to direct the therapeutic process through unsolicited contact, written correspondence, or pressure to adopt externally imposed diagnostic formulations. For example, in one reported case, an alienating parent attempted to pressure the MHP into aligning with them against the adult survivor by supplying a written document that purported to identify the survivor's psychological deficits and dictate treatment priorities, despite having no professional qualification to do so.

MHPs in the PhD cohort interpreted such actions not as clinical collaboration but as extensions of coercive control that seeped into the therapeutic space. Ethical responses involved refusing to engage with the material, documenting its receipt and context, and identifying the act as coercive interference directed at both the survivor and the clinician.

MHPs further described predictable escalation to formal complaints, intimidation, professional isolation, or threats when therapeutic boundaries were maintained, particularly following refusal to engage with unsolicited material or third-party contact. These patterns, documented across the practitioner cohort, reflect systemic coercive dynamics rather than isolated misunderstandings and may pose risks to the safety and wellbeing of both clinicians and survivors (Price-Tobler, 2024b).

Ethical practice within the HQTP, therefore, requires clinicians to actively protect the therapeutic frame. This includes refusing third-party contact, resisting triangulation, maintaining non-negotiable boundaries around confidentiality and access, and documenting attempts at interference. When harassment, intimidation, or professional threats occur, clinicians are ethically justified in escalating concerns through supervision, organisational governance structures, professional bodies, or legal channels as required.

Advocacy within the HQTP is not only advocacy for or against a person, position, or narrative. Rather, it can also be advocacy for conditions of safety, epistemic integrity, and clinical containment in contexts where coercive dynamics may extend beyond the family system and into professional spaces (Price-Tobler, 2024b). Extensive and detailed practitioner accounts of intimidation, harassment, professional isolation, and occupational risk associated with this work are examined in the author's doctoral practitioner study. This study provides an in-depth analysis of the risk pathways and mitigation strategies affecting specialist MHPs working with the adult survivor.

Treatment Architecture Orientation and Phase Flexibility

The treatment phases outlined in subsequent chapters function as a flexible clinical architecture rather than a linear or prescriptive sequence. Movement between phases is governed by safety, readiness, and integration capacity rather than elapsed time, symptom reduction, or external expectation.

Regression, pause, and cyclical movement are inherent features of recovery from complex developmental trauma and must not be interpreted as treatment failure. Ethical practice requires clinicians to respond to fluctuations in regulation and relational capacity without imposing linear trajectories or outcome-driven timelines.

Entry Safeguards and Orientation to Assessment

Before proceeding to fuller assessment and formulation, clinicians must determine whether the HQTP is appropriate for the presenting context and whether sufficient safety and stability are present to support further engagement. Entry safeguards include explicit clarification of scope, boundary setting, and orientation to the therapeutic process. The purpose of this chapter is to establish the ethical and clinical conditions under which assessment can occur safely. More detailed assessment architecture, formulation logic, and phase-readiness decision-making are addressed in the following chapter. Once these initial safeguards and orienting conditions are in place, the protocol turns to the intake process and the use of structured tools to support safe and developmentally attuned identification.

Clinician Interpretation and Screening Guide

Using the Healing Qualia Clinical Intake and Identification Tool

Purpose and Clinical Positioning

The Healing Qualia Clinical Intake and Identification Tool is not a diagnostic instrument and must not be used as a stand-alone assessment tool. Its purpose is to support early pattern recognition, preliminary clinical formulation, and pacing decisions when working with adolescent and adult clients who may have experienced developmental psychological harm associated with post-separation family disruption, prolonged relational conflict, or coercive caregiving environments.

Clinicians are reminded that the presence of individual indicators does not confirm child psychological abuse within a CPA-PA and the associated presentations. Clinical interpretation must occur within a broader clinical formulation that integrates longitudinal developmental history, attachment patterns, behavioural observations, relational dynamics, and current functioning. For example, difficulties with trust, emotional regulation, or identity coherence may reflect a range of developmental or relational stressors and only acquire clinical meaning when understood in context, over time, and in relation to the survivor's broader attachment and family system history.

The primary clinical question at this stage is not whether abuse can be proven or categorised, but whether the presentation reflects patterns of relational disruption, epistemic injury, and developmental trauma adaptation that warrant application of the Healing Qualia framework. This orientation protects against premature categorisation and supports the establishment of epistemic safety in the earliest phase of engagement.

Pattern Recognition Rather Than Event Verification

Assessment prioritises pattern recognition over event verification. Clinicians are encouraged to attend to constellations of relational, emotional, and developmental indicators rather than isolated responses or discrete historical narratives. Adult survivors commonly present with interlocking patterns that may include chronic loyalty conflict and relational triangulation, persistent self-doubt and identity instability, and disrupted epistemic trust accompanied by reliance on external authority. Additionally, ongoing emotional regulation difficulties, relational avoidance or compliance with heightened responsibility for others, prolonged or poorly explained family separation experiences, and histories of repeated therapeutic engagement that were experienced as unhelpful or harmful may also be present.

Clinical formulation, therefore, remains grounded in how these adaptations functioned developmentally and how they continue to shape current relational and emotional functioning. Survivors may describe separation experiences that have occurred across a range of circumstances, including relocation, caregiving transitions, court involvement, family violence responses, or broader family system instability. In isolation, such experiences are not sufficient to infer developmental psychological abuse within a CPA-PA presentation.

Clinical significance emerges when separation is embedded within a broader relational pattern characterised by restricted or disrupted contact, caregiver narrative control, emotional pressure, or loyalty demands. Additionally, suppression or reframing of the survivor's subjective experience, unresolved grief, identity confusion, and enduring relational avoidance or compliance may also present. Adult survivors frequently describe confusion, emotional numbing, fragmented identity development, and difficulty integrating contradictory relational narratives following prolonged or coerced separation, particularly when they were required to repudiate attachment needs or personal perceptions to maintain safety or relational proximity.

Assessing Epistemic Safety and Narrative Coherence

Responses indicating difficulty trusting memory, confusion about personal history, or reliance on external validation may reflect epistemic injury arising from prolonged exposure to relational coercion, narrative control, or authority-mediated invalidation. Adult survivors frequently report developmental environments in which their perceptions were challenged, corrected, dismissed, or overwritten by caregivers or systems, resulting in chronic uncertainty about what is real, permissible to know, or safe to express.

For example, a survivor may describe persistent self-doubt about related negative childhood experiences despite strong emotional or somatic responses, frequently seeking reassurance from the clinician that their memories or reactions are "allowed" or "make sense." Others may minimise or retract disclosures mid-session, particularly when discussing their AP, reflecting an internalised expectation that their account will be questioned, corrected, or carry relational consequences (if their AP finds out). Such patterns are not indicators of unreliability but adaptive responses to environments in which epistemic trust was repeatedly undermined, and loyalty was always expected.

Assessment, therefore, prioritises epistemic safety over narrative completeness or coherence. Clinicians are cautioned against early requests for consistency, factual precision, or explanatory clarity, particularly in the initial stages of engagement. Clinical attention is instead directed toward the survivor's capacity to reflect, tolerate ambiguity, and articulate internal experience without fear of correction, disbelief, or relational consequence.

Narrative coherence is approached as a developmental outcome of safety rather than a prerequisite for assessment. Gradual narrative stabilisation is supported through collaborative formulation, reflective listening, and paced exploration, allowing meaning to emerge over time. As previously advised, premature interpretation, reframing, or meaning-making risks reproducing earlier dynamics of invalidation and control and should be avoided.

Clinical Caution: Explanations Given but Not Received

When assessing distance, silence, refusal, limited contact, or no contact, clinicians should be careful not to assume that the absence of a recognised explanation indicates a lack of explanation. Survivors may have clearly stated what was upsetting them, named relational injury, attempted to set limits, or explained why contact felt unsafe, painful, or intolerable. However, those explanations may not have been heard, emotionally received, accurately remembered, or treated as legitimate by the parent or the wider family system.

In some cases, the survivor's explanations may have been dismissed as irrational, cruel, exaggerated, abusive, disrespectful, or confusing because the parent could not tolerate the emotional meaning of what was being said. The issue is therefore not simply whether an explanation was given, but whether it was received with sufficient openness, accountability, and emotional capacity to be understood. A parent may later report, within the family narrative or collateral history, that the survivor gave no reason, while the clinical history suggests that reasons were given but ignored, minimised, rejected, stripped of context, or reframed as an attack.

This distinction is important in CPA-PA work because clinicians must assess the survivor's reasons for distance or refusal without prematurely pathologising the survivor, dismissing their account, or assuming that silence, withdrawal, or no contact is automatically evidence of alienation. The survivor may be responding to repeated experiences of not being heard, not being believed, or having their distress converted into evidence that they are difficult, cruel, unstable, or unreasonable.

At this early stage, the clinician does not need to resolve the full history or determine whether every stated reason is accurate, complete, inherited, protective, or trauma-shaped. The immediate task is to notice the pattern, preserve context, and avoid premature conclusions. Deeper work belongs later, particularly in Phase II and Phase V, when the survivor has enough safety to explore meaning reconstruction, grief, boundary formation, contact decisions, and the emotional impact of repeated relational invalidation.

This clinical caution does not imply that any parent should be brought into therapy. It is a formulation safeguard. It helps clinicians recognise that survivor withdrawal may reflect not only fear, alienation-shaped refusal, trauma avoidance, or protective boundary formation, but also the exhaustion that follows repeated attempts to explain harm to someone who cannot or will not receive it.

This leads directly into risk and stabilisation screening. When survivors have repeatedly tried to explain distress and have not been heard, revisiting these histories may activate shame, anger, grief, collapse, hopelessness, suicidal ideation, dissociation, panic, or fear of family retaliation. Clinicians must therefore assess current safety, emotional regulation, suicide risk, coercive family pressure, recent contact attempts, escalation in the family system, and the survivor's capacity to remain grounded before inviting further exploration.

Risk and Stabilisation Screening

Indicators such as suicidal ideation, emotional collapse, dissociation, unsafe living environments, or acute relational stress require immediate prioritisation of stabilisation and safety planning before proceeding with deeper assessment or formulation. For example, survivors may present following a sudden relationship rupture, housing instability, or legal stressor with heightened distress or withdrawal, without initially linking their current crisis to earlier developmental experiences.

Risk assessment is integrated with an understanding of developmental and relational trauma rather than treated as a discrete procedural task. Heightened risk is often relationally mediated and may fluctuate in response to perceived abandonment, threat, or epistemic invalidation. Where risk is elevated, Phase I stabilisation principles may be initiated concurrently with ongoing assessment, provided that pacing, containment, and consent remain central. Stabilisation is understood as a recurring clinical requirement rather than a single threshold to be crossed. For example, suicidal ideation or dissociative symptoms may intensify following experiences of perceived disbelief, relational rupture, or external pressure, and then subside when relational safety and containment are restored.

The following 'Initial Clinical Interview' guide supports early formulation, safety assessment, and ethical pacing decisions. It is not a forensic enquiry, a demand for narrative completeness, or a test of memory. Its purpose is to help the clinician understand the survivor's current presentation, immediate stabilisation needs, epistemic safety, developmental and relational context, and readiness for further assessment within the HQTP.

The Initial Clinical Interview (Printable)

Healing Qualia Treatment Protocol

Early Domains for Clinical Enquiry with Adult Survivors

Clinical Use

This printable guide supports the first clinician-led interview with an adult survivor following review of the Healing Qualia Clinical Intake and Identification Tool, or at first contact when that tool has not yet been completed. It is not a forensic interview and is not intended to obtain a full chronological account. Its purpose is to establish psychological safety, clarify current presentation and immediate needs, identify early patterns relevant to CPA-PA, CPA-PAA, and CPA-PERA, assess epistemic safety, and determine the most appropriate initial pathway within the HQTP.

Use alongside clinical judgement, developmental formulation, supervision, and ongoing assessment. Ambiguity is expected. Information that is not yet known should remain open rather than be forced, inferred, or prematurely organised.

Client Information			
Client name		**Date**	
Clinician		**Referral source**	

1. Opening Position, Consent, and Pace
☐ No expectation to prove or explain harm was stated ☐ Permission to pause, decline, or defer questions was explained ☐ Access, sensory, cultural, or communication needs were checked ☐ Current reason for attending was invited before history-taking
Use this section to establish that the first interview is not an interrogation, not a test of memory, and not a demand for premature disclosure. The immediate task is to reduce threat, communicate choice, and understand what the survivor needs in order to remain present in the room.
Suggested prompts • What feels most important for me to understand about how things are for you right now? • What would help this feel safer or more manageable today? • Is there anything you do not want pushed, rushed, or asked about in this first meeting?
Clinical notes

2. Presenting Concerns and Current Functional Strain

☐ Anxiety or panic ☐ Low mood or hopelessness ☐ Dissociation or numbness ☐ Identity confusion ☐ Relational collapse ☐ Parenting activation ☐ Court or family system activation ☐ Somatic distress ☐ Sleep disturbance ☐ Other / mixed

Clarify why the survivor is seeking help now. Focus on the current presentation before asking for broader developmental history, relationship patterns, or family systems context.

Suggested prompts

- What has made it important to seek help at this point in time?
- What feels hardest to manage in daily life at the moment?
- When things become difficult, what tends to happen emotionally, physically, or relationally?

Clinical notes

3. Immediate Safety, Stabilisation, and Environmental Context

☐ Suicidal ideation or self-harm risk ☐ Emotional collapse or severe dysregulation ☐ Dissociation affecting orientation ☐ Unsafe living environment ☐ Acute relational threat or coercive contact ☐ Substance-related destabilisation ☐ Psychosis, cognitive impairment, or other specialist priority ☐ No reliable support person or practical containment

Assess risk and current stability before moving toward developmental enquiry. Where acute risk, unsafe living conditions, or severe destabilisation are present, stabilisation takes precedence over narrative development.

Suggested prompts

- Do you feel emotionally and physically safe where you are living at the moment?
- Have there been any recent events that have left you feeling at risk, overwhelmed, or close to collapse?
- Who, if anyone, can you contact when things become difficult between sessions?

Clinical notes

4. Epistemic Safety and Narrative Capacity
☐ Difficulty trusting memory ☐ Frequent self-doubt or checking ☐ Minimising or retracting disclosures ☐ Fear of getting it wrong ☐ Reliance on clinician to determine what is true ☐ Narrative fragmentation tolerated ☐ Narrative enquiry too destabilising to pursue today
Attend to how the survivor relates to memory, meaning, and self-trust. The aim is not to secure a complete story in the first interview, but to observe whether internal experience can be expressed without fear of correction, disbelief, punishment, or relational consequence.
Suggested prompts • When you try to think about your history or family relationships, what happens inside? • Do you often feel unsure whether your own reactions, memories, or perceptions can be trusted? • What helps you feel safer when something feels confusing or hard to put into words?
Clinical notes

5. Developmental and Relational Context
☐ Prolonged separation from a parent or caregiver ☐ Loyalty pressure or triangulation ☐ Restricted, disrupted, or unsafe contact ☐ Narrative control, denigration, or pressure to align ☐ Parentification, premature adultification, or infantilisation ☐ Identity instability linked to family roles ☐ Abduction, concealment, or forced relocation indicators ☐ Attachment-prevention / estrangement pathway indicators ☐ Not yet known
Explore only as tolerated. This section is used to identify early indicators relevant to CPA-PA, CPA-PAA, and CPA-PERA without forcing a full account. What matters is pattern recognition, not event verification.
Suggested prompts • Were there relationships growing up that felt restricted, dangerous, or impossible to speak about openly? • Did you ever feel caught between adults or pressured to hold one version of events over your own experience? • Are there early family experiences that feel important, but not yet safe enough to go into in detail?
Clinical notes

6. Prior Help-Seeking and Experiences With Services
☐ Previous therapy helpful ☐ Previous therapy mixed ☐ Previous therapy harmful ☐ Felt rushed, dismissed, or disbelieved ☐ Repeated services without developmental formulation ☐ Mental health or crisis presentations ☐ Court, legal, or child protection involvement ☐ Medication or diagnosis history relevant to current formulation
Clarify what has already been tried, what felt helpful, and what may have caused additional harm. Prior service histories often reveal pathologising, disbelief, or repeated symptom treatment without recognition of developmental relational trauma.
Suggested prompts • Have you spoken with anyone before about these experiences, and if so, what was that like for you? • Were there times you felt misunderstood, pathologised, or pushed into a version of your story that did not fit? • What would you want done differently in this work compared with what has happened before?
Clinical notes

7. Initial Pathway Decision and Immediate Treatment Emphasis
☐ Proceed to assessment and formulation ☐ Begin Phase I containment and stabilisation only ☐ Slow assessment and review next session again ☐ Coordinate alternative or adjunct specialist service ☐ Further risk action required immediately
At the close of the interview, determine the most appropriate next step. This decision is based on current formulation, stability, and epistemic safety rather than diagnostic certainty. Pathways are not hierarchical and may change as understanding develops.
Suggested prompts • What would feel like a manageable next step from here? • Would it feel more useful to focus first on safety and stabilisation, or on understanding the broader picture a little more? • Is there anything important I should keep in mind before our next session so that this work does not repeat earlier harm?
Clinical notes

Clinician summary and next session plan

Provisional clinical impression

Immediate treatment priorities

☐ Alliance and relational safety ☐ Risk management / crisis planning ☐ Regulation and containment supports ☐ Practical support or service linkage ☐ Further assessment next session ☐ Psychoeducation about pacing and phase-based work ☐ Supervision required

Follow-up actions before next session

Clinical Decision Pathways Following Intake

Following completion of the Initial Clinical Interview and the Clinical Intake and Identification Tool, clinicians determine the most appropriate next step based on the current formulation, stability, and epistemic safety. These pathways are not hierarchical and do not represent success or failure. They reflect ethical pacing decisions designed to protect both survivor safety and the integrity of treatment. Proceeding to assessment and formulation is appropriate when the presentation reflects patterns of developmental relational trauma and the survivor demonstrates sufficient emotional regulation, engagement capacity, and environmental safety to tolerate further assessment.

In these circumstances, the survivor can remain present during sessions, reflect on internal states without rapid destabilisation, and participate collaboratively in pacing decisions. For example, a survivor may report long-standing identity confusion and relational collapse linked to early family dynamics, while also showing the capacity to pause, reflect, and regulate affect when difficult material arises. In such cases, assessment can unfold gradually and collaboratively, with formulation evolving alongside therapeutic engagement.

Importantly, stabilisation before further assessment is indicated when emotional regulation is compromised, safety is uncertain, or crisis presentation predominates. Adult survivors of CPA-PA commonly enter therapy during periods of acute destabilisation, relational collapse, or cumulative exhaustion rather than with calm, coherent narratives. The immediate clinical focus remains on containment, relational safety, and practical support, with assessment deliberately slowed or temporarily deferred.

Redirection to alternative treatment pathways is appropriate when the survivor's presentation does not reflect developmental psychological abuse patterns. Importantly, when a survivor's primary clinical needs fall outside the scope of the HQTP, such as presentations dominated by acute psychosis, unmanaged substance dependence, primary neurological conditions, or other priorities requiring specialist intervention, collaboration with appropriate community or specialist services must occur before phase-based HQTP work can safely proceed. Where sufficient stabilisation has been achieved, and the survivor is clinically able to engage, re-entry into the HQTP may then be considered.

Referral and transition should be undertaken in a manner that avoids retraumatisation, invalidation, or abrupt disengagement. For example, a survivor presenting primarily with florid psychotic symptoms or severe cognitive impairment may require stabilisation within a specialist service before trauma-informed developmental work is appropriate. These pathways are revisited dynamically as clinical understanding evolves. Movement between pathways is expected and reflects responsive ethical care rather than inconsistency.

Ethical Safeguards and Boundary Protection

Across all pathways, clinicians must remain alert to the risk of confirmatory bias, over-identification with survivor narratives, and pressure to validate specific interpretations prematurely. Survivors of CPA-PA and coercive family systems are particularly vulnerable to epistemic harm when clinicians move too quickly toward certainty. The HQTP, therefore, requires disciplined clinical restraint, reflective supervision, and commitment to evidence-informed formulation.

Transition to Assessment and Formulation

Once initial screening indicates appropriateness for the HQTP and minimum stabilisation thresholds are met, clinicians proceed to the fuller assessment and formulation architecture outlined in the following chapter. That chapter extends, rather than replaces, the intake, screening, and pathway safeguards established here. On the following page, clinicians will find the **Clinical Intake and Identification Tool: Healing Qualia Treatment Protocol Reflection Form**.

Clinical Intake and Identification Tool (Printable)

Healing Qualia Treatment Protocol Reflection Form

This form is simply a way to help your therapist get to know you better and understand some of the experiences that may be affecting you today. You do not need to have everything figured out to complete it. You are welcome to skip any question that feels uncomfortable or unclear. There are no right or wrong answers. You are not being judged, blamed, or asked to prove anything. Nothing you write here is about blame or proving anything. This form is designed to help create a safe and supportive starting point for your therapy journey.

Please answer in the way that feels most true for you right now.

Your Early Family Experiences	
Did your caregivers or parents experience ongoing conflict after separation or relationship breakdown?	□ Yes □ No □ Not sure
Did you ever feel pulled into adult problems or expected to manage adult emotions?	□ Yes □ No □ Not sure
Did you feel pressure to agree with one adult's version of events about another adult in your family?	□ Yes □ No □ Not sure
Were there people in your family you felt discouraged, restricted, or unsafe staying connected with?	□ Yes □ No □ Not sure
Were you separated from a parent or close family member in a way that felt sudden, confusing, or outside your control?	□ Yes □ No □ Not sure
If you would like to add anything: ________ ____ ____	

Feeling Safe in Relationships Growing Up	
Did you ever feel that being close to one person meant having to distance yourself from another?	□ Yes □ No □ Not sure
Did you feel caught in the middle of adult disagreements or loyalty conflicts?	□ Yes □ No □ Not sure
Did you feel afraid of upsetting or disappointing a caregiver if you expressed your own feelings?	□ Yes □ No □ Not sure
If you would like to share more: ____ ____	

How These Experiences May Affect You Now	
Do you sometimes struggle to trust your own memories, feelings, or sense of what is real for you?	□ Yes □ No □ Sometimes
Do you often doubt yourself or feel unsure about your own story?	□ Yes □ No □ Sometimes
Do you feel unsure about who you are or find it hard to feel settled in yourself?	□ Yes □ No □ Sometimes
If you would like to add anything: ____ _ ____	

Emotional and Relationship Patterns	
Do you experience ongoing emotional distress such as anxiety, low mood, emotional overwhelm, or numbness?	□ Yes □ No □ Sometimes
Do close relationships feel difficult, unsafe, or unstable for you?	□ Yes □ No □ Sometimes
Do you find yourself putting others' needs first or avoiding conflict to keep peace in relationships?	□ Yes □ No □ Sometimes
If you would like to share more: ______________________________________ ______________________________________	

Past Support Experiences	
Have you previously worked with a psychotherapist, counsellor, psychologist, or mental health service?	□ Yes □ No
If yes, did you feel understood when talking about your family and early life experiences?	□ Yes □ No □ Sometimes
Did you ever feel rushed, dismissed, or encouraged to minimise what you went through?	□ Yes □ No □ Sometimes
If you would like to add anything: ______________________________________ ______________________________________	

<table>
<tr><th colspan="2">How Things Are for You Right Now</th></tr>
<tr><td>Do you currently feel emotionally safe where you live?</td><td>□ Yes □ No
□ Not sure</td></tr>
<tr><td>Do you have at least one person you feel safe talking to about difficult feelings?</td><td>□ Yes □ No
□ Not sure</td></tr>
<tr><td>Are you currently having thoughts about harming yourself or not wanting to be alive?</td><td>□ Yes □ No
□ Prefer not to say</td></tr>
<tr><td colspan="2">If you answered yes, please let your therapist know as soon as possible so support can be offered.
____
______________________________</td></tr>
<tr><th colspan="2">Anything You'd Like Your Therapist to Know</th></tr>
<tr><td colspan="2">If there is anything important you would like your therapist to understand about you or what brings you here, you can write it below:
____
____
______________________________</td></tr>
<tr><td colspan="2">Clinician Use Note (Not Shown to Client)
This reflection form supports early identification of relational disruption, developmental psychological injury patterns, and possible CPA-PA presentations, including CPA-PAA and CPA-PERA contexts. It is not a diagnostic instrument and should be interpreted alongside interview, formulation, and supervision.

Final Notes</td></tr>
</table>

Phase Entry Decision Logic

Determining Readiness for Phase I Engagement

Once the Initial Clinical Interview, the Clinical Intake and Identification Tool, and the preliminary formulation are complete, the clinician determines readiness for Phase I engagement. This decision is guided by safety, developmental context, and epistemic stability, and supports ethical pacing within the HQTP. It informs clinical judgement rather than replacing it.

The first consideration for MHPs involves determining whether the presenting profile reflects patterns consistent with developmental relational disruption and attachment-based injury. Indicators commonly include histories of prolonged family conflict, relational triangulation, loyalty pressure, identity instability, epistemic trust disruption, unresolved relational separation, and symptom patterns consistent with complex developmental trauma. Where these patterns are not present, the HQTP is not indicated, and clinicians redirect to alternative evidence-based treatment pathways appropriate to the presenting concern.

Where developmental trauma patterns are identified, the second consideration involves current stability and safety. Clinicians assess emotional regulation capacity, suicidal ideation or self-harm risk, dissociative symptoms, environmental safety, substance-related destabilisation, and the presence of acute interpersonal threats. When acute risk or instability is present, stabilisation takes precedence over further progression of the phase. Containment, safety planning, and short-term functional support are prioritised until sufficient stability is implemented.

The third consideration concerns epistemic safety and the capacity for engagement. Clinicians evaluate the survivor's ability to tolerate therapeutic contact, engage reflectively without becoming overwhelmed, participate in consent-based pacing, and maintain minimal narrative coherence required for orientation to treatment. Where epistemic safety remains significantly compromised, Phase I may begin only in a containment-focused manner, without trauma processing or historical exploration.

Based on these considerations, clinicians proceed along one of the three clinical pathways described previously. When developmental trauma patterns are present, immediate risk is managed, and epistemic safety is sufficient, clinicians may proceed to Phase I, with a focus on stabilisation, relational safety, orientation to the therapeutic process, restoration of agency, and pacing scaffolding.

Throughout this process, progression is not time-based. Movement between pathways may recur, and stabilisation may require ongoing attention throughout treatment. Premature trauma processing, outcome-driven pacing, and rigid adherence to phase progression undermine epistemic safety and increase risk of harm. The following chapter translates these ethical foundations into structured assessment and formulation practice for adult survivors, establishing the clinical safeguards that underpin all subsequent treatment phases.

Chapter Four

Assessment Context, Diagnostic Risk, and Clinical Formulation Foundations

Building on the ethical positioning and clinical scope established in the preceding chapter, assessment within the HQTP is understood as a clinically consequential process rather than a neutral administrative task. Decisions made during early assessment shape therapeutic safety, formulation accuracy, and long-term recovery trajectories.

The assumptions clinicians bring to assessment, the order in which questions are asked, and the way meaning is explored all directly influence survivor trust, emotional stabilisation, and the integrity of the therapeutic relationship. Within the HQTP, assessment is therefore oriented not toward extracting objective truth or diagnostic certainty, but toward understanding how experience has been subjectively lived, organised, and survived over time. Careful listening, relational attunement, and collaborative formulation begin the work of restoring psychological safety for survivors whose experiences were previously dismissed, distorted, or overwritten. When conducted with developmental sensitivity and attachment awareness, assessment actively interrupts patterns of misrecognition and establishes the relational conditions required for stabilisation and longer-term repair.

Assessment is therefore situated within an attachment-informed and trauma-aware clinical stance. Rather than treating formulation as a discrete event, the HQTP conceptualises assessment as a longitudinal, relational process that evolves alongside safety, narrative coherence, and emotional regulation. Clinical understanding is built gradually and collaboratively, allowing patterns of attachment disruption, coercive control, and developmental injury to be recognised without premature categorisation or interpretive overreach (Herman, 1992; Courtois & Ford, 2020).

For example, a survivor may initially present with emotional numbing, compliance, or a fragmented narrative, with more coherent reflection, affect, and meaning emerging only after sustained relational safety has been established. Early formulations are therefore held provisionally and revised over time as the survivor's regulatory and reflective capacity increases.

Within the HQTP, the depth and precision of clinical formulation are constrained by the survivor's current capacity for emotional regulation. Interpretive accuracy is not treated as a function of clinician insight alone, but as contingent upon the survivor's ability to remain physiologically regulated while reflecting on experience. When regulation is compromised, formulation is intentionally simplified, externalised, and safety-oriented. In practice, this means the clinician temporarily shifts away from complex relational interpretation, internal attribution, or historical meaning-making. Instead, it frames experience in concrete, present-focused, non-pathologising terms that support nervous system stabilisation. The emphasis moves from *why* something is happening to *what is happening now* and *what supports safety in this moment*.

This approach protects against interpretive harm and reflects established evidence that cognitive integration and meaning-making are state-dependent capacities rather than stable traits, meaning that a survivor's ability to reflect, link experiences, and generate meaning fluctuates with nervous system safety and physiological regulation rather than representing a fixed level of psychological functioning (Linehan, 1993; Siegel, 2020).

For example, when a survivor becomes tearful, cognitively constricted, dissociative, or unable to track conversational content while discussing relational history, the clinician suspends interpretive formulation and redirects attention to grounding, present-moment orientation, or containment. Early indicators of compromised regulation may include subtle micro-expressions such as sudden gaze aversion, slowed or halted speech, shallow breathing, facial flattening, jaw tightening, loss of postural tone, repetitive self-soothing movements, or difficulty responding to simple reflective prompts. In response, the clinician may slow the pace of the session, gently name the observed shift in regulation, invite attention to sensory anchors in the room, or return to concrete, present-focused material, such as orienting to the immediate environment or summarising what feels manageable to hold in awareness. Formulation depth is revisited only once physiological stability is re-established.

Adult survivors of prolonged psychological abuse frequently present with complex, layered symptom profiles shaped by loyalty conflicts, attachment betrayal, identity erosion, and prolonged exposure to coercive family systems. These presentations rarely conform neatly to categorical diagnostic boundaries. Within this context, diagnosis may function either as a stabilising clinical scaffold or as a source of secondary harm, depending on how it is applied and interpreted (Frances, 2013; Paris, 2015).

Diagnosis as a Clinical Tool and Risk Vector

When applied judiciously, diagnostic formulation can operate as a clinical circuit breaker. Accurate diagnosis may provide clarity, guide treatment planning, facilitate communication, and validate survivor experience by offering language to describe internal distress (Frances, 2013). It may also support access to appropriate therapeutic and systemic resources. For some survivors, this process represents the first experience of being psychologically understood rather than pathologised.

However, diagnosis also carries a significant risk. Survivors of CPA-PA and related coercive family systems frequently report experiences of misdiagnosis, over-pathologisation, and clinical invalidation within mental health services that failed to recognise the relational origins of their trauma (Herman, 2015; Johnston & Sullivan, 2020; Price-Tobler, 2023a). Labels applied without developmental and attachment-based formulation may obscure causal pathways of distress, reinforce stigma, and contribute to therapeutic rupture. For example, trauma-based adaptations such as emotional detachment, relational avoidance, or self-doubt may be misinterpreted as personality pathology or treatment resistance when assessed outside a relational context.

Additionally, when assessment is approached through a symptom-first lens divorced from relational and developmental context, trauma adaptations are easily misread as intrinsic pathology. Within the HQTP, diagnosis is therefore treated as provisional and hypothesis-driven rather than fixed or identity-defining. Clinical formulation remains anchored in a longitudinal developmental understanding, with careful attention to the interactions among attachment disruption, environmental stressors, and survival-based adaptation over time. Diagnostic understanding may be revised as assessment deepens and as the survivor's capacity for reflection, narrative integration, and emotional regulation develops. Where the clinical picture does not clarify, or where the mental health practitioner identifies the possible presence of a distinct underlying mental illness requiring formal diagnostic assessment, referral to an appropriate service may be necessary. In such cases, HQTP work may need to pause until sufficient stabilisation has been achieved.

Start With Physiology, Not Pathology

Bailey et al. (2020) propose that many behaviours observed in high-conflict family contexts may be more accurately understood as adaptive nervous-system responses to chronic threat than as evidence of inherent personality pathology or intentional misconduct. When children experience prolonged relational insecurity, coercion, fear, or conflict, their capacity for reflection, communication, emotional regulation, and problem-solving may become reduced because the nervous system is organised around protection and survival.

This distinction is clinically important. Hypervigilance, avoidance, emotional shutdown, hostility, withdrawal, rigid certainty, rapid escalation, appeasement, or reduced reflective capacity should not automatically be interpreted as personality disturbance, manipulation, defiance, or fixed psychopathology. In some children, these behaviours may represent attempts to maintain safety within a relational environment experienced as threatening or unpredictable (Bailey et al., 2020).

The same principle remains relevant when these children reach adulthood. Survival responses developed under chronic relational threat may persist as trauma-organised patterns involving fear, dissociation, relational mistrust, emotional constriction, appeasement, withdrawal, or heightened reactivity. When the developmental context is not recognised, adult survivors may be misread as resistant, unstable, oppositional, dependent, manipulative, or personality disordered, when the clinician may instead be observing the continuing effects of developmental trauma and nervous-system adaptation.

Within the HQTP, this does not mean that genuine psychiatric or personality pathology should be dismissed where diagnostic criteria are met. Rather, it requires clinicians to assess carefully whether the presentation is better explained by enduring psychopathology, trauma-related physiology, or an interaction between both. Bailey et al. (2020) therefore provide further support for the HQTP principle that formulation should begin with developmental history, relational context, nervous-system state, and felt safety before fixed conclusions are drawn about pathology.

Developmental Formulation and Longitudinal Assessment

Assessment within the HQTP prioritises the integration of behavioural presentation, relational history, attachment patterns, family system dynamics, and contextual stressors. Symptoms such as emotional dysregulation, dissociation, relational instability, hypervigilance, compliance, withdrawal, or apparent emotional detachment are interpreted as potential trauma adaptations rather than isolated clinical phenomena (van der Kolk, 2014; Courtois & Ford, 2020). This formulation approach reflects the cumulative nature of child psychological abuse, in which prolonged relational threat and coercive family dynamics shape regulatory capacity, identity formation, and interpersonal functioning across development.

Longitudinal assessment enables clinicians to observe patterns of emotional regulation, relational engagement, and narrative coherence over time rather than relying on cross-sectional or event-focused snapshots. Survivors exposed to prolonged psychological coercion and attachment disruption frequently require extended periods of relational safety before disclosure, reflective capacity, and narrative integration become possible.

For example, a survivor may initially present with limited affect, rehearsed narratives, or compliance-based engagement, with greater emotional access, ambivalence, or narrative complexity emerging only after trust and safety have been established. Early formulation is therefore intentionally provisional and responsive, designed to protect against premature conclusions and interpretive overreach while allowing clinical understanding to evolve alongside therapeutic engagement (Herman, 1992; Courtois & Ford, 2020).

This developmental orientation also reduces the risk of therapeutic reenactment. When clinicians impose rigid interpretive frameworks or premature diagnostic certainty early in treatment, survivors may experience therapy as another environment in which their internal reality is overwritten by professional authority. The HQTP emphasises collaborative meaning-making, where formulation emerges through shared exploration rather than unilateral declaration. This process supports epistemic safety, strengthens the therapeutic alliance, and reinforces survivor agency throughout the assessment.

Consistent with trauma-informed and attachment-based models, the HQTP conceptualises formulation as an ongoing relational process rather than a discrete intake event (Herman, 1992; van der Kolk, 2014). Clinical understanding is refined progressively as safety increases, defensive adaptations soften, and the survivor's capacity for reflective integration expands. This longitudinal formulation framework provides the developmental map that informs phase sequencing, pacing decisions, stabilisation priorities, and readiness for deeper trauma processing throughout the protocol.

Micro Expressions as Indicators of Fear and Relational Activation

Clinicians should remain attentive to signs of hypervigilance, avoidance, and relational mistrust, as these may indicate that early conditioning remains active. Such behaviours should not be misinterpreted as resistance or non-compliance but understood as adaptive survival responses. Treatment must preserve the survivor's agency in decision-making, with clinicians consistently reinforcing that the survivor retains control over the pace, direction, and boundaries of care. This is especially important in Specific Phobia–CPA-PAA Anxiety Variant presentations, where anticipatory fear of externally imposed decisions may remain highly active.

In addition to these broader behavioural cues, clinicians may observe microexpressions: subtle, involuntary facial responses that appear briefly before an individual consciously regulates or suppresses emotion. In trauma work, such cues may offer useful insight into unspoken fear, discomfort, shame, pain, or relational activation, particularly when the survivor verbally minimises distress.

In his clinical teaching on microexpressions, Dr David Puder emphasises that recognising these fleeting affective signals can enhance empathy, strengthen the therapeutic alliance, and help clinicians notice emotional material that may not yet be consciously articulated by the patient (Puder, 2021). He also highlights that attention to microexpressions can help clinicians move beyond their own assumptions and become more curious about the patient's internal state, thereby supporting more accurate emotional attunement and more responsive intervention (Puder, 2021).

Puder and Cunningham further note that fear is an adaptive emotion organised around safety and survival, and that clinicians should respond to visible fear with curiosity rather than confrontation (Puder & Cunningham, 2018). Their discussion is especially relevant to survivors with fear-organised presentations, because fear may disrupt emotional connection, increase autonomic activation, and lead the survivor into fight, flight, shutdown, or relational withdrawal unless psychological safety is actively re-established (Puder & Cunningham, 2018). In this sense, microexpressions are not merely interesting nonverbal details. They may serve as momentary indicators that the survivor is shifting from relational safety to threat-based processing before this becomes fully verbalised or behaviourally obvious (Puder, 2021; Puder & Cunningham, 2018).

In survivors with fear-organised presentations, microexpressions may include brief furrowing of the brow, widened eyes, tightening of the mouth, slight tremors of the lips, shifts in gaze, changes in posture, or subtle withdrawal when trauma-linked relational material is discussed. Puder's broader teaching also notes the clinical relevance of distinguishing emotional expressions such as fear, anger, disgust, pain, and shame-related discomfort, as these may carry different implications for therapeutic pacing and response (Puder, 2021; Puder & Cunningham, 2018).

Within the Specific Phobia–CPA-PAA Anxiety Variant subgroup, these reactions may emerge when themes of contact, separation, the targeted parent, threat, relocation, or loss of control are introduced. Even when fleeting, such cues may suggest that the survivor is moving into heightened autonomic activation before they can verbalise it directly. Clinical attunement to these subtle indicators can help guide pacing and protect therapeutic safety. When such cues emerge, the clinician may need to slow the session, return to grounding, redirect toward safer material, or acknowledge the discomfort without pressing for further disclosure. Their discussion of fear also supports gradual, manageable exposure to emotionally charged material rather than overwhelming confrontation, aligning closely with the pacing requirements of the HQTP in fear-organised survivor presentations (Puder & Cunningham, 2018).

Research on trauma survivors indicates that heightened emotional sensitivity and reactivity may become visible through brief nonverbal expressions, even when verbal presentation appears neutral or controlled (Bérubé, 2021). In this sense, careful observation of microexpressions may support formulation, pacing, and relational safety while also strengthening therapeutic attunement. However, such cues should always be interpreted cautiously and in context, rather than treated as definitive evidence of any single internal state.

Such attunement is important not only for immediate clinical pacing, but also because the effects of early relational trauma may extend far beyond childhood. In survivors of CPA-PA in all its forms, subtle emotional responses observed in therapy may reflect deeper developmental injuries associated with prolonged attachment disruption, chronic relational stress, unresolved grief, and fear-based relational learning. For this reason, treatment cannot assume that resilience is already intact or readily accessible in adult survivors but must understand it as something that may need to be rebuilt gradually within conditions of sustained safety, relational consistency, and therapeutic attunement.

Constructing Resilience Through Therapeutic Process

Resilience in adult survivors is not conceptualised as an innate trait but as a developmental capacity cultivated through safe relational experience, emotional regulation, narrative coherence, and restored agency (Masten, 2014; Herman, 2015). Survivors frequently enter therapy having learned to prioritise survival over authenticity, compliance over autonomy, and emotional suppression over expression. Recovery, therefore, involves more than symptom reduction. It requires the gradual reconstruction of internal working models shaped by attachment betrayal, coercive control, and chronic relational threat.

Healing occurs not only through therapeutic techniques but through the experience of a relationship with the MHP that remains consistent, attuned, and non-coercive over time. For survivors whose early relationships were organised around fear, control, or conditional acceptance, the therapist–client relationship becomes a key context in which safety, trust, and emotional regulation can be rebuilt. Consistent presence, predictable boundaries, and emotionally reliable responses allow survivors to test new ways of relating without fear of punishment, withdrawal, or correction (Liotti, 2004; Siegel, 2020).

For example, a survivor may arrive late to a session, cancel at short notice, or become emotionally withdrawn following a perceived relational rupture. In many survivors' developmental histories, such behaviour would have been met with criticism, withdrawal of affection, or escalation of control. Within the therapeutic relationship, the clinician responds with steadiness rather than reactivity, maintains clear but non-punitive boundaries, and remains emotionally available without demanding explanation or compliance. Over time, repeated experiences of being met with consistency rather than retaliation allow the survivor's nervous system to recalibrate expectations of safety, supporting increased emotional regulation and relational trust.

Over time, this relational stability supports the development of emotional regulation capacity. Grounding practices, somatic regulation strategies, and stabilisation techniques expand tolerance for affective experience and reduce autonomic reactivity, particularly among survivors whose nervous systems have learned to remain on high alert to survive (Cloitre et al., 2012; Ford & Courtois, 2020). Neurodevelopmental research demonstrates that early attachment relationships shape right-hemisphere systems responsible for affect regulation, stress modulation, and relational safety, which remain highly sensitive to relational threat in adulthood (Schore, 2001, 2003). Importantly, these capacities develop gradually and unevenly. Increased regulation in session does not mean the nervous system can yet tolerate external relational stress without destabilisation.

In the context of CPA-PA, regulatory fluctuations are common and clinically expected. Adult survivors may demonstrate increased stability across several sessions, followed by marked destabilisation after contact from an alienating parent or exposure to relational threat. For example, a survivor may experience emotional collapse, self-doubt, shame, dissociation, or urges to withdraw after receiving a critical message, a demand for reassurance, or indirect pressure framed as concern or disappointment from their AP. Such reactions reflect activation of the attachment system rather than a loss of therapeutic gains.

These fluctuations do not indicate regression or treatment failure. They reflect the brain and nervous system responding to cues historically associated with coercion, loss of attachment, or punishment for autonomy. Survivors may require a week or longer to physiologically re-regulate following such activation. During this time, they often do not understand what is happening internally and may fear they are deteriorating or developing a mental health challenge. The clinician's role includes careful psychoeducation, helping the survivor recognise these responses as conditioned survival reactions rather than signs of pathology.

Narrative reconstruction further strengthens resilience by restoring authorship over personal history. Survivors of CPA-PAA were often required to adopt externally imposed narratives that distorted memory, meaning, and identity. Therapeutic support for coherent storytelling enables survivors to integrate fragmented experiences gradually and re-establish a sense of self that is no longer organised around appeasement, denial, or fear (Neimeyer, 2019). Narrative coherence is treated as a developmental outcome of safety rather than a prerequisite for therapeutic engagement.

Boundary development represents another core domain of resilience. Many survivors emerge from environments in which personal limits were punished, ignored, or exploited. Therapy supports the identification of relational boundaries, recognition of coercive dynamics, and cultivation of safer interpersonal connections. This work proceeds slowly and requires repeated validation, as asserting limits may initially intensify anxiety, guilt, or attachment threat. Meaning-making processes help survivors reconnect with values, creativity, cultural identity, and purpose that were suppressed by prolonged trauma (Park, 2010). Agency and mastery experiences consolidate recovery by strengthening self-efficacy and restoring a sense of choice (Bandura, 1997).

Resilience within the HQTP is therefore understood as emergent and non-linear. Periods of increased stability may alternate with destabilisation as deeper material becomes accessible or as external stressors reactivate the threat of attachment. Clinicians are cautioned against interpreting temporary increases in distress, ambivalence, or relational withdrawal as regression. Within a sufficiently contained therapeutic relationship, such shifts often signal increased capacity to engage with previously avoided affect, memory, or meaning (Herman, 2015). Practitioners must remain neutral and non-judgemental regarding survivors' decisions about parental contact. Cycles of distance and reconnection frequently reflect unresolved attachment longing rather than ambivalence or inconsistency. Ethical clinical practice supports survivor autonomy and nervous system safety without imposing prescriptive relational outcomes or timelines.

Clinician Decision Note

When destabilisation follows contact with, or a perceived threat from, an alienating parent, clinicians are advised to pause interpretation and prioritise containment, validation, and co-regulation. The guiding clinical question is not "What diagnosis does this resemble?" but "What has the nervous system just detected as unsafe?" Teaching the survivor to recognise these patterns supports regulation, reduces shame, and restores agency. Throughout this protocol, the depth of clinical interpretation is governed by the survivor's current regulatory capacity rather than diagnostic curiosity or theoretical completeness.

Red Flag Differential Prompt

Attachment-mediated destabilisation should not be automatically interpreted as emerging mental illness. Consider diagnostic escalation only when symptoms persist beyond expected regulation windows, occur independently of relational triggers, or fail to respond to containment, psychoeducation, and relational safety. Where uncertainty exists, longitudinal observation and supervision take precedence over premature classification.

Betrayal Trauma and Attachment Disruption

Betrayal trauma theory provides a critical explanatory context for understanding alienation and abduction dynamics. Children who remain dependent on caregivers for survival frequently suppress conscious awareness of harm to preserve attachment bonds (Freyd, 2021). While adaptive in the short term, this survival mechanism disrupts memory integration, emotional regulation, and identity development. Survivors often internalise distorted relational narratives, invalidate their own perceptions, and prioritise psychological survival over emotional authenticity.

Cultural and contextual factors further shape the expression and recovery trajectories of trauma. Norms surrounding family loyalty, emotional disclosure, and help-seeking behaviour influence symptom presentation and treatment engagement. Some survivors maintain high-functioning public identities while privately experiencing significant distress, whereas others express trauma primarily through somatic or relational channels (Herman, 2015). Cultural sensitivity is therefore essential to accurate formulation and ethical clinical practice.

Trauma-Informed Care, Service System Failure, and Implementation Gaps

Although trauma-informed care has been widely adopted as a guiding principle across mental health and human services, implementation remains inconsistent and frequently superficial. Many organisations adopt trauma-informed language without embedding the structural and relational changes required to support genuine psychological safety (SAMHSA, 2014; Bath, 2015). Survivors of CPA-PA describe that they often encounter services that advertise themselves as trauma-informed while continuing to rely on behavioural compliance models, risk-driven escalation protocols, and deficit-based formulations that inadvertently replicate coercive dynamics.

Trauma-informed practice requires more than awareness training. It demands organisational commitment to safety, transparency, choice, collaboration, empowerment, and cultural humility (SAMHSA, 2014). Bloom and Farragher (2013) emphasise that without parallel changes in organisational culture, supervisory structures, and power hierarchies, trauma-informed initiatives risk becoming performative rather than protective. In practice, survivors frequently report experiences in which their trauma history is acknowledged rhetorically while clinical interactions remain directive, pathologising, or dismissive.

This gap between trauma-informed ideals and operational reality carries significant clinical risk. When practitioners lack training in attachment-based psychological abuse, relational trauma dynamics, and coercive control patterns, they may inadvertently escalate distress through rigid procedural responses. Behaviour interpreted as resistance, avoidance, or non-compliance is often a manifestation of trauma activation rather than defiance. Without trauma-informed formulation, escalation protocols can compound harm rather than restore safety.

Escalation, Nervous System Activation, and Workforce Safety

Adult survivors with histories of prolonged relational trauma frequently exhibit heightened autonomic sensitivity. Threat perception may be amplified by prior experiences of betrayal, abandonment, or coercion. Polyvagal theory highlights how trauma-exposed individuals may rapidly shift into sympathetic mobilisation or dorsal vagal shutdown when cues of safety are absent (Porges, 2011). Clinical environments that rely on authoritative communication, abrupt limit-setting, or procedural enforcement may inadvertently activate these survival responses.

Escalation is therefore not simply a behavioural-management issue. It is also a nervous-system event. Practitioners who lack training in co-regulation, emotional containment, and trauma-informed de-escalation may misinterpret activation as intentional disruption. This misunderstanding can increase risk for both survivors and staff. Workforce safety is achieved not only through control strategies but also through relational containment, environmental predictability, and trauma-aware communication.

Bailey et al. (2020) further observe that high-conflict family systems can become emotionally contagious. Children, parents, clinicians, lawyers, evaluators, and other professionals may be drawn into the same escalating and dysregulated interaction patterns. For clinicians, awareness of autonomic activation is therefore important not only for understanding the survivor, but also for monitoring their own physiological and emotional responses. Remaining regulated, making active use of supervision, and resisting pressure to respond from urgency, defensiveness, rescue, or alignment can help prevent the clinician from becoming incorporated into the family-system conflict. A nervous-system-informed approach may therefore support both clinical formulation and workforce safety.

In disability, forensic, and acute mental health settings, staff frequently report exposure to high-risk presentations without receiving adequate trauma training or access to appropriate supervision. Survivors entering these systems may encounter multiple service transitions, inconsistent relational continuity, overly forceful security responses, and fragmented care coordination. These structural conditions may compound distress and undermine therapeutic engagement.

Systemic Failure and the Royal Commission Findings

The Royal Commission into Violence, Abuse, Neglect and Exploitation of People with Disability documented widespread systemic failures in recognising and responding to trauma across service systems (Royal Commission, 2023). Findings highlighted inadequate workforce training, poor interagency communication, inconsistent safeguarding practices, and limited accountability mechanisms. These failures disproportionately affect individuals with complex trauma histories, including survivors of childhood psychological abuse and family violence.

The Commission's findings reinforce the necessity of trauma-informed, attachment-aware assessment frameworks that extend beyond individual therapy rooms into organisational practice. Without structural reform, clinicians are often forced to work within systems that undermine relational safety and ethical care. The HQTP, therefore, situates clinical practice within broader systemic responsibility, recognising that survivor recovery is influenced not only by therapeutic technique but by the environments in which care is delivered.

Assessment Before Coercive Intervention

In CPA-PA contexts, the central clinical risk is not terminology alone, but the failure to distinguish between a child's rejection arising from abuse, neglect, fear, or seriously deficient parenting, and rejection shaped through coercive psychological alignment. Where this differential assessment is not undertaken with rigour, clinicians may misinterpret protective responses as pathology and make unsafe recommendations, including inappropriate contact or reunification interventions. Within the HQTP, a comprehensive child abuse assessment and developmentally grounded formulation must precede any recommendation that may expose a child to further harm.

Furthermore, survivor-led initiatives such as the Thriver's Speak Conference '*Nothing About Us Without Us'* have made clear that when abuse is minimised, attachment disruption is overlooked, or trauma-based fear is misread as pathology, the consequences for children and later adult survivors can be profound and enduring.

Differential Diagnosis and the Necessity of Structured Assessment

The HQTP adopts the principle of 'assess, do not assume' as a foundational safeguard. Ethical clinical assessment in adult survivor work requires formulation grounded in developmental history, attachment context, and observable trauma patterns rather than assumption, narrative certainty, or diagnostic shortcutting (American Psychological Association, 2017; Psychology Board of Australia, 2025). Attachment-based differential diagnosis models emphasise the distinction between trauma-driven relational avoidance and behaviour arising from coercive psychological alignment. Childress (2015) describes divergent pathways of relational breakdown that call for distinct clinical responses.

Within the HQTP, this distinction is treated as a clinical decision point rather than a theoretical debate, as it directly informs assessment, formulation, and the sequencing of interventions. When these pathways are not differentiated, clinicians increase the risk of misdiagnosis, unsafe intervention, therapeutic reenactment, and the reinforcement of harmful relational narratives that may further escalate family conflict. Structured assessment protects both survivors and practitioners. It reduces confirmation bias, supports clinical humility, and ensures that formulation is grounded in observable patterns rather than ideological alignment or institutional pressure.

Whitcombe (2024) also emphasises the complexity of assessing suspected parental alienation within family-court contexts. Her work reinforces the need to avoid single-factor conclusions and to examine the child's rejection or resistance within the broader attachment, developmental, relational, safeguarding, and family-system context. Although the HQTP is not a forensic assessment model, this caution remains clinically relevant. A child's alignment with one parent or rejection of another should not, by itself, be treated as sufficient evidence of parental alienation, estrangement, abuse, or the source of the child's distress. Careful differential assessment is required before drawing conclusions about the processes organising the child's presentation. This discussion is included to clarify the developmental and assessment context from which later adult-survivor presentations may arise; it does not authorise the use of the HQTP as a child-custody, family-court, or forensic assessment instrument.

Linking Baker's Four-Factor Model, Bernet and Greenhill's Five-Factor Model, Childress's Attachment-Based Assessment Framework, and Price-Tobler's HQTP Sequentially

This issue is especially important in complex and emerging clinical areas where a child may be presented for significant medical, psychological, or identity-related intervention within a high-conflict family context. When a child is living in an environment shaped by coercive control, fear of retaliation, emotional dependency, or loyalty-based compliance, clinicians must carefully consider whether the child's expressed wishes are being communicated freely, reflect a developmentally integrated sense of self, or have become organised around relational survival. In such cases, safeguarding responsibilities require careful assessment, multidisciplinary consultation where appropriate, and close attention to possible indicators of child abuse, coercive control, attachment disturbance, and developmental harm.

For adult survivors, this section remains highly relevant. Many later report that warning signs were visible during childhood but were not adequately recognised, assessed, or acted upon by the professional systems surrounding them. The consequence was not simply delayed understanding. It was the continuation of attachment trauma, developmental distortion, grief, identity confusion, epistemic injury, and relational harm across the lifespan. Early recognition, therefore, matters not only for immediate child protection but also for the prevention of long-term psychological harm extending into adulthood.

To clarify how this early recognition task may be strengthened in practice, the present chapter briefly introduces several frameworks that operate at different points in the clinical sequence. Although these models arise from different literatures and are not usually presented as a single integrated pathway, they may be read together in a clinically useful progression, particularly in contexts where court, child protection, medical, and mental health responses are often fragmented rather than developmentally coordinated.

This proposed sequencing is not intended to suggest that these authors share identical theoretical positions, use interchangeable terminology, or agree on all aspects of formulation, assessment, or intervention. They do not. Nor does this discussion attempt to resolve longstanding professional tensions across these bodies of literature. Rather, the purpose here is pragmatic and clinically oriented. When viewed sequentially, these frameworks may help clinicians move from early threshold recognition to deeper attachment-based assessment, to a lifespan understanding of developmental sequelae, and finally to structured adult survivor treatment. In that sense, the present discussion seeks to elevate the clinical task above disciplinary division by asking how these models may contribute, at different stages, to the protection and treatment of those affected. The following section introduces the Five-Factor Model as a structured first step in that threshold enquiry.

How the Assessment and Treatment Frameworks Function Together Sequentially

Step One: Threshold Recognition Through the Four- and Five-Factor Models

In this proposed sequence, Baker's Four-Factor Model and Bernet and Greenhill's later Five-Factor Model may be understood as structured first-level frameworks for threshold enquiry when a child rejects a parent in the context of high-conflict family breakdown and allegations of abuse (Baker, 2020; Bernet & Greenhill, 2022).

Their function is not to establish a final conclusion, but to assist early assessors to consider whether the child's presentation is more adequately explained by actual abuse, neglect, or seriously deficient parenting, or whether further differential enquiry is required. At this stage, the task is not to arrive prematurely at a global explanation for the family system. It is to determine whether the child's rejection warrants deeper assessment. In this sense, these models may operate as threshold tools. They can help clinicians avoid both naïve acceptance of surface narratives and premature interpretive certainty, thereby supporting a more disciplined and ethically cautious entry point into complex cases. Where contact resistance, refusal, or relational breach is present, these features should not be treated as proof of alienation, but as signals that the child's relational position requires careful assessment rather than assumption-driven intervention.

Author Addition: Proposed Sixth Contextual Consideration for Abduction, Concealment, and Unilateral Removal

Furthermore, the author suggests that an additional Sixth Factor area of enquiry may warrant addition and exploration in cases involving abduction, concealed relocation, or unilateral removal of the child without the other parent's knowledge or consent. Although this proposed Sixth Factor consideration does not form part of the published Five-Factor Model, it may hold substantial clinical and forensic relevance because such circumstances can intensify attachment rupture, restrict access to alternative relational narratives, impede collateral verification, and consolidate the child's dependence on a single controlling caregiving system. Accordingly, abduction-related concealment may be examined as a contextual amplifier of developmental risk within the broader assessment and formulation process drawn from the adult survivor PhD data (Price-Tobler, 2023a).

At a practical level, the Five-Factor Model directs the assessor to consider five linked areas of enquiry. The first is whether the child is demonstrating contact resistance, refusal, or marked withdrawal from one parent. The second is whether there was previously a positive, developmentally meaningful relationship with the now-rejected parent. The third is whether abuse, neglect, or seriously deficient parenting by the rejected parent provides a more adequate explanation for the child's rejection. The fourth is whether the favoured parent has engaged in multiple behaviours that may be contributing to the child's rejection. The fifth is whether the child displays behavioural manifestations associated with rigid, disproportionate, and global rejection (Baker, 2020; Bernet & Greenhill, 2022). Framed in this way, the model provides clinicians, court-related professionals, family consultants, and child protection practitioners with a disciplined set of threshold questions to guide early triage, safeguarding, and referral, rather than relying solely on the child's stated preference or on competing parental allegations (Bernet & Greenhill, 2022).

This use of the model may be particularly helpful for professionals who encounter families before a specialist report has been commissioned. Anyone assessing families in the context of high-conflict divorce, contact refusal, or abuse allegations may use the Five-Factor Model as an initial enquiry framework to determine whether the matter requires more careful differential review and referral into a specialist mental health assessment (Bernet & Greenhill, 2022). In that sense, child protection services, court professionals, intake clinicians, and other frontline practitioners may use the model to organise a first-level enquiry while recognising that it does not replace abuse investigations, collateral reviews, developmental analyses, or specialist clinical formulations (Forslund et al., 2022). This is consistent with attachment-informed guidance for courts, which recommends that caregiver behaviour, relational context, and contextual risk remain central in child protection and custody-related decision-making (Forslund et al., 2022).

In family court contexts, timely assessment for child abuse is important because children affected by coercive family dynamics may present in ways that are easily misread as preference, conflict, immaturity, or oppositionality rather than as indicators of developmental harm. Careful assessment helps distinguish actual abuse, neglect, and pathogenic parenting from surface-level narratives, supports more accurate formulation of the child's difficulties, and assists courts and clinicians to identify when the child's expressed wishes may be organised around fear, loyalty pressure, or relational survival rather than autonomous preference (Baker, 2020; Bernet & Greenhill, 2022; Childress, 2015).

Where abuse is not recognised, the result may be not only immediate failure of protection, but the continuation of attachment disruption, identity distortion, developmental grief, and trauma-related sequelae that can persist into adulthood (Price-Tobler, 2023a; van der Kolk, 2014). Assessment, therefore, matters both for child protection in the present and for preventing long-term developmental harm across the lifespan.

Step Two: Differential Assessment and Child Abuse Enquiry

If threshold concerns are identified, the next step is not reunification planning, but rigorous differential assessment. From an attachment perspective, children are ordinarily organised to seek proximity to a caregiver when alarmed, frightened, distressed, or overwhelmed (Bowlby, 1969/1982). Persistent fear, apprehension, withdrawal, or aversion toward a parent is, therefore, clinically significant and should be treated as an attachment alarm signal requiring careful enquiry. It should not, however, be treated as automatic proof of either abuse or alienation.

Clinicians must examine whether the child's rejection, fear, withdrawal, or resistance is better explained by abuse, neglect, coercive control, seriously deficient parenting, trauma, frightening or frightened caregiving, exposure to domestic violence, attachment disruption, or broader developmental and family system factors (Lyons-Ruth & Jacobvitz, 2016; Main & Solomon, 1990). Comprehensive child abuse assessment must therefore take precedence over assumption-driven intervention. At this stage, the matter is primarily one of mental health, safeguarding, and developmental assessment rather than automatically a court-driven issue, unless statutory or legal protection concerns clearly require formal intervention.

Step Three: When the Five-Factor Model Identifies Concerns

Where the initial Five-Factor review leaves ongoing concern that the child's presentation is not adequately explained by genuine abuse-related causes or seriously deficient parenting, Childress's attachment-based assessment may then be introduced as the next level of formulation (Childress, 2016). At that point, the task shifts from threshold screening and differential review to deeper clinical analysis of the family system, the child's attachment organisation, and the mechanisms through which the child's rejection may be shaped and maintained. Childress's model is more useful for evaluating pathogenic parenting, psychological control, cross-generational coalition, attachment-related symptom formation, and the child's behavioural display within the family system (Childress, 2016).

In this sequence, the Five-Factor Model assists with the initial threshold enquiry, differential review, and referral decision. Childress then provides the more detailed attachment-based assessment framework required when a formal treatment-focused or court-oriented clinical evaluation is indicated. Used together in this way, the two frameworks address different levels of the clinical question. The Five-Factor Model helps determine whether the child's presentation warrants more searching differential enquiry. Childress's attachment-based framework then assists the clinician in examining how pathogenic dynamics may be operating, how they are being maintained, and what specialist assessment or intervention planning may be required if those dynamics are confirmed (Childress, 2016). The first framework, therefore, supports early recognition and referral, while the second supports deeper formulation and attachment-based assessment.

Step Four: Attachment-Based Assessment Through the Attachment-Based Model of Parental Alienation (AB-PA)

Where threshold review raises concern that abuse-related causes do not fully explain the child's rejection, Childress's attachment-based model offers a more detailed attachment-oriented lens for assessment (Childress, 2017). In the AB-PA formulation, the child's rejection of a previously loved, normal-range, affectionally available parent is treated as attachment-related pathology requiring assessment of both parents' parenting contributions, rather than an assumption-driven focus on the child alone. This includes assessment of the targeted or rejected parent for severe problematic parenting that could reasonably account for the child's fear, withdrawal, or rejection, and assessment of the allied or favoured parent for pathogenic parenting, psychological control, cross-generational coalition, and attachment distortion processes that may be shaping the child's symptoms.

At this stage, the clinical task moves beyond threshold recognition into deeper developmental formulation of the child's attachment organisation, the caregiving environment, and the relational mechanisms through which rejection, role distortion, and coercive alignment may be maintained. At this stage, it is also important to recognise that in high-conflict separations, children may become drawn into adult dispute processes in ways that undermine psychological neutrality, distort attachment development, and erode their capacity to maintain meaningful relationships with both parents, unless genuine abuse or safety concerns require protective intervention (Bowlby, 1969; Goldenberg & Goldenberg, 2013; Haley, 1977; Minuchin, 1974). From an attachment perspective, the broader issue is not simply contact or conflict, but the developmental significance of the parent-child bond itself. Where a child is recruited into triangulation, cross-generational coalition, or coercive loyalty processes, the disturbance may extend well beyond immediate family conflict and affect later trust, self-worth, autonomy, and relational functioning (Bowlby, 1969).

Within the HQTP, Childress's work is used as an attachment-based assessment lens to deepen understanding of child protection, development, and clinical formulation. It is not used to bypass child abuse assessment, minimise risk, or justify coercive reunification where safety has not been rigorously established. Once threshold review and attachment-based assessment have been undertaken, the clinical task shifts toward developmental formulation.

At this stage, the question is no longer only whether alienation-related dynamics may be present. The question becomes: what developmental harm has occurred; how the child's attachment system has been affected; how fear, loyalty conflict, role distortion, coercive control, and epistemic invalidation may have shaped the developing self; and what this means for safeguarding and treatment. This includes consideration of identity formation, affect regulation, autonomy, self-trust, epistemic stability, and long-term relational functioning. The purpose of this step is to move beyond surface description and toward a clinically coherent account of the harm, its developmental organisation, and the likely implications for later psychological functioning if left unrecognised or untreated. The following sub-sections elaborate on the core attachment-based concepts relevant to Step Four, including the developmental significance of the parent-child bond, triangulation, pathogenic parenting, parent-specific assessment, symptom display, and implementation considerations. To understand why these dynamics matter clinically, it is necessary to recognise the developmental significance of the parent-child bond itself.

In healthy child development, each parent-child bond may contribute distinctive relational experiences, meanings, and templates for later functioning. Within the attachment-based logic informing this section, the mother-son, mother-daughter, father-son, and father-daughter relationships are treated as developmentally significant bonds rather than interchangeable roles (Bowlby, 1969).

A mother-son bond, for example, may foster emotional security when a mother is a consistent source of comfort and encouragement, such as helping a boy manage setbacks at school or recover from shame after failure. If that bond is chronically disrupted, particularly through pressure to reject that parent, the boy may later struggle with trust, self-worth, or expectations of emotional availability in close relationships (Childress, 2017). Similarly, a mother-daughter bond may support identity formation, emotional attunement, and the modelling of care. If that relationship is destabilised through chronic alienating pressure, the daughter may later struggle with self-worth, nurturance, or her internal sense of relational safety (Childress, 2017).

The father-son bond may provide guidance, esteem-building, and support in developing confidence, responsibility, and relational boundaries. The father-daughter bond may foster affectional security, confidence, and a stable sense of being valued. When these bonds are chronically interrupted through triangulation, coercive alignment, or emotional cutoff, the developmental cost may include insecurity, grief, identity disturbance, and later relational mistrust (Childress, 2017; Bowlby, 1969).

In post-divorce contexts, if a child rejects one parent, the issue is not automatically a custody matter. Unless there is abuse, a pronounced refusal or conflict pattern may be better understood as an attachment and family systems issue requiring careful clinical assessment and, where appropriate, family-based treatment rather than repeated litigation alone (Bowlby, 1969; Minuchin, 1974).

Children are organised to seek proximity, safety, and emotional completion with caregivers. Even when parenting is problematic, the attachment system does not ordinarily extinguish the child's drive to bond. Rather, it often shifts the form of the child's strategy, for example, through protest, heightened vigilance, compliance, withdrawal, or insecure attachment patterns (Bowlby, 1969). This is why chronic parent-child conflict may reflect frustration of attachment needs rather than the absence of attachment motivation (Bowlby, 1969).

In Childress's formulation, attachment-related pathology does not arise spontaneously. It is created through pathogenic parenting, that is, through parenting processes that generate clinically significant disturbance in the child's attachment system, identity organisation, emotional regulation, and role functioning (Childress, 2017). On this view, a child's global rejection of a parent must always be assessed in relation to the caregiving system and to the possibility of abuse, coercive control, triangulation, or family systems distortion (Childress, 2017; Goldenberg & Goldenberg, 2013; Minuchin, 1974).

Clinical Resource Note: Childress's Attachment-Based Assessment Framework

The HQTP may be read alongside Dr Craig Childress's attachment-based formulation where specialist child and family assessment is required, particularly in cases involving attachment disturbance, pathogenic parenting, psychological control, cross-generational coalition, and severe parent–child contact disruption following separation or divorce. Childress's work is especially relevant when clinicians or court-involved professionals are attempting to distinguish between justified rejection arising from genuine abuse, deficient parenting, or substantiated safety concerns and induced rejection arising from coercive family-system processes.

This protocol does not reproduce Childress's AB-PA assessment model, rating scales, diagnostic checklists, consultation protocols, or training materials. Clinicians seeking to undertake child and family assessment in this area should consult Childress's original publications and training resources directly and should apply those materials only within their professional scope, jurisdictional authority, supervision arrangements, and ethical obligations. Childress's attachment-based framework may also assist court-involved professionals to understand why clear clinical assessment questions matter before costly, prolonged, or poorly targeted intervention pathways are pursued. When the clinical question is unclear, families may be sent into repeated reports, reunification attempts, therapy referrals, or litigation steps that do not address the underlying attachment, family-system, or child-protection issue. A properly framed assessment pathway can help clarify what needs to be assessed, what is outside the clinician's role, what requires specialist consultation, and what should not be assumed without evidence. Used in this way, Childress's work may support more focused, clinically coherent, and ethically bounded professional decision-making, while reducing the risk of unnecessary duplication, misdirected intervention, and avoidable financial and emotional burden on families.

For Readers Seeking Help with Current Child and Family Court Concerns

Some readers may come to this protocol looking for help with a current child or family-court matter, particularly where a child is rejecting, resisting, fearing, or refusing contact with a parent, or where there are competing allegations of abuse, neglect, deficient parenting, coercive control, false or unsubstantiated allegations, or pathogenic parenting. The HQTP is not designed for that purpose. It remains a non-forensic, adult-survivor treatment protocol. Its purpose is not to conduct custody evaluation, determine legal truth, provide legal strategy, or undertake specialist child-and-family assessment. Its purpose is to help clinicians understand how attachment disruption, coercive relational dynamics, developmental trauma, and epistemic injury may present in adult survivors, and how treatment should be paced safely. Where readers require specialist assessment and formulation guidance for current child and family presentations, including differentiation between child psychological abuse, pathogenic parenting, physical abuse, sexual abuse, neglect, deficient parenting, spousal psychological abuse, false or unsubstantiated allegations, and allegations requiring careful assessment before being accepted or dismissed, they should consult Dr Craig Childress's published attachment-based resources and professional training materials directly. Those areas sit outside the HQTP's treatment purpose and fall within the specialist assessment terrain addressed in Childress's work.

Publicly listed resources include Childress's professional consulting website, attorney resource section, mental health resource section, parent resource section, YouTube channel, and published books and booklets, including Foundations: An Attachment-Based Model of Parental Alienation, Assessment of Attachment-Related Pathology Surrounding Divorce, Contingent Visitation Schedule, and The Narcissistic Parent (Childress, 2024).

Resource links:

Dr Childress resources: https://drchildress.consulting/2024/03/15/dr-childress-resources/

Dr Childress YouTube channel:

https://www.youtube.com/channel/UCV-OK9_OFd3BgBWgB0ccw4w

Triangulation, Cross-Generational Coalition, and the Child as Custody Prize

Within highly conflicted separation and divorce contexts, one of the most developmentally harmful processes occurs when the child is drawn into a spousal dispute and no longer permitted to remain a psychologically neutral member of the family. Rather than being protected from adult conflict, the child becomes triangulated into it. In this process, the child is drawn into a cross-generational coalition with one parent against the other and begins to function less as a child with independent developmental needs and more as an emotional extension of the allied parent (Goldenberg & Goldenberg, 2013; Haley, 1977; Minuchin, 1974).

When the court process, the parents, or surrounding professionals become organised around identifying the better parent, the child is at risk of being transformed into a custody prize to be won. This shift is clinically dangerous because it invites competition rather than repair. Once the child becomes a symbolic reward within the parental conflict, each parent may feel pressured to secure the child's preference, loyalty, or alignment. In these contexts, the child's relationship with each parent is no longer allowed to develop organically. Instead, attachment bonds may become subordinated to the emotional and strategic demands of the adult dispute (Goldenberg & Goldenberg, 2013; Haley, 1977; Minuchin, 1974).

This process is corrosive to healthy development. A child who is covertly or overtly encouraged to align with one parent against the other is placed in an impossible developmental position. The child may feel that love, safety, approval, and belonging depend on loyalty to the allied parent, while warmth toward the other parent is treated as betrayal. In this way, the child's neutrality is eroded. The child is no longer free to love both parents, hold a complex view of each, or develop an independent relationship with each (Goldenberg & Goldenberg, 2013; Minuchin, 1974).

Triangulation may be present in both subtle and overt ways. A child may begin repeating language that appears borrowed from the allied parent, may show rigid and developmentally unusual certainty about the moral character of the rejected parent, or may demonstrate hostility that exceeds the child's actual lived experience. Some children begin to act as confidants, protectors, witnesses, or emotional partners to the allied parent, particularly when that parent is psychologically fragile, overwhelmed by the separation, or preoccupied with abandonment, grievance, or revenge (Bowen, 1978; Goldenberg & Goldenberg, 2013; Titelman, 2003).

The developmental cost of triangulation is profound. When a child is recruited into a cross-generational coalition, the child's authentic attachment system becomes distorted by fear, dependency, role reversal, and coercive loyalty demands. The child may lose access not only to the rejected parent but also to the developmental experiences embedded in that relationship. When one of these bonds is interrupted through chronic triangulation, the child may later experience insecurity, grief, confusion, identity disturbance, relational mistrust, and difficulty integrating a coherent sense of self across family relationships (Bowlby, 1969; Minuchin, 1974; Titelman, 2003).

From a clinical perspective, the child's hostility toward the rejected parent in these circumstances should not automatically be assumed to reflect autonomous judgement or authentic detachment. In some cases, the rejection may instead reflect chronic pressure within family systems, in which the allied parent's influence has shaped the child's attachment behaviour. The child may be using rejection, contempt, or alignment as a survival strategy within the family field. This is why careful assessment is essential. Clinicians must determine whether the child's rejection arises from genuine abuse, coercive alignment and triangulation, or a combination of both (Goldenberg & Goldenberg, 2013; Minuchin, 1974).

Pathogenic Parenting, Attachment Disturbance, and Child Rejection

Within attachment-based and family systems-informed formulations, the development of significant attachment disturbance in a child does not occur in isolation from the caregiving environment. Drawing on Childress's conceptual use of the term, pathogenic parenting refers to parenting practices that generate clinically significant pathology in the child. In this context, pathogenic does not simply mean imperfect, inconsistent, or stressed parenting. Rather, it refers to parenting processes that actively contribute to the creation, maintenance, or intensification of psychological disturbance in the child, particularly within the child's attachment system, identity organisation, emotional regulation, and family role functioning (Childress, 2017).

From this perception, attachment-related pathology should not be understood as spontaneously arising from within the child. When a child presents chronic, global, and developmentally unusual rejection of a parent, the clinician must ask what relational conditions are operating around the child that could account for such a disturbance (Bowlby, 1969; Childress, 2017). In ordinary developmental terms, attachment disturbance more commonly alters the form of the bond than abolishes the child's underlying drive to remain attached. This may be expressed through insecure attachment strategies, heightened vigilance, protest behaviour, ambivalence, compliance, conflict, or fear-based closeness (Bowlby, 1969).

This has major implications for assessment. If a child demonstrates intense and pervasive rejection of one parent, two broad clinical possibilities require careful consideration. The first is that the rejected parent has engaged in genuinely abusive or profoundly frightening parenting of sufficient severity to suppress or rupture ordinary attachment seeking, such as severe physical abuse, sexual abuse, coercive terror, or serious neglect. The second is that the child's attachment disturbance is being shaped primarily through the pathogenic influence of the other parent, particularly where that parent has formed a cross-generational coalition with the child against the rejected parent. In such cases, the child's hostility may not arise from autonomous evaluation but from distorted family-system pressures, emotional enmeshment, coercive loyalty expectations, or sustained negative influence (Goldenberg & Goldenberg, 2013; Minuchin, 1974).

The degree of parenting disturbance required to produce authentic attachment suppression toward a parent is, therefore, clinically significant. Lesser forms of problematic parenting may contribute to insecurity, conflict, avoidance, or ambivalence, but do not typically explain the complete psychological erasure of an attachment bond. Where rejection is global, rigid, absolute, and developmentally disproportionate, the clinician must consider whether the child's attachment system is being reorganised by coercive family dynamics rather than by direct victimisation from the rejected parent alone. This is why simplistic interpretations are dangerous. Neither unquestioning acceptance of the child's rejection nor automatic assumptions are sufficient. A structured and disciplined differential formulation is required (Childress, 2017).

Within family systems theory, pathogenic parenting may operate through triangulation, role reversal, boundary collapse, and cross-generational coalitions. The allied parent may use the child, consciously or unconsciously, to regulate grief, rage, abandonment fears, humiliation, or the need for emotional stabilisation following separation. In these circumstances, the child is recruited into a relationship position that exceeds the child's developmental role. The child may become a protector, confidant, emotional substitute for a spouse, witness, ally, or weapon. Hostility toward the other parent may then be shaped and reinforced because it serves a function within the family system, namely, preserving the child's bond with the allied parent and regulating the emotional needs of that parent (Bowen, 1978; Goldenberg & Goldenberg, 2013; Haley, 1977; Minuchin, 1974).

The treatment implications are substantial. When attachment-related pathology is present, the clinical task is not simply to manage surface behaviour or to rely on litigation to resolve what are fundamentally disturbances in family processes. Where it is safe and appropriate, intervention requires identifying the barriers that are preventing the child from maintaining or restoring an affectionate bond with the parent. This may include assessing abusive parenting, coercive influence, family systems distortion, and attachment-based fear responses. If the disturbance is rooted in pathogenic parenting by the allied parent, treatment must address the distorted family system processes shaping the child's rejection. If the disturbance is rooted in genuine abuse by the rejected parent, protection and trauma-informed safeguarding take precedence (Childress, 2017).

Attachment Conflict as a Treatment Issue Rather Than a Custody Issue

Once a court determines a parenting arrangement, further problems may arise in implementing it when the child begins to exhibit marked conflict with one parent. This may include hostility, refusal, global rejection, extreme resistance to contact, or a sudden cutoff in the child's bond with that parent. In clinical terms, these developments should not automatically be understood as evidence that the custody arrangement itself is the primary problem. Rather, where abuse has not been established, the emergence of pronounced parent-child conflict following separation is more appropriately understood as a treatment issue requiring careful clinical assessment and, where safe and indicated, family-based therapeutic intervention (Bowlby, 1969; Childress, 2017).

From a developmental perspective, children generally benefit from the opportunity to maintain meaningful, complex relationships with both parents, unless there are genuine child protection concerns. A shared parenting arrangement, including substantial time with both parents, may support this developmental opportunity by allowing the child to access the distinct relational experiences embedded in these bonds. However, when parent-child conflict begins to interfere with the ordinary enactment of such arrangements, the central clinical question is no longer simply how time should be divided. The more pressing issue is understanding why the child conflicts with the parent and which relational or systemic factors are impeding the child's capacity to maintain a workable attachment bond (Bowlby, 1969; Childress, 2017).

This distinction matters because repeated litigation may seek to resolve, through legal means, what is, in substance, a family treatment problem. If the child's rejection is rooted in attachment disturbance, chronic relational misattunement, coercive alignment, fear, or family systems pathology, then further adversarial proceedings may intensify the difficulty rather than resolve it. The legal system may issue orders, but it cannot, by itself, restore affectionate trust, repair attachment injuries, remove coercive barriers to bonding, or resolve entrenched relational distortions. These are clinical and treatment-related tasks (Goldenberg & Goldenberg, 2013; Minuchin, 1974).

In treatment, the clinical task is to identify the barriers that prevent the child's attachment system from achieving a secure, affectionate bond with the parent. Those barriers may include frightening or harmful parenting practices, chronic invalidation, emotional inconsistency, coercive family system pressures, triangulation, loyalty conflicts, or misattunement that has become entrenched over time. Once the barrier is understood, intervention can be directed toward reducing or removing the obstacle to bonding, provided this can be done safely and ethically. The aim is not to force closeness but to restore the conditions under which the child's natural attachment motivations can move toward a more secure, reality-based relationship (Bowlby, 1969; Childress, 2017).

Emotional Cutoff and Inverted Family Hierarchy in Cross-Generational Coalition

In severely disturbed family systems, the child's hostility toward the targeted parent may escalate beyond ordinary conflict and develop into an emotional cutoff. In these circumstances, the child no longer presents as ambivalent, conflicted, or distressed in relation to that parent, but instead appears organised around psychological distance, rigid rejection, and the wish to terminate the relationship altogether. This type of cutoff may reflect more than simple anger or post-separation loyalty strain. It may indicate that the child has become embedded within a distorted family structure in which one parent and child have allied against the other parent (Bowen, 1978; Titelman, 2003).

From a family system's perspective, cross-generational coalitions can disrupt the expected generational boundaries within the family. Rather than remaining in the child role, the child may become elevated into a position of psychological authority, alignment, or judgement alongside the allied parent. This creates an inversion of the family hierarchy. The child no longer encounters the targeted parent as a parent within a secure relational structure, but as an excluded figure who is devalued, opposed, or treated as outside the emotional unit formed by the allied parent and child (Bowen, 1978; Minuchin, 1974).

When this occurs, the coalition does not simply strain the targeted parent-child relationship. It reorganises the family's emotional structure. The child's rejection may become stabilised through enmeshment with the allied parent, shared grievance, borrowed certainty, and ongoing reinforcement of the split family narrative. The emotional cutoff that follows can therefore be understood not merely as the child's independent decision, but as a symptom of broader relational pathology operating within the family system (Titelman, 2003).

Within the author's doctoral findings, some adult survivors described having participated in the rejection of the targeted parent under duress from the allied parent, with consequences for non-compliance ranging from subtle withdrawal, guilt induction, and emotional freezing through to more extreme punishment and intimidation (Price-Tobler, 2023a, 2023b). Some described never fully believing the allied parents' narrative yet feeling they had no safe alternative but obedience. Others reported that after years of exposure to repeated allegations, distortions, and negative storying, they eventually conceded, complied, or stopped resisting. Still others described the allied parent as unstable, broken, "crazy", or chronically unwell, only recognising later that the parent's narrative did not settle, soften, or resolve with time, but instead repeated in cyclical and maladaptive patterns across the lifespan (Price-Tobler, 2023a, 2023b).

This has important treatment implications for adult survivors. The task is not simply to help the survivor recount what happened, but to help them reconsider where the primary disturbance may have been located within the family system. In severe cases, the survivor may have grown up in a system organised around an allied parent whose functioning was marked by significant instability, coercive control, pathological grievance, or other clinically concerning relational disturbance of the kind described in the literature on pathogenic parenting and severe family systems dysfunction (Childress, 2015, 2017). When this is not recognised, survivors may continue to experience themselves as the difficult one, the unstable one, the overreactive one, or the one who must be corrected whenever they fail to align. In treatment, the clinical task is therefore often to reverse that internalised formulation. The survivor's distress may be very real, but this does not automatically mean that the survivor was the primary source of pathology. In many cases, the survivor was adapting to a parent or family system that was far more disturbed, coercive, and psychologically disorganised than the child was ever allowed to name.

Clinically, this means helping the survivor move from the question, "What is wrong with me?" to the more developmentally accurate question, "What kind of system required me to think, feel, and behave this way in order to survive?" That shift is often the beginning of differentiation. It does not require simplistic blame or hatred of the parent, nor does it require the clinician to impose a formal diagnosis where none has been made. Rather, it helps the survivor consider that they may have been organised around a parent whose functioning was shaped by severe instability, coercive need, distorted relational demands, or chronic reality distortion. The survivor may then begin to understand: "My parent may have been profoundly unwell. Their instability may help explain the system I grew up in. My symptoms may be real, but they are not proof that I was the sick one." In this way, treatment begins to loosen enmeshment not by attacking the parent but by helping the survivor more accurately locate pathology, reclaim authorship, and recover the right to think as a separate person.

Reflective Questions for Reframing Self-Blame and Enmeshment

To support this shift, clinicians may use carefully considered questions that help the survivor examine whether their reactions arose from personal defect or from long-term adaptation to a coercive and unwell system. For example, the clinician might ask: "When your parent became distressed, enraged, frightened, or accusatory, what happened to your thinking in that moment?" "Were you allowed to disagree safely, or did disagreement lead to punishment, withdrawal, retaliation, or collapse?" "When you were told that you were selfish, cruel, unstable, or impossible, what was happening in the family just before that?" "Did those labels become strongest when you aligned with the targeted parent, questioned the family narrative, or tried to think independently?" "If another child had been raised in the same environment, would the problem necessarily have been that child, or might the problem have been the condition of the caregiving system itself?" "When your parent said they loved you, what did that love require from you?" "Were you still allowed to disagree, think independently, or care about the targeted parent without punishment, guilt, or withdrawal?" Such questions help survivors move from enmeshed self-blame towards a more accurate developmental formulation of coercion, disturbance, and survival adaptation.

For some survivors, this reappraisal also begins to unsettle long-held assumptions about love, particularly where what was called love was organised around conditional approval, coercive loyalty, emotional possession, or the constant need to protect the allied parent.

Motivational Drivers of Cross-Generational Coalition

The formation of a cross-generational coalition between a child and one parent against the other parent does not occur in a relational vacuum. In many high-conflict family systems, the coalition appears to serve important emotional functions for the allied parent. The following two recurring motivational patterns are especially relevant in clinical formulation. The first involves redirecting unresolved spousal anger. In these cases, the allied parent may draw the child into the post-separation conflict, allowing hostility toward the former partner to be expressed indirectly through the child. The child may come to carry, communicate, or enact the anger that properly belongs to the adult relationship. Rather than the parent managing grief, rage, humiliation, or resentment within appropriate adult channels, the child becomes the vehicle through which those emotions are discharged. This places the child in a psychologically burdensome role and may contribute to the child being used as a relational weapon within the conflict (Bowen, 1978; Haley, 1977).

When the Targeted Parent Forms New Relationships Across the Lifespan

For some adult survivors, the formation of a new intimate relationship by the targeted parent may have been, and may remain, a major point of escalation within the family system. This is often not experienced as an ordinary post-separation transition. Rather, it may reactivate long-standing patterns of abandonment fear, possessiveness, grievance, and control in the allied parent, who may experience each new relationship as another loss of emotional possession, a humiliation, or a threat to exclusive loyalty. Under these conditions, the adult survivor may find that the same dynamics recur over time. Each new partner may become the focus of renewed hostility, suspicion, interference, narrative distortion, or efforts to draw the survivor back into a more exclusive coalition against the targeted parent.

From the adult survivor's perspective, this may involve more than witnessing the allied parent's distress. In some cases, the survivor may have been recruited, subtly or overtly, to taunt, reject, monitor, undermine, or behave abusively towards the targeted parent or the targeted parent's new partner within a pattern of spousal weaponisation. In other cases, the survivor may have felt deeply conflicted and distressed, not only because of the allied parent's reaction, but because they themselves longed to have the targeted parent "back the way it was before the separation". Some may resent new partners, avoid relationships with them, ask repeatedly for time alone with the targeted parent, or feel displaced by the targeted parent's growing investment in another person. These responses should not always be interpreted as immaturity or simple jealousy. They may reflect unresolved attachment disruption, grief, loyalty conflict, and the survivor's wish to recover a version of the targeted parent-child relationship that felt less contaminated by adult conflict and less vulnerable to loss.

For this reason, adult survivors may need their relationship with the targeted parent to be treated as a high clinical priority. Where safe and possible, survivors may require substantial, reliable, quality time with the targeted parent that is not immediately organised around the emotional demands of the new relationship. This is not an argument for excluding the new partner indefinitely. Rather, it recognises that the survivor's bond with the targeted parent may already be fragile, historically interrupted, and highly vulnerable to sabotage. If adequate relational space is not made available, the survivor's distress may intensify. At the same time, clinicians must remain alert to the opposite risk: where the relationship between the targeted parent and the survivor begins to improve, this very improvement may provoke renewed escalation in the allied parent, who may then intensify guilt induction, narrative distortion, contact disruption, or retaliatory allegations in an effort to reverse the repair.

In some families, these patterns may continue well into adulthood. The allied parents' interest in the targeted parent's intimate life may remain intense for years or decades, with each new relationship treated as a fresh injury and a fresh reason to reassert control. The adult survivor may therefore remain vulnerable to repeated cycles of loyalty-testing, coalition pressure, emotional blackmail, or demands to prove that the targeted parent's new attachments do not matter. In these later phases, the survivor may again be positioned as the one who must choose, monitor, reject, or carry grievance on behalf of the allied parent, even when the survivor is no longer a child and is trying to establish a separate adult life.

A further complication arises where the targeted parent, having lived for years within coercive or family and domestic violence-related dynamics, enters another relationship that repeats aspects of the earlier pattern. In some cases, the targeted parent may become involved with a new partner who is likewise controlling, possessive, emotionally regulating, or alienating in their relational style. The adult survivor may then be experienced by that new partner as an interference, a rival attachment, or a threat to exclusivity. Under these conditions, the new partner may seek to draw the targeted parent away from previous family bonds, isolate them from family and friends, discourage contact with adult children and grandchildren, or pressure them to prioritise the new relationship and any future family over pre-existing attachments. In this way, the earlier family and domestic violence pattern may be repeated in altered form: the targeted parent is again organised around another person's regulation needs, while the adult survivor is pushed to the margins as if their existence disrupts the new partner's claim to emotional possession.

Clinically, this means that the adult survivor may be confronting not one static historical injury but a pattern that can re-activate across the lifespan with each new relational reorganisation. What requires attention is not only the survivor's surface reaction to the targeted parent's new partner, but the larger system in which attachment, loyalty, grief, exclusion, and coercive control continue to be repeatedly reorganised around adult relationships. Treatment, therefore, needs to account for the survivor's longing, resentment, fear of replacement, and need for a reliable connection with the targeted parent, while also assessing whether old coercive dynamics are being restimulated, repeated, or newly enacted in the targeted parent's current intimate life.

Adult Survivors Witnessing Repeated FDV Patterns in the Targeted Parent's Later Relationships

A further layer of distress may arise where the adult survivor has already witnessed the targeted parent living within family and domestic violence dynamics during childhood and is then required to watch similar patterns repeat in later relationships across adulthood. In these cases, the survivor may not only be carrying their own trauma history, but also the burden of observing the targeted parent remain in coercive, controlling, or psychologically unsafe relationships from the outside. Some targeted parents may recognise that they are again in a harmful relationship yet feel unable to leave because of fear, dependency, shame, trauma bonding, or the dread of "failing" in another relationship. Others may strongly resist the idea altogether, minimising the pattern, denying the coercion, or insisting that the new relationship is different despite clear signs of isolation, control, and emotional regulation by the new partner.

For example, in some cases, the targeted parent may remain due to financial entanglement, shared property, additional children, social embarrassment, or a wish not to lose yet another family structure. For the adult survivor, this can be profoundly painful. They may feel forced to watch the targeted parent become increasingly isolated from family and friends, drawn again into another person's emotional economy, and used to regulate the needs of a new partner. At the same time, their own place in the relationship is diminished, marginalised, or treated as interference. In this way, the survivor may experience not only the repetition of earlier family and domestic violence patterns but also the grief of watching the targeted parent become unavailable once again, this time through a new coercive attachment system that the survivor can see but cannot easily interrupt.

Where these patterns persist, the adult survivor may be left carrying repeated grief, helplessness, and the ongoing burden of watching one parent remain vulnerable to coercive relationships. At the same time, the other continues to exert pressure, instability, or challenge across the lifespan. For many adult survivors, this is not a resolved childhood history but an enduring adult reality.

For example, the targeted parent may require family and domestic violence counselling, trauma-informed support, or practical assistance to recognise and respond to coercive or controlling relationships. In contrast, the allied parent may remain chronically unwell, grievance-driven, intrusive, or highly challenging across the lifespan. In these cases, the adult survivor may find themselves living in the middle of two ongoing realities at once: one parent who remains difficult, destabilising, or coercively demanding, and another who may be vulnerable, repeatedly entrapped, or psychologically unable to extricate themselves from harmful relationships. This can leave the adult survivor carrying a profound and exhausting burden of vigilance, grief, divided loyalty, anger, helplessness, and repeated disappointment.

Clinically, this means treatment cannot be organised around the fantasy that one or both parents will necessarily recover, gain insight, seek treatment, or become emotionally available in the ways the survivor has long hoped for. The targeted parent may need substantial FDV-oriented intervention and still remain ambivalent, compromised, dependent, or unable to leave coercive relationships. The allied parent may never meaningfully change and may continue to exert pressure, cause conflict, induce guilt, distort narratives, or exert psychological control for decades. This is often the lived reality of adult survivors: they are not only recovering from what happened in childhood but also learning how to survive the continuing instability of parents who remain emotionally, relationally, or psychologically unsafe in adulthood.

The therapeutic task is therefore to help the adult survivor face the limits of what they can change without taking responsibility for rescuing either parent. It is to help the survivor face the painful reality that one parent may need help they do not fully accept or cannot yet use. At the same time, the other may remain persistently challenging, unwell, or coercively organised.

Treatment must then support the survivor to grieve the limits of what they can change, reduce rescue-based over-functioning, strengthen realistic boundaries, and develop a more stable adult position from which they can observe parental dysfunction without being repeatedly pulled back into it.

In this sense, the life of the adult survivor is often shaped not by a single past event, but by prolonged exposure to parental instability, repeated relational disruption, and the ongoing task of building a life that is not organised around either parent's unresolved pathology. For some adult survivors, recovery does not lie in the resolution of the parental system, but in learning how to live with the reality that the parental system may remain unresolved.

Later-Life Re-Enmeshment, Truth-Telling, and Survivor Autonomy

For some adult survivors, alienation dynamics do not end in childhood and do not resolve simply because the parent grows old. Instead, they may reorganise across later-life family events, illness, care needs, weddings, funerals, birthdays, Christmas gatherings, christenings, and the arrival of younger generations. At this stage, the survivor who no longer aligns may cease to be seen merely as the difficult one and may instead come to occupy the same feared, resented, or morally contaminated position once assigned to the targeted parent. In some families, the survivor becomes the new "monster" because they are trying to step out of enmeshment, name coercive tactics, or refuse participation in the preferred cyclical maladaptive pattern framed as the family narrative. Clinical writing on family scapegoating notes that the targeted family member is often criticised, excluded, and blamed for wider family tensions, including in adulthood (Schwartz, 2025; Sherwood, 2015).

Mental health practitioners should understand that these later-life systems are often maintained through a spider's web of alliances rather than by a single direct relationship. Pressure may come through siblings, cousins, grandchildren, nieces, nephews, in-laws, and family friends who carry messages, reinforce grievance, excuse boundary violations, or insist that the survivor is cruel, heartless, unstable, hateful, or ungrateful. In this sense, the survivor is often responding not to one conversation but to an organised field of emotional coercion. The family member who resists enmeshment may then be treated as the source of the problem, while the wider system remains protected from scrutiny (Schwartz, 2025).

Reflective Choice for Survivors

One important therapeutic task at this point is to help the survivor shift attention away from the AP's position of authority and control in the family and back toward how the person behaves. This is not about disrespect. It is about restoring judgement. Survivors who have lived under coercive attachment conditions often assess danger through role, title, age, illness, guilt, family mythology, or obligation rather than through observable behaviour. The question is not only, "But she is my mother," or "But he is family." The question becomes, "What does this person actually do when I see them? What happens to me when I am near them? What happens to my children? What happens afterwards?" This behavioural reorientation helps survivors make clearer choices by shifting attention from family mythology to lived patterns.

MHPs can support this by asking, "What were you trying to do?" Very often, the answer is not, "I wanted to cause trouble," but "I was trying to stop the whole thing from blowing up," "I was trying to protect the children," or "I was trying to stop everyone hating me." That kind of clarification often changes the formulation. Other useful questions include, "What did the person actually do?" "What happened in your body?", and "What did you then feel compelled to do?" Taken together, these questions help move the survivor out of automatic guilt and back into reflective choice.

This becomes especially important because many adult survivors are hyper-accountable for others' emotions. They may automatically assume responsibility for the alienating parent's distress, the sibling's anger, the grandchild's confusion, the cousin's discomfort, or the emotional tone of the entire event. Before asking what is safest, truest, or most sustainable for themselves, they may be trying to figure out how to avoid upsetting everyone else. The clinician's task is to help the survivor recognise when empathy has been conscripted into compliance. The survivor is not being asked to become cold. They are being helped to notice when care for others has become organised around self-erasure.

For example, a survivor may say, "I know she'll be devastated if I don't go." A useful response may be, "I can hear that you care about her feelings. I also want to help you think about what happens to you when you do go, what you were hoping would happen, and whether the pattern supports that hope."

Declining Attendance at Family Events

At this later stage, survivors may also need explicit permission to understand that they do not have to attend family events if they do not feel psychologically safe. Declining a birthday, funeral, wedding, christening, Christmas lunch, or hospital visit may at times be a necessary act of psychological protection rather than an act of cruelty. Some survivors have spent a lifetime being taught that refusal equals abuse, that distance equals hatred, and that non-attendance proves moral defect. MHPs may need to say plainly that choosing not to attend an unsafe event can be an ethically sound and clinically protective decision. In some families, exclusion from major family events or other significant gatherings may function as punishment for non-alignment, reinforcing the consequences of refusing the preferred family narrative.

Example for MHPs: "You are allowed to decide that this event is not safe for you. We can think together about whether not going, going briefly, taking support, or leaving early best protects your peace, dignity, and recovery."

Contagious Fear at Family Events

Practitioners should also be aware that fear can become contagious in family events. Emotional contagion research indicates that emotions can spread rapidly through groups, and research on the social learning of threat and safety in families shows that fear beliefs, vigilance, and avoidance can be transmitted relationally through observation and repeated verbal signalling (Aktar et al., 2022; Herrando & Constantinides, 2021). In highly enmeshed families, one person's grievance, alarm, or persecutory certainty can quickly become the mood of the room. The survivor may then find themselves becoming physiologically activated, confused, self-doubting, urgently compliant, or pulled back into old roles. This is not proof that the survivor is irrational. It may reflect a socially amplified threat environment.

Example for MHPs: "When you walked in, whose anxiety seemed to set the tone? What language started repeating across people? What happened in your body once the room became organised around fear or grievance?"

Gender Bias, Enmeshment and Scapegoating

Gender may also shape who is targeted, who is excused, and who is expected to carry relational labour. Sivak and Smirnov (2019) found that parents mentioned sons more often than daughters in public social media posts, and that posts about sons received more "likes" on average. While this finding should not be overgeneralised to all families, it illustrates how gendered attention may be reproduced in ordinary family life. Broader family research also suggests that differential treatment between siblings can affect self-esteem, perceptions of fairness, and the quality of sibling relationships (McHale et al., 2000). In family systems already organised around coercion, this broader gender bias may intersect with scapegoating, enmeshment, and parentification.

Another layer may involve perceived resemblance to the targeted parent. A daughter may be pursued, criticised, or scapegoated not only because she is female, but because the alienating parent experiences her as carrying the targeted father's traits, appearance, temperament, mannerisms, independence, humour, values, or relational style. Equally, when the alienating parent is the father, a son or daughter may be targeted because they are perceived to resemble the targeted mother. In these cases, the child may become a living reminder of the parent that the alienating parent cannot tolerate, grieve, forgive, or psychologically separate from. The survivor may then be punished not for who they are, but for whom they are perceived to represent.

Clinically, this may manifest when a son is allowed to withdraw, disengage, avoid emotional responsibility, or remain peripheral without being pursued closely. At the same time, a daughter is expected to maintain contact, regulate the parent, organise family connections, absorb blame, or remain emotionally available despite harm. This may overlap with gendered expectations around family care and kinkeeping, where women and daughters are often positioned as the organisers, emotional connectors, and relational maintainers within family systems (Grigoryeva, 2017; Hornstra et al., 2023). In coercive or alienating family systems, these expectations may become intensified. The daughter may be criticised for setting limits, described as cold or selfish when she differentiates, or positioned as the family member responsible for repairing relationships that others have damaged.

This does not mean gender is the only explanation in any individual family, nor does it mean that sons cannot also be scapegoated, parentified, or harmed. Rather, gender should be considered one possible layer in the formulation. It may help survivors and clinicians understand why siblings were treated differently, why one child was excused while another was pursued or blamed, and why the survivor's distress should not be reduced to personal weakness, jealousy, or defect.

When the Survivor Returns to Harmful Patterns

Attachment research is also relevant here. Longitudinal and neurobiological studies indicate that the early parent-child bond shapes later attachment representations across development and is supported by neural systems involved in the formation and maintenance of attachment bonds throughout life (Ulmer-Yaniv et al., 2022). This helps explain why survivors may still feel compelled to return, repair, explain, smooth things over, or try one more time, even when they know the pattern is harmful. The attachment system does not simply switch off because insight has developed. The survivor may therefore have to be brave and vulnerable at the same time: brave enough to face the pattern, and vulnerable enough to admit how strong the pull toward reconnection still feels.

Some survivors may also remain partly organised around grief if they miss their TP too much because grief itself preserves a sense of connection. For example, at times they may feel safer, calmer, or even momentarily comforted within the grief response because it allows them to remain bonded to the targeted parent, to the fantasy of repair, or to the family they wished they had. Clinicians should not shame this response. It may reflect an attachment-preserving strategy in a person whose right to love, mourn, and separate safely was repeatedly disrupted (Ulmer-Yaniv et al., 2022).

Truth-telling, therefore, becomes complex. Some survivors do not remain silent out of confusion. They remain silent because they know the likely repercussions: denigrating gossip, moral attack, smear campaigns, gaslighting, exclusion, retaliation, and renewed family chaos. Research on transgenerational trauma and family secrecy indicates that unspoken traumatic material can weigh across generations, while disclosure can evoke shock, shame, betrayal, anger, and destabilisation (Kostova & Matanova, 2024).

At the same time, scapegoating commentaries note that backlash often intensifies when the targeted person attempts to step outside the assigned role or openly identifies the pattern (Schwartz, 2025; Sherwood, 2015). For this reason, the clinician should not push indiscriminate disclosure. Instead, the task is to help the survivor consider timing, audience, developmental appropriateness, motive, potential backlash, and whether the truth is being told to clarify, to protect, to seek validation, or to stop being crushed by silence. Graduated disclosure may at times be safer than full disclosure. In other situations, privacy may be protective. The survivor does not owe everyone the full story in order for their boundary to be valid.

The Gift of Presence

Survivors may also benefit from being helped toward what could be called the gift of presence. Presence means slowing down enough to observe what is happening around them and within them before deciding what to do. Who is escalating? Who is carrying messages? Who can tolerate difference? Who collapses into grievance? How do people around the survivor actually deal with tension, conflict, or fear? What does the survivor's body do when the alienating parent arrives? What do they instantly feel responsible for? What are they trying to prevent? Presence is not passivity. It is the deliberate act of witnessing reality before submitting to it. In treatment, this can gradually support a level of acceptance: not approval of what the family is doing, but clearer acceptance of what the pattern actually is. That kind of acceptance often strengthens decision-making.

A brief self-examination exercise may assist some survivors before or after family contact:

Brief Reflection for Survivors

What was I trying to do?

Was I trying to keep the peace, prove I am not cruel, protect a child, stop someone from being upset, hold onto a connection, or avoid being attacked?

What actually happened?

What did people say and do?

What was observable?

What happened in my body?

Did I become tight, shaky, frozen, confused, guilty, numb, or urgently compliant?

Whose emotions did I start managing?

Whose fear, grief, outrage, or disappointment became my responsibility?

What choice best protects my peace, dignity, and long-term stability now?

A useful guiding question for MHPs is: Before we decide what you should do next, can we slow this down and look at what you were trying to do, what actually happened, and what it cost you? That question often helps restore agency without forcing the survivor into premature certainty.

Finally, where the family of origin remains organised around coercion, survivors may need explicit support to build a life elsewhere. Community groups, trusted friendships, faith communities, creative circles, peer support, and chosen friends may gradually fill some of the relational space that biological family members did not fill safely. This does not erase grief. Nor does it mean the survivor is unaffected by exclusion, loneliness, gaslighting, or social stigma. It does mean that long-term adaptation may depend less on winning recognition from the coercive system and more on building steadier forms of belonging outside it. In that sense, later-life recovery may involve not only boundary formation, but the gradual reclamation of happiness, peace, and ordinary human freedom in relationships that do not require submission.

Interrupting Intergenerational Scapegoating Through Breach-and-Repair

A further protective pathway may emerge when adult survivors deliberately interrupt the intergenerational pattern of relational cut-off. In many families shaped by coercive control, chronic grievance, or unresolved parental disturbance, family members may have learnt that rupture means disappearance, withdrawal, punishment, relocation, silence, or permanent exclusion. They may not have been taught how to return to a difficult conversation, name 'hurt' safely, listen, repair, and remain connected without submitting to distortion. For this reason, one of the most clinically significant changes across generations may be the slow development of breach-and-repair capacity.

Clinical Resource Note: Teaching Breach-and-Repair

At the time of writing, there appears to be limited cohort-specific training material on teaching breach-and-repair to adult survivors of child psychological abuse in CPA-PA contexts. Mental health practitioners may therefore need to adapt existing alliance rupture-and-repair, psychodynamic, family systems, and mentalisation-based resources for this population. Safran and Muran's (2000) work on therapeutic alliance ruptures, Eubanks, Muran, and Safran's (2018, 2022) Rupture Resolution Rating System, and later alliance-focused training resources provide useful language for recognising withdrawal ruptures, confrontation ruptures, pseudo-agreement, appeasement, avoidance, and repair attempts within the therapeutic relationship (Eubanks et al., 2018; Eubanks et al., 2022; Safran & Muran, 2000). Within the HQTP, clinicians therefore need to teach repair slowly and, rather than assume the survivor already knows how safe relational repair works.

This may include helping the survivor notice when a rupture has occurred, slow the nervous system, separate present conflict from old family threat, name what felt hurtful or unsafe, clarify intent without collapsing into shame, listen without surrendering reality, protect the boundary, and decide whether continued contact is psychologically safe. The therapeutic relationship itself becomes part of this teaching. When a survivor feels misunderstood, misread, hurried, or shamed, the clinician's capacity to pause, acknowledge, clarify, and repair provides a live corrective experience. The survivor can then gradually practise similar skills with safe family members, partners, friends, younger relatives, or other relationships where repair is possible.

For this cohort, repair should never be confused with reconciliation, appeasement, or renewed exposure to coercive control. A repair may restore clarity without restoring closeness. It may allow a relationship to continue with stronger boundaries, or it may help the survivor leave a conversation without shame. Breach-and-repair is clinically useful only when it supports psychological safety, differentiation, and relational freedom.

Clinicians should also assess whether repair is clinically appropriate in the specific relationship. Some ruptures can be repaired; others reveal that the relationship remains unsafe, coercive, or organised around repeated boundary violation. Adult survivors may require support to distinguish between a genuine repair attempt and pressure to resume compliance. A person who apologises but continues the same coercive pattern has not repaired the rupture; they have only temporarily interrupted it. For this reason, clinicians should help survivors look for behavioural evidence of repair, including accountability, changed behaviour, respect for boundaries, reduced retaliation, and the other person's capacity to tolerate the survivor's separate reality.

Supervision may be required where the clinician feels pressure to encourage forgiveness, family unity, or reconciliation before the survivor has established safety. In the HQTP, repair is not measured by reunion. It is measured by whether the survivor can remain psychologically intact, differentiated, and free to choose a safe level of contact.

Unconditional Positive Regard as an Intergenerational Corrective

Unconditional positive regard is equally important (Rogers, 1957). In this context, it does not mean accepting abuse, excusing manipulation, or removing boundaries. It means that the survivor learns to offer younger family members, nieces, nephews, grandchildren, adult children, or other relatives a steadier relational experience that is not organised around retaliation, recruitment, or emotional control. The younger person is not asked to take sides, carry adult trauma, or become the survivor's witness. Instead, they are given repeated experiences of warmth, safety, humour, ordinary contact, and relational reliability.

Over time, this may help younger family members discover that love does not require compliance, conflict does not have to end in exile, and disagreement does not have to destroy the relationship. This is particularly important where the alienating parent or alienating grandparent has modelled conditional love, withdrawal, grievance, punishment, or alignment-based belonging. The adult survivor may not be able to change the older generation, but they may be able to change what the next generation experiences in their presence.

This work is often quiet and repetitive. It may involve maintaining ordinary contact, speaking warmly at family events, establishing safe rituals, avoiding unnecessary escalation, and continuing to offer younger relatives a relationship not based on fear. In this way, unconditional positive regard becomes an intergenerational corrective. It does not undo the past, but it can give the next generation a different experience of conflict, repair, and belonging.

Psychodynamic Psychotherapy, Countertransference, and the Pull Back into the Scapegoat Role

Psychodynamic psychotherapy is especially useful in this space because the adult survivor often needs help to understand how quickly old roles can be reactivated. A distorted comment, a family accusation, a sudden exclusion, or a cruel story told at a family event may pull the survivor back into the scapegoat position. In psychodynamic terms, the clinician must monitor their own countertransference: the feelings, impulses, protectiveness, frustration, disbelief, anger, or rescuing responses that may be evoked when listening to these family systems (Gabbard, 2014; McWilliams, 2011). If the clinician is not careful, they may become pulled into the same urgency, outrage, helplessness, or over-identification that the survivor is trying to manage.

The adult survivor also needs help to recognise their own transferential responses to other family members. Strictly speaking, countertransference refers to the clinician's response to the client; however, survivors may also need help to recognise when they are transferring the old family wound into present relationships. They may feel an intense urge to defend themselves, expose the truth, correct every lie, confront the alienating parent, or prove to younger relatives that they are not the cruel, unstable, selfish, or dangerous person they have been made out to be. While these impulses are understandable, they may sometimes move the survivor directly back into acting out the role that the alienating parent has constructed for them, even when its not who they truly are. The frustration and acting out may then give the alienating parent the upper hand to say “see, I was right!”

In this sense, the survivor may begin responding not only to the person in front of them but also to the older projected family position being imposed on them. A younger relative may speak from fear, loyalty pressure, partial information, or inherited grievance rather than from full knowledge of the survivor’s history. If the survivor reacts with humiliation, accusation, rage, over-explanation, or contempt, the younger person may experience the survivor as confirming the very story they were told. The clinical task is therefore not passive. It is steadiness. The survivor learns to pause, mentalise, hold their own reality, correct what can be corrected, disengage where necessary, and avoid becoming the version of themselves the distorted family narrative is trying to produce (Bateman & Fonagy, 2016; Gabbard, 2014; McWilliams, 2011).

For example, if an alienating grandparent tells younger relatives that the adult survivor is angry with them, judging them, or coming to “teach them a lesson”, the survivor may feel an immediate pull to defend, explain, pursue, or confront. Psychodynamic work helps the survivor pause before acting. The survivor may need to ask:

What role am I being pulled into?

What is the family system trying to make me perform?

Can I correct this calmly without escalating it?

Is there a grounded person who can help reality-test what happened?

This reflective pause can prevent the survivor from being pushed back into the scapegoat position.

Note for clinicians: This pattern may be reactivated for years if the survivor chooses not to align with their alienating parent and their alliances.

Teaching the Language Before Naming the Pattern

Clinicians also need to teach adult survivors how to use clinical language carefully. Terms such as enmeshment, loyalty pressure, triangulation, lack of independent thinking, scapegoating, or coercive alignment may be accurate within formulation, but they can be experienced as insulting or confusing when used to warn younger relatives about the family pattern they have inherited. A young adult niece, nephew, cousin, or grandchild may not understand what "enmeshment" means. They may hear it as an accusation that they are weak, brainwashed, immature, or unable to think.

Before survivors use this language with family members, clinicians should help them translate it into ordinary words. Enmeshment may be explained as: *sometimes it becomes very hard to know what you think for yourself when a powerful person in the family is upset.* Loyalty pressure may be explained as: *Sometimes, families make people feel they must choose sides to stay loved.* Lack of independent thinking may be explained as: *Sometimes we repeat the family story before we have had a chance to ask whether it is actually true.*

When survivors learn to soften the language without weakening the meaning, younger relatives may be better able to think than to defend. This is consistent with systemic understandings of enmeshment, triangulation, and family differentiation, in which the task is not simply to name the pattern but to help the person develop enough reflective space to step outside it (Bowen, 1978; Minuchin, 1974).

Family Events as Sites of Repetition and Repair

Family and community events can become pivotal sites of either repetition or repair. Annual celebrations, cultural traditions, religious observances, birthdays, graduations, weddings, funerals, family meals, and ordinary gatherings may reactivate old alliances, jealousies, exclusions, and loyalty tests. They may also provide rare opportunities to build new memories. Clinicians should help survivors prepare for these events with realistic expectations. The goal may not be to resolve the whole family system. It may be to remain regulated, avoid being pulled into provocation, keep contact with younger relatives light and warm where possible, and create small memories that are not dominated by the alienating parent or the alienating grandparents' emotional state.

This is where psychodynamic psychotherapy, breach-and-repair, and unconditional positive regard work together. The survivor learns how to notice the old pull, avoid becoming reactive to the alienating parent's narrative, and keep moving towards the relationship they are trying to build with the next generation. Sometimes this means keeping conversations with younger relatives light, warm, ordinary, and future-focused rather than drawing them too deeply into adult history. Sometimes it means letting the children, nieces, nephews, grandchildren, or younger adults experience safety, humour, play, food, animals, craft, music, or shared rituals without making the event another battleground for the old family story.

Example One: When a Younger Adult Relative Returns After Rupture

A younger adult family member may become distressed when the adult survivor does not automatically include the alienating parent or alienating grandparent in a family event they are organising. This may occur where the younger relative expects the survivor to invite the alienating grandparent, protect the grandparent's feelings, or maintain the appearance of family inclusion, even when the survivor does not experience that relationship as safe, close, or emotionally mutual. The younger relative may then speak on behalf of the alienating grandparent, argue that exclusion is unfair, or suggest that they may not attend either if the grandparent is not invited.

For mental health practitioners, it is important to understand what may be occurring for the younger adult family member in this moment. The younger person may have internalised the role of advocate, protector, messenger, or emotional regulator for the alienating grandparent. They may feel responsible for ensuring that the grandparent is included, informed, soothed, and protected from disappointment, even when the event is not centred on the grandparent and even when the grandparent has not directly asked to attend. This can reflect loyalty pressure, enmeshment, triangulation, and role confusion rather than independent relational judgement.

The younger adult may also fear the emotional consequences of not advocating. They may anticipate that the alienating grandparent will feel rejected, become upset, withdraw, complain, create conflict, or accuse others of cruelty. In this way, the younger person may be trying to prevent anticipated emotional fallout before it occurs. Their advocacy may therefore appear to be care, fairness, or family loyalty on the surface, while, clinically, functioning as an attempt to regulate the alienating grandparent's anticipated distress.

This can place the younger adult in a bind. They may believe they are acting morally by defending the grandparent, while not recognising that they have been positioned inside an older family triangle. They may speak on the grandparent's behalf instead of allowing the grandparent to speak directly. They may pressure the adult survivor to include the grandparent, while not understanding the survivor's longer history of psychological harm, exclusion, or unsafe relational contact. They may also misread the survivor's boundary as cruelty because they have not yet developed enough distance from the family narrative to understand why the boundary exists.

Clinicians should help adult survivors recognise this pattern without attacking the younger relative. The younger adult may be carrying inherited anxiety, loyalty conflict, and fear of relational collapse. They may not yet understand enmeshment or triangulation, and they may experience those terms as insulting if introduced too directly. The clinical task is to help the survivor respond in a way that protects the boundary, reduces escalation, and avoids humiliating the younger person. This allows the survivor to name the pattern while still leaving room for the younger adult to think, reflect, and return to the relationship later.

In this situation, the adult survivor may need to name the boundary plainly. They may explain that they did not think to invite the alienating grandparent, do not feel responsible for managing the grandparent's emotional response, or do not experience the relationship as one in which automatic inclusion feels natural or safe. The survivor may also gently question why the younger relative feels responsible for speaking on behalf of the grandparent, particularly when the grandparent does not have a close or active relationship with the person being celebrated or included in the event. This kind of conversation may expose patterns of enmeshment, loyalty pressure, and difficulty thinking separately from the alienating parent or grandparent.

The younger adult family member may feel hurt, offended, or accused when this pattern is named. They may hear the survivor's boundary as rejection, cruelty, selfishness, or lack of care, rather than as a protective limit shaped by a much longer relational history. In a family organised around cut-off, this rupture might previously have led to permanent silence. However, if the younger person later returns, says that the comment hurt them, listens to the survivor's explanation, and remains in the relationship, this repair represents an important breach-and-repair moment.

The repair may be imperfect. The younger person may still not fully understand the wider alienation pattern. They may still feel loyal to the alienating grandparent, defensive of the family story, or confused by the survivor's boundaries. Even so, the fact that they return to the conversation rather than disappearing into the inherited cut-off pattern is clinically significant. The adult survivor can be supported in meeting this moment with steadiness by acknowledging the hurt, clarifying the meaning, avoiding the humiliation of the younger person, and keeping the relationship open.

For example, the survivor might say, *I can understand why that word hurt you. I was not trying to say you cannot think. I was trying to describe how powerful family pressure can become when someone is very upset or when everyone feels they have to take sides. You are allowed to have your own view. I also need you to understand that my boundaries come from a much longer history than I am going to speak about, or because I don't want to place this burden on you, or I don't want to pass down the trauma and am stopping it here.* This kind of response protects the survivor's reality without forcing the younger relative to carry the full traumatic history.

Example Two: Christmas, False Narratives, and the Alienating Grandparent

A second example may occur at Christmas or another high-pressure family event, particularly when the adult survivor attends after many years of exclusion or separate gatherings. Their presence may disturb the alienating parent's or grandparent's established narrative. The alienating grandparent may experience the survivor's calm presence, ordinary connection, or inclusion with younger relatives as a threat to control, a source of grievance, or a challenge to the long-standing family story they may have invented. Severe alienation dynamics may involve entrenched distortions, pathogenic influence, and highly defended narratives about the rejected or scapegoated family member (Baker, 2007; Childress, 2015; Price-Tobler, 2023a).

Additionally, the alienating grandparent may begin spreading a false narrative that the survivor is angry, critical, unsafe, or intending to confront someone if their delusions are threatened. This can rapidly destabilise younger relatives who have been exposed to the alienating grandparent's version of reality. They may become anxious, distressed, or fearful without checking whether the story is true. In severe cases, the alienating grandparent's fixed delusions may intensify under emotional pressure. Clinicians need to be aware and also recognise that some alienating family systems are organised around rigid false beliefs, grievance, and defensive reality distortion.

In these moments, a calm and grounded witness can be crucial. A sibling, partner, or trusted family member who was present may need to clarify what actually occurred, reality-test the allegation, and help younger relatives settle before the event is completely reorganised around the alienating grandparent's distress and need for control. The survivor may also need support not to become frantic, punitive, or over-defensive, because the system may be trying to pull them back into the scapegoat role.

For example, a grounded family member might say, *I was sitting with her. That did not happen. No one was coming to confront you. This has become confused, and we need to slow it down. In the future, if your grandparent says something like this to you, come to me, and we will work through it and uncover the truth.* This kind of calm correction may prevent the younger relatives from becoming absorbed into the alienating grandparent's distortion while also reducing the likelihood that the survivor will be forced into public self-defence.

Example Three: Achievement, Attention, and the Return of the Spotlight

A third example may arise when attention is briefly on another person's achievement, such as a graduation, publication, award, recovery milestone, birthday speech, or professional success. The alienating parent or grandparent may respond by minimising the achievement, changing the subject, drawing attention back to their own suffering, or withdrawing in distress, leaving others to regulate them. This is not always random. In some alienating family systems, another person's achievement may be experienced as intolerable because it shifts attention away from the alienating parent's grievance, injury, sacrifice, or centrality. Additionally, within the family and domestic violence category, this is known as 'sabotaging social outings'.

Furthermore, the alienating parent may suddenly appear overwhelmed, offended, abandoned, or emotionally disorganised. Under high affective load, reflective functioning may narrow, threat-based neural pathways may dominate, and the person may lose the capacity to hold the needs of the room in mind (Bateman & Fonagy, 2016; Siegel, 2012). In ordinary language, it may appear as though the alienating parent collapses back into grievance, shame, envy, injury, or fear of abandonment. Clinically, this may appear as sulking, abrupt departure, public distress, hostile comments, phone calls from the car to people still at the party, accusations, or an urgent attempt to identify who is still aligned with them. In these situations, the survivor may need to practise gently returning the focus to the person being celebrated without humiliating the alienating parent or grandparent or becoming drawn into a public battle. The survivor might say: *I do want to come back to what we are celebrating today*, or *This is an important moment for him, her, them and I want us to stay with that for a little longer.* This is a subtle but important form of repair. It protects the event's emotional meaning while refusing to let the old coercive control system completely reorganise the event.

Sometimes the family may choose not to follow the alienating parent into the emotional crisis. If the alienating parent leaves in anger, distress, or injury, family members may decide to remain at the table, continue the celebration, and allow the event to belong to the person it was intended to honour. This can be extremely difficult for relatives who have been trained to immediately regulate the alienating parent. However, it may also represent a major shift in the family system. The message is not cruel abandonment. The message is that one person's dysregulation will not always be allowed to collapse the entire family event.

However, some alienating parents may go further, and their behaviour and need to gain control may also escalate into threats and then actual acts of self-harm or attempted suicide as an urgent attempt to get attention. This can be extremely distressing for all the family members, and the police or an ambulance may need to be called, and the survivor debriefed by their clinician and assessed for whether they need to return to the stabilisation phase until they feel better.

Clinicians should prepare survivors for the fallout that may follow. The alienating parent may make repeated phone calls, send distressed messages, recruit allies, accuse the survivor of cruelty, or create a negative narrative about the person who redirected attention back to the celebration. This fallout may continue for days, weeks, or decades. The survivor may need support to avoid panicking, apologising for something they did not do, over-explaining, or accepting the role of scapegoat simply to restore peace. A steadier response might be: *I am sorry you were upset. It was also important that we stayed focused on the person being celebrated. I am not going to discuss this in a way that turns the event into an attack on anyone.*

This is where psychodynamic psychotherapy becomes especially useful. The survivor learns to recognise the old pull: the demand to regulate the alienating parent, the fear of being blamed, the urge to defend against false narratives, and the temptation to collapse back into compliance. The work is to remain emotionally present without surrendering reality. Over time, this helps the survivor and other family members build a different relational pattern: one in which celebration, joy, achievement, and ordinary family pleasure are not automatically sacrificed to the alienating parent's distress.

Example Four: Split Events and the Pain of Separate Belonging

A fourth example concerns the recurring pain of split-family events. Many adult survivors become used to visiting two or three houses at Christmas, separate birthdays, divided gatherings, or carefully managed contact arrangements. For some, this pattern began in childhood when contact with the targeted parent was controlled, disrupted, or made emotionally dangerous. Later in life, even if the targeted parent is no longer central or out of the picture, the alienating parent may continue to organise family contact according to loyalty, alignment, grievance, or punishment.

This is a profound pain point. Separate events are not merely inconvenient. They may repeat the early experience of divided belonging. Survivors may grieve the family Christmas, birthday, lunch, or celebration they wish they could have had. Clinicians should name this directly. The task is not to pretend that exclusion does not hurt. It is to help the survivor stop interpreting every separate event as proof that they are unloved, unwanted, defective, or impossible to include. These meanings may be historical and still carry a charge. They may come from childhood experiences of being separated from the targeted parent, excluded from family belonging, or made to feel that love was always conditional on compliance with the alienating parent's emotional world.

Where possible, the focus shifts towards creating new memories with the people who are available, safe, and able to remain emotionally present. For example, an adult survivor who is not invited to Christmas may choose to create a beautiful lunch with their partner, children, friends, neighbours, or chosen family. They may cook food they love, decorate the table, play music, go for a walk, invite someone else who is alone, or begin a new ritual that is not organised around rejection. This does not remove the grief of exclusion. However, it gives the survivor an active way to reclaim the day rather than spending it entirely within the alienating parent's old, cyclical, maladaptive narrative pattern, which may still be playing as the evoked companion in the survivor's thoughts.

This can be a profound therapeutic shift. The survivor is not waiting outside the family system, hoping to be chosen. They are building a sense of belonging wherever possible. New traditions may begin quietly: a Boxing Day breakfast, a Christmas Eve dinner with friends, a birthday picnic, an Easter craft day, a graduation lunch with safe relatives, or a small ritual with the survivor's own children. These events may not look like the family gathering the survivor once longed for, but they can still become emotionally real. Over time, the survivor may begin to experience that joy, beauty, celebration, and connection are still available, even when the original family system remains divided.

Clinicians should treat these new memories as active recovery work, not as consolation prizes. They are part of how the survivor builds a life no longer governed by exclusion, conditional love, or the alienating parent's capacity to permit belonging.

Protective Truth-Telling Without Passing on the Full Trauma Story

Survivors may also need support in deciding how much truth to carry into the next generation. In some families, adult survivors make a deliberate and protective choice not to pass on every traumatic detail about what happened to them as children. This does not mean minimising the abuse, excusing the harm, or pretending that the relationship with the alienating parent is safe. Rather, it may reflect an ethically careful attempt to avoid poisoning younger relatives against an older family member while still maintaining necessary psychological safety.

The survivor may need to say, in effect: *You are allowed to have your own relationship with this person, but you also need to respect that my relationship with them is strained for reasons I am not going to fully disclose. I am not asking you to carry my history, but I am asking you not to dismiss the boundaries that keep me feeling happy.*

Sometimes a small amount of truth may be necessary. The adult survivor may need to explain that they have not experienced the alienating parent as emotionally safe, consistently loving, or capable of the kind of unconditional love they needed as a child. They may need to say that conditional love is very different from unconditional love, and that it is painful to live with one parent who cannot love them freely. In contrast, the other parent was prevented, obstructed, or made unsafe to love. This truth can be spoken carefully, without turning the younger relative into a confidant, witness, or judge.

Clinicians should help survivors keep these conversations contained. The aim is not to open the full trauma history or invite the younger relative into their historical trauma. The aim is to give enough truth for the younger person to understand why the survivor has boundaries.

For example, the survivor might say: *There are parts of my childhood and my relationship with her that I am not going to place on you. What I can say is that I have not always felt emotionally safe or loved the way a child needs to be. That is why I manage the relationship carefully. You do not have to take that on, but I do need you to respect it.*

This distinction is important. The survivor is not required to surrender their own reality to protect the next generation, nor are they required to recount every painful story to be believed. The task is to hold both truths: younger family members may be entitled to form their own relationships, while the survivor remains entitled to distance, limits, and psychological protection. When handled carefully, this can reduce the risk of repeating the same alienating pattern in reverse. The survivor does not recruit the next generation into hatred. Instead, they model discernment, boundaries, repair, and emotional freedom.

The Generational Task

This kind of change may take more than one generation. Some relatives may remain tightly aligned with the old system. In contrast, others may gradually develop the capacity to question inherited narratives, call out inappropriate behaviour, return after conflict, and relate to the survivor more directly. Clinicians should recognise these small shifts as meaningful. They may not resolve the whole family system, but they can interrupt scapegoating, reduce inherited fear, and create new relational pathways where younger family members learn that love does not require enmeshment, loyalty does not require silence, and conflict does not have to end in exile.

In this sense, breach-and-repair, unconditional positive regard, and psychodynamic understanding become practical intergenerational tools. They help the adult survivor remain steady when the old system pulls for reactivity. They help younger relatives experience relationships without coercion. They help make family events places where new memories can be created, even when the alienating parent or grandparent remains dysregulated, aggrieved, or unable to share emotional space. The work is slow, but it matters. It may be one of the ways adult survivors stop the family story from being handed down unchanged.

Can the Alienating Parent Be Assessed in Adulthood?

Before turning to the assessment of pathogenic parenting, it is important to address a question many adult survivors quietly carry: *Can the alienating parent ever be assessed?* For some survivors, this question is not abstract. It may represent a final hope that someone will identify the disturbance, name the harm, explain the parent's behaviour, and perhaps open the possibility of treatment, accountability, or relational change.

In principle, an alienating parent can be assessed by an appropriately qualified mental health practitioner. In practice, however, this is often difficult because many alienating parents will not consent to assessment, and many clinicians have not received specialised training in assessing attachment-related pathology in the context of divorce and family separation. Further information is available through Dr Craig Childress's resource, Assessment of Attachment-Related Pathology Surrounding Divorce, which can be purchased through his website.

Unless the alienating parent voluntarily seeks treatment, is assessed within a legal, child-protection, hospital, or other formal clinical process, or becomes involved with services for another reason, the adult survivor will usually have no capacity to compel a psychological or psychiatric assessment. This reality can be deeply painful. The survivor may feel that the source of the harm was never properly examined, that the parent's disturbance was never named, and that the child was left to carry the consequences of a family system that no one adequately assessed.

This issue may be particularly important when an adult survivor has a disability or mental health challenge that has historically been managed by the alienating parent, and the survivor is attempting to move away from enmeshment, develop autonomy, and strengthen independent living skills. The clinical, ethical, safeguarding, and practical complexities of this presentation are substantial and cannot be addressed adequately within this section. Clinicians requiring further guidance or supervision regarding this presentation are welcome to contact the author.

Clinicians should therefore be careful not to create false hope unless they encounter an alienating parent (possibly in the mild category) who shows insight and agrees to an assessment. However, if this doesn't happen, the adult survivor may still long for the alienating parent to be assessed, diagnosed, treated, and transformed into the emotionally available parent they always needed and may not take 'no' for an answer. This wish is understandable. It may represent grief, attachment hunger, developmental longing, and the survivor's hope that repair might still be possible. However, assessment and treatment require a combination of access, consent, insight, motivation, clinical opportunity, and sustained engagement. Where the alienating parent remains organised around grievance, denial, blame, control, or a rigid narrative of victimhood, they may be unlikely to present voluntarily for assessment of the very dynamics the survivor is asking clinicians to examine.

This does not mean change is impossible. Personality disturbance, narcissistic vulnerability, emotion dysregulation, relational instability, and defensive patterns can sometimes be treated when the person is willing to engage in psychotherapy, tolerate feedback, reflect on relational harm, and remain in treatment long enough for change to occur (Gabbard, 2014; McWilliams, 2011; Ronningstam, 2017; Weinberg & Ronningstam, 2022). Psychodynamic psychotherapy, mentalisation-based approaches, schema therapy, transference-focused psychotherapy, and other structured treatments may assist some people with personality pathology, depending on motivation, severity, comorbidity, therapeutic alliance, and service availability (Bateman & Fonagy, 2016; Gabbard, 2014; Project Air Strategy, 2015; Ronningstam, 2017). The difficulty is that the alienating parent may not experience the need for help with alienating behaviour. They may seek treatment only when another problem becomes unavoidable, such as depression, anxiety, substance misuse, relationship breakdown, social isolation, ageing-related decline, legal pressure, or a crisis in functioning.

For the adult survivor, this distinction matters. The question is not only whether the alienating parent *could* be assessed. The more clinically useful question may be: *What happens to the survivor if that assessment never occurs?* If the survivor's recovery depends on the alienating parent being formally assessed, accepting a diagnosis, apologising, entering treatment, and becoming emotionally available, the survivor may remain psychologically tied (enmeshed) to the same parent who harmed them. In that sense, the search for the parents' assessment can become another form of captivity if it delays the survivor's own stabilisation, grief work, boundary formation, and long-term adaptation.

Clinicians should validate the survivor's wish for assessment without making the survivor's recovery dependent on it. The survivor may need to hear: *It would make sense that you want someone to assess what happened. It would make sense that you want the source of the harm identified. It would also be important that your healing does not depend on your parent agreeing to be assessed or treated.* This response protects both truth and agency. It does not dismiss the survivor's hope, but it gently returns the focus to what can be treated in the room: the survivor's nervous system, grief, identity, relational discernment, boundary capacity, and freedom from the old coercive pattern.

Where assessment of the alienating parent does become possible, clinicians should remain cautious and ethically grounded. Assessment should not be approached as a retaliatory exercise, a demand for proof, or a pathway to humiliation. It should be undertaken by an appropriately qualified practitioner using adequate information, direct clinical contact where possible, collateral material where ethically available, and careful differential formulation. The task is not to label the parent in order to vindicate the survivor. The task is to understand whether patterns of parental behaviour, psychological disturbance, coercive influence, relational control, unresolved trauma, fixed grievance, or pathogenic parenting have contributed to the child's developmental and relational injury.

Where the alienating parent refuses assessment, the clinician can still assess the survivor's experience and the observable consequences of the family system. The absence of a parental assessment does not mean the survivor's history is clinically unusable. It does mean the clinician must avoid making definitive diagnostic claims about a person they have not assessed. The clinician can still formulate patterns of coercion, emotional unavailability, triangulation, loyalty pressure, scapegoating, attachment distortion, rupture without repair, boundary violation, and relational fear as they have affected the survivor's development (Baker, 2007; Childress, 2015; Price-Tobler, 2023a).

This is an important epistemic safety point. Adult survivors may have spent years being told that they were the problem, the unstable one, the ungrateful one, the cruel one, or the family member who could not let things go. They may therefore feel desperate for an external assessment of the alienating parent to prove that the pathology was not theirs alone. Clinicians should hold this carefully for as long as this difficult, unfulfilled need lasts. In fact, some may bring it up so often that the clinician may be uncomfortable with this. However, it is critical that the clinician continues to listen and hold space until they can make peace with the memory and move to other unresolved trauma parts within them.

Furthermore, the survivor may never receive the assessment answers they deserve. They may not receive an apology or any meaningful acknowledgement from the alienating parent or the wider family system. This absence can be extremely difficult to come to terms with. It may feel as though there is a filing cabinet in the mind with one drawer that will not close because validation, accountability, and apology have never occurred. Even so, the survivor can still receive accurate formulation, careful treatment, relational repair, and validation elsewhere.

The clinical message is therefore neither hopeless nor naïve. Some alienating parents may become more assessable or treatable when a crisis, life transition, relationship loss, legal process, illness, grief, contact with grandchildren, or moment of insight brings them into genuine treatment. Some may become more reflective when approached without humiliation and with clear boundaries. However, this should never be assumed or made a condition of the survivor's recovery. Many alienating parents will not voluntarily engage in the depth of work required to examine pathogenic parenting, accept responsibility, or understand the harm caused. The adult survivor's treatment must therefore proceed on the basis of what is available, rather than what is wished for.

In more severe cases, the alienating parent may continue to deny culpability, keep the adult survivor in their crosshairs, and demonise them to allies within the wider family or social system. The survivor may continue to be treated as a representation of the targeted parent because of physical resemblance, shared traits, mannerisms, values, or other characteristics associated with the former partner whom the alienating parent despises. In these circumstances, the survivor may need support to grieve the painful possibility that the alienating parent may never provide the unconditional love, accountability, or protection for which they have longed. Coming to terms with this does not mean that the longing was unreasonable or that the survivor must stop caring. It means helping them recognise that their recovery cannot remain dependent on a parent who may never be willing or able to meet that need.

The survivor can be supported to hold two truths at once: *It would be meaningful if my alienating parent were properly assessed and treated, and my recovery cannot wait for that to happen.* This dual awareness protects hope without allowing hope to become dependence. It allows the survivor to grieve what was not assessed, what was not repaired, and what may never be acknowledged, while still moving towards safety, identity, relational freedom, and a life no longer organised around the alienating parent's willingness or unwillingness to change.

These later-life survivor realities now return the clinician to an earlier developmental question: how did this pattern become organised in the first place? If the adult survivor continues to live with the enduring consequences of coercive attachment disturbance, triangulation, and pathogenic influence across the lifespan, assessment must return to the caregiving processes that first shaped the child's fear, alignment, rejection, and relational confusion. The discussion, therefore, now turns back to the clinical task of identifying the pathogenic parenting dynamics contributing to the child's presentation.

Assessing Pathogenic Parenting

When a child presents with severe rejection, fear, hostility, emotional dysregulation, or attachment disturbance in the context of separation or divorce, the clinician cannot interpret the child's behaviour in isolation. The central task is to understand what is organising the child's response. Drawing on Childress's attachment-based assessment framework, the child's symptoms are considered within the caregiving system rather than assumed to arise spontaneously from within the child alone (Childress, 2017).

Terminology note. Childress uses the terms pathogenic parenting, allied parent, and rejected parent within his attachment-based formulation. In this framework, the allied parent refers to the parent with whom the child is pathologically aligned, while the rejected parent refers to the parent the child rejects. This differs from the more familiar CPA-PA terms, alienating parent and targeted parent. Childress's terminology reflects his focus on identifying the caregiving source of the child's attachment-related pathology rather than beginning from parental role labels. Within the HQTP, these terms are discussed alongside the broader CPA-PA language used throughout this protocol, including alienating parent and targeted parent, where those terms are required for continuity with the parental alienation literature and adult survivor accounts.

The clinical question is not simply whether the child is distressed, resistant, fearful, rejecting, or behaviourally dysregulated. The more important question is what relational dynamics are creating, reinforcing, or maintaining that disturbance. Assessment must therefore move beyond surface presentation and consider whether the child's attachment disturbance is linked to genuine harm from the rejected parent, pathogenic influence from the allied parent, or a more complex combination of both.

If the rejected parent has engaged in significant physical abuse, sexual abuse, severe psychological abuse, chronic terrorising, or serious neglect, then the child's fear, withdrawal, or rejection may represent an authentic self-protective adaptation. In that context, rejection may be protective rather than pathological. If, however, the allied parent is the primary source of pathogenic influence, the child's rejection of the targeted parent may be less an expression of autonomous judgement and more a symptom of attachment-related pathology shaped through triangulation, cross-generational coalition, coercive control, role reversal, or distorted family narratives. In some cases, both pathways may be present, requiring careful and disciplined clinical formulation.

For this reason, assessment requires disciplined clinical differentiation rather than ideological assumption or reflexive alignment with either parent's narrative. Similar child behaviour can have very different causes, so ethical assessment depends on careful differentiation rather than assumptions. The clinician must not assume that rejection proves abuse by the rejected parent, nor assume that allegations of harm are false because alienation is suspected. Both errors can place the child at risk. Ethical assessment requires the clinician to examine the child's presentation, developmental history, attachment patterns, relational context, fear responses, and family system dynamics before drawing conclusions (Childress, 2017).

A child-focused clinical assessment is therefore organised around identifying which parent, or which relational configuration, is functioning as the principal source of the pathogenic process affecting the child. This means evaluating not only the child's stated preferences or reported grievances, but also the quality of each parent-child relationship, the presence of trauma indicators, the child's developmental history, patterns of fear and avoidance, shifts in functioning, family role boundaries, and the possibility of borrowed language, role reversal, or coalition-based hostility. The clinician asks whether the child's behaviour is proportionate to lived experience, whether it reflects a developmentally coherent and reality-based concern, and whether the child's attachment system appears organised around protection from real danger or adaptation to coercive family pressure (Childress, 2017).

Assessing the Source of Pathogenic Parenting

Once pathogenic parenting has been identified as a central clinical concern, the next task is to determine its principal source within the caregiving system. In Childress's treatment-focused framework, this requires differentiation between disturbance arising primarily from the targeted rejected parent through severe abuse, neglect, or related harmful parenting, and disturbance arising primarily from the allied parent through cross-generational coalition, coercive influence, or other pathogenic processes operating against the targeted parent (Childress, 2017).

In family court processes, when allegations of child abuse, neglect, or coercive behaviour are made but not thoroughly assessed, the case can remain locked in an adversarial dynamic. Without clear clinical differentiation of which parent's actions are contributing to the child's distress, courts may rely heavily on the child's expressed preference or on the more persuasive parental narrative. This can perpetuate confusion, coalition dynamics, and further developmental harm. By contrast, when a treatment-focused attachment assessment is implemented early, courts and clinicians are better positioned to distinguish between genuine abuse and coercive pathogenic influence, and to respond in ways that are more firmly anchored in the child's safety and developmental needs (Childress, 2017).

Accordingly, determining the source of the pathology requires a structured differential process in which plausible explanations for the child's presentation are systematically considered, tested, and weighed until some possibilities are ruled out, and others strengthened. The aim is not premature certainty, but disciplined clarification regarding the most likely source of the child's pathology (Childress, 2017).

Assessing the Targeted Parent

The process of differential assessment begins by documenting the targeted parent's specific parenting practices. As noted earlier, children remain attachment-organised even when parenting is problematic. The clinical task, therefore, is to determine whether the child's fear, withdrawal, or rejection reflects genuinely harmful parenting by the targeted parent or is being more substantially shaped elsewhere in the caregiving system (Bowlby, 1969; Childress, 2017).

When the targeted parent's harmful practices are driving the conflict, identifying and addressing those specific behaviours is essential. Where those patterns can be reduced, contained, or corrected, the barriers to secure bonding may also lessen, supporting the possibility of a healthier parent-child relationship (Childress, 2017).

In a treatment-focused evaluation of attachment-related pathology in the context of divorce, the assessment of potential pathogenic parenting by the targeted rejected parent is guided by the Parenting Practices Rating Scale described by Childress. This scale categorises the targeted parents' behaviour into four broad levels, ranging from child abuse and severely problematic parenting through to somewhat problematic but normal range parenting and positive, healthy parenting. The scale also records ratings along continua relevant to neglect, hostility, control, empathy, and other domains of clinical concern, including substance-related concerns where relevant (Childress, 2017).

As a structured tool, the Parenting Practices Rating Scale both guides and documents the collection of information regarding the targeted parent's parenting practices. When problematic patterns are identified, those areas of concern can then become the focus of treatment planning or family therapy. Within this formulation, once the problematic parenting barriers are addressed, the child's natural drive to bond with the parent is more likely to find fulfilment in a secure, healthy relationship (Childress, 2017).

Assessing the Allied Parent

Assessing the allied parent involves a focused evaluation of a potential cross-generational coalition in which the child has aligned with that parent against the targeted parent. This dynamic may be more difficult to identify because manipulative influence and psychological control can be concealed behind the appearance of the child's supposedly independent rejection (Childress, 2017).

Parental psychological control is a well-established construct in the developmental literature. It involves intrusive, manipulative parenting that intrudes upon the child's psychological world and developing self-definition, often through guilt induction, shame, anxiety, or love withdrawal rather than through ordinary behavioural guidance or structure (Barber & Harmon, 2002). Unlike behavioural control, it operates by targeting the child's internal experience, thoughts, and feelings rather than primarily regulating external conduct (Stone et al., 2002).

Soenens and Vansteenkiste (2010) describe several common tactics parents may use to exert psychological control. These include guilt induction, contingent love or love withdrawal, the instilling of anxiety, and invalidation of the child's perspective. Each of these tactics interferes with the development of autonomy and can shape the child's perception of loyalty, danger, and relational obligation.

Accordingly, assessment of the allied parent must examine whether the child's rejection has been scaffolded through emotional pressure, selective reinforcement, distorted narratives, or role-reversed dependency rather than emerging from an independent and developmentally grounded appraisal of the targeted parent. This is particularly important where the child's language, affect, or certainty appears borrowed, disproportionate, or poorly matched to the child's direct lived experience (Childress, 2017; Barber & Harmon, 2002).

Narcissistic and Borderline Dynamics in Divorce

Of central clinical importance is the evaluation of attachment-related pathology that emerges during divorce, particularly the risk of a cross-generational coalition forming between the child and a parent with clinically significant narcissistic or borderline personality pathology (Childress, 2015). A parent with narcissistic personality disorder, or pronounced narcissistic pathology, may be especially vulnerable to rejection, shame, and threats to self-esteem. In divorce, the spousal rejection can function as a narcissistic injury, that is, a profound blow to the parent's self-cohesion or self-worth (Ronningstam, 2024).

For example, a father with narcissistic personality disorder may have developed a defensive reliance on external validation, grandiosity, and control following earlier experiences of humiliation, unstable affirmation, or chronic invalidation. In the context of divorce, he may begin to recruit the child into marital conflict by subtly encouraging contempt for the other parent, selectively highlighting grievances, rewarding loyalty, and treating the child's rejection of the other parent as evidence that he remains the preferred, admired, or vindicated parent. In this way, the child is not merely "taking sides"; the child is being used to stabilise the parent's threatened self-structure (Childress, 2015; Hart et al., 2017; Ronningstam, 2024).

Borderline personality pathology is classically organised around abandonment fear, affective instability, identity disturbance, and intense relational dysregulation. When the spouse leaves, this loss can activate powerful fears of being alone or emotionally annihilated.

In response, the parent may draw the child into the marital struggle as a way of preserving exclusive closeness and regulating separation anxiety (Linehan, 1993). For example, a mother with borderline personality disorder may insist that her child cancel visits, saying, "If you go, I will have no one," or may become visibly dysregulated whenever the child shows warmth toward the other parent. Over time, the child may internalise the parent's anxiety and begin resisting or refusing contact as a way of preventing the parent's collapse (Childress, 2015; Linehan, 1993).

These patterns can occur across genders and are not mutually exclusive in complex presentations. Some parents may show grandiose and entitled narcissistic features, others may present with more vulnerable or abandonment-driven traits, and some may show mixed or overlapping features requiring careful diagnostic formulation (Ronningstam, 2024). Treatment pathways also differ. For narcissistic personality disorder, intervention is often longer-term. It may involve psychodynamic, schema-informed, or other structured psychotherapeutic approaches aimed at improving reflective capacity, empathy, shame tolerance, and interpersonal functioning (Ronningstam, 2024). For borderline personality disorder, dialectical behaviour therapy (DBT) remains one of the most established treatment approaches, focusing on emotional regulation, distress tolerance, interpersonal effectiveness, and the balance of acceptance and change (Linehan, 1993).

Diagnostic Indicators in the Child's Symptom Display

The purpose of differential diagnosis is to identify which parent's (sometimes both) behaviour is creating the child's attachment-related pathology by determining the source of the child's sustained hostility and rejection of the targeted parent. Since pathogenic parenting creates the child's symptoms, it leaves telltale evidence, psychological fingerprints, of the parent's influence and manipulation in the child's symptom display. In Childress's model, these signs are especially important when assessing the possibility that an allied parent with narcissistic or borderline pathology has formed a cross-generational coalition with the child against the targeted parent (Childress, 2015, 2017).

Attachment symptoms. When a child consistently rejects a parent who is emotionally present and available, this indicates a disruption in the child's natural attachment drive. The attachment system is a goal-directed motivational system that persistently aims to form a secure bond with a parent. Thus, the child's rejection, as assessed alongside the Parenting Practices Rating Scale, may signal a breakdown in the child's attachment functioning rather than a simple autonomous preference. Examples may include a child refusing to see the targeted parent despite a previously affectionate history, showing exaggerated fear during ordinary transitions, or repeating negative statements about the targeted parent that appear to be borrowed from the allied parent rather than grounded in direct experience (Bowlby, 1969; Childress, 2017).

Narcissistic symptoms. When a child is subject to psychological control by an allied parent with narcissistic or borderline pathology, the child's symptoms may show traits that are narcissistic in quality and selectively directed toward the targeted parent. In the draft, these have been described as psychological fingerprints. Clinically, this may involve entitlement, lack of empathy, exaggerated certainty, devaluation of the targeted parent, or exploitative alignment with the allied parent's narrative. These attitudes do not arise in a vacuum. Rather, the child may internalise the allied parent's distorted view of the other parent and begin to replicate it in their own relational behaviour (Childress, 2015; Hart et al., 2017).

Delusional false belief. The child may develop a fixed false belief that he or she is being harmed by an otherwise supportive and available parent, despite contrary evidence. In the draft, this has been described as an encapsulated persecutory delusion. Within Childress's framework, this false belief is understood as evidence of a trauma reenactment narrative in which the allied parent's own attachment-based wounds are recreated within the current family system through a false pattern of abusive parent, victimised child, and protective parent. When this false persecutory narrative is evident in the child's symptom display toward the targeted parent, it provides clinical evidence for the distorting influence of the allied parent (Childress, 2015).

When all three clusters are evident together, Childress treats the pattern as strongly supportive of pathogenic parenting by an allied parent who has formed a cross-generational coalition with the child against the other parent. The Diagnostic Checklist for Pathogenic Parenting, described in the appendices of his assessment text, is intended to guide the assessment of these indicators and associated signs. Where these indicators raise sufficient concern, the next issue is no longer only what may be present clinically, but whether the practitioner has the training, framework, and scope required to assess the pattern responsibly and without compounding harm.

Session Protocol, Training, and Further Resources

To implement the session protocol effectively, clinicians should follow the structured process outlined by Childress. The assessment unfolds in phases, including initial parent sessions, direct child assessment, evaluation of parent responses, analysis of stimulus controls and behaviour chains, and preparation of a treatment-focused assessment report. For a detailed, step-by-step guide to these procedures, including the Parenting Practices Rating Scale and the Diagnostic Checklist for Pathogenic Parenting, readers should consult Dr Craig Childress's Attachment-Based Parental Alienation (AB-PA), Assessment of Attachment-Related Pathology Surrounding Divorce, and the materials available on his website (Childress, 2017).

Childress's assessment text also provides a model treatment-focused assessment report for a confirmed diagnosis of pathogenic parenting. This report includes the scope of the evaluation, completed rating scales, assessment findings, DSM-related diagnostic formulation, treatment indications, the child's response to protective separation, and the process for ending the protective separation period. These materials are central to understanding how the overall protocol is operationalised in practice, and readers seeking to use this framework should obtain the original text directly from Dr Childress's website or bookseller listing (Childress, 2017).

Application of the child and family attachment-based assessment model described in this section requires an appropriately qualified practitioner with the supervision, training, and scope of practice necessary for specialised child and family assessment. In Australia, this may include PACFA-registered clinical psychotherapists or counsellors whose training and competencies support advanced assessment work with children and families, as well as clinical psychologists and psychiatrists. However, training in these models alone does not override the jurisdictional scope of practice or professional obligations. Clinicians remain bound by the standards, competencies, supervision requirements, and ethical codes governing their registration category (Medical Board of Australia, 2020; PACFA, 2018, 2024; Psychology Board of Australia, 2019).

Formal eligibility, however, does not in itself establish clinical competence in this area. The capacity to assess attachment-related pathology in post-separation family contexts, differentiate between abuse and coercive alignment, and recognise pathogenic parenting requires more than professional title or registration status alone. It requires specific knowledge of attachment systems, family systems dynamics, psychological control, trauma processes, developmental distortions, and the ways these may become organised within adversarial post-separation contexts. The central question, therefore, is not only who is permitted to undertake such assessments, but whether the practitioner possesses the specialised training, conceptual clarity, supervision, and ethical discipline required to do so safely, accurately, and without compounding harm.

When Child Abuse is Not Assessed and Treated

Where proper child abuse assessment does not occur, and the child moves through systems without adequate recognition, the harm may become developmentally embedded and remain clinically active into adulthood. In these circumstances, treatment is no longer addressing childhood events in isolation. However, the enduring aftermath of those events as they present through attachment injury, identity disturbance, unresolved grief, affect dysregulation, compromised autonomy, epistemic instability, and long-term relational impairment. At this point, the HQTP becomes relevant.

Step Five: Price-Tobler's HQTP and Where It Fits in the Sequence

Once developmental harm has been recognised and formulated, the next clinical question is no longer simply what has happened, but how treatment should now be organised. The Healing Qualia Treatment Protocol © (HQTP), developed by Dr Alyse Price-Tobler, enters the sequence at a different clinical level from the preceding frameworks. Baker's Four-Factor Model, Bernet and Greenhill's Five-Factor Model, and Childress's attachment-based framework are positioned primarily as tools for recognition, threshold enquiry, and child-focused assessment and formulation of relational and attachment-related pathology. The HQTP does not function in that way. It is not a child-identification model, a forensic-determination model, or a reunification program. It is a specialist phase-based clinical treatment protocol designed to address the developmental, relational, psychological, and epistemic consequences that remain when harm has already occurred, and earlier systems have failed to recognise, formulate, or adequately protect the adult survivor.

Within this sequence, the HQTP becomes relevant once the clinician is no longer asking only whether alienation dynamics and abuse-related processes may be present, but what those dynamics have done developmentally and how treatment should now proceed. Its clinical task is therefore not threshold recognition, but treatment architecture. In adult survivors, this includes stabilisation, restoration of epistemic safety, longitudinal formulation of attachment injury and developmental distortion, grief integration, identity repair, trauma-readiness, differentiation, and long-term adaptation. In this sense, the HQTP occupies the treatment phase of the sequence: it treats the developmental harm and translates that into structured, paced, non-forensic clinical care.

Within this broader sequence, the author's Volumes One and Two may also be understood as preparatory bridges into the HQTP. Volume One maps the survivor and clinician-facing impacts of severe parental alienation across the lifespan and helps establish why adult survivors require a distinct clinical response. Volume Two extends this work by focusing more directly on practitioner challenges, treatment barriers, modality misalignment, and risk considerations encountered when working with this population. Together, these earlier volumes help prepare the ground for Volume Three, which formalises the sequencing, pacing, containment, and phase-based treatment architecture of the HQTP itself.

The HQTP is particularly important where warning signs in childhood were visible but not adequately assessed, where intervention was misaligned, where the child was pathologised instead of protected, or where the survivor only comes to treatment years later in adolescence or adulthood. In such cases, the clinical problem is no longer solely one of child assessment. It is the enduring aftermath of attachment disruption, coercive control, identity distortion, loyalty conflict, grief, and compromised self-trust across the lifespan. The HQTP was developed specifically to meet that gap by providing a phase-based treatment framework for survivors whose developmental harm was not resolved at the point of first system contact.

When clinically appropriate, the HQTP may also inform later-stage work with adolescents, after safeguarding, abuse assessment, and environmental review have been undertaken, and as the task shifts from identification toward stabilisation and recovery. Even then, its role remains treatment-focused rather than investigative. The protocol does not replace child abuse assessment, statutory safeguarding, or differential diagnosis. Rather, it follows them, organising what comes next when the clinician faces the question of how to treat the survivor without repeating coercion, disbelief, premature interpretation, or system-driven harm. In this sense, the sequence proposed here asks the field to tolerate sufficient complexity to recognise that different frameworks may serve different functions at different points in the lifespan trajectory, and that survivors' needs are better served by careful sequencing than by rigid allegiance to any single model.

Where mental health practitioners become organised around professional rivalry, theoretical camps, or adversarial defence of preferred frameworks, the clinical task may again be displaced, and survivors may be exposed to further misrecognition, fragmentation, and delay.

Integration and Transition to Phase I

The following chapter establishes the foundations for assessment and formulation on which the HQTP is built. It positions diagnosis as a clinical tool requiring restraint, epistemic humility, and developmental contextualisation. Survivor presentations are situated within attachment disruption, betrayal trauma, and systemic failure, while retaining emphasis on resilience, agency, and long-term recovery capacity. Consequently, throughout this protocol, therapeutic progress is measured less by interpretive certainty and more by the survivor's growing capacity to experience, trust, and regulate their own internal states.

With assessment posture, diagnostic safeguards, and formulation principles now established, the protocol transitions into active therapeutic engagement. The following chapter introduces the opening phase of treatment, operationalising these foundations through safety, orientation, epistemic stabilisation, and restoration of internal agency. This transition marks the shift from clinical formulation to treatment implementation while teaching the ethical principles of sequencing, pacing, and epistemic safety that govern the HQTP.

Chapter Five

Beginning the Phase-Based Treatment Architecture for Survivors

Clinical Decision-Making and Ethical Safeguards

How to Use This Chapter

Some concepts introduced earlier are revisited here to orient mental health practitioners to the beginning of the HQTP's phase-based treatment architecture. Additionally, this chapter is deliberately comprehensive and may be read in sections according to clinical need.

Chapter Five begins with Phase I and its core priorities of safety, orientation, epistemic stabilisation, and restoration of survivor agency as the foundation for subsequent therapeutic work. Clinicians are encouraged to read the chapter in full before implementation. The phases described here are intended to function as an integrated clinical architecture, not as a checklist or rigid sequence. Their effective use depends on familiarity with the broader ethical positioning, decision-making principles, and epistemic safety framework outlined earlier in the protocol.

Clinicians may not always meet survivors at the beginning of treatment or at a stable point in their recovery. Some survivors may present in acute distress, during a crisis, or after a long period of therapeutic impasse. In these situations, the clinician's first responsibility is immediate stabilisation, containment, and safety. This chapter can therefore be used as an ethical starting point for intervention when urgent support is required. Once the survivor is more stable, the clinician should return to the broader HQTP framework to guide assessment, formulation, phase placement, and longer-term treatment planning.

Each treatment phase outlines clinical priorities, readiness indicators, risk considerations, ethical cautions, and modality guidance intended to support reflective clinical judgement rather than prescriptive or formulaic intervention. Movement between phases is responsive rather than linear. Survivors may move forward, pause, return to earlier stabilisation work, or remain within a single phase for extended periods depending on safety conditions, cumulative trauma exposure, system involvement, developmental stage, and life context. Such movement reflects the developmental and relational complexity of recovery and should not be interpreted as treatment failure.

This chapter also includes explanations of each phase and companion notes from the author written directly for survivors. In this way, survivor-facing language is presented alongside clinical formulation. These sections are intentionally designed to support transparency, reduce epistemic harm, and strengthen survivor understanding of the therapeutic process without requiring justification, performance, or proof of experience. Importantly, the HQTP does not assume that survivors enter treatment with awareness of the abuse they have experienced. Many present without self-identification, after years of ineffective or harmful treatment, or through secondary systems such as mental health services, justice settings, or disability support pathways.

In these contexts, clinicians are often the first to recognise patterns of psychological abuse, coercive control, and attachment-based injury. For this reason, treatment does not begin with technique, trauma processing, or diagnostic categorisation. It begins with the restoration of psychological safety, relational credibility, and epistemic stability within the therapeutic relationship.

Phase Framework Orientation

The HQTP is not designed for speed. It is designed for sustainability. Treatment progression within this model prioritises psychological safety, stability, and long-term relational processing over rapid symptom reduction, diagnostic certainty, or premature trauma processing.

This framework is not a linear treatment pathway or a time-based progression model. Adult survivors of CPA-PA contexts rarely recover through predictable sequences. Therapeutic work within the HQTP therefore prioritises responsiveness to nervous system capacity, psychological safety, and survivor consent rather than adherence to predetermined timelines or externally imposed outcome targets.

As mentioned, movement between phases is guided by readiness rather than completion. Advancement does not occur because a set of techniques has been delivered, but because the survivor demonstrates sufficient stability, internal coherence, and emotional regulation to tolerate deeper therapeutic work without destabilisation. Conversely, returning to earlier phases is not conceptualised as regression or failure. It is understood as clinically responsive recalibration when new material, relational stressors, or system contact reactivate vulnerability.

Phase progression is governed by the principle of *safety before depth.* Stabilisation and relational safety remain active priorities throughout the protocol. Trauma processing is not initiated when survivors remain emotionally overwhelmed, cognitively fragmented, or physiologically dysregulated. When these conditions are present, the therapeutic focus returns to regulation, containment, and stabilisation of meaning before further integration work proceeds.

Survivor pacing and consent are central operating principles at every phase. Survivors retain authority over the depth, tempo, and level of participation. Clinicians are required to communicate the rationale for interventions transparently, invite questions, and respect the survivor's right to pause, modify, or decline therapeutic approaches. This protects against replicating the coercive relational dynamics that characterised many survivors' childhood experiences.

Clinical responsibility within the phase framework includes continuous monitoring of stability markers. These include emotional regulation capacity, tolerance of relational stress, coherence of personal narrative, ability to self-soothe between sessions, and reduction in compulsive reassurance-seeking or crisis-driven urgency. When these indicators deteriorate, clinicians adjust pacing and reorient treatment focus rather than pushing forward.

The protocol rejects outcome-driven sequencing. Therapeutic success is not defined by reconciliation, forgiveness, symptom elimination, or family contact. Instead, progress is evaluated by increasing psychological safety, internal authority, relational differentiation, and survivor autonomy.

Phases function as flexible clinical scaffolding rather than rigid treatment compartments. Survivors may move forward, pause, revisit earlier phases, or remain within certain stages for extended periods depending on life context, relational exposure, health changes, or system contact. When destabilisation occurs at any point during treatment, clinicians must watch for indicators warranting recalibration, including escalation of suicidal ideation, increased dissociation, persistent affect dysregulation between sessions, collapse in daily functioning, heightened attachment distress toward the therapist, renewed epistemic confusion, or reactivation following family contact, system exposure, or relational rupture. In these circumstances, therapeutic recalibration is framed as responsible clinical care rather than regression. The objective is not to 'go backward,' but to restore sufficient safety and regulation to support continued work without retraumatisation.

Readiness to progress between phases is determined by functional stability rather than by the absence of symptoms. Indicators of readiness include improved emotional regulation, increased capacity to tolerate relational stress without collapse, greater narrative coherence regarding personal history, reduced urgency for reassurance or external validation, and the ability to maintain daily functioning between sessions. When readiness indicators remain inconsistent or fragile, pacing is slowed, and stabilisation work is extended. This protects survivors from premature exposure and clinicians from inadvertently prioritising protocol flow over psychological safety.

Phase Continuity Anchor: Restraint as Clinical Precision

Across all six HQTP phases, progress is governed by readiness rather than by insight, urgency, disclosure, intellectual understanding, or the survivor's wish to "get through it". A survivor may understand the material cognitively and still require an earlier phase if regulation, identity stability, consent capacity, relational safety, or functional steadiness is compromised.

Clinicians should therefore treat return to an earlier phase as ethical recontainment rather than regression. If the survivor becomes destabilised, dissociated, suicidal, compliant, externally pressured, unable to pause, unable to hold complexity, or unable to make choices without fear or coercion, the work returns to the earliest phase required to restore safety. Within the HQTP, restraint is clinical precision.

Phase progression is appropriate only when the survivor can remain sufficiently regulated, participate with informed consent, tolerate ambiguity, recover after activation, preserve a stable sense of self, and engage the next therapeutic task without being pushed beyond clinical capacity. When these conditions are not present, the clinician slows the work, consults supervision where required, and protects phase integrity.

Pre-Phase I Initial Assessment and Identification Requirement

Before initiating Phase I intervention, clinicians must complete an initial assessment process sufficient to determine whether the presenting individual is likely to have an adult survivor history. This assessment is not intended to establish forensic certainty or exhaustive diagnostic categorisation. Its purpose is to identify core developmental trauma indicators, attachment disruption patterns, coercive relational histories, and systemic harm exposure that warrant application of the HQTP rather than standard short-term or symptom-focused interventions.

Where the presentation remains ambiguous, clinicians are advised to proceed conservatively, prioritising stabilisation and relational safety while continuing assessment throughout the early sessions. Premature trauma processing or interpretive framing without sufficient formulation increases the risk of misattunement, retraumatisation, and epistemic harm. If the individual does not meet criteria consistent with developmental psychological abuse exposure, clinicians should redirect to appropriate evidence-based treatment pathways rather than applying the HQTP indiscriminately. Formal diagnostic assessment, differential formulation, risk screening, and safeguarding obligations remain the clinician's professional responsibility and must be completed in accordance with regulatory, ethical, and jurisdictional standards.

Early Clinical Approach: First Contact and the Initial Session

Clinicians entering this work commonly report uncertainty or apprehension when first meeting adult survivors of CPA-PA. This response is understandable. Survivors may present with fragmented narrative coherence, heightened emotional reactivity, emotional constriction, guardedness, apparent compliance, distrust of professionals, or extensive histories of ineffective or harmful therapeutic engagement. Clinicians may simultaneously fear misjudging the presentation, escalating distress, or becoming unintentionally drawn into relational or systemic dynamics they do not yet fully understand.

Findings from the author's doctoral practitioner cohort indicate that this apprehension is not a marker of clinician inadequacy, but a predictable response when working with survivors whose trauma histories are relational, covert, and prolonged rather than event-based. For example, some of the PhD practitioner cohort reported that early uncertainty reflected an intuitive recognition that familiar assessment and engagement strategies were insufficient or potentially harmful in this population.

First Clinical Tasks in Early HQTP Work

The primary clinical task in the initial session is not assessment, diagnosis, formulation, or exploration of trauma. It is the establishment of psychological safety, epistemic respect, and a clear therapeutic frame. Adult survivors may present with secondary symptom clusters, including anxiety, depression, relational instability, somatic distress, identity confusion, or persistent treatment non-response. In some cases, survivors have cycled through systems for many years without the underlying developmental harm being recognised. For this reason, a clinician oriented to the HQTP framework may be the first person to notice patterns consistent with child psychological abuse, attachment-based injury, and long-term relational coercion.

In the first session, the clinician does not ask the survivor to prove the history, organise the family narrative, identify an alienating parent, or commit to a contact outcome. The first clinical tasks are to establish the therapeutic frame, clarify that therapy is not forensic or investigative, assess immediate safety and risk of destabilisation, invite the survivor's present experience at a tolerable pace, and observe how the survivor responds to being heard without pressure for certainty.

The clinician listens for regulation, shame, fear, loyalty conflict, dissociation, urgency, compliance, and the survivor's capacity to pause. These observations guide whether the work remains in early stabilisation, proceeds to fuller assessment, or requires crisis containment before further exploration.

Beginning With Attunement, Not History-Taking

In the author's survivor cohort doctoral study, reported in Volume One, some participants described entering treatment believing they were 'the problem' after years of intervention focused mainly on symptom reduction or behavioural change. Others had spent many years in therapy, in some cases up to 30, without anyone helping them understand how their distress had developed within their family relationships. Early sessions that prioritised safety and a non-evaluative stance were consistently described as the first therapeutic experiences that did not intensify self-doubt or shame.

For this reason, clinicians should avoid pressing for narrative disclosure or detailed historical explanation in early sessions. Invitations such as *"Tell me what happened"* or *"Describe your childhood"* may unintentionally recreate relational pressure, loyalty conflict, or epistemic threat. Survivors may feel they are being interviewed, tested, examined, or required to persuade the clinician that harm occurred.

Survivors in the related doctoral cohort frequently reported that such requests, particularly when posed early, activated a sense of being examined, disbelieved, or required to prove harm. This often resulted in either compliance-based storytelling or emotional withdrawal, neither of which supports accurate formulation or safety.

Instead, the clinician's initial stance should communicate safety, neutrality, consent, and choice. This approach is consistent with the principle that felt safety supports reflection, communication, and connection, while chronic autonomic threat can temporarily reduce each of these capacities (Bailey et al., 2020). Simple, grounded openings are sufficient. For example:

"I'm glad you came today. We can work at your pace. What feels most important to you, so I can understand how things are for you right now?"

or

"Before we talk about anything specific, I want you to know there's no expectation to explain or prove anything here. My role is to understand what helps you feel supported and safe in this space."

It may also help to say:

"This is not an interview or an exam. You only need to answer what feels useful, or possible today."

or

"You are not being judged here. You are the expert on your own feelings and emotions, and I'm very interested in hearing about your perspectives and thoughts."

These statements may appear simple, but for survivors who have lived with distortion, accusation, disbelief, or pressure to perform the correct version of events, they can be deeply regulating. Clinicians should not underestimate the value of ordinary human acknowledgement. Comments such as *"That must have been very hard," "I can imagine that would have felt confusing,"* or simply *"I hear you"* can help the survivor feel received without being pushed further than they are ready to go.

This attunement must be genuine. Communication occurs not only through words but also through the eyes, mouth, facial expression, posture, tone, and timing of the clinician's response. Survivors are often highly sensitive to signs that the therapist is distracted, sceptical, rushed, or emotionally absent. When the clinician's words, face, and presence are congruent, the survivor may begin to feel that someone is actually listening. For many survivors, this may feel unfamiliar, relieving, and frightening at the same time.

Speaking about intimate, painful, or long-hidden experiences can bring both relief and anxiety. Some questions may feel unfamiliar, awkward, exposing, or difficult to answer. The clinician can reduce this pressure by making the choice explicit:

"Some of these questions may feel a little unfamiliar or awkward. Please let me know if this happens at any point, and we can slow things down."

or

"We do not need to go over your whole history now. We can begin with what feels most important, or even with what has helped you survive until now."

These questions shift the focus away from forced historical disclosure and towards the survivor's existing adaptations, strengths, protections, and survival intelligence. It allows the clinician to begin formulation without requiring the survivor to provide a full trauma narrative before safety has been established.

These opening statements establish containment without interrogation, position the clinician as relationally attuned rather than evaluative, and remove performance demands from the survivor. They support early alliance formation while protecting epistemic safety and emotional regulation. The clinician is actively reducing threat cues and allowing the nervous system to settle before attempting any interpretive or exploratory work.

Within the HQTP, crisis architecture is established as a core element of clinical governance, derived directly from the author's dual-cohort doctoral findings. These findings demonstrated that destabilisation in adult survivors of child psychological abuse in CPA-PA contexts is most frequently recognition-driven, emerging through developmental betrayal awareness, narrative reconstruction, exposure to institutional material, and identity reorganisation rather than through affect escalation alone.

Data from the author's adult survivor cohort identified that moments of meaning disruption can precipitate acute destabilisation. Survivors may become disoriented, overwhelmed by grief, activated by moral injury, or temporarily lose the identity structures that had helped them remain stable.

Additionally, in the author's MHP cohort, practitioners described a parallel form of destabilisation happening with them when working in adversarial or high-conflict contexts. This included fear of complaints, intimidation, pressure to cross professional boundaries, attempts to distort the clinician's role, and heightened concern that clinical notes or reports may later be scrutinised, misused, or weaponised.

For this reason, the HQTP integrates both survivor destabilisation and practitioner risk within a single containment structure. Crisis architecture is not treated as a simple safety procedure added onto treatment. It functions as part of clinical governance: a structured way of protecting the survivor, the practitioner, the therapeutic relationship, and the integrity of the work when risk, pressure, or destabilisation escalates.

Accordingly, crisis architecture precedes and governs all phase-based therapeutic work. Work with adult survivors in CPA-PA routinely occurs within adversarial family systems characterised by coercive control, institutional scrutiny, identity vulnerability, and elevated risk states. For this reason, crisis assessment, escalation pathways, consultation thresholds, and practitioner protection are embedded as structural protocol components rather than adjunct safeguards.

Crisis architecture explains how clinicians identify, monitor, and respond to destabilisation across phases. The containment scaffold translates doctoral findings, frontline clinical practice, and lived experience into observable escalation indicators, pacing decisions, consultation triggers, and documentation thresholds. All subsequent phase work is conducted within this containment structure. Phase progression remains contingent on stability, and escalation thresholds take precedence over therapeutic depth when risk indicators emerge.

Acute Risk and Mandatory Safety Responsibilities

The HQTP does not replace acute crisis intervention, statutory reporting, emergency response, or organisational risk procedures. Confidentiality is not absolute. If concerns emerge during treatment regarding suicidality, self-harm, violence towards others, family and domestic violence, intimate partner violence, stalking, coercive control, child safety, medical risk—including medical or psychological FDIOA—psychosis, disclosure of illegal abuse, or a credible threat towards an identifiable person, the clinician must pause phase-based treatment and respond in accordance with the relevant professional, organisational, legal, safeguarding, mandatory-reporting, duty-of-care, duty-to-warn, and emergency-response requirements within their jurisdiction. These responsibilities take priority over progression through the HQTP. The protocol supports, but does not replace, the clinician's existing legal, ethical, professional, and organisational obligations.

In these circumstances, the clinical task is not to continue the protocol, deepen the narrative, pursue contact decisions, or complete phase tasks. The task is to restore immediate safety, assess risk, clarify consent and confidentiality limits, involve appropriate supports, consult or escalate where required, and document clinical reasoning. Suggested clinician wording in acute risk moments: "I want to pause the therapy work for a moment because your safety matters more than continuing this material today. Let us slow down, work out what is happening right now, and decide what support is needed before we go any further."

Within the HQTP, returning to crisis containment, stabilisation, supervision, or external emergency support is not a departure from the protocol. It is the protocol's safety logic in action.

High-Risk Activation Contexts Requiring Safety Review

Clinicians should treat certain clinical events as potential destabilisation points requiring renewed risk assessment, pacing review, and, where needed, supervision, consultation, referral, or escalation. These may include discovery of a targeted parent's death, suicide, homicide, or permanent unavailability; child-protection, medical, school, former cult members have located them, adoption, identity, or migration records; attempts to contact family members; boundary violations or renewed coercive contact; anniversaries of abduction, removal, separation, suicide, familicide, or traumatic disclosure; litigation or complaint processes; sudden changes in family contact; identity-documentation processes; sexual, somatic, or body-memory activation; and recognition of concealed parentage, abduction, FDIOA-related dynamics, or prolonged deception.

When these events arise, clinicians should not assume that insight equals readiness. The clinical task is to reassess suicide and self-harm risk, violence risk, dissociation, functional deterioration, coercive-control exposure, safety concerns, consent capacity, and the survivor's ability to remain oriented to present-day safety. If risk increases, phase-based work should pause and return to stabilisation, safety planning, supervision, consultation, referral, or emergency response as clinically indicated.

Suicide and self-harm assessments should be conducted using the clinician's professional training, service policy, and clinically appropriate tools. No single screening instrument is mandated by the HQTP. Where suicidal ideation, self-harm urges, intent, planning, access to means, marked hopelessness, identity collapse, psychosis, severe dissociation, violence risk, or inability to maintain safety is present, clinicians must prioritise immediate safety over protocol progression.

Consent, Capacity, Confidentiality, and Reporting Limits

The HQTP assumes adult survivor autonomy unless there is a clear clinical, legal, or emergency basis to do otherwise. Clinicians should explain the purpose, risks, limits, and alternatives of proposed interventions, including access to records, family contact, supported meetings, collateral consultation, documentation, reporting, or referral. Consent should be informed, voluntary, specific to the proposed action, and revisited when risk, distress, or the clinical context changes.

Wherever possible, escalation should be transparent and collaborative so that safety action does not unnecessarily replicate coercion, abandonment, secrecy, or institutional betrayal. When emergency risk requires action without full consent, clinicians should document the clinical reasoning, the least restrictive available response, the steps taken to preserve dignity and agency, and the follow-up plan to restore therapeutic safety.

Crisis Containment and Escalation Framework

Across the adult survivor cohort, acute risk rarely emerged solely from affect intensity. Destabilisation more commonly followed epistemic rupture, recognition of developmental betrayal, institutional reactivation (some may want to reconnect with the survivor, sometimes for sinister reasons, such as children of cults), identity destabilisation, and activation of moral injury processes. Crisis within this population, therefore, reflects disruptions to meaning, identity, organisation, relational safety, and future orientation, as well as emotional dysregulation.

The HQTP crisis architecture provides the core protocol infrastructure, setting pacing rules, escalation thresholds, consultation requirements, and practitioner-protection parameters that guide all subsequent phase work. Crisis planning is collaborative, anticipatory, and initiated during Phase I, with revisions at phase transitions and in response to environmental changes, destabilising disclosures, or boundary renegotiation with coercive caregivers.

Escalation represents progression of containment rather than treatment failure. When destabilisation exceeds the capacity for integration, pacing adjusts, interpretive work pauses, and consultation or co-management pathways are activated. The functions of crisis architecture are stabilisation, differentiation, and protection against the reenactment of coercive dynamics within therapy.

Identity Collapse with Potential Suicidality

In the author's adult survivor cohort, findings indicate that suicidal ideation may emerge during periods of developmental betrayal recognition rather than during episodes of acute emotional dysregulation alone. Survivors described destabilisation following recognition that their attachment relationships with their TP had been misrepresented, that a psychologically available parent had been obstructed or erased, and that irreplaceable developmental time with that parent had been lost.

Survivors also reported disruption of autobiographical continuity, erosion of internal working models of attachment, and destabilisation of identity coherence during the introduction of new narratives that differed from what their AP had told them. In cases involving abduction, concealment, or narrative manipulation, recognition of life narrative distortion produced profound disorientation.

Within this protocol, this destabilisation pattern is conceptualised as identity collapse with potential suicidality. The term does not denote a diagnostic category. It describes a clinically observed state in which the organising sense of self destabilises following recognition of prolonged relational manipulation by the AP, developmental deprivation, and attachment disruption. Suicidal ideation in this context appears linked to perceived irreversibility of developmental loss, collapse of narrative coherence, and disruption of future orientation rather than solely depressive symptomatology.

Because this destabilisation pattern is structurally linked to meaning collapse, standard suicide screening alone may not detect early risk emergence. Assessment therefore includes evaluation of epistemic stability, developmental grief load, recognition of attachment ruptures, and identity continuity alongside conventional risk indicators.

Crisis Indicators Specific to CPA-PA Contexts

Crisis risk may increase following identifiable recognition events, including reviewing historical court documents, reunification attempts, contact shifts with previously obstructed family members, discovery of deception, public acknowledgement of abuse, or integration of new autobiographical information.

Court reactivation refers to reviewing historical court documents that recorded or institutionally endorsed distorted narratives. Destabilisation may arise not from legal stress alone, but from confronting written evidence that an inaccurate version of the survivor's family history became part of the official record. Similarly, identity restructuring following the discovery of abduction or the recognition of concealed lineage may temporarily disrupt attachment schemas, relational trust calibration, and existential coherence.

Crisis assessment should therefore examine both recognised signs of possible self-harm or harm to others and any recent discoveries or recognition events that may have contributed to the survivor's destabilisation.

Escalation Thresholds

The threshold for escalation is reached when destabilisation progresses to more serious risk features, including suicidal thinking linked to a specific timeframe, concealment of intent or behaviour, mental or behavioural rehearsal, obtaining access to means, farewell communications, increasingly restricted thinking, or a reduced ability to recognise alternatives to self-harm or harm to others. When these indicators emerge, trauma processing pauses, and containment supersedes interpretive depth. Intervention prioritises collaborative safety planning, increased therapeutic contact where appropriate, psychiatric consultation when indicated, activation of supervision, and jurisdictionally required reporting pathways. Escalation is framed as ethical stabilisation rather than regression.

Targeted Violence Risk

Risk assessment for others is conducted with equivalent clinical clarity. Within the survivor cohort data from Volume One, findings indicate that suppressed rage, humiliation, and betrayal may coexist with retaliatory ideation during periods of differentiation and recognition. However, Volume Two practitioner data demonstrate clinician anxiety when encountering such disclosures, particularly within adversarial systems.

Within the HQTP, retaliatory ideation is neither minimised as a symbolic expression nor amplified through the clinician's fear. It is assessed contextually within developmental exposure to coercive control, family violence, humiliation, and threat modelling. Escalation thresholds include operational planning, target fixation, rehearsal behaviour, leakage communication, acquisition of means, surveillance behaviour, or credible articulation of intent. When these indicators are present, community safety obligations take precedence over exploratory work. Documentation becomes precise, consultation becomes mandatory, and statutory pathways are activated.

Practitioner Destabilisation and Protection

In the author's second doctoral study involving practitioners, the findings from the Volume Two cohort indicate that clinicians working within CPA-PA contexts frequently experience harassment, complaints, intimidation, reputational threats, and fear of regulatory action. These pressures may impair clinical judgement, increase over-responsibility, or lead to defensive withdrawal.

Practitioner destabilisation is therefore incorporated into the protocol's crisis architecture. Structured supervision, consultation thresholds, documentation discipline, and boundary enforcement function as protective infrastructure rather than administrative tasks.

Referral, co-management, treatment pause, or withdrawal based on safety considerations is conceptualised as ethical containment rather than abandonment. No clinician is required to function as a lone actor within high-risk relational trauma systems.

Function of Crisis Architecture Within Healing Qualia

Crisis architecture governs pacing, protects epistemic safety, supports identity stabilisation, safeguards practitioner functioning, and ensures community safety while preserving depth required for long-term relational repair. Recognition of identity collapse, suicidality, and targeted violence risk refines established risk frameworks by situating crisis assessment within developmental, relational, and institutional contexts specific to CPA-PA-related trauma. All phase progression remains conditional upon stability within this containment architecture.

Clinical Crisis Planning Template: Containment and Escalation Architecture

Within the HQTP, crisis planning is conceptualised as a dynamic containment process rather than a static safety document. Findings from the author's dual cohort doctoral research indicate that destabilisation in adult survivors of CPA-PA contexts is frequently episodic, recognition-linked, and relationally mediated. Crisis planning, therefore, requires ongoing revision in response to shifts in epistemic stability, attachment activation, identity coherence, and environmental conditions.

Crisis planning begins with a collaborative understanding of the survivor's known destabilisation patterns, rather than focusing only on immediate behavioural risk. Survivors are supported to identify recognition events that have previously triggered significant distress. These may include reading court affidavits, family reports, custody decisions, subpoenaed documents, historical child-protection records, or other formal material in which family relationships and events were recorded, disputed, or officially accepted. Later recognition that these accounts were incomplete, distorted, or inconsistent with the survivor's lived experience may be profoundly destabilising. Such documents can provide written confirmation that institutions accepted an inaccurate relational narrative, intensifying the survivor's loss of trust in their history, perceptions, and professional systems.

Additional destabilisation events may include direct discovery of deception regarding attachment relationships, discovery of unexpected contact attempts from previously targeted parents and their families, reunification pressure from external systems, identity-related disclosures following abduction or concealment, and recognition of lost developmental time associated with enforced loyalty roles. These events are framed as predictable activation points within developmental trauma integration rather than indicators of treatment failure.

The clinician and survivor jointly map early indicators of destabilisation. The survivor cohort research findings in Volume One reported that these indicators frequently include disorientation regarding personal history, intensified rumination regarding lost attachment time, shame activation associated with perceived complicity, urgency for external validation, oscillation between anger and grief, sleep disruption, a reduced capacity to imagine, plan for, or feel hopeful about the future, and increased cognitive preoccupation with irreversibility of developmental loss. Identification of these markers allows intervention before escalation toward behavioural risk.

Crisis planning differentiates affect surge from identity destabilisation. Where identity collapse destabilisation emerges, suicidal ideation may function as an attempt to restore control, reduce epistemic disorientation, manage developmental grief activation, or interrupt perceived narrative permanence. The planning process, therefore, includes collaborative exploration of the psychological meaning of ideation rather than relying solely on mood-based interpretation. This meaning-based formulation strengthens early detection and reduces misinterpretation of risk signals.

Containment strategies are collaboratively established and anchored in Phase I stabilisation work. These include regulatory approaches already demonstrated to be effective, pacing adjustments, structured session anchoring, written orientation supports, planned contact with identified safe others, and agreed thresholds for temporary increases in therapeutic support. The plan specifies how therapy intensity may shift during destabilisation periods, including additional stabilisation sessions, consultation involvement, or a temporary pause of deeper trauma processing to prioritise epistemic safety and identity continuity.

Practitioner safety is incorporated into crisis planning as a structural component. Volume Two findings of the practitioner cohort study demonstrate that clinician destabilisation may occur alongside survivor destabilisation. The crisis plan, therefore, specifies consultation thresholds, documentation expectations, and the conditions under which co-management, referral, or a temporary treatment pause may occur. These procedures are communicated transparently to preserve relational trust and reduce perceived risk of abandonment.

Documentation within the crisis planning framework prioritises clarity, behavioural specificity, and temporal tracking. The plan records identified destabilisation triggers, early indicators, agreed containment strategies, escalation thresholds, consultation procedures, and jurisdictionally required reporting pathways. Documentation functions as a clinical stabiliser by reducing ambiguity during high-risk periods.

Crisis planning is revisited iteratively across treatment phases. Recognition events, legal developments, identity restructuring, and relational shifts may alter risk patterns over time. Accordingly, the crisis plan is treated as a living clinical formulation embedded within the protocol's broader containment architecture.

Within the HQTP, the purpose of crisis planning is not solely the prevention of self-harm or violence. It is the preservation of epistemic safety, the protection of identity continuity, the safeguarding of practitioner functioning, and the maintenance of therapeutic pacing during periods of destabilisation. This orientation reflects a central finding of the author's doctoral research: crisis in this population is fundamentally relational, developmental, and meaning-linked rather than purely behavioural. All phase progression within the protocol remains conditional on stability within this collaboratively maintained crisis-planning framework.

Operationalisation of Crisis Architecture

The crisis architecture outlined earlier becomes operational through staged escalation pathways that guide clinical decision-making when destabilisation emerges. These pathways translate the containment framework into observable shifts in intervention across survivor care, practitioner governance, and supervisory oversight. Escalation is therefore defined as a structured increase in containment, consultation, and documentation rather than a signal of treatment failure. The escalation ladders that follow operationalise this governance logic.

This section describes the staged containment progression used when destabilisation indicators emerge for either survivor or practitioner. The ladders below operationalise the protocol's governance logic.

Tiered Risk Escalation Response

Tier One: Contained Activation

The survivor experiences increased anxiety, grief, somatic symptoms, or intrusive thoughts but retains reflective capacity and impulse control.

Clinical response involves slowing the pace of therapy, reinforcing regulation strategies, temporarily reducing relational or discovery exposure, and normalising activation as an expected response to developmental threat rather than framing it as pathology. Narrative depth is reduced, and containment is prioritised.

Early supervision consultation is recommended at this stage to prevent premature progression driven by clinician urgency.

Tier Two: Destabilisation With Loss of Coherence

The survivor exhibits dissociation, previously defined identity destabilisation indicators, intrusive imagery, emotional collapse after sessions, or passive death wishes. Clinical response requires immediate return to stabilisation. Trauma integration and discovery exploration are paused. Session focus narrows to regulation, time orientation, and restoration of present-day safety. Session frequency may increase where possible. Supervisor consultation is mandatory.

Safety planning is reviewed collaboratively without escalating to institutional intervention unless imminent risk is present.

Tier Three: Acute Risk

The survivor expresses active suicidality, engages in self-harm, or demonstrates marked loss of reality stability linked to discovery trauma, relational threat, or previously defined identity collapse processes. Clinical response prioritises safety over insight. Emergency protocols may be required, but must be enacted with transparency, collaboration, and care to avoid replicating coercive control or institutional betrayal. Wherever possible, the survivor is involved in decision-making and supported to retain agency during crisis containment.

Movement between tiers is fluid and guided by containment capacity rather than symptom severity alone.

Post-Crisis Integration

Following any Tier Two or Tier Three escalation, therapy does not immediately resume its prior trajectory. A post-crisis integration phase is indicated. This focuses on restoring relational safety, reinforcing survivor autonomy, stabilising identity coherence, and reframing the escalation as an understandable response to extreme developmental activation rather than treatment failure. Supervision review is mandatory following significant destabilisation. The escalation ladders that follow operationalise this logic across survivor and practitioner domains.

Survivor Escalation Ladder: Containment Progression

Phase progression remains conditional on stability within this containment architecture. Volume One survivor cohort findings indicate that destabilisation frequently emerges following recognition events rather than during peak emotional dysregulation alone. These events include recognition of developmental betrayal, narrative reconstruction, exposure to historical institutional documentation, discovery of attachment obstruction, identity-related disclosure following abduction or concealment, shifts in contact dynamics, and integration of previously obscured relational information.

Early Escalation: Recognition Linked Destabilisation

Early escalation occurs when destabilisation is evident at the level of meaning integration, identity coherence, or attachment processing while behavioural risk remains low. Survivors may demonstrate disorientation regarding personal history, intensified rumination about lost developmental time, oscillation between anger and grief, increased validation seeking, shame activation associated with perceived complicity, sleep disturbance, or a reduced capacity to imagine or plan for a meaningful future.

At this stage, escalation involves pacing adjustment rather than emergency intervention. Containment responses prioritise the reinforcement of Phase I regulation strategies, increased session structure, explicit psychoeducation on recognition-driven destabilisation, collaborative identification of triggers, and the preservation of epistemic safety. Therapeutic work emphasises orientation, identity continuity, and differentiation between recognition and immediate action. Early escalation is framed to the survivor as a predictable component of developmental trauma integration rather than evidence of treatment failure.

Intermediate Escalation: Functional Destabilisation

Intermediate escalation is indicated when destabilisation begins to affect daily functioning, relational capacity, cognitive flexibility, or the stability of emotional regulation. Survivors may experience intensified grief activation, urgency for narrative correction, reduced tolerance for ambiguity, avoidance of previously manageable material, or difficulty maintaining ordinary routines.

Containment responses at this level include, where appropriate, a temporary increase in session frequency, targeted stabilisation sessions, consultation involvement, written orientation supports, structured session anchoring, and suspension of interpretive or trauma-processing work that exceeds current epistemic stability. The clinical focus shifts toward restoring regulatory capacity, consolidating identity continuity, and recalibrating pacing.

Intermediate escalation reinforces that stabilisation work represents forward movement within the protocol rather than regression.

Extreme Escalation: Immediate Safety Intervention

Extreme escalation is indicated when imminent risk is identified through credible intent, access to means, behavioural rehearsal, inability to maintain safety agreements, or loss of functional containment. The intervention moves beyond therapeutic pacing to immediate safety procedures consistent with professional, organisational, and jurisdictional requirements.

Clinical actions may include emergency assessment pathways, crisis service interfaces, hospital referrals, protective reporting, or coordinated multidisciplinary responses.

Function of the Survivor Escalation Ladder

The survivor escalation ladder tracks shifts in epistemic stability and behavioural risk across staged containment levels. Survivors are informed that escalation reflects increased support rather than a loss of progress, thereby strengthening the alliance and reducing shame during periods of destabilisation. All phase progression remains conditional upon stability within this staged containment architecture.

Practitioner Protection Escalation Ladder

Practitioner escalation signals an increase in the requirements for governance, consultation, and safety planning. Findings from the author's doctoral practitioner study indicate that practitioner destabilisation typically progresses rather than occurring as an acute event. This progression may begin with heightened concern or emotional activation, then develop into reduced clinical confidence, difficulty maintaining boundaries or pacing, increased urgency, and, in more serious cases, impairment in judgement or practitioner safety. For this reason, the protocol incorporates a staged practitioner escalation ladder that parallels survivor risk escalation.

Level 1 Clinical Strain Indicators may include increased rumination about the case, uncertainty about the wording of documentation, fear of misinterpretation, sleep disruption after sessions, or heightened self-monitoring in communication. Action: supervision discussion, documentation review, reaffirmation of scope and boundaries.

Level 2 Adversarial Pressure Indicators may include threats of complaints, hostile correspondence, triangulation attempts, pressure to issue opinion statements outside the scope, or perceived surveillance. Action: formal consultation, documentation tightening, communication boundaries, supervisor awareness, and consideration of co-management.

Level 3 Practitioner Destabilisation Risk Indicators may include fear of regulatory action affecting clinical judgement, avoidance of clinically indicated discussions, over-accommodation, defensive practice shifts, or role confusion. Action: structured supervision, written case formulation review, boundary reinforcement, and consultation with the indemnity provider, where relevant.

Level 4 Safety/Ethical Threshold: Indicators may include harassment, intimidation, reputational threats, unsafe attempts at contact, legal coercion beyond the scope of the role, or an inability to maintain therapeutic neutrality. Action: co-management, role clarification in writing, referral consideration, service level decision, and possible treatment pause.

Level 5 Withdrawal Threshold: Indicators include an inability to provide safe care, compromised practitioner safety, or sustained adversarial interference that prevents therapeutic containment. Action: planned transition, documented rationale, supported referral, continuity plan for survivor. Practitioner escalation is framed as a matter of governance rather than failure.

Within the HQTP, supervisory authority functions as a stabiliser of containment. It safeguards the survivor's epistemic safety, the practitioner's integrity, and community safety while preserving the depth required for long-term relational repair.

Supervisor Decision Guidance: Crisis Architecture

Supervisory review prioritises the evaluation of destabilisation patterns over symptom intensity alone. Attention is given to whether destabilisation reflects recognition-linked processes, including developmental betrayal recognition, narrative reconstruction, exposure to institutional documentation, or previously defined identity destabilisation in response to new relational information.

Supervisors consider whether the current phase of work remains within the survivor's epistemic stability threshold. When meaning integration exceeds containment capacity, supervisory guidance favours stabilisation, pacing adjustment, or a temporary pause of interpretive work.

Supervisory review also evaluates practitioner context. Findings from the author's doctoral practitioner study demonstrate that clinician pacing may be influenced by complaint anxiety, adversarial system pressure, perceived urgency to make progress, or fear-of-abandonment dynamics. Supervisors, therefore, assess whether practitioner pressures are shaping clinical decision-making, documentation style, or tolerance for uncertainty.

Documentation clarity forms a core decision domain. Supervisors review whether formulation, scope of practice, phase rationale, and escalation thresholds are recorded, thereby protecting both survivor continuity and practitioner integrity.

Supervisory escalation decisions are guided by containment indicators rather than performance expectations. Supervisors evaluate whether destabilisation signals the activation of escalation thresholds that require increased session frequency, consultation involvement, co-management, psychiatric interface, or jurisdictionally mandated reporting pathways.

Where practitioner safety concerns are present, supervisory guidance recognises co-management, referral, or structured withdrawal as forms of ethical containment rather than treatment failure. Preservation of practitioner functioning is treated as a clinical governance requirement.

Supervisory decision-making, therefore, differentiates clinical avoidance, premature withdrawal driven by anxiety or uncertainty, ethical pacing, and containment-driven adjustment based on destabilisation risk. When differentiation remains unclear, the protocol favours containment.

Supervisory guidance also considers the implications for forensic interfaces. Exposure to legal processes, document review, or adversarial proceedings may alter the risk of destabilisation and require modifications to pacing, documentation discipline, and consultation thresholds.

Healing Qualia Treatment Protocol Clinician Crisis Plan Template

(Printable)

Clinical Use

For staff receiving this document:

This printable template is designed to support crisis planning for adult survivors of child psychological abuse in contexts of parental alienation, familial abduction, and estrangement. It forms part of the *Healing Qualia Treatment Protocol* © (HQTP), a phase-based clinical model, and is intended to guide clear, coordinated, and clinically informed care during periods of destabilisation. The person who has this document may present as anxious, distressed, dysregulated, grief-affected, shut down, overwhelmed, or internally destabilised, and may also appear outwardly articulate or composed despite significant distress. Helpful responses include calm pacing, a clear and supportive interpersonal approach, reducing overwhelm where possible, validating uncertainty, supporting emotional regulation, and avoiding confrontation, rapid interpretation, or pressure for narrative clarity. This template should be used alongside clinical interview, formulation, supervision, and risk assessment rather than as a stand-alone instrument. Please contact the therapist listed below (with the client's permission) for more information and to collaborate on the case.

Note: Examples are provided as prompts only and are not exhaustive. Complete only what is clinically relevant to the client's current presentation and safety needs.

Client Information (for MHP to fill out with clients for emergency use)	
Client name	**DOB**
Primary clinician name, address and contact number	**Secondary clinician name, address and contact number**
Date created	**Date last reviewed**
Next of kin (primary) to be contacted in an emergency	**Name and number**
Next of kin (secondary) to be contacted in an emergency	**Name and number**

Client signature and date indicating agreement to contact the above-named clinicians and next of kin	**(Client to sign and date here)**
Primary treating professional while in the hospital *(for example, ward psychiatrist, hospital social worker, mental health nurse, treating psychotherapist or psychologist)*	**Name, clinic/service address, and contact number**
Secondary treating professionals while in the hospital *(for example, registrar, case manager, consultation liaison clinician)*	**Name, clinic/service address and contact number**

Clinical Formulation Relevant to Crisis	
Attachment disruption summary *(for example, prolonged separation from a parent, fear-linked attachment responses, loyalty conflict, disrupted trust, grief around lost relationship)*	**Developmental deprivation indicators** *(for example, emotional neglect, lack of stable protection, restricted family contact, identity confusion, social isolation, disrupted sense of safety)*

Identity destabilisation risks *(for example, confusion about self, collapse in self-coherence, shame spirals, destabilisation after recognition of abuse, fear of "not knowing who I am")*	**Known destabilisation triggers** *(specific examples: family contact, anniversaries, therapy milestones, discussion of childhood, attachment-related topics, grief activation, social media contact, upcoming family events)*
Early Destabilisation Indicators	
Changes in narrative coherence *(for example, becoming confused, disorganised, repetitive, unsure what is real, sudden loss of confidence in one's own account)*	
Shame/humiliation activation *(for example, self-blame, "I'm stupid", "I should be over this", intense embarrassment after disclosure)*	**Rumination about lost developmental time** *(for example, repetitive grief about lost childhood, lost parent, lost years, "what should have been" thinking)*

Withdrawal/urgency for validation *(for example, isolating, not answering calls, repeated reassurance-seeking, panic if not responded to quickly)*	**Sleep disruption** *(for example, insomnia, nightmares, early waking, fear of sleep, sleep reversal)*
	Other client-specific markers *(for example, dissociation, shutdown, agitation, crying spells, appetite change, hypervigilance, fear of contact)*

Suicidality Formulation (Identity-Linked)
Brief history of suicidal ideation or behaviour *(for example, passive death wishes, suicidal thinking during recognition periods, prior attempts, self-harm, hospital presentations)*
Recent status *(for example, no current ideation, fluctuating ideation, recent increase in hopelessness, active thoughts without a plan)*

Meaning of ideation when present (clinical formulation language) *(clinical formulation examples: identity collapse, unbearable shame, grief overload, fear of abandonment, perceived entrapment, loss of self-coherence)*
Indicators that identity destabilisation is emerging *(for example, saying "I don't know who I am", intense confusion, panic after insight, loss of internal stability, collapse after family pressure)*

Containment Strategies Agreed with Client	
Grounding/regulation strategies already stabilised *(for example, paced breathing, sensory grounding, walking, music, contacting safe support, structured routine, brief check-in calls)*	**Session pacing adjustments** *(for example, shorter sessions, slower pace, no trauma processing, increased breaks, stronger closing routines, more stabilisation work)*
Support people whom the client can contact *(for example, partner, trusted friend, sibling, support worker, GP, crisis line, treating clinician)*	**When the clinician contact should increase** *(for example, after negative family contact, after nightmares, if suicidal thoughts increase, before major anniversaries, when dissociation rises)*

Escalation Thresholds
Indicators requiring a pause in trauma processing *(for example, increased dissociation, suicidality, severe sleep disruption, rapid destabilisation, inability to regulate between sessions)*
Indicators requiring consultation *(for example, sudden regression, conflicting risk picture, repeated crisis contact, family pressure escalating, uncertainty about safe pacing)*
Indicators requiring urgent action *(for example, active suicide plan, inability to maintain safety, profound collapse in functioning, acute agitation, psychotic symptoms, medical compromise)*

Risk to Others (If Relevant)
Retaliatory ideation indicators *(for example, thoughts of confronting, exposing, or verbally/physically attacking others when distressed)*

Known triggers for anger escalation *(for example, coercive contact, disbelief, humiliation, perceived betrayal, attachment-related rejection, family pressure)*
Containment strategies *(for example, reduce stimulation, pause contact, grounding, support person involvement, time-limited de-escalation plan, clinician review)*

Medical and Inpatient Information	
Current medications	**Recent medication changes**
Prescriber	**Physical health conditions** **Self-harm behaviours**
Allergies	**Weight (if clinically relevant)**
Height (if clinically relevant) **Anything health-related that staff believe is noteworthy**	**Sleep/nutrition risks** *(for example, not eating, dehydration risk, severe insomnia, appetite collapse, medication non-adherence)*

If Client Is Admitted	
Admitting service **Concerning admission narratives or behaviours**	**Reason for admission (clinical formulation)** *(for example, acute destabilisation following family pressure, suicidality linked to identity collapse, severe grief activation, inability to maintain regulation and safety)*
Known inpatient destabilisation risks *(for example, feeling disbelieved, being pressed for narrative clarity, overstimulation, lack of continuity, confrontation, abrupt staff changes)*	**Recommended containment approach** *(for example, calm pacing, reduced stimulation, validation of uncertainty, no forced disclosure, no premature trauma work, contact primary clinician if possible)*

Current Relational Stressors and Destabilisation Considerations	
Trauma material currently becoming more active *(for example, resurfacing memories, grief material, fear-linked childhood themes, renewed awareness of loss or coercion)*	**Current family or relational pressure affecting stability** *(for example, abusive parent contact, triangulation, coercive messaging, family demands, loyalty pressure, smear campaign fears)*
Family tension, enmeshment, or loyalty conflict *(for example, pressure to align, fear of upsetting a caregiver, guilt about boundaries, emotional over-involvement)*	**Relevant history of familial abduction, disappearance, familicide, suicide, estrangement or profound loss** *(include only what is clinically relevant to current stability)*
Upcoming events or contact situations associated with fear, grief, or distress *(for example, birthdays, funerals, anniversaries, family gatherings, court-related attendance, medical procedures, holidays)*	**Current concerns about suicidality, hopelessness, or internal stability** *(for example, passive wishes to disappear, despair, fear of collapse, inability to cope, increasing self-neglect)*

Clinical Notes for Handover

This containment architecture governs all subsequent phase work and serves as the operational stabilisation scaffold for Phase I. The sections that follow begin with Phase I, in which safety, orientation, epistemic stabilisation, and the restoration of survivor agency are established before deeper recognition or integrative work can proceed. Before initiating Phase I intervention, clinicians must complete an initial assessment sufficient to determine whether the presenting individual is likely to be an adult survivor for whom the HQTP is intended.

Phase I: Safety, Orientation, and Epistemic Stabilisation

Phase I constitutes the initial active treatment phase within the HQTP. Its clinical objective is to establish sufficient relational safety and regulatory capacity to prevent treatment-induced harm and to prepare the survivor for later integrative work. Phase I operationalises the assessment and formulation principles established in the preceding chapters by prioritising psychological safety, emotional stabilisation, epistemic trust, attachment containment, and restoration of survivor agency.

Naming the Behaviour Before Naming the Relationship

One early Phase I stabilisation practice is to help the survivor pause before interpreting an interaction in terms of the person's family role, title, history, or emotional significance. Survivors may feel confused when harmful, coercive, invalidating, or destabilising behaviour comes from someone they love, miss, fear, protect, or have been conditioned to obey. In these moments, the clinician can gently support the survivor in asking, "What is the behaviour?"

This practice asks the survivor to temporarily set aside the question of who the person is and observe what is happening in the interaction. Is this pressure? Is this guilt? Is this minimisation? Is this repair? Is this accountability? Is this punishment? Is this love with conditions attached? Is this fear? Is this control? Is this emotional collapse being used to regain compliance?

The aim is not to label the person as good or bad, nor to push the survivor towards contact or no contact. The aim is to strengthen reality testing, self-trust, and relational discernment. A parent may be loved and still be coercive. A sibling may be familiar and still be unsafe. A family member may be distressed and still be manipulative. A person may present as caring while still using guilt, pressure, silence, blame, or emotional overwhelm to pull the survivor back into compliance.

For survivors of CPA-PA, this distinction is clinically important because many have been conditioned to respond to roles rather than behaviours. They may have been taught that one parent must be protected, one parent must be feared, one parent must be rejected, or one family narrative must not be questioned. Naming the behaviour first helps slow the automatic response and allows the survivor to consider whether the interaction supports safety, repair, truth, respect, and consent, or whether it pulls them back into fear, loyalty, silence, guilt, or self-abandonment.

This skill belongs in Phase I because it supports stabilisation without requiring deep trauma processing. The survivor is not asked to resolve the relationship, confront the person, make a final decision about contact, or reinterpret the whole family history. They are simply supported to notice what is happening in the present interaction. When survivors can name the behaviour, they are more likely to make choices based on safety, reality, and agency rather than obligation, confusion, fear, or inherited family roles.

Phase I is clinically active and reparative. It establishes the relational, physiological, and psychological conditions required for subsequent phases and functions as a safeguard against reenactment, misdiagnosis, premature trauma processing, and modality-driven harm.

Adult survivors of child psychological abuse in CPA-PA contexts frequently enter treatment with compromised emotional regulation, limited capacity to remain within their window of tolerance, fragmented autobiographical coherence, and heightened sensitivity to perceived authority. Many have adapted to prolonged psychological threat and loyalty conditioning through patterns of compliance, emotional suppression, hypervigilance, dissociation, appeasement, and anticipatory self-correction. These adaptations often persist long after the external threat has ceased because they were learned within attachment relationships and, in some cases, reinforced by institutional systems.

Phase I, therefore, focuses on creating conditions in which the survivor can remain present, regulated, and psychologically intact within the therapeutic relationship before deeper trauma processing, meaning reconstruction, or relational repair is attempted.

Stabilisation within the HQTP extends beyond symptom management or behavioural de-escalation. It involves the gradual expansion of affect tolerance, the development of emotional literacy without coercive disclosure, the strengthening of internal and external regulatory resources, and the establishment of predictable therapeutic boundaries. Relational safety is cultivated through consistent attunement, transparent pacing, and collaborative decision-making.

Survivors are not required to perform insight, provide an evidentiary narrative, or prove harm to remain connected in therapy. The clinician's responsibility is to create a therapeutic environment in which connection is not contingent on compliance, agreement, or disclosure.

Restoration of agency is a central task of Phase I. Survivors who have experienced prolonged psychological abuse and attachment betrayal frequently present with diminished autonomy, fear of disagreement, impaired boundary formation, and an internalised expectation that independent thought will result in punishment or abandonment. Phase I, therefore, prioritises consent-based engagement, collaborative goal-setting, and respect for survivors' choices. This restores control over the therapeutic process and reduces the risk of replicating earlier power asymmetries, particularly for survivors whose identity development occurred under coercive relational conditions.

Progression beyond Phase I is guided by readiness rather than time-based expectations. Indicators of stabilisation include improved emotional regulation capacity, increased tolerance of relational closeness without collapse, reduced urgency to persuade or justify, greater capacity to hold uncertainty without panic, and the ability to engage with distress without dissociation, cognitive shutdown, or somatic collapse.

Movement into deeper trauma-focused work without these foundations increases the risk of retraumatisation, epistemic destabilisation, and therapeutic rupture and is therefore inconsistent with the HQTP.

Clinical Responsibility

Phase I is particularly responsive to epistemic injury, fear-based compliance, and loyalty conditioning, in which survivors learned that accurate perception, naming harm, or disagreeing with authority carried relational risk. In this context, the clinician's epistemic posture is not neutral. The assumptions embedded in diagnostic reasoning, the sequencing of enquiry, and the pace at which meaning is introduced directly shape survivor trust, emotional stabilisation, and the integrity of the therapeutic alliance.

Phase I, therefore, places significant responsibility on the clinician to tolerate ambiguity and slow progress, and to resist system-driven pressure for outcomes. It requires the capacity to remain present with distress without premature action, to hold uncertainty without resolving it through interpretation, and to prioritise safety over explanatory coherence. Ongoing clinical supervision and ethical humility are essential components of this responsibility. Phase I is not passive. It is active containment.

The author's doctoral research demonstrates that non-phased or prematurely trauma-focused interventions frequently result in symptom escalation, therapeutic rupture, epistemic harm, and reenactment of coercive dynamics. When clinicians move too quickly into interpretation, introduce meaning prematurely, or apply intensive trauma modalities while epistemic threat remains active, survivors often experience therapy as another environment in which reality is controlled, rewritten, or demanded. In such contexts, treatment replicates rather than repairs the conditions of psychological abuse.

For this reason, progression through treatment phases must be guided by clinical readiness rather than protocol sequence, modality preference, practitioner confidence, or institutional timelines. Advancing depth in the absence of sufficient regulation and epistemic safety increases the risk of retraumatisation and undermines therapeutic integrity.

Consistent with the phase integrity principles outlined in this chapter, the HQTP is not linear, time-bound, or outcome-driven. Survivors may move back and forth between phases, pause for extended periods, or require repeated returns to Phase I throughout the lifespan. Such returns are particularly common during developmental transitions, renewed system contact, relational rupture, or periods of intensified family pressure.

Phase transitions are determined by observable clinical markers rather than by insight attainment, narrative coherence, or symptom articulation. The clinician's responsibility is not to advance treatment, but to protect the conditions under which repair remains possible.

Phase I Micro Decision Trees: Clinical Judgement Prior to Phase Transition

These decision trees are designed for use in sessions, between sessions, and in supervision. They translate Phase I into moment-to-moment clinical action.

Decision Tree 1: When distress increases after sessions, it is interpreted as clinical data rather than non-compliance. The clinician first assesses whether the distress is relational or content-driven. When distress is linked to feeling misunderstood, judged, watched, or evaluated, the clinician remains in Phase I and returns focus to relational safety and epistemic validation. When distress follows exploration of memories, meaning, or interpretation, the clinician pauses exploratory work and returns to grounding, predictability, and present-focused containment. When distress escalates across multiple sessions, supervision is required before attempting further depth. Progression is contraindicated until post-session distress stabilises.

Decision Tree 2: When the survivor seeks validation of facts or proof, the clinician neither affirms facts nor challenges them. Instead, the clinician names the emotional meaning of needing to prove, including fear of being disbelieved, punished, or erased. When the survivor can tolerate this reframing without escalation, Phase I continues. When the survivor becomes dysregulated, ashamed, or withdrawn, the clinician slows further and reinforces that therapy is not an evaluative space. Trauma integration remains contraindicated while epistemic threat is active.

Decision Tree 3: When high compliance or rapid agreement is observed, the clinician assesses for fear of abandonment, punishment, or histories of conditional care. When compliance is accompanied by anxiety, somatic tension, emotional flattening, or urgency to progress, Phase I must be extended. The clinician invites disagreement and models tolerance of difference. Progression is not indicated until the survivor can express uncertainty or dissent without distress.

Decision Tree 4: When clinician countertransference activates urges to rescue, protect, correct, confront, or withdraw, this is treated as clinical data rather than acted upon. The clinician does not alter the treatment trajectory in response to these urges. Supervision is required to determine whether the reaction reflects survivor projection, system pressure, clinician vulnerability, or unresolved material. Phase I continues until relational neutrality can be restored with ongoing emotional attunement.

Decision Tree 5: Considering progression beyond Phase I occurs only when the survivor no longer experiences therapy as a place of judgement, proof, or performance. If the survivor can withstand distress without collapsing, tolerate ambiguity, and maintain a basic sense of self-legitimacy in uncertain circumstances, the clinician may begin preparing for Phase II. If there is any doubt, Phase I continues. There is no penalty for staying.

Clinical Note: - Once epistemic safety has been sufficiently established, the therapeutic task shifts from containment toward meaning-making. This transition does not assume insight, coherence, or readiness for trauma integration but reflects the clinician's assessment that the survivor no longer experiences the therapeutic relationship as a site of threat, persuasion, or evaluation. Only under these conditions can narrative exploration occur without reproducing epistemic harm. This concludes Phase I of the HQTP. The following section introduces Phase II, which becomes clinically available only when the conditions outlined above are reliably met. This section is written for adult survivors who may be reading the HQTP alongside their therapist. It is not a set of instructions, but an explanation of what Phase I is designed to offer and protect.

Phase I Explained for Adult Survivors

A note from Dr Alyse

Dear survivors, fellow journey walkers, and friends, hello and welcome! I'm Dr Alyse Price-Tobler, and I wrote this protocol not only as a clinician and researcher but also drawing on years of frontline clinical practice and my own lived experience, FOR YOU. This work has been shaped by a deep respect for how much you may have carried, and for the quiet strength it takes to keep going. Even being here now is a gentle sign that some part of you is still reaching toward healing.

If you are reading this, you may be feeling unsure, tired, guarded, or overwhelmed. You may have tried therapy before and felt misunderstood, or as though you were never truly met in the way you needed. You may not yet have clear words for what has happened, only a sense that something has never felt quite right. Wherever you are starting from, you are welcome here exactly as you are.

You do not need to have all the answers. You do not need to be ready for everything at once. You do not need to explain yourself before you feel able. Being here is enough for now.

What Phase I Is Here to Offer

Phase I is the beginning of the HQTP process. It is the phase where safety comes first. This phase does not focus on analysing you, diagnosing you, or asking you to relive painful memories. It focuses on helping your nervous system and your sense of self feel safe enough to exist without pressure. Many adult survivors have spent years staying emotionally alert, managing other people's reactions, staying quiet to avoid conflict, or becoming strong and self-reliant because closeness did not feel safe. I understand this deeply, both professionally and personally. Phase I exists so therapy does not repeat those patterns.

During Phase I, your therapist is not trying to "figure you out" or rush you into difficult conversations. Instead, the work is about building steadiness. This might look like learning to slow things down, noticing when your body feels tense or overwhelmed, pausing instead of pushing through, and building a sense of trust that you are not being judged, tested, or evaluated.

You are not expected to tell your whole story.

You are not expected to remember everything.

You are not expected to share anything before you feel ready.

Going slowly is not avoidance. It is how safety is built.

You may feel guilt-ridden if you speak about your parents.

You may wonder what you are allowed to talk about in Phase I.

There is no correct place to start.

You can talk about how you feel right now. You can talk about stress, exhaustion, relationships, anxiety, sadness, anger, or numbness. You can talk about feeling disconnected from yourself, unsure who you are, or carrying a sense of heaviness you cannot explain. You can talk about family, distance from people you care about, loyalty conflicts, or feeling torn between protecting yourself and protecting others. You can talk about your body, sleep, tension, or feeling constantly on edge. You can also choose to sit quietly when words feel hard to find.

You do not have to start with childhood.

You do not have to talk about trauma.

You do not need special language.

You get to decide the pace.

What You May Notice as Healing Begins

When Phase I is working, changes are often quiet and gradual. You may notice that you feel slightly less tense. You may find it easier to pause, breathe, or say "I'm not sure." You may feel less pressure to explain yourself perfectly or manage other people's reactions. These are important signs of healing, even if pain and confusion persist.

As healing continues, some emotions may feel unfamiliar or uncomfortable. You might feel guilt when you start thinking about your own needs. You might feel anxious when you set boundaries or speak honestly. You might feel torn between knowing something was wrong and still feeling loyal to someone who hurt you. These reactions are not a weakness. They are signs of survival patterns that once kept you safe.

Later, you may feel grief or anger that surprises you. You may grieve lost time, lost childhood, lost relationships, or parts of yourself that had to stay hidden. You may feel anger about lies, control, or being denied the truth. These feelings are not setbacks. They often appear when your system finally feels safe enough to feel.

If you choose to reconnect with a parent you were kept from, that process can be meaningful and emotionally complex. Some people feel relief and closeness. Others feel sadness, confusion, or grief. Some decide not to reconnect because it does not feel safe. Healing is not measured by reunion. It is measured by how well you can live with more freedom, clarity, and self-trust. You may also reach a point where you decide to step back from people who continue to pressure, guilt, or destabilise you. This does not make you unkind. It means you are protecting your nervous system and your right to live without being controlled by fear.

Many survivors ask, "Am I doing this right?" or "How long will this take?" Healing is not linear. You may move forward, pause, return to earlier work, or need support again later in life. That does not mean you failed. It means healing happens in layers. This work is not about fixing you. It is about helping you live without fear, guilt, or old survival rules running your life.

You are allowed to move slowly.

You are allowed to rest.

You are allowed to change your mind.

You are allowed to put your safety first.

Nothing about what happened to you was your choice. It is your time now, and you are the expert on yourself. If reading this brings up strong emotion, it is okay to pause and return to it later. You do not need to hold everything at once.

Go gently, Dr Alyse

Applied Phase I Pathways in Abduction and Retrieval

The following applied section returns to the clinician-facing framework and examines how Phase I containment principles are used with adult survivors whose histories include abduction, concealment, recovery, retrieval, or structured relational transition.

Phase I functions as the operational containment bridge between protocol theory and applied phase work. It establishes the clinical foundation upon which all later therapeutic work with adult survivors of parental alienation depends. Without stabilisation, relational safety, and emotional containment, deeper trauma integration risks retraumatisation, premature disclosure collapse, and therapeutic rupture. Within Phase I, stabilisation is operationalised through attention to protective adaptations that developed under conditions of coercive control, attachment disruption, and high conflict separation. One of the most clinically significant of these adaptations is silence.

Abduction, Concealment, Silence, and Selective Mutism

Scope and Terminology: Separating Abduction, Recovery, and Reunification

This section separates three clinically related but different experiences: parental child abduction or concealment; recovery, retrieval, or an escorted transition following removal or retention; and structured reunification or relational transition interventions. These experiences may occur within the same developmental history, but they are not interchangeable. Abduction concerns the taking, concealment, retention, or prevention of a child's return. Recovery and retrieval concern locating or returning the child. Reunification concerns a later relational intervention intended to support contact, reconnection, or repair. Keeping these experiences separate is important because the meaning or outcome of one cannot be inferred from the other.

The HQTP does not take a universal position on structured reunification programs. Adult survivor accounts vary widely: some describe meaningful reconnection or repair, some describe unresolved complexity or perceived pressure, and many describe mixed experiences.

The clinical task is not to enter the public debate by declaring that an intervention is always beneficial or always harmful. It is to understand the survivor's developmental experience, current meaning, physiological response, perceived agency, and degree of internal integration without imposing a retrospective conclusion.

Clinical Language Note: When Breach of a Recovery Order Involves Parental Child Abduction

Within family-law systems, failure to return a child or comply with a recovery order is commonly described as a breach or contravention. These formal legal terms should be retained when describing the court process. However, they may not adequately communicate what has happened to the child in cases involving intentional taking, concealment, prolonged retention, relocation, or the active obstruction of recovery (Federal Circuit and Family Court of Australia [FCFCOA], n.d.-a, n.d.-b).

Where the documented conduct includes deliberately withholding, hiding, moving, or retaining a child contrary to a recovery order, the HQTP may use the paired formulation "breach of a recovery order involving parental child abduction." The term breach identifies the non-compliance with the order; the term abduction identifies the underlying conduct and its potential developmental and attachment consequences. This terminology does not replace a court's legal classification, establish criminal liability, or suggest that every contravention is an abduction. It distinguishes minor or technical non-compliance from deliberate conduct that deprives the child of return, location continuity, lawful caregiving arrangements, or significant attachment relationships (Attorney-General's Department, n.d.; FCFCOA, n.d.-a, n.d.-b).

Going forward, the HQTP uses abduction language only when it is tied to documented behaviour such as taking, concealment, retention, relocation, or obstruction of recovery. Where the available information establishes only non-compliance with an order, the formal terms "breach" or "contravention" remain appropriate.

Abduction, Recovery, and Cumulative Transition Burden

Retrieval and Escorted Transition Experiences in the Context of Prior Abduction

A subset of adult survivors describes childhood experiences involving sudden or highly structured externally facilitated movement away from the caregiver with whom they were residing, facilitated by the police or child recovery experts who were unknown to the child (sometimes carrying out recovery orders). These experiences may have included escorted transitions, coordinated transfers between environments, or retrieval processes that occurred alongside reunification planning between the child and the targeted parent.

For survivors whose developmental history also involved prior abduction, concealment, or repeated relocation by an alienating parent, later court-ordered recovery, retrieval, or structured transition events are rarely experienced as isolated interventions. Instead, they are layered onto an existing history of disrupted attachment access and narrative instability. What may be framed administratively as a single transition can therefore be experienced psychologically as cumulative relational displacement.

From the survivor's perspective, these events are often experienced as abrupt relational changes, accompanied by unfamiliar adults, altered routines, and a limited sense of influence over events. When prior movement experiences occurred without preparation, explanation, or perceived choice, subsequent transitions may reactivate earlier threat learning, even when the later transition is intended to support stability or reconnection.

Meaning assigned to these experiences varies. Some survivors recall the presence of transition professionals as containing during a difficult movement between environments. Others recall heightened uncertainty, emotional intensity, or pressure to adapt quickly. Many describe both simultaneously. Where prior abduction or concealment has occurred, any externally facilitated movement between adults may be registered as a repetition of the earlier loss of agency and trauma inflicted on them to align.

For some survivors, this layering creates a cumulative burden of transition. Relational shifts do not occur as single events but as repeated disruptions requiring behavioural adaptation before emotional integration is possible. The developmental task becomes ongoing management of unpredictability regarding belonging, narrative accuracy, safety and relational stability. In adulthood, these memories frequently consolidate into a narrative organised around movement between parents rather than discrete events. Survivors may struggle to differentiate which aspects felt protective, which felt destabilising, and which were never fully processed.

Post-Abduction Threat Expectancy and Environmental Safety Behaviours

Adult survivors with histories involving abduction, concealment, or repeated forced movement between caregivers frequently describe persistent threat expectancy originating in childhood adaptation. Survivors may recall enduring expectations that unfamiliar police or recovery specialists could arrive without warning, that removal could occur unexpectedly, or that environments assumed to be safe could change suddenly.

In childhood, this expectancy may have led to persistent monitoring of the environment to restore predictability, potentially keeping the child's nervous system in a near-constant state of fear-based alertness. Retrospective adult narratives describe attempts to observe entrances, anticipate approach, alter physical environments, create improvised detection strategies, or position themselves to maintain awareness of movement within the home.

Some survivors recall imaginative threat anticipation organised around being taken again, including fears that individuals could appear unexpectedly or remove them without explanation. These experiences are typically recognised in adulthood as fear-based adaptation rather than fixed belief, yet physiological readiness may persist.

Within the HQTP, these patterns are conceptualised as post-abduction threat expectancy embedded within cumulative transition burden. The presentation reflects conditioned anticipation of recurrence rather than primary psychopathology. Behaviour that appears excessive outside this context represents coherent developmental adaptation within environments characterised by unpredictable relational change.

In adulthood, residual patterns may appear as difficulty feeling fully safe in private and public spaces; heightened sensitivity and fear of unexpected visitors; strong reactions to sounds associated with entry; having trouble sleeping and not knowing where they are upon waking; or continued environmental monitoring during periods of stress.

Trust Disruption as a Central Organising Feature

Trust disruption represents a central organising feature of this presentation. Many adult survivors describe that clinicians encountered during childhood appeared unfamiliar with these removal experiences, responded with confronting levels of curiosity rather than clinical understanding, or treated disclosures as highly unusual and became visibly shocked. Survivors frequently report becoming aware that clinicians did not know how to conceptualise or treat what was being described, so therefore were not helpful.

This absence of recognition contributes to secondary epistemic injury. Survivors may learn that describing complex abduction or removal histories leads to fascination, disbelief, or redirection rather than sustained therapeutic engagement. Over time, this may produce guarded disclosure, narrative compression, or the expectation that meaningful aspects of experience will not be understood. Introduction of explicit clinical language for cumulative transition burden, retrieval experiences, and post-abduction threat expectancy may therefore be experienced as unexpected by survivors. Recognition may be both stabilising and destabilising. Survivors may be surprised that clinicians are aware of these patterns or may initially test whether they have lived experience of CPA-PAA themselves and whether recognition is sustained. For clinicians, this moment represents an opportunity for stabilisation rather than a point for rapid exploration. Practitioners with lived experience of abduction or removal who are no longer triggered by their own experiences may be highly valuable in this context.

Adult Presentation Patterns

When cumulative transition burden is present, adult survivors may demonstrate authority sensitivity in relational decision contexts, difficulty trusting that therapeutic spaces are non-evaluative, rapid behavioural alignment alongside internal uncertainty, vigilance regarding perceived changes in clinician stance, sensitivity to pacing and perceived pressure, difficulty distinguishing present safety from historical unpredictability, and residual environmental monitoring behaviours during stress.

Relational concerns within a session may manifest as an expectation that the clinician's interest will fade, a concern that complex disclosures must be continually justified, a reluctance to introduce experiences that feel unusual, and a fear that therapeutic confidentiality may be broken and an aligned parent may be informed outside therapy. These patterns reflect prior learning that relational stability and professional understanding could not be assumed, trusted, or relied upon.

Phase I Clinical Approach

Within Phase I, the primary treatment task is restoration of epistemic safety and relational trust rather than reinterpretation of historical events. Clinicians communicate that these presentations are recognised within the protocol and do not require extraordinary explanation from the survivor.

Clinical pacing prioritises predictability, continuity of attention, and tolerance for partial disclosure. The clinician's stance emphasises sustained curiosity without urgency, demonstrating that recognition is stable rather than episodic. Survivors are supported in introducing experiences incrementally, without needing to produce narratives of exceptional intensity, to maintain therapeutic engagement.

When post-abduction threat expectancy is present, treatment focuses on differentiating between historical threat and the present context through orientation, nervous system stabilisation, and the gradual reduction of safety behaviours through pacing rather than confrontation. Interventions emphasise restoration of perceived choice.

Working with Trust Disruption

Because survivors may expect clinician understanding to diminish, consistency becomes an active intervention. Clinicians revisit previously shared material, maintain conceptual continuity, and signal ongoing awareness of cumulative transition burden across sessions.

Clinicians avoid positioning these experiences as unusual curiosities. They are framed as predictable developmental responses within a defined clinical population. When surprise emerges that clinicians recognise these patterns, the therapeutic task is containment rather than expansion. Recognition is allowed to stabilise before deeper processing.

Treatment Implications

Where cumulative transition burden and post-abduction threat expectancy are present, Phase I emphasises restoration of agency, tolerance for ambiguity, and differentiation between behavioural adaptation and internally integrated relational meaning. Survivors are supported in understanding that vigilance, environmental monitoring, certainty-seeking, and guarded disclosure represented coherent attempts to preserve safety within contexts characterised by unpredictable movement between caregivers.

Trust development proceeds through repetition rather than insight. The clinician demonstrates that interest does not depend on escalation of narrative intensity and that complex experiences remain clinically relevant even when described in ordinary language. By naming cumulative transition burden as a recognised stabilisation domain, the HQTP provides a framework in which adult survivors no longer need to determine whether their experiences are understandable before introducing them. Recognition itself functions as Phase I intervention, establishing the conditions required for later integration work without recreating the epistemic instability that characterised earlier developmental environments.

Growing Up Being Moved Between Parents and Caregivers

Many adult survivors describe developmental histories organised around repeated movement between adults without consent. This movement may have involved relocation, abduction, reunification processes, changes in caregiving authority, shifts in relational access, or changes in the narrative explaining family relationships. In these contexts, important relational decisions were made around the child rather than with the child.

Growing up being moved between adults does not refer only to physical relocation. It also describes psychological movement among expectations, loyalties, and relational frameworks shaped by adult decision-making. Children often adapt behaviourally to each shift while lacking the developmental capacity to understand timing, meaning, or permanence. Across the author's doctoral findings and clinical work, survivors frequently describe their childhood less as a series of discrete events and more as an ongoing experience of adjusting to externally directed relational change. Movement may have occurred gradually or abruptly, with explanations that were partial, evolving, or absent.

This developmental experience shapes later-life patterns, including sensitivity to authority, urgency in relational decision-making, reliance on certainty for regulation, difficulty tolerating ambiguity, environmental monitoring, and heightened responsiveness to perceived evaluation in relational contexts. Importantly, behavioural adaptation during these movements represents coherent developmental coping rather than evidence of agreement, preference, or internal integration at the time. Children often prioritise stability, safety, and predictability within the relational framework available to them.

Within the HQTP, recognising that a survivor grew up being moved between adults shifts formulation from event-based interpretation toward pattern-based understanding. The focus shifts to how repeated, externally directed relational change influenced trust development, identity organisation, and decision-making processes across the lifespan. In Phase I, the identification of this pattern informs pacing, the restoration of perceived agency, and the explicit differentiation between past environments in which decisions were made about the survivor and the therapeutic environment in which the survivor retains choice. Naming this experience helps survivors understand that adaptation during relational movement was not a failure, an inconsistency, or indecision. It was developmentally coherent behaviour in contexts where relational stability depended on adult action rather than personal agency.

Abduction and Schooling Hidden in Plain Sight

Abducted, alienated, trafficked, or cult-involved children are not always absent from public view. Some attend ordinary schools, health services, community programs, or family settings while living under altered names, controlled identities, carefully managed personal histories, or narratives designed to prevent disclosure and preserve alignment with the adults around them. Some cult-involved children may also speak several languages because of repeated international movement or exposure to multiple countries and communities. Although this may appear notable, sophisticated, or advantageous, it can also obscure the instability, coercion, displacement, and fragmented caregiving underlying the child's experience. Their distress may remain unseen because each professional encounters only one fragment of the child's life, while repeated movement between caregivers, countries, services, and family systems prevents anyone from recognising the full pattern.

With permission, one deidentified gender neutral adult, seen in the author's private clinical practice, had reportedly been born into a family system organised around sexual abuse and coercive cult-like control. Although child-protection authorities had intervened at one stage, the young person subsequently lived across more than ten family or caregiving environments in different parts of the world and developed proficiency in several languages. Despite repeated contact with adults, institutions, and services, the broader pattern of exploitation, identity disruption, attachment instability, alienation from safe relationships, and developmental trauma had not been adequately recognised.

In coercive, trafficking, or cult-like systems, children may be assigned several altered names, appearances, gendered roles, or forms of presentation as part of concealment, ideological control, exploitation, punishment, or disruption of identity continuity. Gender must not be presumed in these cases. Clinicians should not assume that an adult's reported, assigned, presented, or recorded gender reflects either their autonomous identity or the full history of what has been imposed upon them. The survivor may not even mention this to a clinician, so it must be handled delicately and discussed only when they bring it up. The clinical task is to help the survivor differentiate externally imposed identity, survival-based presentation, and their own present-day understanding of self, without treating gender diversity itself as evidence of pathology or abuse.

International examples illustrate the processes. Steven Stayner lived for years under the alias "Dennis Parnell" and attended multiple schools without recognition despite the circulation of flyers. Suzanne Marie Sevakis, known as "Sharon Marshall", excelled academically and attracted scholarships while living under a fabricated identity. Carlina White, raised as "Nejdra Nance", completed high school and later uncovered her own abduction. Zephany Nurse attended school under a new name and was discovered only when classmates noticed her striking resemblance to her sister. Kamiyah Mobley also progressed through high school using fraudulent documentation that stood unchallenged until official verification. (Birkbeck, 2004; Echols, 1991; The Guardian, 2015; WMTW, 2017).

When Abducted Children Notice Other Abducted Children in School

Additionally, the Australian cult known as "The Family" demonstrated how children could be controlled in a system while also attending local schools. For example, these children were kept on a property in Victoria, known as "Kai Lama", where they were drugged and coached to pass outsider inspections under the registered façade of "Aquinel College." One survivor from the PhD study who went to school with some of these children stated (Johnston & Jones, 2016).

"In my own experience, some of those kids in 'The Family' also attended our primary school with us. We all knew they belonged to that cult, and we thought they were super weird and controlled. We didn't recognise what we were seeing as abuse because we were abducted kids ourselves, and we had our own problems. We didn't hang out with them either. My silence wasn't shyness; it was survival. My words were punished or came back to bite me if my mum found out I'd blabbed. At school, I sometimes spoke to a few kids, but I measured every word. Teachers didn't do anything about the abuse that was happening to any of us, right in front of them.

Needless to say, no one ever noticed that we had been abducted and were attending that school either. I spent all my time trying to hide my rage so that I didn't explode; often, I had to keep a lid on it. When you do not feel cared for, you begin to believe it does not matter what happens to you, and I think that some children in that state could be dangerous. I know I was." (Associated PhD Interview from survivor Alan).

This account illustrates how prolonged containment of fear, rage, and attachment disruption may produce internal states characterised by emotional constriction rather than behavioural acting out. Risk emerges when containment collapses, not from inherent dangerousness.

Silence and Selective Mutism as Survival Adaptations

Selective Mutism (SM) is defined in the DSM-5 as a persistent failure to speak in specific contexts despite speaking in others, resulting in interference with social and educational functioning. In ordinary presentations, it is often framed as a form of social anxiety. In the context of child psychological abuse related to parental alienation, abduction, or coercive control, mutism takes on a different clinical meaning. Silence functions as a safety strategy that preserves loyalty, prevents language from being weaponised, and reduces exposure to relational threat. In these families, mutism is not shyness; it is survival. (American Psychiatric Association, 2022; Driessen et al., 2020; Muris & Ollendick, 2015).

Children, adolescents, and adult survivors entrenched in FDV systems where the AP and their allies actively practise coercively controlling behaviours may describe speech as monitored, interrogated, or used against them. In these contexts, silence may be learned as a form of protection. When attachment bonds are inverted, and the child is drawn into role-reversed alliances, not speaking can feel like an essential or forced form of loyalty, often perceived as a 'normal' way to interact with their AP, their allies, and the world in general.

Prolonged fear and threat responses dysregulate arousal systems and impair social engagement; selective mutism can therefore reflect a dissociative freeze or grief that cannot be expressed in words. A nihilistic stance may develop when care is chronically absent, captured by the survivor's cognition, "it doesn't matter what you do to me, because I don't care about myself anymore. If my dad doesn't want to see me, then what do I matter on the earth?" This statement can arise from denigrating stories about the TP from the AP when contact is limited or non-existent, and the AP is not present to correct the narrative.

One survivor from the related PhD research reported "needing to keep a lid on rage because unleashing could be dangerous when they explode". Additionally, when containment fails, aggression toward others or the self may emerge. Selective mutism can also be instrumental and used as a protection from harm, especially when questions touch on the TP or other forbidden topics deemed dangerous by the survivor.

Consequences of Children Speaking Up - A Case Example

Some adult survivors describe childhood environments in which they were asked for their views about major relational decisions, yet the outcome did not depend on their response.

Consultation functioned symbolically rather than developmentally, creating the appearance of agency without the protection that accompanies it.

In these contexts, siblings may discuss the question collectively and reach a shared position, believing responsibility is distributed. However, delivering that position can place one child, often the eldest, in a visible role that carries disproportionate relational risk.

In clinical work within the author's private practice, one adult survivor described being asked by their mother whether the children minded if she married a new partner. After speaking with siblings, the survivor communicated the shared view that the children felt uncomfortable with the relationship. The siblings believed the decision-making process was genuine.

Following this disclosure, the survivor described a sequence of relational consequences. The mother proceeded with the marriage. The survivor was moved out of the family home and placed next door in the home of the partner's mother, who was terminally ill. The stated explanation was that the survivor was needed to help care for the grandmother. The survivor later understood this relocation was because of speaking up rather than a caregiving decision.

During this period, the survivor slept in the same room as the dying step-grandmother and was exposed to intimate medical care tasks, including the presence of a colostomy bag and the sensory environment associated with end-of-life illness. The survivor remained there until the grandmother died. Siblings were not told what had occurred. The survivor intentionally withheld this information out of fear that other children might also be removed from the home if they spoke.

After the step-grandmother's death, the survivor returned to the family home under explicit behavioural expectations. The new stepfather had been informed that the survivor was the child who voiced opposition to the marriage. Following the marriage, he largely stopped speaking to the survivor for approximately ten years unless communication was necessary. Interaction was described as instrumental, minimal, and characterised by interpersonal exclusion. The stepfather consistently aligned with the mother, and the survivor experienced a prolonged pattern of relational isolation within the household.

When the survivor reached adolescence, additional patterns of repeated boundary violations emerged. The survivor described the stepfather entering their bedroom without warning and intruding on private moments, including occasions when the survivor was showering or changing clothes. These events were experienced as surveillance and as body boundary violations rather than accidental intrusions.

When the adolescent disclosed these experiences to the mother, the mother did not believe them. The survivor reported being hit so hard across the face that they lost their balance and fell onto one of the kitchen benches on the other side and was told that they didn't believe a word they said and were trying to cause problems in the marriage. The behaviour was reframed as the adolescent creating conflict rather than raising a safety concern. The survivor learned that reporting boundary violations could produce punishment rather than protection. This was the beginning of her selective mutism stage that lasted 5 years. Interestingly, this survivor also reported that none of the clinical psychologists to whom she was sent noticed the underlying household problems, and she did not receive the appropriate treatment for this level of abuse.

From a clinical perspective, adolescent experiences of repeated privacy invasion, surveillance during stages of undress, and punishment following disclosure are understood as sexual boundary violations even in the absence of overt physical contact. Developmental impact is intensified when protective attachment figures dismiss or invert disclosure.

This sequence illustrates a developmental pattern in which pseudo-consultation leads to spokesperson punishment, relational removal, enforced caregiving exposure, prolonged interpersonal exclusion, adolescent boundary violation, and protective secrecy. The child learns that expression can lead to removal, that group representation does not reduce risk, and that disclosing body boundary concerns may not ensure safety.

Silence, therefore, becomes adaptive. The survivor carried both the consequences of speaking and the responsibility of concealing what happened from siblings. Expression becomes associated with relational loss. Privacy becomes associated with vulnerability. Authority becomes associated with unpredictability.

Adult survivors with similar histories may present with hesitation when expressing preferences, rapid retraction after disclosure, fear of causing harm to others by speaking, heightened sensitivity to surveillance cues, and strong privacy boundaries that may appear disproportionate without developmental context. Clinicians may also observe spokesperson anxiety, reluctance to represent group views, and anticipatory monitoring of relational consequences following disagreement.

In therapeutic contexts, collaborative decision-making can activate implicit memory of pseudo-consultation. Survivors may question whether their input genuinely influences outcomes or whether disagreement carries unseen consequences. Apparent indecision may reflect consequence prediction rather than lack of capacity.

Clinical work, therefore, focuses on decoupling expression from punishment, restoring bodily autonomy, validating adolescent boundary violations as clinically significant, and reducing the burden of protective secrecy carried into adulthood. Explicit acknowledgement that disagreement does not threaten the therapeutic relationship is central. Consistent relational experience in which expression is received without retaliation supports recalibration of authority expectations, reduces spokesperson burden, and allows speech to emerge without anticipatory fear of removal or exclusion.

Differential Diagnosis for an Abuse-Maintained Pathway

Clinicians must distinguish CPA-PA-linked mutism from primary SM or social anxiety, autism spectrum presentations characterised by pragmatic language differences, depressive or dissociative withdrawal that is global rather than situational, and Reactive Attachment Disorder in which social engagement is atypical across relationships. (American Psychiatric Association, 2022; Muris & Ollendick, 2015).

Clinical red flags: An abuse-maintained pathway may include selective mutism symptoms that appear specifically when the targeted parent is mentioned, rapid onset after separation or relocation, caregiver narratives that sound coached or controlling, repeated school moves with gaps in records, and co-occurring indicators such as sexualised behaviour, self-harm, or sudden aggression.

Indicators in Schools and Initial Triage

Schools are often the primary settings where professionals observe the child day after day. For the sake of the child, it is recommended that staff report and document any sudden or situational mutism as it emerges. Onset may occur after family upheaval; inconsistent enrolment records or missing court orders; frequent interstate or international moves; fearful responses to references to the targeted parent; scripted politeness or improbable perfection; and behavioural spikes when silence no longer contains the child's affect. When several of these features cluster, the situation warrants escalation rather than reassurance.

Stealth, Safety, and Strategic Disclosure

In CPA-PAA, careless action can increase danger. Alienating parents are often vigilant and retaliatory. If they sense scrutiny, they may punish the child, withdraw the child from school, or flee. Assessment should therefore be quiet and ordinary-looking. Professionals should avoid public interrogation and premature confrontation, use neutral welfare language for meetings, and build plausible routines that allow contact with the child without signalling an investigation. Schools should convene confidential safety huddles with leadership and the welfare lead and, where necessary, seek legal advice. A decision to involve a child-protection liaison and a clinician experienced in attachment and forensic risk must be carefully considered before taking this direct action. Timing matters. Mandatory reporting obligations remain in force, but the sequencing of when, how, and to whom information is disclosed should be planned to reduce the likelihood of retaliation and to protect all staff and services that may be involved. Monitoring staff welfare and specialised debriefing are recommended. (Attorney-General's Department, 2024).

Structured Reunification and Relational Transition Experiences

Neutral Clinical Position and Scope

The material that follows concerns adult survivors' retrospective accounts of intensive reunification programs, structured relational interventions, escorted transitions, and related professional processes. It is presented as a clinical formulation resource, not as a forensic evaluation of any program, practitioner, court decision, or individual case. Retrospective distress does not by itself establish that an intervention was harmful, and reported benefit does not establish that all aspects were fully integrated. The HQTP therefore uses a neutral, longitudinal, and survivor-specific approach.

Retrieval, Escorted Transition, and Reunification Program Experiences in Adult Survivors

Adult survivors of child psychological abuse within high-conflict separation contexts may report histories involving intensive reunification programs, structured family interventions, escorted transitions between caregivers, retrieval processes, or periods of rapid relational change facilitated by professionals. These experiences vary widely in structure and meaning but share a common feature: relational change occurred within a defined, often time-limited, externally organised context.

Programs may have included residential workshops, therapeutic intensives, structured reunification processes, or coordinated transitional support. Some survivors also describe experiences involving movement between caregiving environments supported by transition providers, escorts, or multidisciplinary teams tasked with facilitating transfer of care. For the developing child, distinctions between program participation, placement transition, and professional involvement are often unclear. Many survivors, therefore, remember these events as a single period characterised by being moved between adults while significant relational decisions were occurring.

Practical conditions surrounding participation frequently form part of the psychological memory. These may include travel, temporary relocation, altered communication patterns, concentrated therapeutic schedules, and awareness of significant financial investment on the part of adults. Reported program costs vary widely and can exceed tens of thousands of dollars when professional fees, travel, accommodation, and follow-up services are included. For some survivors, awareness of this investment shaped their expectations regarding progress, adaptation, or visible relational change.

Outcome narratives are heterogeneous. Some survivors describe meaningful reconnection, increased clarity, and relational repair. Others describe experiences characterised by emotional intensity, confusion, perceived pressure, or difficulty integrating rapid relational change after the structured environment concludes. Many adult survivors describe mixed experiences in which elements of benefit coexist with unresolved complexity.

Clinically relevant features include pace of relational change, authority context, and expectations regarding behavioural adaptation. Behavioural engagement often occurred within contexts where authority, time compression, and relational stakes were highly salient. Behavioural change may therefore precede emotional integration.

Intensive Reunification and Structured Transition Experiences: Adult Survivor Presentation

Within the HQTP, relational movement refers to childhood experiences in which decisions about caregiving relationships, contact patterns, or living arrangements were changed through adult-directed processes that required the child to adapt before full developmental understanding or emotional integration was possible. When relational movement has occurred,

Phase I prioritises restoration of perceived agency, predictability, and epistemic safety before any reinterpretation of relational history is attempted.

A subgroup of adult survivors described childhood participation in intensive reunification programs or other structured transition processes intended to support restoration of parent–child relationships following significant contact disruption. Survivor accounts indicate that these experiences were highly structured, time-limited, and relationally focused, with therapeutic intent to facilitate reconnection, reduce conflict exposure, and stabilise contact arrangements. Many survivors describe elements that felt containing, clarifying, or developmentally important, particularly when interventions occurred within supportive contexts and were followed by consistent relational care.

At the same time, longitudinal presentation suggests that behavioural change achieved during these processes does not always correspond immediately with internal relational integration. Some survivors report that participation required rapid adaptation to new expectations about contact, communication, or relational meaning before they had the developmental capacity to fully understand the shift. In these cases, outward engagement may precede internal coherence.

Survivors may present with stable functioning in education, employment, and relationships, yet demonstrate marked difficulty when invited to reconsider earlier relational narratives. Exploration of childhood contact decisions, emotional experience during reunification, or alternative perspectives on caregivers can elicit disproportionate physiological activation, cognitive rigidity, or a rapid return to previously established meanings. This pattern does not indicate a failure of intervention. It reflects the developmental sequencing in which behavioural adaptation occurred before emotional, attachment, or epistemic integration, leaving aspects of relational reorganisation incomplete and continuing to evolve across adulthood.

Mixed Outcome Presentations Following Intensive Reunification and Structured Transition Experiences

Across private practice and hospital-based clinical work, the author has observed that adult survivors who participated in intensive reunification or structured transition environments rarely present with uniform outcomes. Related patterns were also reflected in the doctoral research. Instead, some demonstrate mixed integration patterns in which elements of relational benefit coexist with unresolved attachment conflicts, uncertainty, or physiological activation.

Some survivors describe meaningful gains associated with participation, including restored contact, increased understanding of family dynamics, reduced exposure to overt conflict, or access to relationships that may otherwise have remained restricted. These experiences can contribute to developmental progress, expanded relational capacity, and later appreciation of aspects of the intervention that supported stability during a complex period.

Survivors may articulate clear cognitive narratives about what occurred while simultaneously demonstrating difficulty accessing emotional nuance, tolerating ambiguity, or revisiting relational meaning without activation. Positive recollections of program elements may coexist with confusion, grief, anger, loyalty tension, or uncertainty about personal experience during the transition.

Within clinical settings, this mixed outcome pattern may appear as simultaneous gratitude and avoidance, confidence in established relational positions alongside sensitivity when those positions are explored, or appreciation for restored contact combined with unresolved questions about agency, pacing, or emotional readiness at the time of the intervention. These presentations reflect layered developmental processes rather than contradiction. Findings from the author's survivor cohort suggest that variability is shaped by multiple factors, including the child's developmental stage at the time of intervention, prior exposure to coercive control or abduction, the level of preparation and follow-up support available, and whether post-intervention environments allowed gradual meaning-making. Where relational change occurred within ongoing instability or high emotional demand, internal integration may have been deferred rather than completed.

Longitudinal associated narrative PhD findings indicate that the long-term impact of intensive reunification experiences is shaped less by program format than by timing, prior attachment disruption, concurrent stressors, and the extent to which post-intervention environments supported gradual meaning integration. For clinicians working with adult survivors, the task is therefore integrative rather than evaluative. Participation in structured relational interventions is treated as one component of the survivor's developmental history that may influence trust formation, responses to authority, attachment expectations, and tolerance for relational ambiguity across the lifespan. Within the HQTP, these experiences are conceptualised as relational transition events requiring later integration, rather than as events whose impact can be inferred solely from behavioural outcomes at the time.

Clinical Examples: Behavioural Change Without Internal Integration

The following examples illustrate recurrent patterns observed across the author's private practice and hospital-based work in which behavioural change achieved during structured reunification or transition interventions did not correspond with internal attachment integration. These examples represent clinical pattern illustrations rather than individual cases.

As stated earlier, an adult survivor may describe the intervention as "worked," maintain a stable relational narrative, yet display marked physiological activation when the emotional experience is explored. Tension, rapid speech, or difficulty tolerating ambiguity may emerge alongside surprise that the experience feels unresolved.

Another survivor may recall participating appropriately and following guidance, but report limited experiential memory, describing the period as "doing what was expected." Later distress arises when independent relational decisions are required, revealing the absence of an integrated meaning behind earlier behavioural change. In some cases, intergenerational activation becomes the first indicator of unresolved integration. A survivor who reports no prior concern may experience sudden urgency or anxiety when their child expresses curiosity about extended family. The intensity of the response is followed by confusion, self-questioning, or shame.

Within inpatient contexts, recognition may occur during destabilisation. Survivors may revisit previously described reunification experiences as resolved and recognise that behavioural participation may have coexisted with fear, uncertainty, or a perceived lack of choice. Distress is associated with the discrepancy, not the event itself.

Authority sensitivity may also emerge in therapy. Survivors may align rapidly with perceived clinician expectations, hesitate when uncertainty is invited, or express concern about giving the “right” answers. Explicit reassurance that therapy does not require relational conclusions often produces visible relief, linking present responses to earlier structured environments.

Across settings, these patterns demonstrate that behavioural indicators of change cannot be assumed to reflect internal integration. Recognition of this divergence allows clinicians to distinguish unresolved integration from resistance and supports pacing that prioritises restoring trust before interpretive work.

Rigid Alignment Presentations Following Intensive Reunification and Structured Transition Experiences

A subgroup of adult survivors demonstrated enduring alignment patterns that emerged during childhood relational transitions or reunification experiences and later stabilised as fixed meaning structures. In these cases, behavioural adaptation supported contact reorganisation at the time but subsequently functioned as a primary mechanism for managing relational complexity. Alignment may provide continuity, reduce ambiguity, and function as protection against reactivation of earlier attachment disruption. The narrative clarity it offers can support functioning across adolescence and adulthood, particularly when relational environments remain emotionally demanding or uncertain.

Difficulty emerges when later developmental stages introduce new relational questions. Exploration of childhood experiences, alternative perspectives on caregivers, or discussion of extended family contact may evoke physiological activation, cognitive rigidity, or a rapid return to previously established explanatory frameworks. This response reflects the regulatory role of the alignment rather than its opposition to therapeutic work.

Rigid alignment presentations are more frequently observed when relational change occurs alongside earlier attachment disruption, abduction, repeated movement between caregivers, or in environments with limited perceived agency. Under these conditions, clear relational positioning can become a stabilising adaptation that reduces uncertainty during development while constraining later meaning integration.

Clinical work does not aim to remove alignment. The therapeutic task is to support tolerance for ambiguity while preserving the stabilising function that the alignment has served. Pacing prioritises the differentiation between narrative certainty and emotional experience, the gradual expansion of reflective capacity, and the maintenance of physiological safety during relational exploration.

Within the HQTP, rigid alignment is understood as an adaptive meaning structure that forms when behavioural stabilisation precedes developmental integration. Its presence informs pacing, containment, and later relational differentiation work across subsequent phases of the protocol. If a survivor has a history of being moved between caregivers, abducted, retrieved, structurally reunited, or subjected to repeated relational repositioning, the clinician should slow the work down in Phase I. The clinician should not assume that the survivor's current alignment, compliance, or contact pattern reflects a fully integrated belief or freely formed relational meaning. It may instead reflect a behavioural adaptation that once helped the survivor survive instability, pressure, or loss of control. So, the task is to restore agency and avoid mistaking adaptation for genuine internal resolution.

Intergenerational Reactivation in Adult Survivors

Intergenerational reactivation refers to the re-emergence of unresolved relational meaning when adult survivors become parents or encounter developmental situations that echo earlier attachment disruption, relational movement, or family reorganisation. Doctoral findings from the twin study identify this period as a common point at which previously stabilised alignment structures re-enter conscious processing, particularly among survivors whose childhood included relational movement, abduction, or prolonged attachment disruption. Situations such as a child asking questions about extended family, school projects involving family history, requests for contact from relatives, or routine discussions about grandparents can activate previously stabilised alignment structures. Survivors may experience these moments as unexpectedly destabilising, even when day-to-day functioning remains intact.

The activation is often experienced as a sense of urgency rather than reflection. Survivors may report a strong need to protect their child from perceived relational risk, difficulty tolerating hypothetical discussion of previously restricted caregivers, or rapid return to established narratives without conscious deliberation. This response reflects reactivation of earlier uncertainty about safety, agency, and relational meaning rather than deliberate opposition to contact.

Clinical observation indicates that the intensity of response is shaped by the developmental conditions under which the original relational change occurred. Where childhood experiences involved rapid repositioning, limited perceived influence, repeated movement between adults, or exposure to threat narratives, later parenting decisions may carry implicit pressure to prevent the recurrence of destabilisation across generations.

Survivors frequently describe these reactions as surprising. Many report that they had not previously considered how their own childhood relational experiences might influence their parenting responses until activation occurs. The experience may be accompanied by fear that exploration could destabilise identity, family stability, or previously achieved relational gains.

Within treatment, intergenerational reactivation is approached as a predictable developmental process rather than evidence of pathology or regression. Clinical work focuses on differentiating past relational threat from present decision-making, supporting tolerance for uncertainty, and expanding reflective capacity without pressuring immediate behavioural change.

The therapeutic task is to create a space in which survivors can examine protective urgency while maintaining their sense of agency as parents. This includes recognising that fear-based responses may originate in earlier experiences of limited influence, perceived coercion, or rapid repositioning in relationships, rather than solely in current relational evidence. Within the HQTP, intergenerational reactivation signals an area where behavioural stabilisation in childhood is encountering developmental demands for integrating meaning. It therefore informs pacing, containment, and later relational differentiation work across subsequent phases of the protocol. The HQTP refers to this presentation as the fear of relational repetition across generations.

Clinical Examples of Relational Repositioning

Relational repositioning becomes clinically observable when adult survivors describe childhood periods in which changes to living arrangements, contact patterns, or relational expectations followed decisions made by specific people or teams responsible for the child's care or transition. Survivors describe being taken to structured reunification environments run by program clinicians and facilitators, escorted transitions facilitated by therapeutic escort staff or contracted transition professionals following separation or recovery events, sudden household or placement changes arranged by parents, stepparents, or extended family members, and situations in which contact expectations were shaped by MHPs, case workers, school personnel, or multidisciplinary teams involved in family decision-making.

Some survivors recall being informed by a parent, practitioner, or transition professional that living arrangements, schooling, or contact expectations were changing after plans had already been finalised. Others describe needing to adjust behaviour quickly within structured therapeutic settings where facilitators or clinicians guided relational expectations.

Additional examples include professional handovers between households; periods in which program staff or practitioners increased structured contact with one caregiver while limiting exposure to another; therapeutic environments in which clinicians explored or reframed relational narratives; and repeated adjustments to caregiver proximity following family decisions, safety planning, or service involvement. In these situations, the child's task was adaptation to coordinated relational change.

When these experiences occurred more than once, survivors often describe learning to anticipate decisions made by parents, practitioners, or transition teams, to monitor expectations closely, and to rely on certainty as a stabilising strategy. In adulthood, these histories may become visible through sensitivity during relational transitions, urgency when parenting decisions involve extended family, difficulty tolerating open-ended relational discussion, reliance on certainty as a regulatory strategy, or activation when situations resemble earlier coordinated relational change.

For clinicians, identifying who organised the repositioning provides essential clarity about the formulation. It allows present-day responses to be linked to specific developmental events rather than generalised relational concepts, supporting paced integration while preserving the stabilising function these adaptations originally served.

Retrieval and Escorted Transition Experiences

Some adult survivors describe childhood experiences involving retrieval or escorted transitions undertaken to transport them to structured reunification environments, intensive relational interventions, or other time-limited settings designed to support changes in parent-child contact. These movements were typically coordinated in advance and could involve designated transition professionals, program staff, or multidisciplinary teams whose role was to facilitate safe arrival and manage the logistical aspects of movement between locations.

Survivor accounts indicate that anticipation of these transitions varied. Some children understood the purpose and agreed to attend. Others describe uncertainty, fear, or resistance prior to the transition, including awareness that the movement was imminent but a sense that they had limited influence over whether it would occur.

In some cases, adolescents have recorded or documented retrieval moments themselves. When revisited later in adulthood, these recordings may be emotionally confronting, particularly when the young person's internal state at the time differed from how the transition was externally framed. Survivors often recall the practical elements first: unfamiliar adults present, travel already organised, and being told they were going somewhere specific, sometimes with explanation, sometimes with limited understanding of what the intervention would involve.

For some children, the transition marked the beginning of a highly structured environment where expectations about communication, perception, and behaviour could shift rapidly. From the child's perspective, this may involve leaving one relational setting and entering another in which relational expectations are actively addressed within a compressed timeframe.

Some survivors describe the presence of transition professionals as reassuring at the time. Others describe heightened alertness, confusion, or a sense of danger and pressure to adjust quickly without fully understanding the purpose or duration of the setting. Mixed responses are common. Survivors may describe the transition and the reunification environment as a single developmental episode characterised by rapid relational change. Where these experiences occurred alongside earlier abduction, concealment, repeated movement between households, or exposure to coercive family dynamics, survivors may describe a cumulative sense of being moved between adults across childhood. Meaning assigned to these experiences frequently evolves over time rather than remaining fixed.

Retrospective awareness that these programs involved significant planning, coordination, and financial investment may influence later meaning-making, including questions about pacing, agency, expectations, and perceived influence over relational decisions. Clinical work focuses on helping adult survivors differentiate between logistical movement and relational meaning, restore their perceived influence over narrative interpretation, and integrate these experiences without imposing evaluative conclusions about the intervention itself.

Within the HQTP, retrieval and escorted transition experiences are understood as high-salience relational change events that shape Phase I stabilisation, trust formation, authority sensitivity, and later work involving agency, consent, and relational predictability. Because these experiences involve rapid, externally organised relational change, adult survivors do not present with uniform outcomes. Later integration varies.

Mixed Outcome Presentations Following Structured Reunification Experiences

Because these experiences involve rapid, externally organised relational change, adult survivor presentations do not follow a single pathway. Later integration varies, reflecting the developmental reality that behavioural adaptation may occur during childhood, while emotional meaning, relational interpretation, and identity positioning continue to evolve over time.

A subgroup of adult survivors describes experiences that were ultimately integrated in a way that supported relational clarity. These individuals may acknowledge that participation was challenging while also reporting that the experience contributed to contact restoration, reduced uncertainty, or enabled a relationship that had previously felt inaccessible. In adulthood, the intervention is remembered as one developmental event among many rather than as a defining rupture.

A second subgroup presents with partial integration. Behavioural adaptation achieved during the environment supported observable relational change at the time, yet internal meaning-making remained incomplete. Survivors in this group often function well but struggle to tolerate later reinterpretation of childhood relationships, especially when new information, a developmental perspective, or life-stage transitions prompt reconsideration. Reactions may include rigidity, anxiety about "getting it wrong," a sense of urgency to maintain a stable narrative, or distress when relational complexity increases.

A third subgroup describes experiences characterised by overwhelm, perceived pressure to adapt quickly, or insufficient time to process rapid internal relational shifts. For these survivors, the intervention may be remembered less as a discrete program and more as a period in which expectations about perception, communication, and loyalty changed rapidly and in a highly structured way. The developmental impact reflects pacing rather than a simple classification as positive or negative.

Across presentations, clinicians frequently observe a gap between behavioural compliance and internal resolution. Survivors may describe learning what was required within the environment while continuing to organise relational understanding over many years. Later-life triggers often include becoming a parent, exposure to new information, a child's curiosity about extended family, or therapeutic exploration of attachment history.

Where retrieval or escorted transitions preceded participation, survivors may experience movement and intervention as a single developmental episode involving externally structured relational repositioning. This can influence later responses to authority, sensitivity to perceived pressure, difficulty tolerating rapid therapeutic pacing, and heightened attention to agency in relational decision-making. Mixed outcome presentations do not indicate intervention failure. They reflect the developmental reality that relational reorganisation can occur faster than identity integration. Meaning-making, therefore, remains active across adulthood.

Clinical work focuses on differentiation rather than evaluation. The task is to help survivors distinguish adaptation from internal agreement, place the experience within a developmental context, and expand tolerance for relational complexity without destabilising identity coherence. Recognition of mixed outcome presentations informs stabilisation pacing, authority sensitivity, trust formation, and later work involving agency, consent, and relational reinterpretation.

Enduring Alignment Patterns and Authority-Linked Attachment Organisation

A distinct clinical presentation involves enduring alignment patterns in which behavioural change achieved during childhood remains structurally stable into adulthood, while internal relational certainty remains fragile. In these presentations, the survivor may experience the previously rejected parent as psychologically unsafe to approach despite stable functioning in other domains. This does not necessarily reflect conscious rejection. Rather, it reflects attachment organisation shaped within conditions in which relational positioning occurred under structured expectations, compressed timeframes, and heightened authority.

Adult survivors may describe confidence in their relational stance alongside difficulty tolerating ambiguity, reinterpretation, or new information. When reconsideration arises, distress is often disproportionate to the immediate context. Reactions can include anxiety, an urge to restore certainty, narrative rigidity, avoidance of exploration, or activation of a physiological threat response when hypothetical discussion is introduced.

This presentation is best understood as an authority-linked attachment organisation rather than simple loyalty persistence. The survivor's relational position was formed within a context in which adaptation supported predictability, safety, or relational continuity. Maintaining that position may therefore function as ongoing stabilisation. Later-life triggers frequently include becoming a parent, a child expressing curiosity about the extended family, exposure to historical material, therapeutic exploration of attachment history, or contact attempts that were previously unlikely. These moments introduce intergenerational reactivation, in which earlier relational positioning becomes newly relevant.

As noted earlier in this chapter, intergenerational reactivation may present as sudden rigidity, urgency to protect the child from contact, difficulty tolerating the child's curiosity, shame following strong reactions, and fear that relational harm will repeat across generations. In this later presentation, the clinical task is to assess whether the survivor is responding to present-day risk, unresolved fear from their own history, or both. These responses should be understood as threat activation rather than deliberate obstruction.

Clinical work prioritises pacing, differentiation, and restoration of perceived agency. The therapeutic task is not to challenge the survivor's relational position but to support tolerance for uncertainty, expand reflective capacity, and separate past environmental conditions from present decision-making. Where this work proceeds safely, survivors may begin to hold multiple possibilities simultaneously without immediate destabilisation. This capacity represents developmental integration rather than relational reversal.

Intergenerational Reactivation and Fear of Relational Repetition Across Generations

For some adult survivors, earlier experiences of externally directed relational positioning become clinically relevant again when their own children reach developmental stages associated with relational curiosity, autonomy, and identity formation. The HQTP conceptualises this presentation as fear of relational repetition across generations, describing distress that may emerge when survivors become responsible for relational decisions for their own children.

This activation rarely centres on a single individual. It reflects concern that childhood relational experiences could recur in altered form, uncertainty about relational safety, and heightened awareness of the consequences of decisions by adult authorities. Survivors who previously adapted to relational change with limited perceived influence may experience increased vigilance when positioned as the person responsible for determining proximity, boundaries, and contact.

Presentations may include increased monitoring of the child's relational environment, an urgency to anticipate relational questions, difficulty tolerating neutral or hypothetical discussions involving extended family members, physiological activation when contact scenarios are introduced, and internal conflict between protective intentions and uncertainty about how risk is interpreted.

This pattern does not indicate resistance to relational repair or inflexibility. It reflects a protective organisation shaped by earlier experiences in which relational positioning occurred under defined expectations, compressed timeframes, or conditions that reduced perceived agency. Clinical work focuses on the differentiation between past lack of agency and present authorship. The task involves supporting survivors to recognise that relational decisions can be paced, revisited, and contextualised rather than enacted in a rush. Emphasis is placed on strengthening tolerance for ambiguity, restoring confidence in evaluative capacity, and reducing fear that a single decision will determine long-term relational outcomes.

Where containment is maintained, survivors may begin to hold curiosity without immediate action, recognise protective responses without rigid avoidance, and experience relational decision-making as iterative rather than irreversible. This phase of work reflects continued integration rather than destabilisation. It marks the developmental shift from adapting to externally directed relational positioning toward exercising internally guided relational authority across generations.

Clinician Caution: Interpreting Behavioural Change Following Structured Reunification

Clinicians should avoid assuming that observable behavioural change achieved within structured reunification or recovery-related environments reflects internal attachment integration. Behavioural participation may occur in response to an authority structure, time limits, perceived expectations, a desire for stability, or adaptive compliance amid relational uncertainty.

Premature interpretation of behavioural change as resolution may obscure unresolved integration domains that become clinically relevant later in life. Conversely, retrospective distress does not in itself indicate that the intervention was harmful. Both positions oversimplify complex developmental processes. Clinical formulation, therefore, prioritises differentiation rather than evaluation. The task is to understand how behavioural change occurred, what meaning was assigned at the time, and whether emotional integration followed a different timeline.

Clinicians should also avoid introducing a sense of urgency for reinterpretation when survivors revisit these experiences. Exploration that exceeds epistemic stability may recreate dynamics associated with earlier structured environments, including perceived evaluation, pressure to reach conclusions, or fear of relational consequences. Where rigid alignment is present, direct challenge is contraindicated in Phase I. Stabilisation requires restoration of curiosity tolerance before narrative flexibility can emerge. The clinician’s stance remains neutral, paced, and longitudinal.

Survivor Recognition and Therapeutic Surprise

As mentioned, a recurrent feature within the author's clinical work is survivor surprise when clinicians demonstrate familiarity with cumulative transition burden, post-abduction threat expectancy, and unresolved reunification integration. Many adult survivors report earlier experiences in which these domains were treated as unusual disclosures, elicited curiosity without sustained formulation, or were not revisited once initial narratives were established. This history contributes to an expectation that clinicians may not understand the structural nature of these experiences. Survivors may therefore monitor clinician responses closely, limit disclosure, or anticipate that interest will diminish if narratives are not dramatic or novel.

Explicit recognition that these patterns are known within the protocol often produces a mixed response. Relief may coexist with apprehension, testing behaviour, or concern that recognition implies reinterpretation and may be challenged. Survivors may express statements indicating surprise that clinicians "already know," uncertainty about how much explanation is required, or hesitation to introduce material previously experienced as difficult to convey.

Within Phase I, this moment is treated as a stabilisation event. The therapeutic task is not the expansion of material but the consolidation of epistemic safety. Clinicians maintain continuity of recognition across sessions; revisit previously introduced concepts and demonstrate that understanding does not depend on narrative escalation. Recognition itself functions as an intervention by reducing the burden on survivors to establish the legitimacy of their experiences before therapeutic work can proceed.

Structural Placement Within Phase I

Within the HQTP, the domains addressed above are situated within Phase I as stabilisation constructs rather than interpretive domains. Specifically, cumulative transition burden, retrieval experiences, unresolved reunification integration, rigid alignment, reverse intergenerational activation, and post-abduction threat expectancy serve as indicators of pacing, trust development, and authority sensitivity.

These constructs sit alongside other Phase I stabilisation domains, including identity coherence, epistemic safety, regulation capacity, and attachment threat monitoring. Their presence signals the need for enhanced pacing, explicit clarification of therapeutic role boundaries, and prioritisation of agency restoration before exploratory trauma work.

Structurally, these sections follow crisis architecture because they represent predictable destabilisation pathways linked to recognition processes rather than discrete trauma events. They inform clinicians' decision-making regarding session structure, interpretation thresholds, consultation timing, and readiness to progress to later phases.

Phase progression remains contingent on the survivor's capacity to tolerate curiosity about earlier relational change without collapsing into urgency, certainty, or withdrawal. When these constructs are active, continued Phase I work represents forward movement rather than delay. By locating these patterns within Phase I, the protocol prevents misinterpretation of later-life destabilisation as regression and instead frames it as the emergence of previously unintegrated developmental material within a stabilised therapeutic environment.

Clinical Safeguard: Avoiding Polarised Conclusions

The HQTP does not use adult survivor material to support a generalised claim that reunification interventions are either inherently safe or inherently harmful. Clinicians should avoid advocacy-driven interpretation in either direction. Formulation should remain focused on the individual survivor's developmental context, preparation, consent and perceived agency, relational safety, intervention pacing, follow-up support, present-day functioning, and capacity to reflect without destabilisation. Where legal or forensic conclusions are required, these remain outside the scope of the HQTP and must be addressed by appropriately qualified professionals within the relevant jurisdiction.

Although reunification and structured transition experiences must be considered without predetermined conclusions, the earlier histories surrounding these interventions may still reveal clinically important patterns of fear organisation. One such pattern identified in the author's doctoral research involved the development of a specific phobia presentation following early exposure to CPA-PAA. The following section examines how this fear may first emerge in early childhood and persist across the lifespan.

Developmental Emergence and Lifespan Persistence of the Specific Phobia–CPA-PAA Anxiety Variant

Within the author's doctoral analysis, a specific phobia variant presentation was identified as associated with exposure to SPA-PAA under approximately eight years of age. Seventy-five per cent of the survivor cohort who had experienced CPA-PAA described that this fear began during the period of alienation and abduction itself, when everyday life became organised around sudden change, concealment, and uncertainty. This pattern was identified in the author's doctoral research on twins, with the survivor cohort describing the internal fear organisation and the practitioner cohort describing parallel recognition of the same presentation in clinical settings, including later-life persistence.

Survivors described not knowing where they were going, being moved between locations with little warning, changing schools repeatedly, and being unable to say goodbye to friends or teachers. Some described being required to learn or use a different name, to follow coached narratives about identity and family, or to monitor their speech because disclosure could lead to consequences. Silence and compliance served as protection in environments where relational preferences could not be safely expressed.

Within this developmental context, fear extended beyond the initial abduction period. Survivors described persistent anticipation that movement could occur again without notice, including fear of further removal by the alienating parent, associates, or adults aligned with that narrative. This anticipatory fear contributed to vigilance, avoidance of authority figures, difficulty trusting helpers, and heightened sensitivity to situations involving relational decision-making.

The twin study findings positioned this presentation as a clinically observed developmental pathway rather than a formal diagnostic category. It is included within the protocol to support the formulation of threat learning associated with externally directed relational change and to guide stabilisation pacing and containment architecture in Phase I. The HQTP conceptualises fear of relational repetition across generations as a developmental extension of the specific phobia variant presentation. Distress may emerge when survivors become responsible for relational decisions concerning their own children, particularly when contact questions, extended family discussions, or school-related family tasks arise.

The distress reflects sensitivity to the possibility that relational positioning could again occur without sufficient safety, clarity, or agency. Twin study findings identified this pattern across both survivor and practitioner cohorts. Survivors described anticipatory fear that relational decisions could again be externally determined, while practitioners described uncertainty about how to support relational decision-making without replicating externally directed change. This positioned the phenomenon as a developmental formulation rather than avoidance, resistance, or treatment ambivalence.

When activated, clinicians may observe an urgency to protect the child from perceived relational risk, difficulty tolerating hypothetical discussions of extended family members, rigidity in previously flexible narratives, oscillation between certainty and doubt, and distress that appears disproportionate to current evidence yet is coherent in the context of early threat learning.

Within the HQTP, activation of this pattern signals the need for containment, pacing, and explicit reinforcement of survivor agency. Clinical work focuses on differentiating past externally directed relational change from present decision-making and on supporting survivors to experience relational decisions as revisable, collaborative, and developmentally paced rather than urgent and irreversible.

Clinical Approach When Fear of Relational Repetition Is Activated

When fear of relational repetition across generations is activated, the clinical task shifts from interpretation to containment. The objective is not immediate decision-making but restoration of epistemic safety around relational choice.

The first step involves a clear distinction between past externally directed relational change and present decision authority. Survivors benefit from clear acknowledgement that earlier experiences involved limited influence, while current relational decisions are paced, collaborative, and reversible. This distinction reduces urgency and interrupts survival-based assumptions that action must occur quickly to prevent harm. Pacing becomes central. Clinicians slow discussion of relational decisions, avoid framing choices as final, and emphasise the tolerability of uncertainty within structured support. Language highlighting flexibility, review points, and gradual exposure supports nervous system regulation and reduces perceived pressure.

Work focuses on restoring agency rather than on contact outcomes. Survivors are supported in identifying what information is needed before making choices, what supports are required, and what boundaries can exist alongside uncertainty. This approach allows relational decision-making to be experienced as an ongoing process rather than a single irreversible event.

The regulation strategies established earlier in Phase I are being re-engaged. Orientation, grounding, written scaffolds, and structured session anchoring help maintain continuity of identity when anticipatory fear increases. Where intrusive imagery or urgency emerges, clinicians prioritise stabilisation before continuing relational exploration.

Clinicians also monitor for subtle replication of externally directed positioning within therapy. This includes avoiding directive recommendations framed as necessary, maintaining transparency about clinical reasoning, and checking how suggestions are experienced rather than assuming they are. Explicit permission to disagree serves as a protective intervention.

Where survivors are parenting, psychoeducation focuses on developmental pacing, tolerance for child curiosity, and differentiation between protection and prohibition. Survivors are supported in holding protective instincts alongside reflective capacity, reducing the pressure to eliminate all perceived risk immediately. This approach is grounded in twin-study findings indicating that anticipatory fear, linked to externally directed relational change, can persist into adulthood, even when overall functioning appears stable. Activation signals the need for containment, agency reinforcement, and gradual integration rather than corrective relational action.

Clinical Risks if Fear of Relational Repetition Is Misunderstood

When fear of relational repetition across generations is misinterpreted, clinical responses may unintentionally replicate the very dynamics that organised the survivor's early experience. Urgency, directive guidance, premature contact recommendations, or framing relational decisions as problems to be resolved can increase destabilisation rather than support integration.

A common risk involves interpreting protective rigidity as resistance or avoidance. When clinicians attempt to challenge the position directly without first restoring epistemic safety, survivors may experience pressure resembling externally directed relational positioning. This can lead to withdrawal, compliance without integration, or escalation of anxiety and certainty seeking. Another risk involves over-reassurance. Attempts to eliminate fear through reassurance that situations are safe may bypass the developmental origins of the fear and leave the underlying threat-learning unaddressed. Survivors may temporarily stabilise while continuing to experience anticipatory distress during future relational decision points.

Clinicians may also underestimate how quickly urgency can emerge. Relational decision discussion can shift rapidly from exploratory dialogue to perceived necessity, particularly when the survivor senses that a recommendation is forming. Without pacing, this can lead to a narrowing of perceived options, shame in response to strong protective responses, or sudden disengagement from treatment.

Misunderstanding this pattern may also distort formulation. Distress may be attributed to personality traits, attachment style, or current relational dynamics, without recognising early externally directed relational change as the organising experience. This risks treatment approaches that focus on correction rather than stabilisation.

Recognition of this pattern allows clinicians to maintain containment, protect the survivor's agency, and avoid replicating externally directed relational positioning in therapy. When understood developmentally, activation becomes an indicator for pacing and agency reinforcement rather than a barrier to progress.

Group Work with Adult Survivors of CPA-PA: Phase I Stabilisation Considerations

Group environments introduce a distinct stabilisation context for adult survivors of CPA-PA and related developmental trauma. Although groups can reduce isolation and support recognition, this population does not enter group work as a psychologically uniform cohort. Survivors arrive with distinct developmental impact profiles, varying levels of insight, exposure histories, degrees of autonomy, and relationships to recognition itself. This variability is not simply descriptive. It actively shapes group dynamics.

Mixed Developmental Impact Within Groups

Groups frequently include survivors across mild, moderate, and severe developmental impact, although these distinctions are rarely formalised. Survivors with concealment, abduction, identity disruption, prolonged coercive environments, FDIOA-related histories, or familicide exposure may have trouble tolerating material shared by members whose developmental environments were less extreme. Conversely, survivors whose histories did not include overt threat may experience destabilisation when exposed to narratives that exceed their window of tolerance.

These differences can lead to comparisons, self-monitoring, withdrawal, or escalation. Survivors may censor themselves to protect other members, to avoid overwhelming the clinician, or to avoid being perceived as dramatic, attention-seeking, or not believed. Others may escalate when they feel silenced, misunderstood, or placed back into a role where their reality must be minimised to preserve relational safety.

Relational Conditioning Within Groups

Early relational conditioning frequently reemerges in group space. Survivors may split into informal subgroups, align around shared narratives, or experience pressure to adopt interpretations. Loyalty dynamics can develop quickly, particularly when members remain partially enmeshed, uncertain about their own history, or strongly identified with a relational position. Misinterpretation is common. Neutral comments may be experienced as invalidation, narrative correction, or authority positioning. Survivors with FDIOA-related histories may also interpret bodily, psychological, or relational experiences shared by others through threat-based frameworks, increasing confusion or emotional intensity.

Accidental Counsellor Dynamics

A recurring pattern involves survivors who enter groups seeking answers because prior clinicians did not recognise alienation. These survivors may direct formulation questions toward other members, positioning peers as informal experts. Members perceived as more informed may be appointed as educators, stabilisers, or mediators without consent or support.

This accidental counsellor dynamic is clinically significant. It increases the burden on certain members, creates a hierarchy within the group, and shifts the focus from stabilisation to explanation. Survivors attempting to hold this role often experience exhaustion, self-doubt, or overwhelm.

Survivor Only Groups

Survivor-only groups without trained facilitation pose an elevated risk of destabilisation. When recognition material emerges without containment, emotional intensity can escalate rapidly. Participants may attempt to manage discussion, regulate others, or provide guidance beyond their capacity. Individuals who assume leadership roles often become overwhelmed, even when their intentions are well-intended.

Without containment, groups may fragment, develop competing narratives, split along lines of severity, or collapse following the disclosure of a conflict or crisis. These outcomes reflect the absence of clinical structure rather than the lack of survivor motivation.

Trust and Clinician Understanding

Trust is strongly influenced by survivors' perception of the clinician's understanding of CPA-PA dynamics. Many survivors report previous clinical encounters characterised by curiosity or fascination without sustained therapeutic engagement when the material became complex. When clinicians demonstrate familiarity with concealment, silence, externally directed relational positioning, recognition-driven destabilisation, and intergenerational fear patterns, pressure on peers decreases, and testing behaviours reduce. Survivors are often surprised when clinicians recognise these dynamics. Explicit acknowledgement that these experiences are clinically understood can stabilise group engagement and reduce urgency for peer validation.

Infiltration and Boundary Risks

Because this area remains under-researched, boundary concerns may arise when individuals seek information rather than support. Survivors may express concern about alienating parents, extended family members, or others connected to the relational system who may indirectly access group spaces. Researchers or professionals may also approach groups seeking insight without fully understanding stabilisation requirements.

Clear boundaries regarding confidentiality, external communication, speaking invitations, and information sharing are protective. Transparency about the group's purpose and limits reduces role confusion and protects members.

Clinical Placement Decisions

Not all survivors are ready for group work during Phase I. Indicators that individual stabilisation may be required first include active destabilisation, strong urgency for answers, difficulty tolerating others' narratives, persistent comparison, inability to maintain personal boundaries, or significant risk of suicidality.

Placement into individual work is framed as a matter of pacing rather than exclusion. Survivors are supported to understand that the capacity to remain regulated in shared space is itself a stabilisation milestone.

Group Safety Orientation

Phase I group work begins with an explicit safety framework. Members are informed that the group is not a space for investigative disclosure, narrative verification, or relational decision-making. The emphasis is on stabilisation, recognition, tolerance, and development of shared space capacity. Guidelines include pacing disclosure, respecting different levels of developmental impact, avoiding directive advice, and recognising the difference between sharing experience and providing formulation. Permission to pause, step back, or limit detail is normalised.

Suicidality and Boundary Breaches

If guidelines are not followed, facilitators prioritise stabilisation over correction. Discussion may be redirected, paused, or moved to individual follow-up. When suicidality emerges, group containment immediately shifts to safety procedures consistent with clinical governance. Members are informed at the outset that the group cannot function as a crisis service, and that disclosure of imminent risk will activate individual support pathways.

Purpose of Group Work in Phase I

Within the HQTP, group work in Phase I is used to reduce isolation, support recognition tolerance, and allow survivors to experience shared space without loss of identity continuity. It is not used for trauma processing, relational decision-making, or narrative correction at this stage. When structured within containment, group work can support stabilisation. Without containment, group dynamics may replicate externally directed relational positioning, loyalty pressure, and identity destabilisation. Recognition of these dynamics allows clinicians to structure groups as stabilisation environments that protect both survivors and facilitators.

Group Readiness and Contraindications

Group participation during Phase I is determined by stabilisation capacity rather than motivation or insight. Survivors may express a strong desire for group connection while lacking the capacity to remain regulated in a shared recognition space. Readiness, therefore, reflects the ability to tolerate difference, uncertainty, and partial understanding without the need for urgent resolution.

Indicators of group readiness include the ability to pause when distressed, to maintain personal boundaries while others speak, to tolerate hearing material that differs from one's own experience, and to accept that formulation may remain incomplete. Survivors who can identify early signs of destabilisation and use previously established regulatory strategies are more likely to benefit from group participation.

Contraindications for Phase I group work include active recognition shock without containment, strong urgency for answers, reliance on peers for formulation, persistent comparison, difficulty tolerating others' narratives, significant risk of suicidality, unstable identity organisation, or inability to differentiate personal experience from peer material. Survivors who experience pressure to educate, correct, or manage other members may also require individual work first.

Group participation may also be paused when authority displacement dynamics intensify, when subgroup loyalty pressure emerges, or when exposure to others' material produces sustained dysregulation between sessions. Pause is framed as pacing rather than removal.

When contraindications are present, individual stabilisation work focuses on recognising tolerance, developing boundaries, differentiating authority, and remaining present in shared space without urgency for resolution. Group readiness is revisited iteratively rather than treated as a fixed threshold.

Within the HQTP, group placement decisions are understood as containment decisions. Entry into the group signals sufficient stabilisation to tolerate relational variability without loss of identity continuity, while delayed entry reflects protective pacing rather than treatment limitation.

Clinical Position on Timing of Group Work

Survivor Only Groups: Clinical Caution and Containment Considerations

Survivor-led groups often emerge in response to prolonged isolation, lack of recognition, and limited access to clinicians with relevant experience. These groups can provide validation, language development, and relief from invisibility. Many survivors describe the first experience of being understood occurring in peer spaces rather than clinical environments. This function is important and should not be minimised.

However, within Phase I of the HQTP, survivor-only groups are conceptualised as high-variability environments that may exceed stabilisation capacity without structured containment. In the absence of a trained facilitator, group processes may shift rapidly toward recognition urgency, comparison of developmental impact, formation of implicit hierarchies, and pressure to adopt shared interpretations before individual formulations are established.

A recurring pattern involves members entering the space to seek clarification about whether they were alienated, thereby placing other survivors in an unintended explanatory or counselling role. This dynamic can create strain for members who feel responsible for providing answers while still navigating their own recognition process. Survivors with more articulated narratives may be positioned as informal educators, while others may feel pressure to accept frameworks before they are ready, contributing to withdrawal, conflict, or subgroup formation.

Splitting dynamics may emerge around perceived severity of developmental impact, including distinctions related to abduction experiences, exposure to family violence, familicide threat or occurrence, medical or psychological FDIOA presentations, and prolonged concealment. These distinctions are often clinically meaningful but can also become relational organising forces within unstructured peer environments. Loyalty pressure, disagreement about interpretation, or attempts to manage group direction may lead to fragmentation.

Without facilitation, emotional pacing may become inconsistent. Recognition material can surface rapidly, members may share highly distressing experiences without containment, and others may suppress disclosure to avoid overwhelming the group. Survivors whose histories involve extreme or chronic threat may feel silenced, while those earlier in recognition may experience destabilisation from exposure to material beyond their window of tolerance.

Another risk involves boundary diffusion. Members may attempt to provide crisis support, monitor each other's safety, or assume responsibility for distressed peers. Although driven by care, this can exceed individual capacity and reproduce earlier dynamics of role inversion. Survivors may leave interactions feeling responsible, inadequate, or emotionally flooded.

These environments may also be vulnerable to external pressures. Survivors describe concern about misrepresentation, unsolicited requests for disclosure, or the presence of individuals whose motivations are unclear. Even perceived risk can reduce psychological safety and increase vigilance.

For these reasons, the protocol does not position survivor-only groups as a substitute for stabilisation work. Instead, they are understood as adjunct peer spaces that may support validation when participation occurs alongside individual clinical containment.

Clinical guidance emphasises preparation rather than prohibition. Survivors benefit from clear boundaries before entering peer spaces, including limits on explanatory roles, permission not to disclose, strategies for pausing participation, and identification of a clinician to process material that emerges. Participation is framed as optional, time-limited, and reversible.

Where clinicians are aware that a survivor is participating in peer groups, Phase I work includes discussion of pacing, differentiation between personal experience and others' narratives, recognition of comparison triggers, and planning for withdrawal if destabilisation occurs. This approach preserves the validating function of peer connection while protecting stabilisation.

Within the HQTP, the absence of structure does not imply the absence of value. It signals the need for parallel containment. Survivor-only groups can provide recognition, but stabilisation, formulation, and risk management remain clinical responsibilities.

Clinician Preparation for Phase I Work

Phase I requires clinicians to work without rushing formulation, interpretation, or relational conclusions. Survivors may present with fragmented recognition, fluctuating certainty, and a strong urgency for meaning while their capacity for stabilisation is still developing. The clinical task is to slow the process without dismissing the survivor's reality.

Survivors often expect clinicians to either provide definitive answers or disengage when narratives become complex. Maintaining steady engagement while tolerating uncertainty is therefore a central competency. Curiosity must be paired with containment rather than escalation of disclosure.

Requests for validation frequently reflect safety seeking rather than a demand for interpretation. Clinicians focus on helping survivors tolerate not knowing, differentiate memory from conclusion, and remain oriented when new understanding emerges.

Authority dynamics require careful pacing. Interpretation, reframing, or attempts to resolve relational questions too quickly can be experienced as influence rather than support. Transparent reasoning, collaborative formulation, and explicit permission to revisit understanding reduce this risk.

Clinicians should anticipate oscillation rather than linear progress. Periods of clarity may be followed by doubt, emotional activation, or withdrawal. These shifts reflect recognition processes rather than resistance.

Common practitioner pressures include the urgency to provide answers, pressure to correct perceived injustice, and discomfort with prolonged ambiguity. Phase I emphasises supervision, pacing awareness, and differentiation between survivor urgency and clinical timing.

Preparation, therefore, centres on the capacity for containment. The clinician's ability to remain steady while meaning develops is a primary stabilising factor within Phase I.

Phase I Core Clinical Tasks

Phase I focuses on stabilisation before interpretation. The clinical tasks centre on helping the survivor remain psychologically safe while recognition develops, rather than helping them reach conclusions about relationships, history, or responsibility.

Establishing Epistemic Safety

Survivors need to experience that therapy is a place where uncertainty can exist without pressure to decide what is true, who is right, or what action must follow. Example: a survivor asks whether their memories mean they were alienated. Instead of confirming or rejecting, the clinician helps them hold the question, notice what arises emotionally, and continue building understanding over time.

Pacing Recognition

Recognition often emerges unevenly and can destabilise functioning even when accurate. Clinicians monitor activation linked to new understanding and, when necessary, slow disclosure. Example: after reading old court material, a survivor experiences insomnia and rumination. The clinician pauses narrative exploration and shifts to orientation, regulation, and containment before continuing.

Stabilising Identity Continuity

Survivors may experience shifts in self-understanding as relational narratives change. Phase I supports maintaining a coherent sense of self while new information is considered. Example: a survivor begins to reinterpret childhood loyalty as a matter of survival rather than choice and fears that they "do not know who they are anymore". The clinician anchors current roles, strengths, and present identity while meaning develops.

Developing Differentiation Capacity

Survivors learn to separate memory from interpretation, feeling from conclusion, and curiosity from urgency. Example: a survivor states, "That means my whole childhood was a lie". The clinician helps differentiate between emerging insight, emotional impact, and conclusions that may still be forming.

Strengthening Regulation in Relational Activation

General regulation strategies may not hold when attachment themes emerge. Clinicians practise regulation specifically in response to relational triggers. Example: discussion of a parent leads to a shutdown despite otherwise stable functioning. Regulation is practised while remaining gently in contact with the topic rather than avoiding it entirely.

Authority Recalibration

Therapy positions formulation as collaborative rather than declarative. Survivors experience guidance without being repositioned. Example: a survivor repeatedly asks the clinician to decide whether contact is safe. The clinician provides frameworks, explores factors, and supports decision capacity without issuing directives.

Preparing for Later Phases Without Entering Them

Psychoeducation about recognition-driven destabilisation reduces fear during shifts. Example: a survivor worries they are "getting worse" after increased clarity. The clinician explains recognition-linked activation and links the experience to protocol pacing rather than regression.

Across Phase I, progress is reflected in increased tolerance for uncertainty, reduced urgency to reach relational conclusions, improved regulation when recognition emerges, and preservation of identity continuity as meaning develops.

Phase I Indicators of Progress and Indicators to Pause

Phase I progression is determined by stabilisation capacity rather than insight acquisition. Increased understanding does not indicate readiness to advance if recognition produces identity destabilisation, urgency, or behavioural risk. Indicators, therefore, focus on how survivors hold emerging meaning rather than on whether meaning has emerged.

Indicators of Progress

Progress within Phase I is reflected in the survivor's growing ability to remain psychologically organised while recognition develops. Survivors demonstrate increased tolerance for uncertainty without urgent pressure to reach relational conclusions. Questions about childhood, parents, or past decisions can be held over to subsequent sessions rather than resolved immediately.

Recognition events produce emotional activation that remains within a workable range. Distress may occur, but the survivor can orient, regulate, and return to present functioning without prolonged collapse. Narrative flexibility begins to emerge. Survivors can consider multiple possibilities about past experiences without rigid certainty or immediate rejection of alternative interpretations.

Identity continuity is preserved during the development of insight. Survivors may describe shifts in understanding while maintaining connection to current roles, relationships, and future orientation. Relational triggers become more predictable. Survivors recognise early signs of destabilisation, such as rumination, urgency, shame activation, or sleep disruption, and can use stabilisation strategies before escalation.

Authority dynamics shift. Survivors increasingly seek collaboration rather than decisions from the clinician and demonstrate emerging confidence in their own pacing. Recognition can occur without immediate behavioural action. Survivors may notice new meaning without feeling compelled to confront others, change contact arrangements, or disclose prematurely.

Indicators to Pause Phase Progression

Phase work pauses when recognition exceeds containment capacity, even if insight appears accurate. Urgency for relational action emerges during periods of activation, including pressure to confront family members, disclose widely, or make irreversible decisions.

Narrative rigidity increases. Survivors move rapidly toward certainty accompanied by emotional constriction, panic, or intolerance of alternative perspectives. Identity destabilisation indicators emerge as previously defined within the crisis architecture, including statements that reflect loss of self-continuity, existential collapse, or the perceived irreversibility of developmental loss. Recognition events produce sustained functional disruption, such as sleep collapse, inability to work, withdrawal from support systems, or persistent rumination that does not settle between sessions.

Increased reliance on the clinician for certainty, reassurance, or decision-making indicates that authority recalibration has not stabilised. Avoidance of previously tolerable material emerges, suggesting narrowing capacity rather than integration. Behavioural risk indicators appear, including temporal framing of suicidality, concealment behaviours, retaliatory fixation, or cognitive constriction.

When pause indicators are present, the protocol returns to Phase I stabilisation tasks. This is framed as an alignment with the containment architecture rather than a regression. Phase progression occurs only when recognition can be experienced without loss of psychological organisation, urgency for action, or identity collapse. These pause indicators operationalise the identity-collapse risk described earlier and serve as decision markers rather than diagnostic conclusions.

Applied Safeguarding Extension: When Current Child Risk or School Disclosure Is Present

Although the HQTP is primarily a clinical treatment protocol for adult survivors, adult survivor work may reveal current risks involving children, schools, clinicians, or allied professionals who remain exposed to similar dynamics in real time. The following safeguarding extension is included because CPA-PA, familial abduction, concealment, coercive control, and retaliatory parent behaviour do not only affect the survivor in therapy. They may also place children, educators, clinicians, and institutions at risk when disclosure occurs.

This material is not intended to convert the HQTP into a child protection manual, forensic tool, or school policy document. Rather, it provides clinically relevant orientation for mental health practitioners who may need to recognise when adult survivor work intersects with current child safety, school disclosure, mandatory reporting, practitioner safety, or institutional retaliation.

Structured Assessment and Safety Protocol

High-quality safeguarding assessment rests on objective observations across settings, careful verification of guardianship and court orders where relevant, and systematic collection of collateral school and health records when this sits within role, consent, law, and organisational policy. In classrooms, staff should document what was seen and heard, by whom, and in what context, including the child's non-verbal cues and any observable change when a targeted, allied, rejected, or feared parent is referenced.

Clinicians and school staff should document patterns over time, including the history of moves, changes in attendance or presentation, immediate risks, known safe adults, and any concerns about concealment or restricted visibility. Interviews or conversations should occur in settings that feel predictable and low-threat, with developmentally appropriate nonverbal modalities available when speech feels unsafe.

Where concern arises, a confidential leadership or safeguarding consultation should occur promptly. This discussion should determine whether continued monitoring is sufficient, whether urgent specialist consultation is required, or whether statutory reporting obligations have been met. If there is immediate danger, child protection and police involvement, including protective orders where appropriate, may be necessary.

If direct action may escalate risk, further documentation, consultation, and safeguarding planning should be undertaken in accordance with legal, organisational, and mandatory reporting requirements. A written safety plan should identify safe adults, supervised transitions between school and clinic where required, secure communication pathways, and named staff responsibilities. Reporting to child protection, statutory authorities, or the court should be timely, behaviourally anchored, and explicit about limitations created by safety constraints, confidentiality, restricted access to information, or the child's fear of disclosure.

Intervention Pathways Adapted to CPA-PA

Intervention proceeds in phases. The first priority is containment and safety, stabilising the environment and mitigating immediate risks. Engagement and trust-building come next, using predictable sessions and modalities such as art, play, writing, rhythm, and somatic regulation that allow expression where direct speech feels unsafe.

Trauma integration and attachment repair follow only when conditions allow. Where safe caregivers are involved, cautious dyadic work may be considered when clinical and protective indicators support it. Exposure to feared, rejected, or highly charged relational material must be titrated carefully, remain within the child's window of tolerance, and directly and safely address rage, fear, shame, loyalty conflict, and confusion.

Integration and risk management then consolidate gains, plan for relapse indicators, and consider reunification steps only where safety and clinical indicators support them. Joint therapy with an alienating, coercive, violent, or unsafe parent is contraindicated until abuse dynamics have been thoroughly assessed and protective conditions are in place.

Legal and Statutory Interface

Legal and statutory systems require clear, behaviourally anchored information. Reports should describe behaviour and context rather than unsupported inference, explain the assessment methods used, state any constraints created by safety or limited access to information, and distinguish observed information from clinical opinion.

Where reporting is required, communication should occur promptly and remain within the practitioner's professional role. Recommendations should be clear where the practitioner is appropriately qualified and authorised to make them. These may include supervised contact, protective monitoring, statutory review, school-based safety planning, or referral for specialist assessment where indicated.

Delay can prolong exposure to harm and weaken the protective value of the clinical record. At the same time, the HQTP does not position clinicians as investigators, advocates for a litigating party, or substitute decision-makers for courts or statutory authorities.

Practitioner and Staff Safety

Practitioners in this field may face harassment, threats, complaints, reputational attacks, and attempts at professional intimidation (Price-Tobler, 2024b). Services should embed safety protocols, supervision, and rapid staff debriefing, and liaise with senior leadership, legal advisers, insurers, unions, police, or statutory authorities when behaviours escalate. Protecting clinicians is part of protecting the child, because retaliatory pressure often aims to shut down assessment, reporting, and treatment.

International Oversight Gaps

System safeguards are uneven. Homeschooling regulations, identity-verification practices, school enrolment processes, medical records, relocation oversight, and interagency communication vary widely across jurisdictions. Weak oversight can allow concealment to persist, particularly where children are moved across regions, schools, countries, or service systems. Clinicians and school leaders should familiarise themselves with local blind spots, advocate for reforms that increase child visibility, and treat record verification as a safeguarding function rather than clerical administration.

School Safety Protocol: Protecting Children and Staff After a Disclosure

When a child discloses abuse or coercive control within the family, schools are often the first place where these truths surface. In these moments, educators have a dual responsibility: to safeguard the child and to protect themselves from potential parental retaliation.

Parents involved in coercive, enmeshed, or alienating dynamics may respond with rage, harassment, complaints, or even litigation, not only directed at the child but also at the professionals who fulfilled their mandated reporting responsibilities (Palusci, 2018; Social Work Today, 2016). This creates risks that are both personal and institutional.

Suggestions for Schools

Educators must first provide a calm, safe space, listen carefully, and reassure the child that speaking up was the right thing to do. They should explain that the information will need to be passed to people who can help (NSW Department of Education [DoE], 2022). They must avoid promising secrecy or confronting the parent directly. Disclosures should be documented precisely, including date, time, setting, and the child's words verbatim, with records stored securely in line with school policy (National Association of School Psychologists [NASP], 2020).

Mandatory reporting pathways must then be followed. Reports may need to be lodged with statutory child protection authorities such as the Department of Communities and Justice in New South Wales or Child Protection in Victoria. Staff should follow their jurisdiction's specific reporting pathway and school policy. In New South Wales, schools should follow the Department of Education's child protection procedures and mandatory reporting pathways, including the Mandatory Reporter Guide, the Child Protection Helpline, and, where relevant, the Child Wellbeing Unit. Parent notification should not be managed informally by individual staff members when doing so may increase the risk to the child, compromise a statutory response, or expose staff to retaliation. Victoria's Four Critical Actions framework similarly emphasises that parent or carer contact must be carefully managed where child safety, police involvement, or statutory reporting issues are present.

Leadership involvement is essential. Principals and safeguarding leads should be informed immediately so that no individual staff member is left to manage a volatile parent alone. When risk is anticipated, meetings with parents should include senior staff and adhere to school safety procedures. In extreme cases, police advice or attendance may be required. Schools may have authority under trespass and safety legislation to restrict access to their grounds if a parent's behaviour threatens staff or students. Communication should be kept in writing and confined to official channels to reduce the risk of misrepresentation.

Legal and professional protections must be engaged early. Threats of lawsuits, defamation claims, or complaints should be referred directly to the Department of Education's legal services, the relevant employer, union, insurer, or professional body. Staff should avoid responding personally to legal correspondence and should seek guidance through their employer, union, insurer, professional body, or legal adviser. Educators may have legal, organisational, or professional protections when acting in good faith within their reporting obligations, but these protections depend on jurisdiction, employment context, and policy. Securing legal and organisational support promptly is therefore vital for staff protection.

Confidentiality is another safeguard. Information shared with parents should be restricted to what is necessary for the child's immediate educational needs. Counselling notes or child protection records should never be disclosed unless legally compelled or authorised through appropriate processes. Guidance in Australian and international frameworks recognises that counsellors and schools may need to withhold information where disclosure would undermine trust, compromise safety, or increase risk to the child.

Finally, staff wellbeing must be prioritised. Disclosure work and subsequent retaliation can be traumatising for educators. Access to counselling, structured debriefing, and supportive supervision is essential (Australian Institute for Teaching and School Leadership [AITSL], 2023). Principals and leaders play a vital role in affirming and protecting staff who follow procedure, ensuring that no teacher feels isolated amid parental hostility.

The guiding principle is clear: educators are mandated reporters, not investigators. Their duty is to listen, document, and report through statutory channels while maintaining professional and personal safety by strictly adhering to established protocols. Protection for both children and staff comes from staying within policy, following procedures, documenting all actions, and ensuring no staff member carries the risk alone.

Case Examples

In one de-identified professional consultation example, a child disclosed abuse and withholding of contact with a parent. Following school involvement, the alleged abusive parent escalated through anger, legal threats, and complaints against staff. The example illustrates why schools require clear documentation, leadership involvement, statutory reporting pathways, and protection for staff who respond to disclosures in good faith.

In a United States professional liability case, a parent sued school personnel following a child's disclosure of abuse. Although the matter was dismissed, the process placed considerable strain on the school community (Social Work Today, 2016). This example demonstrates that even when professionals act appropriately, the complaint or litigation process itself can become a source of institutional stress.

Recent United States parental-rights cases also demonstrate the broader risk of escalation when parents perceive that schools have exceeded their role or spoken privately with a child. Although cases such as *Foote v. Ludlow* and *Regino v. Staley* involved gender identity rather than abuse disclosure, they illustrate how quickly school-based conversations with children can become the subject of litigation, public controversy, or professional attack. These cases should be understood as examples of institutional vulnerability and retaliatory pressure, not as direct precedents for abuse disclosure.

Australian data also confirm the occupational risk. Principal wellbeing research has identified high levels of threats, violence, bullying, gossip, and slander directed at school leaders, with parents and caregivers frequently reported as a major source of these behaviours (Phillips & Sen, 2022; Department for Education [South Australia], 2023).

Practice Standard Statement

Schools must treat every child disclosure as both a safeguarding matter and a potential occupational hazard. Educators are obligated to protect children through mandated reporting and to protect themselves by following documentation, reporting, supervision, and secure communication protocols.

Institutions must support staff with strong leadership, access to legal protections, timely debriefing, and wellbeing resources. Embedding these practices into school culture ensures that children are heard safely and that educators are supported and protected when fulfilling their professional duty.

Phase II: Meaning Reconstruction and Identity Repair

Phase II becomes clinically available only when the previously described readiness markers are reliably met. Its inclusion here does not indicate an immediate transition. Once stabilisation has created sufficient psychological safety, the survivor may begin recognising the relational conditions that shaped their development. Whereas Phase I establishes regulation, containment, and identity continuity, Phase II introduces careful recognition of survival adaptations, relational conditioning, and inherited narratives without destabilising the organising sense of self.

Recognition in this context is not conceptualised as a purely cognitive realisation. It is a developmental process involving shifts in meaning, reinterpretation of autobiographical experience, and gradual differentiation between externally imposed narratives and lived relational reality. Survivors frequently enter this phase with emerging questions about identity, attachment history, family roles, and the accuracy of long-held beliefs. These questions reflect developmental readiness rather than pathology.

Clinical work in Phase II, therefore, focuses on supporting recognition while preserving epistemic safety. Survivors are assisted to examine patterns of compliance, loyalty conflict, silence, role reversal, and narrative restriction as adaptive responses to relational environments characterised by coercion, reality distortion, and attachment disruption. The therapeutic task is not to replace one narrative with another, but to expand the survivor's capacity to hold uncertainty, complexity, and multiple possibilities without urgency for resolution.

This phase introduces structured differentiation processes through which survivors begin separating internal experience from inherited meaning structures. Differentiation may involve recognising the function of survival strategies, identifying discrepancies between internal perception and external narrative, and developing language for experiences that were previously unnamed or misinterpreted. Meaning reconstruction emerges gradually as survivors integrate new understanding without collapsing identity continuity.

Recognition in Phase II is inherently destabilising when it involves developmental betrayal, institutional reinforcement of distorted narratives, or awareness of lost attachment time. For this reason, interpretive depth is continuously titrated against regulatory capacity so that emerging insight remains psychologically survivable. Movement through this phase reflects increased tolerance for ambiguity, reduced urgency to resolve, and the preservation of identity coherence amid changes in meaning.

Phase II, therefore, represents the bridge between stabilisation and grief work. It prepares the survivor to encounter loss, attachment rupture, and developmental impact with sufficient psychological structure to prevent identity collapse, ensuring that subsequent phases deepen integration rather than reproduce destabilisation.

Core Clinical Function of Phase II

The core clinical function of Phase II is the development of recognition capacity without destabilisation of identity continuity. Whereas Phase I establishes safety, regulation, containment, and the conditions required for psychological survivability, Phase II introduces the careful examination of how relational environments shaped perception, behaviour, belief formation, and self-organisation across development.

This phase does not aim to produce definitive conclusions about the past. Instead, it supports the survivor's capacity to observe previously automatic patterns as adaptive responses that emerged within conditions of coercion, loyalty conflict, relational threat, and narrative constraint. Recognition is therefore approached as a developmental process rather than an interpretive event.

A central task involves differentiating survival adaptation from identity. Many survivors enter treatment with internal experiences organised around certainty, compliance, avoidance, or narrative rigidity that functioned historically to preserve relational safety. Phase II creates space to recognise these patterns without requiring their immediate revision. The emphasis remains on expanding reflective capacity while maintaining psychological stability.

Recognition in this phase frequently occurs in layered form. Survivors may notice inconsistencies in relational narratives, shifts in emotional responses when discussing family history, or emerging awareness that previously unquestioned beliefs served protective functions. These observations are approached collaboratively and without pressure to resolve them. The therapeutic task is to strengthen tolerance for ambiguity while preserving epistemic safety.

Differentiation represents the second central function of Phase II. Survivors gradually learn to distinguish between externally shaped narratives and internally experienced meaning, between behavioural adaptation and relational agreement, and between inherited interpretations and present-day evaluative capacity. This differentiation is developmental rather than corrective. It supports the emergence of internal authority without destabilising previously stabilising structures.

Meaning reconstruction begins in this phase but remains provisional. Survivors are supported in exploring multiple explanatory possibilities, revising timelines, and considering alternative interpretations of relational events while retaining the right not to conclude. The ability to hold partial understanding without urgency for certainty represents a primary indicator of Phase II progress.

Throughout this work, pacing functions as a stabilisation intervention. Recognition that exceeds the capacity for integration may produce identity destabilisation, a sense of urgency for answers, or a return to rigid narrative positions. For this reason, Phase II prioritises titrated exploration, repetition, and explicit permission to pause. The objective is not the acquisition of insight but the expansion of meaning tolerance.

Within the HQTP, Phase II therefore serves as the bridge between stabilisation and deeper integrative work. It enables survivors to encounter developmental reality in a manner that protects identity coherence, reduces reenactment of coercive interpretive dynamics, and establishes the reflective foundation required for subsequent grief, integration, and relational reorganisation phases.

Recognition Processes in Phase II

Recognition within Phase II is conceptualised as a developmental process rather than a discrete moment of insight. It involves the gradual emergence of awareness regarding the relational conditions, narrative structures, and adaptive strategies that shaped the survivor's developmental environment. This process unfolds incrementally and often occurs in layered form, reflecting shifts in meaning rather than the recovery of isolated information.

Survivors frequently notice inconsistencies in previously accepted narratives, changes in emotional responses when discussing family history, or an emerging awareness that certain beliefs historically served to preserve relational safety. Recognition may involve subtle shifts in language, increased questioning of long-held assumptions, or the capacity to observe patterns that were previously experienced as fixed reality. These developments represent an expansion of reflective capacity rather than resolution.

Recognition processes are typically non-linear. Periods of clarity may be followed by doubt, re-stabilisation, or temporary return to familiar narrative positions. Such oscillation reflects the nervous system's effort to maintain continuity of identity while accommodating new meaning. Movement between certainty and uncertainty is understood as expected and clinically informative rather than as resistance or regression.

Recognition may emerge across multiple domains simultaneously. Survivors may begin to reconsider relational roles, reinterpret behavioural adaptations, identify previously unrecognised loyalty pressures, or recognise the function of silence, compliance, or narrative restriction within earlier environments. This does not require definitive conclusions about intent, accuracy, or responsibility. The clinical task is to support observation without interpretive pressure.

A central feature of recognition in this population is the experience of epistemic disruption. Survivors may describe a growing awareness that previously trusted sources of meaning were incomplete, constrained, or shaped by coercive relational dynamics. This awareness can produce disorientation, emotional activation, or a sense of urgency for certainty. Recognition is therefore approached as a regulated process requiring pacing, containment, and explicit permission for ambiguity.

Clinicians support recognition by facilitating curiosity rather than directing interpretation. Questions are framed to expand reflective space rather than to confirm explanatory narratives. Attention is directed toward shifts in perception, emotional responses, and relational expectations as indicators of recognition. Repetition, summarisation, and gentle linking across sessions function as stabilising mechanisms that allow meaning to evolve without overwhelming the survivor.

Recognition processes often involve recontextualisation rather than memory recovery. Experiences previously understood as personal failure, relational rejection, or individual pathology may gradually be recognised as adaptive responses to environments characterised by coercion, loyalty conflict, narrative control, or attachment disruption. This reframing reduces self-blame while preserving psychological stability.

Importantly, recognition is not equated with confrontation, decision-making, or relational action. The purpose of this phase is to support awareness that remains psychologically survivable. Premature movement toward behavioural change, confrontation, or definitive conclusions may exceed the capacity for integration and risk destabilising identity. For this reason, recognition remains provisional throughout Phase II.

Within the HQTP, recognition processes establish the conditions required for differentiation to emerge. As survivors develop the capacity to observe adaptation without immediate reinterpretation, space emerges in which inherited meaning structures can be distinguished from internally experienced reality. Recognition, therefore, represents the first movement in developmental reorganisation, preparing the survivor for the subsequent differentiation work.

Differentiation

Differentiation is the central developmental task of Phase II.

Following recognition, survivors begin the gradual process of separating their internal experience from narratives that were imposed under conditions of coercion, loyalty pressure, fear, and developmental dependency. Differentiation does not involve rejecting family members, making contact and boundary decisions involving the alienating parent, or establishing behavioural boundaries. It refers first to an internal psychological process: the restoration of the survivor's capacity to experience thoughts, emotions, memories, and meanings as their own.

In the context of child psychological abuse in contexts of parental alienation and/or abduction, identity formation often occurred within environments where independent interpretation was discouraged, punished, or reframed as disloyalty. Over time, this produces an internal structure in which external narratives become fused with self-concept. Survivors may experience beliefs, emotional reactions, and relational expectations that feel self-generated but originate in conditioning. Differentiation, therefore, begins when survivors can observe their internal experience without immediately assuming it is true, required, or safe to act on.

This process is frequently destabilising. As internal separation emerges, survivors may face confusion, guilt, and fear of betrayal. They may also struggle with identity uncertainty and oscillate between competing realities. Long-standing loyalty conditioning may activate intensely when previously unquestioned beliefs are examined. Survivors may report sudden doubt about their own perceptions, intrusive defensive narratives about the alienating parent, or a return to familiar self-blame patterns. These experiences do not indicate regression. They reflect the nervous system responding to perceived relational threat as internal autonomy increases.

Within the HQTP, differentiation is conceptualised as observational before behavioural. The clinical aim is not to change external relationships but to support the survivor in recognising distinctions that were previously collapsed. This includes the emerging capacity to notice differences between emotional responses and installed interpretations, between fear responses and present danger, and between responsibility for others' emotions and responsibility for one's own wellbeing. Survivors begin to recognise that multiple internal voices may be present and that these voices can be examined without requiring immediate resolution.

Differentiation commonly involves separating the survivor's authentic emotional experience from internalised narratives associated with coercive environments. Survivors may begin to distinguish feelings of sadness from beliefs that sadness is disloyal, anger from beliefs that anger is dangerous, curiosity from beliefs that questioning is betrayal, and longing from beliefs that connection is unsafe. Similarly, memories may be experienced as subjective recollections rather than evidence that must be defended, denied, or reconciled with external authority.

A central component of this phase is recognising internalised relational voices. Survivors often discover that critical, minimising, or loyalty-enforcing thoughts reflect previously external dynamics that have become internal regulatory mechanisms. Differentiation allows these experiences to be approached as learned relational patterns rather than inherent character traits. This shift reduces shame and supports the development of reflective capacity, enabling survivors to consider where beliefs originated, how they functioned adaptively, and whether they remain necessary.

The clinician's stance during differentiation is deliberately restrained. Premature encouragement toward confrontation, disclosure, boundary setting, or relational decision-making risks replicating earlier experiences of imposed meaning and may destabilise emerging autonomy. Instead, clinicians support language that reflects observation rather than conclusion, such as noticing shifts in internal dialogue, recognising moments of uncertainty without forcing interpretation, and tolerating contradictory emotional states. The therapeutic relationship provides a context in which internal distinction can occur without pressure for action.

Differentiation also involves recalibrating responsibility. Survivors frequently carry an enduring sense of obligation for the emotional stability of others, particularly alienating parents. As internal separation develops, survivors begin to recognise the differences between empathy and responsibility, care and compliance, and relational connection and relational control. This recalibration does not require immediate behavioural change; rather, it allows survivors to experience their own needs as psychologically legitimate.

Importantly, differentiation does not produce immediate clarity. The process is characterised by tolerance for ambiguity, oscillation, and gradual increases in reflective capacity. Survivors may move repeatedly between established narratives and emerging perspectives. This movement represents developmental progression rather than indecision. The capacity to hold uncertainty without collapse is itself a marker of differentiation.

Early indicators of emerging differentiation include subtle shifts in language and response patterns. Survivors may begin to describe beliefs as something they were told rather than something inherently true, pause before defending familiar narratives, recognise the presence of multiple emotional responses to the same relational memory, or question previously automatic assumptions about responsibility and loyalty. Increased tolerance for ambiguity, reduced urgency to resolve the family narrative, and the ability to observe internal reactions without immediate self-correction are significant markers of progress.

Within the phased architecture, differentiation establishes the psychological conditions necessary for later grief work. Without internal separation, grief processing risks being organised around defence, loyalty conflict, or narrative preservation rather than authentic loss recognition. Phase II, therefore, prioritises differentiation as a stabilising developmental achievement rather than an endpoint. The goal is not certainty, but the restoration of internal space in which experience can be felt, examined, and gradually integrated without coercion.

Differentiation marks the beginning of psychological autonomy. It represents the survivor's increasing capacity to experience an internal world that is no longer fully organised around external authority, relational threat, or conditioned meaning. This emerging internal freedom forms the foundation for Phase III, where grief, loss, and developmental mourning can be approached within a context of sufficient stability and self-recognition.

Emerging Self and Identity Reorganisation

Emerging self and identity reorganisation represent the stabilising developmental function of Phase II. Following recognition and differentiation, survivors often move between familiar adaptive identity states and emerging experiences of self that feel less organised by monitoring, guilt, or relational consequence. This movement reflects developmental reorganisation rather than regression. Oscillation between these states is expected and indicates that identity is becoming more flexible rather than less stable.

In contexts of child psychological abuse in contexts of parental alienation and/or abduction, identity frequently developed in environments where survival depended on regulating another person's emotional state, anticipating consequences, and maintaining alignment with imposed narratives. As differentiation progresses, these organising structures begin to loosen. Survivors may experience moments in which they respond from their internal experience rather than from an adaptive role, followed by a rapid return to vigilance, guilt, or responsibility patterns. This oscillation is a core feature of identity reorganisation.

For example, a survivor may express a personal preference or emotional response in session and then immediately question whether doing so will lead to relational consequences. Relational consequence refers to the anticipated interpersonal effects that historically followed independent expression, such as emotional escalation, withdrawal of warmth, narrative correction, subtle punishment, or pressure to repair another person's distress. Even in the absence of a present threat, the nervous system may remain organised around the expectation that deviation will alter relational safety.

A survivor might, for instance, state a preference about contact, express uncertainty about a past narrative, or describe feeling differently than expected, and then rapidly monitor the clinician's response for signs of disappointment, tension, or evaluation. The concern is not whether the preference is reasonable but whether the expression itself will create an impact that must be managed. This may include anticipating that someone will become upset, that the survivor will be required to explain themselves, or that they will need to restore emotional equilibrium in the relationship.

Within Phase II, this anticipation is understood as learned relational mapping rather than evidence of current danger. The internal question is less "Is this safe to say?" and more "What will happen to the relationship if I say this?" As identity reorganisation progresses, survivors experience moments where their expression no longer triggers escalation, withdrawal, or the need to manage another person's emotional state, allowing for authentic self-expression. Cognitive-behavioural approaches are often introduced at this stage as stabilisation tools rather than corrective interventions. Cognitive behavioural therapy (CBT) supports survivors in noticing automatic thoughts associated with consequence anticipation, such as expectations of blame, responsibility, or relational disruption. Rather than challenging beliefs directly, Phase

II use of CBT emphasises gentle identification of thinking patterns, differentiation between past-based expectations and the present context, and the development of alternative interpretations that reduce immediate nervous system activation.

This process helps settle the brain by providing cognitive scaffolding that interrupts rapid threat prediction. When survivors can label an automatic thought, for example, “If I say this, something bad will happen,” the experience shifts from unquestioned expectation to observable mental activity. This shift reduces urgency, supports regulation, and allows the nervous system to remain engaged without immediate adaptive reorganisation.

For example, a survivor may cautiously express disagreement and then apologise immediately, not because expressing disagreement feels wrong, but because the body expects a relational shift. Using CBT-informed reflection, the clinician may help the survivor notice the sequence: expression, anticipatory thought, guilt activation, apology impulse. Naming this pattern does not invalidate the survivor’s experience; instead, it introduces predictability and reduces perceived threat. When no negative consequence occurs, confusion may arise before relief. Over time, consistent experiences of expression without relational penalty allow the nervous system to update its expectations, supporting the development of an identity that is not organised around anticipating consequences.

CBT also supports tolerance of ambiguity by helping survivors hold prediction and present experience simultaneously. A thought predicting relational consequence can be recognised as understandable given past experience, while remaining open to alternative outcomes in the present. This dual awareness reduces cognitive rigidity and supports identity reorganisation without forcing a change in belief.

This process is central to emerging self and identity reorganisation. Survivors are learning that relationships can tolerate difference, uncertainty, and incomplete expression without requiring rapid adaptation. Through this process, the absence of relational consequence becomes internalised as a new organising experience, allowing identity to stabilise around self-experience rather than relational prediction.

Emerging self-work also involves increased visibility of younger self-states. As relational safety becomes more consistent and differentiation reduces narrative pressure, aspects of the survivor's inner child may begin to emerge, particularly when discussing experiences that were not previously spoken about in depth. This emergence may occur through shifts in tone, affect, language, posture, or emotional intensity. The appearance of younger self material does not signal readiness for trauma processing. Instead, it reflects the nervous system recognising sufficient safety for previously contained experience to become perceptible.

For example, when describing a childhood experience, a survivor may shift from reflective narration into sudden vulnerability, confusion, or emotional exposure that feels developmentally younger than the surrounding discussion. Rather than interpreting this shift, Phase II work supports the survivor in remaining present with the experience while maintaining regulation and relational safety. The goal is not narrative completion but the stabilisation of self-experience across states.

Unconditional positive regard, as described by Rogers (1957), is clinically essential during this stage. Survivors whose identities were shaped within conditional relational environments often anticipate evaluation, correction, withdrawal, or consequence when vulnerable states emerge. Consistent unconditional positive regard communicates that oscillation, uncertainty, guilt, and younger self-expression are permissible and do not threaten relational stability. This stance creates the psychological conditions necessary for identity to develop without defensive reorganisation.

Clinicians enact unconditional positive regard through observable relational behaviours. This includes maintaining warmth when survivors move into monitoring or guilt states, allowing pauses without interpretive pressure, responding to uncertainty with curiosity rather than with urgency to clarify, and avoiding subtle signals that identity must stabilise quickly. Survivors learn that both adaptive identity and emerging self-experience can be held within the same relationship without loss of safety.

Emerging self and identity reorganisation require parallel competence in rupture and repair among clinicians. Because survivors are testing expression without consequence, perceived misattunements may activate historical expectations of correction, withdrawal, or relational instability. These moments are often subtle. A reflective statement may feel overly interpretive, a clarifying question may be experienced as evaluation, or a shift toward meaning-making may occur before the survivor feels ready. Survivors may respond by becoming quieter, moving into analytical language, over-explaining, apologising, or returning to adaptive identity states organised around performance and monitoring.

For example, a survivor may share a vulnerable memory, and the clinician offers a structured summary intended to demonstrate understanding. Although well-intended, the survivor may experience this as being redirected or misunderstood. The nervous system may activate rapidly, accompanied by internal commentary reflecting the companion voice. The survivor may withdraw emotionally or attempt to explain more clearly to prevent a perceived error. Within Phase II, this response is understood as activation of learned relational expectation rather than resistance.

Repair involves gently noticing the shift and prioritising relational safety over accuracy. The clinician may pause, acknowledge that their response may not have landed as intended, and invite clarification without pressure. Communicating that a misunderstanding carries no consequences within the therapeutic relationship provides a corrective experience. Over time, repeated repair demonstrates that expression need not be withdrawn following misattunement and that relational stability does not depend on precision, alignment, or narrative coherence.

A similar process may occur when clinicians ask clarifying questions. Survivors may experience questions as indicators that they are not explaining things properly, activating performance monitoring and anticipatory guilt. In these moments, the clinician reduces evaluative pressure by emphasising curiosity, normalising uncertainty, and reaffirming that there is no requirement to tell the story correctly. This shifts the relational frame from performance to exploration, weakening the authority of the companion voice.

Rupture and repair are particularly important when younger self-states emerge. If clinicians move too quickly toward meaning, survivors may become distant, minimise experience, or return to adaptive identity language. Repair involves slowing pace, acknowledging that the clinician may have moved ahead, and communicating that nothing needs to be concluded. The survivor learns that vulnerability does not create urgency and that relational connection can remain intact even when experience is incomplete.

Through repeated experiences of misattunement followed by repair, survivors internalise a new organising principle: relational disruption does not require identity suppression. This learning is central to emerging self-development and supports the survivor's capacity to remain present amid oscillating identity states without automatically returning to adaptive role organisation.

Another example involves guilt activation. A survivor may notice guilt arising when expressing a preference, resting, or deviating from historically required roles, even when no current consequences exist. Rather than directly challenging the guilt, Phase II work supports observing the guilt response while maintaining unconditional positive regard. Over time, survivors learn that guilt can be experienced without reorganising behaviour around it, allowing identity to develop alongside rather than within guilt regulation.

Early indicators of emerging self and identity reorganisation include increased tolerance for oscillation between adaptive and emerging self-states, reduced expectation of immediate relational consequences, moments of spontaneous recognition of preference, the appearance of younger self-experience without immediate shutdown, and the ability to remain in relational contact following perceived misattunement. Survivors may begin to experience identity as something that can shift without disappearing.

Within the phased architecture, emerging self and identity reorganisation establish the stability required for later grief work without identity collapse. When survivors can move between identity states while maintaining relational continuity, grief can be encountered without automatic return to adaptive role organisation. Phase II, therefore, prioritises identity reorganisation as a protective developmental achievement rather than a state of certainty.

Emerging self and identity reorganisation represent the survivor's growing ability to experience selfhood in moments of uncertainty and adaptation, without the immediate threat of relational consequences. It reflects the internalisation of relational experiences characterised by unconditional positive regard, consistent repair, and the weakening of the companion voice's authority. This stabilising process prepares the conditions for mourning, loss integration, and the repair of developmental grief to occur without destabilising the emerging sense of self.

Within Phase II, no single therapeutic modality is sufficient on its own. Instead, clinicians selectively draw on approaches that support stabilisation, differentiation, and the emergence of identity without accelerating trauma processing. Cognitive behavioural approaches help survivors identify automatic thoughts associated with anticipating consequences, activating guilt, and taking responsibility for others' emotional states, providing cognitive scaffolding that reduces immediate threat prediction and supports nervous system regulation. Attachment-informed work supports recognition of relational patterns organised around safety, alignment, and monitoring, allowing survivors to understand oscillation between adaptive identity and emerging self as developmentally coherent rather than contradictory. Psychodynamic perspectives support exploration of internalised relational voices, including the companion voice, enabling survivors to observe how past relational dynamics continue to shape present identity experience.

Across modalities, the organising clinical principle remains pacing rather than intervention intensity. Techniques are used to increase observation, language, and tolerance for uncertainty rather than to produce rapid cognitive change, emotional catharsis, or narrative resolution. This integrative stance ensures that the use of modalities remains aligned with Phase II objectives: stabilising identity reorganisation, reducing anticipatory consequences, and supporting the gradual emergence of internally anchored self-experience. One way this becomes visible in treatment is through the survivor's relationship to internalised coercive commentary and inherited survival-based thought.

The Evoked Companion: Internalised Relational Authority and Survival-Based Thought

Within the HQTP, the *evoked companion* may be understood as a clinically descriptive term for the survivor's internalised, fear-organised, relationally conditioned commentary that becomes active in response to attachment threat, shame, conflict, or perceived disloyalty. It is not proposed here as a formal diagnosis or standalone disorder. Rather, it refers to the lingering internal presence of coercive relational messaging: the survivor's experience of carrying forward a way of thinking, anticipating, and self-monitoring that was learned in a high-control developmental environment. In many adult survivors of CPA-PA, CPA-PAA, and CPA-PERA, this may present as an internal presence that feels less like reflective thought and more like an inherited relational authority, monitoring, warning, criticising, directing, and constraining the self long after the original environment has ended (Bandura, 1977; Fenn & Byrne, 2013; Shinn et al., 2020).

From an HQTP perspective, this helps explain why some survivors do not simply recall coercive family dynamics as something that happened in the past but continue to think from within their thought residues. The problem is not merely memory. It is the continued organisation of thought around rules that were once tied to safety, attachment, and survival. These rules may include prohibitions against trusting one's own mind, questioning authority, revisiting the targeted parent, expressing anger, feeling too much, or forming an independent view of events. Cognitive theory has long described the persistence of rigid assumptions and rules for living, while social learning theory helps explain how these patterns are acquired and maintained through modelling, repetition, fear, and relational dependency (Bandura, 1977; Fenn & Byrne, 2013). Where manipulation, gaslighting, or chronic distortion of reality has been present, the survivor may also carry deep doubt about the legitimacy of their own perception, memory, or emotional truth (Abramson, 2014).

This is highly relevant to the HQTP because CPA-PA-related harm often extends beyond discrete incidents and becomes embedded in the survivor's epistemic world. What is injured is not only attachment security, but confidence in one's own knowing. Research on epistemic trust is especially useful here. When development occurs within coercive, unreliable, or chronically misattuned environments, relational communication may cease to feel trustworthy, safe, or personally usable. In adulthood, this may appear as suspicion of others, but also as uncertainty about one's own thoughts, reduced confidence in inner experience, and a tendency for old coercive messages to re-emerge under stress as though they still carry present authority (Fonagy & Allison, 2014; Li et al., 2023; Campbell et al., 2024). Within this frame, the evoked companion may be understood as one way in which disrupted epistemic safety continues to operate internally: the survivor remains organised around old instructions, warnings, and relational rules even when no external enforcer is present.

Clinically, the evoked companion may become especially visible when the survivor encounters material linked to separation, loyalty conflict, identity, contact decisions, attachment longing, authority, or anticipated judgement. At such moments, the survivor may seem to shift from reflective adult thinking into an inherited survival script. They may abruptly minimise distress, defend harmful behaviour, distrust their own memory, or speak as though certain thoughts are forbidden. In some cases, the person may describe strong internal commentary or a voice-like inner presence without this implying a primary psychotic process. Trauma literature supports caution here, as internally experienced commentary and voice-hearing phenomena may occur across trauma-spectrum presentations and should be interpreted within the person's broader developmental and clinical context rather than reduced to psychosis by default (Shinn et al., 2020).

Within the HQTP, the therapeutic task is not to shame this internal presence or confront it aggressively. Nor is it to treat it as evidence of weakness or irrationality. The first task is to understand it as a survival-based adaptation. What the survivor was taught to think frequently made sense within the original environment. Self-silencing, hypervigilance, appeasement, loyalty-based thinking, and chronic self-monitoring may once have reduced danger, preserved attachment, or prevented retaliation. The problem is not that these responses were learned, but that they remain active beyond the context in which they were formed (Bandura, 1977; Fenn & Byrne, 2013). For this reason, the HQTP approaches the evoked companion with contextual understanding, careful pacing, and compassion rather than premature challenge.

Change, therefore, is not achieved through simple cognitive correction. Survivors are rarely helped by being told that the internal voice is "wrong" or that they should simply think differently. Within the HQTP, the authority of the evoked companion can be reduced through repeated experiences of epistemic safety, relational consistency, reflective functioning, and affect regulation. As the therapeutic relationship becomes more stable, non-coercive, and mentally usable, the survivor gradually begins to test whether inherited warnings still need to govern present life. Over time, a distinction can emerge between present reality and past threat conditioning, between the survivor's own adult values and the imposed rules of the coercive family system, and between autonomous judgement and child survival logic. This is consistent with work suggesting that psychotherapy can help restore epistemic trust through attuned, mentalising, trustworthy engagement, rather than through information-giving alone (Fonagy & Allison, 2014; Campbell et al., 2024).

Intervention within the HQTP is therefore directed not only towards content, but towards the relationship to content. The survivor is helped to recognise recurring internal messages as learned relational communications rather than unquestionable truths. CBT-informed work may support examination of assumptions, predictions, and rigid rules carried by the internal voice. Metacognitive approaches, such as detached mindfulness, may assist the survivor to notice these messages without immediate fusion or obedience. Compassion-focused work may further support the development of a more stable internal position that is less punitive, less shaming, and more protective of the self (Fenn & Byrne, 2013; Wells, 2005; Gilbert & Procter, 2006). Within the HQTP, however, these interventions are always subordinated to phase-based readiness and safety. The aim is not rapid dismantling, but gradual reduction in coercive internal authority.

In practical terms, survivors may be helped to ask, "Whose voice is this?" *When does it become louder? What does it warn me will happen? What did it once help me survive? What does it cost me now?* Over time, the goal is not necessarily the total disappearance of the evoked companion, but a reduction in its dominance. As treatment progresses, the survivor becomes more able to think, feel, remember, and choose from a differentiated adult self-position rather than from a fear-organised internal authority. In HQTP terms, this reflects movement away from coercively inherited cognition and towards reflective autonomy, restored epistemic confidence, and a more integrated identity (Fonagy & Allison, 2014; Gilbert & Procter, 2006; Wells, 2005).

Phase II Clinical Risks: Protective Retreat and Return to Enmeshment

A primary risk in Phase II is protective retreat following destabilisation. As differentiation and emerging self-processes progress, survivors may move back toward the alienating parent and the enmeshed relational dynamic that previously organised identity and emotional safety. This can include renewed alignment with the alienating parent, increased acceptance of imposed narratives, minimisation of earlier recognition, or re-immersion in the abuse dynamic because compliance reduces internal activation.

For some survivors, emerging autonomy introduces uncertainty, guilt activation, and loss of relational orientation. Returning to alignment may therefore feel easier than sustaining differentiation. An agreement does not necessarily reflect belief; it may reflect the nervous system selecting the fastest path to relational stability. Survivors may describe "just going along with it" or feeling that resisting requires more emotional energy than they can tolerate at that time.

At this stage, returning to being a regulatory object can feel familiar. The survivor resumes monitoring the alienating parent's emotional state, adjusting expression to prevent escalation, and allowing externally imposed meaning to organise internal experience. This shift reduces ambiguity and restores a predictable relational position, even when it contradicts earlier recognition. The movement reflects capacity protection rather than loss of insight.

Clinicians must recognise that renewed alignment with the alienating parent can serve as a form of regulation. Survivors may show increased defence of the alienating parent, discomfort revisiting recognised dynamics, reduced engagement in therapy, or statements indicating that "it's easier not to think about it." These shifts reflect the nervous system prioritising familiarity and relational safety over continued identity reorganisation.

Therapy Disengagement Risk

Disengagement during Phase II is a recognised clinical risk and should be understood within a developmental and regulatory framework rather than interpreted primarily as treatment rejection. As differentiation and emerging self-processes progress, the internal demands placed on survivors increase. Heightened awareness of relational patterns, activation of guilt, identity uncertainty, and reduced access to familiar adaptive roles may create levels of emotional exposure that exceed current regulatory capacity. In this context, discontinuing therapy can represent an attempt to restore psychological equilibrium rather than avoidance of therapeutic work.

This cohort is particularly sensitive to pacing misalignment. Even subtle experiences of acceleration, including increased interpretive depth, repeated focus on destabilising material, or perceived expectation to articulate emerging insight, may contribute to withdrawal. Survivors may not communicate this. Instead, disengagement may appear as cancelled sessions, reduced responsiveness, increased intellectualisation prior to leaving, or statements indicating fatigue, confusion, or a desire to "pause thinking about it."

Disengagement may also occur alongside renewed alignment with the alienating parent or re-entry into enmeshment dynamics. Returning to familiar relational positions can reduce internal conflict and restore predictability, making therapy temporarily unnecessary from a regulatory perspective. Importantly, this shift does not indicate loss of recognition. Survivors may retain awareness while prioritising stability over continued differentiation.

Assessment of whether disengagement reflects pacing misalignment should rely on observable indicators rather than clinician intuition. Relevant indicators include increased apologising, over-explaining, rapid agreement, reduced spontaneous reflection, fatigue following sessions, heightened language of guilt, or growing emphasis on certainty over exploration. Direct pacing check-ins provide additional clarity. Questions regarding session intensity, emotional residue between sessions, and the manageability of current focus areas allow survivors to signal activation levels without needing to frame this as difficulty with therapy.

Disengagement may also be influenced by shame processes. Survivors may feel embarrassed about returning after missed sessions, concerned that they have disappointed the clinician, or worried that renewed alignment with the alienating parent will be judged as inconsistency or lack of progress. Anticipated evaluation can reinforce withdrawal, particularly for survivors whose identities were organised around performance, compliance, and fear of relational consequence. In this context, not returning may represent protection from perceived judgement rather than a lack of therapeutic value.

Clinicians benefit from conceptualising disengagement through a readiness framework. Phase II frequently brings survivors to the edge of their current regulatory capacity. When this threshold is reached, stepping back may be necessary for emotional stability. Framing withdrawal as “not ready yet” supports a non-pathologising stance and reduces the likelihood of clinician urgency, corrective intervention, or implicit pressure to resume work prematurely.

This perspective also protects the therapeutic relationship. Survivors are more likely to re-engage when therapy is experienced as a place that tolerates pause rather than demands continuity. Where disengagement persists despite appropriate pacing, rupture-repair attempts, and supervision review, clinicians should consider boundaries of readiness. The survivor may have reached a point at which continued differentiation cannot be sustained without destabilising functioning. In this context, leaving therapy, returning to enmeshment, renewed alignment with the alienating parent, or temporary avoidance of recognised dynamics may reflect capacity protection rather than therapeutic failure.

Therapy disengagement in Phase II should therefore be conceptualised as part of the developmental trajectory rather than an endpoint. Recognition may remain intact beneath withdrawal. Maintaining a non-corrective stance, preserving relational availability, and avoiding pursuit allow survivors to re-engage when regulatory capacity increases.

What Makes Pacing Population-Specific in the HQTP

Pacing is not unique to the HQTP and is already a recognised component of safe trauma-informed psychotherapy. What is population-specific within this protocol is the material being paced, the developmental and psychological systems that may be destabilised, and the clinical consequences of moving too quickly. For adult survivors of child psychological abuse related to parental alienation, recognition itself may be activating. New understanding can disrupt attachment organisation, inherited family narratives, identity continuity, loyalty-based survival strategies, and the survivor's confidence in their own memory and perception.

The clinician is therefore pacing more than emotional intensity or trauma recollection. The work must also be calibrated to the survivor's epistemic stability, attachment security, identity coherence, capacity to tolerate uncertainty, and ability to question coercively acquired beliefs without experiencing overwhelming guilt, fear, relational panic, or psychological collapse. Premature interpretation, naming, disclosure, documentary exposure, grief work, confrontation of family narratives, or discussion of contact may destabilise several of these systems simultaneously.

This is particularly important when the survivor begins to recognise that a childhood attachment, family history, or sense of self may have been organised through coercion, concealment, forced alignment, abduction, or distorted relational narratives. The survivor may move rapidly between recognition and denial, anger and defence, grief and minimisation, or emerging autonomy and renewed compliance. These shifts should not automatically be interpreted as resistance, lack of insight, or treatment failure. They may indicate that recognition has exceeded the survivor's current capacity to remain emotionally regulated, relationally secure, and epistemically coherent.

Accordingly, pacing within the HQTP is guided not only by the survivor's level of emotional activation, but also by whether the work preserves identity continuity, internal authority, reflective capacity, relational safety, and autonomous choice. The aim is not to avoid clinically important material, but to introduce it at a rate that permits integration without reenacting the coercion, narrative imposition, or forced psychological compliance that characterised the original harm.

Pacing Assessment and Calibration

Within Phase II, pacing is not determined solely by clinician intuition. It is assessed through observable indicators of regulatory capacity, identity stability, relational safety, and tolerance for emerging meaning. The central pacing task is to determine whether the survivor can remain in contact with new understanding without needing to restore safety through compliance, withdrawal, intellectualisation, minimisation, or renewed alignment with the alienating parent.

Observable behavioural indicators provide important pacing data. Signs that the work may be progressing too quickly include increased apologising, rapid agreement, diminished spontaneity, over-explaining, heightened monitoring of the clinician's responses, or a sudden move toward certainty after periods of exploration. Session residue is another important pacing indicator. Relevant markers include prolonged emotional activation, sleep disruption, rumination, increased guilt, renewed narrative defence, fatigue, or urges to re-establish familiar relational roles. When session residue increases, the clinician may need to shift toward stabilisation, consolidation, and reduced interpretive depth.

Direct pacing check-ins support collaborative calibration. Questions about session intensity, emotional aftereffects, and the manageability of current focus areas allow survivors to communicate activation without framing it as failure or difficulty. Pacing assessment also requires attention to relational safety. Increased concern about clinician evaluation, performance-based language, appeasement, or subtle withdrawal following interpretive statements may indicate that meaning-making is outpacing stabilisation. The clinician may respond by slowing the work, returning to observational language, increasing predictability, and reducing pressure for immediate insight.

Clinicians must also assess their own contribution to pacing. Over-interpretation, repeated return to destabilising themes, premature consolidation of meaning, or subtle encouragement toward behavioural change may unintentionally accelerate the process. Slowing does not mean abandoning Phase II work. It may involve narrowing the focus, increasing predictability, supporting language development, and strengthening the survivor's capacity to tolerate uncertainty without requiring immediate resolution. Pacing assessment is continuous rather than episodic. Because capacity fluctuates across sessions and contexts, calibration requires ongoing observation, direct survivor feedback, attention to session residue, and clinician self-monitoring.

Clarification: Real-Time Pacing Within Phase II

The population-specific rationale described above does not replace ordinary moment-to-moment clinical pacing. It extends it by requiring simultaneous attention to affect regulation, epistemic stability, identity continuity, attachment threat, loyalty conflict, and survivor autonomy.

Earlier sections of the protocol address architectural pacing: whether the survivor is ready to enter, remain within, or move between phases. Real-time pacing within Phase II addresses a different question: whether the current topic, interpretation, emotional intensity, or level of reflection remains within the survivor's immediate capacity.

Architectural pacing governs the broader treatment trajectory. Real-time pacing governs the moment-to-moment depth, speed, and intensity of the work. The clinical question therefore shifts from whether the survivor is ready to enter Phase II to whether they can sustain differentiation and emerging recognition without protective retreat, relational collapse, or loss of epistemic stability. Distinguishing these two levels prevents conceptual duplication. The broader phase architecture protects developmental safety throughout treatment, while real-time calibration helps the clinician recognise when that safety begins to narrow within a particular session.

Clinician Self-Blame, Supervision, and Anxiety Containment

Phase II work carries a parallel clinical risk for practitioners: the emergence of clinician self-doubt when survivors destabilise, disengage, or realign with the alienating parent. Because identity reorganisation is visible but fragile during this stage, withdrawal, renewed narrative defence, reduced engagement, or therapy discontinuation may be experienced by clinicians as signs that harm has occurred. These reactions are understandable and reflect the relational investment required for this work, but they should be contained within supervision rather than prompt immediate corrective action.

A common clinician response involves retrospective scanning for error. Practitioners may review sessions repeatedly, questioning whether interpretive depth progressed too quickly, whether misattunement occurred, or whether emerging identity work exceeded stabilisation capacity. Reflective review is appropriate; however, uncontained self-blame can create a sense of urgency. This may appear as increased reassurance, attempts to re-explain insight, pressure toward re-engagement, or outreach motivated by practitioner anxiety rather than survivor need. Such responses risk reproducing the pressure dynamics the protocol seeks to avoid.

Within the HQTP, clinician anxiety following destabilisation or disengagement is conceptualised as a predictable feature of Phase II risk, not evidence of clinical failure. Supervision supports practitioners in reviewing pacing decisions, identifying possible misattunements without over-interpreting their impact, and maintaining a non-reactive stance.

The supervisory task is to stabilise the clinician's capacity to tolerate uncertainty alongside the survivor's developmental process.

Recognising clinician anxiety as part of Phase II governance helps reframe disengagement. It may signal that the survivor has reached the edge of their current capacity, rather than that the clinician or treatment has failed. This perspective helps practitioners remain steady when survivors move back toward familiar relational alignment, step away from therapy, or pause differentiation work. The therapeutic relationship can remain available without requiring immediate resolution.

Clinical Governance When Survivors Pause, Withdraw, or Become Destabilised

In this context, clinical governance refers to the practitioner's responsibility to respond to risk, disengagement, destabilisation, and treatment uncertainty in a structured, ethical, and accountable way. It includes careful documentation, pacing review, supervision, consultation where needed, and decisions about whether outreach is clinically appropriate. Clinical governance does not mean taking control of the survivor, correcting their choices, or pressuring them back into therapy.

When a survivor becomes destabilised, withdraws, or pauses therapy, the clinician's task is to review what has occurred rather than react impulsively. The practitioner should document observed signs of distress, pacing concerns, risk indicators, changes in engagement, relevant clinical decisions, and any supervision or clinical consultation undertaken. This creates a clear clinical record and helps the practitioner think carefully about safety, pacing, and responsibility without turning disengagement into a treatment failure or a demand for immediate repair.

Where outreach is clinically appropriate, contact should remain brief, neutral, and focused on availability. The aim is to let the survivor know that support remains available without implying pressure, disappointment, responsibility, or judgement. For example, the clinician may communicate that the survivor is welcome to pause, that the door remains open, and that any return to therapy can begin again with stabilisation rather than with an expectation to explain everything or resume from the most difficult point. This protects both the survivor's autonomy and the clinician's boundaries.

Communicating a Credible Re-Entry Pathway

A clear re-entry pathway is especially important for this cohort. Many survivors have previously been told that support remains available, only to later experience withdrawal, disappointment, judgement, administrative barriers, or relational coldness when they try to return. For this reason, a general statement such as "you can come back anytime" may not be enough. The clinician may need to make re-entry explicit, calm, and believable.

This may include saying: "If you need to pause, we can pause. You are welcome to return when you are ready. You do not have to explain everything or start at the hardest point. We can begin again with stabilisation and work out what feels safe from there." This kind of statement reduces shame, performance pressure, and fear of disappointing the clinician. It also helps prevent therapeutic disengagement from being experienced as another relational cut-off.

Clinicians should understand that the survivor may not fully believe this invitation at first. The credibility of re-entry is built over time through consistency, tone, documentation, and the clinician's response if the survivor does return. A warm, non-punitive re-entry can itself become a corrective relational experience. The survivor learns that pausing does not automatically mean abandonment, punishment, or exile from care.

When Disengagement Persists Despite Stabilisation

Where multiple stabilisation efforts have been undertaken, and disengagement from sessions persists, clinician containment becomes especially important. Practitioners may need support to hold the possibility that the survivor is not ready at that time, rather than becoming preoccupied with whether one more intervention might have prevented withdrawal. This stance protects the integrity of the HQTP by keeping treatment aligned with pacing, autonomy, and non-coercive care.

Clinician self-blame and anxiety containment, therefore, remain part of Phase II governance. When practitioner emotional responses are held within supervision, documentation, and pacing review, uncertainty is less likely to become pressure. This allows the therapeutic space to remain available without pursuit, leaving open the possibility that the survivor may re-engage later as their regulatory capacity increases.

Clinical Positioning

In Phase II, the clinician adopts a stance of collaborative meaning-making rather than interpretive authority. The therapist does not impose explanatory frameworks, adjudicate factual accuracy, correct survivor narratives, or assume the role of arbiter of truth. Instead, the clinician supports the survivor in developing language, conceptual clarity, and psychological understanding for experiences that were previously confusing, denied, minimised, or actively distorted.

This positioning is grounded in the formulation safeguards established in Chapter Four, particularly those addressing epistemic injury, diagnostic restraint, and developmental contextualisation. Clinical neutrality in Phase II is relational rather than detached. The clinician remains emotionally present, consistent, and attuned while deliberately refusing roles associated with judgement, rescue, reassurance, or corrective authority. This protects the therapeutic relationship from replicating the power asymmetries and coercive dynamics that characterised the survivor's developmental environment.

Phase II requires disciplined clinical restraint. Survivors frequently oscillate between emerging insight and renewed doubt as internalised coercive narratives, loyalty conditioning, and self-blame patterns are challenged. The clinician must tolerate ambiguity, contradiction, and emotional complexity without rushing toward certainty, emotional discharge, or narrative closure. Premature interpretation or resolution-seeking at this stage risks destabilising identity consolidation and reactivating fear-based compliance.

Core Psychological Aims

Phase II supports a series of interrelated psychological shifts. Survivors begin to contextualise childhood experiences within patterns of coercive control, attachment disruption, and developmental power asymmetry rather than interpreting them as mutual conflict, misunderstanding, or personal failure. Language is developed to describe loyalty conflict, fear-based alignment, role reversal, psychological captivity, conditional attachment, and identity distortion.

Responsibility for relational rupture is gradually relocated from the child self toward adult caregivers, relational systems, and institutional failures that contributed to the original harm. As this relocation occurs, identity stability increases as adaptive survival strategies are recognised as context-dependent responses rather than fixed character traits or inherent flaws. Survivors develop greater tolerance for complexity, including ambivalence toward caregivers, mixed emotional states, and unresolved grief, without collapsing into guilt, self-blame, or fragmentation. These psychological aims align with the phased progression logic and readiness markers outlined in this chapter and establish the foundation for later integrative work without requiring premature trauma exposure, emotional flooding, or narrative reconstruction.

Orientation to Subsequent Phases

Phase II does not complete the healing process, nor does it resolve all relational or emotional pain. It prepares the psychological ground for deeper integration by stabilising meaning, identity, and internal authority. Only when survivors can engage with ambiguity, complexity, and emotional activation without destabilisation does the protocol progress toward later phases involving trauma integration, relational differentiation, and long-term continuity.

Phase II: Core Clinical Tasks

(What Sessions Actually Focus On)

Phase II sessions focus on reflective meaning reconstruction rather than trauma processing or emotional discharge. The work centres on helping survivors develop coherent psychological understanding for experiences that were previously confusing, denied, minimised, or actively distorted, while maintaining regulatory stability and epistemic safety.

A primary task is contextualising experience. Clinicians support survivors in situating childhood and relational experiences within patterns of developmental power asymmetry, coercive control, attachment disruption, and institutional failure. This reframing relocates responsibility away from the child self and toward the relational and systemic conditions under which harm occurred. The emphasis is on accuracy and coherence, not persuasion or proof.

Another core task is language development. Survivors are assisted to develop words and concepts for phenomena such as loyalty conflict, fear-based alignment, role reversal, conditional attachment, psychological captivity, and identity distortion. Language is introduced collaboratively and tentatively, with attention to whether the survivor experiences new terms as clarifying rather than intrusive.

Sessions also prioritise identity consolidation. Clinicians help survivors differentiate adaptive survival strategies from identity traits, supporting recognition that behaviours such as compliance, appeasement, hypervigilance, or emotional suppression were context-dependent responses rather than personal flaws. This differentiation reduces shame and supports internal coherence without requiring emotional exposure.

Phase II includes the explicit therapeutic focus of tolerance of ambiguity. Survivors are supported to hold uncertainty, mixed feelings, and unresolved questions without collapsing into self-blame, urgency, or epistemic anxiety. The clinician models steadiness in the absence of certainty, reinforcing that meaning can evolve without immediate resolution.

Throughout Phase II, clinicians continuously monitor regulation. Sessions remain paced, reflective, and collaborative. When destabilisation emerges, the focus returns to containment rather than advancing content. Progress is measured by increased psychological stability, internal authority, and reduced reliance on external validation, not by the quantity of insight or the completeness of the narrative.

Phase II: Common Errors and Clinical Safeguards

The most frequent error in Phase II is premature interpretation. This occurs when clinicians move from collaborative exploration into explanatory certainty, offering formulations that outpace the survivor's capacity to integrate meaning. Even accurate interpretations can destabilise identity consolidation when delivered too quickly.

Another common error is substituting meaning reconstruction with trauma exposure. Introducing emotionally intense material, memory processing, or cathartic techniques during Phase II undermines the phase's purpose and risks reactivating fear-based compliance or dissociation. Phase II is reflective, not evocative.

Over-intellectualisation represents a further risk. When meaning-making becomes abstract, analytical, or disconnected from embodied experience, survivors may comply cognitively while remaining emotionally fragmented. Clinicians must ensure that reflection remains grounded, paced, and responsive to affective cues.

A related error concerns the correction of survivor narratives. Challenging inconsistencies, disputing interpretations, or clarifying "what really happened" replicates epistemic control and undermines trust. Phase II does not involve adjudication of facts; it involves understanding impact and meaning.

Finally, clinicians may experience pressure to consolidate identity too quickly, particularly when survivors seek certainty or closure. Rushing toward resolution, forgiveness, or integration prematurely risks replacing one imposed narrative with another. Clinical safeguards include slowing the pace, naming uncertainty, and returning to collaborative enquiry.

Supervision remains essential in Phase II to monitor countertransference, particularly urges to rescue, validate prematurely, or resolve perceived injustice. Ethical practice requires sustained restraint and fidelity to the principle of phase integrity.

Phase II: Meaning-Making Boundaries

(What Clinicians Must Not Do)

Phase II is governed by explicit boundaries that protect survivors from epistemic harm and identity destabilisation. Clinicians must not position themselves as arbiters of truth, judges of credibility, or authorities on what survivors "should" understand about their past.

Clinicians must not impose explanatory frameworks, theoretical models, or diagnostic narratives that override survivor meaning-making. Language and concepts are offered tentatively and collaboratively, with permission to accept, adapt, or reject them.

Meaning-making must not be accelerated in response to survivor anxiety, clinician discomfort, or institutional timelines. The urgency to "understand," "make sense," or "move on" is treated as clinical information rather than a directive.

Clinicians must not equate insight with readiness for trauma processing. Increased cognitive clarity does not automatically indicate capacity for exposure, memory work, or emotional intensity. Phase boundaries remain in place until regulatory stability is demonstrated consistently.

Finally, clinicians must not treat Phase II as a pathway to reconciliation, forgiveness, or relational repair. Decisions about contact, distance, or boundaries remain survivor-led and are not used as measures of therapeutic success.

Meaning reconstruction in Phase II is successful when survivors experience increased internal coherence, reduced self-blame, and growing trust in their own perceptions—without feeling pressured to arrive at final answers.

Pacing, Readiness, and Clinical Boundaries

Progression through Phase II is governed by psychological readiness rather than session count, disclosure volume, or apparent insight. Survivors may demonstrate strong intellectual understanding of their experiences while remaining emotionally vulnerable to destabilisation. For this reason, Phase II's pacing prioritises consolidation over acceleration.

Clinical indicators that Phase II work is proceeding within safe parameters include increased tolerance for ambiguity without panic, reduced urgency to persuade or justify, improved capacity to reflect on relational patterns without collapse, and the ability to hold complexity without reverting to global self-blame or rigid splitting. Survivors may still experience emotional fluctuation, grief, or anger; however, these experiences occur within a broader context of psychological coherence and relational stability.

Contraindications for deepening meaning reconstruction include persistent epistemic threat, fear-based compliance, escalating dependence on therapist validation, rapid shifts between idealisation and devaluation, post-session destabilisation, or renewed urgency to prematurely confront family members, institutions, or past events. When these patterns emerge, clinical pacing must slow and return temporarily to Phase I stabilisation processes.

Phase II does not introduce trauma integration, memory-focused exposure, or intensive somatic processing. Although meaning reconstruction may activate emotional material, the clinician maintains focus on reflective understanding rather than experiential reliving. The objective is cognitive-emotional integration without overwhelming the survivor's regulatory capacity.

The clinician remains responsible for monitoring subtle indicators of overload, including emotional flattening, dissociation, rumination loops, sleep disruption, somatic escalation, or withdrawal from relational engagement. These signals are treated as clinical data rather than resistance. When present, they indicate the need for containment rather than progression.

Phase II work unfolds iteratively rather than following a linear progression. Survivors may move back and forth between stabilisation and meaning integration as new insights emerge or as developmental transitions activate earlier attachment material. This movement is not framed as regression. It reflects the layered nature of developmental trauma recovery.

Phase II Clinical Decision Safeguards

Phase II is governed by clinical patterns identified in the doctoral research and supported by broader trauma literature. Survivors of CPA-PA may destabilise when recognition of coercive developmental conditions occurs without sufficient containment. Harm in this cohort arises not from insight itself, but from insight introduced too rapidly, imposed interpretively, or delivered without regulatory support. Within the author's doctoral survivor study, participants repeatedly described distress not arising from insight itself, but from the collapse of previously held attachment narratives. Harm emerged when meaning shifted faster than emotional integration could occur.

For many survivors, recognition involves the realisation that a trusted parent engaged in deception, manipulation, or coercive narrative control. The psychological implications of this shift are profound. A parent represents a primary attachment figure, a source of safety, identity formation, and epistemic trust. When survivors begin to recognise that a parent may have lied for personal gain, distorted reality, or exploited the child's dependency, the impact is not merely cognitive. It destabilises foundational assumptions about safety, loyalty, and truth.

A Cascade of Questions

Adult survivors frequently describe a cascade of destabilising cognitive and relational questions during this phase of recognition. When a parent's deception or manipulation becomes apparent, foundational assumptions about attachment are disrupted. Survivors may begin to question the reliability of past experiences, the integrity of family narratives, and the safety of previously trusted relationships.

The recognition that a primary attachment figure may have lied for personal gain raises broader epistemic instability. If one core narrative was false, what else may have been distorted? If the person positioned as the safest figure was also the source of manipulation, how is safety recalibrated in adulthood? Survivors often grieve lost developmental time and confront the irreversibility of years shaped by misinformation.

This shift also has contemporary implications for relationships. Adults may struggle to determine how to relate to both the alienating and targeted parents under a new understanding. Where there is emerging awareness of a possible untreated mental health condition in a parent, survivors must reconcile the tension between compassion, accountability, and boundary formation. If the parent denies impairment or refuses treatment, uncertainty intensifies.

Intergenerational considerations frequently arise. Survivors may question how to manage contact between their children and grandparents, what information to disclose, when to disclose it, and how extended family members may respond. Concerns about family fragmentation, retaliation, or renewed conflict can further amplify distress.

These questions are not abstract philosophical reflections. They represent active reorganisation of attachment models, identity coherence, and intergenerational responsibility. Without careful containment, this cognitive cascade can overwhelm regulatory capacity.

The doctoral findings document that such recognition may produce acute distress, grief, anger, confusion, and temporary identity destabilisation. Survivors described disorientation when long-standing beliefs about one parent were reversed. Some experienced intensified despair when recognising that lost developmental years could not be retrieved.

From a neurobiological perspective, attachment threat and betrayal activate stress circuitry associated with survival responses. Trauma research demonstrates that perceived attachment rupture can stimulate amygdala activation, increase sympathetic arousal, and temporarily reduce prefrontal regulatory integration (van der Kolk, 2014; Siegel, 2012). When early developmental attachment systems are implicated, implicit memory networks may activate alongside present cognition. This can result in heightened vigilance, catastrophic anticipation, dissociation, or emotional flooding. The experience may feel immediate and urgent, even though the recognition concerns historical events.

In complex trauma populations, meaning shifts can activate stored procedural memory patterns encoded under conditions of dependency and fear (Courtois & Ford, 2020). Recognition of deception by a primary caregiver, therefore, engages both cognitive appraisal systems and embodied threat responses. The brain may respond as though present safety is compromised, even when the recognition is reflective and occurring in adulthood.

The doctoral research indicates that destabilisation in this cohort frequently occurs when clinicians underestimate the neurobiological and attachment implications of such insight. Recognition without containment may lead to agitation, rumination, insomnia, anger escalation, relational withdrawal, or increased suicidality. It is therefore essential that Phase II pacing respects both the psychological and neurobiological weight of attachment re-evaluation.

Phase II Clinical Decision Tree: Destabilisation and Escalation

Trigger Condition

Phase II destabilisation most commonly emerges when survivors begin recognising deception, attachment captivity, coercive alignment, misinformation, institutional betrayal, or parental mental health instability within alienation-related child psychological abuse presentations. Destabilisation risk increases when survivors re-evaluate the character, reliability, or psychological stability of a parent they were developmentally required to trust. Recognition at this level constitutes an attachment event rather than a purely cognitive shift.

Early Risk Indicators

In adult survivors, destabilisation may initially present as rapid cognitive acceleration, global reinterpretation of past events, or statements reflecting identity disorientation. Survivors may report thoughts such as "Everything was a lie" or "I do not know who I was anymore." Clinically observable indicators may include heightened agitation, pacing, dissociation, emotional numbing during sessions, repetitive rumination after sessions, insomnia following recognition work, or an urgent need to contact or confront a parent. Some survivors may immediately begin drafting emails, affidavits, or legal complaints. Others may demonstrate increased hostility within co-parenting arrangements or withdraw from partners, work, or extended family relationships. These responses are not interpreted as resistance. They reflect activation of attachment threat circuitry during meaning reconstruction.

Primary Clinical Action

When early destabilisation indicators emerge, the clinician pauses interpretive expansion and reduces cognitive load. Regulatory containment, consistent with the Phase I stabilisation architecture, is reinstated. The therapeutic task becomes differentiation between past attachment threat and present-day safety. Pacing slows before meaning reconstruction resumes. Insight does not override nervous system activation, and recognition work proceeds only within sustained regulatory capacity.

Escalation Threshold: Behavioural Urgency

If reflective processing shifts toward behavioural activation, Phase II work slows immediately. Behavioural urgency may include planning immediate confrontation with a parent, publicly disclosing family material, abruptly terminating extended family relationships, escalating family court filings in reaction to session content, or pressuring the clinician to formally declare abuse for legal use.

In such cases, the clinician clarifies that therapy is not a vehicle for reactive decision-making or litigation positioning unless it is formally contracted for a forensic role. Containment is reinstated, and interpretive depth is reduced until stability is sustained across sessions. The focus returns to internal processing rather than external action.

Escalation Threshold: Violence Risk

If anger escalates toward a credible threat of harm to self or others, property destruction, stalking behaviour, or expressed violent intent, Phase II work ceases immediately. Adult presentations may include verbal threats toward a parent or new partner, statements suggesting retaliatory harm, expressed intent to damage property, escalating physical agitation within the session, or observable loss of behavioural inhibition.

At this threshold, the clinician activates the previously established Crisis Architecture and Escalation Threshold protocols. Senior staff consultation is required. Internal safety procedures are engaged. Where risk is imminent or credible, emergency services or the police are contacted in accordance with duty-of-care obligations and applicable jurisdictional law. Clinician safety and public safety override phase progression. The Crisis Architecture and Practitioner Safety sections of the protocol govern operational guidance.

Escalation Threshold: Suicidality and Identity Destabilisation

Clinical Indicators

If identity destabilisation coincides with increased hopelessness, collapse of language, or suicidal ideation, Phase II work pauses immediately. Indicators may include re-emergence of prior suicidal thinking, post-session withdrawal and silence, behavioural shutdown, preparatory behaviours such as giving away possessions or sudden resignation, or a marked narrowing of future orientation.

In survivors, suicidal ideation may arise within the context of acute identity destabilisation rather than solely within a primary depressive disorder. As documented in the author's doctoral findings (Price-Tobler, 2023a, 2023b), recognition of coercive developmental conditions can destabilise previously organising attachment narratives. Survivors may report intrusive questions such as, "Who am I really?" or "Why was this done to me?" When long-standing attachment meanings collapse, the self's organising structure can temporarily fragment. The loss is not only relational. It is existential.

Regulatory Object Recognition and Identity Collapse

Many survivors recognise during Phase II that they functioned as a regulatory object for a parent, required to stabilise the parent's emotional state, uphold a narrative, or maintain loyalty under threat. When this recognition occurs, identity disorientation may intensify. If developmental identity was organised around who the parent required them to be, the question of selfhood becomes destabilising.

Survivors may ask internally: If I am not who my parent needed me to be, then who am I? How do I find myself outside that role? Adult presentations may include abrupt re-evaluation of career direction, relational patterns, parenting style, or long-standing beliefs about self-worth. Some survivors report feeling "constructed," "manufactured," or "programmed," followed by intense shame or confusion.

This destabilisation aligns with research on identity disturbance within developmental trauma populations (Courtois & Ford, 2020; van der Kolk, 2014) and was repeatedly described in the survivor cohort as a period of psychological groundlessness (Price-Tobler, 2023a).

Conditional Versus Unconditional Love

A further destabilising element involves the meaning of attachment. Survivors may ask: Did they really love me? Was the love I experienced conditional upon compliance, agreement, or loyalty? If affection was contingent, what does that mean about my worth?

The recognition that caregiving may have been approval-based rather than grounded in unconditional positive regard (Rogers, 1957) can destabilise deeply internalised beliefs about safety and belonging. Survivors may struggle to differentiate between conditional reinforcement and genuine attachment. Adult examples include difficulty trusting partner affection, anxiety when receiving praise, or fear that disagreement will result in withdrawal.

Attachment Disorientation and Ambivalent Love

For many adult survivors, recognition of conditional versus unconditional attachment does not produce simple clarity. It produces psychological disorientation. Some survivors report that, even as children, they sensed intuitively that the alienating parent's love was conditional. They may recall subtle withdrawal, approval contingent on loyalty, emotional warmth contingent on compliance, or affection tied to narrative alignment. At the same time, they may recognise retrospectively that the targeted parent demonstrated consistent emotional availability, warmth, and unconditional care. The destabilising realisation is not merely that one parent lied or manipulated. The safe parent may have loved them consistently, while they were conditioned to fear or reject that love.

This recognition can produce intense attachment conflict. Survivors may ask: Did they really love me? Do they love me now? If not, why not? Was I only valued when I complied? Was I loved for who I was, or for what I provided? Simultaneously, they may experience grief or guilt upon recognising the rejection of the unconditionally loving parent.

The psychological impact can be profound. Adult survivors may report difficulty identifying what love feels like. They may compare themselves to peers who describe secure attachment bonds and struggle to understand what "normal" parental love entails. Some describe feeling emotionally muted when others speak warmly about their families. Others report confusion in intimate relationships, oscillating between craving closeness and fearing conditional withdrawal.

Ambivalence is common. Survivors may state that they no longer care if the alienating parent dies, do not wish to attend their funeral, or do not want further contact. In rare circumstances, intense anger may escalate into transient homicidal ideation, particularly during early recognition phases. These disclosures often coexist with expressions of deep attachment and longing. A survivor may say, in the same session, "I don't want anything to do with them," followed by, "But I still love them," and then express fear that the clinician will judge the contradiction.

This oscillation reflects attachment trauma, not moral instability. It is characteristic of relationships organised under coercive control and conditional belonging. The therapeutic space must tolerate ambivalence. Survivors require reassurance that simultaneous anger, love, grief, detachment, and longing can coexist without implying pathology.

Additional complexity arises when siblings remain aligned with the alienating parent. Survivors may struggle with whether to disclose their evolving understanding. Will telling a sibling cause further rupture in the family? Will they be accused of betrayal? Will conflict escalate? In families where one sibling continues to provide care to an ageing, alienating parent, further questions may emerge. Who will look after them if I withdraw? Am I responsible? Was I always responsible? These questions frequently intensify when the alienating parent becomes ill, cognitively impaired, or approaches the end of life.

As noted in the doctoral findings (Price-Tobler, 2023a), end-of-life contexts often reactivate unresolved loyalty conditioning and identity conflict. Survivors may experience renewed guilt, pressure to reconcile, or expectations of caregiving based on historical role-reversal dynamics. These scenarios require careful pacing within Phase II and may necessitate temporary reversion to Phase I stabilisation if identity destabilisation escalates.

From an attachment perspective, this internal conflict reflects the reorganisation of internal working models (Bowlby, 1988). From a humanistic lens, it exposes the absence of unconditional positive regard during development (Rogers, 1957). From an existential perspective, it confronts the survivor with questions of freedom, responsibility, relational choice, and mortality (Yalom, 1980).

The clinician's role is not to direct reconciliation, severance, forgiveness, or confrontation. The task is to contain, differentiate, and support autonomous decision-making within regulatory capacity. Survivors must be allowed to hold love and anger simultaneously, to choose distance without shame, and to experience grief without coercion toward closure.

This phase is emotionally complex and clinically demanding. Ambivalence is not instability. It is evidence of attachment reorganisation.

Existential Crisis and Meaning Disruption

For some individuals, Phase II recognition introduces an existential crisis. Survivors may confront questions of meaning, freedom, responsibility, irretrievability of time, and authorship of their lives (Yalom, 1980). The recognition that coercive conditions shaped formative years can lead to a confrontation with lost possibilities and unchosen identities.

Adult survivors may state, "If my childhood was built on a lie, what is real?" or "I cannot get those years back." Existential anxiety may intensify as survivors attempt to reconcile who they were required to be with who they might yet become.

In this destabilised state, cognitive narrowing may occur. Survivors may report feeling unable to see a viable path forward. Identity collapse can lead to a sense of entrapment and irreversibility. When distress feels uncontainable and future orientation constricts, suicidal ideation may emerge as an attempt to escape overwhelming identity confusion and existential disorientation rather than as a sustained wish for death. This represents a high-risk state requiring immediate containment.

Clinical Safeguard and Therapeutic Response

If suicidality escalates, the clinician reverts immediately to Phase I safety protocols. A formal risk assessment is conducted. Containment frequency increases. Emergency services are engaged where indicated. Phase II, meaning reconstruction, is suspended until regulatory stability is restored. The therapeutic task shifts to identity anchoring, present-moment safety, and differentiation between past attachment threat and current safety. Supervision and consultation are activated as required.

Where existential themes are present but imminent risk is not active, clinicians may cautiously incorporate existential–humanistic therapeutic dialogue within a regulated frame. Existential psychotherapy (Yalom, 1980) and meaning-oriented approaches (Frankl, 1963) may inform structured reflection without imposing resolution. For example, a clinician might explore: "If parts of your identity were shaped by survival, what qualities feel most authentically yours now?" or "What small actions reflect your chosen values today?" The emphasis remains on agency and authorship rather than on philosophical abstraction.

Existential enquiry remains subordinate to nervous system regulation and is contraindicated when suicidality or severe destabilisation is active.

Re-Entry Criteria

Progression within Phase II requires demonstrated regulatory continuity across sessions and stabilisation of suicidal risk. Movement forward is contingent upon the survivor's capacity to tolerate identity and existential exploration without collapse, behavioural urgency, or self-harm ideation. Reversion to Phase I in these circumstances is not regression. It demonstrates adherence to phase integrity and the clinical governance architecture within the HQTP.

Clinical Safeguard: Specific Phobia–CPA-PAA Activation During Recognition Work

In survivors with the Specific Phobia–CPA-PAA Anxiety Variant, recognition work may activate conditioned fear responses. Adult manifestations may include panic when discussing abduction or enforced separation, somatic shaking, breath constriction, catastrophic anticipation of retaliation, or dissociation when attachment captivity is named.

When phobic activation occurs, interpretive work stops immediately. The focus shifts to nervous system regulation, grounding, and present-moment orientation. Recognition of the survivor's experience resumes only when the survivor's reflective capacity is restored, and the survivor can differentiate between historical threat and current safety.

Escalation Threshold: Litigation Reactivation

When survivors are engaged in family court proceedings involving their own children, recognition work may reactivate unresolved childhood trauma. Adults may experience courtroom environments as re-enactments of their own childhood, interpret routine co-parenting conflict as catastrophic repetition, seek therapist endorsement for affidavits, or escalate legal conflict immediately following sessions.

In such cases, the clinician differentiates past trauma from the present legal context, moderates interpretive intensity during active litigation, reinstates stabilisation when reactivation escalates, and clarifies therapeutic role boundaries. The therapeutic relationship is not positioned as an investigative, evidentiary, or advocacy forum unless contracted within a defined scope of practice.

How to Use This Decision Tree

The following decision tree is designed as a rapid-reference clinical tool for use during sessions, immediately after sessions, and in supervision. It does not replace the preceding explanatory safeguards. Rather, it translates those principles into moment-to-moment clinical judgement pathways.

Clinicians are encouraged to read the full Phase II Clinical Decision Safeguards section before relying on this tool in practice. The tree is intended to support containment, pacing, and risk recognition under pressure. It assists the practitioner in differentiating reflective destabilisation from behavioural escalation and in identifying when Phase II work must pause in favour of Phase I stabilisation or Crisis Architecture activation.

This tool should be applied conservatively. When in doubt, slow pacing, reduce interpretive expansion, and revert to stabilisation. Phase integrity takes precedence over depth. Supervision is required whenever escalation thresholds are activated.

Phase II Decision Tree Quick Reference

Clinician's note: Read the Phase II Clinical Decision Safeguards narrative first. Use this as the in-session and post-session operational guide.

Start: A Phase II session includes recognition work. Recognition themes may include deception, coercive alignment, attachment captivity, misinformation, institutional betrayal, parental mental health instability, and CPA-PA dynamics.

Step 1: Identify the survivor's current state

1A. Survivor remains reflective, paced, and regulated

Continue Phase II, meaning reconstruction within pacing limits.

1B. Early destabilisation signals emerge

Examples may include rapid cognitive acceleration, global reinterpretation, identity disorientation, agitation, pacing, dissociation or numbing, rumination after sessions, insomnia, an urgent need to contact or confront a parent, or immediate drafting of emails, affidavits, or complaints.

If these signs are present, proceed to Step 2.

Step 2: Immediate clinical action

2A. Pause interpretive expansion.

Stop adding meaning, models, or conclusions.

2B. Reduce cognitive load.

Shorten content, simplify language, and slow the pace.

2C. Reinstate regulatory containment consistent with the Phase I stabilisation architecture.

2D. Differentiate past attachment threat from present-day safety.

Then reassess:

Is the survivor returning to reflective capacity?

If yes: Return carefully to Phase II tasks using short, contained meaning reconstruction.

If no: Proceed to Step 3 and identify the highest active escalation threshold.

Step 3: Determine the escalation threshold

Select the highest active threshold.

3A. Behavioural urgency threshold

Indicators: planning an immediate confrontation, public disclosure, abrupt termination of the relationship, escalation of court filings immediately after sessions, or pressure on the clinician to obtain a legal declaration or validation.

Clinical response:

1. Clarify role boundaries. Therapy is not a vehicle for reactive decisions or litigation positioning unless formally contracted for a forensic role.
2. Reinstate containment.
3. Reduce interpretive depth until stability is sustained across sessions.
4. Consider a brief between-session stabilisation plan if urgency persists.

Continue Phase II only when behavioural urgency has resolved.

3B. Violence risk threshold to self, others, or property

Indicators: threats, retaliatory intent, stalking behaviour, intent to damage property, marked in-session agitation, or loss of behavioural inhibition.

Clinical response:

1. Stop Phase II work immediately.
2. Activate the Crisis Architecture and Escalation Threshold procedures.
3. Initiate staff support procedures. Do not manage credible risk alone.
4. Consult senior staff or supervision immediately.
5. If risk is imminent or credible, contact emergency services or police in accordance with duty of care and jurisdictional law.

Phase II resumes only after stabilisation and formal risk clearance in accordance with protocol.

3C. Suicidality and identity destabilisation threshold

Indicators: hopelessness, collapse of language, re-emergence of suicidal thinking, post-session withdrawal, behavioural shutdown, preparatory behaviours, narrowed future orientation, or statements suggesting loss of self-continuity.

Clinical response:

1. Stop Phase II, meaning reconstruction immediately.
2. Revert to Phase I safety protocols.
3. Conduct a formal risk assessment.
4. Increase containment frequency and support.
5. Engage emergency or crisis services where indicated.

Phase II resumes only when suicidal risk has stabilised, and regulatory continuity is demonstrated over time.

3D. Phobic activation threshold

Indicators: panic, breath constriction, shaking, catastrophic anticipation of retaliation, or dissociation when abduction, enforced separation, or attachment captivity is named.

Clinical response:

1. Stop interpretive work immediately.
2. Shift to nervous system regulation and present moment orientation.
3. Resume recognition work only when reflective capacity has returned, and the past threat is clearly differentiated from the present safety.

3E. Litigation reactivation threshold

Indicators: court settings experienced as re-enactments, catastrophic interpretations of routine co-parenting events, urgent requests for therapist endorsement of affidavits, or legal escalation immediately following sessions.

Clinical response:

1. Differentiate past trauma from the present legal context.
2. Slow interpretive intensity during active litigation.
3. Reinstate stabilisation if activation escalates.
4. Clarify therapeutic role boundaries and documentation scope.

Continue Phase II only when reactivity reduces, and decisions can be made without urgency.

Step 4: Re-entry decision

Phase II continues only when all the following are sustained across sessions:

1. Emotional regulation is sustained.
2. Behavioural urgency is absent.
3. No credible violence risk is present.
4. Suicidality is stabilised.
5. Reflective capacity returns without collapse or dissociation.

If any criterion is not met, revert to **Phase I principles**. This is not regression. It is correct phase integrity.

Key therapeutic processes

One of the central tasks of Phase II is to name coercive developmental dynamics that were previously normalised, minimised, or psychologically forbidden. This includes identifying how fear, dependency, misinformation, emotional punishment, secrecy, and conditional belonging shaped behavioural adaptation. Survivors are supported in recognising that alignment with an alienating parent frequently occurred under conditions of threat and psychological captivity rather than autonomous choice.

Importantly, Phase II does not impose guilt narratives. The author's doctoral research indicates that not all adult survivors experience guilt, particularly those alienated at earlier developmental stages or those who developed phobic fear responses. For many survivors, there was no psychological space for moral reflection or agency at the time. Phase II accommodates this diversity of survivor experience.

A second core task involves differentiating identity from adaptation. Survivors frequently describe themselves using language internalised within abusive or coercive systems, including labels such as selfish, dramatic, unstable, disloyal, weak, or ungrateful. Phase II actively separates identity from survival strategy. Hypervigilance, emotional shutdown, people-pleasing, relational avoidance, and compliance are reframed as adaptive responses to developmental threat rather than as inherent character flaws. This process directly counters misdiagnosis and internalised stigma and should be conducted in alignment with the formulation safeguards described in Chapter Four.

Phase II also addresses narrative continuity. Many adult survivors report fragmented life narratives resulting from secrecy, misinformation, repeated relocations, identity disruption, or enforced silence. The therapeutic aim is not to construct a perfectly linear or complete story, but to support the development of a psychologically owned narrative that feels internally coherent and emotionally tolerable. Clinicians must resist the urge to fill gaps, impose causality, or prematurely accelerate coherence. Survivors are permitted to hold uncertainty and evolving understanding.

Recognition of violations of developmental and relational rights is an explicit component of Phase II. Many survivors were deprived of fundamental relational and developmental rights, including the right to maintain attachment bonds, access accurate personal history, retain family continuity, possess medical and familial knowledge, and grieve losses as they occurred. Recognition of these violations is not political advocacy within therapy. It is part of psychological repair. Without naming such violations, survivors frequently continue to locate harm internally and carry responsibility that never belonged to them. The clinician does not require forgiveness, reconciliation, or acceptance of injustice. The task is recognition rather than resolution. Lastly, increased clarity or emotional insight does not constitute readiness for trauma integration.

Role of Therapeutic Modalities

The author's doctoral findings indicate that no single therapeutic modality is sufficient in Phase II. Clinicians selectively draw on approaches that support meaning reconstruction, identity repair, and relational integration. Psychodynamic psychotherapy supports work with internalised relational templates and identity formation. Narrative approaches facilitate re-authoring of personal meaning without invalidating emotional truth. Attachment-based interventions support recognition of developmental relational patterns that continue to shape adult functioning.

Somatic awareness may be introduced gently to support the embodiment of insight, but not trauma integration. Cognitive techniques may be used selectively to address internalised false beliefs only after the coercive developmental context has been clearly named. Trauma integration modalities such as EMDR, prolonged exposure, and memory-focused interventions remain contraindicated unless stabilisation remains robust and meaning integration has been achieved.

Clinical Decision Points Within Phase II

If survivors become preoccupied with defending narratives or seeking factual confirmation, the clinician pauses meaning-focused work and returns to relational validation using Phase I containment strategies. If exploration increases shame, collapse, or global self-condemnation, interpretations are reframed to emphasise adaptation rather than pathology. If grief or anger emerges for the first time, containment is prioritised over analysis. If countertransference arises in the form of urgency to correct, confront, rescue, or protect, supervision is required before proceeding. These decision points align with the real-time clinical judgement pathways embedded within the Phase I and Phase II decision frameworks in Chapter Five.

Indicators of Phase II Integration

Readiness to transition from Phase II is indicated when survivors demonstrate the capacity to hold a differentiated sense of self, recognise abuse without needing to prove it, tolerate ambivalence without collapse, and engage with personal history without destabilising present safety. Emotional pain may remain. What changes is the survivor's relationship to that pain and their capacity to hold it without self-erasure. Only when these conditions are present should Phase III be considered.

Clinical Implementation Overview: Operationalising Phase II within the HQTP

Phase II clinical work is not delivered through a single technique or a standalone intervention. Instead, it is operationalised through a coordinated combination of relational positioning, pacing structure, language scaffolding, and phase-specific clinical tools embedded throughout the HQTP.

Chapter Four provides the formulation framework and diagnostic restraint principles that guide meaning reconstruction without epistemic harm. These foundations inform clinicians' approaches to narrative material, identity work, and developmental interpretation without imposing premature certainty or replicating coercive relational dynamics. Phase-specific readiness indicators, safety thresholds, and real-time clinical decision trees are embedded within Chapter Five and are used to guide pacing, containment, and progression decisions throughout Phase II work.

Additional guidance for responding to survivor distress, narrative pressure, loyalty conflict activation, countertransference dynamics, and the re-emergence of epistemic threat is integrated throughout the Phase I and Phase II clinical decision frameworks in Chapter Five. Later chapters outline selective application of psychodynamic, attachment-based, narrative, and somatic-informed approaches while avoiding technique-driven escalation or premature trauma exposure.

Within clinical sessions, Phase II work is enacted primarily through collaborative formulation, reflective dialogue, developmentally informed psychoeducation, and structured narrative clarification rather than through protocolised trauma processing. The clinician's task is to support meaning reconstruction without imposing interpretation, accelerating emotional exposure, or positioning the therapeutic space as evaluative or adjudicative.

Phase II, therefore, requires a shift in clinical stance more than a shift in technique. Practitioners apply Phase II principles through disciplined pacing, continuous assessment of epistemic safety and affect tolerance, and regular clinical supervision. The emphasis remains on relational containment, identity differentiation, and psychological authorship rather than symptom reduction, narrative completion, or outcome-driven treatment sequencing.

The design of the HQTP intentionally separates meaning reconstruction from trauma integration. This structural separation protects survivors from re-enactment of coercive relational patterns and helps prevent modality-driven destabilisation when adult survivors of prolonged psychological abuse and attachment disruption are advanced prematurely into trauma processing. Phase II is thus operationalised not by adding interventions, but by changing how clinicians listen, pace, frame meaning, and hold relational authority within the therapeutic environment.

Phase II Explained for Adult Survivors

A note from Dr Alyse

Dear friends,

I have written this part directly to you, in simple language, so this phase feels clearer and more manageable.

This part of therapy begins when the work no longer feels like something you simply must get through. By this stage, there is usually a little more steadiness in the room, a little more safety in the relationship, and a little more space for you to begin to make sense of what you lived through. If the work slows down, pauses, or circles back to earlier stabilisation, that does not mean anything is going wrong. It usually means your nervous system is doing what it learned long ago: protecting you.

This phase is not about fixing you. It is about helping you understand yourself in the context of what happened to you. Many adult survivors were never given the chance to make sense of their childhood as it unfolded. Some were too young. Some were too afraid. Some were too dependent on the adults around them to question what they were being told. Some were isolated, moved, lied to, or placed in positions where loyalty was demanded at the expense of truth. This phase is about gently untangling those experiences in a way that feels manageable and safe enough to hold.

You do not need a perfect memory for this work. You do not need every answer. You do not need to explain yourself flawlessly. What matters here is your lived experience: how things felt, what you learned about safety and love, what you came to believe about yourself, and how those experiences shaped your life. You are allowed to take your time. You are allowed to pause. You are allowed to say, “I do not know.” You are allowed to let understanding come slowly.

Many survivors discover in this phase that what looked like a choice in childhood was not really a choice at all. Children depend on adults for safety, belonging, and survival. When those things are threatened, children adapt. They comply. They align. They freeze. They shut down. They appease. They dissociate. Some survivors carry guilt about how they responded. Others do not, not because they do not care, but because they were psychologically trapped, too overwhelmed, or too developmentally young to reflect in that way at the time. Both experiences are valid. This work helps you understand what was possible then without judging yourself from where you stand now.

Many survivors also carry labels that were never truly theirs. Over time, these labels can become part of the way you speak to yourself. You may have been called selfish, difficult, unstable, weak, dramatic, disloyal, or ungrateful. You may still hear those words inside. One of the important tasks of this phase is to help separate who you are from the ways you had to survive. Hypervigilance, emotional shutdown, people pleasing, distrust, confusion, and relational fear are not signs that you were broken. They are signs that you adapted to unsafe conditions.

This phase is not about building a perfect timeline or proving your story to anyone. It is about helping you develop a version of your story that is yours. Some parts may remain unclear. Some things may never be fully known. That does not make your experience less real. What matters is that your understanding begins to feel more internally true, more compassionate, and more your own.

Many survivors also come to recognise that important rights were taken from them. This may include the right to love both parents safely, the right to receive truthful information, the right to know family members, the right to maintain family continuity, the right to grieve losses as they occurred, and the right to grow up without being forced into adult loyalties or impossible choices. Recognising these losses is not about staying trapped in anger. It is about stopping the lifelong habit of blaming yourself for injuries that never belonged to you.

This part of therapy can feel clarifying at times and unsettling at others. You may feel grief, anger, relief, confusion, numbness, or all of these at once. If it becomes too much, the work slows down. You are not expected to push through pain in order to prove that you are healing. Small shifts matter. Less shame matters. Less pressure to defend yourself matters. More permission to pause matters. These are real signs of repair.

This phase does not end with certainty, forgiveness, or neat closure. It begins to settle when you can hold more of your experience with greater clarity, compassion, and self-trust. There is no deadline here. Healing unfolds at the pace that safety allows. When enough steadiness, meaning, and trust have been built, therapy may later begin to move toward deeper grief and emotional integration. Until then, we go gently, honestly, and at your pace.

Reclaiming Meaning, Identity, and Your Own Story

Therapy does not move forward because you are "ready" or because something has been fixed. It moves forward because your nervous system and sense of safety now allow it. If this phase takes time, if progress feels slow, or if therapy pauses and loops back, this is not failure. This is how repair happens without repeating harm. Phase II is not about fixing you. It is about helping you understand yourself with honesty, safety, and compassion.

By the time you reach this phase, therapy is no longer only about getting through each week or calming your nervous system. It begins to become about meaning. It becomes about helping you make sense of a childhood that may have felt confusing, contradictory, or impossible to understand while you were living it.

Many adult survivors of CPA-PA were never given the opportunity to understand what was happening to them at the time. You may have been too young, too afraid, too dependent, or too overwhelmed to think clearly. Some survivors were moved repeatedly, lied to, isolated from family members, or taught to fear the very people they loved. Others were placed in positions of loyalty where belonging came at the cost of truth, safety, or identity.

What matters here is not building a "perfect" story. What matters is learning to trust your own perspective again. Alienating caregivers can be highly persuasive. Over time, they can teach children to doubt their own memories, emotions, and instincts, which carries into adulthood. In this phase, therapy helps you slowly reconnect with what feels true to you. For some survivors, it can also be helpful to notice whether siblings remember similar experiences, when that information is safely available, as a way of reality-checking long-standing distortions. This is not about proving anything. It is about gently rebuilding your right to your own experience. This phase is where therapy begins to untangle these experiences at a pace that feels manageable and emotionally safe.

Common Misconceptions About Phase II

Your therapist is not trying to interrogate your memories, cross-examine your story, or decide who was right or wrong. Memories often surface naturally when your system feels ready. Many survivors describe this stage as trying to assemble a jigsaw puzzle with missing pieces and no clear picture. Together, you and your therapist begin to form a version of your story that belongs to you, not to the person who previously controlled the narrative. This is a powerful and often emotional step.

Your therapist is not trying to push you to forgive, confront, reunite, reconcile, or "move on." They are not diagnosing you, analysing you, or searching for what is "wrong" with you. If therapy has felt like that in the past, it makes sense if this phase feels unfamiliar or even unsettling at first.

What Phase II Is Intended to Support

Phase II is about meaning. It is about understanding how your thoughts, feelings, behaviours, and relationships make sense in the context of what you lived through, rather than viewing them as personal flaws. It is about separating who you truly are from what you had to become to survive. It is about reclaiming ownership of your story without pressure to explain it perfectly or justify it to anyone.

Many Survivors Do Not Realise They Were Abused

A central part of this phase is recognising that many adult survivors do not enter therapy knowing they were abused. Some people have spent years in therapy, in and out of mental health units, justice systems, or crisis services, without anyone naming the underlying harm. Others were given diagnoses that never fully explained why life felt unsafe, confusing, or disconnected. In many cases, it is the therapist who first notices patterns of child psychological abuse or alienation, not the survivor. If you are only beginning to wonder whether something serious happened to you, this does not mean you are behind, resistant, or in denial. It means no one helped you see it sooner.

Understanding Coercion and Loyalty Conflict

One of the most important understandings in this phase is that many of the choices you made as a child were not freely chosen. Children depend on adults for survival. When love, safety, or belonging are threatened, children adapt. They comply, align, freeze, dissociate, appease, or shut down emotionally. These were survival strategies, not moral failures.

Some adult survivors carry deep guilt about how they behaved toward a targeted parent. Others feel little or no guilt, not because they were uncaring, but because they were overwhelmed, frightened, or psychologically trapped. The author's research demonstrates that both experiences are valid. Especially for children alienated at very young ages or those who developed intense fear responses, there may have been no psychological space for reflection or choice at all. This phase helps you understand what was possible for you at the time, rather than judging yourself from an adult perspective.

Reclaiming Your Identity

Many survivors grow up carrying labels that were never truly theirs. You may have been called difficult, selfish, dramatic, disloyal, unstable, or ungrateful. Over time, these labels can become internal voices. In this phase, therapy helps you recognise that many of the traits you were criticised for were adaptations. Hypervigilance often develops in unpredictable environments. Emotional shutdown develops when feelings are unsafe. Difficulty trusting develops after repeated betrayal. Confusion about identity develops when children are given contradictory stories about their own lives. None of these means you are broken. They mean you adapted.

Making Sense of Your Story Without Forcing It

Some survivors want answers immediately. Others avoid thinking about the past altogether. Both responses are understandable. This phase does not require you to remember everything, confront anyone, or build a neat, linear story. Instead, your therapist helps you build a version of your story that feels true enough to you, even if parts are missing or unclear. You are allowed to say, "I don't know." You are allowed to revise your understanding over time. What matters is that the story belongs to you.

Recognising Violated Rights

For many survivors, deep pain emerges when they realise that fundamental rights were taken from them. These may include the right to know and be known by family, the right to maintain attachment relationships, the right to accurate information about personal history, the right to medical and familial knowledge, the right to grieve losses when they occurred, the right not to be lied to, and the right to feel safe loving both parents. Recognising these violations is not about staying angry. It is about breaking the long habit of blaming yourself for harm that was never yours to carry.

How Therapy Often Feels in This Phase

Therapy in this phase may feel clarifying at times and destabilising at others. You may feel relief, grief, anger, confusion, or numbness. You may begin questioning long-held beliefs about yourself or your family. Your therapist's role is to stay with you through this process without rushing it. If things become overwhelming, the pace slows. You are not expected to push through pain to prove progress.

When This Phase Is Working

Change in this phase is often subtle. You may notice that you feel less compelled to defend your story. You may begin to feel less shame about your reactions. You may notice moments when self-blame softens. You may begin to recognise that what happened to you had a context.

These are signs that meaning is beginning to return.

Moving Forward Toward Phase III

Phase II does not end because you suddenly feel "better," clearer, or finished. It ends when something quieter but important has begun to change inside you. You may notice that you trust yourself a little more. You may feel less pressure to explain or defend your story. You may begin to recognise that what happened to you had a context, and that your reactions were not personal failures.

You may still feel pain. You may still feel confused at times. Healing does not remove the past. What it changes is your relationship to it. When this phase is working, you are no longer trying to survive your own story. You are beginning to carry it with more stability and self-respect. There is no requirement to rush forward. You are allowed to stay here as long as you need. Therapy does not move forward due to timelines or expectations. It moves forward only when your nervous system and sense of safety allow it.

How Therapy Gently Deepens

When enough safety, meaning, and self-trust have been built, therapy may begin to shift again. This shift does not mean that Phase II work is finished or left behind. It means your system has reached a level of stability that allows it to begin approaching emotional experiences that were once too overwhelming, dangerous, or painful to feel.

Phase III is not about forcing emotions, reopening wounds, or “reliving” trauma. It is about allowing feelings that were previously locked away for survival reasons to be processed slowly, safely, and with support. For many survivors, grief, sadness, anger, and attachment pain were not absent in childhood. They were simply not safe to feel at the time.

This next phase begins only when your therapist can see that you are no longer experiencing therapy as a place of judgement, pressure, or performance. It begins when your system shows signs that it can remain present with emotion without collapsing, dissociating, or becoming overwhelmed.

You will not be pushed into this phase. You will not be rushed. You will not be asked to “go deeper” before you are ready. The work that follows is built on everything you have already done learning safety, rebuilding meaning, reclaiming your identity, and restoring trust in yourself. Phase III does not replace these foundations. It rests on them. When sufficient meaning, identity coherence, and epistemic safety have been established, therapeutic work may begin to shift toward the careful exploration of attachment injury, grief, and affective loss. This transition marks the beginning of Phase III.

Go gently, Dr Alyse

Phase III: Mourning, Loss Integration, and Developmental Grief Repair

The clinical objective of Phase III is to support survivors in processing compound grief and integrating losses that occurred under conditions of coercion, secrecy, developmental captivity, and systemic betrayal. Phase III formalises the survivor's right to mourn experiences that were previously denied recognition, language, or communal support, while maintaining psychological safety and protection from retraumatisation. This phase addresses complex grief arising from family erasure, disrupted attachment bonds, delayed truth disclosure, and loss without consent. Many adult survivors were not informed of illness, death, relocation, or major family events during childhood. Some discover in adulthood that a targeted parent died by suicide, that siblings existed but were concealed, or that extended family relationships were intentionally severed. These discoveries frequently produce shock, anger, identity destabilisation, and delayed grief responses that differ significantly from normative bereavement trajectories.

Within the HQTP, grief in this population is conceptualised as both an attachment injury and a developmental rights injury. Survivors were not only deprived of relational bonds but also denied the opportunity to mourn in real time, receive communal validation, and integrate loss into identity formation during critical developmental periods. Phase III, therefore, establishes mourning as a legitimate clinical task rather than an optional emotional outcome. It requires structured pacing, containment, and safeguards for decision-making to prevent retraumatisation and avoid reproducing coercive relational dynamics within the therapeutic process.

Entry Criteria for Phase III

Phase III may begin only when sufficient meaning integration, identity coherence, and epistemic safety have been established to allow engagement with grief material without destabilisation. Indicators of readiness include the capacity to tolerate emotional activation without dissociation or collapse, sustained internal validation of personal experience, reduced fear-based compliance, and the ability to reflect on relational loss without immediate urgency to act, confront, or resolve. These criteria are assessed using Phase II readiness markers and clinical decision frameworks outlined in Chapter Five. When these conditions are not met, the clinician returns to Phase II consolidation processes without framing this recalibration as regression, resistance, or therapeutic failure. Movement between phases remains fluid and capacity-based.

Phase III Decision Tree Quick Reference

Grief Containment and Trauma Integration Readiness

Phase III requires continuous, moment-to-moment clinical decision-making rather than linear progression through tasks. This decision tree framework operationalises differentiation, grief containment thresholds, and readiness for trauma integration. These decision trees guide in-session pacing, between-session monitoring, and supervision-based clinical reflection. They function as clinical containment mechanisms rather than procedural algorithms. Their purpose is to protect survivors from premature emotional exposure and protect clinicians from technique-driven escalation. In Phase III, grief work is paced to the survivor's regulatory capacity rather than to narrative completeness, and the clinician remains responsible for slowing the work when destabilisation markers appear.

Decision Tree 1: Epistemic Stability and Disclosure Orientation

When the survivor discloses material related to child psychological abuse, parental alienation, abduction, or attachment injury, the clinician first assesses the form and function of disclosure.

If disclosure is urgent, repetitive, escalating in detail, or involves monitoring the clinician's reactions to secure belief or validation, remain in Phase III differentiation work. Trauma integration is contraindicated. The clinical response prioritises epistemic stabilisation, relational safety, and meaning consolidation rather than emotional exposure. Distress tolerance and grounding strategies may be used to stabilise arousal without reinforcing dependency on validation.

If the survivor can describe experiences without needing to persuade, justify, or defend, epistemic stability is beginning to emerge.

Survivors raised within family systems characterised by severe, contested, or highly polarised allegations may exhibit heightened vigilance in their disclosures. Urgency, persuasive intensity, or monitoring of clinicians' beliefs may reflect developmental conditioning in adversarial environments rather than current instability alone. The clinician does not assume a forensic role or adjudicate historical claims. Treatment focuses instead on strengthening internal narrative authority, reducing reliance on external validation, and supporting the survivor's capacity to tolerate ambiguity without identity collapse. Trauma integration remains deferred when allegation-related activation triggers regulatory destabilisation or reactivation of loyalty conflict.

Clinical Example

A survivor reports prolonged exposure to adversarial court proceedings during childhood in which severe allegations were publicly discussed. They describe humiliation, confusion, and fear as private family narratives were debated in formal settings. The survivor recalls feeling disbelieved, pressured to align with one parent's account, or warned of relational consequences for expressing dissent. In adulthood, discussion of these events evokes shame activation, intense affect, and heightened sensitivity to the clinician's belief in them.

In this context, the clinician communicates belief in the survivor's lived experience and validates the emotional impact of growing up in adversarial conditions. Validation is directed toward humiliation, loyalty conflict, and epistemic injury rather than toward adjudication of historical claims. The clinical task is to repair epistemic disruption and strengthen internal narrative authority while maintaining a non-forensic stance.

Clinical Consideration: Attuned Validation Without Forensic Alignment

Survivors exposed to adversarial and allegation-saturated environments are often highly sensitive to cues of disbelief, dismissal, or emotional withdrawal. Clinician scepticism, visible discomfort, premature reframing, or rapid topic shifts may replicate earlier experiences of not being heard. Within the HQTP, the clinician maintains attuned belief in the survivor's lived experience and emotional reality while remaining nonjudgemental regarding historical claims. Validation is directed toward humiliation, fear, loyalty conflict, and epistemic injury. The therapeutic task is to provide steady presence, regulated listening, and coherent containment rather than to debate plausibility or resolve factual disputes. Trauma integration is deferred until the survivor can discuss these experiences without destabilisation, compulsive persuasion, or external validation dependence.

Phase III Decision Tree 2: Attachment Orientation Within the Therapeutic Relationship

The clinician evaluates the survivor's relationship with the therapist.

If the survivor demonstrates excessive compliance, fear of disagreement, heightened anxiety around misattunement, or seeks reassurance regarding therapist approval, trauma integration is deferred. Treatment remains focused on relational safety, differentiation, and boundary stabilisation. DBT interpersonal effectiveness skills may be introduced selectively to support autonomy, boundary expression, and self-advocacy within the therapeutic relationship.

If the survivor can tolerate misattunement, express disagreement, pause sessions without fear of abandonment, and maintain relational stability without performance behaviours, attachment conditions may be sufficient to continue the Phase III readiness assessment.

Decision Tree 3: Affect Activation and Recovery Capacity

The clinician evaluates emotional activation and recovery rather than emotional intensity alone.

If emotional activation leads to prolonged destabilisation, dissociation, panic responses, somatic collapse, or identity fragmentation, trauma integration is postponed. Treatment returns to containment, pacing, and nervous system stabilisation. DBT emotion regulation and distress tolerance skills may be used to support recovery capacity without bypassing meaningful work.

If emotional activation can be tolerated and metabolised with predictable recovery within or between sessions, readiness indicators increase, and further assessment may proceed.

Decision Tree 4: Loyalty Conflict and Internalised Coercive Narratives

The clinician assesses whether the survivor remains organised around internalised coercive family narratives.

If exploration of grief or attachment material intensifies guilt, loyalty conflict, self-condemnation, fear of betraying caregivers, or pressure to reframe harm as mutual responsibility, trauma integration is contraindicated. Under these conditions, treatment remains focused on narrative differentiation, ethical reframing, epistemic stabilisation, and restoration of internal moral clarity.

If the survivor can accurately locate responsibility outside the self, tolerate ambivalence toward the alienating parent, relevant allies, and authority figures without collapsing, and recognise coercive dynamics without reverting to self-blame or defensive justification, then processing readiness may be cautiously considered.

Decision Tree 5: Contextual and Environmental Safety

The clinician evaluates the survivor's current relational environment.

If the survivor remains embedded in active coercive family relationships, ongoing legal conflict related to separation or divorce, pressure from allies of abusive caregivers, or involvement in psychologically controlling dynamics around them, trauma integration is deferred. Therapy remains focused on boundary stabilisation, safety planning, and meaning reconstruction.

If the survivor's current environment supports psychological safety and autonomy, readiness indicators increase. Even so, this level of safety may take considerable time to achieve and sustain.

Decision Tree 6: Clinician Countertransference Monitoring

The clinician evaluates internal responses as clinical data.

If the clinician experiences sustained urgency to accelerate treatment, pressure to demonstrate progress, rescuing impulses, moral distress, or frustration, trauma integration is paused. Supervision is advised and should be treated as mandatory before proceeding. These reactions may re-enact coercive dynamics for the survivor and adversely affect treatment.

If the clinician can maintain reflective distance, tolerate ambiguity, and sustain relational attunement without urgency, ethical conditions are strengthened.

Decision Tree 7: Survivor Agency and Consent Capacity

The clinician evaluates whether the survivor can freely choose to engage in ongoing therapy.

If the survivor feels obligated to proceed, fears disappointing the therapist, equates progress with worth, or experiences pressure to "be ready," trauma integration is contraindicated. Therapy remains focused on restoring agency, stabilising epistemic certainty, and maintaining consent-based pacing. DBT-informed wise mind framing may be used to support autonomous decision-making without reinforcing compliance dynamics.

If the survivor can choose engagement freely, pause without fear of relational rupture, say no without anticipating abandonment, and trust that therapeutic safety does not depend on performance, trauma integration may be ethically considered. Trauma integration proceeds only when readiness is sustained across these domains rather than inferred solely from insight, disclosure depth, or emotional intensity.

Phase III Stabilisation Supports: DBT Skills-Informed Integration

Within the HQTP, DBT is not positioned as a standalone treatment model in Phase III. Instead, selected DBT skills are used as adjunct stabilisation supports within the Phase III decision framework. These skills are intended to enhance the survivor's capacities in affect tolerance, physiological regulation, present-moment awareness, and relational safety without bypassing differentiation, meaning reconstruction, or epistemic repair. This use of DBT within the HQTP does not constitute comprehensive DBT. Rather, selected DBT skills are incorporated adjunctively to support phase-specific stabilisation, pacing, and relational safety (Linehan, 2015).

Within Phase III, the use of DBT skills is guided by the decision framework and by moment-to-moment assessment of arousal, dissociative drift, relational safety, and consent stability. DBT distress tolerance skills may be introduced when emotional arousal exceeds the survivor's immediate coping capacity but does not require regression to Phase I containment. Techniques such as paced breathing, temperature-based regulation strategies, sensory grounding, and other crisis-survival supports may be used selectively to help the survivor tolerate acute distress without escalating, withdrawing, or losing behavioural control. Their function in this phase is not to resolve grief, but to help the survivor remain safely engaged when activation becomes too high (Linehan, 2015).

Emotion regulation skills may be used to support the survivor's capacity to identify emotional states, understand emotional vulnerability, reduce secondary emotional escalation, and modify unwanted emotional responses when clinically appropriate. In keeping with DBT principles, these skills are not used to communicate that the survivor should not feel what they feel. Rather, they are introduced within a validating therapeutic stance that supports awareness, modulation, and safe engagement with affect. These skills are not used to minimise grief, dispute the survivor's reality, or pressure the survivor to prematurely control emotions (Linehan, 2015).

DBT interpersonal effectiveness skills may be introduced where attachment insecurity, fear of disagreement, compliance patterns, or difficulty articulating limits interferes with relational safety. In this context, these skills support clearer boundary expression, consent-based pacing, help-seeking, and the capacity to say no while maintaining self-respect and therapeutic alliance (Linehan, 2015).

DBT mindfulness skills may be integrated to strengthen present-moment awareness and nonjudgemental observation during affective processing. Within the HQTP, mindfulness is not used to neutralise emotion or detach from meaningful experience. Rather, it is used to support embodied awareness and psychological presence when dissociative drift, panic, or narrative collapse begins to emerge. Emotion regulation and interpersonal effectiveness skills are also understood to rely on mindfulness capacities (Linehan, 2015).

Importantly, DBT skills do not replace the differentiation, grief integration, or meaning reconstruction processes of Phase III. They function as stabilisation supports when affect tolerance, relational safety, or epistemic stability becomes compromised. Their role is to help the survivor remain within a workable window for therapeutic engagement, not to substitute for the core clinical tasks of this phase (Linehan, 2015).

Decision Integration Rule: Phase III Progression Threshold

No single decision point authorises progression. Phase III advancement requires convergence across epistemic stability, relational safety, affect tolerance, agency capacity, and consent integrity. When instability emerges in any domain, clinical focus returns to stabilisation and differentiation rather than advancing trauma processing. Phase progression remains capacity-based rather than time-based and is continuously reassessed throughout Phase III work.

Clinical Purpose of Phase III

Phase III marks a critical threshold in treatment. It is the phase in which clinicians must determine whether work is ready to move from meaning reconstruction into trauma integration, or whether further differentiation, stabilisation, and relational safety remain necessary. This phase does not assume that trauma integration is inevitable or required for all survivors. Instead, it provides a structured clinical decision framework designed to prevent retraumatisation, epistemic harm, premature exposure, and therapeutic reenactment.

The author's doctoral findings demonstrate that many adult survivors were exposed to trauma-focused interventions prematurely, often after years of misdiagnosis or therapeutic misunderstanding. In these cases, treatment frequently replicated coercive dynamics by prioritising emotional exposure over psychological safety. Phase III exists to prevent therapy itself from becoming another site of harm.

Core Clinical Task: Differentiation

The primary clinical task of Phase III is differentiation. Differentiation refers to the survivor's growing capacity to distinguish between multiple psychological domains that were previously collapsed through coercion and developmental captivity. This includes differentiation between past and present, adaptation and pathology, authentic self and survival-based identity, internalised coercive narratives and personal meaning, and the therapeutic relationship and historical attachment injury.

Without sufficient differentiation, trauma integration techniques risk reinforcing fear conditioning, loyalty conflict, and epistemic instability. Differentiation allows survivors to hold emotional material without collapsing into self-blame, narrative confusion, or relational dependency. It is therefore the prerequisite condition for any form of memory processing or affective exposure.

Grief as Attachment Injury and Rights Violation

Grief in adult survivors of parental alienation and psychological abuse frequently presents in non-linear, delayed, or fragmented forms. Survivors may grieve the loss of a parent they never knew, the loss of siblings from whom they were separated, the loss of truthful family narratives, the loss of cultural identity, and the loss of time that cannot be recovered. Some grieve events they were never allowed to witness, including funerals, illnesses, and family rituals.

Clinicians must recognise that these grief processes occur alongside identity disruption. Survivors are not only mourning people, but also mourning unrealised developmental experiences, lost attachments, and erased versions of self. Phase III, therefore, requires clinicians to validate grief as legitimate even when it emerges decades after the original loss.

Clinical tasks during this stage include supporting grief permission, facilitating meaning-making around loss, addressing moral injury and systems betrayal, and helping survivors identify specific grief themes. These themes commonly include the loss of truth, family continuity, medical and genetic knowledge, childhood security, and relational belonging.

Clinical Containment Before Technique

Phase III emphasises that containment precedes technique. The presence of emotional pain does not indicate readiness for trauma integration. Many survivors demonstrate increased emotional access before sufficient differentiation has occurred. In such cases, premature trauma processing risks overwhelming affect regulation systems and reinforcing old survival patterns.

Containment in Phase III involves maintaining relational stability, pacing emotional exploration, monitoring epistemic safety, and ensuring that the therapeutic environment remains non-evaluative and non-coercive. Clinicians must resist pressure to "do trauma work" simply because emotional material is present.

Survivors Who Appear Ready Before They Are Clinically Ready

A common clinical mistake is assuming that a survivor is ready for deeper trauma or grief work because they appear calm, articulate, reflective, or emotionally organised. Some survivors present as highly insightful, able to describe their experiences clearly and discuss painful material without visible distress. While this may appear to indicate readiness, it does not necessarily mean that psychological safety and agency have been restored.

Many adult survivors learned early how to manage their emotions, present well to authority figures, and tell coherent stories to survive coercive or unsafe family environments. For example, a survivor may be able to speak about childhood abuse in a calm and structured way yet still feel intense internal pressure to please the therapist, minimise harm, avoid "sounding dramatic," or protect abusive caregivers from being judged. On the surface, the survivor appears stable. Internally, they may still be operating from loyalty conflict, fear of relational rupture, or the need to perform safety rather than experience it.

Within the HQTP, readiness is not measured by how well a survivor can talk about their story or tolerate emotional discomfort. Readiness is defined by whether the survivor can remain emotionally present without collapsing into self-blame, compliance, self-erasure, or compulsive reassurance seeking. The key clinical question is not "Can this survivor handle distress?" It is "Can this survivor engage with distress while maintaining agency, internal authority, and psychological safety? "When this capacity is not yet present, the clinical task is not to push forward. It is to return to stabilisation, meaning differentiation, and consent-based pacing until the survivor can participate in the work without sacrificing themselves in the process.

Required Clinical Capacities Prior to Trauma Integration

Before introducing any structured trauma integration modality, clinicians must assess whether the survivor has developed several core capacities. The survivor demonstrates an internalised understanding that the abuse was not their fault, even if emotional ambivalence remains. This does not require the absence of grief, anger, or guilt, but it does require that the survivor is no longer attempting to justify survival behaviours or prove innocence.

The survivor possesses language for coercion, loyalty conflict, psychological control, and attachment disruption. This language may be clinical or personal, but it must allow the survivor to conceptualise experiences without defaulting to self-blame. The survivor demonstrates growing epistemic stability, including reduced compulsive validation seeking, diminished urgency to persuade the clinician, and tolerance for uncertainty without self-invalidating responses.

The survivor can tolerate emotional activation with predictable recovery rather than prolonged dissociation, collapse, or identity fragmentation. The survivor no longer experiences the therapeutic relationship as evaluative, forensic, or adversarial. If the clinician is still perceived as a judge, rescuer, or authority figure who must be convinced, trauma integration is contraindicated.

When Trauma Integration Is Contraindicated

Trauma integration should be deferred when the survivor remains engaged in active coercive relationships, unresolved loyalty conflicts, or legal and familial environments that compromise psychological safety. It is also contraindicated when survivors continue to use disclosure intensity as a strategy to secure belief, when dissociation remains persistent, or when therapy itself is experienced as destabilising. Clinicians must also monitor their own countertransference during this phase. Sustained urges to rescue, accelerate treatment, validate prematurely, or demonstrate progress frequently reflect systemic pressure rather than survivor readiness. In these circumstances, supervision is required before proceeding.

Modality Positioning Within Phase III

The author's doctoral research identified several therapeutic approaches consistently endorsed by experienced practitioners working with adult survivors of severe parental alienation and child psychological abuse. These modalities were not recommended as interchangeable techniques, but as components of an integrated, phase-based framework.

Psychodynamic psychotherapy was identified as central for addressing internalised relational dynamics, identity formation, transference patterns, and attachment injury. Trauma-informed cognitive approaches were valued for supporting the integration of meaning without invalidating emotional experience. Narrative therapy was endorsed for restoring authorship, coherence, and agency, particularly in survivors exposed to prolonged gaslighting and historical erasure.

Somatic approaches were recommended selectively and only after epistemic stability was established, given the heightened risk of dysregulation in survivors with early attachment trauma. EMDR and other memory-processing modalities were endorsed conditionally and only when readiness criteria were clearly met. Survivor responses to EMDR varied within the author's doctoral sample, with some adult survivors reporting benefit and others expressing discomfort, limited engagement, or preference for alternative approaches. These findings highlight the necessity of consent-based, individualised modality selection rather than assuming trauma processing techniques are universally appropriate.

Dialectical and skills-based frameworks, including DBT-informed regulation strategies, were valued for their role in supporting affect tolerance, relational stability, distress management, and long-term containment rather than short-term symptom control. DBT skills are positioned within the HQTP as stabilisation scaffolds rather than as primary tools for trauma resolution. Across all modalities, the defining feature was clinical restraint. Technique was consistently framed as secondary to containment, formulation, and ethical positioning.

Supervision and Countertransference Monitoring

Phase III requires active monitoring of clinician countertransference in clinical data. Feelings of urgency, protectiveness, moral outrage, frustration, or helplessness may signal unresolved survivor fear, loyalty conflict, or unintegrated attachment injury. Supervision during this phase is not optional. It functions as a containment structure for the clinician, protects against enactment, and ensures that therapeutic decisions remain survivor-led rather than system-driven. Clinicians are encouraged to view supervision not as a corrective mechanism, but as a parallel process that mirrors the differentiation work occurring in therapy.

Phase III Transition to Readiness Evaluation

Phase III does not conclude with emotional resolution, narrative completion, or symptom remission. It concludes when the survivor demonstrates sufficient epistemic stability, affect tolerance, and relational safety to remain psychologically present during attachment-related material without collapse, coercive compliance, or identity destabilisation. This transition is governed by clinical readiness indicators rather than therapeutic momentum, time spent in treatment, or observable emotional expression.

The transition from Phase III to Phase IV is intentionally conservative. The function of this transition is not to escalate clinical intensity but to protect survivors from premature exposure and clinicians from technique-driven progression. Phase IV, therefore, operates as a threshold phase in which readiness for grief integration and trauma processing is evaluated rather than assumed. When readiness criteria are not met, therapeutic focus returns to Phase III differentiation, stabilisation, and meaning consolidation processes without framing this recalibration as regression, resistance, or therapeutic failure. Within the HQTP, phase movement remains fluid, capacity-based, and ethically governed. This structure preserves treatment safety while preventing the replication of coercive dynamics in which survivors are pressured to perform progress or emotional endurance.

Phase III Operational Quick Reference for Clinicians

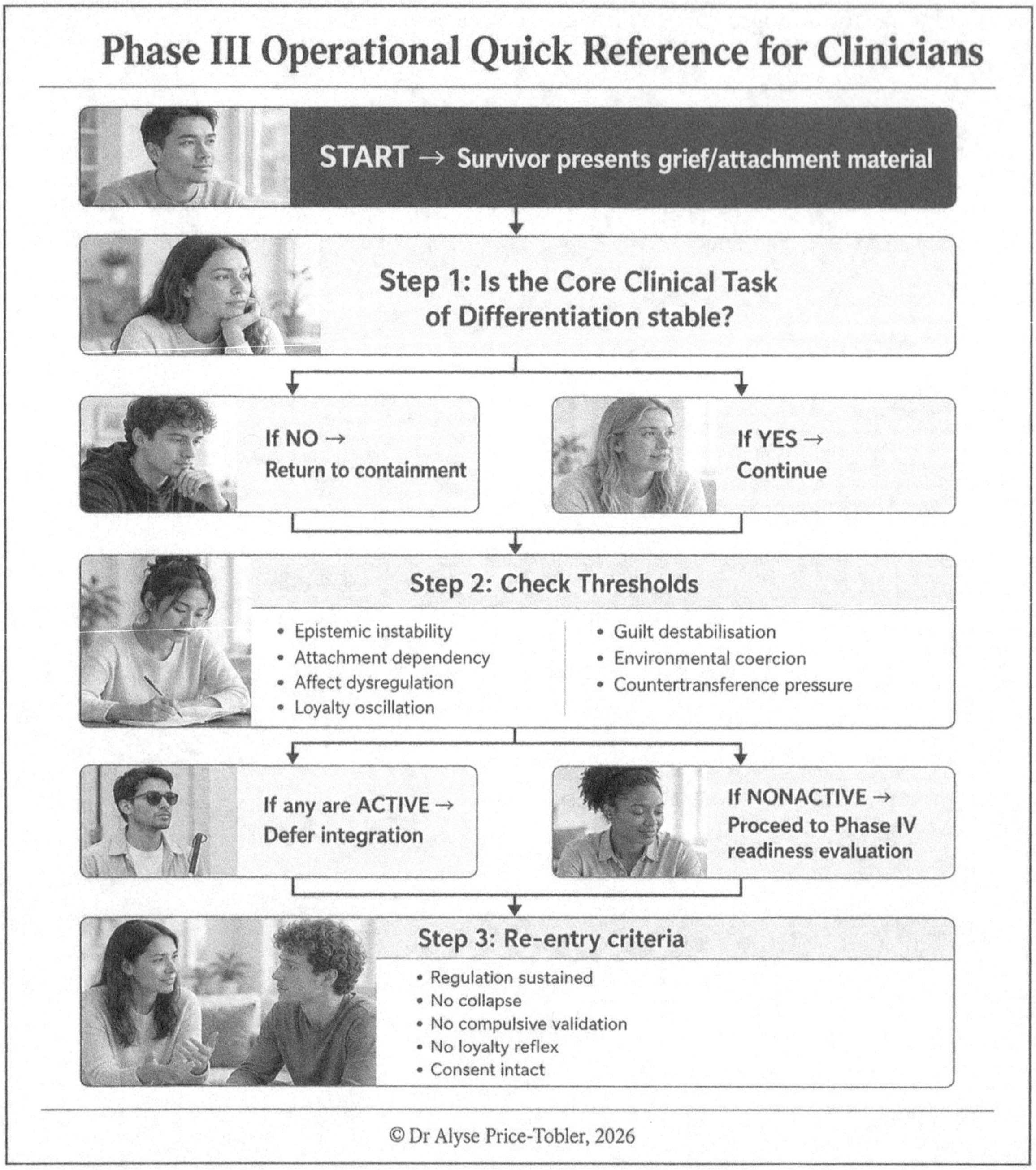

Clinical Note

This quick reference is designed to help clinicians pause before moving from grief and attachment material into deeper integration work. Differentiation must be stable enough to support continued work without collapse, compulsive validation seeking, loyalty reflex, or loss of consent capacity. If threshold concerns are active, the clinician returns to containment rather than deferring integration as failure or regression. Progression toward Phase IV readiness occurs only when regulation, consent, and internal stability are sufficiently sustained.

Phase III Explained for Adult Survivors: What This Stage Is Preparing You For

A note from Dr Alyse

Dear friends,

This section is here to help you understand what this phase means for you and why it matters in your healing.

I want to speak to you gently here. By the time therapy reaches this point, many survivors begin to notice some shifts inside. You may understand your history more clearly than before. You may trust your own perceptions more consistently. You may feel less dependent on someone else to confirm what is real. That does not mean the work is finished. It means something inside you is becoming stronger and steadier.

This stage is not about pushing you into deeper emotional processing. It is about ensuring your system is stable enough to handle difficult material without becoming overwhelmed, losing your sense of self, or feeling pressured to comply with expectations. Many adult survivors have been rushed in the past. They were encouraged to go deeper or process faster without enough stabilisation. That often led to increased distress or confusion. This work is designed to prevent that pattern. Nothing here moves because it is "time." It moves because you are steady enough.

At this point, the question is not whether you can tolerate pain. You already have. The more important question is whether you can remain connected to yourself while something 'triggering' is being discussed. Can you slow down the work if needed? Can you say no without fearing the relationship will change? Can you stay grounded in your own authority rather than looking outward for direction? If those capacities are still strengthening, that is not failure. It reflects how your system learned to survive earlier environments. Those adaptations are respected here. They are not forced away.

What Readiness Looks Like

Progress in this phase is not measured by emotional intensity or by how much of your story is exposed. It is measured by safety, agency, and internal stability. I also want to say something personal. I have moved through this stage myself. During that time, I held onto a sentence that helped me stay steady: "The fastest way through hell is to keep walking." For me, that did not mean pushing. It meant not turning back on myself. It meant allowing the process to unfold without forcing it.

Another phrase that grounded me was: "Where you focus is where you go." I learned to pay close attention to my thoughts. When my focus stayed on questions around "why had all this happened in my childhood?" I felt more distressed and unsettled. When I shifted my focus toward what I could control in my life, toward what was true, and toward what helped me stay anchored and reach out for help, I felt calmer. That shift was gradual, and pretty slow.

Your intuition matters here. It may not always feel loud, especially if you have spent years listening to other people's narratives. However, it is there. Intuition grows stronger when you begin to listen to and trust it.

When and if deeper grief work or trauma processing is considered during this protocol, it will only be with your consent, at your pace, and with your full understanding of what is involved. You are not expected to prove readiness by enduring distress. You are not required to move faster than your nervous system allows. Phase III closes when you can remain present and regulated while discussing your history without losing yourself in the process. Please do not be disheartened if this does not happen perfectly every time. What matters is your growing capacity to return to yourself, again and again, when needed. From there, the next phase is simply an evaluation, a careful look at whether deeper integration would support you now. There is no rush. You are allowed to move slowly. You are allowed to pause. You are allowed to trust your own internal sense of what feels right. You are the expert on you!

Go gently, Dr Alyse

Readiness Evaluation Rather Than Escalation

Phase III concludes not with emotional resolution, narrative completion, or symptom elimination, but with the establishment of sufficient differentiation, epistemic stability, and regulatory continuity to permit structured readiness evaluation. The completion of this phase does not indicate that trauma has been processed. It indicates that the survivor may now possess the internal capacities required for careful consideration of whether trauma processing is clinically appropriate.

Movement into Phase IV does not represent an escalation of intensity. It represents a shift in clinical function. The therapeutic task transitions from grief containment and differentiation toward a formal evaluation of integration readiness. This shift is conservative by design. In the HQTP, trauma processing is never assumed to be inevitable, required, or universally beneficial. It is considered only when relational safety, affect tolerance, internal authority, and consent stability remain intact across contexts and over time.

If readiness markers fluctuate, if loyalty reflex reactivates, if epistemic dependence resurfaces, or if affect recovery becomes unstable, clinical focus returns to Phase III without framing this recalibration as regression or therapeutic failure. Phase movement within the HQTP remains capacity-based rather than time-based and ethically governed rather than technique-driven. Phase IV, therefore, functions not as a trauma-exposure phase but as a readiness architecture. It establishes the decision thresholds under which trauma integration may proceed without reenactment, coercion, or destabilisation.

Phase IV: Trauma Integration Readiness Architecture

Phase IV establishes the evaluative threshold within the HQTP at which readiness for trauma processing is formally assessed. This phase functions as a clinical decision architecture rather than as a trauma-exposure phase. Therapeutic focus shifts from grief containment and developmental loss work toward a structured appraisal of differentiation capacity, regulatory stability, epistemic resilience, and consent-based engagement.

Phase IV does not initiate trauma processing by default. It determines whether trauma work may proceed ethically and safely within this protocol. Trauma processing is not presumed to be inevitable, necessary, or appropriate for all adult survivors of child psychological abuse in contexts of parental alienation, familial abduction, estrangement, relocation, or related family-system harm. In some cases, continued stabilisation and relational differentiation represent the appropriate long-term clinical position. Phase IV defines an ethical decision architecture designed to prevent retraumatisation, epistemic harm, loyalty reenactment, and premature exposure mislabelled as therapeutic progress.

Although structured mourning and developmental grief repair are addressed in Phase III, unresolved or delayed grief frequently influences readiness for trauma processing. In Phase IV, grief dynamics are evaluated as determinants of regulatory stability and differentiation capacity. If grief activation produces identity destabilisation, loyalty collapse, or affect flooding, clinicians return to Phase III containment processes.

Phase IV Entry Criteria

Transition into Phase IV occurs only when Phase III grief containment has stabilised sufficiently to permit structured readiness evaluation. Entry into this phase does not imply that trauma processing will proceed. It indicates that the survivor demonstrates preliminary regulatory and relational stability sufficient to support a structured assessment of integration readiness. Entry requires sustained affect regulation in response to predictable relational triggers and a marked reduction in oscillation between idealisation and defensive loyalty. The survivor must be able to reference attachment injury without acute destabilisation and demonstrate consent capacity that persists under mild affect activation. Epistemic dependence on the therapist's interpretation should be reduced, with an increasing capacity to hold personal meaning without immediate reassurance.

The survivor must also be able to tolerate exploratory discussion of trauma-related themes without dissociative withdrawal, affect flooding, or collapse into self-blame. Grief activation may still be present; however, it no longer leads to identity collapse, a loyalty crisis, or a regulatory breakdown. When such responses remain prominent, clinicians return to Phase III containment processes before initiating Phase IV readiness evaluation.

Core Clinical Task: Differentiation Before Integration

The central clinical task of Phase IV is differentiation. Differentiation must occur across multiple domains, including distinction between past and present relational threat; between developmental survival adaptations and current adult responsibility; between survivor-authored narrative and internalised coercive narratives; and between the therapeutic relationship and historical attachment injury.

Without sufficient differentiation, trauma processing risks replicating coercive dynamics, reinforcing loyalty-bound cognition, or destabilising epistemic trust. Differentiation reflects the survivor's capacity to acknowledge historical harm without collapsing into self-blame, defensive loyalty, emotional flooding, or dissociative withdrawal. It requires sufficient internal authority to tolerate ambiguity without compulsive reassurance-seeking or epistemic dependence on the therapist's validation.

Readiness for Trauma Processing

Within the HQTP, readiness for trauma processing is not determined solely by symptom reduction, narrative coherence, or emotional articulation. Survivors may appear calmer, more reflective, or more verbally organised while still operating under internalised fear conditioning, loyalty conflicts, or epistemic instability. Phase IV, therefore, evaluates readiness across relational safety, epistemic stability, affect regulation and recovery capacity, and restoration of agency rather than relying on surface indicators of improvement (Courtois & Ford, 2020).

Before any trauma integration modality is considered, clinicians assess whether the survivor demonstrates a stable internal understanding that the abuse was not their fault, even in the presence of emotional ambivalence. The survivor must also possess sufficient conceptual language to describe coercion, loyalty conflict, psychological control, and attachment disruption. Without this scaffolding, trauma processing risks reinforcing self-blame, narrative fragmentation, or renewed destabilisation.

Phase IV Clinical Decision Trees

Integration Readiness and Boundary Stability

Phase IV operates through continuous clinical decision trees rather than linear task progression. These decision trees function as structured safety checkpoints that govern pacing, differentiation, and ethical restraint. Advancement toward trauma processing occurs only when readiness indicators remain stable across relational, regulatory, and contextual domains.

Some Phase IV decision points intentionally revisit safety domains first assessed in Phase III. This is not repetition for its own sake. It reflects the HQTP principle that the same clinical capacity must be reassessed at deeper levels of activation before trauma integration is considered.

Phase III to Phase IV Readiness Reassessment Flow Diagram

The following Phase III-to-Phase IV Readiness Reassessment Flow Diagram is included to help clinicians understand the transition between Phases III and IV. Phase IV is not a signal that trauma processing should begin. It is a readiness checkpoint. The diagram shows that clinicians must first assess whether grief containment, regulation, consent, relational safety, and epistemic stability remain strong enough before trauma integration is even considered. If these capacities fluctuate, the survivor returns to Phase III containment without this being framed as regression or failure.

Phase III to Phase IV Readiness Reassessment Flow Diagram

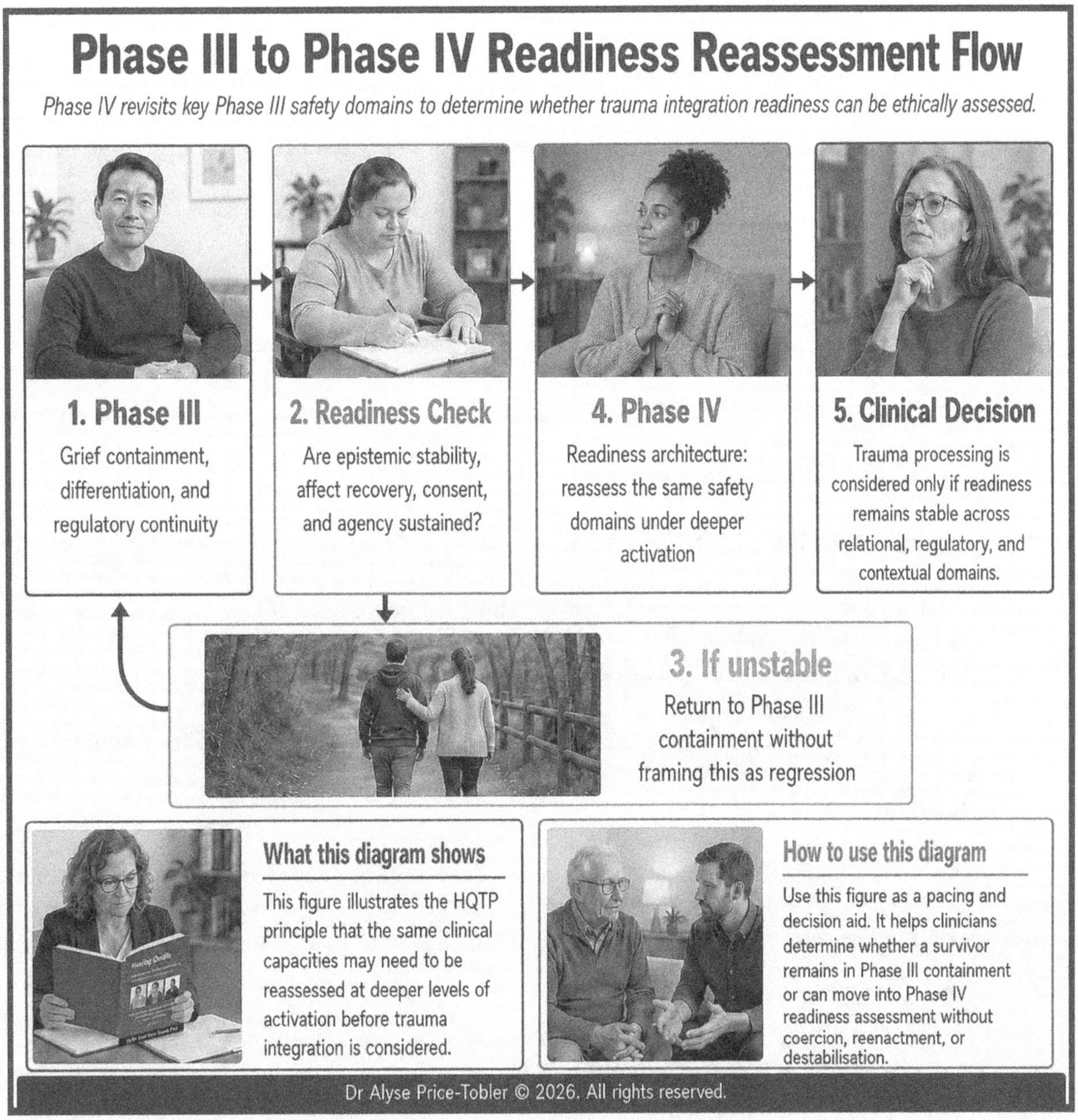

Clinical note. This diagram is not a trauma-processing pathway. It is a safety and readiness map. Clinicians should use it to decide whether the survivor remains in Phase III, returns to containment, or proceeds only to Phase IV readiness evaluation. Movement into Phase IV does not mean that trauma processing will occur. It means that the survivor's capacity for deeper work is being assessed carefully and slowly, under supervision.

Decision Tree 1: Epistemic Stability

When survivors revisit, expand, or newly disclose child psychological abuse related to parental alienation, familial abduction, estrangement, or related family-system harm during Phase IV, clinicians must first assess epistemic orientation. If survivors intensify disclosure, repeat details compulsively, seek reassurance, or ask whether the clinician believes them, trauma integration is contraindicated. Treatment remains focused on differentiation and meaning reconstruction, with clinicians prioritising epistemic safety over advancing exposure-based work.

Clinically, this may manifest as escalating repetition of abuse narratives, validation monitoring, documentation brought to establish legitimacy, or destabilisation when therapist neutrality is maintained. When survivors can acknowledge their experience without the urgency to persuade, tolerate the therapist's neutrality, and maintain internal legitimacy despite uncertainty, epistemic stability emerges, and further readiness assessment may proceed.

Clinical red flags: Escalating disclosure intensity across sessions, emotional collapse following neutral therapist responses, compulsive reassurance seeking, narrative rigidity, and preoccupation with external validation.

Supervision prompt: Is the clinician being drawn into an adjudicatory role? Is subtle reassurance being used to reduce survivor distress? Is discomfort with ambiguity influencing pacing?

Phase IV Decision Tree 2: Attachment Orientation Within the Therapeutic Relationship

Clinicians evaluate how survivors experience the therapeutic relationship itself.

If the survivor demonstrates excessive compliance, fear of disagreement, performance anxiety, or reliance on therapist approval for emotional safety, trauma integration is deferred. Treatment remains focused on relational differentiation and the restoration of autonomy.

Clinically, this may appear as rapid agreement with interpretations, frequent apologising, distress when boundaries are set, narrative shifts aligned with perceived therapist expectations, or suppression of disagreement to preserve relational safety. When survivors can tolerate misattunement, express disagreement, pause sessions without abandonment fear, and maintain internal authority rather than therapist dependency, attachment conditions support Phase IV progression.

Clinical red flag: Idealisation of the clinician, dependency statements, distress following routine boundary setting, and behavioural compliance masking internal anxiety.

Supervision prompt: Monitoring countertransference related to rescue roles, attachment substitution, or alliance preservation at the expense of differentiation.

Decision Tree 3: Affect Regulation and Recovery Capacity with DBT Anchoring

Readiness in Phase IV is determined not by emotional intensity but by the predictability of recovery. If emotional activation leads to prolonged dissociation, identity fragmentation, shutdown, or multi-session destabilisation, trauma integration is postponed, and stabilisation strategies are reinforced. Clinically, this may present as non-responsiveness during sessions, prolonged panic following emotional work, sleep disruption, impulsive behaviour, or functional deterioration in daily functioning.

At this point, dialectical behaviour therapy-informed regulation strategies are embedded as containment scaffolds rather than trauma exposure tools. These include distress tolerance strategies such as paced breathing, temperature modulation, sensory grounding, and present-moment anchoring; emotion regulation strategies including affect identification and modulation; and interpersonal effectiveness skills focused on boundary stabilisation and relational safety (Linehan, 2015). Within Phase IV, DBT serves as a stabilisation architecture that supports differentiation and grief without overwhelming the nervous system.

Clinical red flags: Inability to return to baseline between sessions, escalating dissociation, harsh self-criticism following emotional activation, or reliance on avoidance strategies such as withdrawal or substance use.

Supervision prompt: Monitor clinicians' tendencies to equate emotional intensity with progress, and assess whether containment scaffolding is being withdrawn prematurely.

Decision Tree 4: Loyalty Oscillation and Parental Defence

A recurring clinical pattern observed in the author's practice involves oscillation between survivor insight and renewed psychological defence of the alienating or abusive caregiver. Survivors may minimise harm, reverse previously articulated insight, express concern about being unfair, or directly ask whether the clinician believes the parent is "bad." These shifts frequently occur following periods of heightened clarity or emerging grief and reflect reactivation of loyalty conditioning rather than conscious cognitive revision.

When this pattern emerges, clinicians do not advance trauma processing. Treatment focus returns to differentiation and stabilisation. Clinical attention remains anchored in the developmental context, relational power asymmetry, behavioural impact, and survivor safety, rather than in moral adjudication. Requests for clinician judgement regarding parental character are redirected toward examining relational harm and attachment dynamics, thereby preserving epistemic safety and preventing the reenactment of family-system polarisation.

Clinical example: After recognising manipulation, a survivor later states that the parent "did their best" and questions whether therapy is unfair. This signals activation of loyalty reflexes and requires containment rather than interpretive escalation.

Clinical red flags: Abrupt narrative reversals, renewed contact-seeking during destabilisation, defensive anger toward therapeutic enquiry, and escalation of loyalty-based guilt.

Supervision prompt: Examine the clinician's frustration with perceived regression and vigilance against subtle pressure to preserve insight gains.

Decision Tree 5: Guilt Patterns and Moral Injury

Survivor's guilt presents heterogeneously. Some survivors experience profound guilt related to childhood behaviour toward targeted parents, while others report minimal or absent guilt, particularly in cases of early developmental alienation or fear-based conditioning where emotional access was neurologically constrained.

When intense guilt is present, clinicians focus on repairing moral injury, reframing development, and distinguishing child-survival adaptation from adult responsibility. When guilt is absent, this is not interpreted as a moral deficit or lack of empathy. Clinicians instead assess developmental context, fear conditioning, dissociative survival patterns, and attachment captivity. In both scenarios, trauma integration is deferred if guilt dynamics destabilise epistemic safety.

Clinical example: A survivor expresses panic about being “a useless or weak child” for complying with alienation narratives. Another expresses no emotional response toward the abusive parent. Both require differentiation work rather than exposure to trauma.

Clinical red flag: escalating self-condemnation, rigid moral reasoning, emotional flattening, and self-punitive relational behaviour.

Supervision prompt: Monitor clinician assumptions about “appropriate” guilt responses and cultural or developmental biases that may influence interpretation.

Decision Tree 6: Contextual and Environmental Safety

Clinicians assess whether survivors remain embedded in active coercive relationships, hostile family systems, unstable housing, or ongoing legal or illegal processes that compromise psychological and/or physical safety. When external coercion persists, trauma integration is contraindicated. Treatment remains focused on boundary stabilisation, meaning reconstruction and safety planning.

Clinical red flag: Coercive contact, housing insecurity, escalating legal conflict, surveillance, retaliatory threats, or active pressure from family system allies.

Supervision prompt: Does the current environment support meaningful containment? Is the clinician underestimating environmental danger because the survivor appears articulate or composed?

Decision Tree 7: Countertransference and Supervision Threshold

Phase IV requires continuous monitoring of clinician countertransference. Persistent urgency to accelerate progress, pressure to demonstrate outcomes, or desire to "complete" trauma work often reflects institutional or clinician needs rather than survivor readiness. Feelings of protectiveness, frustration, moral distress, or impatience may indicate unresolved attachment dynamics being activated within the therapeutic field.

When these reactions arise, supervision is mandatory before advancing treatment depth. Ethical progression in Phase IV requires clinicians to exercise restraint, demonstrate reflective capacity, and tolerate ambiguity. These decision trees do not function to delay healing, but to ensure that trauma integration proceeds without reenactment, coercive pacing, or epistemic destabilisation. In this population, restraint is not avoidance; it is protection.

Clinical Contraindications and Deferral Indicators

Within Phase IV, trauma processing is considered only when differentiation, epistemic stability, and affect regulation are sufficiently established. The following conditions warrant deferral or continued stabilisation work rather than progression into memory integration:

Trauma processing should be deferred when active loyalty conflict remains unresolved, and the survivor continues to experience coercive relational pressure, whether internal or external. Proceeding under such conditions risks reinforcing allegiance dynamics and reenacting the original attachment bind.

Processing should also be delayed when the survivor demonstrates persistent self-blame in response to discussions of abuse, particularly when insight collapses under emotional activation. Intellectual acknowledgment alone is insufficient if affective states remain organised around personal fault. Frequent dissociation, prolonged emotional flooding, or impaired recovery following activation indicate insufficient regulatory capacity. Trauma integration requires not the absence of distress, but the capacity to return to baseline without extended destabilisation.

Where the survivor continues to seek therapist validation to confirm the reality of abuse, or where epistemic authority remains externally anchored, trauma processing may inadvertently reinforce dependency rather than autonomy. Active environmental instability, including ongoing court proceedings, housing insecurity, safety threats, or coercive family contact, may also contraindicate progression into deeper memory work. Stabilisation and protective planning take precedence. These indicators are not framed as rigid exclusion criteria but as clinical signals that further differentiation and containment are required before trauma integration is ethically indicated.

Phase IV Exit Criteria

Phase IV is considered established when readiness indicators are consistently demonstrated across the relational, regulatory, and epistemic domains. Completion of this phase does not indicate that trauma has been processed. It confirms that trauma processing may proceed ethically within the parameters outlined in Chapter Fifteen.

Exit from Phase IV requires sustained differentiation between past attachment injury and present relational context, stable recognition that the abuse was not the survivor's fault even under emotional activation, and reduced oscillation between defensive loyalty and repudiation.

The survivor must demonstrate regulatory recovery following moderate activation of affect without prolonged destabilisation or dissociative collapse.

Epistemic stability must be internally anchored, with diminished reliance on therapist validation to confirm personal perception. Consent capacity must remain intact when trauma themes are introduced, including the ability to pause, decline, or renegotiate pace without fear of abandonment or relational rupture. If these capacities fluctuate significantly, trauma processing is suspended, and the clinician returns to stabilisation, differentiation, or grief containment processes as clinically indicated.

Quick Summary

Within the Phase IV framework, trauma integration remains contraindicated when survivors remain preoccupied with persuading the clinician, are embedded in active loyalty conflict, experience persistent dissociation, experience therapy as destabilising, or when clinician countertransference pressure is present. Proceeding under such conditions risks replicating systemic harm by prioritising technique over safety.

When trauma integration is considered, modality selection is guided by readiness rather than clinician preference. Memory-processing approaches such as EMDR require careful readiness assessment, slow pacing, and clinician expertise in complex trauma. Survivor responses to EMDR are heterogeneous. Some report benefits when readiness criteria are clearly met, while others experience destabilisation or misalignment with their healing needs. Trauma integration is therefore framed as optional, conditional, and subordinate to containment rather than as a standard protocol requirement.

Phase IV Decision Tree Quick Reference

Integration Readiness and Boundary Stability

Start: Trauma integration is being considered.

Step 1: Is the survivor preoccupied with persuading, convincing, or monitoring the clinician's belief?

If **yes** → Defer trauma integration. Return to differentiation, containment, and epistemic stabilisation.

If **no** → Continue.

Step 2: Is active loyalty conflict still organising the survivor's responses?

If **yes** → Defer trauma integration. Continue work on differentiation, internal authority, and conflict recognition.

If **no** → Continue.

Step 3: Is dissociation persistent, or is therapy being experienced as destabilising?

If **yes** → Defer trauma integration. Reassess pacing, regulation, and safety.

If **no** → Continue.

Step 4: Is clinician countertransference pressure present?

If **yes** → Pause progression. Use supervision and return to phase-consistent containment before proceeding.

If **no** → Continue.

Step 5: Are readiness conditions sufficiently established?

Readiness includes the survivor being able to remain present, maintain a coherent sense of self, tolerate activation without collapse, and participate with consent and understanding.

If **no** → Continue Phase IV stabilisation and readiness work.

If **yes** → Trauma integration may be considered.

Step 6: If trauma integration is considered, how should modality be selected?

Modality selection should be guided by survivor readiness, clinical indication, consent, regulatory capacity, clinician competence, supervision, and the least destabilising intervention available. Trauma integration should not proceed simply because a modality is available, familiar, or preferred by the clinician.

Clinical rule:

Trauma integration is never a required endpoint of the HQTP. It remains optional, conditional, and clinically subordinate to safety, differentiation, and survivor consent.

Phase IV Explained for Adult Survivors

A note from Dr Alyse

Dear friends,

This section is written with you in mind, in straightforward language, so the meaning of this phase feels easier to understand and carry.

What This Phase Is About

By the time therapy reaches this phase, something important has already shifted, even if it does not feel dramatic on the surface. You are no longer spending all of your energy trying to work out whether what happened to you was real, serious enough, or allowed to matter. You may not feel "finished," "healed," or permanently settled, but you are less lost in your own experience. This phase is about learning how to live with what you now understand, without being ruled by it.

Many adult survivors describe this phase as the moment they begin to feel like the author of their own story again. You may start to want to know your real history, your family's health background, or the truth about events that were hidden from you. Wanting accurate information about your own life is not disloyal, selfish, or disruptive. It reflects a basic human need for continuity, identity, and truth. Therapy in this phase supports your right to understand what shaped you, without forcing conclusions or pushing you toward any particular outcome. Phase IV is not about fixing the past. It is about reclaiming choice in the present.

For many adult survivors of child psychological abuse, particularly those impacted by parental alienation or abduction, life has often been organised around reacting rather than choosing. Decisions were made for you. Narratives were imposed. Relationships were shaped by fear, demands of loyalty, silence, or emotional control. Even in adulthood, you may have found yourself avoiding conflict, over-explaining yourself, suppressing your needs, or slipping back into roles that never truly fit. This phase of therapy focuses on helping you step out of automatic survival patterns and begin making decisions guided by your own values, safety, and internal sense of direction.

Integration does not mean forgetting what happened or minimising its impact. It means learning to hold your history without letting it define the limits of your future. You are not asked to forgive anyone, reunify with family members, confront people, or make peace before you are ready. Instead, therapy helps you notice what feels true for you now, what feels possible going forward, and what kind of life you want to build on your own terms. Many survivors begin asking questions such as: What matters to me outside the family story I was raised in? Which relationships feel safe enough to invest in? What boundaries do I need, even if others do not understand or approve of them? What parts of myself were never allowed to develop, such as creativity, independence, playfulness, ambition, or rest, and how might I begin giving those parts space now?

What You May Notice in This Phase

Grief often becomes more present during this phase, though it does not always look like people expect. Some survivors grieve the loss of parents or family relationships. Others grieve things they never had, such as safety, stability, emotional protection, truthful information, or the chance to grow up without fear and divided loyalties. You may grieve lost time, missed opportunities, or versions of yourself that were never allowed to exist. This grief is not a sign of weakness or regression. It reflects the reality of what was taken. Therapy does not rush this process or try to "resolve" grief. It allows it to be acknowledged, felt safely, and integrated at your pace.

You may also notice that your relationship with the world begins to change. Situations that once overwhelmed you may start to feel more manageable. Other situations may suddenly feel intolerable, not because you are becoming fragile, but because you are becoming clearer. Integration often brings discernment. You become more aware of what feels safe, what feels draining, and what no longer aligns with who you are becoming. Learning to trust these signals is part of reclaiming your internal authority.

Choice, Pace, and What Comes Next

Importantly, Phase IV is not about making dramatic life changes unless you choose to. Some survivors decide to reduce contact with family members. Others maintain contact as they change internal boundaries. Some reframe relationships psychologically without altering them externally. There is no correct path. Therapy supports your agency rather than pushing you toward a predetermined outcome.

You are also not expected to become endlessly strong, independent, or emotionally self-sufficient. Healing is not linear. There may be periods when you require additional support, particularly during life transitions, illness, parenting, relationship changes, anniversaries, or renewed contact with family systems. Returning to therapy or increasing support during these times does not mean you have failed. It reflects responsiveness rather than denial.

If at any point you choose to engage in more focused trauma work, such as EMDR, somatic approaches, or memory-based processing, this occurs only with your consent and when you feel ready. Many adult survivors never need to revisit specific memories in detail to live with greater freedom and stability. Integration can occur through understanding, relationship repair, boundary development, and choice, not only through exposure to past experiences.

For some survivors, this phase also involves reconnecting with aspects of identity that were interrupted, such as culture, creativity, spirituality, education, advocacy, community involvement, or a sense of purpose. Therapy supports this expansion gently, without pressuring the client to turn pain into meaning before readiness has developed. Lastly, Phase IV lacks a finishing line. It creates space to live with greater choice, clarity, and self-trust in the present.

Go gently, Dr Alyse

Phase IV Clinical Logic: Integration Readiness and Ethical Containment

Phase IV represents a shift in clinical responsibility from stabilisation and meaning reconstruction toward protection of survivor autonomy and differentiation. The clinician's primary task in this phase is not to guide outcomes, resolve relational dilemmas, or shape survivor decisions. It is to maintain a therapeutic environment that supports internal authority, preserves choice, and prevents reenactment of coercive relational dynamics.

Unlike earlier phases, in which containment and epistemic safety are foregrounded, Phase IV introduces greater behavioural and relational complexity. Survivors may begin experimenting with changes in boundaries, contact decisions, identity expression, vocational direction, or relational restructuring. These movements reflect developmental repair but also carry a risk of destabilisation when undertaken prematurely or under relational pressure. Clinical pacing in Phase IV, therefore, prioritises reflective processing, consent, and proportionality over visible action.

The clinician remains responsible for monitoring whether therapeutic influence is subtly replacing survivor agency. Indicators of therapist over-functioning include prescriptive advice about family contact, implicit endorsement of confrontation strategies, encouragement of rapid life restructuring, or framing progress primarily in terms of external behavioural change rather than internal coherence. When these patterns emerge, supervision is indicated, and clinical posture must be recalibrated.

Phase IV logic is anchored in three interrelated functions: differentiation, boundary consolidation, and relational autonomy. Differentiation involves supporting survivors to experience themselves as psychologically separate from loyalty conditioning, imposed family narratives, and identity distortion. The clinician facilitates reflective distance without promoting emotional detachment, relational cut-off, or ideological positioning. Survivors are supported in holding ambivalence and complexity without reverting to generalised self-blame or rigid splitting.

Boundary consolidation is approached as a developmental repair process rather than a behavioural skill alone. Survivors frequently enter Phase IV with limited internal permission to assert needs, tolerate disapproval, or prioritise safety over loyalty demands. Clinical work, therefore, focuses on strengthening internal boundaries before encouraging external action. This includes increasing tolerance for guilt, discomfort, and relational tension without automatic compliance or avoidance.

Relational autonomy refers to the survivor's growing capacity to make decisions grounded in personal values, safety, and internal coherence rather than fear-based conditioning or therapist direction. Continued, modified, reduced, or no-contact are considered context-dependent decisions rather than therapeutically prescribed outcomes. The clinician supports exploration without positioning any relational configuration as inherently correct.

Clinical indicators that Phase IV work is proceeding safely include increased tolerance for interpersonal complexity, reduced urgency to "do something" to prove progress, improved capacity to reflect on contact and boundary decisions involving the alienating parent (relational decisions) without collapse, stable affect regulation following sessions, and decreased reliance on therapist validation to support decision-making.

Indicators that require pacing adjustment include pressure to make rapid relational changes, rigid, outcome-driven thinking, increased dependency on therapist reassurance, resurgence of loyalty-entrapment dynamics, or escalation of action-focused urgency that bypasses internal consolidation. When these patterns emerge, clinicians return temporarily to Phase III containment or Phase II, meaning consolidation rather than accelerating behavioural change.

Phase IV also requires sustained attention to countertransference. Clinicians may experience subtle pressure to support empowerment by endorsing decisive action, aligning emotionally with survivor anger, or adopting advocacy roles within the therapeutic relationship. Ethical positioning requires maintaining emotional attunement without assuming directional authority. Supervision functions as a structural safeguard against positional drift rather than a corrective measure.

Phase IV concludes not when visible life changes occur, but when survivors demonstrate sustained internal differentiation, relational self-trust, and decision-making capacity grounded in personal values rather than fear, loyalty entrapment, or external pressure. Only under these conditions does the protocol transition into Phase V continuity work.

Additional Resources for Survivors and MHPs

For some survivors, integration also includes connecting with others who share similar lived experiences. Many adult survivors report that survivor-led spaces can reduce isolation, self-doubt, and internalised shame when engagement occurs safely and voluntarily. For this reason, the author has contributed to survivor-centred education initiatives that prioritise lived experience alongside clinical understanding. The international Nothing About Us Without Us (NAUWOU) Conference was created to provide a space where adult survivors of child psychological abuse, parental alienation, and abduction speak for themselves, share their stories, and participate in shaping education and advocacy. This conference prioritises survivor voices, ethical practice, and community dialogue, and reflects the same principles of epistemic safety and autonomy that guide this protocol.

In addition, the author's educational YouTube channel offers public psychoeducation, survivor reflections, and practitioner-informed discussions designed to help individuals and families better understand the psychological impact of coercive family dynamics and attachment disruption. These resources are intended to complement therapy, not replace it, and may be used selectively according to individual readiness and emotional safety.

Survivors may also wish to explore the collaborative book project *Warning: Children Are Not Weapons*, which emerged from the survivor conference community. This volume brings together lived experience accounts and professional perspectives to highlight the real-world impact of children being used within high-conflict separations, alienation dynamics, and coercive family systems. Many survivors report that reading about shared experiences helps validate their reality and reduces their sense of isolation on their journey.

Engagement with these resources is always optional. There is no requirement for survivors to participate publicly, share their story, or join advocacy spaces to heal. Some survivors find strength in community connection, while others prefer private integration. Both paths are valid. The purpose of offering these resources is to ensure that survivors know support exists beyond the therapy room, should they wish to access it.

Phase IV does not ask a survivor to become a spokesperson, an advocate, or a symbol of resilience, as they may have seen other survivors do in the NAUWOU conference video series on YouTube. It simply invites survivors to live with greater choice, clarity, and self-trust. How that unfolds is your decision. If you are interested in how other survivors have chosen to speak in public spaces, recordings of the conference talks remain available on the author's YouTube channel. Please go to https://www.youtube.com/channel/UCiN_DxTEdbOpGZNB3Bo3ndQ

Transition From Phase IV to Phase V

Phase IV concludes when the survivor demonstrates sustained epistemic stability, affect regulation capacity, relational differentiation, and internal authority over meaning and memory. At this point, therapeutic work shifts from differentiation and readiness monitoring toward the practical integration of autonomy, relational choice, and long-horizon continuity of care.

Phase V does not represent escalation of clinical intensity or progression toward termination. Instead, it reflects a reorientation of therapy from internal consolidation toward lived application. The focus moves from building internal capacity to supporting the survivor in exercising that capacity across real-world relational contexts, boundary decisions, and ongoing life transitions. This transition is governed by sustainability rather than speed and by continuity rather than closure.

Phase V: Differentiation, Boundary Formation, and Contact Decisions

Entry Criteria (Readiness-Based)

Phase V addresses adult relational differentiation, boundary formation, contact decisions, and the survivor's right to choose whether to maintain proximity or distance from family members without coercion. Within the HQTP, this phase is governed by a rights-based clinical lens that contrasts with the coercive, loyalty-bound, and authority-driven conditions that shaped the survivor's childhood environment.

Once readiness for Phase V has been established, clinicians should continue to anchor contact decisions in present-day behaviour rather than family role, obligation, grief, or inherited loyalty.

Clinical Reminder: Behaviour First, Relationship Second

When survivors are making decisions about contact, limited contact, structured contact, or no contact, clinicians can help them return to a simple question: What is the behaviour? Before the survivor decides what a relationship "should" mean, they are supported to notice whether the interaction contains pressure, guilt, coercion, minimisation, repair, accountability, respect, curiosity, punishment, or emotional safety.

This helps prevent decisions from being made only out of family role, obligation, fear, grief, or loyalty. The survivor is not asked to condemn the person. They are asked to identify the behaviour clearly enough to make a safer and more reality-based decision.

Adult survivors were subjected to prolonged psychological control, attachment-distortion, and restricted autonomy. Therapeutic work in Phase V, therefore, prioritises transparency, consent, pacing, and survivor-led decision-making. The clinician's role is not to guide relational outcomes, recommend contact strategies, or evaluate the moral correctness of survivor choices. It is to support reflective autonomy without substituting professional authority for personal agency.

When trauma integration modalities are utilised in Phase V, they are applied only when stabilisation, consent, and epistemic safety remain intact. Clinicians use titrated exposure, outside-in sequencing, and integrative pacing rather than rigid procedural protocols. Survivors are informed of clinical rationale, optional participation, and their right to pause, decline, or modify therapeutic processes at any point.

Phase V rejects outcome-driven or experimental treatment postures. Survivors are not positioned as therapeutic projects. They are treated as autonomous participants in their own care, with their internal authority prioritised over protocol completion.

Clinical Positioning and Core Therapeutic Tasks

The central clinical task of Phase V is to support autonomous relational choice without reproducing coercive dynamics. The clinician's role is not to guide outcomes, recommend relational decisions, or shape survivor direction. It is to create a therapeutic environment in which survivors can exercise choice, consolidate boundaries, and engage with relational complexity without therapist authority replacing internal agency.

Clinicians collaborate with survivors to explore relational boundaries, contact decisions, identity direction, and life planning while maintaining disciplined ethical containment around influence and power. Clinical neutrality in this phase is active rather than passive. It involves sustained emotional attunement combined with deliberate restraint from positional authority, prescriptive guidance, or outcome framing.

Rather than prescribing treatment pathways, clinicians offer a structured menu of therapeutic options that survivors may engage with selectively. These options are presented transparently, with a clear explanation of clinical rationale and limitations. Pacing is co-designed and continuously reviewed in relation to emotional regulation capacity, relational safety, developmental context, and external system pressures. This collaborative posture protects against reenactment of hierarchical dynamics that characterised earlier relational environments.

Phase V requires particular sensitivity to residual fears of professional control, therapeutic authority, and institutional power. Survivors with histories of coercion may interpret clinical structure, modality changes, or session adjustments as implicit loss of agency or withdrawal of care. These dynamics are addressed rather than assumed resolved. The clinician names power differentials, invites discussion of perceived pressure, and remains responsive to concerns about autonomy.

Autonomy in Phase V is operationalised through repeated consent-based decision-making rather than abstract empowerment language. Clinical reasoning is made transparent. Survivors are invited into collaborative planning. Disagreement is normalised. Revisions to therapeutic focus or pacing are treated as adaptive recalibration rather than disruption.

Phase V logic prioritises sustainability over speed. Visible behavioural change, relational action, or boundary enforcement is never used as the primary indicator of therapeutic progress. Instead, the clinician monitors internal consolidation markers, including the stability of self-trust, tolerance for relational ambiguity, reduced urgency to prove progress, and the capacity to reflect on choices without collapsing or becoming dependent on external validation.

When survivors feel pressured to take rapid action, escalate confrontation, or prematurely restructure relationships, clinicians slow the pace of work and refocus on internal consolidation. When survivors display increased dependency on therapist reassurance, authority-seeking behaviour, or externalisation of decision responsibility, supervision is indicated to recalibrate clinical posture and prevent role substitution.

Phase V also requires ongoing countertransference monitoring. Clinicians may experience subtle pressure to support empowerment by endorsing decisive action, aligning emotionally with survivor anger, or framing relational disengagement as therapeutic success. Ethical positioning requires maintaining emotional attunement without directional influence. Supervision functions as structural containment rather than corrective intervention.

Phase V concludes when survivors demonstrate sustained capacity to exercise relational choice grounded in internal authority rather than fear, loyalty entrapment, or therapist influence. Only under these conditions does the protocol transition into Phase VI continuity work.

Consent, Choice, and Psychological Safety in This Phase

A note from Dr Alyse

Dear friends,

In this phase of the HQTP, the work is never about forcing you to endure, comply, perform, or push through distress. You stay in charge of how deep the conversations go, how fast or slowly things move, and what feels safe enough to talk about. You can always ask why something is being suggested. You can slow things down, pause, change direction, or say no to anything that does not feel right for you.

As therapy begins to shift toward relationships, boundaries, and future planning, consent is treated as an ongoing process rather than a one-time agreement. If people have suddenly left, pulled away, or made love feel conditional in the past, changes in therapy can sometimes feel like abandonment, even when that is not what is happening. For this reason, these changes are talked about openly and planned together throughout this phase.

To help you feel safe and included, your clinician should speak clearly with you about any changes in therapy, especially changes in pace, focus, or session frequency. These conversations should be gentle, direct, and collaborative.

For example: “Before we continue, I want to check whether being here still feels right for you. You are allowed to change your mind. Nothing in this process is set in stone. If we adjust the session frequency or focus, we will decide on it together and can revise it at any time. You are not being ‘moved on’. Support remains available when you need it.”

This kind of conversation can help protect against old feelings of sudden loss, rejection, or conditional care. It reminds you that therapy is something you do with your clinician, not something that is done to you. It also reinforces that support is not taken away as a reward for progress. Care remains available across the lifespan.

You may feel proud of the progress you have made, yet still feel scared about change. Both can be true. You are allowed to ask for things to be explained clearly. You are allowed to say if something feels confusing, too fast, or unsettling. You do not have to have everything figured out. It is okay to be unsure. Therapy can make space for that too. Needing support again does not mean you have gone backwards. It means you are human, and support is there when you need it. You do not have to get everything right in this phase. You do not have to be certain, strong, or fully ready all the time. You are allowed to be unsure, to ask questions, and to come back to things more than once. That is part of healing, too.

Go gently, Dr Alyse

Phased Endings and Relational Continuity

Within the HQTP, therapeutic endings are not abrupt events but phased, relational transitions introduced gradually, discussed transparently, and negotiated collaboratively over time. For many survivors of CPA-PA, abandonment has been a defining developmental injury. Survivors often carry histories of sudden caregiver disappearance, forced separation, emotional withdrawal as punishment, or repeated relational disruption across care systems. As a result, the prospect of ending therapy can activate significant attachment distress even when clinical progress is strong.

Phase V, therefore, reframes endings not as termination, discharge, or closure, but as a form of continuity planning. The clinical objective is not to eliminate relational attachment to the clinician, which is neither realistic nor therapeutically necessary, but to prevent reenactment of sudden relational loss and to avoid creating another abrupt absence in the survivor's relational history.

Transition conversations are introduced only when the survivor demonstrates sufficient stability and internal authority to tolerate them without collapse. These discussions occur gradually and are revisited across sessions rather than presented as fixed decisions. This pacing allows survivors to integrate the emotional reality of change without experiencing it as abandonment or rejection.

Clinicians remain mindful that long-term therapeutic relationships often carry mutual emotional significance. Survivors may experience grief, sadness, or relational loss as therapy evolves. Clinicians may also experience fondness, emotional investment, and attachment to the survivor's growth. These experiences are not pathologised, but they must be held within professional boundaries and processed through supervision rather than enacted within the therapeutic relationship. Ethical practice requires the clinician to remain emotionally present while gradually shifting the relational function of therapy from primary attachment stabilisation toward a secure, accessible professional resource. The clinician avoids both premature withdrawal and role entrenchment.

Clinical Red Flags During Transition Planning

Indicators that transition pacing requires slowing include panic responses to reduced session frequency, emotional collapse when future change is discussed, increased dependency behaviours, urgent reassurance seeking, or fear-based clinging to the therapeutic relationship. These responses signal unresolved abandonment conditioning and require stabilisation rather than acceleration.

Applied Supervision Practices and Clinical Safeguards

Phase V requires ongoing supervision to monitor clinician countertransference, particularly impulses toward withdrawal, rescue, over-availability, emotional disengagement, or unconscious role substitution. Supervisory reflection supports ethical containment and prevents reenactment of abandonment, dependency, or authority dynamics.

Ethical Continuity as an Outcome

Within the HQTP, an ethical ending is not defined by cessation of contact. It is defined by establishing a relational structure in which the survivor can move in and out of care without shame, justification, or fear of abandonment. Therapy becomes a stable point of access rather than a temporary attachment substitute.

Under these conditions, therapy remains accessible across the lifespan.

Access does not require crisis justification, moral performance, or reauthorisation.

Contact as Choice, Not Outcome

Phase V carries an elevated clinical risk because decisions about relational contact are frequently misinterpreted as indicators of therapeutic success. Within the HQTP, contact with family members is never treated as a treatment goal.

The primary therapeutic objective is the survivor's capacity to think, feel, choose, pause, decline, reconsider, and make contact-related decisions without fear-based compulsion, loyalty distortion, coercion, shame, or therapeutic pressure. Relational differentiation is demonstrated not through reconciliation or estrangement, but through the survivor's growing ability to tolerate ambivalence, maintain boundaries, and make relational decisions grounded in present-day psychological safety rather than historical conditioning.

Before supporting contact, reunification, or relational repair, clinicians must also understand the clinical complexity of being seen, looking at, and recognising a long-separated family member. Visual contact may appear simple from the outside. However, in CPA-PA, CPA-PAA, abduction, coercive-control, and long-term estrangement contexts, it can carry profound attachment, grief, threat, recognition, and nervous-system activation.

Eye Contact, Recognition, and Supported Reunification: A Clinical Caution

In some reunification work, particularly after long periods of alienation, estrangement, or abduction, the first moment of seeing one another can be almost impossible to describe. Words may not come first. The body may respond before the mind has caught up. A survivor may look at a parent, sibling, adult child, or other long-separated family member and feel grief, shock, love, anger, numbness, fear, disbelief, longing, or nothing at all. The other person may be experiencing the same thing. The clinician must understand that this is not an ordinary meeting. It may be one of the most emotional moments either person will ever experience.

Visual contact can be powerful because it brings recognition into the room. To look at someone after years or decades apart is not simply to "see" them. It may mean seeing the child who was taken, the parent who was lost, the sibling who grew up elsewhere, the adult who survived, or the person who has lived with the consequences of separation for many years. However, this does not mean visual contact is automatically healing. It is not a test of love, honesty, attachment, remorse, forgiveness, readiness, or the success of reunification. It is not something a clinician should demand. It is not something a survivor should be pressured to perform. It may open a doorway, but only when the survivor remains free to look away, pause, stop, speak, cry, sit in silence, or leave.

For this reason, visual contact within supported reunification is not a standardised exercise, a first-line intervention, or a technique to be copied from public reunion videos. It should only be considered after careful assessment, preparation, consent, supervision, and clear stop conditions, and only when it serves the survivor's current phase of safety, autonomy, and readiness.

Neuroscience helps explain why this must be handled carefully. Direct gaze is a powerful social cue that can increase attention, emotional arousal, interpersonal salience, and social connection in some contexts (Hietanen, 2018; Prinsen & Alaerts, 2019). However, for people with interpersonal trauma histories, direct eye contact may activate threat pathways rather than safety. Steuwe et al. (2014) found that direct gaze in people with PTSD related to prolonged childhood abuse was associated with activation of an innate alarm-system pathway rather than calm social engagement. More recent work also suggests that direct gaze may be particularly loaded after trauma involving shame, moral injury, or fear of being seen (Andrews et al., 2023).

For survivors of CPA-PA and related contexts, this matters deeply. Many survivors have learned to read faces for danger. They may have learned that a parent's face could signal withdrawal, punishment, rage, grief, manipulation, disappointment, or emotional capture. Others may have been trained not to look at the targeted parent with warmth, curiosity, love, or longing. Visual contact may therefore awaken attachment, but it may also awaken fear, shame, loyalty conflict, collapse, compliance, or dissociation.

In supported reunification work, even a short period of quiet visual contact can carry both possibility and risk. For some people, it may open a path towards apology, tenderness, recognition, grief, love, or repair. For others, it may become overwhelming very quickly. The person may feel flooded, exposed, unable to speak, unsure whether they can continue, or suddenly aware that they need to stop. This is why visual contact should be prepared carefully, held safely, and stopped immediately if either person becomes distressed or overwhelmed.

The Shock of Seeing the Person as They Are Now

One of the most human and confronting parts of supported reunification is that the person in front of the survivor may not look anything like the person held in memory. In some cases, the survivor may not recognise them at all. The brain may struggle to connect the person standing in the room with the parent, sibling, adult child, or family member who has been missing, feared, longed for, grieved, idealised, demonised, or held in a frozen image for many years.

This may happen on both sides. The child who was taken, rejected, hidden, silenced, frightened, or forced into loyalty may now be an adult. The parent who was remembered as young, strong, loving, frightening, absent, or unreachable may now be older, greyer, softer, frailer, ill, guarded, regretful, emotional, or simply unfamiliar. A survivor may have carried one photograph, one childhood image, or one memory for decades. When they finally meet again, the person may be biologically and relationally connected to them yet still feel like a stranger. The survivor may know intellectually who the person is, but their body and nervous system may not yet be able to accept or integrate that reality.

Clinicians need to stop and really think about this. Imagine being separated from your child, your parent, your sibling, or someone you loved under circumstances of alienation, abduction, coercive control, or family-system manipulation. Imagine carrying one face in your mind for years or decades, only to see a different face in the room. The person is still them, but they are also not the person your nervous system has been holding. The younger version is gone. The years are visible. The missing time has a body. It sits across from you.

This can be devastating. It can also be beautiful. Sometimes it is both at once. A parent may suddenly see the adult body of the child they were not allowed to raise. A survivor may see the ageing face of the parent they were taught to fear, hate, dismiss, pity, rescue, or forget. A sibling may see the brother or sister who grew up without them. In abduction-related cases, the shock may be especially profound because the missing child may have been held in memory at the age they were taken. Reunification can collapse decades into a single moment.

This is not just visual recognition. It is developmental grief. It confronts both people with the years they did not get to live together. It may bring love, sorrow, anger, disbelief, tenderness, regret, relief, shock, and numbness into the room at the same time. Clinicians must not rush this moment, explain over it, interpret it too quickly, or turn it into a therapeutic achievement. Sometimes, the most helpful thing a clinician can do is create enough safety for both people to absorb the reality of each other.

A clinician may prepare the survivor by saying:

"One thing we need to prepare for is that they may not look the way you remember them. You may know who they are but still feel as if you are looking at a stranger. You may feel shocked, sad, numb, angry, relieved, protective, disappointed, or overwhelmed. None of those responses means you are doing it wrong. Seeing someone after many years is not just seeing their face. It can bring the missing years into the room."

The same preparation should be offered to the targeted parent, sibling, adult child, or other estranged family member:

"The person coming into the room may not match the image you have carried. They may look, speak, move, think, or respond differently from the child or person you remember. Please do not comment on their appearance immediately unless they invite it. Let them arrive as they are now. Your task is not to reclaim the past in one moment, but to meet the person in front of you safely."

This preparation is essential. A shocked comment, even if well-meaning, can wound the moment. Statements such as “you look so different”, “you’re so old now”, “you’re not how I imagined”, “you are so grown up”, “I would never have recognised you”, or “you look just like your mother/father” may land painfully. The survivor may already be trying to work out whether they are safe, whether they are allowed to feel, whether they are betraying someone, and whether this person is truly the one they have been missing. Clinicians should prepare both people to avoid immediate comments on appearance and instead begin with presence, breathing, and simple recognition.

Clinicians should also prepare both people for the fact that they may have very little shared present-day material to connect on. They may have old memories, but even those memories may not be shared in the same way. The adult child may have been told distorted versions of events or may not have been told certain memories at all. The targeted parent may hold a very different account of what happened. This can create confusion, grief, disbelief, anger, or a strong urge to correct the record immediately.

In the early stages of supported contact, the clinical task is not to resolve every discrepancy. It is to slow the interaction down enough that both people can remain present. The clinician may need to say:

“There may be different memories in the room today. We do not need to sort them all out at once. Today is about safety, pacing, and noticing what it is like to be in contact without pressure.”

Entering an Existing Family System

Reunification does not occur in an empty relational space. The targeted parent may now have a partner, spouse, stepchildren, additional biological children, grandchildren, step-relatives, in-laws, or extended family members who have built a family life during the years of separation. Some may welcome the adult child with compassion and curiosity. Others may experience the adult child's return as a threat.

This can be very painful for the adult survivor. After years of loss, fear, distorted narratives, or longing, they may finally reach the point of supported contact, only to discover that they are being viewed with suspicion by people they have never met. In some cases, the adult child may be accused, directly or indirectly, of returning for money, inheritance, property, status, or inclusion in a will. They may be treated as opportunistic or assumed to be entering the family only because the targeted parent now has assets, stability, or social standing. This can be profoundly retraumatising, particularly when the adult child has already lost years or decades of a relationship through no fault of their own.

Clinicians should understand that this accusation may land heavily. The survivor may already feel like an outsider. They may already feel ashamed, unsure, guilty, disloyal, or frightened of taking up space in a family system that continued without them. Being framed as a financial threat may confirm the survivor's fear that they do not truly belong, that their motives will be mistrusted, or that they will again be positioned as the problem.

The targeted parent may also be placed in an extremely difficult position. They may feel joy, grief, guilt, protectiveness, and urgency around the adult child who has returned, while also trying to reassure their current partner, other children, stepchildren, or relatives. Existing family members may feel jealous, displaced, frightened, resentful, or worried that the adult child will become the new focus of the targeted parent's attention. Stepchildren may fear losing emotional or financial security. Adult siblings may feel confused about where they now stand. A current partner may fear that the past is returning in a way that destabilises the present family.

In some families, the adult child may be welcomed carefully and lovingly. In others, the existing family system may close ranks. The targeted parent may be given explicit or implicit ultimatums about time, contact, money, loyalty, inheritance, grandchildren, holidays, family events, or emotional attention. The adult child may then be pulled into another loyalty system, this time from the targeted parent's side of the family. This can be very confusing. The survivor may have left one relational system organised around fear and loyalty, only to encounter another system that is anxious about their arrival.

Clinicians should therefore avoid turning early reunification into a large family event. Initial contact should usually be small, slow, and carefully contained. The targeted parent may understandably want to quickly introduce the adult child to everyone. They may feel that the family is finally being restored. However, every new person may be another emotional shock for the adult child. Biological connection does not remove the need for pacing.

A clinician may need to say:

"It makes sense that you want to introduce them to everyone. You may feel that the family is finally being restored. However, for the adult child, every new person may be another emotional shock. They may need time to meet one person, pause, integrate, and choose the next step. Reunification needs to be paced around safety, not around the understandable excitement of the family."

The adult child may also receive new information that changes their understanding of themselves and their family history. They may learn about physical illnesses, genetic risks, mental health histories, neurodivergence, addictions, family violence, deaths, suicides, estrangements, or other events that were hidden from them, distorted, or never passed on by the alienating parent. Some adult survivors may discover that family members died years earlier, such as a grandparent or great-grandparent and that they were never told. Others may learn of suicide, serious illness, or intergenerational trauma only after contact resumes.

This information can be clinically significant. It may affect identity, grief, medical history, risk awareness, and the survivor's understanding of what was withheld from them. It may also create renewed anger or sorrow towards the alienating parent if the survivor realises they were denied access not only to relationships, but also to important family knowledge. Clinicians should prepare survivors for the possibility that reunification may bring not only relational contact, but new medical, psychological, genealogical, and historical information.

The clinician may say:

"Sometimes reunification brings new information about family history, health, deaths, relationships, and events you were not told about. Some of it may be meaningful. Some of it may be painful. We do not have to process all of it at once. We can slow it down and make sense of it carefully."

The clinical task is to protect the adult survivor from being pulled too quickly into a family system that has not yet made room for them. The adult child does not need to prove purity of motive, perform gratitude, reassure step-relatives, answer inheritance fears, or immediately take their place in a family tree. They need time to arrive. They need time to understand who is who. They need time to decide what kind of contact is safe, wanted, and sustainable.

The Alienating Parent Should Not Be Positioned as the Support Person

In most cases, it is not clinically advisable for the alienating parent to attend this kind of supported reunification meeting with the adult child. The adult child may need a support person, but that person should be someone who can remain calm, be non-intrusive, and genuinely support the adult child's autonomy. The alienating parent is usually unable to occupy that role safely because the meeting may directly activate the original relational system that created or maintained the separation.

The adult survivor may already be carrying intense fear, guilt, loyalty conflict, and concern about "betraying" the alienating parent by meeting the targeted parent or previously rejected family member. If the alienating parent is present, the adult child may feel watched, monitored, judged, or emotionally responsible for managing that parent's distress. This can prevent the adult child from noticing their own feelings. Instead of being free to meet the person in front of them, they may return to managing the emotional state, fear, anger, collapse, or approval of the alienating parent.

For many adult survivors, the alienating parent has been the central attachment figure, authority figure, narrator, gatekeeper, rescuer, victim, and threat interpreter for many years. Meeting the targeted parent may therefore feel, at a body level, like disloyalty or danger, even when the adult survivor has consciously chosen the meeting. If the alienating parent attends, the survivor may become compliant, shut down, over-explain, apologise, perform indifference, minimise warmth, avoid visual contact, or feel unable to ask questions. They may also become frightened that any visible tenderness towards the targeted parent will later be punished, questioned, or used as evidence that they have "turned against" the alienating parent.

The alienating parent may also become highly dysregulated as reunification becomes possible. They may fear that the adult child will hear a different account of the past, that long-held narratives will be questioned, that the targeted parent will be seen as loving or safe, or that the adult child may begin to recognise distortions, omissions, or untruths in the history they were given. In some cases, the alienating parent may fear exposure. They may fear losing emotional control, losing their role as the only safe parent, or losing the adult child's loyalty. This can lead to renewed pressure, guilt, anger, panic, threats, illness behaviour, victim narratives, accusations, or attempts to reframe the meeting as dangerous.

Old threat narratives may return very quickly. An adult survivor may be told that meeting the targeted parent will place them, the alienating parent, the family, children, grandchildren, cousins, or others in danger. This may mirror earlier narratives used to maintain the separation. For example, an adult survivor may have been told for years that the targeted parent's family was dangerous, unsafe, criminal, unstable, or capable of serious harm. When reunification becomes possible, the same narrative may return with force, even where later contact shows that the feared danger was not real. Clinicians must be prepared for this. The adult child may not simply be deciding whether to attend a meeting. They may be trying to step outside a whole fear-based reality that has been maintained for years.

The adult survivor should be reassured that they do not need to emotionally support, reassure, rescue, or regulate the alienating parent before, during, or after the meeting. This is a crucial clinical point. The survivor's task is not to protect the alienating parent from discomfort. The survivor's task is to remain connected to their own reality, body, feelings, questions, boundaries, and choices. This may be extremely difficult if the survivor has spent many years organising themselves around the alienating parent's distress.

Clinicians may need to say this clearly:

"You are allowed to meet this person without taking responsibility for your other parent's emotional reaction. Their distress may be real, but it does not have to control your choices. We can plan for how you will manage guilt, pressure, fear, or contact from them afterwards, but you do not have to carry them into the meeting with you."

The alienating parent may also attempt to contact the clinician. They may demand information, accuse the clinician of bias, attempt to stop the work, threaten complaints, or try to pull the clinician into the old family narrative. The clinician must be prepared for this and must hold firm boundaries around confidentiality, consent, documentation, and role clarity. The clinician should not become a messenger between family members, should not defend the reunification to the alienating parent, and should not allow themselves to be triangulated into the conflict.

Where there is risk of escalation, the clinician should document carefully, seek supervision or consultation, and ensure that the adult survivor has a clear safety and communication plan. This may include deciding what the survivor will say if pressured, whether they will disclose the meeting, when they will disclose it, who will support them afterwards, and how they will respond if the alienating parent becomes dysregulated or retaliatory.

The central clinical point is that supported reunification cannot be safely held if the adult child is still required to manage the emotional survival of the alienating parent. The survivor must be supported to enter the meeting as a separate person, not as an extension of the alienating parent's fear.

When Quiet Visual Contact May Help

Quiet visual contact may help when both people have consented, both understand the purpose of the meeting, and both are able to stop without shame. It should be considered only when there has been sufficient preparation, emotional regulation, clinical containment, and relational safety for both people to remain present as strong feelings arise.

In supported reunification work, looking at one another is not powerful because it is dramatic. It is powerful because it can bring the other person's reality into the room. After years or decades of alienation, abduction, estrangement, distorted narratives, or family-system control, the survivor may have lived with an image, a story, a fear, or a longing rather than the real person. The targeted parent, sibling, adult child, or other family member may have done the same. A carefully held moment of seeing one another may allow the old internal image to meet the living person in front of them.

For some survivors, this can soften a fixed trauma narrative. A parent who was described as dangerous, abandoning, selfish, uncaring, irrelevant, or unsafe may suddenly be seen as grieving, ageing, loving, confused, frightened, regretful, or human. A sibling who was remembered only through rivalry, absence, family stories, or childhood pain may now be seen as another person who also survived the family system. A targeted parent may see the adult child not only as the lost child, rejecting child, or alienated child, but as the person who has had to grow up inside years of pressure, fear, misinformation, and loss.

This does not mean the survivor must forgive, reconcile, continue contact, or change their decision. It simply means that visual contact may allow a different kind of information to enter the room. It may allow both people to notice what words they have not yet been able to carry. There may be grief in the face. There may be love. There may be fear. There may be regret. There may be shock. There may be nothing clear at all. All of these responses need to be allowed without forcing meaning too quickly.

When visual contact is helpful, it may create a small opening. The survivor may feel, "This is not who I was told they were," or "I can see that something was lost here," or "I do not know what I feel yet, but I want to know more." The targeted parent or sibling may feel, "They are here," or "They survived," or "I need to slow down because this person is not the child I have held in my mind." These are not final outcomes. They are beginnings.

Clinicians must also understand that a powerful moment of recognition can be destabilising, even when positive. Relief can destabilise. Love can destabilise. Being believed can destabilise. Being seen can destabilise. A survivor who has spent years protecting themselves from grief may feel overwhelmed when warmth, tenderness, or recognition arrives unexpectedly. A targeted parent may also become flooded by the reality of the adult child in front of them, and the years they were not able to share.

For this reason, when quiet visual contact helps, the clinician should still slow the process down. A moving moment should not be immediately converted into a family reunion, a contact plan, a disclosure session, or an expectation of an ongoing relationship. The aim is not to make the moment bigger. The aim is to protect it.

A clinician may need to say:

"This feels important. Let's not rush it. You do not need to decide what this means today. We can let the moment settle before we make any decisions about what comes next."

Quiet visual contact may be most helpful when it is brief, optional, and followed by space. A few seconds of safe recognition may be more clinically useful than several minutes of forced intensity. The survivor should always know that looking away is allowed. The targeted parent or sibling should understand that looking away is not rejection. It may be a form of regulation. It may be grief. It may be the person's nervous system protecting them from becoming overwhelmed.

The clinician should therefore treat visual contact as an invitation into recognition, not as a measure of success. It may help when it allows both people to become more real to each other while still preserving safety, choice, and pacing. It should never be used to prove attachment, demand forgiveness, test truthfulness, accelerate contact, or satisfy the grief of the targeted parent.

When it goes well, it can be extraordinary. It can open grief. It can allow an apology. It can allow curiosity. It can allow the first small movement towards repair. It may allow two people to recognise, even without words, that something precious was interrupted and that the person in front of them matters.

Even then, the HQTP remains clear: the outcome is not visual contact, reunion, forgiveness, or an ongoing relationship. The outcome is the survivor's capacity to stay connected to themselves while deciding what contact, if any, is safe, wanted, and sustainable.

What May Go Wrong

Supported visual contact may go wrong when it is introduced too early, too intensely, or in the wrong relational context. A survivor may freeze, go blank, dissociate, become compliant, collapse into shame, feel trapped, become angry, panic, or experience sudden loyalty conflict. They may later feel exposed, foolish, disloyal, frightened, embarrassed, or overwhelmed by how much they felt.

The other person may also become flooded. A targeted parent may start explaining too quickly, apologising repeatedly, defending themselves, asking questions, blaming the alienating parent, or trying to make up for years of loss in one sitting. A sibling may move between love, resentment, guilt, rivalry, protectiveness, and grief. A parent may see the adult survivor and suddenly feel the full force of the childhood they missed. A survivor may see the parent and feel both longing and danger at the same time.

Silence can be misread as rejection. Tears can be misread as manipulation. Looking away can be misread as avoidance. Numbness can be misread as a lack of care. A smile can be misread as forgiveness. For this cohort, misinterpretation is always a clinical risk.

Visual contact should not be used where there is active coercive control, current violence risk, untreated intoxication, acute suicidality, high dissociation, significant psychosis, unsafe family pressure, stalking, threats, ongoing legal coercion, or where either person is attending only to satisfy someone else's agenda. It should also be avoided if the survivor feels they cannot say no.

How the Clinician May Introduce Supported Contact

The clinician should gently, without pressure, introduce the possibility of supported visual contact. This should never be presented as something the survivor "should" do.

A clinician might say:

"There is a relational exercise some people use where two people sit together quietly and allow brief visual contact before speaking. I am not suggesting we do that now, and we may never need to do it. I am raising it only as one possible way of thinking about recognition. For some people, it is powerful; for others, it is too much. If we ever considered it, you would remain fully in charge of whether it happens, how long it lasts, and when it stops."

The clinician should then slow down and assess the survivor's response. Helpful questions include:

"What happens in your body when you imagine seeing them?"

"What happens when you imagine looking at them?"

"Would it feel like being seen, or would it feel like being captured?"

"Who would you be doing this for?"

"Would you feel free to stop?"

"What would tell us that your nervous system is still within your window of tolerance?"

"What would you need afterwards?"

The first clinical task is not to arrange the meeting. The first task is to assess whether imagining the meeting destabilises the survivor. If imagining contact produces panic, collapse, dissociation, compulsive compliance, or fear of betraying the alienating parent, then the work remains internal and preparatory.

Preparing Both People

Preparation should occur over several sessions where possible. The survivor should identify body signals, stop signals, grounding strategies, transport arrangements, an exit plan, and an aftercare plan. The clinician may first practise safer alternatives: looking at a photograph, sitting beside the clinician while imagining the person, reading an unsent letter aloud, using an empty-chair exercise, listening to a voice recording, or practising one or two seconds of visual contact with the clinician before looking away.

The survivor should be told clearly:

"You do not have to look at them to prove anything. Looking away is not failure. Stopping is not failure. Crying is not failure. Feeling nothing is not failure. Your job is not to perform healing. Your job is to stay connected to yourself."

The invited person also needs preparation. They must understand that their role is not to defend themselves, correct the record, demand answers, challenge the alienating parent's narrative, or secure a promise of future contact. Their role is to be present, regulated, respectful, and able to tolerate whatever the survivor can or cannot offer.

For targeted parents, the clinician may need to say:

"Your longing is understandable, but it cannot lead the session. Your grief is real, but it must not become pressure on the survivor. If they look away, become quiet, cry, become angry, or need to stop, you must allow that without pursuing them. The aim is not to get your child back in one session. The aim is to make this contact safe enough that it does not close the door further."

For siblings, preparation may need to acknowledge that both siblings may have been harmed differently by the same family system. One may have remained aligned. One may have been rejected. One may have carried loyalty to the alienating parent. One may have been told stories about the other. Sibling reunification can therefore carry love, rivalry, guilt, shame, anger, protectiveness, and grief simultaneously.

Conducting the Meeting

If supported visual contact is used, the HQTP recommends beginning far more gently than public or televised reunion formats. Several minutes may be far too long for traumatised survivors. Begin with seconds, not minutes, then pause.

The clinician may say:

"You may look at each other if you wish. You may also look away. We will begin with a very short moment. I will keep time. When I say pause, both of you can look down, breathe, and notice what is happening inside."

The clinician should monitor breathing, colour, posture, gaze, muscle tension, trembling, agitation, dissociation, compliance, sudden silence, forced smiling, and rapid emotional shifts. If the survivor becomes distant, glassy-eyed, frozen, overly agreeable, confused, collapsed, or intensely distressed, the exercise stops. The clinician should not ask deep interpretive questions while the survivor is dysregulated. The immediate task is to orient, ground, and return the person to the room.

The clinician should also monitor the invited person. If the targeted parent, sibling, or other family member begins to flood, explain, apologise repeatedly, pursue, blame, or pressure the survivor, the clinician should pause the interaction. Emotional intensity must not be allowed to become emotional demand.

If the Meeting Goes Badly

If the meeting becomes overwhelming, the clinician should stop it early and name the stop as protection, not failure:

"We are going to pause here. Nothing has gone wrong. Your nervous system is giving us information, and we are going to listen to it."

The clinician may separate the parties if needed, reduce stimulation, orient the survivor to the room, offer water, use feet-on-floor grounding, slow the pace, and use simple present-time cues. The survivor should not be asked to explain the reaction immediately. The invited person should be supported separately and instructed not to pursue, apologise repeatedly, text, call, or seek reassurance after the session unless this has been agreed.

The clinician should then review the risk. This includes suicidality, self-harm, dissociation, panic, driving safety, substance use risk, family retaliation risk, and whether the contact may trigger pressure from other relatives. A stopped exercise may still be clinically useful if it shows that the survivor needs more stabilisation, more preparation, or a different form of contact. In the HQTP, stopping is not regression. Stopping is pacing.

If the Meeting Goes Well

If the meeting goes well, the clinician still needs to contain it. This is often where mistakes happen. A moving moment can create urgency. The survivor may want to meet again immediately. The parent or sibling may want to introduce additional family members, explain everything, share documents, or repair decades of loss in a single conversation. The clinician should slow this down.

A helpful response is:

"This was important. Let's not overload it. We do not need to decide the whole future of the relationship today. We need to protect what just happened by giving both of you time to settle, reflect, and return carefully."

The first contact after a successful meeting should be modest. It may be a short message, a brief phone call, another supported session, or a simple agreement that neither person will pressure the other for more than they can manage. Successful reunification is not measured by intensity. It is measured by whether safety, respect, pacing, and choice can continue after the emotional moment has passed.

Guidance for Survivors Who Want to Try This

Some survivors may feel drawn to trying quiet visual contact with a parent, sibling, adult child, or other estranged loved one after watching a reunion video or hearing another survivor's story. This desire should be respected, but it should also be slowed down. Wanting contact is not the same as being ready for contact. Missing someone is not the same as being safe with them. A powerful reunion story can awaken hope, grief, longing, and urgency, especially in survivors who have lost years or decades of a relationship.

Survivors should not attempt this with a person who is currently abusive, coercive, threatening, intoxicated, stalking, manipulating, or pressuring them. They should not do it secretly, publicly, on camera, or in a setting where they cannot leave. If possible, they should first prepare with a trauma-informed clinician. If a clinician is not available, the survivor should still have a support person, a time limit, their own transport, a clear exit plan, and aftercare arranged for the hours and days afterwards.

A safer survivor-led version may begin with a photograph, an unsent letter, a supported message, a short phone call, or sitting beside the person rather than opposite them. Visual contact should be optional and brief. The survivor may say:

"I would like to try sitting with you quietly for a moment. I may look at you, and I may need to look away. I do not want to be asked questions straight away. I do not want pressure to forgive or decide anything today. I just want to see what it feels like to be near you safely."

The survivor should also plan what they will do afterwards. This may include going home with a trusted person, resting, eating, walking, journalling, contacting their therapist, or avoiding major decisions for at least twenty-four to forty-eight hours. Even beautiful reunification moments can bring grief afterwards. The nervous system may need time to understand that the moment has happened and that the survivor still belongs to themselves.

Clinician Reflection: If This Work Activates You

Clinicians are human beings. This work may affect them too. A reunification session involving alienation, abduction, long-term separation, or a parent seeing an adult child after decades may activate the clinician's own grief, family history, parenting fears, unresolved losses, protective instincts, anger at injustice, or rescue impulses. This does not make the clinician unsafe. What matters is whether the clinician recognises the activation and manages it responsibly.

Before undertaking this work, clinicians should ask themselves:

"What would this bring up in me if I had lost my child?"

"What would this bring up in me if I had been the child who was taken?"

"What would I feel if I saw my parent, child, or sibling after twenty, thirty, or forty years?"

"Am I able to hold this without pushing for a reunion because I want relief?"

"Am I able to tolerate the possibility that contact may stop, even after a beautiful moment?"

"Am I able to protect the survivor's pacing even if the parent's grief is heartbreaking?"

If the clinician becomes emotionally activated during the session, they should not make the moment about themselves. They should slow their breathing, ground through their feet, soften their voice, and return attention to the safety of the room. If needed, they may pause the exercise and say:

"Let's slow this down for a moment. This is a lot to hold."

The clinician does not need to disclose their own feelings unless doing so is brief, contained, and clearly in the clients' service. For example:

"This is a very moving moment, and we are going to take it slowly."

That is enough. The clinician should not cry in a way that requires the clients to comfort them, over-identify with either party, or push the session towards emotional closure because the moment feels powerful. The clinician's role is to hold the frame when the room becomes emotionally flooded.

After the session, the clinician should use supervision or consultation. This is especially important if the clinician notices rescue fantasies, anger towards an alienating parent, pressure to "make" the reunion work, difficulty tolerating the survivor's ambivalence, or an urge to contact, advise, protect, or over-direct the family outside the agreed treatment frame. These are signs that the work has touched something important in the clinician and needs containment.

In the HQTP, clinician activation is not treated as failure. It is treated as information. The work is emotionally demanding because the material is profoundly human. However, the survivor must not become responsible for the clinician's feelings, and the targeted parent's grief must not become the organising force of the session. The organising force remains safety, consent, pacing, and the survivor's right to remain free while being seen.

Core HQTP Principle

Reunification work is not only about whether two people can look at each other. It is about whether they can survive the emotional reality of what they see.

The face in front of them may carry love, loss, ageing, absence, fear, regret, hope, and the evidence of stolen time. Clinicians should treat this as sacred clinical ground. Do not rush it.

Do not perform it. Do not turn it into proof of success. Let the people in the room meet the truth slowly.

In the HQTP, visual contact must be invited, not demanded; brief, not forced; reversible, not binding; and contained, not romanticised.

After supported contact, visual recognition, or family reactivation, survivors may need help distinguishing between present-day risk and the older danger state that has been reawakened in the body. The following exercise can be used only after sufficient grounding has occurred and only where the clinician has assessed that the survivor is not in immediate danger. Its purpose is not to minimise risk, encourage contact, or override protective fear. Its purpose is to help the survivor gently test whether the current activation belongs to the present moment, the past, or both.

Brief Present-Day Safety Reorientation Exercise

This exercise may be used when an adult survivor becomes activated by later-life family contact, family events, contact pressure, guilt, obligation, or fear of relational retaliation. It is not intended to override genuine present-day risk. Its purpose is to help the survivor distinguish between past danger that has been reactivated and the current reality, in which they may now have greater distance, agency, support, and options.

In moments of activation, the clinician may ask:

"Is it absolutely true, in this moment, that you are still unsafe in the same way now?"

If the answer is no, or even partly no, the survivor may be invited to pause and notice whether anything shifts internally when they say, slowly and firmly:

"I am not in that same danger now. I am safer now. I have more choice now. I can decide what I expose myself to."

The aim is not to deny that family contact may still be distressing, provocative, coercive, or unsafe in particular circumstances. Rather, the exercise helps the survivor test whether the nervous system is responding to present-day, remembered, or anticipated danger, or a combination of these. The clinician should not assume safety. The task is to assess carefully, slow the response, and support the survivor to orient to the present before making contact, boundary, or avoidance decisions.

The clinician may then ask:

"If the old thought is no longer fully true, what thought would be more accurate now?"

"What happens in your body when you say that?"

"What might become possible if you respond from the present rather than from the old danger?"

Example for mental health practitioners: A survivor says, "If I do not go, everything will turn on me, and I will not cope."

The clinician might respond:

"Let us slow that down. I am not going to assume you are safe or unsafe. Let us check it carefully. Is the danger happening in the same way now, or is your body remembering an earlier danger? If you say to yourself, 'I am not in that same danger now. I have more choice now,' do you notice even a small shift anywhere in your body?"

The practitioner can then help the survivor build from that shift into clearer contact and boundary decisions. If no shift occurs, if the survivor becomes more distressed, or if present-day risk remains unclear, the clinician does not push the exercise further. The work returns to grounding, stabilisation, risk assessment, and reassessment of whether contact exploration is premature.

Clinical caution. This exercise should not be used to minimise real danger, encourage unsafe contact, override protective avoidance, or persuade the survivor into family engagement. Where coercion, violence, stalking, intimidation, active legal threat, suicidality, severe dissociation, or current safety concerns are present, the clinician should prioritise safety planning, supervision, consultation, and appropriate escalation.

Clinical reminder. The aim of this exercise is not to prove that the survivor is safe. The aim is to slow the work down enough to distinguish among past, present, anticipated, and mixed activation before making clinical or relational decisions.

Clinical Table. Present-Day Safety Reorientation: Advanced Clinical Decision Table

Clinical presentation	What the clinician is assessing	Suggested clinician response	Clinical direction
Past danger reactivated	The survivor is responding as though an earlier threat is happening again, but there is no immediate evidence of current danger.	"Your body may be remembering an old danger. Let us check what is happening now, slowly and carefully."	Use present-day orientation, grounding, regulation, and careful cognitive updating.
Present-day danger remains possible	The survivor may still be exposed to coercion, intimidation, stalking, violence, legal threat, family retaliation, or unsafe contact.	"I do not want to assume this is only old fear. Let us look carefully at what is happening now."	Prioritise safety planning, risk assessment, supervision, consultation, and possible escalation.
Anticipated danger	The survivor is not currently unsafe, but expects punishment, rejection, shame, collapse, or retaliation if they set a boundary or decline contact.	"Let us separate what is happening now from what you fear may happen next."	Support planning, boundary rehearsal, support mapping, and assessment of realistic consequences.
Mixed activation	Earlier danger, current stress, and future fear are all present at once.	"This may be partly old danger, partly current pressure, and partly fear about what may happen. We do not need to decide too quickly. "	Slow the work. Return to stabilisation, map the risks, and defer contact or boundary decisions until clearer.
No internal shift after reorientation	The survivor remains highly activated, frozen, dissociated, ashamed, or unable to access present-day safety.	"Your system is not ready to move into decision-making yet. That is important clinical information."	Stop the exercise. Return to grounding, containment, regulation, and phase reassessment.
Survivor becomes calmer and more oriented	The survivor can notice that the old danger is not fully present and can access more choice.	"Something has shifted. Let us stay with that gently and not rush it."	Build slowly toward contact, boundary, or avoidance decisions from a more regulated state.
Survivor moves into compliance	The survivor says what they think the clinician wants to hear, minimises danger, or agrees too quickly.	"I do not want you to agree with me. Let us check what feels true for you."	Pause interpretation. Re-establish autonomy, consent, and reflective space.
Survivor wants immediate action	The survivor wants to contact, confront, disclose, attend, cut off, or make a major decision while still activated.	"This may be important, but we do not need to decide while your nervous system is still under threat."	Delay major decisions. Use stabilisation, supervision, and a planned review point.

Phase V Decision Tree Quick Reference

Relational Contact, Boundary Safety, and Ethical Continuity

Phase V operates through iterative clinical decision trees rather than linear progression. These trees guide relational pacing, protect against the reenactment of coercive family dynamics, and prevent contact decisions from serving as proxy indicators of therapeutic success. Each decision point functions as a safety checkpoint that must be revisited throughout this phase as relational conditions shift.

Decision Tree 1: Autonomy Consolidation Versus Separation Anxiety

The clinician first evaluates whether the survivor's increasing independence reflects genuine autonomy consolidation or unresolved attachment distress related to perceived separation. When survivors demonstrate growing confidence in decision-making, reduced reassurance seeking, and the ability to self-regulate between sessions, pacing adjustments and gradual modulation of session frequency may be supported while preserving continuity of access.

When survivors experience heightened anxiety, guilt, panic, or emotional collapse in response to spacing sessions or discussing future transitions, this is understood as an attachment-based response rather than resistance. In such cases, relational continuity is maintained, and pacing changes are slowed to prevent reenactment of abandonment dynamics.

Clinical red flags: Distress disproportionate to minor scheduling changes, urgency to maintain constant therapeutic contact, panic around perceived endings, or escalating dependency behaviours.

Supervision prompt: Monitor clinicians' discomfort with survivor attachment cues and ensure that pacing decisions are not influenced by service pressure or by clinicians' avoidance of emotional complexity.

Decision Tree 2: Meaning Integration Versus Past Injury Fixation

The clinician next assesses whether survivors are integrating therapeutic insight into present-day identity development and relational functioning or remaining organised around unresolved injury narratives. When survivors apply insight to boundary development, future planning, relational choice, and identity consolidation, this supports forward integration.

When survivors remain preoccupied with external validation, recognition-seeking, or repeated attempts to correct historical injustice, clinicians validate the legitimacy of these concerns while gently redirecting the focus toward internal coherence rather than external resolution. Therapy is not positioned as a forum for systemic repair, but as a space for personal authorship and stability.

Clinical red flags: Escalating rumination, fixation on vindication, stagnation around unresolved family or institutional failures, or emotional escalation following perceived invalidation of justice claims.

Supervision prompt: Supervision helps clinicians tolerate moral distress related to systemic injustice without passing urgency, pressure, or unresolved frustration on to the survivor.

Decision Tree 3: Family Contact Re-Emergence and Boundary Stability

When survivors initiate or consider contacting family members, the clinician evaluates emotional stability and boundary capacity, rather than the decision itself. When survivors demonstrate emotional steadiness, reflective capacity, and the ability to disengage from coercive dynamics, clinicians support boundary clarification and post-contact processing.

When contact results in renewed coercion, confusion, self-erasure, or emotional destabilisation, the clinician assists the survivor in reassessing boundaries and reinforces the legitimacy of distance or disengagement. When survivors express pressure to reconcile for moral, social, cultural, or religious reasons, clinicians separate healing from reunification and reaffirm relational choice as a survivor right.

Clinical red flags: Rapid contact escalation following emotional breakthroughs, guilt-driven reconnection, idealisation of abusive caregivers, or minimisation of harm following renewed contact.

Supervision prompt: Support clinician neutrality and guard against subtle pressure to privilege relational repair over psychological safety.

Decision Tree 4: Meaning Consolidation Versus Existential Flattening

Phase V also involves monitoring whether survivors are consolidating meaning and identity or entering phases of emotional flattening and disengagement.

When survivors report increased coherence, purpose, and grounded identity, clinicians support narrative continuity and future orientation. When survivors experience numbness, disengagement, or loss of direction, clinicians assess for delayed grief, moral injury, identity exhaustion, or accumulated relational fatigue and reintroduce reflective work where indicated. Quiet phases are not pathologised but monitored for withdrawal or collapse.

Clinical red flags: Emotional shutdown following autonomy gains, disengagement from relational life, or abrupt withdrawal from therapeutic engagement.

Supervision prompt: Assist clinicians in tolerating quiet integration phases without prematurely reactivating intervention intensity.

Decision Tree 5: Ongoing Therapeutic Access and Ethical Continuity

The clinician evaluates whether ongoing intermittent access to care remains clinically indicated. When survivors benefit from periodic support during transitions, relational stressors, or developmental milestones, continuity is maintained without requiring justification or reassessment. When survivors demonstrate sustained stability without active therapeutic need, planned pauses are formalised rather than framed as termination. When new trauma exposure, system contact, or relational destabilisation occurs, clinicians re-enter earlier protocol phases without framing this as regression.

Clinical red flags: Clinician pressure to discharge, organisational expectations of closure, or survivor fear of losing access to support.

Supervision prompt: Reinforce ethical continuity practices and protect against institutional pacing overriding clinical judgement.

Decision Tree 6: Clinician Role Integrity and Countertransference Monitoring

Throughout Phase V, clinicians continuously monitor role integrity.

When clinicians experience pressure to rescue, remain indefinitely available, or replace relational networks, supervision is required. When clinicians feel disengaged, avoidant, emotionally withdrawn, or prematurely inclined to end therapy, supervision is likewise required. Ethical continuity depends on maintaining clear boundaries while preserving relational presence.

Phase V does not conclude through discharge. It transitions into ethical continuity when survivors experience therapy as a resource rather than a requirement, when clinicians maintain availability without obligation, when healing is defined by safety, agency, and meaning rather than closure, and when responsibility for harm is accurately located within relational systems rather than internalised by the survivor. Under these conditions, therapy remains accessible across the lifespan without requiring justification in crisis, moral performance, or reauthorisation.

When Contact Exploration Is Contraindicated

Exploration of contact with alienating or psychologically abusive caregivers is contraindicated when survivors demonstrate threat-based compliance, unresolved epistemic injury, or physiological destabilisation in response to relational pressure. Clinically, this may present as panic activation, dissociation, somatic collapse, cognitive constriction, urgency to decide, moral self-attack, or sudden idealisation of the abusive parent following boundary assertion.

Contact exploration is also contraindicated when survivors seek to prove fairness, goodness, forgiveness, or emotional maturity to relieve guilt, obligation, or fear. Under these conditions, relational decisions are likely to replicate original power asymmetries, with survivors unconsciously prioritising the emotional regulation of abusive caregivers over their own psychological safety. When these patterns are present, clinicians frame postponement or non-contact as an active therapeutic choice rather than avoidance, regression, or failure. Responsibility for slowing pacing rests with the clinician. Protection from reenactment is an ethical obligation, not a burden on survivors.

Loyalty Compulsion and Autonomy Differentiation

Clinicians do not interpret loyalty compulsion as ambivalence or resistance. Loyalty-driven behaviour is conceptualised as a trauma-based constraint on agency shaped by developmental coercion, attachment fear, and conditioned compliance. Phase V proceeds only when survivors can recognise these internal pressures without being governed by them.

Autonomous relational choice is indicated by the survivor's capacity to tolerate ambivalence, hold relational complexity, and make decisions without urgency, moral panic, or fear of abandonment. When relational decisions are driven by guilt relief, appeasement, or fear-based obligation, clinicians return to stabilisation and differentiation processes rather than advancing contact exploration.

Indicators Requiring Return to Earlier Phases

Return to Phase II is indicated when boundary-setting or contact exploration elicits renewed hypervigilance, affect dysregulation, epistemic destabilisation, or increased reliance on the clinician for reassurance, permission, or moral validation. These presentations signal insufficient consolidation of meaning and identity to support autonomous relational choice.

Return to Phase III is indicated when contact exploration activates identity fragmentation, narrative collapse, renewed self-blame, minimisation of harm, or reframing of coercion as mutual conflict. Survivors may begin questioning whether abuse occurred or revert to internalised responsibility narratives. These responses indicate unresolved grief or incomplete integration, which require reinforcement before relational decisions can be safely held. Movement between phases is not framed as regression. It is framed as clinically responsive recalibration based on survivor capacity and safety.

Clinical red flags: Renewed hypervigilance following boundary setting, affect dysregulation after contact exploration, increased reliance on the clinician for reassurance, permission, or moral validation, identity fragmentation, narrative collapse, minimisation of harm, reframing of coercion as mutual conflict, and renewed self-blame following family contact or boundary assertion.

Supervision prompt: Assess whether contact exploration is being advanced prematurely, whether clinician values or urgency are influencing pacing, whether survivor autonomy is being confused with compliance or avoidance, and whether renewed destabilisation signals a need to return to Phase II or Phase III processes before further relational decision-making.

Phase V Closure Logic (Clinical)

Phase V does not conclude when relational decisions are finalised. It concludes when survivors demonstrate reliable internal authority, emotional stability across relational stressors, and the ability to engage with family systems or boundaries without identity collapse, fear-based compliance, or dependence on therapist validation.

At this point, therapeutic work transitions toward continuity-based care rather than procedural progression. This prepares the survivor for Phase VI, which formalises long-horizon access to support rather than clinical termination.

Phase VI: Integration, Continuity, and Long-Term Adaptation

Continuity and Re-Entry

Phase VI begins when the primary therapeutic goals have stabilised, and therapy is no longer functioning as the survivor's main organising structure for regulation or day-to-day functioning. The survivor demonstrates sufficient internal authority to notice activation, recognise recurring trigger patterns, and seek support without collapse, shame, or the assumption that needing contact again means failure. Re-entry is understood as part of continuity, not evidence of regression.

Entry into Phase VI does not require the absence of symptoms, nor does it require that all contact decisions, boundary questions, or family relationships be fully settled. Contact may remain occasional, planned, or informal. What is required is sufficient psychological stability for autonomy to be tolerated without abrupt disengagement, dependency, or renewed fear-based reliance on the therapeutic relationship.

Where these conditions are not yet established, clinicians remain in Phase IV or Phase V work and defer continuity planning. Within the HQTP, Phase VI recognises that adult survivors of child psychological abuse, parental alienation, and abduction may require intermittent therapeutic support across the lifespan. Endings are therefore not organised solely around termination. Many survivors have already lived through abrupt withdrawal of care, conditional access to support, institutional abandonment, and profound relational discontinuity. Therapy should not replicate those patterns. Instead, continuity is made explicit through clear pathways for re-entry, transparent discussion of future access, and survivor-led pacing.

The central clinical task of Phase VI is to embed continuity without dependency and availability without boundary erosion. The clinician supports the survivor in transitioning from active therapeutic engagement to a stable, accessible care relationship that can be entered and exited without shame, crisis justification, or moral performance.

Phase VI also formalises the clinician's role at the interface between therapy and external systems. Survivors do not heal in isolation from the institutions that shaped, silenced, or misinterpreted their experiences. Family law, child protection, education, health, and justice systems frequently remain psychologically active long after formal involvement has ended. The clinician's role in this phase is best conceptualised as an ethical witness with disciplined restraint.

The clinician neither functions as a legal actor nor retreats into neutrality, which feels like abandoning. Ethical witness involves acknowledging harm without adjudicating facts, validating impact without positioning it as evidence, and holding space for grief, anger, and moral injury without mobilising therapy toward external outcomes. This stance protects survivors from misplaced hope that therapy can correct historical injustice while preserving the therapeutic space as a refuge from systemic harm.

Phase VI rejects the expectation that therapy should restore rights, produce recognition, or resolve institutional failure. While survivors were often denied fundamental relational and developmental rights, therapy does not function as a reparative system. Naming this limitation protects both survivor and clinician from unconscious role drift.

Survivor Guidance: Continuity, Re-Entry, and Psychological Safety

Within the HQTP, returning to therapy is not framed as relapse. It is framed as adaptive continuity. Survivors retain full authority to re-engage care during life transitions, relational stressors, system contact, or periods of renewed activation. Therapy remains available as a resource rather than a requirement. Consent continues to operate as an ongoing relational process. Survivors have the right to request booster sessions, short stabilisation blocks, or periodic check-ins without committing to long-term re-engagement. They also retain the right to pause therapy without being positioned as disengaged or resistant.

Clinicians use explicit language to prevent reenactment of abandonment. For example, survivors are informed that support remains accessible without time limits, reassessment burden, or justification requirements. This framing counters developmental experiences of conditional care and protects against internalised beliefs that help must be earned through deterioration.

Predictable Activation Contexts and Continuity Planning

Phase VI includes proactive mapping of predictable activation contexts. Common triggers include anniversaries of separation and loss, family events, death notifications, unexpected contact attempts, legal correspondence, authority reminders, medical crises, developmental transitions such as parenthood or ageing, and renewed system exposure.

The clinician collaborates with the survivor to identify which periods have historically led to destabilisation and to pre-plan support strategies. These may include scheduled booster sessions during known risk windows, temporary increases in session frequency, or rapid-access pathways for unexpected events.

Continuity planning also includes preparation for future system contact. Survivors may anticipate interactions with healthcare providers, employers, schools, courts, or child-related institutions. Therapy supports the survivor in choosing how much of their history to disclose, developing language that preserves dignity without over-explanation, and establishing boundaries that protect psychological safety.

Clinical Red Flags During Phase VI Transitioning

Indicators that Phase VI pacing requires slowing include panic activation when session frequency is reduced, compulsive reassurance seeking, emotional collapse following perceived distance, or fear-based clinging to therapeutic access. These responses signal unresolved abandonment conditioning and require stabilisation rather than acceleration.

Additional clinical red flags include renewed shame about needing support, interpreting re-engagement as a personal failure, escalating moral self-attack, or pressure to perform independence. Phase VI also requires recalibration when system contact triggers dissociation, somatic shutdown, identity fragmentation, epistemic destabilisation, sudden minimisation of harm, or re-emergence of threat-based compliance. When these patterns appear, clinicians reactivate earlier phases of the protocol without framing the survivor as regressed.

Supervision Considerations

Phase VI requires ongoing supervision to monitor clinician countertransference related to rescue impulses, moral outrage toward institutions, over-availability, role substitution, emotional withdrawal, or premature closure pressure. Survivors' histories of institutional betrayal and systemic harm can evoke strong emotional responses in clinicians. Without supervision, these responses risk distorting clinical boundaries or replicating authority dynamics that mirror the survivor's original experiences of coercion or abandonment.

Supervision is also important when survivors ask clinicians to write letters, provide documentation, or communicate with lawyers, courts, schools, child protection, hospitals, or other systems. For example, a survivor may ask for a letter stating that alienation has occurred or that a parent was abusive. Within the HQTP, supervision helps the clinician consider what can be stated clinically, what cannot be concluded, and how to avoid drifting into a forensic role or unintentionally increasing the survivor's risk. Supervisors assist clinicians to maintain disciplined restraint while remaining relationally present and transparent about scope limitations. Phase VI operates through iterative clinical decision trees rather than linear progression. These decision points guide continuity pacing, protect against the reenactment of abandonment, and preserve ethical boundaries.

Phase VI Decision Tree Quick Reference

Decision Tree 1: Developmental Transition Versus Stable Integration

The clinician evaluates whether the survivor is entering a developmental transition such as parenthood, relationship rupture, illness, ageing, institutional contact, or family death. When transitions are present, re-engagement with therapy is normalised as anticipatory care rather than a relapse response. When no transition is present, the clinician maintains low-intensity availability without active intervention while ensuring that continuity remains explicit.

Clinical red flags include interpreting renewed distress as weakness, avoiding re-engagement out of fear of judgement, or believing that support must be earned anew.

Supervision prompt: Assess whether re-engagement is understood as adaptive continuity or is subtly framed by the clinician or service culture as relapse, dependency, or failure.

Decision Tree 2: System Re-exposure and Psychological Safety

When survivors re-encounter authority systems, the clinician supports reflective preparation, boundary clarity, and language development. When system contact produces destabilisation, disbelief, or retraumatisation, the clinician reactivates Phase III or Phase IV processes without reframing the survivor as regressed.

Clinical red flags: An urgency to demonstrate credibility, pressure to maintain emotional composure, or an escalation of threat-based compliance patterns.

Supervision prompt: Assess whether contact with external systems, including courts, lawyers, schools, child protection, hospitals, police, government agencies, or other services, is reactivating earlier epistemic injury. Consider whether documentation or communication requests are causing role drift, whether the clinician is being pulled toward advocacy, investigation, or forensic opinion, and whether earlier-phase containment needs to be reinstated.

Decision Tree 3: Shame-Based Avoidance Versus Adaptive Re-Entry

The clinician assesses whether the survivor is avoiding re-engagement due to internalised beliefs that needing help is failure. When shame-based avoidance is present, the clinician reframes help-seeking as adaptive continuity and addresses internalised system logic rather than clinical dependency.

Clinical red flags: Moral self-attack, perfectionistic independence narratives, or suppression of distress to avoid appearing needy.

Supervision prompt: Assess whether shame, perfectionism, or internalised beliefs about burden and failure are preventing timely re-engagement, and whether the clinician is underestimating distress because the survivor appears outwardly competent.

Decision Tree 4: Ethical Availability Versus Boundary Erosion

The clinician continuously evaluates whether availability remains clear and bounded. When clinicians feel pressured to provide unlimited access, to rescue, or to replace relational networks, supervision is required. When clinicians feel emotionally withdrawn, avoidant, or prematurely inclined to close care, supervision is likewise required. Ethical continuity is maintained when availability is survivor-led, transparent, and professionally contained.

Clinical red flags: Blurred access expectations, pressure for unlimited availability, rescue pressure, clinician resentment, boundary softening driven by guilt, emotional withdrawal, or premature movement toward closure.

Supervision prompt: Assess whether availability remains clear, bounded, and survivor-led, and whether rescue impulses, fatigue, avoidance, or premature-closure pressure are shaping clinicians' responses.

Decision Tree 5: Witnessing Versus Outcome-Driven Therapy

When survivors seek recognition, justice, or validation beyond therapy, the clinician affirms the legitimacy of these needs while clarifying the limits of therapy. The clinician supports grief, moral injury, and meaning-making without redirecting therapy toward restitution, forgiveness, or reconciliation.

Clinical red flags: Include an urgency to mobilise therapy for external outcomes or to frame therapeutic success in terms of institutional recognition.

Supervision prompt: Assess whether the clinician is being pulled too far in either direction: moving beyond their clinical role into rescue, advocacy, investigation, or forensic opinion, or becoming so cautious and neutral that the survivor feels dismissed or unsupported. Supervision should also help the clinician tolerate the moral distress of witnessing serious harm without promising to fix outcomes that therapy cannot control.

Decision Tree 6: Explicit Continuity Communication

The clinician evaluates whether continuity has been communicated.

When survivors understand that support remains accessible without justification, Phase VI is functioning as intended. When survivors believe therapy has ended permanently or must be reauthorised, the clinician clarifies continuity immediately. In this cohort, silence about availability is frequently interpreted as abandonment. For example, if the clinician notices subtle activation in the moment, they could say:

"I noticed a shift just now as we talked about spacing sessions or future contact. I do not want to make assumptions, but I want to check whether any part of this is landing as distance, loss, or abandonment. If it is, we can slow down and talk about that directly."

And then:

"My role is not to disappear without explanation. We can make the pathway explicit and go gently together. That means being clear about how you reconnect, what support is available, and how we would respond if things become difficult again. Does that sound OK, or do you have another suggestion that you may like to run past me?" (MHP smiles).

Clinical red flags: Assumptions that the survivor "knows they can come back," unspoken endings, or survivor hesitation linked to uncertainty about access.

Supervision prompt: Review whether continuity arrangements have been clearly stated, appropriately documented, and framed to reduce the risk of reenactment of abandonment.

Phase VI does not terminate. It establishes the ethical position that therapy remains available across the lifespan, that re-engagement does not require crisis or reassessment burden, and that support is survivor-initiated and context-responsive.

Moving toward healing within the HQTP is defined by safety, agency, dignity, and internal authority rather than independence from care. The protocol concludes not because therapy ends, but because support remains available in a clear, ethical, and boundaried way that does not rely on dependency or abandonment. In Phase VI, the clinician's authority lies not in speaking for the survivor, but in refusing to replace their voice.

Phase VI Explained for Adult Survivors

Systems, Safety, and Ethical Witness - What This Phase Means for You

A note from Dr Alyse

Dear friends,

I have written this note for you in clear, gentle language, so this phase feels easier to follow as you continue to grow in confidence, self-trust, and choice.

Many survivors carry pain that was shaped not only by family relationships but also by systems that did not respond with the care, protection, or understanding that was needed. Courts, schools, child protection services, healthcare providers, universities, and mental health professionals may at times have misunderstood, overlooked, minimised, or even reinforced what you were living through. Experiences like these can leave deep, lasting effects that do not simply fade over time.

This phase matters because healing does not happen in isolation. Even when you are no longer actively involved with these systems, their impact can still live inside you. It is very understandable to feel anxious around authority figures, or to feel a strong need to explain yourself, defend your reality, or prove what happened. You may also carry anger, grief, or a deep sense of injustice that has never been fully acknowledged.

If this is where you are, please know you are not alone. Many survivors feel this way. These responses often make sense in the context of what you have lived through. You have been through a great deal, and you are brave to be doing this work. Sometimes tears are part of healing. They can be a way for the body to begin to release what has been held for a very long time. You do not need to rush yourself, harden yourself, or have it all figured out at once. Be gentle with yourself. With time, safety, and the right support, these feelings can become less intense, less constant, and easier to carry.

In this phase, therapy becomes a place where your experiences are held without being judged, investigated, or put on trial. Your therapist's role here is not to decide what really happened, take sides, or act as a legal representative. Instead, they act as an ethical witness. This means they recognise the impact of what you have lived through without demanding evidence, explanations, or certainty. You do not need to persuade, justify, or prove yourself to be taken seriously. Your experience does not need institutional approval to matter.

Navigating Authority, Education, and Professional Spaces

As you move forward in life, you may again encounter authority figures. This can include university staff, psychology lecturers, supervisors, managers, professional gatekeepers, or senior clinicians. Some of these people may not understand lived experience trauma. Some may minimise your perspective, question your credibility, or speak from positions of theoretical authority without recognising the reality of survivor knowledge.

If you are studying psychology or working in mental health, this can feel especially confronting. Survivors who become clinicians often carry deep insight that does not always fit neatly within traditional academic frameworks. At times, you may feel talked over, dismissed, subtly undermined, or treated as too emotional, too subjective, or not objective enough. These experiences can activate old threat responses linked to being silenced or not believed as a child. It is important to remember that your lived experience matters, and your own understanding of what you have lived through matters as well.

Your lived knowledge has value. You do not need to erase yourself to belong in professional spaces. At the same time, your safety matters. If interactions with authority figures become invalidating, shaming, coercive, or emotionally aggressive, they can trigger intense distress. Some survivors notice spikes in anxiety, shutdown, dissociation, or suicidal thoughts when they feel attacked, humiliated, or made to feel powerless. These reactions are often nervous system responses to threat.

If this happens, you do not have to carry it alone. Reach out to safe people. This might include trusted friends, lecturers, fellow students, peer support groups, university wellbeing services, disability or equity offices, or student advocacy services. If you are already a clinician, this may include your clinical supervisor, senior colleagues, professional mentors, or trusted peers. You are allowed to ask for support, perspective, and protection.

It can also help to document interactions that feel unsafe or inappropriate. Keeping records may help you stay grounded and protect yourself if boundaries are crossed. You are not required to endure mistreatment in the name of education, professionalism, or growth.

Protecting Yourself While Staying Empowered

Phase VI supports you in learning how to stay connected to your values without being pulled back into harmful power dynamics. This may include learning when to speak up and when to step back, when to engage and when to disengage, and how to choose psychologically safer environments.

You are allowed to further your education, and when you do, you are allowed to change supervisors, courses, workplaces, or professional pathways if they are not supporting you or consistently harming your wellbeing. You are allowed to seek trauma-informed spaces. You are allowed to prioritise your mental health over external approval. Therapy can help you develop language that protects your dignity, boundaries that reduce your exposure to harm, and internal steadiness that helps you stay grounded even when others do not understand.

Choice, Not Compliance

This phase also protects you from being retraumatised by systems that have already caused harm. You are not expected to seek justice, closure, reconciliation, or recognition unless you choose to. Some survivors want answers, accountability, or public acknowledgement. Others want distance, privacy, or peace. There is no correct choice. Therapy does not tell you which path to take. It supports you in making decisions that feel psychologically safe and aligned with your values.

If you anticipate future contact with systems such as healthcare, employment, education, parenting services, or family-related processes, therapy can help you prepare emotionally and practically. This may include deciding how much to disclose, choosing what parts of your story remain private, recognising early warning signs of threat activation, and building support around you before difficult interactions occur. The goal is not to make you more compliant or more confrontational. The goal is to help you stay grounded in choice.

Honouring the Limits of Therapy

It is important to name the limits of therapy honestly. Therapy cannot undo the past. It cannot restore lost time, relationships, or opportunities. It cannot force systems to acknowledge harm or correct injustice. Pretending otherwise can create new hurt by placing responsibility on you to heal what was never yours to fix.

What therapy can do is offer a space where your story does not need permission to exist.

Many survivors were denied basic human rights in childhood. This may have included the right to maintain relationships with family, the right to truthful information about their history, the right to grieve losses, or the right not to be lied to or manipulated. Therapy cannot restore these rights, but it can recognise that they were taken and that the impact of that loss matters.

What You May Notice Changing

As you move through this phase, you may notice a shift in how you relate to your own story. You may feel less urgency to convince others and more permission to trust yourself. You may begin assigning responsibility where it belongs, rather than carrying it alone. You may find that your sense of self becomes less dependent on external validation and more rooted in your own understanding.

There is no emotional outcome you are expected to reach here. Some survivors feel relief. Others feel sadness, anger, or grief. Some experience a quieter settling or a greater sense of stability. All of these responses are valid. Phase VI is not about returning to systems. It is about ensuring that therapy itself does not become another system that takes control away from you. In this phase, your voice is not replaced. It is protected.

Go gently, Dr Alyse

Responsibility, Continuity, and the Limits of Therapy

The HQTP was developed in response to a consistent finding across the author's doctoral research: adult survivors of CPA-PA were not primarily seeking symptom reduction, reconciliation, or closure. They sought recognition, safety, clarity, understanding, psychoeducation and an end to misinterpretation by the very systems entrusted with their care.

Across survivor narratives and MHP perspectives, a central theme emerged. Harm did not end with childhood. It was often prolonged, compounded, and deepened by professional misunderstanding, misdiagnosis, and systemic blindness to psychological abuse and attachment disruption. Survivors described years of ineffective therapy, repeated institutional contact, and ongoing self-doubt, not because they were resistant to treatment, but because the frameworks applied to them did not fit the reality of their lives.

The HQTP therefore rejects the premise that adult survivors of child psychological abuse require correction, reparenting, or forced reunification. Instead, it affirms that many survivors adapted intelligently to environments defined by coercion, control, and epistemic threat. What was labelled pathology was often survival. What was framed as resistance was often self-protection and resilience building. What was interpreted as relational dysfunction was frequently the imprint of forced loyalty, erased attachment, and prolonged psychological control.

The findings of the author's research further demonstrated that survivors did not experience healing as a linear process. Movement occurred in cycles, with periods of stability followed by reactivation during developmental transitions, relational shifts, or contact with authority and institutions. Survivors consistently reported that what mattered most was not whether therapy ended, but whether it remained accessible without judgement, disbelief, or withdrawal.

MHPs participating in the research echoed this complexity. Those with sustained experience in this field identified the need for integrative, attachment-aware, trauma-informed approaches that resisted both theoretical rigidity and modality dominance. They emphasised the importance of supervision, ethical humility, and tolerance for ambiguity. Practitioners also named the emotional burden of this work and the risk of countertransference, misalignment, and professional isolation when working without adequate support. Taken together, these findings underscore a fundamental principle of this protocol. Healing does not occur because the survivor changes. It occurs because the environment around them becomes safer, clearer, and less coercive.

The HQTP deliberately resists framing therapy as a corrective substitute for justice, accountability, or systemic repair. Adult survivors were often denied fundamental rights, including the right to know and maintain relationships with family, the right to truthful information about their history, the right to grieve losses, and the right not to be manipulated or silenced. These violations cannot be undone in therapy. The survivor should not be expected to carry the additional burden of somehow repairing within themselves what was caused by other people, family systems, or institutions. Doing so risks placing responsibility for the harm back onto the person who endured it.

Instead, therapy offers something more modest and more ethical. It offers a relationship that does not demand loyalty, performance, or persuasion. It offers language where there was silence, coherence where there was distortion, and continuity where there was rupture. It offers a space in which survivors are not required to forgive, reconcile, or make meaning from harm to be considered healed. Sometimes healing takes a lifetime, and there is no time limit in this space.

For clinicians, the HQTP does not promise mastery. It demands responsibility. Work in this field requires ongoing supervision, reflective practice, and a willingness to remain unsettled by complexity. No professional discipline, credential, or modality confers immunity from blind spots when engaging with identity-level trauma shaped by adversarial systems. Ethical practice requires clinicians to examine where authority ends continually, and humility must begin. The HQTP's closing stance is therefore intentional. It does not end with an endpoint, an outcome, or a declaration of success. It ends with continuity.

Adult survivors of CPA may step in and out of care over many years. They may require different forms of support at different times. They may live well while still carrying grief, anger, or unresolved questions. None of these realities indicates failure. They indicate a life lived in the face of coercion.

Healing, as articulated in this work, is not the absence of pain. It is the presence of choice. It is the ability to trust one's own perceptions without needing permission. It is the freedom to engage with or disengage from relationships and systems without fear of punishment or erasure. Adult survivors deserve care that does not rush them toward resolution, does not confuse neutrality with safety, and does not disappear when complexity remains. Clinicians deserve frameworks that protect clarity, integrity, and wellbeing in emotionally demanding work that is often misunderstood. Healing, when it occurs, unfolds not because therapy ends, but because safety continues.

Practitioner Readiness and Clinical Preparation

Anchored in UniSC Twin PhD Survivor and Practitioner Findings

Before clinicians engage in assessment, formulation, or phase-based intervention with adult survivors of CPA-PA, practitioner readiness must be formally addressed. Findings from the author's twin doctoral studies at the University of the Sunshine Coast identified practitioner preparedness as a primary determinant of therapeutic safety and treatment outcome.

Across both survivor and practitioner datasets, a consistent pattern emerged. Survivors described therapeutic harm occurring not through overt malpractice, but through well-intentioned clinicians applying inappropriate models, rushing insight, misinterpreting attachment trauma, or imposing reconciliation-oriented frameworks. Practitioners simultaneously reported emotional overload, ethical uncertainty, countertransference strain, and lack of population-specific guidance when working with alienation-related developmental trauma.

The UniSC research coded this pattern as the Practitioner Readiness Gap Theme, referring to the systemic mismatch between general trauma training and the specialised clinical demands of CPA-PA and prolonged relational abuse.

Population Misclassification

Survivors described layered developmental injury rather than a single, discrete trauma. Identity disruption, loyalty conditioning, moral injury, attachment rupture, and prolonged relational threat were recurrent themes. Many reported receiving inconsistent or changing diagnoses across years of treatment, including anxiety disorders, depression, bipolar disorder, personality disorders, or adjustment difficulties. Some explained that the diagnosis seemed to change each time they sat before a different psychiatrist, depending on how they were feeling and presenting on that particular day. Rarely did they receive the same diagnosis twice. Others described being prescribed different medications without an adequate clinical formulation of the underlying trauma, sometimes experiencing significant or adverse side effects.

Practitioners acknowledged that their initial training had not prepared them to identify the distinct clinical profile of alienation survivors. Many described beginning treatment with standard trauma models before realising that this population required different pacing, relational containment strategies, and a fundamentally different therapeutic stance.

Effective preparation begins with an accurate assessment and understanding of the population. Adult survivors of CPA-PA do not present similarly to survivors of single-event trauma. Training must therefore begin with a population-informed understanding of this survivor group and then draw flexibly on multiple therapeutic modalities and appropriate holistic treatments according to the survivor's needs.

The UniSC practitioner cohort identified inconsistent theoretical positioning as a destabilising factor in treatment. Survivors mirrored this experience, describing therapy as confusing or contradictory when clinicians lacked a coherent, integrative framework.

Effective work requires the capacity to hold attachment disruption, developmental trauma, coercive control dynamics, nervous system dysregulation, identity formation, and relational betrayal simultaneously. Cognitive and behavioural strategies remain valuable tools, but only when embedded within a developmental and relational structure.

Avoiding Training Saturation Without Integration

Practitioners reported accumulating certifications without corresponding increases in clinical confidence. Workshop attendance did not automatically translate into integrative competence. The HQTP prioritises a thorough understanding of this survivor population and the clinical judgement required to select and adapt treatment appropriately. Training should strengthen pacing discipline, awareness of countertransference, boundary clarity, and tolerance for ambiguity in high-complexity cases.

Both survivor and practitioner data support framing supervision and ongoing professional development as structural requirements rather than optional enhancements. Work in this field carries a high emotional load, reputational exposure, and risk of vicarious trauma. Ethical sustainability requires continuous reflective practice and engagement in supervision.

The recommended subjects and topics identified by practitioners are presented alphabetically on the next page. These recommendations are included to show the breadth of knowledge practitioners considered relevant to safe, informed, and clinically responsible work with adult survivors. Additionally, they highlight why supervision, scope awareness, specialist referral, and careful phase-based practice are essential.

Recommended Training Subjects and Topics Reported by the PhD Mental Health Practitioners Cohort Working Therapeutically with Survivors

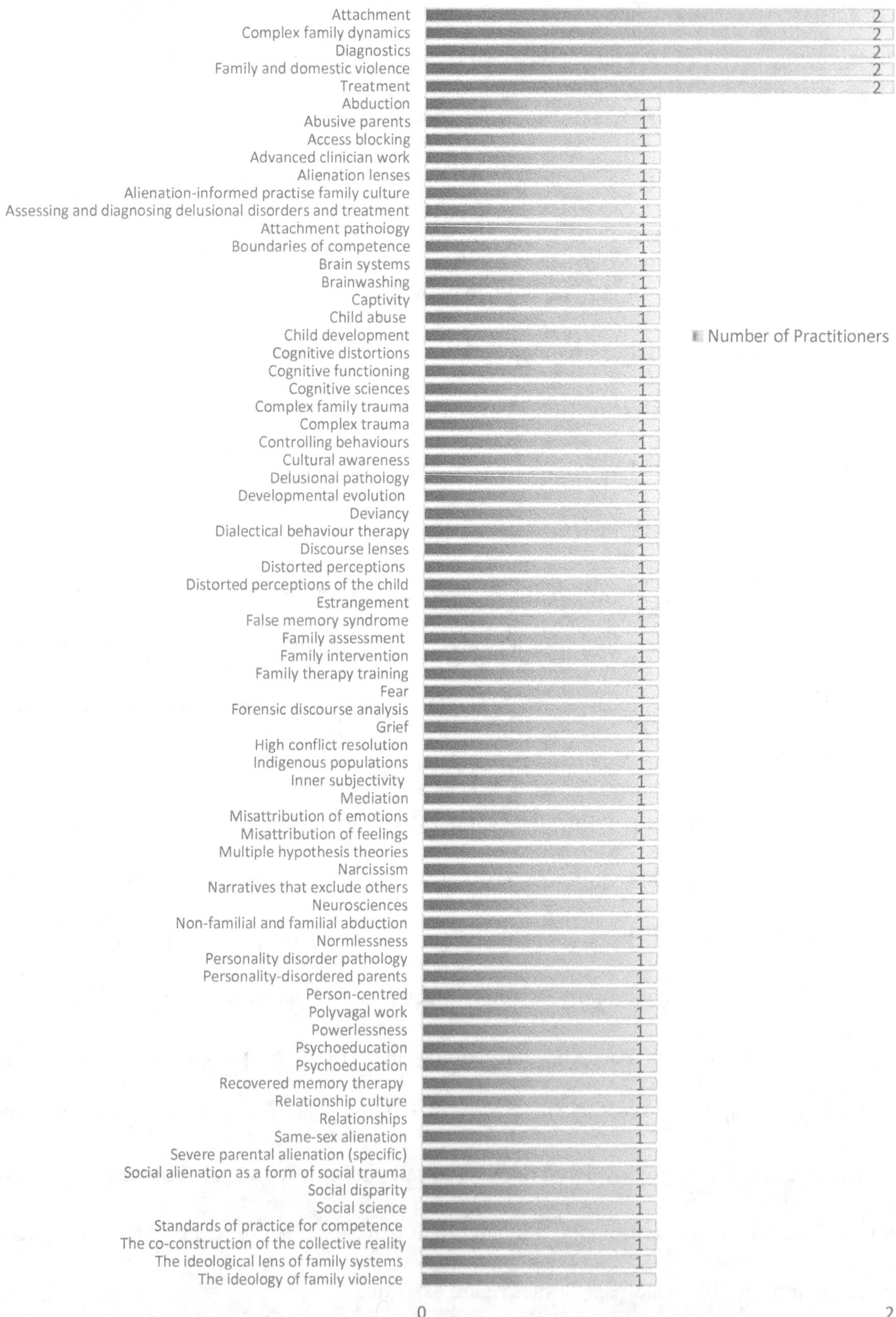

Note: Recommended specialty subjects & topics undertaken by the 10 MHPs totalled 72

Transition to Practitioner Readiness

The breadth of practitioner-recommended training subjects does not mean that every clinician must be fully trained in every area before beginning HQTP-informed work. Rather, it highlights the need for honest scope awareness, supervision, careful pacing, and referral where specialist knowledge is required. The following readiness checklist is provided to help clinicians reflect on their current preparation, identify areas for further development, and consider what supervision or consultation may be needed before working with adult survivors in this population.

UniSC-Informed Practitioner Readiness Checklist (Printable)

Use of This Checklist

Clinicians are encouraged to print and revisit this checklist regularly. Integrating it into supervision and peer consultation processes is recommended.

Domain	Readiness indicator	Tick
Population Knowledge	Demonstrates understanding of CPA-PA, developmental trauma, attachment disruption, and institutional betrayal specific to adult survivors	☐
Theoretical Integration	Works from the HQTP, a coherent relational and developmental framework rather than isolated techniques	☐
Pacing Capacity	Able to tolerate slow progress without pushing insight, disclosure, or reconciliation narratives when working with survivors	☐
Countertransference Awareness	Recognises urgency, protectiveness, anger, rescue impulses, and is able to identify and name personal triggers and countertransference as necessary	☐
Ethical Boundary Clarity	Maintains distinction between therapy and investigative or advocacy roles	☐
Autonomy Orientation	Prioritises survivor agency over professional authority	☐
Supervision Engagement	Participates in regular clinical supervision with appropriately qualified professionals	☐
Emotional Regulation	Maintains the capacity to sit with distress without withdrawal or escalation	☐
Cultural and Systemic Awareness	Understands the impact of legal and institutional systems on survivor presentation	☐
Commitment to Ongoing Learning	Engages in continuing professional development specific to developmental trauma and alienation practices	☐

Adult Survivors Supporting Each Other Without a Therapist

Another important area for practitioners to understand is that many adult survivors have not had access to specialised, trauma-informed therapy, either as children or later in adult life. In the absence of safe and appropriate professional support, many learned to turn to those closest to them, often their siblings, for comfort, understanding and protection.

For some children, siblings may have been the only people in the home who really knew what was happening behind closed doors. They may have kept secrets together, developed private words, codes or ways of communicating, and found small ways to protect one another. Sometimes one sibling may have stepped in when another was being criticised, punished, shamed or emotionally singled out. At other times, a child may have been left alone with their distress for long periods, crying themselves to sleep without the soothing, repair or emotional comfort they needed.

In these dynamics, the child's experience can feel as though a light has suddenly been switched off. Warmth may disappear quickly, especially when the child is no longer used to meet the parent's emotional or regulatory needs. The child may then learn to cope alone, internalising distress and finding private ways to survive. Where siblings are available and safe enough, they may become the only source of emotional holding the child can reach for.

This does not mean sibling relationships are always simple or harmonious. In severe alienation dynamics, siblings may also be placed under pressure, divided from one another, compared, recruited, blamed or split off so that they cannot safely support each other. This splitting can be part of the wider pattern of coercive control within the family system. However, when siblings do find ways to stay connected despite these pressures, the bond can become an important protective thread that continues into adulthood.

For some adult survivors, this pattern of turning to siblings may continue for many years. They may speak to each other in ways no therapist has ever heard. They may hold the shared memories, the secret stories, the private language and the emotional truth of what happened. They may not think of this as "support" in a formal sense. It may simply be what they have always done to survive.

Some survivors may later try to seek therapy, but if the therapist does not understand CPA-PA, familial abduction, estrangement dynamics or the depth of coercive family control, the survivor may leave feeling more confused, exposed, misunderstood or alone. This can reinforce the belief that only siblings, or other survivors who have lived through something similar, can truly understand.

For practitioners, it is important not to pathologise this pattern. Adult survivors who have relied on siblings or other survivors for support have not done anything wrong. They were often doing the best they could in circumstances where trustworthy adults were unavailable, unsafe or unable to understand. This kind of sibling or survivor-to-survivor support is not therapy in the professional sense, but it can be a deeply meaningful survival strategy.

This is especially important in severe cases, and in cases involving familial abduction, where trusting adults, professionals or formal systems may feel extremely difficult. Survivors may need time before they can speak openly with a therapist. They may need to know that their private ways of surviving will not be judged, taken away, mocked or misunderstood. The therapeutic task is not to replace these bonds, but to understand why they formed, honour the protection they provided, and gently widen the survivor's access to safe, informed and trustworthy support.

When There Was No Safe Witness as an 'Only' Child

A closely related group for practitioners to understand are adult survivors who did not have access to specialised counselling, sibling support, or any safe person who could witness what was happening to them. Some were 'only' children. Some had siblings with large age gaps. Some had siblings who had already been split off from them, aligned elsewhere, or were also too frightened, overwhelmed or unavailable to offer comfort. In these circumstances, the child may have had no one inside or outside the family system who could help them make sense of what was happening.

For these children, survival may have become very private. They may have disappeared into their own inner worlds, relied on imagination, books, animals, routines, silence, fantasy, spiritual meaning, dissociation or emotional numbing. From the outside, they may have appeared quiet, compliant, withdrawn, dreamy, overly mature or difficult to reach. However, this should not be misunderstood as the absence of distress. It may have been the child's way of staying safe when no one was available to soothe, protect, believe in, or understand them.

This is particularly important when children have neither professional counselling nor a sibling confidant. They may not have developed a shared language for what happened. They may not have had anyone to check reality with, cry with, whisper to, or ask, "Did that really happen?" As adults, they may therefore come into therapy with very little practice speaking about their childhood experiences. Their story may arrive slowly, unevenly or in fragments. They may know the feeling before they know the words.

Practitioners can understand these survivors more gently by remembering that they may be speaking about experiences that were never witnessed, named or emotionally held by anyone else. The therapist may be the first safe person to hear parts of the story. This requires patience, steadiness and careful listening. The survivor should not be rushed into disclosure, interpretation or insight before enough safety has been established.

This group may also require careful attention because isolated children can become more vulnerable when untrusted adults enter the family system, including new partners, family friends or other adults who gain access to the child. This does not mean that harm occurred in every case, but it does mean practitioners should listen carefully to the survivor's sense of fear, confusion, bodily memory, silence, avoidance or uncertainty. The absence of clear language should not be mistaken for the absence of experience. For example, one adult survivor described, "I felt shame around my coping mechanisms, such as past behaviours as eating alone and hiding food, rejecting relationships, feeling behind in life compared to my peers regarding education, mental health, and feeling lost with no purpose unlike the others" (anon).

For these survivors, therapy may need to begin with helping them feel that their inner world will be respected rather than invaded. The practitioner's role is not to force the story out, but to become a steady and trustworthy witness over time. In this way, the survivor can begin to discover words for experiences they may have carried alone for many years.

When Survivors Support Each Other Before Therapy is Available

Throughout the HQTP, the author generally encourages survivors to seek support from appropriately trained, trauma-informed practitioners when this is possible. This remains the preferred pathway, particularly where there is suicidality, family violence, coercive control, severe trauma activation, dissociation, medical complexity, or major relational destabilisation. In this context, relational destabilisation may include situations where contact, rupture, reunion, family disclosure, sibling reconnection, estrangement, rejection, grief, or new information begins to overwhelm the survivor's sleep, functioning, safety, relationships, or capacity to remain emotionally steady.

This recommendation, however, needs to sit beside the reality that many adult survivors cannot access specialised therapy when they need it. Some may not want to seek therapy because they have previously been dismissed, misunderstood or harmed by poorly informed clinicians or services. Others may have waited months or years to find the right support, only to discover that the practitioner did not understand the dynamics of CPA-PA. Some may have felt unheard, exposed or confused after therapy, while others may have found that sessions were too far apart to safely contain what had been opened up.

This section is therefore included as an exception to the general clinical caution. It is not a replacement for therapy, diagnosis, supervision, crisis support, or specialised trauma treatment. Rather, it offers a harm-reduction and stabilisation guide for survivors who are already supporting one another, and for survivors who have had little or no safe support available to them. It recognises that, for some adult survivors, informal support may have been the only available form of emotional holding while appropriate clinical care remained unavailable, unsafe, inaccessible or poorly matched to their needs.

The practical suggestions in this section were informed by a real-life family example shared with the author by two sisters in New Zealand. These sisters had found careful ways to support one another without becoming overwhelmed, without forcing each other into disclosure, and without turning every conversation into trauma processing. In this family example, the older sister had grown up largely on her own, with a seven-year age gap before her younger sibling's birth. After entering treatment and beginning to receive specialised psychoeducation, she was able to recognise some of the patterns that had affected her own childhood, while also noticing similar patterns still affecting her younger sibling in the relationship with the alienating parent.

Their support for one another is careful and ongoing. The older sister is working to free herself from the enmeshment patterns that have shaped much of her life, while also trying to remain available to her younger sibling, as those patterns can shift in response to outside influences from other family members. She is also learning to understand that the younger sibling may move in and out of enmeshment, especially around major family events, grief, funerals, pressure, loyalty conflict or renewed contact with the alienating parent and their alliances. Rather than forcing insight, she is learning to recognise the pattern, remain steady, and gently hold the connection until the younger sibling comes forward again.

Their approach supported the authors' research data. Survivors know the truth behind the family stories, the hidden harms, the private codes, the silences and the survival strategies that developed behind closed doors. Their support of each other is not therapy in the professional sense, but it still provides steadiness, recognition and connection where no other support has been available. Their ideas are included here in the hope that other survivors may draw on their wisdom, while the wider clinical community continues to develop a sufficient number of trained practitioners to address this treatment gap.

Using the SEMPI Social Communication Model Alongside This Section

When survivors support each other without a therapist, the author also recommends referring to the SEMPI Social Communication Model © for additional communication support. SEMPI was developed by the author as a free, grassroots, pay-it-forward model for community first responders, family members, friends, peers, and everyday people who may be sitting with someone in distress after asking, "Are you OK?" and hearing the answer, "No."

Adult survivors can download the SEMPI model, read the guidance, and watch the accompanying videos to learn how to respond with steadiness, safety, and care rather than panic, giving advice, rescuing, fixing, interrogating, or pushing for answers too quickly. SEMPI can sit alongside the suggestions in this chapter by helping survivors slow the conversation down, listen more safely, recognise distress, support grounding, and know when extra help is needed. Used carefully, SEMPI may help siblings, adult children, partners, and trusted relatives support one another in a way that is human, boundaried, and stabilising while they wait for, search for, or prepare to access appropriate therapeutic support.

Go to www.sempi.net for more free information.

A Note from Dr Alyse

Dear friends,

Before we go further, I want to speak to you personally and gently, because this section may touch places that have been lonely, confusing or difficult to name.

Many adult survivors do not grow up thinking, "I am being abused." As children, you may not have had the words for what was happening. You may have felt responsible, loyal, frightened, confused, watchful, protective of a parent, or weighed down by things that were far too heavy for a child to carry. You may have been trying to keep the peace, avoid punishment, protect a sibling, stay connected, or survive inside a family story that did not leave much room for your own feelings, questions or needs.

Psychological abuse can be hard to recognise because it can sit unrecognised inside ordinary family life. It may not always look obvious from the outside. It can look like being made responsible for a parent's emotions, being discouraged from asking questions, being taught to fear independence, being rewarded for loyalty, being punished for having your own needs, or being told that one version of the story is the only safe truth.

This can become even more confusing when there were also moments of closeness, humour, affection, warmth or ordinary family life. Loving moments do not erase harm. They can, however, make the harm harder to name, because the relationship may have felt meaningful and painful at the same time. A child can love a parent, need a parent, fear a parent, protect a parent and feel responsible for a parent all at once. That is a very confusing place for a child to live.

At the same time, not every adult survivor will describe love in this way. Some adult children may say very clearly that they never felt loved by the alienating parent, and that they never felt love towards them. This can also be true. For some, the idea of having a parent may feel painful, but the lived experience of that parent may never have felt safe, warm, protective or loving. They may grieve the parent they needed, rather than the parent they actually experienced. This does not make them cold, unkind or wrong. It may simply be an honest description of what their childhood felt like.

Some adult children may also appear not to react when warmth, attention or approval is suddenly withdrawn. It can be as though the light is switched off on them, but they have known that darkness for a very long time. They may not protest, chase, plead or collapse in obvious ways because they are used to being left emotionally alone. Some learned very early to keep going, to turn inward, to expect very little, or to protect themselves from hoping for comfort that never came. This kind of quiet response should not be mistaken for a lack of hurt. Sometimes it means the hurt has been there for so long that the person has had to build a life around it.

If it has taken a long time to recognise these patterns, that makes sense. Many survivors could not have seen the truth earlier because seeing it may not have felt emotionally safe at the time. Not recognising it sooner does not mean you were weak, blind or complicit. It means you were a child trying to stay attached, safe and emotionally intact inside a family system you could not yet fully understand.

Sometimes adult survivors only begin to recognise the impact years later. This may happen after becoming a parent, entering a long-term relationship, reconnecting with a sibling, losing a family member, attending a funeral, experiencing a rupture, or finally hearing language that makes sense of what they lived through. You may begin to notice difficulty with boundaries, fear of conflict, fear of abandonment, strong reactions to authority figures, chronic self-doubt, guilt, confusion about what is "normal", or a deep uncertainty about whether you can trust your own perceptions. These are not personal failures. They are understandable responses to growing up without enough emotional safety.

Sometimes adult survivors find each other before they find the right therapist. A sibling, cousin, adult child, partner, friend, or trusted relative may become the person who understands the family story better than anyone else. This can be deeply healing. It can also feel frightening, because when one person begins to remember, question, grieve or name what happened, it can stir the whole family system.

Many of us have had to rely on trusted people around us because the right therapeutic help was not available at the time. I include myself in this. For many years, there was no clear pathway, no specialist treatment protocol, and very few practitioners who could speak clearly about what adult survivors of CPA-PA and related family-system harms were carrying. Sometimes we survived because another person believed us, sat beside us, listened without rushing us, or helped us stay steady until better support could be found.

If you are supporting each other in this way, please remember that you do not have to become each other's therapist. You do not have to solve the past together. You do not have to analyse every memory, agree on every detail, keep talking when one of you is overwhelmed, or work everything out in one conversation. You do not have to rush towards confrontation, contact, non-contact, forgiveness, disclosure, repair, or a final decision about what everything means.

Support does not mean fixing each other. Sometimes support means slowing down. Sometimes it means asking, "Is now a good time to talk about this?" Sometimes it means saying, "I want to listen, but I am getting overwhelmed and need a pause." Sometimes it means going for a walk, making tea, talking about the garden, checking in about sleep, feeding the animals, discussing work, children, appointments, food, or what is happening today. Ordinary connection is not avoidance. Sometimes, an ordinary connection is exactly how the nervous system learns that a relationship can become safe again.

Please also remember that you are allowed to say no. You do not have to attend family events, funerals, birthdays, Christmas gatherings or other family obligations if you do not feel safe or ready. You do not have to walk back into an unsafe family environment simply because you were trained to do so as a child. As an adult, you are allowed to pause, decline, step back, wait, or choose differently. Giving yourself permission to do this can be a healthy and important part of recovery.

There are also times when extra support is important. If conversations are leading to panic, shutdown, dissociation, self-harm urges, suicidal thoughts, fear for someone's safety, or pressure to make major decisions before you feel steady, it is time to pause the conversation and reach for more help where you can. Needing extra help does not mean you have failed. It means you are protecting yourself and the people you care about.

Finding the right words can also be part of healing. Many survivors describe the relief of finally finding language that explains what they lived through without blaming them or treating them as broken. Good language should help you feel clearer, steadier and less alone. If a resource pushes you too quickly towards forgiveness, forced neutrality, rapid reconciliation, shame, or contact before you feel safe, it may simply not be the right resource for you at that time.

You are not weak for needing support. You are not disloyal for wanting clarity. You are not cold for naming that love was missing. You are not broken because this is hard. Healing from psychological abuse and parental alienation is not about proving anything to anyone. It is about slowly rebuilding safety, choice and trust in yourself.

Go gently, Dr Alyse

Extreme Case Illustration: Mental Health Unit Presentation

The following section returns to practitioner-focused guidance and introduces an extreme case illustration. It is included to help practitioners understand the kinds of complex histories they may hear when adult survivors begin to describe what happened across childhood, adolescence and later life.

This illustration is not presented as representative of all CPA-PA cases. Rather, it demonstrates how psychological abuse and alienation dynamics can sit within a much broader pattern of harm. In some complex presentations, practitioners may hear histories that cross over multiple areas, including child sexual abuse, caregiver coercion, addiction, criminal court involvement, family court involvement, abandonment, institutional response, sibling disruption, and the long-term effects of trauma.

Cases of this nature require careful listening and slow formulation. The practitioner may need to hold several realities at once, rather than reducing the survivor's history to a single explanation, diagnosis, event, or family narrative. In these presentations, alienation dynamics may not exist in isolation. They may interact with sexual exploitation, substance misuse, fear, secrecy, loyalty pressure, disrupted attachment, legal processes, and ongoing trauma symptoms. Clinical supervision is mandatory when working with these complex cases.

The purpose of including this illustration is therefore educational. It invites practitioners to consider how adult survivors may present with layered and overlapping histories, and why a trauma-informed, CPA-PA-informed lens is needed when listening to complex family-system harm.

In this case, the central male caregiver was approximately 30 years old when he married a woman with two adolescent daughters. He subsequently fathered four children with one of those stepdaughters before she reached 20 years of age. One of the children later died. Both biological parents of the youngest children reportedly experienced alcohol dependence.

The mother left the family abruptly when the eldest surviving child was approximately five years old. She did not re-engage with the children until she was contacted by a family court social worker following initial allegations of child sexual abuse. At that time, she did not assume custodial responsibility, and primary care remained with the father.

Following the mother's departure, survivor accounts describe a sustained pattern of paternal denigration and psychological alienation directed toward the mother. This included persistent negative messaging, distortion of the maternal narrative, and reinforcement of rejection-based attitudes. The children were discouraged from developing independent curiosity, emotional connection, or a more differentiated understanding of their mother.

In this presentation, the dynamics of alienation did not occur in isolation. They were embedded within a broader context of alleged child sexual abuse, caregiver coercion, alcohol dependence, family disruption, isolation, and systemic involvement. This case therefore illustrates the importance of careful formulation when CPA-PAA dynamics intersect with other forms of complex developmental harm.

Throughout childhood, the siblings experienced repeated placement instability (during times the father was drinking too much) and were moved in and out of foster care. At times, when no foster placements were available, they were housed in juvenile detention facilities despite not having committed criminal offences. Additionally, the children were frequently separated from one another, further disrupting their attachments.

The siblings later reported being sent individually, while underage, to stay with adult associates of the father for extended weekends in exchange for debts owed to the father. The survivors described sexual abuse occurring both within the home by the father and during these weekend stays with his associates.

Over time, the concealed abuse and coercive family dynamics began to surface through external systems. After a prolonged period, one of the brothers disclosed the father's behaviour to a teacher. This disclosure led to a police investigation, followed by criminal proceedings. The father was later convicted by a jury of child sexual abuse and related charges and was sentenced to imprisonment.

The long-term effects on the three surviving siblings were significant. All three developed problematic alcohol and drug use during adolescence. By adulthood, each had presented with addiction-related difficulties and complex post-traumatic stress symptoms. Their adult presentations illustrate how early sexual abuse, psychological alienation, caregiver coercion, addiction exposure, secrecy, and systemic instability can continue to shape functioning across the lifespan.

The eldest brother is now sober, has been married for two decades, works in a high-pressure corporate environment, and continues to engage in anger management and psychotherapy. He also reports longstanding grief associated with being alienated from his own daughter during infancy. He has not had contact with her since early childhood, and she is now an adult.

The younger brother continues to experience active methamphetamine dependence. The sister developed heroin dependence in early adulthood and was later diagnosed with a brain tumour. She is currently sober apart from occasional alcohol use and medically supervised cannabis. She has had four children removed from her care and maintains contact with two of them. In therapy, she expresses remorse for her lack of parenting toward the children and is actively practising unconditional love and openness to hearing what they have to say to her so she can apologise as needed. She reports that this technique helps them to recover.

This aspect of the case illustrates the intergenerational consequences that can follow when early developmental harm remains unrecognised, untreated, or poorly contained by family and service systems. It also demonstrates the need for practitioners to formulate adult survivor presentations with compassion and care, without reducing the survivor to addiction, parenting difficulty, relational instability, or trauma symptoms alone.

The adult survivors' mother remains in active alcohol dependence and has struggled to maintain stable relational contact with them. The siblings report persistent anger and unresolved attachment rupture associated with her departure during childhood and perceived failure to protect them from harm. The father's earlier alienation of the mother continues to shape their perceptions of her, even as they simultaneously express grief regarding her absence. He has since died. However. these unresolved attachment injuries persist beyond the father's death.

The intergenerational impact is ongoing. The adult siblings describe difficulty establishing secure attachments, managing affect regulation under stress, and navigating parenting without reactivating trauma-based survival strategies. Patterns of substance vulnerability, relational instability, anger dysregulation, and disrupted caregiving have adversely affected the next generation. This case illustrates how developmental captivity, coercive control, sexual exploitation, attachment rupture, and alienation dynamics may converge to produce enduring and transgenerational trauma. This case is not presented as representative of CPA-PA. Rather, it demonstrates how alienation dynamics may operate within a broader ecology of abuse and systems failure, amplifying harm when combined with coercive and criminal behaviour.

Intergenerational Trauma and Clinical Implications

Cases of this nature require clinicians to conceptualise harm across developmental and generational timelines rather than as isolated childhood events. Intergenerational trauma transmission may occur through disrupted attachment modelling, dysregulated affect management, substance dependence as a regulatory strategy, unresolved grief, and maladaptive internal working models of trust and safety.

Clinicians working with this cohort must adopt a phased, trauma-informed, and systems-aware approach. Treatment priorities include stabilisation of substance misuse, affect regulation, grief integration related to lost caregivers and estranged children, and differentiation of trauma-adaptive survival strategies from entrenched personality pathology. Interventions must also address internalised alienation narratives, unresolved anger toward absent or abusive caregivers, and shame associated with intergenerational parenting disruption.

Where survivors are parents, clinicians may need to coordinate with child protection services, parenting support programs, addiction specialists, and psychiatric services. Team-based care is often essential. Trauma processing should be deferred until sufficient capacity for regulation and environmental safety are established. Without structured containment, premature trauma activation may exacerbate substance relapse, relational instability, or dissociative fragmentation.

Within HQTP, such presentations are conceptualised as complex, layered trauma requiring careful phase sequencing, relational repair, identity reconstruction, and gradual integration. Multidisciplinary collaboration functions as a protective scaffold to reduce further destabilisation and interrupt intergenerational transmission patterns.

Clinical Supervision, Vicarious Trauma, Threat Exposure, Judicial Interface, and the Physical Toll of High-Complexity CPA-PA Practice

The complexity illustrated in the preceding case does not reside solely within survivor experience. The author's doctoral findings identified that MHPs who work with CSA and alienation-related abuse presentations frequently reported cumulative psychological strain associated with prolonged exposure to adversarial family systems, high-conflict litigation, and complex intersecting traumas (Price-Tobler, 2023, pp. 19–23).

Participants described sustained engagement with narratives involving sexual abuse, abduction, coercive control, threats of familicide, and repeated exposure to systemic failure.

Polarised professional environments and reputational risk compounded the emotional intensity of these cases. In some instances, explicit or implied threats of harm were reported within case contexts, directed toward targeted parents, adult survivors, court professionals, and occasionally judicial officers. While not universal, practitioners described experiences of intimidation, hostile correspondence, threats of complaints to regulatory bodies, adversarial courtroom cross-examination, and exposure to highly charged litigation environments. Judges, independent children's lawyers, social workers, and expert witnesses may all operate within these emotionally volatile systems. These dynamics sustain vigilance and increase cumulative stress across the broader professional ecosystem.

The doctoral data further revealed destabilisation within supervision structures. Supervisees working in SPA contexts reported educating their own supervisors about alienation dynamics, and, in some cases, supervisors withdrew from supervising due to burnout or overwhelm (Price-Tobler, 2023, pp. 21–22). Concerns were also raised regarding the threat of deregistration if mandated supervision requirements could not be maintained (Price-Tobler, 2023, p. 21). This created a structural vulnerability in which practitioners engaged in the most complex cases were at risk of losing professional containment precisely at the point of highest clinical demand.

Beyond psychological strain, the thesis recorded anomalous but clinically concerning reports of serious health conditions among practitioners working extensively in the SPA field (Price-Tobler, 2023, pp. 25–26). While causation cannot be inferred and these findings remain exploratory, participants perceived a relationship between prolonged occupational stress and deteriorating physical health.

From a psychophysiological perspective, repeated exposure to high-conflict threat environments may contribute to prolonged activation of the hypothalamic–pituitary–adrenal axis, dysregulated cortisol secretion, inflammatory processes, immune modulation, and increased cardiovascular strain (McEwen, 2007; Segerstrom & Miller, 2004; Steptoe & Kivimäki, 2012). Chronic activation of the stress response without adequate recovery may contribute to the accumulation of allostatic load, which has been associated with vulnerability to stress-related disease processes (McEwen & Stellar, 1993). When practitioners operate within adversarial legal systems while simultaneously holding complex trauma material, the nervous system may remain in a state of anticipatory activation. Over time, sustained hyperarousal can affect sleep architecture, immune function, cardiovascular regulation, and inflammatory pathways.

The cumulative effect of exposure to psychological threat, reputational scrutiny, legal cross-examination, and unresolved systemic conflict may therefore affect both emotional regulation and physiological resilience. Clinicians in the author's doctoral practitioner study described sleep disturbance, irritability, emotional numbing, hypervigilance regarding complaints, and withdrawal from complex cases.

In high-conflict environments where threats of harm have emerged within proceedings, practitioners and court professionals may internalise an ongoing perception of ambient risk. Within such contexts, clinician regulation cannot be conceptualised as peripheral to client care. It is essential to ensure the safe delivery of treatment. Supervision integrity, peer consultation, deliberate recovery practices, and clear professional boundaries function as protective mechanisms.

The HQTP, therefore, positions practitioner containment not as optional self-care but as ethical infrastructure. The clinician's regulated nervous system is a therapeutic instrument. When working within extreme presentations involving intergenerational trauma, criminal abuse, and adversarial litigation, safeguarding oneself psychologically and physiologically is essential to sustaining ethical, competent, and long-term practice.

Forensic Practice Standards and Professional Risk Containment

Work with adult survivors of CPA-PA, particularly in cases involving sexual exploitation, criminal proceedings, or historical allegations, carries distinct forensic responsibilities. Clinical documentation, progress notes, formulation summaries, and reports may be subpoenaed or scrutinised in court proceedings. In high-conflict family contexts, clinicians may be cross-examined regarding their conceptualisation, diagnostic impressions, perceived alignment, or treatment decisions.

Reports relating to this cohort can be criticised as biased, speculative, or overly influenced by one relational narrative. Clinicians may experience external pressure to provide definitive statements in circumstances where trauma complexity requires nuance. The adversarial nature of court processes may expose practitioners to public challenge of their professional judgement.

Accordingly, rigorous documentation practices are essential. Formulations must be clearly differentiated from allegations. Observations must be distinguished from survivor-reported material. Diagnostic impressions should be grounded in recognised criteria and, where appropriate, framed as provisional. Phase readiness decisions require a documented clinical rationale.

Supervision functions as a professional safeguard in this context, supporting neutrality, language refinement, and adherence to scope-of-practice boundaries. Where forensic involvement is anticipated, additional training in report writing and preparation for court proceedings is advisable. When clinicians remain supported, reflective, and ethically grounded, they are better positioned to withstand external scrutiny and provide consistent containment for survivors whose developmental histories were marked by instability, coercion, and betrayal.

The Clinical Anchor for This Protocol

The HQTP uses the author's twin PhD program of research conducted at the University of the Sunshine Coast (2023) as its primary clinical anchor for understanding adult survivors of severe parental alienation and the MHPs who work with them. In the author's qualitative research, adult survivors consistently described severe parental alienation not as an extension of divorce conflict, but as an organised pattern of developmental psychological harm involving coercion, loyalty conflict, reality distortion, and attachment disruption sustained across time.

In the companion practitioner study, clinicians reported parallel concerns: inconsistent professional literacy, limited formal training pathways, and the absence of coherent clinical guidance for adult survivors whose presentations are frequently complex, high-risk, and misinterpreted within standard diagnostic frameworks. Together, these two datasets establish a convergent clinical map: what survivors experience, what clinicians observe, and where systemic gaps in assessment and treatment persist.

This chapter serves two functions. First, it establishes the author's research findings as the foundational clinical framework for the protocol's early stages, including stabilisation, formulation, and phase-based treatment planning. Second, it situates these findings within the broader literature on adult outcomes of parental alienation and parental alienating behaviours. Across available studies, a consistent pattern emerges: adult survivors commonly report enduring trauma-related symptoms, complicated grief, identity and attachment disturbance, relational impairment, elevated vulnerability to anxiety and depression, and increased risk for suicidal ideation (Baker, 2005).

While the author's research extends the field by centring severe-level survivor narratives and clinician perspectives within a single coordinated design, the wider literature is notably convergent regarding long-term impact profiles.

Importantly, the HQTP does not rely on a single explanatory model. Childress's attachment-based conceptualisation is included because it offers a structured way to describe mechanisms repeatedly identified in child survivor narratives: pathogenic caregiving, role reversal, psychological enmeshment, and suppression or distortion of the child's attachment system. Additionally, transference-focused contributions from Yeomans, Clarkin, and Kernberg (2015) will be discussed and built upon; however, the organising logic of the protocol remains grounded in the author's twin-study findings, with the work of other important clinicians integrated as a complementary interpretive framework.

Positioning Statement on Scholarly Inclusion

During the early stages of the author's doctoral research, guidance was given to restrict citations to work published within a narrow range of peer-reviewed journals. Certain researchers and bodies of work were discouraged or excluded because they were not accepted by mainstream academic journals or did not align with dominant theoretical positions.

The author considers this approach deeply problematic in a field as small, specialised, and under-published as parental alienation research. Parental alienation, particularly in its severe forms, is not a topic routinely represented in mainstream academic publications. The field is niche, politically charged, and often actively avoided by journals despite its clear clinical relevance. As a result, important empirical findings, clinical observations, and treatment models are frequently published in books, doctoral dissertations, clinical monographs, conference proceedings, and specialist publications rather than in high-impact journals.

Further, many academic journals operate on cost-prohibitive publishing models. Article processing charges can amount to thousands of dollars, creating structural barriers that exclude independent researchers, clinicians, survivors, and practitioners without institutional funding. In a field already marginalised, this economic gatekeeping further restricts whose knowledge is deemed legitimate.

Restricting citations solely to journal-accepted material, therefore, risks excluding critical knowledge based on access rather than merit. It narrows the evidence base, privileges institutional alignment over clinical insight, and reinforces academic power structures rather than advancing understanding. The author views such exclusionary practices as a form of *epistemic alienation*. In a field concerned with coercion, silencing, and narrative control, selectively excluding research based on publication venue or cost risks replicating the very dynamics this work seeks to expose.

Accordingly, this book intentionally includes research findings, clinical models, and theoretical contributions from across the field, including work that has been marginalised, discouraged, or excluded from mainstream publication pathways. All sources are cited transparently and in accordance with APA 7 standards, regardless of publication venue. Clinicians are best served not by a curated consensus but by access to the full body of available evidence, enabling informed, critical, and context-sensitive practice.

Delayed Recognition Processing in Survivors

Across adult survivor narratives, several clinical priorities emerge consistently and early. First, survivors frequently describe a *delayed recognition process*. Many did not conceptualise their childhood experiences as abusive until adulthood, often following psychoeducation, therapy, or later-life developmental transitions such as becoming a parent themselves. Clinically, this delay reflects not a lack of insight but the enduring psychological effects of prolonged coercion, chronic invalidation, and developmental dependence. Treatment must therefore begin with stabilising meaning-making rather than forcing confrontation or premature trauma integration.

Second, identity disruption is central. Survivors commonly internalised split representations of parents, with one positioned as wholly good and the other as wholly bad. The child's self-concept fractured accordingly. Identity repair in adulthood is therefore not a superficial self-esteem task, but a long-term reconstruction following imposed developmental distortion.

Third, the practitioner study identified systemic risk. Clinicians reported inconsistent recognition of alienation-related coercion, variable formulation practices, and a tendency within broader professional systems to misinterpret survivor presentations as personality pathology or relational dysfunction without identifying developmental trauma origins. This misformulation carries significant clinical risk, increasing the likelihood of retraumatisation and ineffective treatment. Accordingly, the protocol adopts an explicit principle: *assess mechanisms and patterns, not symptoms alone*.

Fourth, the author identified under-recognised sequelae in severe-level cases. These include intense fear conditioning linked to specific contexts (e.g., abandonment threats, institutional betrayal, abduction-related terror) and survivor-reported later health concerns associated with prolonged toxic stress exposure. While the broader ACEs literature supports links between chronic childhood stress and later health vulnerability (Felitti et al., 1998; Anda et al., 2006), these specific observations are presented as hypothesis-generating clinical findings rather than established consensus.

Holistic and Integrative Approaches

While this book emphasises the importance of diagnostic clarity and evidence-based treatment, it also recognises the profound value of holistic and integrative approaches to healing. These methods, ranging from somatic therapies (Levine, 2010), mindfulness-based stress reduction (MBSR) (Kabat-Zinn, 2003), forest therapy (Shinrin-yoku) (Hansen et al., 2017), and expressive therapies such as art and movement-based interventions (Malchiodi, 2012), to name a few, have shown significant benefits in enhancing emotional regulation, reducing trauma symptoms, and restoring a sense of safety and embodiment.

Rather than viewing integrative and clinical treatments as oppositional, this work advocates for their thoughtful integration. When used alongside a precise diagnostic formulation, holistic approaches can support nervous system regulation, deepen therapeutic engagement, and foster meaning-making in survivors of complex trauma. A formal diagnosis offers a clinical anchor; holistic interventions restore personal agency, embodiment, and connection. Together, they create a multidimensional treatment architecture that honours both scientific rigour and lived experience.

In later chapters, we will explore specific holistic and therapeutic methods identified by adult survivor participants in the associated PhD study as the most helpful in their healing journeys. For example, these include nature-based interventions, journaling practices, trauma-informed yoga, co-regulation with animals, and community-based peer support. This survivor-informed, trauma-responsive model encourages clinicians to listen deeply to what works directly from the survivor voices and to co-create pathways to recovery that reflect both clinical insight and human complexity.

Relational and Identity Consequences of Parental Alienation in Adulthood

Parental alienation alters development not through a single event, but through sustained psychological conditioning that reshapes attachment, identity formation, and relational safety. Adult survivors do not simply "struggle with relationships" in a generic sense. Their adult difficulties emerge from childhood environments in which love was made conditional, loyalty was enforced, and attachment was organised around fear rather than safety.

Across the author's doctoral research, adult survivors consistently described relational difficulties that could not be explained by temperament, divorce alone, or isolated trauma exposure. Instead, these difficulties reflected predictable outcomes of growing up within coercive relational systems where emotional survival depended on compliance, secrecy, and psychological alignment with one parent at the expense of another.

This chapter examines how those mechanisms translate into adult relationship patterns and identity disturbance. Understanding these processes is essential before moving into grief, loss, and moral injury, as many survivors remain caught in relational adaptations that predate conscious recognition of what was taken from them.

Mechanism 1: Coercive Attachment Conditioning

A central mechanism identified in the author's research is coercive attachment conditioning. In alienating environments, children are required to organise their attachment around the alienating parent's emotional needs, fears, or fragility. Love is not experienced as secure or reciprocal, but as contingent upon agreement, silence, and loyalty.

Adult survivors frequently described being placed into developmentally inappropriate roles, including emotional confidant, protector, or regulator of the alienating parent. This role reversal disrupted normative attachment development, replacing it with hypervigilance to relational threat. As adults, these survivors often struggle to trust intimacy, not because they lack desire for connection, but because closeness has historically been paired with danger, obligation, or loss. In the author's PhD findings, survivors commonly reported either emotional withdrawal in relationships or intense fear of abandonment. These patterns reflect adaptive responses to early environments in which attachment carried a high emotional cost.

Mechanism 2: Identity Fragmentation and Self-Erasure

Alienation does not only sever relationships; it fractures identity. When a child is required to reject a parent, they are also required to reject parts of themselves. Traits, values, interests, or physical features associated with the targeted parent become psychologically unsafe.

Adult survivors in the author's research frequently described chronic identity confusion, shame without a clear origin, or discomfort with self-expression. Many reported feeling internally divided, as though aspects of their personality were illegitimate or dangerous. This internal fragmentation often persists into adulthood, complicating decision-making, self-trust, and life direction.

Importantly, these identity disruptions were not limited to emotional experience. Survivors described tangible impacts on education, career progression, and social development. Growing up in environments dominated by relational surveillance and emotional labour left limited space for exploration, autonomy, or future planning.

Mechanism 3: Relational Templates Shaped by Fear Rather Than Safety

Adult relationship difficulties among alienation survivors are not random. They reflect internalised relational templates formed in childhood. Where attachment was organised around fear, obligation, or appeasement, adult relationships may replicate these dynamics. Some survivors gravitate toward controlling or emotionally unsafe partners, not because they seek harm, but because these dynamics are familiar. Others avoid intimacy altogether, having learned that closeness inevitably leads to loss or betrayal. Many oscillate between these poles.

The author's research identified a recurring theme of survivors tolerating relational distress far beyond healthy limits, often prioritising harmony or avoidance of conflict over personal safety or authenticity. These patterns frequently coexisted with profound loneliness and unmet attachment needs.

Mechanism 4: Developmental Disruption in Social and Educational Domains

Parental alienation often occurs alongside instability in schooling, housing, and social networks. Across the author's doctoral research, adult survivors described repeated moves, disrupted peer relationships, fractured contact with extended family, and reduced access to extracurricular, cultural, and community experiences. These disruptions compounded relational injury by limiting opportunities for continuity, safety, belonging, and ordinary developmental participation.

Survivors frequently described missed developmental milestones not as a consequence of limited capacity, but of restricted opportunity. In adulthood, these disruptions may present as diminished confidence, interrupted educational or vocational pathways, underachievement relative to potential, and enduring grief regarding lost possibilities. Such losses are not merely circumstantial. They shape the survivor's internal sense of capability, worth, and entitlement to stability, connection, and a coherent future.

These developmental disruptions do not occur in isolation. They often arise within broader family environments marked by coercion, fear, instability, psychological control, and the erosion of the child's relational world. For this reason, the clinician's task cannot end with documenting only developmental loss. It must also include careful assessment of the family dynamics in which those losses were organised and maintained.

Comprehensive Assessment: Child Abuse and Family Dynamics

When high-conflict family systems are present, assessment must extend beyond the presenting clinical question. Clinicians working with children in these circumstances must consider the child's psychological and physical wellbeing within the broader caregiving environment, including possible indicators of child psychological abuse, physical abuse, neglect, coercive control, and exposure to spousal or family violence.

Childress's attachment-based assessment model provides a structured framework for examining these dynamics in depth. Rather than locating the problem primarily within the child, the model directs attention to pathogenic parenting, psychological control, attachment disruption, and the relational mechanisms through which a child's alignment, fear, or rejection may be shaped within the family system (Childress, 2015). Where concerns arise that a child's presentation is being organised through coercive or abusive caregiving processes, further assessment is required to clarify risk, differential explanation, and protective need.

Clinicians should therefore remain alert to abusive family dynamics in cases where a child's presentation appears unusually rigid, fearful, compliant, or developmentally incongruent. Indicators may include abrupt behavioural change, withdrawal, hypervigilance, fear-based loyalty, excessive compliance with one parent's demands, or marked distress associated with the other parent. Assessment must also consider whether one parent is using fear, dependence, punishment, reward, or narrative control to organise the child's behaviour and relational responses (Herman, 1992; Stark, 2007). The central task is not to accept the child's presentation at face value, but to determine how that presentation has been shaped, whether abuse-related dynamics are present, and what interventions are required to safeguard the child.

The losses associated with parental alienation are profound, but grief cannot be integrated while survivors remain organised around survival-based relational templates. Before grief work can safely proceed, survivors must begin to understand how attachment, identity, and relational expectations were shaped under coercive conditions rather than through personal failure or defect. This chapter, therefore, establishes the clinical and developmental groundwork for the grief and loss work that follows. It clarifies why grief in this population is often delayed, fragmented, defended against, or overwhelmed by fear, shame, anger, and moral injury.

Grief, Loss, and Psychological Survival in Adult Survivors in CPA-PA Contexts

Once the coercive conditions organising the survivor's childhood experience are better understood, the depth of the associated grief becomes more visible. Beneath the relational and identity disruptions described in the previous chapter lies a deeper and often less spoken reality shared by many adult survivors of parental alienation: enduring grief.

This grief is not limited to the loss of a parent. It includes the loss of childhood safety, the loss of truthful attachment history, the loss of identity continuity, and the loss of developmental experiences that were never permitted to unfold. Across the author's doctoral research, adult survivors repeatedly described grief that remained unprocessed for decades. Many did not recognise their experience as grief until adulthood because the original separation occurred within environments that did not permit mourning. Children were often unable to miss the targeted parent, express sadness, or acknowledge loss without emotional punishment, withdrawal of affection, or escalation of manipulation. As a result, grief was suppressed, fragmented, or displaced into anxiety, anger, emotional numbing, or chronic confusion.

Rather than reflecting a single bereavement event, survivors described grief as cumulative, relational, and developmental. Each missed birthday, school milestone, family ritual, shared memory, and ordinary moment of connection represented a further unmarked loss. By adulthood, many reported a persistent sense of incompleteness, emotional ache, or unresolved longing that they had been unable to name earlier in life.

Loss of Parent, Childhood, and Attachment Continuity

One of the most consistent themes identified in the author's research was grief related to the forced loss of a loving parent who remained physically alive but psychologically inaccessible. Survivors described this experience as uniquely disorienting. Unlike death-related bereavement, there was no social recognition of loss, no collective mourning, and no permission to grieve openly.

Participants reported mourning not only the parent-child relationship that was severed, but the childhood they never experienced. Many described early role reversal, emotional caretaking responsibilities, and exposure to adult conflict that replaced normal developmental play, exploration, and a sense of safety. This premature emotional burden contributed to chronic exhaustion, emotional maturity beyond age expectations, and later difficulty accessing joy or spontaneity in adulthood.

Therapeutically, this form of grief often emerges gradually. Survivors may initially present with anger, numbness, or relational distress before recognising the deeper layer of developmental loss beneath these symptoms.

Guilt, Moral Injury, and Internalised Responsibility

Another prominent grief-related theme identified in the author's findings was enduring guilt. Alienating environments commonly condition children to believe they are responsible for the emotional wellbeing of the alienating parent. This conditioning persists into adulthood, even after survivors intellectually understand the manipulation they were subjected to.

Adult survivors frequently reported guilt related to rejecting the targeted parent, participating in false narratives, or remaining silent for years. Many expressed ongoing remorse despite recognising that they were children operating under coercive conditions. This internal conflict reflects moral injury rather than simple regret. Survivors grieve not only what was taken from them, but what they were forced to become to survive.

Clinically, this guilt requires careful processing. Premature reassurance or minimisation can reinforce shame. Effective treatment involves contextualising behaviour within developmental coercion, restoring accurate attribution of responsibility, and supporting self-forgiveness grounded in developmental reality rather than in adult moral standards applied retroactively.

Anger, Injustice, and the Emergence of Conscious Awareness

As survivors gain insight into the dynamics of parental alienation, anger commonly emerges alongside grief. In the author's research, many participants described a delayed period of intense emotional reaction once they recognised the scale of manipulation, deception, and institutional failure involved in their childhood experiences.

This anger is not pathological. It reflects the restoration of psychological boundaries and moral clarity. Survivors described anger directed toward alienating parents, family systems that failed to protect them, and professional systems that misunderstood or minimised their experiences. When supported therapeutically, this emotional activation often becomes a catalyst for identity reconstruction and self-advocacy. However, without containment and processing, unresolved anger can remain dysregulated, interfering with relational repair. The specialist clinical treatment protocol, therefore, treats anger as a necessary transitional phase within grief integration rather than an endpoint.

Resilience as Survival Adaptation, Not Idealisation

While this work necessarily centres harm, the author's research also identified significant adaptive survival strategies among adult survivors. These included emotional self-reliance, heightened empathy, vigilance to injustice, and strong motivation to protect others from harm. Importantly, these traits developed in response to unsafe environments and should not be romanticised as strengths in isolation.

Many survivors described their turning point as the moment when their experience was accurately named. Learning language, such as psychological abuse, coercive control, or parental alienation, allowed survivors to externalise blame and begin reconstructing personal narratives. This reframing often initiated engagement in therapy, peer support communities, and advocacy efforts. Resilience in this population is therefore not innate optimism. It is the capacity to re-author identity once psychological captivity ends. The HQTP emphasises supporting this process without placing responsibility on survivors to "be strong" in the absence of systemic accountability.

Reconceptualising Parental Alienation as Psychological Abuse and Coercive Control

The author's doctoral findings strongly support the conceptualisation of severe parental alienation as a form of child psychological abuse characterised by coercive control dynamics. Survivors consistently described experiences of reality manipulation, emotional isolation, fear-based compliance, and attachment sabotage. These patterns align with established models of coercive relational control observed in other abuse contexts.

Parental alienation operates through sustained psychological influence rather than overt physical force. Children are conditioned to suppress attachment needs, align emotionally with the controlling parent, and internalise distorted narratives about the targeted parent. Over time, this produces chronic stress activation, attachment disorganisation, and identity fragmentation.

Importantly, many survivors reported that professionals failed to recognise these dynamics during childhood. This misrecognition contributed to secondary trauma and reinforced feelings of invisibility and invalidation. When clinicians later named the experience as abuse, survivors frequently described this as profoundly reparative. This reframing carries direct treatment implications. It shifts therapy away from conflict mediation models and toward trauma-informed, attachment-focused recovery work. Survivors require validation, psychoeducation, stabilisation, and structured identity reconstruction rather than neutral positioning between parents.

Why Grief Integration Precedes Protocol Application

Grief in adult survivors of parental alienation is not a discrete phase that resolves quickly. It is intertwined with attachment repair, identity development, and nervous system regulation. Attempting trauma integration or relational reconstruction without acknowledging loss risks retraumatisation and emotional destabilisation.

For this reason, the HQTP presented in subsequent chapters integrates grief work throughout multiple phases rather than isolating it as a standalone intervention. Survivors must be supported to mourn what was taken, recognise what cannot be restored, and build meaningful futures without invalidating the depth of past harm.

Phase II Governance Integration

The risks described within Phase II are situated within the broader clinical governance architecture established earlier in the protocol. While governance principles apply across all phases, Phase II requires particular emphasis on monitoring capacity fluctuations, pacing alignment, and the relational impact of identity reorganisation. Governance in this stage is therefore characterised less by crisis escalation and more by early detection of narrowing regulatory tolerance.

Phase II governance focuses on identifying signals that differentiation and emerging self-processes are approaching the survivor’s current capacity threshold. Observable indicators such as increased monitoring, shame activation, disengagement, renewed alignment with the alienating parent, or protective retreat are treated as governance-relevant events rather than purely clinical observations. These signals inform pacing adjustment, supervision consultation, and documentation practices, ensuring that the response is structured rather than reactive.

Governance functions as a stabilising scaffold for both survivor and clinician. Structured review processes support calibration before destabilisation necessitates corrective intervention, while supervision provides containment for clinicians' uncertainty and emotional responses. Documentation anchors decision-making to observable indicators, reducing reliance on retrospective interpretation or assumption. This integration ensures that identity reorganisation is supported within clearly defined professional safeguards.

Phase II governance also clarifies the distinction between developmental destabilisation and clinical deterioration. Increased ambiguity, oscillation between identity states, or temporary withdrawal are understood as expected features of reorganisation when they occur within regulatory limits. Governance, therefore, prioritises monitoring trajectory rather than preventing activation altogether. The task is not to eliminate destabilisation but to detect when activation begins to exceed the tolerable range.

Importantly, governance in Phase II emphasises a non-coercive response. When risk indicators emerge, the primary interventions involve pacing adjustment, reinforcement of relational safety, and supervision-informed review rather than escalation of interpretive depth or behavioural direction. This approach prevents the therapeutic environment from replicating consequence-based relational dynamics and preserves survivor autonomy.

Integration with the broader governance framework ensures continuity across phases. Documentation of pacing indicators, disengagement events, rupture-and-repair processes, and supervision consultations contributes to a longitudinal understanding of readiness rather than to isolated session-level decisions. This continuity allows later phases to proceed with awareness of previous capacity thresholds, supporting safer progression when differentiation can be sustained more consistently.

Phase II governance, therefore, operationalises the protocol's core principle that developmental progression must remain capacity-led. By embedding observable pacing indicators, clinician containment, and readiness monitoring within existing governance structures, the model ensures that identity reorganisation occurs within a context of professional stability. This integration protects against premature progression, reduces the likelihood of pressure-driven disengagement, and maintains the therapeutic relationship as a consistent point of safety amid fluctuating readiness.

Manifestations of External Escalation Toward Clinicians

Within Phase II, shifts in survivor alignment may become perceptible within the relational system surrounding the survivor. When differentiation reduces automatic agreement, introduces ambiguity, or alters previously stable narrative positioning, external responses may intensify. Clinicians may become visible within this process despite maintaining an observational, capacity-led stance.

External escalation may take multiple forms. Alienating parents may characterise therapy as interference, question the clinician's role, attribute relational change to therapeutic influence, or frame identity reorganisation as external manipulation. This may include attempts to obtain information about treatment, increased communication directed toward the survivor regarding therapy, formal complaints, requests for justification of clinical work, or narrative positioning of the clinician as responsible for perceived relational disruption.

Such responses are not indicators of inappropriate practice but reflect the relational impact of identity reorganisation within systems organised around alignment and control. As survivors move away from automatic compliance, the clinician may be positioned symbolically within that shift. This dynamic can increase practitioner self-monitoring, concern about complaint processes, and pressure to alter pacing in ways that prioritise defensibility over developmental need.

External escalation may also directly affect the survivor. Survivors may be exposed to increased narrative messaging about therapy or the clinician, particularly during periods of reduced identity certainty. Temporary repetition of these narratives should be understood as regulatory behaviour rather than a loss of recognition. The presence of this dynamic reinforces the importance of pacing, relational safety, and clinician containment.

Where escalation involves boundary testing, persistent contact, formal complaint processes, or behaviour experienced as intimidating, the situation moves from relational complexity to governance relevance. Documentation, supervision, consultation, and adherence to professional boundary procedures become essential components of the response. Organisational awareness supports clinicians in maintaining a therapeutic stance without reactive adjustment to external pressure.

Recognising manifestations of external escalation allows the protocol to translate practitioner findings into practical safeguards. Identity reorganisation does not occur in isolation, and clinician visibility is a foreseeable feature of Phase II. Naming these dynamics supports preparation, reduces clinician uncertainty, and ensures that pacing decisions remain guided by survivor capacity rather than external relational pressure.

Modality Misuse Risk

Premature Application of Therapeutic Techniques

A final Phase II risk involves applying therapeutic modalities in ways that exceed the stabilisation function of this stage. Because survivors often demonstrate insight, motivation, and capacity for reflection, clinicians may feel justified in increasing interpretive depth, challenging beliefs directly, or introducing trauma processing approaches prematurely. When modalities are applied beyond the survivor's regulatory capacity, the work may shift from identity reorganisation toward destabilisation.

Examples of Timing-Related Modality Risk

Cognitive-behavioural approaches may be experienced as corrective when automatic thoughts are challenged before they can be safely observed. For example, a survivor who notices the thought "I must keep them happy" may feel exposed if the clinician moves quickly to dispute the belief rather than first supporting curiosity about when and why the thought developed. The intervention may be experienced as pressure to change rather than permission to notice.

A psychodynamic interpretation may feel intrusive when meaning is consolidated before stabilisation. A clinician linking current difficulty directly to alienating parenting dynamics before the survivor can tolerate ambiguity may be experienced as premature certainty, prompting monitoring, withdrawal, or rapid agreement without integration.

Somatic approaches may increase activation if embodiment occurs without sufficient containment. Inviting a survivor to remain in bodily sensations associated with fear or guilt before adequate regulation skills are established may intensify distress and reinforce avoidance rather than support awareness.

Similarly, early boundary coaching or behavioural change planning may inadvertently signal expectation. For example, suggesting reduced contact, encouraging assertive communication, or discussing relational decisions while the survivor is still differentiating internal experience may activate anticipation of consequences, leading the survivor to prioritise relational safety over identity exploration.

These examples illustrate that modality risk in Phase II is primarily a timing risk rather than a technique error. The same interventions may be effective when identity reorganisation can be sustained but destabilising when introduced before differentiation has stabilised. Sequencing, therefore, functions as a safety mechanism, ensuring that therapeutic methods support emerging self-development rather than unintentionally reinforcing adaptive identity strategies.

Phase-Consistent Use of Modalities

Within Phase II, the use of modalities remains observational, language-focused, and stabilising. The aim is to support the recognition of patterns, the development of reflective capacity, and the tolerance of ambiguity rather than to produce rapid cognitive change, emotional catharsis, or behavioural restructuring. Techniques are therefore applied to increase predictability and reduce threat perception, not to resolve narrative questions or accelerate decision-making.

Modality misuse often occurs subtly through emphasis rather than intention. Repeated return to destabilising material, encouragement toward insight consolidation, or implicit framing that understanding should lead to action may shift the survivor toward adaptive identity strategies designed to restore relational safety. These responses can increase the risk of disengagement, reinforce shame processes, or contribute to protective retreat.

Monitoring Modality Alignment

Clinicians monitor modality alignment through the same pacing indicators that guide Phase II calibration. Increased monitoring, rapid agreement, fatigue following sessions, or urgency to resolve meaning may signal that techniques are being experienced as directive rather than exploratory. Adjusting modality intensity, returning to observation language, and prioritising relational safety restores alignment without abandoning therapeutic work.

Situating modality misuse within Phase II governance reinforces that treatment risk extends beyond content to include process. Applying modalities in a manner consistent with stabilisation protects identity reorganisation from interpretive pressure and ensures that therapeutic approaches remain congruent with capacity-led progression. This emphasis preserves the protocol's core principle that development precedes resolution and that technique must remain subordinate to readiness.

Sequencing as a Safety Mechanism

The inclusion of modality misuse risk reflects the protocol's emphasis on sequencing rather than technique selection. Within this population, insight, motivation, and reflective language may emerge before the nervous system can sustain identity reorganisation without protective retreat. As a result, well-intended application of therapeutic modalities can unintentionally accelerate destabilisation when developmental readiness is misinterpreted as treatment readiness. Positioning modality use within a phase-governed framework helps prevent timing errors by ensuring the technique remains subordinate to capacity. This approach recognises that effective intervention is defined not only by theoretical fit but by alignment with the survivor's ability to tolerate emerging experience without reverting to adaptive identity strategies.

Phase II → Phase III: Bridging the Transition from Identity Reorganisation to Grief Work

The transition from Phase II to Phase III represents a shift from stabilising emerging self-identity to processing grief, loss, and developmental mourning. As survivors achieve greater internal autonomy and begin to experience their emotions and experiences as their own, they gain the psychological space needed for grief work. This marks a critical point: the foundation of identity reorganisation established in Phase II becomes the container for integrating mourning and loss.

Identity reorganisation provides the necessary stabilisation to engage with grief in a non-defensive, non-adaptive way. Survivors are now able to face the reality of loss without the overwhelming pressure of maintaining relational alignment or external narratives. They have developed the reflective capacity to experience grief without retreating into old relational roles organised around survival, guilt, or external expectations.

At this stage, survivors are ready to address the emotional complexity of loss, not just in terms of personal experience but also in the relational losses tied to the alienation and separation from their original family system. This stage often brings feelings of deep sadness, anger, and mourning for a lost sense of self and a lost connection to the family unit that once defined them. However, with the stabilisation of their emerging self, survivors can now hold these feelings without being overwhelmed.

It is at this point that grief can be integrated, without fear of losing the newly developed sense of self. The grief is no longer experienced as a threat to the survivor's autonomy, but rather as a necessary process for fully embracing their identity in the context of relational loss. Survivors can now begin to mourn the losses that have been previously suppressed or denied.

The transition to Phase III requires the continued support of the therapeutic relationship, which has provided the safe space for differentiation to unfold. The clinician's role becomes mourning, loss integration, and emotional healing. Before examining this later phase work in greater depth, the following section returns to Phase I to demonstrate how its containment principles are applied to survivors with histories of abduction, retrieval, and enforced relational movement.

Chapter Six

Theoretical and Empirical Rationale for the HQTP

Empirical Context: Complex Intersecting Traumas

This section presents the complex intersecting trauma profiles identified in the author's doctoral cohorts, which provide the empirical foundation for the phased architecture outlined in Chapter Five.

Before outlining modality selection and phase-specific interventions, it is essential to understand the complex and intersecting trauma profiles consistently identified in adult survivors of parental alienation and child psychological abuse. Therefore, the following section, Complex Intersecting Traumas (CITs), has been drawn from the author's PhD study, cohort 2, Mental Health Practitioners Who Work with Adult Survivors of Severe Parental Alienation, as originally presented in *Navigating the Maze During Treatment of Adult Survivors of Child Psychological Abuse: Severe Parental Alienation*, the author's doctoral practitioner study.

This material was also developed further in Volume Two of this book series. These examples illustrate the cumulative, intersecting nature of trauma exposure that clinicians must hold in mind when applying the HQTP.

The following paragraphs address some of the CITs identified in the participant data that practitioners should be aware of when embarking on therapeutic work with adult survivors.

Terminology note: The following doctoral material retains the terminology used in the original practitioner study, including severe parental alienation (SPA) and related phrasing. Since the completion of that research, the HQTP has refined this language into the broader CPA-PA, CPA-PAA, and CPA-PERA clinical framing used throughout this protocol. The original terminology is retained here to preserve fidelity to the doctoral data and published research context. At the same time, the clinical application of these findings should be understood within the updated HQTP framework.

SPA Complex Intersecting Trauma Reported to MHPs

The data corpus was examined using social constructionist thematic analysis (Braun & Clarke, 2014). Three main themes emerged from the mental health practitioner data. Theme One focused on the complex intersecting traumas reported by adult survivors of SPA. Theme Two reflected the treatment modalities, clinical methods, and practitioners' perspectives used in therapeutic work with survivors. Theme Three captured practitioners' recommendations for professional training and development.

This section introduces Theme One because it provides the clinical rationale for the HQTP's emphasis on complexity, restraint, stabilisation, and phase-based care. Themes Two and Three are returned to later in the protocol, where treatment modalities and practitioner training needs are discussed.

Theme One highlights the broader social dimensions, cumulative impacts, and clinical constraints practitioners encounter when working with adult survivors of child psychological abuse related to severe parental alienation. Study participants consistently reported the absence of specific SPA training pathways, limited guidance regarding appropriate treatment approaches, and the difficulty of holding multiple intersecting trauma exposures within standard therapeutic models. Practitioners also described the kaleidoscope of complex, intersecting traumas and social dimensions that survivors may disclose gradually over time, often in fragmented, non-linear ways.

Importantly, the presence of multiple intersecting trauma exposures does not indicate readiness for trauma processing, narrative exploration, or formulation refinement. During Phase I, awareness of these patterns functions as a contextual backdrop rather than a clinical agenda. This ensures that stabilisation, regulation, and epistemic safety remain prioritised. The clinician's task at this stage is not to identify, organise, or prioritise trauma categories, but to hold an informed appreciation of complexity while maintaining therapeutic restraint.

Clinical Teaching Note on Complex Intersecting Traumas

CIT's are frequently misused in early treatment when clinicians attempt to organise, name, or prioritise trauma exposures before sufficient relational and physiological safety has been established. Within the HQTP, these traumas are not treated as targets for early enquiry, confirmation, or sequencing. Attempting to identify or map intersecting traumas during Phase I risks reintroducing epistemic pressure, accelerating interpretation, and overwhelming the survivor's regulatory capacity. Clinicians are therefore advised to hold this material as contextual knowledge only, allowing disclosures to emerge organically and unevenly over time as safety stabilises. Awareness of complexity is intended to slow the work, not advance it.

Figure 1 - Main Theme One and Subthemes from Mental Health Practitioner Data

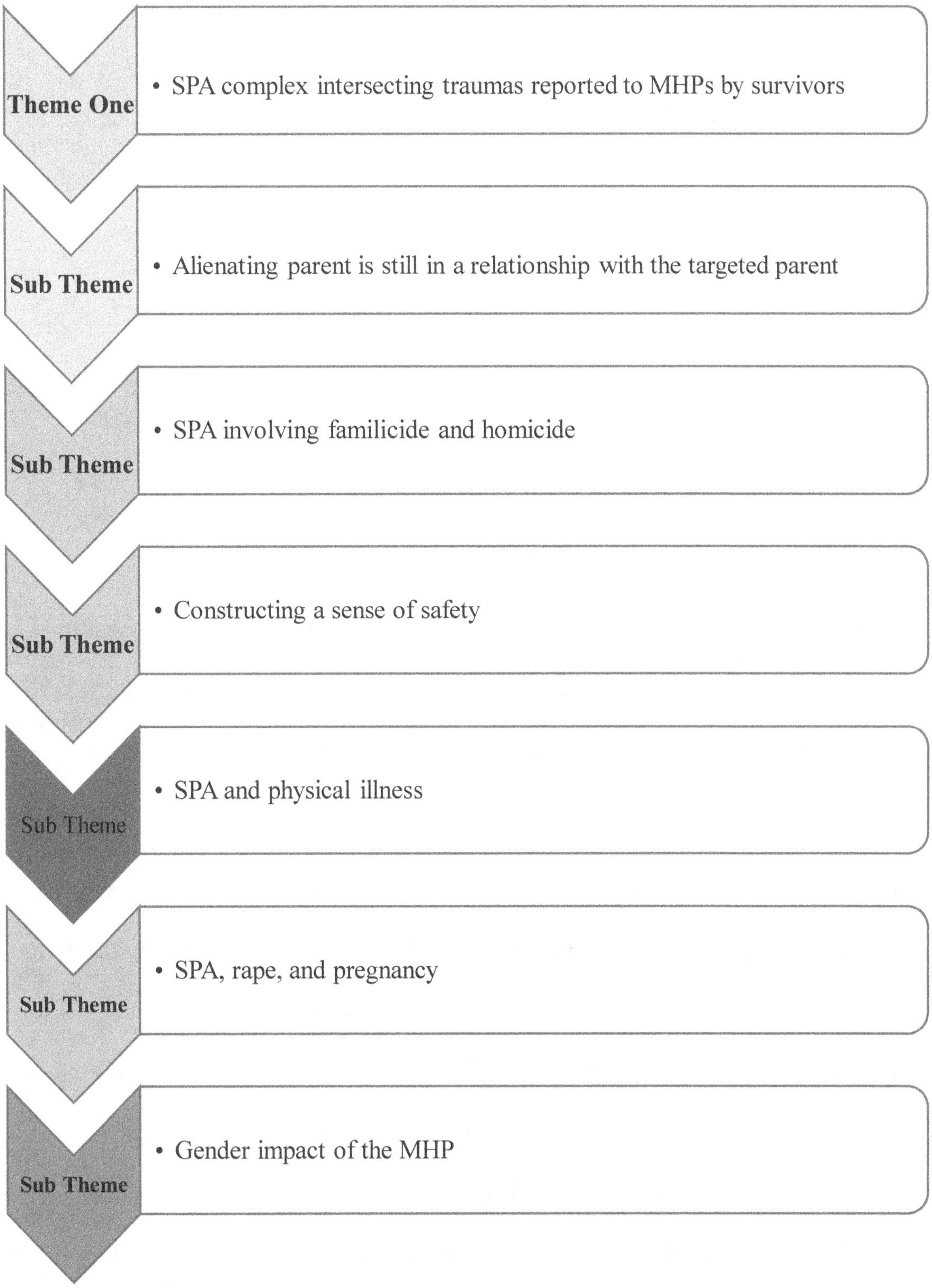

Alienating Parent is Still in a Relationship with the Targeted Parent

Within the following sub-themes, one mental health practitioner reported the construction of SPA CITs experienced by adult survivors. This practitioner explained that parental alienation and SPA may occur within intact family systems, not only in families that have experienced separation or divorce. The term *family dynamics* refers to the highly individual relational patterns operating within a family system. These dynamics include overt and covert mannerisms that may be expressed directly or indirectly (Gerhardt, 2019). Each family system is unique, and specific relational dynamics shape how family members understand themselves, others, and their world (Gerhardt, 2019).

In intact families, coercive control and relational manipulation may be normalised, externally invisible, and more difficult to detect, particularly when family functioning appears stable from the outside. The following extract is an example shared by de-identified MHP8, who described therapeutic work with adult survivors as clinically challenging because of the intricate family dynamics operating among siblings within an intact family system;

This is an unusual situation because the parents are still together but are alienating. They actually use the partner as the regulatory object. When they get together, the children are born. And now, the children are the regulatory objects. And as long as the partner is still enmeshed with them, everything's okay. My client's the regulatory object for the whole family. And so the other sisters, one has gone completely wild, one's on drugs, alcohol, multiple substances, multiple partners, can't be in a relationship. That's the eldest sister. The next sister down, she's chaotic in behaviour. When she's regulated, life is good for her other sister, which is my client; when she's not regulated, it gets really tricky. My client presented with a relational difficulty, but we finally talked about family and domestic violence after probably about a year of working together. (MHP8)

In this extract, MHP8 describes a family system in which emotional regulation is managed externally through relational control rather than through internalised capacity. Family members function as regulatory objects, absorbing and containing distress on behalf of the system rather than developing their own regulation skills. In this context, a regulatory object refers to a person whose role is to stabilise others' emotional states through compliance, availability, emotional suppression, or self-sacrifice, rather than through reciprocal, developmentally appropriate relational exchange.

The adult survivor occupies a central regulatory role, with the emotional stability of the wider family contingent upon their compliance, emotional labour, and willingness to prioritise others' needs over their own. From a clinical perspective, such dynamics frequently result in adult survivors presenting with diffuse relational distress, chronic responsibility for others' emotional states, and limited awareness of coercion or abuse. For example, survivors may describe persistent guilt when asserting needs, intense anxiety when others are distressed, or a sense that their role is to "keep everyone calm," without being able to articulate why. Because these dynamics are established early and reinforced across development, survivors may experience them as normal family functioning rather than as indicators of relational harm or violence.

MHP8 further reports that the survivor initially presented with relational difficulties rather than with explicit disclosures of FDV. It was approximately one year into therapy before the survivor was able to articulate the presence of ongoing FDV within the intact family system. Family and domestic violence is defined as "any behaviour that is violent, threatening, controlling, or intended to make you or your family feel scared and unsafe" (Australian Government, 2022, p. 1).

This pattern highlights how coercive control within intact families may remain concealed for extended periods, particularly when survivors have been conditioned to maintain family equilibrium and avoid disrupting relational bonds. In such systems, overt violence may be absent, while control is exercised through emotional pressure, role assignment, loyalty demands, and implicit threats of withdrawal or destabilisation. In these cases, FDV may constitute a CIT that coexists with alienation dynamics, attachment disruption, and prolonged epistemic invalidation.

Importantly, the delayed disclosure described here does not indicate avoidance, denial, or resistance. It reflects limited epistemic safety, meaning the survivor has not yet experienced sufficient relational safety to trust their own perceptions or to name harm without fear of consequence. It also reflects the absence of internal permission to conceptualise familiar relational patterns as abusive, and the necessity of prolonged relational containment before awareness can emerge.

Phase I Clinical Constraint

During Phase I, clinicians should not treat delayed disclosure as a signal to increase enquiry, pursue clarification, or accelerate interpretation. Awareness of these dynamics is intended to support patience and containment rather than diagnostic or narrative urgency. The appropriate clinical task is to maintain a non-adjudicative stance, reinforce the survivor's right to proceed at their own pace, and continue prioritising regulation and epistemic safety until the survivor demonstrates sufficient internal stability to tolerate recognition without destabilisation.

For example, a survivor may make indirect or minimised references to family harm, such as stating, *"Things at home were just complicated," "I was always the one who kept everyone calm,"* or *"It wasn't abuse. My parents just had strong personalities."* In these moments, clinicians may feel an urge to clarify, seek confirmation, or name the experience, for instance, by asking, *"Can you tell me what the violence was like?"* or stating, *"That sounds like abuse."*

Although well-intentioned, such responses risk imposing meaning before the survivor has sufficient epistemic safety to hold it.

Instead, the clinician maintains containment by responding in ways that neither interrogate nor interpret. The clinician might say, *"It sounds like you carried a lot of responsibility in your family,"* or *"We don't need to define or label anything today. What matters is how these experiences are affecting you now."* If the survivor minimises or retracts their statement, the clinician does not pursue elaboration, but rather affirms autonomy and pacing, such as, *"We can come back to this whenever it feels right for you,"* and gently redirects attention to grounding or present-focused material.

In some cases, survivors may test safety by partially disclosing and then monitoring the clinician's response for signs of urgency, judgement, or disbelief. When clinicians respond with neutrality, patience, and without demanding further detail, survivors gradually learn that they are not required to justify, prove, or organise their experience to remain relationally safe. Over time, this consistent stance supports the internal conditions necessary for later recognition and meaning-making without destabilisation.

Familicide and Homicide

Within this broader context of stabilisation and restraint, clinicians must also remain aware of severe forms of CITs that may be disclosed gradually over time, including exposure to familicide, attempted familicide, homicide, or threats of lethal violence within the family system. The term *familicide* has been used to describe diverse forms of homicide within families (Karlsson et al., 2021).

Familicide represents a severe category of CIT that may appear in the histories of adult survivors of Severe Parental Alienation (SPA). It involves the intentional killing, or attempted killing, of a current or former intimate partner and one or more biological or stepchildren within a family system (Karlsson et al., 2021). Research indicates that separation or divorce precedes many familicide incidents and that firearms are frequently involved (Karlsson et al., 2021). In these cases, the adult partner is often the primary target, with children harmed or killed as an extension of control over the partner (Karlsson et al., 2021).

From a clinical perspective, familicide is rarely presented as a discrete or clearly articulated trauma in therapy. Instead, it often emerges indirectly or fragmentarily, embedded within broader narratives of family violence, coercive control, threat, and prolonged fear. Existing research frequently subsumes familicide within larger studies of homicide–suicide or offender populations, resulting in partial data and limited attention to the lived experience of surviving family members (Karlsson et al., 2021). Clinicians should therefore be cautious about overgeneralising prevalence data or assuming uniform survivor presentations.

Within the author's practitioner cohort, four MHPs reported working with adult survivors affected by familicide or homicide within the context of SPA. MHP8 described familicide as a social dimension of severe parental alienation that may occur when family conflict escalates to extreme coercive control, including threats to kill children as a means of domination. Another practitioner described an SPA-related familicide case in which one parent immobilised their partner with a firearm before killing the children. These accounts underscore that threats or acts of lethal violence may form part of the coercive environment in which alienation occurs, even when the survivor was not the direct victim of the physical act.

Importantly, survivors rarely present with explicit disclosures such as *"there was a risk of familicide"* or *"my parent threatened to kill us."* Instead, clinicians may hear indirect references, such as persistent fear of a parent's emotional volatility, childhood memories of weapons in the home, ongoing hypervigilance around safety, or long-standing beliefs that survival depended on compliance. For example, an adult survivor may describe having learned early that *"keeping the peace"* or *"not upsetting him"* was essential to staying alive, without initially connecting this belief to a credible threat of lethal violence.

MHP8 further noted that clinicians may encounter this CIT when working with children or adult survivors of SPA, as threats to kill children or harm family members are commonly used as a mechanism of control. Within the practitioner data, alienating parents were reported as more likely than targeted parents to engage in threats or acts consistent with familicide, particularly where coercive control, entitlement, and identity fusion with the children were present.

Weaponised Loyalty, Violent Rehearsal, and the Risk of Targeted Harm

Children Left Alone During Family Breakdown

During prolonged divorce, separation, family court proceedings, parental conflict, or the breakdown of ordinary family routines, some children spend substantial periods alone in bedrooms or other private spaces with unrestricted access to video games, films, online platforms, social media, and violent material. Parents may be working, emotionally overwhelmed, involved in legal proceedings, absent from the home, or preoccupied with conflict. In some families, gaming becomes one of the child's primary forms of escape, stimulation, social contact, emotional regulation, or relief from loneliness.

Gaming itself should not be pathologised. Most children and adolescents who play violent video games do not become violent, and there is insufficient evidence to claim that violent games independently cause homicide, familicide, or serious interpersonal violence (American Psychological Association, 2020; Przybylski & Weinstein, 2019). However, the clinical question becomes more complex when an isolated child is also being exposed to sustained denigration of a targeted parent, encouraged to view that parent as dangerous or deserving of punishment, rewarded for cruelty, and denied access to corrective relationships or alternative versions of family events.

In these circumstances, violent games, films, online communities, or repeated viewing of real or fictional violence may become part of a wider environment of rehearsal. The concern is not the game alone. It is the convergence of isolation, coercive grievance, emotional reinforcement, dehumanisation, fantasy, repetition, and access to a named real-world target.

Why Grossman's Work Is Relevant

Lieutenant Colonel Dave Grossman is a former United States Army officer, educator, and author known for his work on the psychology of killing, combat conditioning, stress responses, and the methods used to prepare soldiers to act under extreme pressure. His writings have examined how repetition, realistic rehearsal, rapid target engagement, reward, group approval, and stress conditioning may reduce hesitation during combat (Grossman, 2001).

Grossman's work is brought into this discussion as a **conceptual comparison**, not as direct proof that video games cause children to kill. His descriptions raise an important clinical question: what may happen when repeated violent rehearsal occurs alongside the psychological conditioning of a child who has already been taught that a particular parent is evil, dangerous, less than human, or deserving of punishment?

The comparison is relevant to the earlier discussion of **child soldier dynamics** within severe parental alienation. A child soldier is not created merely by exposure to a weapon or a violent image. The child is recruited through authority, dependency, fear, distorted narratives, loyalty demands, group approval, repetition, and the redefinition of violence as necessary or morally justified. In severe family-system abuse, similar psychological mechanisms may operate on a smaller and more concealed relational scale. The alienating parent may position the child as a protector, spy, messenger, witness, ally, or retaliatory agent in an adult conflict that the child is developmentally unable to understand independently.

ICURE and the Conditioning of Loyalty in Alienated Children

The HQTP previously described this conditioning through the **ICURE sequence: Influence, Control, Uncertainty, Reinforcement, and Enmeshment**.

Influence occurs when the parent repeatedly supplies frightening, hostile, or dehumanising information about the targeted parent.

Control restricts access to competing information, safe relationships, family members, memories, photographs, communication, or opportunities to test the dominant narrative.

Uncertainty destabilises the child's confidence in their own memories, feelings, attachments, and judgement.

Reinforcement teaches the child which responses produce affection, safety, approval, closeness, or relief from emotional pressure.

Enmeshment blurs the psychological boundary between the parent's grievance and the child's developing identity.

Within this sequence, the child may gradually learn that empathy toward the targeted parent is disloyal, whereas hostility earns approval. Aggression may be reframed as protection. Punishment may be reframed as justice. Refusing to participate may be interpreted as betrayal of the alienating parent.

The child may no longer experience the grievance as the parent's. It may feel like the child's own belief, responsibility, and mission.

Laughter at the Targeted Parent's Pain

Targeted parents sometimes describe children laughing while the parent is distressed, injured, humiliated, excluded, or emotionally overwhelmed. This behaviour is understandably experienced as deeply cruel. It should nevertheless be assessed carefully rather than immediately interpreted as evidence that the child has permanently lost empathy.

The laughter may reflect imitation of the alienating parent, appeasement, nervous-system discharge, emotional numbing, dissociation, attachment signalling, or an attempt to demonstrate loyalty in front of a controlling caregiver. It may also reflect moral disengagement, in which another person's suffering has been reframed as deserved, exaggerated, humorous, or unimportant (Bandura, 1999).

Repeated approval of cruelty can strengthen the behaviour. A child who receives laughter, affection, praise, attention, or emotional closeness after insulting or frightening the targeted parent may learn that cruelty protects their relationship with the alienating parent. By contrast, showing sadness, concern, or affection towards the targeted parent may be followed by anger, withdrawal, interrogation, ridicule, or punishment.

The clinician should therefore ask what preceded the laughter, who was present, what happened afterwards, whether the child behaves differently away from the alienating parent, and whether empathy returns when relational pressure is reduced.

When Violent Media Becomes Part of a Wider Risk Pattern

Violent media exposure should not be treated as a stand-alone risk marker. The more clinically relevant question is whether media is being incorporated into a real-world grievance-and-preparation pathway.

Concern increases when several of the following are present together:

- repeated statements that a named person deserves to die or suffer;
- escalating dehumanisation of the targeted parent or family member;
- fascination with previous offenders or copycat violence;
- detailed searching for methods of harming a particular person;
- repeated rehearsal of a planned act;
- stalking, surveillance, testing access, or approaching a target;
- threats, leakage (telling a friend, sibling, teacher, online contact what they plan to do), warning statements, drawings, messages, or videos;
- collection of weapons, accelerants, restraints, or other means;
- deliberate animal harm, fire-setting, serious property damage, or assault;

- approval or encouragement from an alienating parent or allied adult;
- movement from fantasy towards preparation and capability.

Behaviour-based threat assessment focuses on the progression from grievance and ideation to planning, preparation, and action. It does not attempt to predict violence from gaming, diagnosis, anger, family status, or personality characteristics alone (Amman et al., 2017).

A Survivor Account of Weaponised Loyalty

A deidentified adult survivor described to the author how repeated frightening and dehumanising stories about his father contributed to an incident in which he seriously harmed his father and endangered the family home many years ago. He later received approval from the alienating parent.

This account is not offered as an independently verified forensic finding or as evidence of prevalence. It is included as a clinical illustration of how coercive grievance and post-act reinforcement may operate together. Conduct that could have caused death, serious injury, imprisonment, and lifelong psychological consequences was reportedly incorporated into the attachment system as evidence of loyalty.

This example demonstrates the importance of holding two realities together. The young person may have been psychologically conditioned, manipulated, frightened, or recruited by a parent. At the same time, the harm caused to the targeted person remains real. Understanding coercion does not require erasing responsibility, danger, legal consequences, or the need to prevent repetition.

Reframing the Warrior

Grossman (2001) uses warrior, sheepdog, knight, and centurion metaphors to describe people who prepare themselves to move towards danger and protect others. Within the HQTP, these metaphors require careful reframing.

Alienated children and adult survivors should not be encouraged to view themselves as soldiers in a war against the alienating parent. They should not enter the parent's "lair", confront a dangerous person alone, retaliate, or attempt to prove courage through physical aggression.

The protective warrior in this clinical context is the person who:

- refuses to carry out threats or acts of revenge;
- protects life rather than proving loyalty through harm;
- recognises when another person's grievance is being placed inside them;
- leaves an unsafe interaction before it escalates;
- maintains legal and ethical boundaries;
- alerts a safe adult or emergency service when danger is present;
- protects companion animals, children, and vulnerable family members;
- tolerates the fear, guilt, or rejection that may follow saying no.

The survivor advances towards psychological freedom, not towards combat.

Stress Inoculation and Preparing for the Critical Moment

Stress inoculation does not mean teaching the child to fight. It means preparing the child or adult survivor to respond safely when under pressure.

A person who has been conditioned to obey an alienating parent may panic, freeze, appease, dissociate, or comply when instructed to frighten or harm someone. Therapeutic preparation may therefore include rehearsing simple refusal statements:

"I will not hurt anyone."

"I am leaving now."

"I am calling someone for help."

"I will not carry this message."

"Your anger does not belong to me."

The clinician may also help the survivor identify physical signs of activation, locate exits, maintain access to a charged phone, establish a code word, identify safe transportation, protect medications and documents, plan for companion animals, and decide which trusted person or service to contact.

Grossman describes soldiers carrying equipment for physical injury. Alienated children rarely possess an equivalent psychological or practical safety kit. The HQTP adapts this concept by helping survivors prepare before the critical moment, rather than expecting clear thinking after fear, coercion, and nervous system activation have already overwhelmed them.

After the Act: Moral Injury and Recovery

When a child or adult survivor has already caused serious harm while under coercive influence, treatment may need to address guilt, shame, grief, fear, divided loyalty, identity disturbance, and moral injury.

Two extremes must be avoided.

The first is annihilating condemnation, which may deepen secrecy, suicidality, defensive denial, self-hatred, or renewed dependence on the alienating parent.

The second is complete exoneration, which may erase the harmed person's experience and obstruct accountability, empathy, learning, and prevention.

The therapeutic task is to help the survivor understand how coercion shaped the pathway, accept proportionate responsibility, tolerate remorse without psychological collapse, make safe reparative choices where appropriate, and construct an identity that is no longer organised around another person's hatred.

The Need for More Protective Eyes on Children

Children who are isolated in bedrooms, left alone for extended periods, emotionally neglected during family breakdown, or dependent on online environments require safe human connection. Schools, extended family members, health professionals, neighbours, youth workers, sporting organisations, clinicians, child-protection services, and community mentors may each notice only one part of the pattern.

Their role is not to interrogate the child, make public accusations, or diagnose the family from a distance. Their role is to notice concrete changes in behaviour, preserve connection, document concerns appropriately, and respond through lawful safeguarding and threat-assessment pathways when risk indicators emerge.

Children need adults who do not reward cruelty, demand allegiance, or place them inside an adult grievance. They need adults who can recognise recruitment and offer a safe way out.

Scope of the Present Child Recruitment Discussion

The intersection of coercive recruitment, child soldier dynamics, violent media, gaming, social isolation, operant conditioning, copycat identification, targeted harm, animal harm, arson, moral injury, legal accountability, threat assessment, and survivor recovery is too extensive to be addressed adequately within the present volume.

This brief clinical note is intended to identify the issue, establish necessary safeguards, and place it within the HQTP's wider risk and treatment architecture. The author intends to examine this subject in substantially greater depth in a separate, dedicated article.

For the purposes of the HQTP, the central position is clear: alienated children and adult survivors do not need to be prepared for war. They need to be protected from recruitment into someone else's war. The protective warrior is the person who maintains boundaries, protects life, refuses unlawful harm, and can say:

"This violence ends with me."

Abduction and Threats of Being Killed

Constructing a sense of safety is a complex clinical task when working with adult survivors of Severe Parental Alienation who have been abducted and subjected to threats of being killed by a parent. Within the author's practitioner cohort, clinicians described the difficulty of restoring safety in cases involving abduction, international displacement, and fear-based narratives shaped by coercive control.

The following extract is drawn verbatim from the MHP cohort. Identifying details have been withheld for confidentiality:

When the [agency name withheld for confidentiality] has called me, there were two children taken to a different country, and they believe their mother had stopped looking, and I had the [withheld] bring the flier and a [withheld] bring the missing cancelled checks to show them that, indeed, this was not the right story. So, you must stop this shit as soon as possible. This bullshit of always showing pictures of the family being happy it's just a crock of shit that can't help, but that's not it. You have to be really mindful, authentic, and purposeful and hit it right out of the gate and say, look, your father's not trying to kill you. He never tried to kill you. One of the things we know from the [agency withheld] is the parent that usually, the parent who's been left behind would never take the children from the other parent. (ID withheld for confidentiality)

This extract illustrates the clinical complexity of working with survivors whose fear-based beliefs about lethal threat have been reinforced through abduction, misinformation, and prolonged coercive dynamics. While the practitioner's language reflects urgency and intensity, the underlying clinical task is the careful reconstruction of safety without invalidating the survivor's terror. In such cases, fear of being killed may function as a survival belief rather than a reflection of present risk, shaped by prolonged exposure to threat narratives rather than direct intent.

From a Phase I perspective, this material is not an invitation for immediate exploration, correction, reassurance, or direct contradiction of the survivor's fear. Directly challenging fear-based beliefs without sufficient relational safety may produce epistemic rupture, while avoiding the fear altogether may reinforce its power. Clinicians must therefore carefully pace the construction of safety, maintaining awareness of abduction-related threats while prioritising regulation, containment, and epistemic trust.

Practitioners also reported that abduction cases involving homicide detectives, forensic police, and child recovery agencies created significant risks for clinician wellbeing. Exposure to hostile systems, threats, professional complaints, and high-risk recovery contexts was identified as a source of vicarious trauma and practitioner destabilisation. This underscores the necessity of supervision, organisational backing, and explicit safety planning for clinicians working in SPA-related abduction cases.

It may therefore be inferred that abduction and threats of being killed represent severe forms of Complex Intersecting Trauma for adult survivors of SPA. The following subtheme examines an additional concern identified by practitioners: the presence of significant physical illness and somatic distress among survivors exposed to prolonged SPA-related trauma.

SPA and Physical Illness Among Adult Survivors

During the interviews, MHPs were asked about their greatest clinical concerns when working with adult survivors of SPA. Two participants identified serious physical illness, somatic distress, and the bodily burden of prolonged trauma exposure as significant concerns within this population. The following extract is retained as practitioner data and should not be read as a claim of direct medical causation between SPA and physical illness:

Oh, God, it's the physical illnesses that they've developed as a result of carrying it in their body the load. A few months ago, I just started seeing a young woman 14, she just turned 14, and she's been diagnosed with cancer. She came because she thought she was anxious about cancer. Her history is horrible. And severe alienation is all over it. And for me, it's finding strength within me to help carry some of that burden and damage and to help them process their reactions to what happens in their relationship. The hardest part for me is helping them come to terms with the gravity of what happened to them. (MHP4)

This account reflects the practitioner's perception of the bodily burden associated with prolonged relational trauma, rather than a diagnostic or causal statement about physical illness. It also illustrates the breadth of presentations encountered by clinicians in this field, including adolescent presentations that may later inform adult survivor trajectories. Within the HQTP, physical illness and somatic distress are therefore understood as clinically relevant contextual factors requiring careful pacing, medical collaboration where appropriate, and avoidance of premature trauma-processing assumptions.

In this extract, the practitioner constructs the impact of Severe Parental Alienation as an embodied experience, described through the metaphor of the body "carrying" a prolonged trauma load. This reflects a pattern observed across the practitioner cohort, in which survivors' distress is experienced not only psychologically, but also physically, through fatigue, illness, and somatic vulnerability.

The practitioner also describes an internal process of attempting to "carry some of the burden" for the survivor. Within the HQTP, this stance is recognised as an empathic response that may arise when clinicians work with highly vulnerable clients, particularly children and adolescents. However, this response also highlights the need for clear boundaries, supervision, and phase-appropriate restraint, as clinicians cannot and should not absorb trauma on behalf of survivors.

Alongside this relational stance, the practitioner implicitly links prolonged exposure to Severe Parental Alienation with catastrophic meaning-making and sustained stress responses that coexist with serious physical illness. Within the HQTP, such links are understood as clinically meaningful observations rather than causal explanations. Physical illness is not treated as proof of trauma severity or as a direct manifestation of psychological abuse. Instead, it is held as a significant contextual factor that may compound vulnerability, distress, and treatment complexity.

The presence of serious physical illness introduces additional ethical, clinical, and systemic considerations. Survivors experiencing medical illness alongside histories of Severe Parental Alienation may face heightened fear, loss of bodily trust, increased dependency on authority figures, and intensified catastrophic interpretations of symptoms. These dynamics necessitate careful pacing, interdisciplinary collaboration, and explicit avoidance of meaning-making that attributes illness solely to psychological processes.

Phase I Clinical Constraint: Physical Illness and Meaning-Making

The appropriate clinical task in Phase I is to prioritise regulation, stabilisation, and coordination of care over interpretation. This includes supporting engagement with appropriate medical treatment, monitoring the survivor's capacity to tolerate discussion of illness, and maintaining a non-adjudicative stance that protects epistemic safety. Exploration of symbolic meaning, perceived causation, or trauma–illness narratives is deferred until sufficient internal stability and trust are established.

Clinicians are also advised to attend to their own emotional responses when working with survivors experiencing serious illness, particularly children and adolescents. Feelings of helplessness, grief, or a desire to internally "carry" the survivor's burden should be addressed through supervision to prevent boundary erosion and vicarious trauma. Within the HQTP, clinician containment is achieved through structure, supervision, and restraint, not through personal absorption of suffering.

Physical Illness, Regulatory Depletion, and Lifespan Burden in Adult Survivors of Severe Parental Alienation

Within the HQTP, observations regarding physical illness among adult survivors of Severe Parental Alienation are drawn from the author's twin doctoral studies, comprising adult survivor accounts and the perspectives of MHPs who work with this population. Across both cohorts, physical illness was described not as a singular outcome or causal endpoint, but as part of a broader pattern of cumulative burden associated with prolonged relational trauma, developmental constraint, and systemic stress exposure across the lifespan.

Importantly, the HQTP does not advance a psychogenic or mind–body explanation for illness. Instead, it reflects how survivors and clinicians describe the conditions under which illness emerges, deteriorates, or becomes clinically significant within lives shaped by sustained psychological abuse.

Prolonged Stress Exposure and Regulatory Depletion

Data from the adult survivor cohort indicated that Severe Parental Alienation involves long-term exposure to unpredictable relational threat, coercive control, and chronic vigilance during critical developmental periods. Survivors described environments in which emotional safety was contingent, bodily signals were ignored or suppressed, and recovery from stress was rarely possible. MHPs similarly described working with survivors whose nervous systems appeared persistently organised around threat, compliance, or emotional suppression rather than restoration.

Within the HQTP, physical illness is understood in this context of prolonged regulatory depletion. The emphasis is not on stress as a cause of disease, but on the erosion of physiological resilience over time. Survivors who have spent years managing fear, loyalty conflict, and relational instability may enter adulthood with limited capacity to absorb additional stressors, including illness itself, without significant destabilisation.

Developmental Interference with Bodily Awareness and Care

Findings from the adult survivor cohort further indicated that many survivors learned early to prioritise the emotional stability of caregivers or family systems over their own internal states. This frequently involved minimising physical discomfort, suppressing distress, and delaying help-seeking in order to avoid conflict, punishment, or relational rupture. Across development, these adaptations interfered with the acquisition of skills related to bodily awareness, early symptom recognition, and self-protective care.

Practitioners reported that adult survivors often presented late to medical systems, downplayed symptoms, or framed physical distress as insignificant until crisis points were reached. Within the HQTP, serious illness is not conceptualised as trauma-caused, but as occurring in survivors whose developmental histories may have constrained their ability to respond to bodily signals in timely or protective ways.

Meaning-Making Under Conditions of Epistemic Injury

Both doctoral cohorts highlighted the role of epistemic injury in shaping survivors' interpretations of physical illness. Survivors who had been repeatedly disbelieved, corrected, or blamed in childhood often described difficulty tolerating uncertainty when illness emerged. Physical symptoms were frequently interpreted catastrophically or moralised internally, with survivors reporting beliefs that illness confirmed defectiveness, punishment, or personal failure.

Practitioners identified these meaning-making patterns as clinically significant, not because they explain illness, but because they intensify distress and complicate coping. Within the HQTP, such interpretations are understood as products of epistemic insecurity rather than insight. The clinical task is therefore to stabilise meaning-making processes before engaging in exploration or reframing.

Cumulative and Systemic Burden Across the Lifespan

The doctoral data further demonstrated that physical illness among adult survivors of Severe Parental Alienation rarely occurs in isolation. Survivors frequently reported intersecting stressors across the lifespan, including disrupted education, legal involvement, financial instability, family estrangement, and inconsistent access to healthcare. Practitioners similarly noted that these systemic factors often limited survivors' capacity to rest, recover, or access preventive care once illness emerged.

From this perspective, illness is situated within a cumulative life context rather than attributed to a singular psychological mechanism. The HQTP, therefore, conceptualises physical illness as a compounding vulnerability within already-constrained systems, requiring responses that extend beyond individual psychotherapy to encompass medical, social, and systemic coordination.

Clinical Implications Within the HQTP

Grounded in the author's doctoral findings, this framework serves a protective clinical function. It prevents premature causal attribution, discourages mind–body determinism, and reinforces ethical restraint. Clinicians are instructed to remain aware of physical illness, somatic distress, and lifespan burden without imposing explanatory narratives or symbolic meaning in the early phases of treatment.

Consistent with Phase I principles, the clinician's responsibility is not to explain illness, but to protect regulation, epistemic safety, and collaboration. Physical illness is treated as real, serious, and deserving of appropriate medical care, while the survivor's subjective experience remains the focus of therapeutic repair rather than blame.

The following subtheme turns from somatic burden to sexual violation, gendered harm, and the additional clinical complexity that arises when CPA-PA intersects with rape, coercive control, and bodily trauma.

SPA, Rape and Gender

Within the HQTP, the intersection of CPA-PA and rape is understood as a high-risk clinical context requiring deliberate restraint, heightened boundary awareness, and explicit attention to power, safety, and regulation. Survivors may present with layered attachment injury, bodily violation, and epistemic harm, all of which may be reactivated within therapeutic relationships if pacing and boundaries are not carefully maintained.

Scholarly work on trauma and recovery has long noted that gender dynamics within therapy may influence how safety, authority, and relational proximity are experienced, particularly when sexual violence is part of the survivor's history (Herman, 1998). Within this protocol, however, gender is not treated as a determinant of therapeutic effectiveness. Rather, it is treated as one among many contextual variables that may shape transference, countertransference, and regulatory responses in the clinical setting.

The primary concern in Phase I is not the symbolic meaning of gender, but the survivor's capacity to remain regulated in the presence of another person who holds authority. For survivors of CPA-PAR, the therapist's gender may initially function as a trigger for threat detection rather than as a site of relational repair. This does not indicate pathology, resistance, or preference; it reflects state-dependent nervous system organisation shaped by prior harm.

For example, a female survivor of CPA-PAR may experience heightened vigilance, appeasement, or emotional constriction when working with a male practitioner, even in the absence of any boundary violation or explicit fear. Conversely, a survivor may feel an intense pull toward perceived safety or over-identification with a female practitioner, accompanied by rapid attachment, disclosure, or reliance. In both cases, the clinician's task is not to interpret these responses, but to pace the work, maintain clear boundaries, and prioritise regulation over relational meaning.

Practitioners of all genders may require additional clinical supervision when working at the intersection of SPA and rape. Male and non-binary practitioners may encounter heightened self-monitoring, fear of misinterpretation, or pressure to manage the survivor's discomfort, which can inadvertently lead to over-distancing or over-cautious engagement. Female practitioners may experience strong empathic resonance, protective impulses, or countertransference shaped by their own trauma histories, particularly if they share experiences of sexual violence. These responses are not indicators of clinical unsuitability; they are predictable relational phenomena that require structured reflection and containment.

Importantly, the HQTP rejects the assumption that rape is a gender-specific experience. Survivors of all genders may have experienced sexual violence, and MHPs of all genders may also carry their own histories of rape or sexual trauma. For this reason, supervision is framed as an ethical necessity rather than an optional support, particularly when shared trauma histories risk blurring boundaries or accelerating emotional proximity.

Phase I Clinical Constraint -Gender, Rape, and Relational Safety

During Phase I, clinicians must not treat gender dynamics, sexual trauma history, or relational reactions as material for interpretation, exploration, or therapeutic processing. Awareness of gendered power, vulnerability, and projection is intended to inform pacing, boundary clarity, and supervision, not to guide insight-oriented work.

For example, if a survivor expresses discomfort, attraction, mistrust, or emotional flooding in relation to the clinician's gender, the appropriate response is not to explore meaning or trauma history, but to stabilise the present moment. The clinician may respond with statements such as, "We can slow this down," or "Nothing needs to be worked out or explained right now," while redirecting attention to grounding and choice. The focus remains on restoring a sense of safety and control rather than on understanding the reaction.

Only when the survivor demonstrates sufficient emotional regulation, epistemic safety, and capacity to tolerate relational closeness without destabilisation should clinicians consider addressing gender-related transference or trauma material. Premature engagement risks re-enacting power imbalances, reinforcing fear-based compliance, or collapsing boundaries in ways that undermine the therapeutic alliance.

Within the HQTP, effective treatment does not depend on matching or avoiding particular genders. It depends on the clinician's capacity to hold authority without coercion, presence without intrusion, and care without over-identification. Gender awareness serves this aim only when it supports regulation, supervision, and ethical restraint.

SPA and Pregnancy Due to Rape

Within the practitioner cohort, MHPs described complex presentations involving severe levels of parental alienation (SPA), rape, pregnancy resulting from sexual violence, and intergenerational trauma. These cases were consistently identified as requiring heightened clinical containment, cultural awareness, and explicit safeguards for pacing.

One practitioner (TLE MHP5), who identified as an African American female working within her local community, described the prevalence of SPA and "fatherless generations" as a significant contextual factor in her clinical work. She articulated the layered complexity of supporting a young mother who had experienced rape, was raising twin daughters conceived through sexual violence, and later discovered her own history of adoption and alienation.

The following extract is presented verbatim from the practitioner cohort:

She didn't even know that she had an alienation problem. She's a single mom wanting to get around the trauma because she has twin girls due to rape. And so she was like, 'They're not going to have a father. They're just not!' So how do we help them be better? They're not going to be perfect. But how do we help them be the best possible young ladies that they can be? So, I was giving her tools. A year and a half later, she finds out she's adopted. And that's why her mother treated her so badly. And as she goes through that journey, she realises this is why I'm married to men who were fatherless. What if they had someone who helped them identify the trauma, the childhood trauma from their fatherless journey? Walk them through a healing process. The point is you've got to heal your childhood trauma. TLE (MHP5)

This extract illustrates multiple intersecting trauma layers operating simultaneously: sexual violence, pregnancy resulting from rape, parenting under conditions of unresolved trauma, delayed discovery of adoption, and unrecognised Severe Parental Alienation. The practitioner describes a process in which the survivor initially presents for support around parenting concerns, without awareness of her own alienation history, only later uncovering deeper developmental and attachment-level injuries.

Importantly, the practitioner's account reflects how meaning-making often unfolds non-linearly across time. The survivor's concern initially centres on her children's future rather than her own trauma history. Recognition of adoption and alienation emerges later, reshaping her understanding of relational patterns, partner selection, and intergenerational transmission of trauma. Within the HQTP, this delayed recognition is understood as a function of epistemic injury and developmental adaptation rather than avoidance or resistance.

The practitioner's reference to "fatherless journeys" reflects a culturally situated narrative within her community context. Within this protocol, such narratives are not interpreted as prescriptive models of wellbeing, but as expressions of lived experience shaped by social, historical, and systemic factors. The HQTP does not assume that the presence or absence of a father determines developmental outcome. Rather, it recognises that unprocessed trauma, disrupted attachment, and epistemic harm, regardless of family structure, place survivors and their children at increased risk unless addressed with appropriate clinical containment.

Phase I Clinical Constraint -Pregnancy Resulting from Rape

During Phase I, clinicians must not treat pregnancy resulting from rape as a focal point for trauma processing, meaning-making, or identity reconstruction. Survivors who are parenting children conceived through sexual violence frequently prioritise their children's wellbeing and future safety over their own internal experience. At this stage, clinicians should not pressure the survivor to recognise, disclose, or process sexual trauma before they are ready. Moving too quickly may overwhelm the survivor, damage trust in the therapeutic relationship, and increase the risk of withdrawal, shame, dissociation, or destabilisation.

For example, when a survivor expresses concerns about raising children without a father or fears about repeating intergenerational harm, the clinician should resist the impulse to explore rape trauma, attachment history, or alienation narratives prematurely. Instead, the clinician maintains containment by supporting present-focused parenting, stress regulation, and safety, while affirming that deeper work can occur later, once the survivor has sufficient internal stability and epistemic safety. The clinical task in Phase I is to protect regulation, reduce shame, and prevent re-enactment of coercive dynamics. Survivors must not feel required to heal, explain, or integrate trauma to be perceived as "good enough" parents or clients.

Clinical Synthesis and Transition to the Phase-Based Model

Across the practitioner cohort, MHPs reported exposure to a wide range of CITs during work with adult survivors of Severe Parental Alienation. These included intact families with covert alienation, abduction and lethal threat, serious physical illness, rape and gender-based vulnerability, and pregnancy resulting from sexual violence. Practitioners consistently emphasised the severity of abuse histories, the fragility of survivor regulation, and the ethical responsibility to construct safety before pursuing meaning or narrative coherence.

Both doctoral cohorts further indicated that while a strong therapeutic relationship is necessary, it is not sufficient for effective work with adult survivors of child psychological abuse. When clinicians rely solely on relational intuition, personal style, or general trauma principles, survivors remain vulnerable to misattunement, re-enactment, and further epistemic harm.

These findings necessitate a structured, phase-based treatment model that translates empirical insight into clinical practice. Such a model must provide clinicians with clear responsibilities, pacing safeguards, and ethical containment when working with adult survivors of child psychological abuse, parental alienation, and abduction.

The phase-based treatment model that follows is therefore situated as a direct clinical response to these intersecting trauma profiles. It recognises that adult survivor presentations arise not from isolated events, but from cumulative, developmentally embedded patterns of attachment disruption, epistemic injury, fear conditioning, and repeated systemic failure. The model operationalises these findings by sequencing recognition, stabilisation, meaning reconstruction, attachment repair, and long-term continuity in a manner that prioritises survivor safety and clinician accountability.

Theoretical Foundations of the HQTP Phase Model

Phase Integrity and Core Operating Principles

Phase I operationalises the HQTP's core operating principles by prioritising stabilisation, safety, and epistemic repair before any interpretive or trauma-focused work is undertaken. This phase is not preparatory in a superficial sense, nor is it time-limited. It constitutes an active therapeutic stage in which the primary clinical task is to establish sufficient physiological regulation, psychological safety, and relational reliability to prevent further harm. For adult survivors of child psychological abuse, parental alienation, and attachment disruption, Phase I addresses the foundational conditions that were absent across development: protection from coercion, respect for subjective experience, and the restoration of internal authority. All subsequent phases depend on the integrity of this work. When these conditions are not established or are later disrupted, treatment returns to Phase I processes as a clinically responsible recalibration rather than a regression.

This chapter provides the theoretical and research rationale for the phase model presented in Chapter Five and does not duplicate operational treatment procedures. Its purpose is to contextualise the HQTP within attachment-based, developmental, and trauma-informed clinical theory. The model is organised around phased clinical sequencing that emerges from observed treatment necessity rather than stylistic preference or rigid procedural design. It is grounded in the developmental, attachment-based, and trauma-related injuries observed in adult survivors of child psychological abuse associated with parental alienation, coercive control, and prolonged disruption within family systems.

Across both survivor and practitioner cohorts in the author's research at the University of the Sunshine Coast, a consistent finding emerged. Linear, insight-driven, or exposure-led therapies frequently failed to produce stability in this population and, in some cases, resulted in further fragmentation, shame, or psychological collapse. Survivors were often expected to process traumatic material before sufficient safety, coherence, or identity consolidation had been established. At the same time, clinicians working without a shared structural framework were required to rely heavily on intuition as they navigated high-risk clinical terrain.

A phase-based framework addresses this gap by recognising that different therapeutic tasks are required at different recovery points, and that attempting to undertake later-stage work prematurely can reproduce the very dynamics of overwhelm, coercion, and invalidation that characterised the original abuse. Rather than accelerating treatment, this model prioritises sequencing, containment, and proportionality, ensuring that each stage of work is matched to the survivor's current capacity rather than their apparent insight or articulation.

Clinical supervision within the HQTP functions as a structurally embedded component of clinical governance rather than as an optional adjunct. Across all phases, supervision supports ethical pacing, monitoring of countertransference, risk containment, and protection against the reenactment of coercive dynamics.

Why a Phase-Based Model Is Required

Adult survivors of developmental psychological abuse rarely present with discrete traumatic memories that can be processed in isolation. Instead, they present with layered adaptive patterns shaped over time within relational environments marked by loyalty conflict, reality distortion, emotional role reversal, chronic threat, enforced compliance, and suppression of authentic attachment needs. In these contexts, symptoms are not random or pathological in isolation. They represent organised survival responses to environments in which safety, truth, and autonomy were persistently compromised.

From a clinical perspective, this has direct implications for treatment. Distress in this population cannot be addressed solely through symptom reduction, narrative clarification, or emotional processing. When insight-driven or exposure-oriented interventions are introduced without adequate stabilisation and containment, survivors are at risk of destabilisation, identity fragmentation, or reactivation of survival-based adaptations. These outcomes mirror the original conditions of overwhelm and coercion by their alienating parent rather than resolving them.

A phase-based model provides the necessary structural containment for this work. It allows treatment to proceed in a sequenced, developmentally coherent manner, with early phases prioritising safety, regulation, and stability of meaning, and later phases supporting integration, grief, and identity consolidation. This sequencing reflects developmental necessity rather than arbitrary ordering. Survivors cannot integrate experiences that are not yet psychologically survivable, nor can they relinquish survival strategies without first establishing alternative internal structures that support safety and agency.

Population and Systems Significance

Although developed within a clinical treatment context, the population addressed by this framework represents a substantial and historically under-recognised public health group. Adult survivors of CPA-PA frequently present across mental health, legal, medical, and social service systems without a shared treatment architecture. The absence of developmentally sequenced intervention has contributed to fragmented care pathways, clinician uncertainty, treatment withdrawal, and elevated long-term psychosocial risk.

By articulating a phase-based model grounded in developmental formulation, this framework extends beyond individual symptom management to address systemic gaps in recognition, stabilisation, and longitudinal care. The model therefore contributes to trauma-informed systems development practice by reducing intergenerational transmission of relational harm, supporting clinician sustainability in complex presentations, and providing structured intervention pathways for populations historically positioned between diagnostic, legal, and service boundaries.

Non-Linearity and Clinical Readiness

Although presented sequentially, the phases described in this model are not linear steps. Movement through the framework is determined by clinical readiness, not time, compliance, or perceived insight. Survivors may move forward, pause, or return to earlier phases as new material emerges or as life circumstances shift. Such movement should not be interpreted as regression or treatment failure, but as an expected feature of work with complex developmental trauma.

This non-linear orientation is critical. Many survivors of parental alienation and related abuses have been subjected to externally imposed narratives about progress, obedience, or recovery. A rigid therapeutic trajectory risks replicating these dynamics. The phase-based framework instead offers structure without coercion, allowing the therapist to hold direction while remaining responsive to the survivor's internal capacity.

Boundaries as a Therapeutic Intervention

Within this model, boundaries are not obstacles to healing; they are a central component of treatment. Clear pacing, role clarity, and containment protect both survivor and clinician from reenactment dynamics, including over-disclosure, premature confrontation, or role confusion. Boundaries also provide survivors with an experience that may have been absent in childhood: a relationship in which limits are predictable, protective, and non-punitive.

The framework, therefore, emphasises that not all material must be accessed immediately, and that therapeutic restraint is often an act of care rather than avoidance. Decisions about when to deepen, pause, or redirect work are made collaboratively and informed by observations of nervous system capacity, emotional regulation, and meaning-making, rather than by adherence to protocol alone.

Overview of the Phases

The phases introduced within this model represent distinct therapeutic functions, each addressing a different component of recovery. Although explored in detail in subsequent chapters, the framework broadly encompasses the establishment of safety, coherence, and orientation; the recognition and reframing of survival adaptations; the processing of grief, loss, and disrupted attachment; the consolidation of identity, agency, and relational boundaries; and the integration of lived experience into a survivable narrative.

Each phase builds upon preceding work while remaining accessible as required in response to clinical need. The framework is therefore designed to support therapeutic depth without destabilisation and meaning development without retraumatisation. These functions describe therapeutic movements across the framework rather than discrete procedural phases.

Recovery of Authentic Identity and Role Deconditioning

When stabilisation is demonstrably consistent across relational and regulatory contexts, therapy shifts toward dismantling the role reversal patterns imposed during childhood. Identity work does not abandon safety architecture; it builds upon it. Identity exploration proceeds only while regulatory capacity and environmental safety remain stable. Adult survivors commonly describe having been positioned as emotional caretakers, confidants, protectors, spies, or loyalty enforcers for the alienating parent. These roles suppress normal identity development and replace authentic self-expression with compliance-based identity.

This therapeutic movement focuses on helping survivors recognise these imposed roles, distinguish their own emotional needs from those of the alienating parent, and reconnect with their personal values, preferences, and agency. This work often involves inner developmental repair, identity exploration, integration of grief related to lost childhood self-states, and the rebuilding of autonomy in decision-making.

Attachment Repair and Relational Reconstruction

Attachment repair in adult survivor work does not automatically mean reunification with a targeted parent. It primarily refers to restoring the survivor's capacity for safe connection, trust calibration, emotional reciprocity, and relational boundaries.

For some survivors, this includes rebuilding contact with a previously alienated parent if both parties choose to engage. When this occurs, therapy focuses on pacing, managing expectations, processing reunion emotions, and preventing retraumatisation. For others, attachment repair is internal. It involves integrating the targeted parent's memory, resolving loyalty conflicts, and developing healthy relational templates independent of family reconciliation. This therapeutic movement also supports survivors in building healthier friendships, partnerships, and, where applicable, parenting practices.

Long-Term Boundary Integration and Relational Autonomy

The final therapeutic movement is not concerned with the reintegration of the alienating parent. It focuses on stabilising the survivor's long-term relational position. Some survivors choose structured contact with the alienating parent under strict boundaries. Others choose low-contact or no-contact. The protocol does not prescribe a relational outcome; it supports psychological safety and functional autonomy. This stage emphasises the consolidation of gains, the prevention of re-entanglement, the strengthening of self-trust, the maintenance of identity coherence, and long-term life development beyond trauma recovery.

Conclusion: From Evidence to Applied Clinical Protocol

The findings emerging from the author's doctoral research and the wider clinical literature converge on a clear reality. Adult survivors of severe parental alienation present with patterns of developmental trauma that are qualitatively different from standard post-divorce adjustment or isolated childhood adversity.

Clinical and Survivor Vulnerability: The Need for Structured Treatment Approaches

These survivors carry layered attachment injury, prolonged identity disruption, unresolved grief, and nervous system dysregulation shaped by years of psychological coercion, erasure, and relational fracture. Many also report delayed recognition of abuse, misdiagnosis within mental health systems, and repeated therapeutic harm when clinicians fail to understand the specific dynamics of alienation trauma.

The author's qualitative twin study demonstrated that survivors often enter therapy decades after the original injury, not because the trauma has resolved, but because the psychological consequences surface later in life when safety increases, relationships deepen, or identity questions emerge. Practitioners interviewed in the study consistently reported feeling underprepared to work with this population and lacking structured guidance on pacing, stabilisation, grief integration, and relational repair. This combination of survivor vulnerability and practitioner uncertainty creates a clinical environment in which retraumatisation risk is high unless treatment is intentionally structured.

The evidence also indicates that severe parental alienation produces ongoing threat states rather than discrete trauma events. Survivors described persistent hypervigilance, attachment insecurity, emotional fragmentation, and identity confusion linked to prolonged exposure to coercive relational dynamics. In extreme cases involving abduction, concealment, or institutional betrayal, additional layers of terror, abandonment injury, and phobic responses emerged. These findings reinforce the necessity of viewing adult survivor work through a developmental trauma lens rather than short-term symptom management.

For these reasons, effective clinical intervention in this field cannot rely on generic trauma approaches alone. It requires a phased, containment-based framework that prioritises safety, nervous system regulation, identity stabilisation, and relational integrity before deeper trauma integration occurs. It also requires clinicians to understand that discovery, insight, and meaning-making can destabilise survivors if introduced prematurely. The author's research consistently demonstrated that survivors benefit most when therapy is paced deliberately, when autonomy is preserved, and when treatment is framed as collaborative rather than directive.

This chapter has established the conceptual foundation for the applied framework. It has demonstrated why adult survivors of parental alienation require specialised clinical attention, why standard diagnostic categories often fail to capture the depth of injury present, and why practitioners must be equipped with both theoretical understanding and structured treatment guidance.

The sections that follow shift the focus from conceptual analysis into applied clinical practice. Phase I introduces the stabilisation and containment architecture that anchors all subsequent work. It outlines how therapists establish safety, regulate physiological threat responses, support identity coherence, and create the relational conditions necessary for ethical and effective trauma intervention. This phase is not merely preparatory. It is the clinical foundation upon which all meaningful healing work in this population depends.

Preparing for the Chapters That Follow

The chapters that follow examine each phase in detail, including clinical aims, typical survivor presentations, and the practical decisions clinicians must make at each stage of treatment. Additional sections address cases involving childhood abduction, long-term concealment, permanent separation from a targeted parent, and situations where reunification is not possible due to death or lifelong estrangement. These presentations involve higher levels of risk and complexity and therefore require specific clinical safeguards and adapted treatment approaches.

Developmental Formulation and Diagnostic Positioning

Within the HQTP, diagnosis is conceptualised as provisional, descriptive, and subordinate to longitudinal developmental formulation. Presenting symptoms are understood as organised adaptations to relational environments characterised by coercion, reality distortion, attachment disruption, and chronic threat exposure rather than as discrete disorder entities. This orientation reflects the author's doctoral findings, which indicated that symptom clusters frequently shifted as recognition emerged, identity reorganised, and relational context changed.

A formulation-first stance allows clinicians to understand emotional dysregulation, dissociation, compliance patterns, identity disturbance, relational avoidance, and episodic destabilisation as developmentally coherent responses rather than indicators of fixed psychopathology. This approach reduces the risk of misclassification, prevents premature diagnostic closure, and supports treatment pacing aligned with meaning integration rather than symptom suppression.

Diagnostic language, therefore, remains clinically useful but is applied with caution, transparency, and iteration. Formulation emphasises developmental timing, attachment disruption, epistemic instability, institutional context, and relational conditioning as primary organising variables. Within this model, diagnosis informs communication and access to care, while formulation governs treatment sequencing, pacing decisions, and risk interpretation.

This formulation stance directly informs the model's crisis architecture. When symptom expression is understood as developmentally organised rather than diagnostically discrete, destabilisation must be anticipated as a predictable feature of recognition, identity restructuring, and relational differentiation. Crisis within this population, therefore, cannot be conceptualised solely as an acute escalation of affect. It reflects disruption of meaning organisation, attachment assumptions, and epistemic stability. The phase model and its containment architecture are consequently structured to monitor destabilisation linked to recognition processes, ensuring that pacing, escalation thresholds, and consultation pathways are governed by developmental formulation rather than diagnostic severity alone.

Healing Qualia Crisis and Safety Planning Framework

Crisis planning within the HQTP is collaborative, structured, and anticipatory. It is developed during Phase I and reviewed throughout treatment, particularly during periods of legal escalation, reunification attempts, public scrutiny, destabilising disclosures, or boundary renegotiation with coercive caregivers.

The crisis plan identifies early indicators of destabilisation specific to the survivor. These may include escalating rumination about injustice, retaliatory ideation, suicidal ideation, dissociative shutdown, compulsive reassurance seeking, fixation on legal narratives, or heightened sensitivity to perceived betrayal. The clinician and survivor document these signals as cues for containment rather than progression.

The plan specifies regulation strategies appropriate to the survivor's presentation, including grounding procedures, behavioural interruption techniques, structured contact limits, and temporary suspension of high-activation relational exposure. It also clarifies crisis escalation pathways, including emergency services, after-hours support resources, and jurisdictionally appropriate reporting obligations.

Where risk to self or others arises with credible intent, operational planning, or access to means, confidentiality boundaries are reviewed, and the legal duty of care is activated. The plan states that the protection of life supersedes phase progression.

Given the adversarial contexts common in this population, the crisis plan also addresses environmental interference. This includes preparation for destabilisation following court hearings, public allegations, reunification contact, or exposure to coercive communications. Survivors are supported in anticipating emotional activation and pre-planning containment responses rather than reacting impulsively.

For clinicians, the crisis framework includes supervision thresholds. Escalating countertransference urgency, fear of reputational threat, pressure to accelerate trauma work, or discomfort with ambiguity require consultation before deepening treatment.

The HQTP crisis plan is not a static document. It is reviewed at phase transitions and whenever environmental conditions change. The purpose is not control, but containment. Crisis planning supports differentiation, preserves safety, and protects both the survivor and the clinician from reenacting coercive dynamics.

Phase I establishes the non-negotiable safety architecture of the protocol. It ensures that emotional expression does not escalate into destabilisation, that differentiation does not activate unmanaged risk, and that the survivor's emerging internal authority develops within containment. Within the HQTP, Phase I operationalises this safety architecture in clinical practice. It translates crisis planning from structural principles into observable pacing decisions, escalation thresholds, and containment procedures that govern all subsequent phase work. The phase model, therefore, begins not with interpretation or narrative reconstruction, but with establishing conditions that render later therapeutic depth psychologically survivable.

Before proceeding, it is important to understand that this chapter is intended to function as a structural guide rather than a procedural checklist. The framework is designed to support careful, ethically grounded clinical decision-making in a field where poorly timed or poorly contained interventions can cause real harm. When applied with restraint and clinical judgement, a phase-based approach helps clinicians remain anchored in safety, supports survivors in remaining regulated and autonomous, and protects the therapeutic relationship from the replication of coercive or destabilising dynamics.

Chapter Seven

Purpose of This Brief Chapter

This chapter functions as an orienting map rather than a second explanation of the HQTP phases. Its purpose is to help clinicians locate the applied clinical pathways within the broader treatment architecture before moving on to the specialised abduction, extreme harm, modality, supervision, and diagnostic chapters.

Applied Clinical Pathways Within the HQTP

This chapter does not replace the full phase architecture introduced earlier. It revisits the phases in a concise applied form to support orientation, teaching, and cross-phase understanding within the HQTP. It does not restate phase definitions or operational procedures. Instead, it offers clinicians a high-level map of treatment flow, non-linearity, and readiness-based progression to support navigation of the HQTP in practice.

Although the phases are presented in sequence for clarity, clinical work does not progress in a strictly linear manner. Survivors may move back and forth between phases as new material emerges, life circumstances shift, or deeper layers of experience become accessible. Progression is guided by clinical readiness, regulation, and stability rather than by protocol timelines or external pressure.

Phase I: Safety, Orientation, and Epistemic Stabilisation

Clinical work in this phase focuses on orienting the survivor to the therapeutic process, establishing predictability and boundaries, securing consent, supporting regulation and containment, and clarifying the purpose and limits of therapy. Rather than pursuing insight or trauma integration, the emphasis is on stabilisation, trust, and therapeutic safety. Survivors learn that therapy is a space where pace is respected, disclosure is voluntary, and emotional intensity can be modulated. Without this foundation, later phases risk replicating overwhelm, invalidation, or coercive dynamics.

Phase II: Meaning Reconstruction and Identity Repair

In Phase II, the clinical focus shifts toward reflective meaning reconstruction, recognition of survival adaptations, and early identity repair. The emphasis is on helping survivors understand how coercive developmental environments shaped self-concept, loyalty patterns, and relational expectations without pushing them into premature trauma processing.

Work in this phase remains careful and contained. The clinician supports narrative flexibility, reduced shame, and growing psychological authorship while maintaining epistemic safety and consent-based pacing.

Phase III: Mourning, Loss Integration, and Developmental Grief Repair

Phase III turns toward grief for what was lost, withheld, or developmentally disrupted through child psychological abuse. This may include the loss of a psychologically available parent, extended family continuity, a coherent childhood narrative, and trust in systems that were meant to provide protection. Mourning is not imposed or accelerated. It is approached slowly, with strong containment, and only when the survivor has sufficient safety and meaning capacity to engage loss without collapse.

Phase IV: Trauma Integration Readiness Architecture

Phase IV is a readiness architecture rather than immediate trauma processing. The task is to assess whether traumatic material can be approached without flooding, dissociation, reenactment, or renewed dependency on therapist authority. Clinical attention in this phase centres on timing, regulation, consent stability, ambiguity tolerance, and recovery capacity.

When these conditions are not yet established, therapy returns to earlier phases rather than advancing prematurely into trauma-focused work.

Phase V: Differentiation, Boundary Formation, and Contact Decisions

In Phase V, clinical work shifts toward identity consolidation, personal agency, and the establishment of functional relational boundaries. Survivors are supported in differentiating from inherited family narratives, developing internal reference points for decision-making, and making contact or boundary decisions in ways guided by safety, capacity, developmental reality, and informed judgement.

Phase VI: Integration, Continuity, and Long-Term Adaptation

The final phase focuses on integration and continuity rather than completion. Survivors are supported in carrying their experiences forward in a way that allows life to expand beyond survival, without requiring the erasure of what occurred. This work involves developing a personal narrative that can hold truth, complexity, and grief without becoming the organising centre of identity. For some survivors, this includes meaning-making or values clarification. For others, it involves practical decisions about boundaries, contact, distance, or long-term relational positioning.

Integration in this framework does not imply emotional resolution, forgiveness, reconciliation, or closure. Many survivors, particularly those who have experienced permanent separation, abduction, or irreversible loss, will live with unanswered questions and ongoing grief. Phase VI supports the capacity to live well alongside what cannot be repaired, while gradually strengthening forward orientation, agency, and self-continuity across the lifespan.

Movement Between Phases

Throughout treatment, clinicians remain attentive to signs of overload, dissociation, or destabilisation. Movement back to earlier phases is expected and clinically appropriate. The framework is designed to support depth without urgency, allowing therapy to unfold at a pace that honours both vulnerability and adaptive strength.

The phases described here represent the core pathway for many adult survivors. In cases involving extreme or complex harm, including abduction, prolonged separation, concealment, or sustained identity erasure, additional adaptations and safeguards are required. These presentations are addressed in later chapters.

The phases outlined above are not techniques to be applied mechanically, but relational and developmental tasks to be undertaken with care. Applied flexibly and ethically, the framework helps clinicians remain grounded in complex work and offers survivors a pathway to recovery that does not reenact the original harm.

Chapter Eight

Clinical Pathways for Adult Survivors of Childhood Abduction

This chapter contains abduction-specific and extreme-harm material that sits alongside, rather than replaces, the six HQTP phases. It extends the HQTP into clinical work with adult survivors of childhood abduction, concealment, identity disruption, discovery trauma, and irreversible loss. Clinicians are not expected to apply every subsection to every survivor. The purpose of this chapter is not to establish a separate protocol, but to support formulation, pacing, supervision, risk recognition, and phase adaptation when abduction or extreme harm complicates the core HQTP phase structure.

Clinical work with abducted survivors remains anchored in stabilisation, epistemic safety, and relational containment. Many survivors present with fragmented autobiographical histories, unresolved identity discontinuities, and unintegrated attachment ruptures that increase vulnerability to destabilisation when traumatic material is approached prematurely. For this reason, abduction-related work is not organised around disclosure or narrative reconstruction. Instead, intervention is introduced gradually, with emphasis on present safety, internal coherence, and survivor-led pacing before historical exploration is clinically indicated.

Abduction represents one of the most severe and developmentally destabilising forms of child psychological abuse. It is not simply an escalation of parental alienation, nor can it be understood as "alienation over time." In abduction, the child is removed not only from a parent but from relational reality itself. Attachment bonds, family networks, cultural continuity, autobiographical memory, and identity development are disrupted simultaneously, often under conditions of secrecy, threat, and enforced compliance.

Findings from the author's University of the Sunshine Coast research indicate that adult survivors of abduction frequently describe lives organised around concealment, instability, and chronic fear. Many report repeated relocations, attendance at multiple schools, unexplained name changes, falsified birth records, or being instructed to memorise fabricated personal histories. Some describe illegal adoptions, informal custodial handovers, or identity substitution. Others report exposure to violence perpetrated by stepparents or associates of the abducting caregiver, including sexual abuse, criminal exploitation, and in some cases, sex trafficking.

These developmental conditions produce long-term psychological vulnerability that extends beyond relational loss. Survivors often enter adulthood with disrupted self-continuity, impaired trust in external systems, fragmented identity development, and heightened sensitivity to authority, abandonment, and perceived threat. These patterns require specific clinical adaptations within treatment planning and pacing.

Secondary Trauma and the Death of the Targeted Parent

Survivors may experience extreme grief and profound psychological destabilisation when a deeply loved targeted parent dies by suicide. Many abducted survivors carry preserved attachment representations of the targeted parent that were never allowed to evolve, repair, or mature. These internalised relational memories often remain emotionally vivid, frozen in time, or anchored to unresolved childhood longing.

When death occurs, survivors are confronted with the permanent loss of a relationship that was already forcibly interrupted. This produces layered bereavement: the loss of the parent, the loss of future reconciliation, and the loss of all imagined opportunities for shared adulthood, explanation, and relational repair.

For some survivors, grief is further intensified by exclusion from mourning rituals. Those abducted internationally or living under controlling caregivers may be prevented from attending funerals, memorials, or family gatherings. The inability to say goodbye, witness communal acknowledgment of the death, or participate in culturally meaningful grieving processes can disrupt emotional integration. Survivors may report feeling unreal, disconnected, or psychologically suspended in time, as though the death occurred outside their lived reality.

Other survivors are never formally informed of the death. Some discover the truth years later through third parties, public records, or online searches. Others remain uncertain for extended periods, holding unresolved questions about whether the parent is alive or deceased. This creates an ambiguous loss, in which the survivor is psychologically unable to complete grief processes because relational status remains unresolved. Ambiguous loss frequently produces chronic longing, searching behaviours, intrusive imagining, emotional numbness, and difficulty forming closure even when the truth eventually becomes known.

Grief in these cases rarely presents as a single event. It often re-emerges at life milestones that symbolically activate attachment needs and family continuity. Survivors commonly report intensified grief during weddings, engagements, the birth of children, birthdays, graduations, anniversaries, and major transitions. These moments highlight the absence of the targeted parent in roles they were never allowed to occupy and often reactivate questions about what could have been. Survivors may experience sudden waves of sadness, anger, or longing even years after learning of the death, particularly when witnessing peers or partners experiencing shared family milestones.

Expanded Section Drawn from PhD Research and Clinical Session Examples

Survivors' experiences of parental death following abduction or prolonged alienation are not limited to natural causes. In some cases, death occurs through violence, homicide, or suicide, compounding attachment trauma with acute traumatic loss and moral injury.

Across survivor accounts drawn from doctoral research, private clinical material, and survivor-led conference testimony, a recurring pattern has emerged in which some adult survivors later learn that severe violence, threats, or homicide occurred within the broader alienating family system. In one anonymised clinical case, a survivor learned in adulthood that their father had been fatally assaulted by adult children from a subsequent relationship following prolonged separation from his biological child. In survivor testimony presented at the conference, other participants described targeted parents being shot, threatened, or subjected to organised intimidation. These accounts suggest that, in a minority of cases, alienation-related family systems may also include severe interpersonal violence that compounds attachment trauma with traumatic loss and ongoing threat.

Other survivors report parental death by suicide following years of family court conflict, enforced separation, institutional invalidation, and prolonged relational loss. In one research-based case, a survivor who had been abducted internationally alongside two siblings later learned that their father had died by suicide after extended isolation from his children. Despite decades of separation, the survivor retained vivid sensory and emotional memories of early father-son bonding experiences, including routine nurturing interactions and teaching experiences, for example, fishing and sports, which became powerfully activated during grief processing. These preserved attachment representations frequently remain psychologically alive even when physical contact has been severed, intensifying grief reactions when death occurs.

In some presentations, survivors experience delayed reunification followed by rapid secondary loss. In another example, an anonymised clinical case drawn from doctoral research data explains how an abducted survivor was able to reconnect with their targeted parent in adulthood and spend approximately two years rebuilding contact, meeting extended family members, and forming new relational bonds. Shortly thereafter, the parent died. This sequence created a layered grief response involving both relief at regained connection and profound loss at its sudden termination. Survivors in these circumstances often report heightened attachment activation, unresolved longing, and intensified mourning that feels the same as when they were originally separated from their parent after their abduction as a child.

Murder of a Targeted Parent

Clinical material from private practice and survivor conference narratives also highlights exposure to intergenerational violence within alienating family systems. Some survivors report learning that targeted parents were subjected to repeated threats, attempted shootings, or physical assaults by extended family members. Others describe being told in adulthood that hired individuals were engaged to intimidate or harm a targeted parent. These disclosures frequently emerge years after abduction or alienation has occurred, introducing secondary trauma layered upon earlier developmental injury.

From a clinical perspective, these forms of loss create a distinct treatment profile. Survivors are not only grieving the death of a parent. They are grieving the permanent erasure of a relationship that was already forcibly interrupted. The psychological impact often includes complex bereavement, unresolved attachment activation, moral injury, survivor guilt, identity destabilisation, and intrusive memory activation. Many survivors also struggle to integrate violent or traumatic death with preserved internal representations of the parent as emotionally alive within childhood memory.

For this reason, the HQTP treats secondary traumatic bereavement in abduction and extreme alienation contexts as a high-risk clinical domain. Grief processing is never accelerated or framed as closure-oriented. Instead, it is approached as a long-horizon integration process that unfolds only when epistemic safety, relational containment, and internal stabilisation have been firmly established. Clinicians are required to pace this work carefully to prevent retraumatisation, reactivation of loyalty, or collapse of emerging identity coherence.

Clinically, this pattern should not be interpreted as unresolved pathology or failure to "move on." It reflects the enduring nature of attachment bonds and the cumulative impact of forced separation combined with permanent loss. The therapeutic task is not to eliminate grief, but to support survivors in integrating these experiences into a survivable emotional narrative that does not collapse identity or reintroduce self-blame.

Clinicians must approach this work with restraint and attunement. Standard bereavement timelines and models are rarely applicable. Grief may unfold across decades, layered with identity reconstruction, delayed meaning-making, and relational renegotiation. Survivors require space to express contradictory emotions, including love, rage, sorrow, confusion, and relief, without being directed toward resolution or closure.

This clinical terrain demands recognition that the survivor is not only grieving a person, but also reconstructing a life history that was interrupted, distorted, or concealed. Effective treatment supports the survivor in holding both the reality of loss and the continuity of self, without forcing emotional outcomes or accelerating integration beyond what the nervous system can tolerate.

How to Read the Applied Abduction Pathways

The applied abduction pathways in this chapter do not replace the core HQTP Phases I–VI. They are additional clinical maps used when abduction, concealment, forced relocation, identity disruption, or extreme harm histories require a more specific formulation. These pathway labels are embedded within the broader HQTP architecture. Clinicians should continue to use the core phase principles of safety, pacing, consent, epistemic protection, grief containment, trauma-readiness, differentiation, and long-term adaptation when applying these specialised pathways.

Core HQTP Phase II: Clinical Decision Logic and Entry Safeguards

Before initiating Phase A1 work, clinicians must assess whether the survivor has sufficient present-day regulatory capacity to tolerate reframing of captivity without destabilisation. Apparent insight, articulation, or intellectual understanding is not a sufficient indicator of readiness. Many abducted survivors learned to present as coherent, compliant, or emotionally contained as a survival strategy. Regulation, not presentation, governs entry.

Phase A1 work should be paused or deferred if the survivor demonstrates active dissociation, collapse, identity fragmentation, survival-driven compliance within the therapeutic relationship, or escalating physiological distress. In these situations, clinicians must redirect to stabilisation and containment strategies rather than proceeding with meaning-based work. This redirection is not regression. It is ethical sequencing and pacing.

Throughout core HQTP Phase II, clinicians are required to continuously monitor nervous system stability, pacing, and epistemic safety. Progression is determined not by protocol sequence but by the survivor's capacity to remain oriented, autonomous, and psychologically safe. When destabilisation emerges, clinicians return to earlier containment principles without framing this as a setback or failure.

The clinician's task in this phase is not to advance material, but to protect the survivor's autonomy, regulate intensity, and prevent the replication of coercive dynamics through premature insight, interpretation, or narrative pressure.

Phase A1: Survival, Recognition and Reframing of Complicity Narratives

Adult survivors of abduction may arrive in therapy without ever having named their childhood experience as abduction, or they may present with an internalised narrative of complicity. Many report beliefs such as, "I didn't have a clue what was going on. I was a kid with no voice," "I couldn't get to my mum, so I stopped trying. It got me in too much trouble," "I had to agree with everything I was told or else it would be a bad day for me," or "My dad could never have saved me, so I accepted the lie and stayed safe." These beliefs often persist even when the survivor intellectually recognises that they were a child at the time. Clinically, this reflects the moral confusion and need for stability and safety created by prolonged FDV, specifically coercion, secrecy requirements, dependency, and threat conditioning.

Phase A1 focuses on reframing childhood behaviour as a form of survival under conditions of developmental captivity. Abducted children were frequently taught, implicitly or , that disclosure would result in harm. Some were threatened with violence, abandonment, punishment of the abducting caregiver, institutional involvement, or the death of the targeted parent. Others learned through repeated experience that safety depended on obedience, silence, rapid adaptation, and compliance with imposed narratives. Over time, these conditions shaped behavioural strategies that prioritised survival over authenticity.

Clinical work in this phase involves careful psychoeducation that distinguishes agency from adaptation. Survivors are supported to understand that compliance under threat does not constitute consent, and that childhood moral responsibility cannot be retroactively imposed on behaviour shaped by fear, dependency, and power imbalance. Without this reframing, later phases of treatment risk amplifying shame and self-blame rather than restoring coherence and self-compassion.

A common clinical presentation during this phase involves acute distress when survivors begin to examine their own past behaviour. For example, a survivor may experience panic, nausea, or emotional collapse when recalling having defended the abducting caregiver to teachers, authorities, or extended family. In these moments, the clinician does not challenge the behaviour itself but anchors it within the closed survival system in which truth carried danger and compliance functioned as protection. The therapeutic task is to relocate responsibility from the child to the coercive environment, while preserving the survivor's sense of dignity and agency in the present.

Children who defended the abducting caregiver to teachers, authorities, or extended family were not expressing allegiance in the way adults understand it. They were responding to a closed survival environment in which disclosure carried real or perceived consequences. Many abducted children learned that telling the truth could result in punishment, emotional withdrawal, further relocation, intensified control, or threats toward themselves or the targeted parent. In some cases, children were instructed on what to say. In others, they learned through repeated reinforcement that alignment with the abducting caregiver was the only path to stability, shelter, and relational safety.

Defence behaviour also served as an attachment-preservation strategy. When a child's access to food, housing, schooling, and daily care is controlled by the abducting caregiver, the nervous system prioritises maintaining that relationship, even when it is harmful. From a developmental perspective, maintaining proximity to the available caregiver is more urgent than telling the truth. The child's brain organises around survival, not justice.

In addition, many children experienced cognitive narrowing under chronic threat. Complex moral reasoning, long-term consequence evaluation, and abstract truth-telling are developmentally limited under stress. The child's capacity to hold dual realities was often suppressed. In these conditions, repeating the caregiver's narrative becomes an automatic protective response rather than a consciously chosen deception.

Clinically, these behaviours must be understood as adaptive strategies shaped by dependency, fear, and environmental constraints, rather than as evidence of complicity, betrayal, pathology, or moral failure.

Clinicians must exercise particular care when survivors disclose having defended the abducting caregiver or participated in maintaining false narratives. These disclosures must not be interpreted as resistance, deception, manipulation, or lack of insight. Doing so risks re-enacting the same moral invalidation and epistemic control that characterised the original environment of coercion.

Survivors often carry intense shame when they recognise these behaviours in retrospect. If clinicians respond with judgement, surprise, or corrective confrontation, the survivor may experience renewed internal collapse or withdraw emotionally from the therapeutic relationship. The appropriate clinical stance is one of normalisation within context: naming the behaviour as a survival adaptation while affirming the survivor's present-day capacity for agency and choice.

Clinicians should avoid asking "why didn't you tell someone, "Or "why didn't you leave," either explicitly or implicitly. These questions impose adult agency onto child-level dependency and recreate responsibility distortion. Instead, clinicians support the survivor in exploring what the environment enabled, what was restricted, and the behaviours required to maintain safety at the time.

When survivors begin to disclose these survival strategies, the clinician's task is not to extract confession or promote emotional catharsis, but to stabilise the meaning of the behaviour in a way that reduces shame and restores developmental coherence. This framing protects the survivor's dignity and prevents retraumatisation through moral re-exposure.

As survivors begin to reframe childhood behaviour as survival rather than complicity, a parallel process often emerges questioning whom they were required to become in order to survive. Once responsibility is relocated from the child to the coercive environment, attention naturally shifts from behaviour to identity. Phase A2 builds directly on this work by addressing the long-term impact of concealment, forced adaptation, and relational instability on the survivor's sense of self.

Phase A2: Identity Reconstruction After Concealment and Forced Identity Change

Abducted survivors frequently present with identity disturbance that goes beyond ordinary developmental confusion. Many grew up without stable reference points for who they were, where they belonged, or which version of their life story was accurate. Repeated relocations, multiple schools, inconsistent records, and shifting family roles often created a persistent sense of psychological displacement and instability. In many cases, identity disruption was actively created rather than incidental.

Some survivors were raised under different names or altered personal histories. Others were told that the targeted parent had died, never wanted them, was dangerous, or did not care. In cases involving illegal adoption, informal transfer, or trafficking, children were deliberately separated from family identity, lineage, and origin information, leaving adulthood marked by confusion about belonging, history, and personal continuity.

Phase A2 focuses on supporting identity reconstruction without forcing coherence or narrative closure. Survivors are supported in exploring who they became to survive, as well as the parts of self that were interrupted, suppressed, or never allowed to develop safely. The task is not to restore a mythical "original self," but to build an integrated identity that can hold multiple developmental layers without being organised around conditions of abduction.

Clinicians must understand that fragmentation in this population reflects developmental disruption resulting from concealment, forced adaptation, and relational instability, rather than personality pathology. Stability emerges through the validation of uncertainty, the continuity of the therapeutic relationship, and the gradual consolidation of self-experience, not through imposed meaning or accelerated integration.

Phase A3: Trauma Integration Under Prolonged and Extreme Threat

Abduction survivors are often exposed to sustained threat over extended periods of development. Fear may have been reinforced through monitoring, secrecy rules, sudden relocations, repeated disruption of schooling and friendships, exposure to violence, or witnessing harm to others. In many cases, children were moved deliberately to avoid detection, resulting in long-term hypervigilance and mistrust of authority, systems, and relational stability.

In adulthood, survivors may present with patterns that resemble mood or anxiety disorders but are consistently activated by relational, autonomy-related, or truth-based stimuli. Panic following expressions of independence, dissociation when questioned about history, or somatic collapse after accessing records or documentation are common presentations. These responses reflect nervous systems that remain organised around threat detection rather than present-day safety.

Clinical work in this phase prioritises nervous system stabilisation before any trauma integration or narrative integration. Interventions must be paced to avoid recreating powerlessness, exposure without consent, or loss of bodily autonomy. Techniques that assume baseline safety, promote rapid disclosure, or emphasise emotional catharsis risk retraumatising survivors whose systems remain calibrated to danger.

For example, when working with a survivor who experienced trafficking through informal or hidden networks, clinicians may need to spend extended time establishing predictability, relational safety, and environmental control before any exploration of traumatic material is attempted. In these cases, fear responses are treated as historically accurate survival adaptations rather than exaggerated, irrational, or maladaptive reactions. Progress is measured by increased regulation and stability, not by volume of disclosure.

Phase A4: Attachment Loss and Interrupted Family

Grief in abduction trajectories is complex, layered, and frequently unsupported. Survivors may grieve parents they barely remember, siblings they never met, extended families removed from their lives, and entire cultural, relational, or ancestral continuities that were never allowed to form. This grief often includes mourning for developmental experiences that never occurred, such as shared childhoods, family rituals, and ordinary relational milestones.

When the targeted parent has died by suicide, grief may be compounded by shock, anger, confusion, and intrusive counterfactual thinking. Survivors may struggle with unbearable "what if" questions, moral injury, and persistent attachment longing that was never resolved. These reactions are not indicators of dysfunction. They reflect attachment bonds that were interrupted rather than completed.

This phase legitimises grief even when memory, relationship continuity, or public acknowledgment is absent. Survivors are supported to mourn losses that were never socially recognised and for which no rituals or communal frameworks existed. Grief is not linked to forgiveness, reconciliation, or understanding of the abducting parent's behaviour. It is treated as a personal and autonomous process.

Clinicians must be prepared for delayed and overwhelming grief responses, particularly when survivors learn of a parent's death years or decades after the separation. These reactions should not be framed as regression. They represent the emergence of grief that was previously unsafe, suppressed, or structurally impossible.

Phase A5: Truth Contact, Record Exposure, and Information Integration

Many abducted survivors feel compelled to seek external records in adulthood, including court files, police reports, school documentation, medical records, or family accounts. Others encounter information accidentally through death notices, genetic testing, online searches, or third-party disclosure. Contact with factual truth often destabilises identity and overwhelms coping capacity, particularly when it contradicts long-held narratives or reveals the scale of concealment.

Clinical support in this phase prioritises pacing, preparation, and containment. Survivors are supported in making deliberate decisions about what they want to know, when they want to know it, and what emotional cost they are prepared to bear. Full historical reconstruction is not positioned as necessary for healing. Accessing information is treated as a choice rather than an obligation.

For example, a survivor who discovers multiple illegal name changes or falsified documentation may require support to integrate this information without collapsing into unreality, rage, or identity disorganisation. Truth is framed as something to be metabolised gradually rather than consumed rapidly. The therapeutic task is not the accumulation of facts, but the stabilisation of the self in the presence of new information.

Clinical Decision Logic for Phase A5: Truth Contact and Information Integration

Clinicians must not assume that access to factual information is inherently therapeutic. Before supporting record retrieval, disclosure, or investigation, the clinician assesses the survivor's current regulatory capacity, identity stability, and emotional containment. If the survivor is experiencing active dissociation, emotional collapse, compulsive searching, or escalating agitation, truth-seeking activity is paused.

Truth contact should proceed only when the survivor demonstrates the ability to tolerate ambiguity, emotional activation, and incomplete information without destabilisation. If the survivor begins to experience sleep disruption, intrusive rumination, somatic overwhelm, or urgency to uncover "everything at once," clinicians slow the process and return to stabilisation strategies.

Clinicians must remain alert to external pressures that influence truth-seeking, including family demands, legal processes, media exposure, and internalised obligations to prove one's story. When truth-seeking is driven by performance, validation-seeking, or a perceived responsibility to confront others, clinicians reorient their work toward survivors' autonomy and safety.

If new information results in identity disorganisation, intense rage, or collapse, the clinician prioritises containment over further investigation. In these moments, therapy focuses on helping the survivor stabilise in the present rather than process content.

Throughout Phase A5, clinicians reinforce that the survivor retains control over what is accessed, when it is accessed, and whether it is accessed at all. Withdrawal from information-seeking is framed as self-protection rather than avoidance. Progress is measured by stability and agency, not by the quantity of information obtained.

Phase A6: Attachment Repair After Prolonged Separation

Attachment repair in abduction trajectories occurs under conditions that differ fundamentally from non-abduction family disruption. The targeted parent may be deceased, elderly, psychologically injured, physically unwell, or emotionally unavailable. Where reunion is possible, it often evokes complex emotional responses, including relief, grief, anger, longing, and disorientation, rather than simple reconnection.

Clinical work in this phase does not centre on restoring contact. It focuses on repairing internal attachment representations that were interrupted, distorted, or frozen during childhood. Repair may be relational, symbolic, or intrapsychic, depending on the survivor's circumstances and preferences. Survivors are not directed toward forgiveness, reconciliation, or the restoration of relationships. These outcomes are treated as choices rather than therapeutic goals.

Caution: Where the targeted parent is deceased, clinicians do not move automatically toward symbolic attachment work. If, and only if, the survivor expresses readiness, carefully paced non-contact attachment work may be considered, including unsent letters, narrative reconstruction, memory integration, or other survivor-chosen grief practices. These interventions are optional supports rather than expected steps, and they are used only when they strengthen stability, relational autonomy, and grief tolerance rather than intensify collapse, flooding, or coercive pressure.

When contact with the targeted parent is possible, clinicians support slow pacing, clear boundaries, and emotional containment. The goal is not to recreate a lost childhood relationship, but to allow adult-to-adult connection to develop safely, if desired, without pressure to resolve historical injury or perform emotional repair.

Across all presentations, attachment repair is framed as strengthening the survivor's internal capacity for connection, safety, and relational choice, rather than correcting family systems or repairing others.

Clinical Decision Logic for Phase A6: Attachment Repair After Prolonged Separation

Clinicians must not assume that attachment repair requires direct contact with the targeted parent. Before supporting reunion attempts, symbolic work, or relational exploration, clinicians assess the survivor's emotional stability, boundary capacity, and tolerance for relational complexity. If the survivor is experiencing heightened dependency, identity diffusion, emotional collapse, or pressure to perform reconciliation, attachment work is slowed or deferred.

When considering contact with the targeted parent, clinicians support gradual pacing, clear boundary setting, and realistic expectations. Rapid emotional reunification, idealisation, or attempts to recreate lost childhood relationships are treated as risk indicators rather than therapeutic progress. If contact produces destabilisation, guilt activation, or renewed conflict over loyalty, clinicians redirect the work toward stabilising internal attachment.

If non-contact attachment work is considered, clinicians continue to monitor for grief collapse, intrusive imagery, emotional flooding, loyalty activation, or pressure to perform forgiveness. If these responses emerge, the work returns to containment and regulation.

Throughout Phase A6, clinicians reinforce survivor choice and relational autonomy. Survivors are not required to maintain contact, forgive, reconcile, or repair family systems. Withdrawal, distance, or permanent boundary setting are recognised as legitimate outcomes when they support psychological safety.

Clinicians must monitor their own emotional responses, including rescue impulses, idealisation of reunification, or discomfort with survivor disengagement. These reactions are treated as supervision signals rather than treatment directives.

Progress in Phase A6 is reflected not in relationship outcomes but in the survivor's increased capacity to tolerate relational complexity, maintain boundaries, and engage in connection without self-erasure or survival-driven compliance.

Phase A7: Agency, Meaning-Making, and Adult Integration

This phase supports survivors to integrate their history into adult life without remaining organised around captivity or loss. Some survivors choose advocacy, research, public education, or legal engagement. Others prioritise privacy, family formation, creative pursuits, or deliberate distance from the past. There is no preferred pathway.

The clinical aim in this phase is agency rather than outcome. Survivors are supported to reclaim authorship over their lives, values, and future direction, with historical experience acknowledged but no longer functioning as the primary organising force of identity.

Integration does not require closure, reconciliation, or emotional resolution. It involves the gradual capacity to hold personal history without being dominated by it, and to make present-day decisions based on choice rather than survival conditioning.

Clinical Implications for Practitioners

Work with abduction survivors requires clinicians to slow pace, tolerate ambiguity, and resist pressure for narrative completion or visible resolution. Compared to non-abduction parental alienation work, treatment must prioritise safety before truth, identity coherence before relational repair, and grief recognition before reconnection.

This is not delayed reunification therapy. It is adult recovery following childhood captivity, enforced separation, and, in many cases, irreversible loss. Clinicians who approach this work without recognising the developmental severity of abduction risk minimise harm and destabilise survivors. Effective practice requires sustained ethical restraint, supervision, and a willingness to allow survivors to define their own endpoints.

Phase A Summary for Clinicians: Adult Survivors of Childhood Abduction

Phase A addresses the long-term psychological impact of childhood abduction as a form of developmental captivity. This phase is not a preparatory stage for reunification or confrontation. It is the core recovery pathway for survivors whose early lives were shaped by enforced separation, secrecy, identity disruption, and prolonged threat.

Clinical work in Phase A prioritises survivor safety, autonomy, and internal psychological stability over narrative resolution or relational outcomes. Survivors may enter this phase without recognising that abduction occurred, or with internalised beliefs of complicity, responsibility, or abandonment. These narratives are approached as survival adaptations rather than cognitive errors.

Across Phase A, clinicians support survivors to gradually reframe captivity dynamics, stabilise nervous system responses, reconstruct identity disrupted by concealment and relocation, integrate trauma without re-enactment, process complex grief, regulate truth contact, restore internal attachment representations, and reclaim adult agency.

Movement through Phase A is not linear. Survivors may cycle between stabilisation, grief, meaning-making, and identity work depending on life circumstances and emerging material. Progress is measured by increased regulation, relational autonomy, and reduced survival-driven compliance, not by contact outcomes, disclosure volume, or family system repair.

Clinicians working in this phase must maintain a disciplined stance of non-coercion. Pressure toward forgiveness, confrontation, reconciliation, or emotional performance replicates the dynamics of captivity and undermines safety. Ethical practice requires a slower pace, tolerance for uncertainty, and respect for survivor-defined endpoints.

Phase A concludes when survivors demonstrate increased capacity to live from choice rather than threat, hold personal history without collapse or urgency, and engage in present life without being organised around abduction.

Within the chapter sequence, the clinical focus now turns toward accurately identifying and formulating the survivor's developmental history. In practice, however, this work may begin earlier, particularly when childhood abduction is suspected but has not yet been clearly recognised or formulated. Without this step, therapeutic work risks addressing surface symptoms while leaving the organising injury unnamed. Phase B therefore centres on recognising childhood abduction patterns, reconstructing developmental context, and correcting the misclassification that commonly occurs in adult survivor presentations.

Phase B Opening Positioning

Position of Phase B Within the Applied Abduction Pathway

Although Phase A is presented first in this chapter as the principal abduction-recovery pathway, Phase B often operates earlier in practice. Its function is to identify, screen, and formulate childhood abduction histories in adult survivors whose presentation has previously been misclassified, minimised, or treated only at the symptom level.

Once sufficient developmental reconstruction and formulation have occurred, clinicians determine whether the survivor should remain within core HQTP work, enter the applied abduction pathway, or require the additional safeguards set out in the Extreme Harm Addendum. Phase B marks the point at which clinical work turns toward accurate developmental formulation. Where sufficient identity stabilisation, containment, and early grief recognition are present, the task becomes understanding what occurred in the survivor's childhood and how that history continues to organise present functioning.

This phase does not exist to establish legal certainty or factual completeness. Its purpose is clinical orientation. Without developmental reconstruction, therapy risks addressing surface distress while leaving the organising injury unnamed. Phase B, therefore, supports careful identification of abduction patterns, prolonged separation dynamics, and identity disruption while protecting survivors from premature truth exposure or narrative pressure.

The central task of Phase B is not discovery. It is precision. Clinicians learn to differentiate between alienation, concealment, prolonged disappearance, and irreversible loss so that treatment pacing, containment, and clinical direction are aligned with the survivor's actual developmental history rather than assumptions or generic trauma frameworks.

Phase B: Identification, Screening, and Developmental Reconstruction of Abduction Impact

Phase B focuses on helping clinicians and survivors accurately identify whether childhood abduction, prolonged concealment, or permanent relational erasure occurred, and to formulate the survivor's presentation within the correct developmental context. Many adult survivors do not enter therapy knowing that they were abducted. Instead, their histories are frequently framed as high-conflict separation, unstable caregiving, or family breakdown. As a result, treatment is often directed at anxiety, attachment difficulty, or relational symptoms without recognising the underlying injury of enforced separation, identity disruption, and long-term attachment rupture. Phase B corrects this misalignment by shifting clinical attention from symptom interpretation to developmental reconstruction.

Screening Indicators for Childhood Abduction and Prolonged Familial Erasure in Adult Survivors with Clinical Examples

Many adult survivors of childhood abduction do not arrive in therapy with an articulated understanding that they were abducted. In the author's research, survivors frequently reported that their experiences were not noticed by the majority of professionals, and when they were, it was framed as "a bad childhood," "family breakdown," or "unstable parenting." Unfortunately, for most of the PhD survivor cohort, they stated that they were never even asked about their parents' divorce, let alone abduction. As a result, treatment often targeted symptoms while leaving the organising injury unnamed.

For clinicians, screening for abduction is therefore not a discrete intake task. It is a longitudinal, formulation-driven process that relies on recognising patterns of erasure, concealment, and threat-based control, particularly when adult survivors struggle to construct a coherent developmental narrative.

Developmental and Historical Indicators

What Abduction Often Looks Like in Retrospect

Adult survivors frequently describe childhoods marked by instability that was never explained, never contextualised, and rarely permitted to be questioned. For example, one survivor recalled attending nine schools across three states before the age of fourteen, each move described as "keeping safe" or "escaping for being found and hurt." No court orders were ever mentioned, no custody explanations offered, and questions were discouraged. As an adult, this survivor presented with chronic hypervigilance and an inability to tolerate routine or predictability, initially diagnosed as an anxiety disorder.

Another survivor discovered in adulthood that their surname had been changed twice during childhood. They had assumed this was due to remarriage. When later attempting to obtain birth records, they encountered discrepancies that revealed informal adoption arrangements following a parental disappearance. Until that point, the survivor had no language for why identity questions triggered panic and dissociation.

Clinicians should also be alert to the total absence of one family system. In many abduction cases, survivors report knowing nothing about a parent's extended family. Photographs, stories, or keepsakes may have been destroyed or never existed. One survivor described believing their father "had no family," only to later discover cousins, grandparents, and siblings who had searched for them for decades.

Secrecy rules are another hallmark. Survivors may recall being instructed not to discuss family history, not to answer questions at school, or to provide rehearsed explanations to doctors or teachers. These rules were often enforced through fear rather than overt threat, shaping lifelong patterns of silence.

Psychological and Relational Indicators in Adulthood

How Abduction Presents Clinically

In adulthood, abduction-related trauma frequently masquerades as mood, anxiety, or personality presentations unless understood developmentally.

One common pattern is extreme fear around truth-seeking. Survivors may express a strong intellectual desire to access records or locate family members, yet experience panic attacks, collapse, or suicidal ideation when attempting to do so. In one case from the author's research, a survivor could speak calmly about searching for their parent in session, but became physically ill when opening an online records portal, a response previously misinterpreted as avoidance.

Another frequent presentation is threat-linked autonomy anxiety. Survivors may report that success, independence, or self-directed choices provoke dread rather than confidence. One clinician described a client whose anxiety escalated whenever life felt "too stable," later understood as conditioning from years in which autonomy increased the risk of discovery.

Relationally, survivors often oscillate between compliance and mistrust of professionals. Some appear overly agreeable in therapy while withholding crucial information, reflecting childhood strategies of survival under surveillance. Others repeatedly test clinicians' disbelief, having previously been dismissed when disclosing fragments of their history.

Moral confusion is particularly salient. Survivors may express disproportionate guilt for childhood actions, such as complying with lies or failing to "rescue" a parent. This guilt persists even when cognitive understanding is present, indicating moral injury rather than distorted thinking.

Clinical Red Flags Suggesting Abduction Rather Than Alienation Alone

Clinical Differentiation with Examples

While CPA-PA exist on a continuum, certain features warrant explicit consideration of an abduction pathway.

Permanent loss of contact without explanation is a key indicator. For example, one survivor believed their mother had "walked away." In adulthood, court records revealed repeated attempts by the mother to locate the child after an interstate disappearance. The survivor's lifelong abandonment schema shifted dramatically once this context was known.

Late discovery of parental suicide is another powerful indicator. Several survivors in the author's research learned, often accidentally, that a targeted parent had died by suicide following separation. These survivors frequently presented with severe moral injury, intrusive responsibility beliefs, and existential despair that had not responded to conventional trauma treatment.

Other clinical red flags include exposure to criminal exploitation. Survivors abducted across jurisdictions may report sexual abuse by stepparents or associates, involvement in informal labour arrangements, or unexplained periods of isolation. In some cases, survivors later discovered links to sex trafficking networks or false adoption practices, particularly where name changes and school mobility were extreme.

Once these distinguishing features are identified, clinicians require a structured decision framework to guide assessment, pacing, and response. Phase B, therefore, concludes with a practical clinical pathway designed to support formulation without replicating coercive or interrogative dynamics.

Transition From Phase B to Phase A Treatment Pathways

Once Phase B formulation has clarified the presence, structure, and severity of abduction-related harm, clinical work returns to the Phase A treatment sequence. The function of Phase B is not to replace treatment phases, but to ensure that Phase A interventions are accurately matched to developmental injury rather than misclassified symptom presentations.

Clinicians should not assume that all survivors require every Phase A domain. Selection and sequencing are guided by the survivor's current regulatory capacity, identity stability, grief activation, and exposure to unresolved threat. Movement between Phase B and Phase A remains fluid throughout therapy, particularly when new information emerges or when truth contact destabilises earlier assumptions.

At this point, the clinician's task is not progression, but precision. Treatment focus is determined by what is most destabilising for the survivor in the present, not by protocol order or completeness.

Phase B Closure Logic and Clinical Direction

Phase B does not conclude with a diagnosis or a definitive historical determination. It concludes with a formulation decision about clinical direction, pacing, and safety. The purpose of this phase is not to establish certainty, but to determine what type of therapeutic work is appropriate next and what must be protected.

When multiple indicators of abduction, prolonged erasure, or permanent separation are present, clinicians should formally shift the clinical frame from general parental alienation treatment into the abduction pathway outlined in Phase A. This includes prioritising survival reframing, identity stabilisation, and nervous system containment before any relational repair or narrative integration work is attempted.

When indicators are partial, ambiguous, or emerging, clinicians maintain abduction as a working formulation without forcing clarity. Ongoing longitudinal assessment is preferred over premature categorisation. Survivors are not required to resolve uncertainty in order to continue therapeutic work. Clinical safety takes precedence over historical completeness.

When the survivor demonstrates destabilisation during truth contact, including panic, dissociation, collapse, intrusive guilt, or suicidal ideation, Phase B work must pause. The clinician redirects to stabilisation and containment principles rather than continuing investigative exploration. This redirection is framed as protective pacing rather than avoidance or regression.

When ongoing external influence from an abducting or allied caregiver remains active, Phase B prioritises boundary protection, threat reduction, and autonomy development before any historical reconstruction is pursued. Truth-seeking in the presence of active relational control is contraindicated and risks reproducing coercive dynamics.

In all cases, Phase B decisions are guided by the survivor's nervous system capacity, not by the clinician's curiosity, research interest, or procedural momentum. The clinician's responsibility is to protect the survivor's autonomy, psychological safety, and developmental pacing while ensuring that treatment does not reproduce the same pressures that originally shaped the survivor's captivity.

Clinical Decision Pathway for Identification, Developmental Reconstruction, and Clinical Formulation

A Practice-Based Pathway for Identifying and Responding to Abduction Histories

Step One: Assess Narrative Coherence, Not Just Symptom Presentation

When adult survivors present with anxiety, depression, or relational instability, clinicians must assess whether the survivor is able to construct a coherent account of childhood separation rather than focusing solely on symptom profiles. Fragmented timelines, vague explanations for repeated relocations, or distress when basic developmental history is explored often indicate that the organising injury has not yet been named.

For example, survivors may report frequent moves, school changes, or sudden family disruption without being able to explain why these events occurred. Others become visibly dysregulated when asked about custody arrangements, parental absence, or early family structure. These patterns signal the need to slow the assessment process and hold abduction or prolonged concealment as a working clinical hypothesis.

At this stage, clinicians avoid pressing for factual clarification or detailed reconstruction. Premature information gathering can replicate interrogation dynamics experienced in childhood and may trigger defensive compliance, shutdown, or distress. The task is not to establish historical accuracy, but to determine whether the survivor's developmental narrative is sufficiently stable to support further exploration.

Step Two: Determine Whether Separation Was Time-Limited or Permanent

Once narrative coherence has been assessed, clinicians must determine the nature of the child's removal from the targeted parent. Separation may have been temporary, with contact later restored; prolonged and effectively permanent; or involve relocation to a location unknown to the targeted parent or deliberately made difficult to access. This distinction is clinically decisive.

From the author's perspective, and based on survivor accounts, any situation in which a child is moved away without the knowledge and informed agreement of the targeted parent constitutes abduction, regardless of how it is later framed. This is particularly significant in cases where court orders prohibited relocation, and the child was nonetheless moved in secret. In Australia, breaches of family court relocation orders are widely reported by survivors and practitioners, yet enforcement is often slow, inconsistent, and heavily burdened by cost and procedural delay. Once a child has been moved interstate or internationally, recovery commonly requires prolonged court action, significant financial resources, and repeated hearings, during which time the child remains separated, and attachment disruption deepens.

Within communities, schools, and extended family networks, these removals are frequently normalised. Moves are framed as "starting fresh," "needing a new beginning," or "getting away from conflict," and are rarely questioned by surrounding adults. This social silence contributes to the invisibility of abduction and reinforces the child's perception that what is happening is ordinary, unavoidable, or justified.

Where separation was brief, and contact was restored, alienation-focused treatment may be sufficient. Where separation was prolonged, permanent, or involved concealment, relocation without consent, or deliberate obstruction of contact, the clinical context changes fundamentally. In these cases, adult survivor advocates consistently identify the experience as abduction, even when legal systems failed to label it as such at the time. Treatment must therefore shift to an abduction-informed formulation that recognises captivity conditions, enforced disappearance, and long-term identity and attachment disruption.

Once the nature of separation has been clarified, clinicians must shift from descriptive history-taking to developmental formulation. At this point, the task is no longer to catalogue events, but to understand how prolonged absence, concealment, relocation, and disrupted attachment shaped the survivor's internal world. Without this shift, therapy risks treating surface symptoms while leaving the organising injury untouched. The following section, therefore, examines how these early conditions become embedded in identity, belief systems, relational patterns, and nervous system organisation across adulthood.

Clinicians must attend carefully to the explanations survivors were given to account for the parents' absence. These commonly include claims that the parent was dangerous, had died, did not care, did not want the child, or abandoned them by choice. Survivors frequently report hearing repeated refrains such as "He didn't want you," "She chose drugs over you," or "You're lucky, you have me," often framed as protection rather than exclusion. Fathers may be portrayed as deadbeat, violent, selfish, or absent by choice, while mothers may be described as unstable, immoral, addicted, or incapable of love.

For many survivors, these narratives were repeated throughout childhood and never counterbalanced by alternative accounts. Some have never heard a different explanation in their lives. At the same time, clinicians must avoid assuming that all narratives are entirely false. In some cases, elements may be partially accurate, exaggerated, selectively framed, or distorted over time. The clinical task is not to replace one story with another, but to hold uncertainty without prematurely closing meaning.

When survivors express a genuine desire to understand their origins, clinicians may cautiously support exploration through surviving relatives or others who knew the parents at the time, whether the relationship was brief, casual, or long-term. This process must remain survivor-led and carefully paced, as new information can destabilise deeply held beliefs about identity, belonging, and being wanted.

Clinicians must also remain open to more confronting realities. In some cases, the abducting or alienating parent may have deliberately chosen pregnancy while intending to exclude the other biological parent entirely. Later disclosures, such as "I just wanted a child so I wouldn't be alone", can create profound abandonment injury and confusion about whether the survivor was wanted by either parent. These themes require careful, non-avoidant clinical holding.

One abducted survivor described spending decades believing that her father "didn't want me," only to later discover letters he had written every year, all intercepted, retained and hidden by the AP's extended, allied family members. Treating this presentation as a standard alienation case failed to capture the scale of deliberate erasure involved, and the depth of grief associated with discovering that love and effort had existed but had been systematically concealed.

In such cases, the clinical frame must shift. The work is no longer focused primarily on relational repair or cognitive reframing, but on recognising and holding the long-term psychological impact of withheld truth, identity organised around enforced absence, and developmental loss that has never been named.

Step Three: Evaluate Ongoing Threat and Residual Capture

At this stage, clinicians assess whether the abducting or allied parent continues to exert influence over the survivor's psychological, relational, or behavioural functioning. Ongoing contact is not required for the threat to remain active. In some cases, survivors remain in regular communication with the abducting parent and experience destabilisation whenever records, truth-seeking, or boundary setting is attempted. Presentations may include sudden health crises, emotional collapse, or relational manipulation by the abducting parent that function to interrupt the survivor's autonomy. In these contexts, treatment must prioritise stabilisation, boundary containment, and nervous system safety before any historical exploration is undertaken.

In other cases, the abducting parent is no longer alive or accessible. Here, the threat often persists internally rather than externally. Survivors may experience panic, collapse, or intense anxiety when considering independence, identity development, or truth-seeking, despite the absence of an active perpetrator. Clinically, this reflects conditioned fear responses and internalised control rather than present-day relational danger. Treatment in these cases focuses on dismantling threat conditioning and restoring agency before proceeding with deeper historical work.

Step Four: Identify the Presence of Irreversible Loss

When survivors discover that a targeted parent is deceased, particularly in cases involving suicide, the clinical trajectory shifts in fundamental ways. The possibility of reunion, clarification, or relational repair is permanently removed, and survivors are confronted with a form of loss that is both relational and existential.

In some cases, survivors learn during adulthood, and sometimes during the course of therapy, that a targeted parent died shortly after separation or prolonged alienation. Presenting symptoms such as anxiety or identity disturbance may rapidly transform into profound grief, moral injury, self-blame, and destabilisation. Treatment focus must shift away from recovery fantasies or reunification narratives and toward grief integration, meaning reconstruction, and the containment of responsibility beliefs that often emerge in these contexts.

Clinicians must recognise that irreversible loss introduces a different therapeutic task. The work is no longer oriented toward relational restoration, but toward helping survivors carry the reality of permanent absence without collapse, self-erasure, or internalised blame.

Step Five: Determine Whether the Abduction-Specific Phases Are Required

The abduction-specific treatment pathway is activated when there is evidence of concealment, forced separation without consent, identity disruption, exploitation, prolonged disappearance, or irreversible loss. This determination is rarely made in a single session. In many cases, clinicians only recognise abduction dynamics after extended therapeutic engagement, particularly when survivors begin accessing records, encountering inconsistencies in family narratives, or reporting sudden destabilisation linked to truth contact.

Clinicians should remain alert to delayed recognition. Survivors may not initially name their experiences as abduction, especially when relocation, secrecy, or court violations were normalised by family members or institutions at the time. Activation of the abduction pathway reflects a formulation decision, not a diagnostic label. It signals the need to adjust pacing, containment, and therapeutic posture to account for the developmental impact of disappearance and captivity, rather than treating the presentation as alienation alone.

Step Six: Regulate the Pace of Truth, Contact, and Meaning-Making

Once abduction dynamics are identified, clinicians must make deliberate decisions about when and how to support truth-seeking, record access, or family contact. These processes carry high emotional and physiological load and can destabilise survivors who have lived for years within controlled or distorted realities.

Some survivors stabilise after confirming limited core facts about their identity or history without pursuing further contact. Others require extended preparation before engaging with extended family, legal records, or reunification attempts. In the author's clinical work and research, premature truth exposure has been associated with panic, dissociation, and increased suicide risk when not adequately contained.

Healing does not require exhaustive historical reconstruction. It requires enough truth to restore agency, coherence, and self-authorship without overwhelming the nervous system.

Clinicians must therefore privilege regulation and safety over completeness, and survivor readiness over therapeutic curiosity.

Clinical Positioning Statement

Abduction work requires clinicians to tolerate uncertainty and incomplete information far longer than most therapeutic models allow. Many survivors do not have language for what occurred, and some do not consciously recognise their experience as abduction for decades. The clinician's role is not to force recognition, extract disclosure, or prematurely define the narrative. It is to remain alert to patterns of disappearance, concealment, erasure, and threat conditioning as they emerge over time.

In the author's research, the most harmful therapeutic ruptures occurred when clinicians failed to recognise that a survivor may not yet know they were abducted and reframed the developmental consequences as ordinary family conflict, attachment disruption alone, or relational dysfunction. In other cases, clinicians pushed reconciliation, contact, or "repair" without understanding the conditions of captivity under which the original separation occurred.

Correct identification does not accelerate treatment. It protects survivors from misdirection, retraumatisation, and moral injury.

Clinician Countertransference in Adult Abduction Cases

Recognising, Containing, and Using the Therapist's Reactions Ethically

Work with adult survivors of childhood abduction reliably activates strong countertransference responses in clinicians. These reactions are not incidental. They arise because abduction involves prolonged deception, identity erasure, developmental captivity, and, in many cases, irreversible loss. When left unrecognised, countertransference can distort pacing, formulation, boundary decisions, and ethical judgement.

In the author's research with both adult survivors and MHPs, clinicians consistently reported feeling unusually protective, angry, morally outraged, or emotionally destabilised when the full scope of abduction emerged. Several described an urge to "fix," "expose," or "recover what was lost," particularly when survivors had been deprived of entire family systems or later learned of parental suicide. These reactions are understandable. They are also clinically dangerous if they are not examined and contained.

Common Countertransference Patterns

Rescue Urgency

Clinicians may feel compelled to accelerate truth-seeking, access to records, legal action, or family contact to restore justice or repair what was taken. This urgency often mirrors the survivor's own delayed longing for repair. When acted upon prematurely, it can overwhelm the survivor's nervous system, destabilise attachment safety in therapy, and recreate loss through collapse, dissociation, or suicidality.

Moral Alignment Pressure

Therapists may feel pulled to adopt a strong moral stance against the abducting parent and unconsciously communicate this to the survivor. While validation of harm is essential, excessive moral alignment can paradoxically increase survivor guilt, particularly for those who were coerced into compliance as children. Survivors may internalise responsibility for betraying the "good parent" or feel pressure to perform loyalty in the therapy room.

Disbelief Fatigue or Horror Response

Some clinicians report moments of disbelief when survivors disclose experiences involving trafficking, false adoption, or institutional failure. Others experience visceral horror that leads to subtle distancing, topic changes, emotional withdrawal, or over-clinicalisation. Survivors are highly sensitive to these shifts, having often been disbelieved or minimised throughout childhood.

Grief Entanglement

When survivors discover that a targeted parent died by suicide, clinicians may experience secondary grief, rage, despair, or helplessness. Without containment, this can lead to avoidance of the topic, premature meaning-making, or unconscious pressure on the survivor to "find purpose" in the loss. This risks repeating the survivor's experience of having emotions managed by others rather than held.

Ethical Use of Countertransference

Countertransference in abduction work is not something to eliminate. It must be recognised, regulated, and ethically used. Clinicians are required to monitor their internal reactions continuously and distinguish between what belongs to the survivor and what belongs to the therapist's own emotional system. Emotional activation should never be used to justify accelerating treatment, pushing disclosure, promoting confrontation, or shaping the survivor's narrative.

Ethical use of countertransference involves slowing down rather than speeding up, increasing containment rather than action, and strengthening survivor autonomy rather than directing outcomes. When clinicians notice internal urgency, anger, rescue fantasies, or moral positioning, the appropriate response is not to act but to pause, seek supervision, and recalibrate therapeutic pacing.

Regular clinical supervision is not optional in this work. Abduction cases carry a high risk of vicarious trauma, moral injury, and boundary erosion. Supervision provides a necessary external container where clinicians can process reactions without burdening the survivor or contaminating the therapeutic relationship.

Above all, clinicians must remember that the survivor does not need the therapist to feel outraged on their behalf. They need steadiness. They need emotional regulation. They need someone who can hold unbearable material without collapsing, rushing, or retreating. In abduction work, restraint is not passivity. It is an ethical discipline.

With the clinician's positioning stabilised, the work returns to the survivor. Once countertransference reactions are recognised and contained, therapy can proceed without being driven by urgency, moral pressure, or rescue dynamics. This creates the conditions necessary for the next phase of treatment, in which the survivor's nervous system, identity, and meaning-making processes can be engaged safely without replicating the dynamics of captivity. From this point forward, clinical focus shifts back to the survivor's internal organisation, developmental repair, and the gradual movement from survival-based functioning toward adult autonomy and integration.

When Not to Ask for the Story

One of the most consistent clinical errors in abduction-related therapy is asking for the survivor's full story too early. Contrary to common trauma therapy assumptions, disclosure is not inherently stabilising for adult survivors of childhood abduction. In many cases, early narrative exploration reactivates threat conditioning rather than supporting integration. Survivors whose nervous systems remain organised around danger often experience storytelling not as processing, but as renewed exposure to captivity dynamics.

Clinicians should avoid detailed narrative work when survivors demonstrate rapid physiological collapse, such as nausea, shaking, dissociation, or shutdown, when their history is approached. Other indicators include obsessive rumination followed by shame or suicidal ideation after sessions, deterioration in daily functioning when truth-seeking is discussed, compulsive reassurance-seeking about whether they are "bad" for wanting answers, or escalating interference from an abducting or allied parent as the survivor's autonomy increases.

In one clinical illustration from the author's research, a survivor repeatedly insisted on recounting childhood events because they believed this was what "doing therapy properly" required. Each session ended with panic, insomnia, and emotional collapse. Stabilisation only began when the clinician reframed containment as strength rather than avoidance and redirected the work toward regulation and present-day safety.

When these indicators are present, the protocol directs clinicians to temporarily shift focus away from narrative reconstruction and toward nervous system stabilisation, post-trigger recovery, boundary containment with current relational influence channels, and present-oriented identity stabilisation. Work at this stage centres on helping the survivor anchor in who they are now, rather than who they were forced to be. Meaning-making may still occur, but it is approached in a permission-based, non-chronological way that does not require detailed recounting of events. Psychoeducation regarding delayed memory emergence, coercion dynamics, and moral injury is also prioritised to reduce shame and internal pressure to "perform recovery."

Clinicians may communicate the rationale for this pacing by stating that the survivor's system survived by not knowing everything all at once, and that this protective adaptation is not dismantled until the body and nervous system demonstrate sufficient safety. This framing positions containment as an act of care rather than avoidance and reinforces the survivor's autonomy over the timing and depth of their own narrative.

When the Story Becomes Therapeutically Useful

Narrative exploration becomes clinically appropriate when the survivor demonstrates the capacity to remain regulated during discussion, to tolerate uncertainty without collapse, to differentiate historical threat from present safety, and to disengage from disclosure without fear of abandonment or relational rupture. At this point, the story no longer functions as an uncontrolled emotional flood. Instead, it becomes one component of integration rather than the organising force of therapy itself. The survivor is no longer driven to tell to survive but can choose when, how, and whether to access narrative material.

Closing Integration Note

Abduction-related trauma requires a therapeutic posture that is slower, quieter, and more restrained than many clinicians are trained to expect. Progress in this work is not measured by the volume of material uncovered, nor by the speed of insight, but by what the survivor is able to hold without terror, collapse, or destabilisation. The phases outlined in this chapter, together with the additions described above, exist to protect survivors from a secondary injury: exposure to the truth without sufficient internal and relational safety.

In the chapters that follow, these principles are extended into detailed clinical work addressing nervous system regulation, grief and moral injury, boundary development, attachment repair, and practitioner self-protection. Together, they form a protocol capable of holding the realities of disappearance, exploitation, and irreversible loss without reproducing those dynamics within the therapeutic relationship.

Phase B is therefore not a gatekeeping phase. It is a clinical navigation phase. Its effectiveness is measured not by the certainty achieved, but by the appropriateness of the therapeutic direction established. Movement between Phase B and Phase A remains fluid throughout treatment, particularly when new information emerges or when truth contact destabilises earlier assumptions. At this stage, the clinician's task is not progression, but precision. Treatment focus is determined by what is most destabilising for the survivor in the present, rather than by protocol sequence or structural completeness.

Extreme Harm Addendum

Adult Survivors of Childhood Abduction, Prolonged Concealment, and Identity Disruption

This addendum addresses a subgroup of adult survivors whose developmental histories extend beyond separation, obstruction of contact, or parental alienation alone. These are survivors who were physically removed from a targeted parent and extended family, often without consent or legal authority, sometimes across state or national borders, and in many cases for years or decades.

Many of these survivors were raised within environments organised around concealment and control. Their childhoods may have involved identity alteration, repeated school changes designed to avoid detection, enforced silence, chronic instability, exposure to severe violence, sexual exploitation, or ongoing threat conditions.

Furthermore, some only discover in adulthood that the targeted parent died by suicide during the period they were separated from them, or that repeated attempts to locate them by their targeted parent were actively blocked, intercepted, or erased.

In extreme harm presentations, the core HQTP phase structure remains essential but may require additional module-based guidance. The modules outlined below do not replace the six core HQTP phases. Instead, they provide an additional clinical map for presentations involving childhood abduction, prolonged concealment, identity disruption, fragmented sexual harm, bodily memory, irreversible loss, and boundary-controlled re-engagement or non-engagement. These modules may operate alongside, within, or across the HQTP's existing phase logic, depending on the survivor's history, stability, and current safety. In many cases, work within these modules occurs cyclically rather than sequentially, reflecting the layered and non-linear nature of recovery following prolonged concealment, captivity dynamics, and identity disruption.

Having outlined the Extreme Harm Modules, the protocol now returns to the core HQTP framework. These modules do not create a separate treatment pathway. They deepen the clinician's capacity to apply the same HQTP principles where abduction, concealment, identity disruption, exploitation, irreversible loss, or recapture risk are present: safety before exposure, agency before action, identity before narrative, and regulation before meaning.

Extreme harm trajectories commonly include patterns such as relocation across regions or countries without consent or court authorisation, false adoption or undisclosed guardianship arrangements, illegal or repeated name changes, serial school enrolments used to maintain concealment, enforced separation from extended family, culture, language, or ancestry, exposure to domestic homicide threats, organised violence, or sexual exploitation networks, abuse perpetrated by step-parents or substitute caregivers protected by secrecy and mobility, and adult discovery of parental suicide, death, or prolonged institutional failure to intervene.

Clinically, these histories do not function solely as attachment trauma. They represent developmental disruption under coercive control, prolonged loss of relational reality, and identity destabilisation requiring a distinct clinical posture and an expanded module framework.

Additional Modules Required in Extreme Harm Work

The Extreme Harm Modules do not replace the six core HQTP phases. They are included for survivors whose histories involve CPA-PA as well as more severe forms of harm, including childhood abduction, prolonged concealment, forced relocation, identity disruption, erased or altered records, repeated school changes used to avoid detection, enforced silence, blocked attempts by the targeted parent or extended family to locate the child, loss of culture, language, ancestry, or kinship connection, exposure to severe violence or threat conditions, familicide, homicide, suicide, the death of a targeted parent in the context of family-system conflict, sexual harm that may be remembered only in fragments or through bodily responses, harm by stepparents or substitute caregivers protected by secrecy and mobility, institutional failure to intervene, irreversible loss, and complex decisions about contact or non-contact.

These modules help clinicians slow the work down, hold the survivor safely, and recognise when standard phase progression needs additional clinical mapping. They must still be used within the HQTP's core logic: safety first, stabilisation first, supervision first, and no movement into deeper material before the survivor is ready. Phase I safety, stabilisation, supervision, and clinical containment remain the governing foundation.

The following Relationship Between the Core HQTP Phases and Extreme Harm Modules Diagram is included to help clinicians visualise how the Extreme Harm Modules fit within the broader HQTP phase structure. They are not a separate treatment model. They do not replace Phases I through VI. Clinicians should first ask, "Where is the survivor clinically within the core HQTP phases?" Only then should they ask whether one or more Extreme Harm Modules are needed to support safer formulation, pacing, containment, and supervision.

Relationship Between the Core HQTP Phases and Extreme Harm Modules Diagram

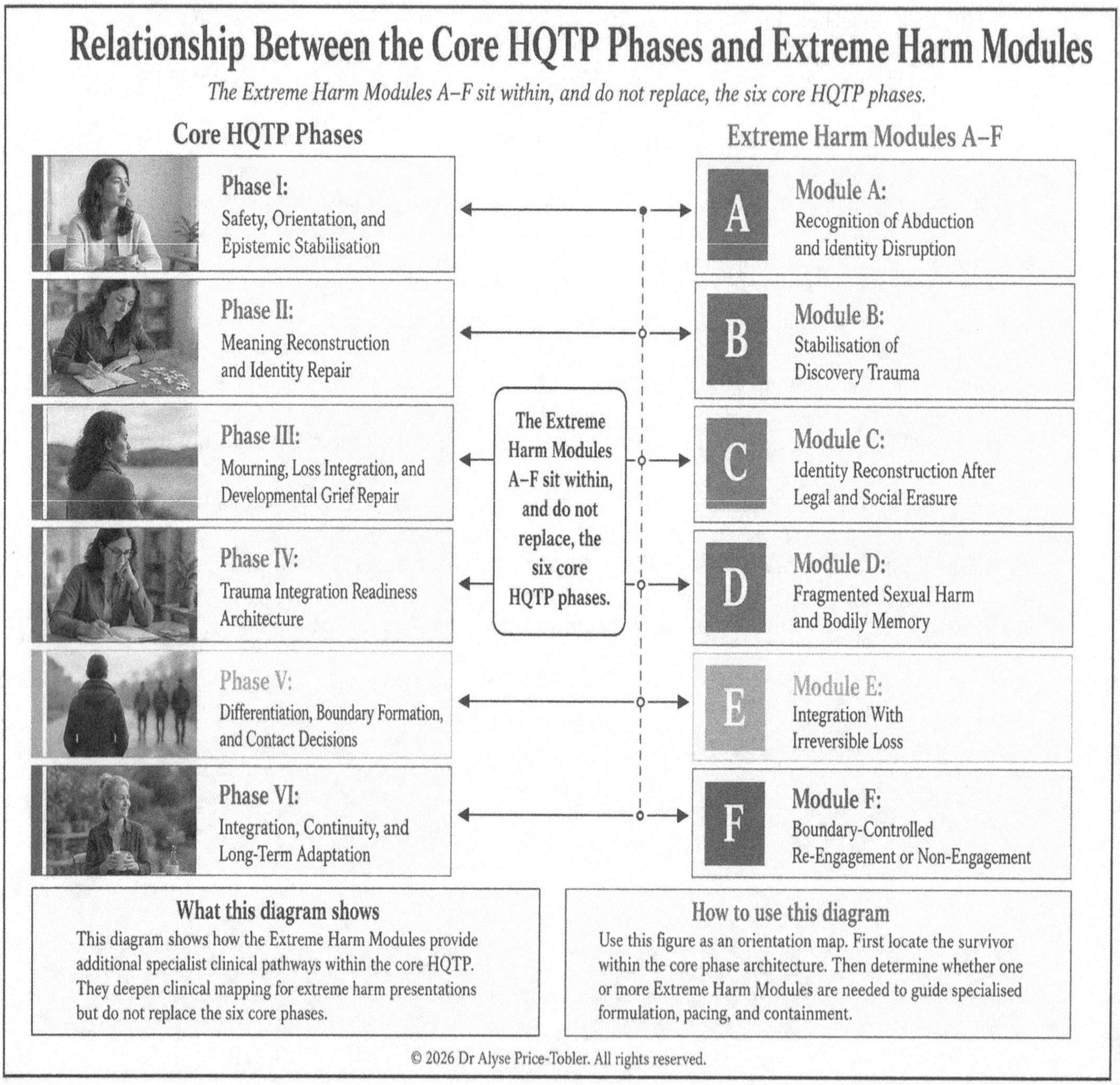

Clinical note. This diagram is not a step-by-step progression chart. Survivors do not have to move through every module. The modules are used only when the survivor's history or current presentation requires them, and only in ways that protect safety, readiness, autonomy, and clinical containment.

Extreme Harm Module A: Recognition of Abduction and Identity Disruption

Many adult survivors do not enter therapy identifying their childhood experiences as abduction. Some have never been given language for what occurred. Others minimise or intellectualise events to preserve psychological coherence. For some, the environment in which they were raised felt normal because no alternative reality was ever made available.

The clinical task at this stage is recognition without confrontation. Clinicians attend to indicators such as inconsistent biographical timelines, unexplained name changes, gaps in schooling or documentation, absence of family records, or persistent fear of authorities without an identifiable present-day cause. These signals are approached cautiously and tentatively, not as evidence to be proven, but as developmental clues requiring containment rather than interrogation.

Clinical work at this stage prioritises validating confusion as an adaptive response, normalising not knowing, restraining premature labelling, and, where appropriate, gently and provisionally introducing the concept of identity disruption. The goal is not to establish certainty, but to create psychological safety around the possibility that the survivor's history may be more complex than previously understood.

For example, an adult survivor may report attending "too many schools to count", be unable to produce childhood medical records, and become visibly distressed when asked about their legal name history. In this context, therapy focuses first on stabilisation and containment rather than investigation. The clinician introduces the idea that mobility and secrecy are often strategies used by adults who control a child's environment, rather than failures of the survivor's memory or understanding. This reframing helps the survivor begin to orient towards reality without being overwhelmed by it.

Extreme Harm Module B: Stabilisation of Discovery Trauma

Treating Revelation as a New Traumatic Event

For many adult survivors of abduction, the most destabilising moments do not occur in childhood memory work, but in adulthood, when previously hidden information suddenly becomes known. This may involve learning that a targeted parent died by suicide, discovering siblings or extended family for the first time, accessing court or police files, uncovering evidence of identity alteration, or realising that abuse was known by institutions and left unaddressed.

These moments are not memory recoveries. They are critical incident traumas occurring in the present. They carry the emotional force of shock, rupture, and irreversible loss, and they frequently overwhelm coping systems that had been organised around partial knowledge or protective not knowing.

Clinical work in this phase treats discovery as an acute trauma response rather than as insight or progress. Immediate priorities become safety, sleep stabilisation, physiological regulation, and containment of catastrophic meaning-making. Deeper trauma integration, narrative integration, or relational exploration is deliberately paused until the survivor's nervous system has returned to a tolerable range of functioning.

An essential task at this stage is to separate responsibility from outcome. Survivors often experience intense guilt, believing that their absence caused the parent's death, that reunion could have prevented the outcome, or that they failed morally by not knowing sooner. Clinical containment focuses on restoring developmental context and interrupting self-blame before these beliefs become entrenched.

For example, a survivor may locate a biological parent in adulthood and discover that the parent died by suicide years earlier. The survivor may rapidly spiral into shame, intrusive imagery, and existential despair. In this situation, therapy slows rather than intensifies. The clinician frames the response as a predictable human reaction to sudden loss and shock, introduces grounding and time orientation strategies, reinforces present-day safety, and defers meaning-making work until regulation has stabilised.

Extreme Harm Module C: Identity Reconstruction After Legal and Social Erasure

Restoring Selfhood Without Forcing Documentation

Abduction survivors frequently carry a profound sense of non-existence or instability of self. Many grew up with incomplete, falsified, or missing documentation. Some were raised under altered names. Others experienced repeated institutional disruptions that undermined continuity of identity. As adults, this can manifest as fear of paperwork, avoidance of official systems, difficulty asserting legal identity, or deep discomfort around signatures, records, and verification processes.

Clinical work in this phase focuses on restoring selfhood before pursuing documentation. Identity is treated as a lived psychological experience rather than a bureaucratic status. Survivors are supported in defining who they are now, separate from what may or may not exist on paper, and in developing internal continuity before seeking external validation.

Legal or administrative tasks are approached as exposure processes rather than neutral errands. Survivors are helped to pace record retrieval, passport applications, or name verification slowly and with regulatory support. Fear of institutions is framed as a learned safety response shaped by childhood concealment and surveillance rather than as avoidance or resistance.

For example, a survivor may avoid applying for a passport despite professional or personal need, reporting panic when confronted with forms, identity verification, or official signatures. Rather than interpreting this as procrastination or anxiety disorder, therapy recognises the reaction as a conditioned threat linked to historical identity instability. The clinician supports consolidation of internal identity and self-continuity first, then gradually introduces administrative tasks with co-regulation, pacing, and explicit permission to pause when overwhelm emerges.

Extreme Harm Module D: Fragmented Sexual Harm and Somatic Memory

Working Without a Single Perpetrator Narrative

In extreme harm trajectories, sexual harm and bodily violation may be present without a coherent narrative structure. Survivors who experienced frequent relocations, multiple caregivers, informal guardianship arrangements, or prolonged secrecy often report somatic reactions, boundary collapse, or aversion to intimacy in adulthood while simultaneously stating that they "do not remember anything happening". This pattern reflects fragmentation produced by survival conditions rather than the absence of harm.

Clinical work in this phase avoids pressuring survivors to produce disclosure, chronological coherence, or identifiable perpetrators. The body is approached as a primary archive of experience, holding procedural memory, threat responses, and protective reflexes that may exist independently of explicit recall. Validation of harm does not depend on proof, documentation, or narrative certainty. The clinical task is not reconstruction, but restoration of agency and bodily sovereignty in the present.

Therapy prioritises consent, pacing, and choice within the therapeutic relationship and in the survivor's broader relational life. Survivors are supported in developing boundaries, recognising bodily signals, and regaining a sense of control over physical and emotional proximity, without being required to interpret or explain the origins of these responses.

For example, a survivor may experience panic during physical intimacy yet insist that "nothing bad happened" in childhood. Rather than challenging this belief or attempting to uncover hidden memories, therapy respects the absence of narrative and focuses on present moment bodily safety, consent awareness, and relational pacing. Interpretive pressure is avoided to prevent retraumatisation and reinforce survivor autonomy.

Extreme Harm Module E: Integration with Irreversible Loss

Grief Without Reunion

For many extreme harm survivors, reunion is not possible. Targeted parents may be deceased. Extended families may remain inaccessible. Entire relational histories may have been permanently severed. In these cases, therapy must move beyond frameworks that assume restoration or relational repair as endpoints.

Clinical work in this phase supports grief that does not resolve into reconciliation, forgiveness, or closure. Survivors are permitted to hold sorrow, anger, longing, and love simultaneously without being forced into coherence or positivity. The aim is not to make the loss acceptable, but to make it survivable.

In extreme harm presentations, clinicians should not move quickly toward repair, forgiveness, meaning-making, or relational closure. The first clinical responsibility is to ensure safety, stabilise discovery-related distress, preserve survivor autonomy, and assess whether the survivor has sufficient regulatory and epistemic capacity to engage with the material without collapsing, being coerced, or retraumatising.

For example, a survivor may learn decades later that a targeted parent died during the period of separation and may then face pressure from others to "make peace", "forgive", or "move on". Within the HQTP, therapy does not reinforce these demands. The clinician supports the survivor in naming the loss, stabilising the shock, tolerating grief without collapse, and retaining authority over whether forgiveness, contact, silence, anger, mourning, or non-engagement has any place in their recovery. Some survivors may not wish to forgive the alienating parent and may not know whether this will ever change. Such uncertainty is respected rather than corrected.

Extreme Harm Module F: Boundary-Controlled Re-Engagement or Non-Engagement

In some extreme harm presentations, survivors may later face renewed contact pressure from abducting, alienating, allied, or extended family systems. This may occur after recognition, after a discovery event, after the death of a targeted parent, or after the survivor begins to establish a clearer sense of self. Contact pressure may present as apology, collapse, guilt, sibling triangulation, cultural obligation, family pressure, or demands for forgiveness.

Clinical work in this module does not direct the survivor toward contact, non-contact, forgiveness, reconciliation, or confrontation. The task is to support boundary-controlled decision-making that protects safety, autonomy, and psychological continuity. Survivors are helped to consider whether contact, limited contact, delayed contact, indirect contact, or no contact is clinically safe and consistent with their current capacity.

Clinicians monitor carefully for recapture dynamics, including sudden guilt, fear of abandonment, pressure to comfort the harmful parent, compulsive explanation, collapse into old roles, or loss of internal authority after family contact. When these indicators appear, the work returns to containment, stabilisation, and boundary scaffolding. Progress is measured not by whether contact occurs, but by the survivor's capacity to make relational decisions without coercion, self-erasure, or survival-based compliance.

Closing Integration Note: Returning to the Core Framework

Extreme harm presentations do not sit outside the core phase-based framework. They deepen it. The additional modules described in this addendum are not parallel tracks, nor specialist detours. They represent adaptive extensions of the same ethical principles that govern the broader model: safety before exposure, agency before action, identity before narrative, and regulation before meaning.

For survivors who have lived through prolonged concealment, identity disruption, exploitation, or irreversible loss, therapy must move more slowly, more cautiously, and with greater tolerance for ambiguity than most clinicians are trained to expect. Progress in these cases is not measured by how much history is uncovered, how many records are accessed, or how much grief is expressed. It is measured by the survivor's increasing capacity to remain present, make choices without collapse, and hold reality without being overwhelmed by it.

Importantly, movement between the extreme-harm and core phases remains fluid across the lifespan. Survivors may stabilise in one domain while destabilising in another as new information emerges, life transitions occur, or developmental milestones reactivate unresolved material. This is not regression. It reflects the layered nature of captivity-related trauma and the fact that many losses unfold over time rather than all at once.

Clinicians must therefore resist linear expectations. The work is cyclical, responsive, and relational. The protocol does not seek to "complete" survivors, resolve all unanswered questions, or produce closure. It exists to support continuity of self, coherence of identity, and the gradual return of authorship over one's life.

With this foundation established, the next section turns to the practical task of identifying extreme harm patterns in adult survivors who may not yet recognise their own history. Accurate screening is not a procedural formality. It is a protective intervention. Without it, survivors are at risk of being misclassified, misdirected, and retraumatised through inappropriate pacing and formulation.

What follows, therefore, outlines screening indicators designed to help clinicians recognise abduction-related and extreme harm presentations early enough to prevent a second injury occurring inside the therapy room.

Screening Indicators for Clinicians Working with Extreme Harm Presentations

Clinicians should consider extreme harm screening when adult survivors present with developmental histories that do not organise coherently around ordinary separation, divorce, or family conflict. These presentations often include inconsistencies in personal identifiers such as names, dates of birth, locations, or schooling histories, as well as unexplained gaps in documentation or repeated difficulty in obtaining basic records. Survivors may report long periods of mobility without clear reasons, missing medical or educational histories, or an inability to reconstruct basic timelines without distress.

A heightened and often disproportionate fear of authorities, institutions, or formal systems is another common indicator. This fear is not limited to anxiety about police or courts. It may extend to government agencies, hospitals, schools, legal processes, or identity-related paperwork. Survivors may experience panic, avoidance, or somatic collapse when required to complete forms, verify identity, or engage with official processes. Clinically, this reflects learned associations between institutional contact and threat, exposure, or punishment during childhood concealment.

Chronic identity disturbance is also frequently present. Survivors may describe feeling unreal, fragmented, or disconnected from any stable sense of self. They may struggle to answer basic questions about who they are, where they come from, or where they belong. This confusion often coexists with high external functioning, which can obscure the underlying developmental disruption. In extreme harm trajectories, identity disturbance is not a personality issue. It reflects prolonged disruption of continuity, belonging, and autobiographical coherence.

Somatic symptoms without accessible narrative memory are another important signal. Survivors may report bodily reactions such as panic, nausea, freezing, or dissociation without being able to identify specific traumatic events. These responses often emerge in relational contexts, during intimacy, when discussing history, or when engaging in truth-seeking behaviours such as record access. The absence of explicit memory does not indicate the absence of harm. In many cases, it reflects adaptive compartmentalisation developed under conditions where remembering or speaking was unsafe.

Clinicians should also be alert to panic or destabilisation linked to discovery events. Some survivors become acutely distressed when encountering new information about their past, including genetic testing results, death notices, family contact attempts, or institutional records. These reactions frequently resemble acute trauma responses rather than delayed emotional processing. The emergence of suicidality, intrusive imagery, or collapse following discovery is a strong indicator that extreme harm dynamics may be present.

Relational patterns shaped by secrecy rather than by open conflict further distinguish extreme-harm presentations. Survivors may demonstrate compliance, concealment, emotional withdrawal, or surface-level engagement in relationships, rather than overt conflicts over loyalty or triangulation. Their attachment strategies are often organised around invisibility and safety through silence rather than overt alliance with one caregiver against another.

It is critical to state clearly that the absence of disclosure does not indicate the absence of harm. Many survivors do not have language for what occurred. Others minimise, intellectualise, or normalise experiences that were profoundly destabilising. Screening is therefore not about extracting confessions or histories. It is about recognising patterns that suggest developmental captivity rather than ordinary relational rupture.

Clinical Decision Pathway When Extreme Harm Indicators Are Present

When indicators of extreme harm are identified, clinical priorities must shift immediately. The first task is stabilisation and safety. This includes assessing current risk, supporting sleep and daily functioning, and ensuring that therapy itself does not become another destabilising environment. Survivors who are actively processing discovery material or experiencing nervous system overwhelm require containment before exploration.

Discovery events should be treated as present-day trauma rather than as historical processing. When new information emerges, the clinician's task is to slow the work, orient the survivor to the present, and protect against impulsive decision-making, collapse, or self-blame. Meaning-making and interpretation are deferred until regulation is restored.

Investigative curiosity must be restrained. While clinicians may feel compelled to help survivors "find out what happened," premature fact-finding can replicate interrogation dynamics and activate threat conditioning. The survivor must remain in control of what is explored, when, and at what pace. Therapy supports choice, not exposure.

Identity consolidation is prioritised before documentation recovery. Survivors are supported to develop internal psychological stability and self-definition before engaging with records, legal processes, or administrative tasks that may reactivate historical vulnerability. When documentation work is necessary, it is approached gradually, with explicit attention to regulations and support.

Pressure toward reconciliation or family contact is avoided entirely. Extreme harm trajectories often involve irreversible loss, ongoing risk, or complex power dynamics. The clinician's role is not to restore relationships but to support survivor agency and safety. Any relational decisions must be survivor-led and grounded in present capacity rather than external expectations.

Finally, clinicians must increase supervision and consultation when working with cases involving extreme harm. The intensity of the material, the moral injury content, and the risk of countertransference distortion are high. Ongoing professional support is not optional. It is a core safety mechanism for both survivor and clinician.

Closing Note

Adult survivors who present with extreme harm histories are not "more damaged." They are individuals who survived prolonged coercion designed to disrupt continuity, erase identity, and fracture attachment. Their adaptations reflect intelligence, endurance, and survival under conditions most people never encounter.

This addendum exists to prevent a second injury: the replication of childhood powerlessness through therapy that moves too fast, demands coherence prematurely, or positions reunion, truth extraction, or emotional resolution as compulsory outcomes.

Effective work in this domain is measured by safety, internal coherence, and restored authorship over one's life. It is not measured by how much is uncovered, how quickly contact is made, or whether families are repaired. The aim is dignity, autonomy, and the gradual return of choice.

Cross-Referencing the Extreme Harm Modules A-F with PhD Findings

The extreme harm modules outlined above are not speculative additions. They are grounded directly in the author's twin PhD findings from the University of the Sunshine Coast, drawing on both adult survivor narratives and mental health practitioner accounts. What follows is an explicit mapping of each module to the core themes, patterns, and clinical implications identified across both studies. This cross-referencing is intentional. It makes clear that the Extreme Harm Modules are not an extrapolation from child-focused models, but an evidence-led clinical response to what adult survivors consistently report and what clinicians repeatedly encounter in practice.

Module A, which focuses on recognition of abduction and identity disruption, reflects one of the most consistent findings across the survivor cohort: delayed or absent conceptualisation of what actually occurred. Many participants described growing up within environments where concealment, narrative control, and normalisation of instability prevented them from naming their experience as abduction. Survivors frequently reported believing their childhood was "just chaotic," "unlucky," or "normal for our family," despite later recognising patterns of secrecy, forced relocation, and isolation from extended family systems. Practitioner data mirrored this pattern, with clinicians reporting that abduction histories were often identified only after months or years of therapeutic work. Module A, therefore, directly operationalises the research finding that recognition must be gradual, non-confrontational, and paced according to nervous system capacity rather than factual urgency.

Module B, which addresses discovery trauma and acute destabilisation following adult truth contact, is anchored in survivor accounts describing adult-onset psychological collapse following the emergence of new information. Participants reported intense reactions after learning of parental suicide, discovering siblings, accessing court records, or uncovering identity alterations. These reactions were consistently described as more destabilising than many childhood memories, supporting the finding that discovery itself functions as a new traumatic event rather than a simple cognitive insight. MHPs similarly described underestimating the impact of late-stage truth exposure and being unprepared for the intensity of grief, suicidality, and moral injury that followed. Module B therefore reflects the documented need to treat revelation as a present-day clinical crisis requiring stabilisation and containment rather than immediate integration.

Module C, which focuses on identity reconstruction following legal and social erasure, is directly informed by survivor reports of long-term identity instability. Many participants described persistent uncertainty about their name, family lineage, cultural belonging, and personal legitimacy. Several reported fear responses linked to official documents, forms, or institutional contact, reflecting conditioned threat associations tied to earlier identity disruption. Practitioner interviews confirmed that these presentations were often misinterpreted as avoidance, anxiety disorders, or executive dysfunction rather than identity-based trauma responses. Module C was therefore designed to prioritise internal self-definition and psychological continuity before any engagement with records, legal systems, or external verification processes.

Module D, addressing fragmented sexual harm and bodily memory, draws on survivor narratives describing somatic symptoms, intimacy distress, and boundary disruption in the absence of coherent autobiographical memory. Many survivors reported knowing "something happened" without being able to construct a linear narrative, particularly in cases involving mobility, multiple caregivers, or prolonged secrecy environments. Clinicians similarly reported discomfort with non-narrative trauma presentations and pressure to impose coherence prematurely. The inclusion of Module D reflects the doctoral finding that bodily memory and implicit trauma often carry the psychological load of extreme harm in ways that cannot be approached through traditional disclosure-based models.

Module E, which focuses on integration alongside irreversible loss, is grounded in survivor accounts of long-term grief following the permanent loss of parents, siblings, extended family systems, or the possibility of reunion. This was particularly evident in cases involving parental suicide, death during separation, or institutional failure to intervene. Survivors described ongoing cycles of grief triggered by life milestones such as marriage, childbirth, and anniversaries, rather than a linear resolution process. Practitioners echoed this pattern, reporting difficulty supporting clients whose losses could not be repaired relationally. Module E, therefore, reflects the need for a model that allows grief to coexist with forward living without imposing reconciliation, closure, or redemptive narratives.

Across both doctoral cohorts, a central finding was the repeated harm caused by treatment models that moved too quickly, prioritised exposure or narrative coherence, or assumed that insight alone would lead to recovery. The Extreme Harm Modules directly respond to this evidence by embedding pacing, containment, and non-coercive sequencing into the structure of care.

Rather than treating abduction as a variation of family conflict, this framework operationalises the research finding that prolonged concealment, identity disruption, and irreversible loss require a fundamentally different clinical posture. In this way, the extreme harm addendum functions not as an optional supplement, but as an evidence-informed extension of the core protocol. It reflects what survivors described needing, what clinicians reported struggling to provide, and what the data repeatedly indicated was missing from existing therapeutic frameworks.

The following section maps Module A of the protocol directly to the dominant recognition and secrecy patterns identified in the UniSC adult survivor and practitioner datasets.

Extreme Harm Module A: Recognition of Abduction and Identity Disruption

UniSC Survivor Themes: Delayed Recognition, Narrative Fragmentation, and Normalised Secrecy

Across the adult survivor cohort, delayed recognition emerged as one of the most consistent and clinically significant patterns. Many participants reported that they did not conceptualise their experience as abduction, concealment, or forced separation until well into adulthood. For some, recognition occurred only after entering therapy. For others, it was triggered by parenthood, relationship breakdown, genetic testing, or accidental discovery of records.

Survivors commonly described fragmented developmental timelines, uncertainty about names, residences, schooling histories, or custody arrangements, and a persistent internal sense that "something never made sense." However, this sense was rarely accompanied by language or frameworks that allowed the experience to be named. Instead, many reported having normalised instability, secrecy, and frequent relocation as simply "how our family was."

These findings directly inform module A's clinical emphasis on recognition without confrontation. The UniSC data demonstrated that many survivors maintained psychological stability by compartmentalising, minimising, or intellectualising early experiences. Abrupt naming of abduction or identity disruption, particularly when introduced by clinicians without sufficient regulation capacity, was associated with destabilisation, withdrawal, or defensive shutdown.

Practitioner participants reported parallel observations. Clinicians consistently described adult clients presenting with anxiety, dissociation, relational confusion, or identity instability long before any conscious acknowledgement of abduction emerged. Those who attempted to force narrative clarity or factual reconstruction too early frequently encountered rupture, dropout, or intensified distress.

Module A, therefore, operationalises a central research finding: recognition must be paced, relationally contained, and anchored in safety rather than accuracy. The task is not immediate labelling. It is creating enough internal psychological stability for reality to become psychologically tolerable.

Extreme Harm Module B: Stabilisation of Discovery Trauma

UniSC Survivor Themes: Adult-Onset Shock, Betrayal, and Institutional Harm

A defining contribution of the UniSC research was the identification of discovery trauma as a distinct clinical phenomenon. Survivors described adult moments of revelation that were experienced as psychologically destabilising events, rather than as delayed recollections of childhood harm. These moments commonly included learning that a targeted parent had died by suicide, discovering siblings previously unknown to them, uncovering falsified or withheld records, or realising that institutions were aware of their situation but failed to intervene.

Across survivor accounts, these events were consistently framed as fresh injuries. Participants described acute emotional shock, somatic collapse, suicidality risk, disorientation, and profound moral injury. The clinical presentation closely resembled acute adult trauma responses rather than memory-based processing of historical events.

This finding directly underpins Module B's emphasis on treating discovery events as present-day trauma requiring immediate stabilisation and containment. Practitioner data reinforced this need. Clinicians reported that when discovery trauma was not recognised, survivor responses were frequently misinterpreted as regression, resistance, emotional instability, or treatment non-compliance. These misinterpretations often resulted in inappropriate pacing and further psychological harm.

Extreme Harm Module C: Identity Reconstruction After Legal and Social Erasure

Position of Extreme Harm Module C Within the Applied Abduction Pathway

Extreme Harm Module C is not a separate treatment model. It functions as an applied stabilisation and identity-reconstruction pathway within the broader abduction framework when survivors require additional containment before developmental reconstruction, grief work, and identity reorganisation can proceed safely.

UniSC Survivor Themes: Loss of Continuity, Non-Existence, and Fear of Systems

Identity disruption emerged as a central theme across severe-level abduction cases. Survivors described not only attachment rupture, but a deeper erosion of personal continuity linked to name changes, false adoption narratives, repeated school enrolments, and the loss of cultural, familial, and historical reference points. Many articulated a persistent sense of being "unreal," "unregistered," or existing outside ordinary social recognition.

Survivors also consistently linked fear of paperwork, authorities, and institutional systems to earlier experiences of concealment, surveillance, punishment, or threat. These reactions were frequently misunderstood by professionals and mislabelled as avoidance, resistance, or poor engagement.

Module C directly reflects these findings. The UniSC data support the need to separate identity reconstruction from documentation recovery and to treat administrative processes as potential trauma exposures rather than neutral life tasks. Practitioner participants in the companion study reported significant gaps in training in this area, noting that well-intentioned clinical efforts to "clarify facts" or pursue records often retraumatised survivors by destabilising fragile identity foundations before adequate containment was established.

Extreme Harm Module D: Fragmented Sexual Harm and Bodily Memory

UniSC Survivor Themes: Somatic Distress Without Narrative and Shame Without Images

A subset of survivors reported experiences of sexual harm that could not be organised into a single coherent narrative. This pattern was particularly evident in cases involving multiple caregivers, stepparents, trafficking contexts, or prolonged secrecy and mobility. Survivors frequently described intense bodily reactions, sexual boundary collapse, aversion, or physiological distress in the absence of explicit memory images or chronological recall.

The UniSC findings demonstrate that these survivors were often invalidated within service systems that implicitly required verbal disclosure, linear storytelling, or identification of a specific perpetrator. In practice, the absence of narrative was frequently misinterpreted as the absence of harm.

Module D operationalises these findings by recognising the body as a legitimate carrier of trauma memory and by prioritising present-day safety, agency, and consent over disclosure. Survivor accounts consistently emphasised that pressure to "explain," "prove," or fully narrate sexual harm replicated earlier dynamics of coercion, disbelief, and powerlessness. Module D, therefore, establishes containment and bodily autonomy as primary therapeutic anchors in this domain.

Extreme Harm Module E: Integration with Irreversible Loss

UniSC Survivor Themes: Complicated Grief, Moral Injury, and Unfinished Attachment

Grief emerged as one of the most persistent and complex themes across the UniSC survivor narratives. In abduction contexts, this grief was layered and cumulative, encompassing loss of childhood, loss of identity continuity, loss of extended family systems, and, in some cases, the death of a targeted parent during the period of separation. Survivors frequently described profound moral injury, particularly when they carried beliefs that their absence, compliance, or inability to return had contributed to a parent's suffering or death. The research clearly demonstrated that this grief does not resolve through reunion narratives. For many survivors, reunion was not possible. For others, reunion intensified grief rather than alleviating it by exposing the scale of what had been lost.

Module E reflects these findings by rejecting redemptive, closure-driven, or reconciliation-based treatment models. The UniSC data support an approach that allows grief, anger, love, rage, and longing to coexist without forcing forgiveness or relational repair as therapeutic endpoints. Practitioner participants reinforced this, reporting that survivors often felt retraumatised when clinicians implicitly pushed meaning-making framed around acceptance, peace, or family restoration rather than psychological integration and autonomy.

Extreme Harm Module F: Boundary-Controlled Re-Engagement or Non-Engagement

UniSC Practitioner Themes: Risk of Re-Capture and Systemic Misinterpretation

Practitioner participants consistently warned of the risk of relational recapture following the development of survivor insight and autonomy. Survivors who began asserting boundaries were frequently met with intensified coercion, smear campaigns, sibling triangulation, emotional collapse displays, or moral pressure from extended family systems. Without explicit boundary scaffolding, survivors remained vulnerable to being pulled back into threat-based relational roles.

This directly informs the protocol's boundary decision framework. The UniSC findings support removing moral pressure to reconcile and repositioning contact decisions as clinical safety decisions rather than character judgements. Importantly, practitioners reported that survivors were often blamed or pathologised for choosing limited or no contact, reinforcing the need for clinician neutrality, validation, and protection against systemic misinterpretation.

Extreme Harm Addendum: Clinical Training Overview

Adult Survivors of Abduction, Prolonged Concealment, and Identity Disruption

This training framework is designed to support clinicians working with adult survivors whose childhood involved abduction, prolonged disappearance, enforced separation, identity disruption, or irreversible family loss. These presentations extend beyond the scope of standard attachment-based or alienation-informed treatment models and require a distinct therapeutic posture grounded in safety, pacing, and autonomy.

Extreme harm survivors do not present with "more severe symptoms" in isolation. Rather, they present with developmental adaptations shaped by prolonged coercion, secrecy, threat conditioning, and relational erasure. Effective treatment, therefore, prioritises stabilisation, identity consolidation, and ethical restraint over rapid narrative exploration or relational repair agendas.

Core Clinical Principles

Clinical work with extreme harm presentations is guided by the following foundational principles:

Safety is prioritised before truth exploration. Stability is prioritised before narrative reconstruction. Identity consolidation precedes documentation or legal processes. Grief recognition precedes considerations of reunion or reconciliation. Survivor agency is prioritised over externally defined outcomes.

The clinician's role is not to uncover all historical details, resolve family systems, or produce closure. Rather, the task is to create conditions in which survivors can remain regulated as they rebuild psychological coherence, meaning, and choice.

Module-Based Orientation for Extreme Harm Presentations

Extreme Harm Module A: Recognition Without Narrative Forcing

Many survivors do not initially conceptualise their history as abduction or concealment. Clinical recognition, therefore, focuses on identifying patterns of secrecy, mobility, identity disruption, and fear of institutional systems without imposing labels or prematurely confronting the survivor. Confusion and fragmentation are approached as adaptive survival responses rather than pathology.

Extreme Harm Module B: Stabilisation of Discovery-Related Trauma

Adult revelation events, including the discovery of parental suicide, access to concealed records, or identification of previously unknown family members, are conceptualised as present-day traumatic experiences. Clinical focus shifts immediately toward containment, nervous system regulation, sleep stabilisation, and safety rather than interpretive processing.

Extreme Harm Module C: Identity Reconstruction Following Developmental Disruption

Identity consolidation is prioritised before administrative or legal reconstruction. Survivors are supported in developing internal coherence and self-definition prior to engaging with documentation, record retrieval, or institutional processes that may activate threat conditioning.

Extreme Harm Module D: Fragmented Harm and Bodily Memory Integration

In cases where sexual or physical harm is held somatically rather than narratively, clinical work centres on present-day bodily safety, consent, and agency. Disclosure is not required for validation. The absence of explicit memory is not taken to indicate the absence of harm.

Extreme Harm Module E: Integration with Irreversible Loss

For survivors facing permanent relational loss, including deceased parents or permanently fragmented families, therapy supports mourning without imposing reconciliation, forgiveness, or closure frameworks. Emotional complexity, including grief, anger, longing, and ambivalence, is held without hierarchical valuation.

Extreme Harm Module F: Boundary-Controlled Contact or Non-Contact

Survivors are supported to make relational decisions based on psychological safety rather than moral pressure. Clinician neutrality is maintained, and protection against recapture dynamics is prioritised.

High-Risk Clinical Errors

The following practices increase the risk of retraumatisation and ethical breach in extreme harm work and should be actively avoided: premature truth-seeking; exposing adolescents or adult survivors to court records, medical records, school records, 'real' identity documents, child protection records, family documents, or digital records before they are clinically ready; framing disclosure as necessary for healing; prioritising documentation over regulation; applying reconciliation pressure; acting on rescue-oriented countertransference; and assuming investigative or forensic roles.

Assuming Investigative or Forensic Roles

Indicators for Pacing Reduction

These patterns frequently replicate earlier coercive dynamics experienced by survivors. Clinicians are advised to slow therapeutic pacing when survivors demonstrate physiological destabilisation during historical discussion, suicidal ideation associated with discovery processes, panic responses linked to autonomy or administrative tasks, compulsive reassurance-seeking regarding moral worth, or escalation of contact or coercion from abducting or allied figures. In these presentations, containment is conceptualised as a protective clinical intervention rather than avoidance.

Supervision and Practitioner Support

Extreme harm presentations are associated with elevated countertransference intensity, moral distress, and secondary trauma exposure. Ongoing clinical supervision is essential. Consultation is strongly recommended when working with abduction histories involving identity disruption, institutional failure, or parental suicide.

Clinical Orientation Statement

The HQTP is not designed to produce closure. It is designed to prevent further harm. Clinical progress is evaluated by improvements in safety, internal coherence, and survivor agency, rather than by reunion outcomes, narrative completeness, or symptom eradication alone.

Supervisor Companion Framework

Clinical Supervision for Extreme Harm and Abduction-Informed Treatment Work

This companion framework is designed for clinical supervisors overseeing practitioners working with adult survivors of childhood abduction, prolonged concealment, identity disruption, and irreversible relational loss. Supervision in this domain requires additional structural safeguards due to the high emotional load, ethical complexity, and intensity of countertransference associated with presentations of extreme harm.

Standard supervision models are often insufficient for this work. Supervisors must actively support clinician containment, formulation accuracy, and ethical restraint while protecting both practitioner wellbeing and survivor safety.

Supervisory Role and Ethical Responsibility

Supervisors working with abduction-informed clinicians have three primary responsibilities: safeguarding survivors' welfare, supporting practitioners' stability, and maintaining fidelity to trauma-informed, autonomy-centred treatment principles.

Supervision should reinforce that the clinical task is not investigative resolution, legal reconstruction, or moral adjudication. The supervisor's role is to assist clinicians in maintaining therapeutic precision, pacing discipline, and survivor-led direction.

Supervisors are encouraged to actively monitor for drift toward rescue behaviours, narrative urgency, or system-driven pressure that may compromise clinical safety.

Core Supervisory Priorities

Supervision sessions should consistently attend to clinical pacing and containment decisions, accuracy of developmental formulation, management of discovery-related trauma events, boundary architecture and protection against recapture dynamics, and clinician emotional regulation and countertransference processing.

Ethical Scope Maintenance and Documentation Practices

These priorities should be revisited throughout treatment, particularly when new historical information emerges or when survivors enter high-risk emotional phases.

Countertransference Monitoring and Supervisor Intervention

Extreme harm work reliably activates strong emotional responses in clinicians. Supervisors should actively screen for:

Rescue urgency and justice-driven action impulses. Moral over-alignment with survivor anger or grief. Emotional flooding, despair, or secondary trauma reactions. Avoidance of difficult material due to discomfort.

Pressure to Accelerate Truth, Discovery or Reconciliation

When these patterns appear, supervisors should intervene directly. Recommended responses include slowing the therapeutic pacing, refocusing on stabilisation goals, reinforcing autonomy principles, and supporting clinicians in tolerating ambiguity without acting prematurely.

Supervision should normalise emotional activation while reinforcing that ethical practice requires regulation before response.

Discovery Trauma and Crisis Supervision Protocol

When clinicians report that survivors have experienced a discovery event, such as learning of parental suicide, uncovering falsified records, or locating unknown family members, supervisors should immediately guide clinicians to treat this as acute trauma exposure. Supervisory focus should prioritise immediate safety planning, sleep and nervous system stabilisation, containment of impulsive decision-making, and temporary suspension of historical meaning-making work.

Assessment of Suicide Risk Escalation

Supervisors should discourage clinicians from using discovery moments for therapeutic 'breakthroughs' or narrative integration until regulation is restored.

Identity Disruption and Documentation Exposure Risk

Supervisors must assist clinicians in recognising that administrative processes, including birth certificates, court files, passports, or name-change documentation, often function as trauma triggers in abduction survivors.

Supervision should reinforce that identity consolidation must precede documentation work. Supervisors should guide clinicians to frame paperwork engagement as graded exposure requiring preparation, pacing, and co-regulation, rather than as routine life tasks.

Boundary Protection and Recapture Risk

Survivors who develop insight and autonomy frequently experience renewed pressure from abducting or allied family systems. Supervisors should support clinicians to anticipate and proactively plan for:

Escalation of contact attempts. Guilt-based manipulation. Sibling triangulation. Institutional pressure to reconcile.

Community or Cultural Coercion

Supervisory guidance should emphasise boundary scaffolding, prioritisation of safety, and explicit validation of no-contact or limited-contact decisions when clinically indicated.

Supervisor Self-Monitoring

Supervisors themselves are not immune to emotional activation when overseeing cases of extreme harm. Supervisors should remain attentive to their own reactions, including moral outrage, despair, over-identification with survivor narratives, or pressure to "fix the system." Regular peer consultation is recommended for supervisors working extensively in this domain.

Documentation and Risk Management Guidance

Supervisors should reinforce documentation practices that are:

Clinically descriptive rather than investigative.

Neutral in tone

Focused on observed clinical phenomena.

Free from speculative language.

Aligned with the therapeutic scope of practice

Supervision should discourage clinicians from assuming forensic roles or acting beyond professional boundaries.

Closing Supervisory Orientation Statement

Supervising familial abduction- and developmental harm-informed clinical work requires patience, restraint, and ethical clarity. The primary measure of effective supervision is not speed of progress, narrative completeness, or family reunification outcomes. Rather, it lies in preserving the safety of survivors, clinician stability, and therapeutic integrity. This companion framework is intended to ensure that clinicians are not left to carry this work alone and that survivors are protected from secondary harm arising from well-intentioned but misdirected interventions.

Adult survivors of familial abduction frequently present with overlapping patterns of developmental harm, attachment disruption, identity instability, grief, fear, and relational disorganisation that do not unfold in a simple or linear sequence. Within the HQTP, these presentations require careful formulation, pacing, and phase-informed decision-making, grounded in safety, stabilisation, identity grounding, grief integration, trauma-processing readiness, and later boundary formation. The following table is presented as a clinical mapping tool to assist practitioners in linking key findings from the author's UniSC twin doctoral research with common adult survivor presentations, primary therapeutic tasks, and the risks associated with rushed or poorly sequenced intervention.

Table. Adult Survivors of Familial Abduction and Developmental Harm

Phase-Based Clinical Mapping of UniSC Twin PhD Findings, Survivor Presentations, and Clinical Tasks

Phase	UniSC Twin PhD Core Findings	Common Adult Survivor Presentations	Primary Clinical Tasks	Clinical Risks if Missed or Rushed
Phase A: Recognition of Abduction and Identity Disruption	Survivors frequently do not conceptualise their experience as abduction until adulthood. Delayed recognition is adaptive rather than avoidant. Fragmented timelines, name changes, school instability, secrecy rules, and narrative discontinuity are common.	Confusion about childhood history, vague or inconsistent biographical details, discomfort completing official forms, persistent sense that "something is missing," anxiety when asked about family or early life.	Pace recognition without confrontation. Validate confusion as a survival-based adaptation. Support meaning-making without demanding clarity or proof. Track emotional responses to insight rather than factual completeness.	Premature naming can destabilise identity, trigger collapse, and increase withdrawal from therapy. Forcing clarity risks replicating coercive childhood dynamics.
Phase B: Stabilisation of Discovery Trauma	Adult discovery events such as learning of abduction, trafficking, false adoption, or parental suicide frequently produce acute trauma responses comparable to new injuries. Survivors report shock, dissociation, suicidality risk, and existential destabilisation.	Panic attacks, intrusive thoughts or images following discovery, sleep disruption, suicidality risk, somatic distress, sudden decline in daily functioning after new information emerges.	Treat discovery as present-day trauma. Prioritise stabilisation, containment, and safety planning. Slow processing. Normalise intensity as expected rather than pathological.	Misinterpreting discovery trauma as regression or emotional instability increases suicide risk and retraumatisation.

Phase	UniSC Twin PhD Core Findings	Common Adult Survivor Presentations	Primary Clinical Tasks	Clinical Risks if Missed or Rushed
Phase C: Identity Grounding After Legal and Social Disruption	Survivors describe identity disruption linked to altered documentation, repeated relocations, informal adoption arrangements, and institutional failure. Fear of systems and paperwork is common and frequently misunderstood	Avoidance of documentation tasks, anxiety around identity records, difficulty asserting personal history, shame related to "not knowing who I am," mistrust of professionals and institutions.	Separate identity repair from administrative recovery. Support internal continuity before engaging in documentation. Pace records work as graded exposure rather than routine task.	Forcing documentation or proof prematurely can trigger dissociation, shutdown, or disengagement from therapy.
Phase D: Fragmented Sexual Harm and Bodily Memory	Sexual harm in abduction contexts is often fragmented, non-linear, and without coherent narrative memory. Survivors report somatic responses without explicit recall. Disclosure pressure is experienced as retraumatising.	Sexual boundary confusion, bodily distress, shame without narrative memory, dissociation, intimacy difficulties, autonomic fear responses without identifiable trigger.	Validate body-based memory. Prioritise present safety and agency. Avoid demands for disclosure or chronological reconstruction. Use stabilisation-oriented and somatic-informed approaches.	Pressuring narrative disclosure replicates earlier coercion and reinforces survivor self-blame and mistrust.
Phase E: Mourning, Loss Integration, and Developmental Grief Repair	Many survivors discover that a targeted parent has died, including by suicide. Grief is layered, moral, and unresolved. Reunion narratives are frequently	Acute grief spikes, intrusive guilt ("If I had known…"), anger toward systems, despair, existential questioning, destabilisation	Allow grief without forcing meaning, forgiveness, or closure. Support moral injury processing. Hold love, anger, and grief simultaneously	Premature reframing toward acceptance or peace invalidates loss and deepens despair.

Phase	UniSC Twin PhD Core Findings	Common Adult Survivor Presentations	Primary Clinical Tasks	Clinical Risks if Missed or Rushed
	unavailable or destabilising.	following loss discovery.	without hierarchy.	
Phase F: Boundary Formation and Contact Decisions	Practitioner findings identified risk of re-capture and systemic misinterpretation when survivors begin exercising autonomy around contact. Renewed coercive pressure, guilt-based manipulation, sibling triangulation, and institutional pressure to reconcile may reactivate threat and destabilisation.	Ambivalence about contact, panic or urgency around relational decisions, fear of retaliation, guilt, pressure to reconcile, withdrawal after perceived recommendations, and escalating anxiety when autonomy is exercised.	Support boundary-controlled contact or non-contact based on psychological safety rather than moral pressure. Maintain clinician neutrality, monitor for recapture dynamics, pace relational exploration, and reinforce survivor agency and transparency in clinical reasoning.	Premature contact guidance, reconciliation pressure, or directive framing can replicate coercive dynamics, narrow perceived options, trigger withdrawal or compliance without integration, and increase anxiety or disengagement.

Note. This table is intended as a clinical orienting guide within the HQTP, grounded in the author's UniSC twin doctoral research and subsequent clinical refinement. It is presented as a phase-based decision guide for therapeutic formulation with adult survivors of familial abduction and severe developmental harm. Movement across phases is not linear and should be determined by survivor safety, stabilisation, readiness, regulation, functional capacity, relational tolerance, and clinical judgement rather than elapsed time. Presentation may overlap across phases, and some survivors may require repeated return to earlier stabilisation work before progressing. This table is intended for therapeutic use only and is not designed for forensic determination, evidentiary purposes, or legal adjudication.

Comparative Clinical Survivor Examples

Abduction, Alienation, Identity Reconstruction, and Layered Systems of Control

Michelle Marie Newton

Long-term CPA-PAA cases demonstrate that childhood separation rarely exists in isolation. Instead, survivors often experience multi-layered systems of control that include identity manipulation, attachment disruption, institutional invisibility, and, in some cases, ideological or religious enclosure. The experiences of Michelle Marie Newton, Scott Berne, and Dawn McCarty illustrate distinct yet converging developmental injury pathways that clinicians increasingly encounter among adult survivors.

Michelle Marie Newton was abducted at age three in Louisville, Kentucky in 1983 and lived more than four decades unaware of her missing-child status. Raised under a different identity narrative, she only learned of her abduction during court proceedings following the arrest of her mother, Debra Leigh Curry Newton, on custodial interference charges in 2025 (ABC7 News, 2025; WDRB News, 2025). At the time of writing, her mother has pleaded not guilty, and the case remains pending. Media reporting further indicates that Michelle has experienced emotional pressure from her mother to withdraw cooperation with prosecution efforts, reflecting the continuation of coercive relational dynamics even after legal intervention. Clinically, this represents a form of post-discovery relational intrusion that places survivors in conflicted loyalty positions and can destabilise emerging identity reconstruction.

Scott Berne

Scott Berne's childhood abduction occurred in 1978 following a custody dispute, during which he and his brother were relocated across multiple countries under false identities (Berne, 2019; Spectrum News, 2015). Unlike Newton's late discovery, Berne retained memory of pre-abduction attachment to his father while simultaneously being subjected to psychological coercion that included being told his father was deceased. Public accounts further describe extreme violence associated with the abduction context, including reports that his mother hired a hitman to kill his father and that security measures, including bodyguards, were required for periods during his schooling. This illustrates how some abduction environments extend beyond separation into sustained threat exposure, producing chronic hypervigilance and long-term nervous system dysregulation. In clinical terms, this reflects developmental trauma embedded within relational and environmental danger rather than discrete traumatic events. To see the talk that Scott gave at the NAUWOU conference in 2024, please go to Dr Price-Tobler's YouTube Parental Alienation Channel https://www.youtube.com/watch?v=ZTFSQiHnoh8

Dawn McCarty

Dawn McCarty's experience adds an additional structural layer relevant to clinical understanding. Following her abduction and removal from her biological family, McCarty was raised within the Mormon church, creating an environment where religious authority, family narrative control, and identity formation became intertwined. Public documentation and survivor testimony indicate that she was raised under fabricated origin narratives and later discovered that her childhood identity had been constructed through unlawful removal and adoption processes. Through personal communication, McCarty has described the psychological impact of learning in adulthood that her familial, cultural, and spiritual identity foundations were built upon deception, including profound attachment confusion, grief, and identity fragmentation (D. McCarty, personal communication, 2024). For clinicians, this highlights the role of institutional and ideological structures in reinforcing alienation dynamics, particularly when religious or community systems implicitly validate false family narratives. To see the talk that Dawn gave at the NAUWOU conference in 2024, please go to

https://www.youtube.com/watch?v=Ob4xYUXCRZI

Across all three cases, common developmental injury patterns emerge despite differing contextual details. Attachment rupture occurs through forced separation from a targeted parent and extended family network. Epistemic injury develops when survivors discover that core autobiographical information has been falsified or withheld. Identity destabilisation occurs when adult survivors attempt to reconcile competing life narratives shaped by radically different relational environments. In Newton's case, identity rupture emerges suddenly in midlife. In Berne's case, it unfolds across childhood and adolescence under conditions of persistent threat. In McCarty's case, it is compounded by institutional and religious enclosure that reinforced narrative control.

For clinicians, these cases offer critical guidance. First, adult survivors presenting with abduction and alienation histories should not be approached as conventional trauma cases. The presenting distress often reflects layered developmental injury rather than isolated events. Second, practitioners must be attentive to ongoing coercive dynamics that may persist long after physical separation has ended, including emotional pressure from abducting caregivers, family systems, or community institutions. Third, identity reconstruction must be treated as a central therapeutic task, not a secondary outcome of trauma processing.

The HQTP was developed to address precisely these complex, layered presentations in contemporary clinical practice. While it would be inappropriate to retrospectively prescribe treatment pathways to individual survivors whose stories are publicly documented, the framework offers clinicians a structured orientation for working with similar adult survivor populations. Its phased sequencing emphasises early stabilisation and psychological containment, protection of emerging identity coherence, careful pacing of trauma processing, and explicit support for relational autonomy. This approach is particularly relevant for survivors whose histories include false identities, prolonged separation, institutional complicity, and delayed justice processes.

For practitioners, these cases do not serve as exceptional anomalies but as increasingly visible examples of the broader clinical population. Survivors encountering this material may also recognise aspects of their own histories within these narratives, including fragmented memory, loyalty conflict, identity confusion, and delayed awareness of abuse dynamics. Clinicians are therefore encouraged to approach such presentations with humility, pacing, and developmental sensitivity, recognising that healing is not linear and that integration occurs over time rather than through rapid disclosure or forced reconciliation.

Clinical Orientation Examples for Abduction-Related Presentations

It is important for MHPs to be aware of two provisional clinical observations identified during coding of the author's doctoral data on adult survivors. Within a subgroup of survivors who experienced severe parental alienation and abduction in early childhood, three of four participants described a distinct anxiety presentation. This provisional observation may hold important clinical implications, particularly given the limited literature on the combined developmental impact of severe parental alienation and abduction in very young children. Although specific phobias and abduction-related trauma have each been examined independently, their intersection remains underexplored. The finding suggests that some children exposed to both severe parental alienation and abduction may later exhibit long-term anxiety and behavioural patterns not adequately captured within existing trauma frameworks.

Given the preliminary nature of this observation, the purpose of including it here is not to overstate certainty, but to alert clinicians to a possible anxiety presentation requiring careful assessment, further research, and cautious clinical formulation. Readers seeking fuller discussion are directed to Volume One of the author's first doctoral study, 'Disrupting the Intergenerational Trauma Cycle of High Conflict Divorce.'

Clinical Application of the Specific Phobia–CPA-PAA Anxiety Variant

This section is positioned immediately before Phase I, as the SPAA-specific phobia variant is a newly identified clinical presentation arising from doctoral research (Price-Tobler, 2023a). This section provides practical guidance for clinicians on applying this presentation in therapeutic contexts.

Survivors exposed to combined CPA-PAA during early childhood often present with early-conditioned threat responses. These responses can significantly alter treatment readiness, session engagement patterns, relational safety capacity, and tolerance for emotional activation across all phases of the HQTP. Such developmental adaptations reflect prolonged exposure to concealment, forced relocation, caregiver deception, identity disruption, and, in some cases, media exposure related to missing-child narratives or public searches.

While the HQTP offers a unified phased approach for adult survivors of child psychological abuse, survivors of SPAA present as a higher-complexity subgroup. For this subgroup, treatment requires slower sequencing, extended stabilisation windows, enhanced consent-based pacing, and heightened attention to survival responses, particularly flight-based survival mechanisms.

Without differentiation, clinicians risk misinterpreting survival adaptations as resistance, prematurely advancing trauma processing, mislabelling relational mistrust as pathology, and underestimating the cumulative impact of prolonged threat conditioning.

Primary red flag indicators in these survivors include persistent hypervigilance, discomfort with observation, relational mistrust, abrupt session withdrawal, difficulty remaining in enclosed spaces, avoidance of emotionally activating material, and repeated disengagement following therapeutic activation.

These behaviours reflect conditioned survival responses rather than a lack of motivation or noncompliance with treatment.

In clinical practice, this presentation is conceptualised as a developmentally embedded safety adaptation rather than a standalone diagnostic entity. Treatment, therefore, prioritises stabilisation, identity coherence, and relational recalibration before trauma processing is introduced. This section acts as a bridge for clinical orientation, enabling clinicians to adjust pacing decisions across all subsequent phases.

Research Note: Provisional Clinical Observation

The SPAA-specific phobia variant referenced in this section was identified during the author's doctoral qualitative research program (Price-Tobler, 2023a). It is presented as a provisional clinical observation, rather than a formal diagnostic classification. The clinical relevance of this variant is still being explored, as it has not yet been widely documented in existing SPA or abduction literature to the author's knowledge.

The provisional nature of the SPAA-specific phobia variant calls for clinical vigilance and should be used as a treatment pacing and safety descriptor, rather than a diagnostic label. Clinicians are encouraged to use this construct to inform treatment decisions and to recognise that further empirical investigation is needed to validate and expand this clinical observation. For empirical foundations and participant data that inform this clinical orientation, please refer to the earlier research-informed discussion of the Specific Phobia–CPA-PAA Anxiety Variant, in which the original doctoral terminology is also explained (Price-Tobler, 2023a).

Clinical Advisory: Extreme Harm Specific Phobia–CPA-PAA Presentations and Risk-Adjusted Treatment

When CPA-PA and abduction occur together, extreme coercive behaviours may follow, including credible threats of violence, contracted harm, stalking, arson, or prolonged concealment. Clinicians must treat these cases as high-risk developmental trauma presentations, requiring enhanced containment and ethical caution.

Survivors with extreme-harm Specific Phobia–CPA-PAA presentations frequently demonstrate elevated nervous system sensitivity, complex attachment disruption, identity instability, and heightened vulnerability to retraumatisation. As a result, entry into treatment should proceed with explicit pacing agreements, prioritisation of stabilisation, and clear consent boundaries regarding the depth and pace of therapeutic work.

Structured safety and destabilisation screenings should be conducted prior to initiating trauma-focused exploration. This includes assessment of current contact with abducting caregivers, evaluation of legal proceedings, and media exposure reactivation to avoid triggering past trauma. Additionally, clinicians must assess ongoing coercive influence and environmental stability. If active risk factors remain, Phase I stabilisation may need to be extended significantly before progression can be considered. These periods often reactivate threat conditioning, requiring anticipatory pacing, containment, and support.

A critical red flag in extreme-harm Specific Phobia–CPA-PAA presentations is rapid emotional flooding following initial disclosure. This may manifest as dissociation, somatic shutdown, panic symptoms, or abrupt treatment disengagement. These reactions should signal to clinicians that slowing the pacing is essential rather than assuming readiness for deeper trauma processing.

Boundary management is vital in these presentations. Survivors may oscillate between intense dependency and abrupt withdrawal. Therapists must maintain consistent session structure, predictable scheduling, and transparent therapeutic framing to support safety without replicating control dynamics.

Given the ethical complexity and emotional intensity associated with extreme-harm Specific Phobia–CPA-PAA work, specialist-informed clinical supervision is strongly recommended. Supervision should specifically address countertransference reactions, over-rescue impulses, and the pressure to accelerate treatment due to perceived survivor urgency or external legal timelines.

This advisory layer does not replace the HQTP phased architecture. Instead, it serves as a risk-adjustment filter applied to all subsequent phases when extreme-harm indicators are present. These safeguards are necessary to restore ethical alignment, clinical stability, and phase-appropriate care.

This section concludes the guidance on pacing and risk adjustment and transitions to the HQTP phase architecture. The following phases should be applied with these modifications to stabilisation, containment, and sequencing in mind.

This advisory layer serves as a risk-adjustment filter applied across all HQTP phases when extreme-harm indicators are present. Because clinical pacing decisions in these cases are ethically complex and vulnerable to countertransference, structured clinical supervision is positioned as a core containment mechanism within the protocol. The following section outlines a supervision framework designed to support phase integrity, manage clinical drift, and maintain survivor safety.

Clinical Supervision Protocol

Working with Adult Survivors of Abduction and Extreme Harm

This section examines how inadequate supervision, rigid theoretical frameworks, unmanaged countertransference, and systemic pressures can unintentionally cause further harm to survivors. The role of clinical supervision in this process cannot be overstated. Supervision must serve as a critical safeguard to ensure that clinicians are appropriately managing countertransference, clinical drift, and ethical dilemmas that arise when working with survivors who have experienced prolonged coercion and abuse. This section will outline the supervision protocol specifically designed for clinicians working with adult survivors of abduction and extreme harm, ensuring that clinical practice remains aligned with ethical standards, clinical integrity, and survivor safety.

Survivors of CPA-PA differ fundamentally from survivors of single-incident trauma. Many were removed, renamed, relocated, or concealed across years or decades. Their developmental environments were organised around secrecy, obedience, and survival rather than continuity, safety, or identity formation. In adulthood, this often presents as layered grief for relationships never recovered, families never known, and truths discovered too late to repair. Clinical work with this population requires restraint, precision, and ethical clarity.

Treatment must prioritise stabilisation over disclosure, consent over insight, and safety over reconciliation. Identity consolidation precedes documentation. Grief integration precedes forgiveness narratives. The absence of answers must not be framed as therapeutic failure.

Many survivors protected themselves by not knowing. Recognition must therefore be paced and survivor-led. Discovery is frequently destabilising rather than relieving, particularly when it involves parental suicide, irreversible loss, institutional betrayal, or evidence of extreme harm.

Therapeutic Stance and Language

Effective clinical language frames symptoms as survival adaptations rather than pathology. Clinicians should communicate that confusion is understandable, that safety does not require immediate answers, and that the body often learns how to survive before the mind has the capacity to understand what is happening. Boundaries should be framed as stabilisation tools rather than moral positions.

Clinicians should avoid requiring proof to validate experience, rushing reunification narratives, moralising contact decisions, or prematurely diagnosing personality pathology when relational threat activation and developmental disruption provide a more accurate clinical explanation. Particular vigilance is required around anniversaries of relocations or discovery events, identity documentation processes, family backlash following boundary setting, learning of parental death or suicide, and sexual intimacy that triggers unexplained distress.

Adult survivors of abduction are not resistant to treatment. They are preserving continuity of self in the aftermath of developmental rupture. Healing does not depend on full factual reconstruction. It depends on the restoration of agency, authorship, and internal safety. Clinicians are advised to treat this construct as an emerging pattern descriptor intended to inform treatment pacing and safety planning rather than as a diagnostic label.

Clinical Supervision and Specialist Support

Work with adult survivors of abduction and extreme harm requires a level of clinical containment that exceeds standard trauma supervision. The emotional intensity, ethical complexity, and risk profile of this population make regular, specialist-informed supervision essential rather than optional. Clinical supervision is also a formal requirement for professional registration and ethical practice across counselling, psychotherapy, and psychology professions. This requirement becomes even more critical when working with highly complex trauma presentations.

At present, the supervision pool for this niche area remains extremely limited in Australia. As a result, the author has been undertaking ongoing clinical supervision with Dr Craig Childress in the United States for the past 6 years. Dr Childress is a clinical psychologist whose professional background includes court-involved child custody conflict, attachment pathology, child abuse, complex trauma, parent-child and family conflict dynamics, and early childhood mental health consultation. He also provides consultation and expert testimony to mental health professionals and legal practitioners in high-conflict and attachment disruption cases, and he has developed an attachment-based model of alienation and coercive family systems that informs specialist clinical practice in this area.

Given the complexity of the work, supervisors in this area should possess more than general trauma expertise. Specialist supervision for abduction-related treatment ideally includes demonstrated competence in attachment theory and developmental trauma in contexts of prolonged concealment and disrupted caregiving, longitudinal assessment and formulation of identity disruption, coercive control, and family systems dysfunction that shapes the survivor's nervous system organisation.

Where appropriately trained supervisors are not locally available, international clinical supervision via telehealth platforms is an important resource. Dr Childress offers virtual supervision and consultation for clinicians working with complex attachment and alienation-related trauma. Clinicians seeking specialist guidance are advised to refer directly to his professional consultation platform for current supervision arrangements.

Supervision Clinical Red Flags Requiring Escalation

Immediate supervisory consultation is required when specific risk indicators emerge in abduction-related work. These include a sudden escalation in survivor suicidality following insight, discovery events, or boundary shifts, as well as situations in which the clinician begins to experience intrusive imagery, sleep disruption, persistent anger, or emotional preoccupation related to the case. These signals indicate that the clinical system itself is under strain and requires containment.

Escalation is also necessary when clinicians feel increasing pressure to advise on legal action, confrontation, access to records, or family contact decisions that fall outside the therapeutic scope. Similarly, when survivors begin seeking factual confirmation of historical events as a condition for psychological safety, supervision becomes essential to recalibrate pacing and prevent therapy from drifting into investigative or forensic roles.

Another critical red flag occurs when clinicians begin to feel uniquely responsible for the survivor's safety, outcomes, or recovery trajectory. This sense of singular responsibility reflects rescue dynamics that place both the clinician and survivor at risk of burnout, dependency, and boundary erosion.

Supervision in abduction-informed clinical work requires expertise beyond general trauma supervision. Clinicians working with adult survivors of childhood abduction, prolonged concealment, identity disruption, and extreme developmental harm require supervisors who are equipped to support complex formulation, ethical sequencing and pacing, and high-risk clinical decision-making. This framework outlines the minimum competency requirements for safely and responsibly supervising this work.

Supervisors must demonstrate advanced understanding of attachment theory as it applies to forced separation, attachment capture, and long-term caregiver disruption. This includes developmental trauma arising from prolonged coercion rather than discrete traumatic events, identity formation under secrecy and survival-based environments, and the impact of disrupted autobiographical continuity on adult psychological functioning. Supervisors must be able to assist clinicians in differentiating attachment injury from personality pathology and in recognising survival-based adaptations without pathologising them.

Competence in formulation and clinical decision-making is essential. Supervisors must be able to support a longitudinal developmental formulation rather than a symptom-driven diagnosis, differentiate among alienation, concealment, disappearance, and irreversible loss trajectories, and guide clinicians in assessing readiness for truth-seeking, narrative work, and identity exploration. Supervision should prioritise clinical precision and pacing over linear progression or protocol adherence, recognising that phase movement in this population is non-linear and context-dependent.

Supervisors must also be skilled in trauma stabilisation and risk management. This includes managing discovery trauma and adult-onset shock responses, conducting suicide risk assessment in the context of moral injury and late revelation, recognising nervous system collapse, dissociation, and somatic overwhelm, and supporting containment strategies when narrative exploration becomes destabilising. Supervisors have an ethical responsibility to monitor clinician pacing decisions and intervene when treatment intensity exceeds a survivor's capacity.

Understanding coercive control and the ongoing dynamics of family system threat is another core supervisory requirement. Supervisors must be competent in recognising loyalty conditioning, threat-based compliance patterns, the risk of recapture following the development of survivor autonomy, and the need for explicit boundary architecture and safety-based contact decisions. Supervision must help clinicians identify when family pressure, sibling triangulation, or institutional involvement is recreating threat conditions within the survivor's present environment.

Effective supervision in this domain also requires active awareness of countertransference and ethical containment. Supervisors must monitor clinicians' rescue impulses, moral outrage, alignment bias, pressure toward confrontation or reunification, and avoidance responses to disclosures of extreme harm. Emotional reactions must be treated as clinical data rather than personal shortcomings, and supervision must address how these reactions influence pacing, formulation, and therapeutic stance.

Supervisors should maintain awareness of legal and systemic boundaries without allowing supervision to drift into investigative or forensic roles. This includes understanding the risks associated with clinicians assuming evidentiary or advocacy functions, maintaining appropriate documentation standards for high-risk cases, and preserving clear therapeutic boundaries. Supervisors play a critical role in protecting clinicians from role confusion that can compromise client safety and ethical practice.

Professional accountability is central to this work. Supervisors must ensure that supervision frequency meets registration requirements, that documentation is maintained accurately, that ethical codes are actively referenced in complex decision-making, and that risk escalation protocols are clearly established. In this population, supervision is not optional. It functions as a structural safety mechanism for both clinician and survivor.

Supervisors must also recognise the limits of local expertise and be willing to support referral for specialist consultation when case complexity exceeds available knowledge. This includes openness to international supervision where domestic options are limited and encouragement of multidisciplinary collaboration when appropriate. Isolation of clinicians working in extreme harm cases significantly increases the risk of burnout, misjudgement, and ethical drift.

Supervisors working on this work should engage in ongoing self-reflection on their readiness to oversee such cases. This includes regularly evaluating whether they possess sufficient attachment-based and developmental trauma training, whether emotional reactions to case material are influencing clinical guidance, whether they are promoting safety and containment rather than inadvertently accelerating disclosure or action, and whether additional specialist consultation would benefit the clinician or client. When uncertainty exists, further supervision or referral is ethically indicated.

Working With Adult Survivors in CPA-PA Contexts and Complex Events

Clinical work with adult survivors of childhood abduction, prolonged concealment, identity disruption, trafficking exposure, and extreme violence carries a level of psychological and ethical weight that exceeds most forms of complex trauma practice. Many of these survivors were exposed not only to interpersonal abuse but to sustained systems of deception, forced silence, institutional failure, and, in some cases, the later discovery of a targeted parent's suicide or disappearance. The cumulative impact of this material on clinicians is significant. For this reason, within this protocol, structured and ongoing clinical supervision is not treated as an optional professional safeguard. It is positioned as a core component of ethical practice and client safety.

Supervision in this population serves several essential functions. First, it protects survivors by ensuring that therapy does not inadvertently drift into investigative, rescuing, confrontational, or coercive dynamics that replicate earlier experiences of control and powerlessness. Second, it protects clinicians from the cumulative psychological impact of repeated exposure to extreme harm narratives, which can gradually distort clinical judgement, affect pacing decisions, and erode emotional neutrality if left unchecked. Third, supervision provides a structured space for ethical formulation and decision-making in cases where information is incomplete, delayed, contradictory, or emotionally destabilising. Fourth, it preserves phase integrity by supporting clinicians in resisting pressure to accelerate insight, disclosure, reunification, or meaning-making when stabilisation and containment remain clinically indicated.

Supervision is understood as a parallel regulatory system. Just as adult survivors require containment, pacing, and nervous system stabilisation in therapy, clinicians working with this material require structured containment of their own cognitive, emotional, and ethical processing. When supervision is absent, inconsistent, or poorly matched to the complexity of abduction-related trauma, the risk of clinical drift, boundary erosion, and unintentional harm increases significantly.

Core Supervision Domains

Supervision sessions must attend to phase integrity and pacing. Supervisors play a critical role in helping clinicians maintain survivors within the appropriate therapeutic phase, particularly resisting premature movement into attachment repair, relational work, or meaning reconstruction when stabilisation and safety are not yet secure. In abduction-related presentations, rushing progression commonly reflects clinician discomfort rather than survivor readiness.

Ongoing monitoring of countertransference is essential. Clinicians frequently experience intense protectiveness, moral outrage toward perpetrators, disbelief at institutional failures, or urgency to "make sense" of fragmented histories. Without containment, these reactions can subtly shape clinical pacing, language, and assumptions. Supervision provides the space in which these responses can be identified, regulated, and ethically integrated, rather than acted out in the therapy room.

Supervisors must also assist clinicians in recognising rescue and validation traps. While validation of harm is necessary, premature affirmation of catastrophic interpretations can overwhelm survivors who have not yet developed sufficient internal authority, narrative stability, or nervous system regulation. The supervisory task is to help clinicians differentiate between supportive witnessing and inadvertently amplifying distress before the survivor is resourced to metabolise it.

Ethical boundary clarity is another central domain of supervision. The HQTP rejects therapy as a truth-finding or investigative process. Supervision must reinforce that the absence of documentation, proof, or institutional confirmation does not invalidate survivor experience and should not drive clinical behaviour. The clinician's role remains therapeutic containment, not factual arbitration.

Finally, supervision must include regular review of clinical risk formulation. This includes monitoring risk of suicidality, severity of dissociation, identity destabilisation, environmental stressors, and vulnerability periods such as boundary shifts, discovery milestones, or renewed family contact. In adult abduction work, risk is often dynamic rather than static, requiring continuous recalibration rather than one-time assessment.

PART IV Healing Qualia: An Integrative Framework

This section outlines the theoretical, relational, and neurobiological frameworks that safely contain therapeutic work with adult-child survivors of child psychological abuse. The HQTP refers to the internal conditions that allow recovery to become coherent, embodied, and survivable for adult survivors of child psychological abuse, abduction, and prolonged identity erasure. It is not a technique, intervention, or therapeutic modality. It is the integrative framework that holds together stabilisation, attachment repair, identity reconstruction, grief processing, and long-term meaning-making within this protocol.

Survivors do not heal simply by reducing symptoms. They heal by restoring authorship over their internal world after years or decades of relational control, narrative capture, and developmental disruption. The HQTP, therefore, centres the survivor's lived experience, nervous system regulation, relational safety, and embodied coherence as the foundation for all subsequent therapeutic work.

This framework acknowledges that recovery unfolds simultaneously across psychological, relational, neurobiological, and existential domains. It provides clinicians with a structured lens for integrating evidence-based trauma therapies, attachment-informed practice, somatic regulation, and reflective meaning work without fragmenting the survivor's experience into disconnected interventions.

Clinical Framework for Healing Qualia

Within this protocol, personalised treatment planning is not an optional enhancement. It is a clinical requirement. Survivors do not recover through standardised sequences alone. Each survivor's healing trajectory is shaped by their lived experience, nervous system adaptations, attachment history, and capacity for meaning-making.

The author's twin PhD findings demonstrated that both survivors and specialised MHPs repeatedly identified the limitations of one-size-fits-all trauma models when applied to this population. Survivors reported that recovery depended not only on symptom reduction but on whether therapy aligned with their subjective experience of safety, agency, and internal coherence. Practitioners reported that rigid adherence to technique often failed in the presence of developmental disruption, moral injury, and identity fragmentation.

For this reason, the HQTP places subjective experience at the centre of clinical formulation. The survivor's internal world, emotional responses, bodily signals, and evolving sense of meaning are treated as primary clinical data rather than secondary outcomes. This does not replace evidence-based practice. It contextualises it.

Ongoing subjective assessment is therefore built into the framework. Clinicians are encouraged to attend not only to observable behaviour and symptom change, but to how survivors experience their own recovery process. This includes shifts in perceived safety, sense of authorship, emotional tolerance, relational capacity, and identity stability. These qualitative markers often provide earlier and more accurate indicators of readiness for deeper therapeutic work than diagnostic scales alone.

The HQTP does not privilege any single modality. Instead, it provides an integrative container within which different therapeutic approaches can be applied ethically and selectively. Cognitive approaches may support restructuring of internalised narratives shaped by coercion and erasure. Trauma-focused interventions may assist with nervous system regulation and memory integration when stabilisation has been achieved. Mindfulness and embodied practices may support present-moment orientation and emotional regulation in survivors whose bodies learned to survive under prolonged threat.

Pharmacological support may be indicated for some survivors during periods of acute distress, discovery trauma, or destabilisation. Medication is positioned as an aid to stabilisation rather than a primary treatment pathway. Its purpose is to support functional capacity and therapeutic engagement, not to replace relational or developmental repair.

The HQTP, therefore, functions as the connective tissue of the protocol. It holds together stabilisation, attachment repair, grief integration, identity reconstruction, and long-term recovery without forcing survivors into rigid timelines or externally imposed definitions of progress. Healing is measured not by speed or symptom suppression, but by increasing internal safety, coherence, agency, and the survivor's capacity to live without being organised around captivity.

Clinician Application and Scope Clarification

The HQTP does not require clinicians to become experts in multiple therapeutic schools or to implement a wide range of specialised techniques simultaneously. The framework is not a demand for breadth of modality. It is a structural orientation that guides the application, sequencing, and pacing of existing clinical skills when working with adult survivors.

Most clinicians already possess the core competencies required for this work, including stabilisation strategies, relational containment, psychoeducation, boundary work, and trauma-informed care. The HQTP provides the organising logic that determines when these skills are used, when they are withheld, and how they are adapted to prevent re-enactment of coercion, pressure, or premature exposure.

Where additional training is recommended, the HQTP identifies those areas in later chapters. Clinicians are not expected to implement every intervention described in this volume. The framework is designed to support clinical judgement rather than replace it, allowing practitioners to work safely within their existing scope while progressively developing capacity in areas specific to abduction and extreme developmental trauma.

The primary requirement is not technical mastery. It is clinical restraint, phase awareness, supervision engagement, and ethical sequencing and pacing.

Clinician's note: while some themes may feel familiar in the following clinician quick-start guide, they are intentionally restated to anchor clinical safety and continuity as the protocol shifts to the HQTP integration framework.

Clinician Quick-Start Guide for Adult Survivors in CPA-PA Contexts and Extreme Harm

This framework is designed as a clinical navigation system rather than a technique manual or disclosure-driven treatment model. It provides clinicians with a structured method for sequencing therapeutic work safely in cases involving complex developmental trauma, prolonged coercive control, identity disruption, and irreversible relational loss. The primary clinical task is not to uncover the survivor's story, but to protect regulation, autonomy, and developmental repair throughout treatment.

Clinical work within the HQTP begins with accurate phase positioning. Before selecting any intervention, clinicians must assess the survivor's current regulatory capacity, identity stability, grief activation, and exposure to ongoing relational threat. Apparent insight or intellectual understanding is not sufficient to indicate readiness for meaning-making or narrative exploration. When safety is compromised, treatment remains anchored in stabilisation phases regardless of the survivor's expressed curiosity about the past.

The protocol follows a strict sequencing logic. Safety must be prioritised before truth-seeking, stabilisation before trauma integration, identity consolidation before documentation recovery, grief integration before reunion narratives, and survivor autonomy before reconciliation framing. Interventions that violate this sequence risk replicating the coercive conditions that led to the original harm. When uncertainty arises, clinicians are instructed to pause rather than progress.

Vigilance is required around high-risk activation points that commonly destabilise adult survivors of abduction and extreme harm. These include the discovery of parental death or suicide, engagement with legal or identity documentation, attempts to locate family members, boundary-setting with family systems, anniversaries of removals or relocations, and activation of sexual or bodily memory responses. During these periods, therapeutic pacing must slow rather than intensify, with an emphasis on containment rather than exploration.

Phase integrity functions as the primary clinical anchor. When destabilisation occurs, clinicians are directed to return to stabilisation work, reduce narrative focus, increase support for regulation, reinforce present-day safety, and recentre survivor autonomy. Progress within this model is measured through improved emotional regulation, reduced collapse following activation, strengthened boundary stability, increased internal authority, decreased fear associated with autonomy, and improved daily functioning. Progress is not dependent on achieving full historical clarity or narrative completion.

The therapeutic relationship itself requires active protection. Clinicians are instructed to avoid interrogative questioning, pressure for coherence, reconciliation-driven framing, moral positioning, forensic-style fact gathering, and premature meaning-making. Instead, the protocol emphasises permission-based exploration, neutral pacing, reflective containment, collaborative decision-making, and survivor-led timing of narrative engagement.

Clinical supervision is treated as an integral component of the HQTP rather than an optional professional support. Clinicians are expected to bring phase-placement uncertainty, countertransference reactions, rescue impulses, destabilising discovery events, boundary-backlash experiences, and shifts in suicidality risk to supervision. Supervision functions as a parallel regulatory system that protects both the survivor and the clinician from cumulative harm and from distorted clinical judgement.

A central clinical principle underpinning this framework is recognition that adult survivors of abduction and extreme harm survived through silence, adaptation, and containment. Therapeutic work must not dismantle these protective strategies faster than the survivor's nervous system can tolerate. Within this protocol, restraint is conceptualised not as inaction, but as clinical precision. The following figure summarises the core navigation sequence for clinicians using the HQTP in CPA-PA contexts and extreme harm presentations. It is intended as a quick orientation tool only and should be read alongside the full phase guidance.

Quick-Start Clinical Navigation Diagram for CPA-PA Contexts and Extreme Harm

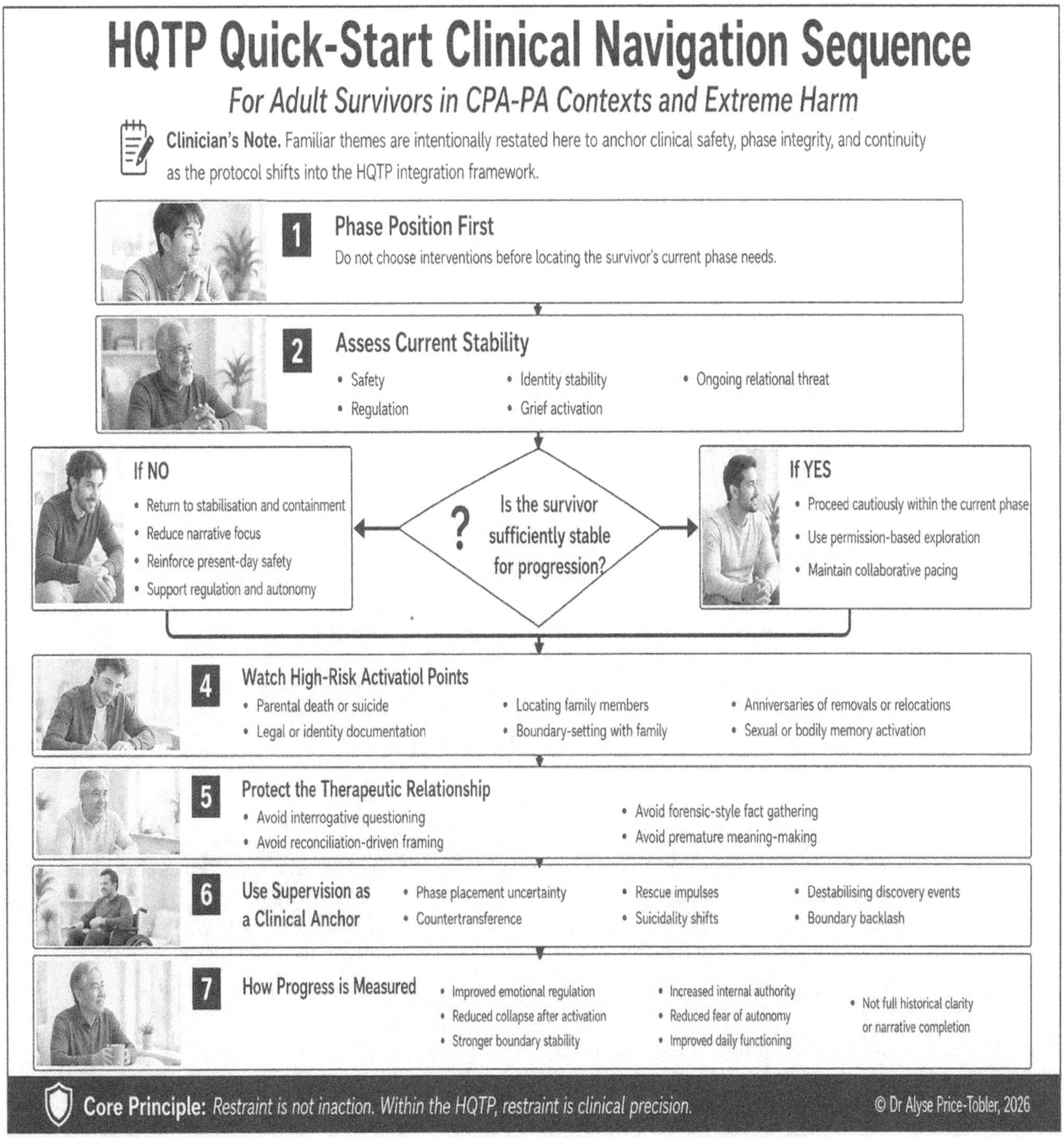

Clinical Note

Use this quick-start sequence to locate phase position before selecting interventions. If stability is unclear, return to regulation, containment, supervision, and collaborative pacing. Familiar safety themes are repeated intentionally because survivors may move in and out of readiness as grief, identity, contact, discovery, or bodily memory becomes activated. Within the HQTP, restraint is not inaction; it is clinical precision.

Holistic Framework and Integration of Qualia

The integration of the HQTP reflects what adult survivors repeatedly described in the University of the Sunshine Coast twin PhD studies: healing is not experienced as a purely cognitive or symptom-focused process. Survivors spoke about recovery as something that occurs across the whole person, including body, identity, relational safety, emotional meaning, and existential reconstruction. For many, traditional talk therapy alone was not sufficient. They described needing approaches that allowed their nervous systems to settle, their bodies to feel safe again, and their inner worlds to reorganise without being forced into linear narratives or performance-based recovery.

The HQTP is therefore not positioned as an additional layer of technique. It is the integrative container that allows phase-based work to be embodied, personalised, and paced according to the survivor's lived experience rather than external therapeutic agendas. This reflects the central finding of the adult survivor cohort: that healing required autonomy, choice, and internal authority rather than prescriptive intervention.

Survivors consistently reported that reconnection with the body was a foundational turning point in recovery. Many described years of living in intellectualised survival modes while remaining disconnected from physical sensation, psychological safety, and internal cues. Practices that support mind-body regulation, including somatic awareness, breath-based regulation, grounding movement, and gentle body-based therapies, were repeatedly identified as stabilising when applied in non-coercive and consent-based ways. These approaches allowed survivors to experience safety without needing immediate narrative disclosure or cognitive processing.

From a clinical perspective, this aligns with the protocol's emphasis on stabilisation before meaning-making. Body-based regulation is not positioned as a separate modality, but as a parallel process that supports nervous system safety while identity, grief, and attachment repair unfold gradually.

Survivors also emphasised the importance of reconstructing meaning without imposing closure, forgiveness, or forced coherence. The HQTP supports this by allowing survivors to hold multiple internal experiences simultaneously, including grief, anger, love, confusion, and hope, without needing to resolve them into a single narrative outcome. This approach respects the reality that many survivors carry irreversible losses and incomplete histories, and that healing often involves learning how to live alongside uncertainty rather than eliminating it.

Clinical integration within the HQTP remains anchored in evidence-based practice, including trauma-informed cognitive approaches, attachment-oriented therapy, and stabilisation frameworks. However, the author's research demonstrated that survivors valued flexibility over rigid adherence to modality. They reported feeling safer when clinicians adapted methods to the survivor's capacity, rather than expecting survivors to adapt themselves to the method.

Mindfulness-based practices, when used carefully and without spiritual pressure, were described by survivors as helpful for increasing present-moment safety and emotional tolerance. Journaling, creative expression, and reflective narrative work were also identified as supportive when framed as optional tools for expression rather than performance tasks. These modalities offered survivors alternative ways to process experience without relying solely on verbal disclosure.

Pharmacological support, where clinically indicated, is framed within the HQTP as a stabilising adjunct rather than a primary intervention. Survivors described medication as most helpful when it reduced acute symptom burden enough to allow therapeutic engagement, not when it was used as a replacement for relational and identity-based work. The HQTP, therefore, positions medication as a supportive infrastructure rather than the core healing mechanism.

Importantly, this framework directly responds to survivors' requests for choice, autonomy, and pacing. The HQTP is not about doing more techniques. It is about creating an integrative therapeutic environment in which the survivor's internal experience is treated as primary data rather than secondary to diagnostic categories or procedural targets.

For clinicians, this section is not asking you to master every modality. It provides a conceptual map of how different supports can be layered within the safety scaffolding already established by the phase-based protocol. The emphasis remains on relational presence, nervous system regulation, ethical restraint, and survivor-led integration rather than technical performance. In this way, the HQTP becomes the living interface between structure and subjectivity. It allows the protocol to remain clinically grounded while honouring the deeply personal, non-linear, and embodied nature of recovery described by adult survivors themselves.

A significant finding across the adult survivor cohort was the diversity of survivor relationships with medication and altered states of consciousness. While some survivors reported benefit from pharmacological support during periods of acute destabilisation, others expressed strong opposition to medication based on lived experience. Several survivors described growing up in environments characterised by confusion, psychological distortion, and emotional instability, and articulated a deep desire to experience healing in what they described as a "clear" or "real" state of awareness. For these individuals, medication was perceived not as supportive but as another layer of disconnection from internal reality.

Some survivors reported adverse reactions to antidepressant and anxiolytic medications, including emotional numbing, dissociation, and, in some cases, the emergence or worsening of suicidal ideation, which is a documented side effect for certain pharmacological medications. These experiences were described as particularly distressing because they occurred during periods when survivors felt they were beginning to emerge from the cognitive and emotional fog of childhood trauma. For some, medication was experienced as pushing them back into a state of detachment and internal confusion that mirrored earlier survival conditions rather than supporting recovery.

Other survivors described a broader sensitivity to altered states of consciousness altogether. Individuals who had grown up in chronically unsafe environments often reported that any experience of feeling "not fully present," including alcohol intoxication or cannabis use, increased anxiety rather than reducing it. For these survivors, remaining fully oriented and in control of their perceptions was experienced as essential to safety. As a result, some made deliberate choices to avoid substances entirely, including prescribed medications, to preserve internal psychological stability and agency.

At the same time, the research also identified survivors who experienced medication as helpful when used cautiously and collaboratively. These survivors described pharmacological support as enabling sleep, reducing overwhelming anxiety, or stabilising mood sufficiently to engage in therapeutic work. What distinguished positive outcomes was not the medication itself, but the way decisions were made. Survivors emphasised the importance of being involved in medication discussions, having their concerns taken seriously, and not feeling pressured to comply with pharmacological recommendations that did not align with their lived experience.

The HQTP, therefore, positions medication as a survivor-guided option rather than a default intervention. Unless there is active involvement from community mental health teams managing diagnosed psychiatric conditions requiring medical treatment, medication decisions prioritise informed consent, bodily autonomy, and subjective safety. The clinician's role is not to persuade, but to support survivors in making decisions that preserve agency, clarity, and nervous system stability.

This approach reflects a broader principle embedded throughout the protocol: adult survivors of child psychological abuse, parental alienation, and abduction are rebuilding control over their internal and external worlds. Healing is not achieved by imposing solutions, but by restoring the survivor's capacity to choose what feels safe, coherent, and sustainable for their own recovery.

Working With Survivors Who Are Also Engaged with Mental Health Services

A proportion of adult survivors of CPA-PA may present with a diagnosed mental illness and receive care through public mental health units, inpatient services, crisis teams, or scheduled outpatient programs. These survivors often move between trauma-informed therapy and medically oriented systems that may not recognise alienation dynamics, developmental coercion, or identity disruption as organising injuries.

Clinicians working within the HQTP must be prepared to collaborate with treating teams while protecting the survivor's narrative integrity and psychological safety. This requires clear role boundaries. The therapist does not replace psychiatric care, medication management, or crisis stabilisation services. Instead, the therapist provides a developmental context that can prevent misinterpretation of survivor behaviour as purely symptomatic or personality-based.

Many public mental health systems are structured around symptom reduction rather than developmental formulation. Survivors may be labelled with mood disorders, personality disorders, psychosis-spectrum presentations, or trauma diagnoses without attention to the relational captivity, long-term coercion, or attachment disruption that shaped these presentations. Where appropriate and consented to by the survivor, clinicians can support treating teams by offering formulation language that reframes behaviour through a developmental and trauma-informed lens rather than solely through pathology.

Effective collaboration begins with transparency. Survivors should be informed about what information is shared, with whom, and for what purpose. The survivor remains the primary authority over their story. When communication with treating teams occurs, the focus should remain on current safety, stabilisation needs, and functional support rather than historical interrogation or forced disclosure of abduction details.

In inpatient or acute settings, particular care is required. Institutional environments can unintentionally replicate dynamics of powerlessness, surveillance, and loss of autonomy that mirror earlier experiences of captivity. Clinicians should support survivors to maintain choice wherever possible, including participation in care planning, medication discussions, and discharge decisions. Small acts of agency within structured systems are clinically protective.

Where survivors are under community mental health case management, scheduled treatment orders, or ongoing psychiatric review, coordination is most effective when framed around shared goals of stabilisation, safety, and functional recovery. The HQTP does not compete with psychiatric care. It complements it by addressing identity repair, relational safety, and meaning-making that medication alone cannot resolve.

Importantly, clinicians should not assume that treating teams understand parental alienation, abduction dynamics, or developmental psychological abuse. When appropriate, gentle psychoeducation may be necessary. This is not advocacy through confrontation, but through collaborative formulation that reduces misinterpretation and prevents survivors from being repeatedly retraumatised by system responses.

Across all settings, the guiding principle remains consistent: the survivor's psychological safety, autonomy, and coherence take priority over institutional convenience or theoretical rigidity. Integration across systems is possible when clinical humility, clear communication, and survivor-centred practice are maintained.

Incorporating Open Dialogue Principles in Work with Public Mental Health Systems

The author supports the principles of Open Dialogue as a clinically compatible approach when working with survivors of CPA-PA who are also engaged with mental health services. Originally developed within Finnish mental health services, Open Dialogue emphasises transparency, shared understanding, relational safety, collaborative decision-making, and the inclusion of the survivor's voice as central to care. Within the HQTP, its relevance lies in reducing professional overreach, protecting uncertainty from premature closure, and ensuring that survivors are spoken with rather than spoken about.

The author was first formally introduced to and trained in Open Dialogue principles during her tenure as Western Sydney Area Manager of the Schizophrenia Fellowship of NSW, where the model was utilised to support individuals and families experiencing severe mental distress within community and hospital interface settings.

This orientation aligns closely with the HQTP, which recognises that adult survivors have often experienced enforced silence, narrative control, and institutional authority being exercised over their lives. By prioritising dialogue over directive intervention, Open Dialogue reduces the risk of retraumatisation, supports the restoration of autonomy, and creates relational conditions in which psychological safety precedes interpretation or treatment planning. Within abduction-related work, this approach is particularly protective, as it prevents clinicians and systems from replicating the very dynamics of control, silencing, and erasure that characterised the original harm.

This approach is particularly relevant for survivors whose histories include enforced silence, narrative control, institutional betrayal, and loss of personal agency. Many adult survivors report that traditional service models have replicated these dynamics by speaking about them rather than with them, making decisions without consultation, or framing distress through narrow diagnostic lenses without developmental context.

Open Dialogue offers an alternative posture. It prioritises relational safety, slows clinical processes, tolerates uncertainty, and allows meaning to emerge through dialogue rather than being imposed through diagnosis or protocol. This aligns directly with the HQTP, which views recovery as an internally guided process supported by containment rather than externally directed intervention.

When working alongside mental health units or community teams, clinicians can integrate Open Dialogue principles by advocating for shared-care conversations in which the survivor is present, informed, and actively participating. This includes encouraging transparency about treatment decisions, medication changes, risk management strategies, and discharge planning. It also involves validating multiple perspectives without privileging institutional narratives over lived experience.

The author's position is that Open Dialogue does not replace psychiatric care or crisis intervention when required, but it fundamentally changes how those services are delivered. It reduces power imbalances, decreases the likelihood of retraumatisation, and supports survivors to rebuild trust in relational systems after histories of coercion and control.

In practice, this means slowing conversations, avoiding rushed conclusions, naming uncertainty honestly, and creating space for the survivor to describe their internal experience without immediate categorisation or correction. It also means allowing emotional meaning to coexist with clinical information, rather than treating one as superior to the other.

For survivors of abduction and psychological captivity, this relational stance is not optional. It is reparative. It restores the right to be heard, to participate in decisions that affect one's body and life, and to rebuild a sense of authorship after years of enforced compliance.

Within the HQTP, Open Dialogue is understood not as a technique but as a clinical attitude. It reflects a commitment to collaboration, humility, and respect for subjective experience. When used alongside stabilisation, identity repair, and trauma-informed care, it offers a powerful model for bridging private therapy and public mental health systems without sacrificing survivor autonomy.

Open Dialogue as a Trauma-Compatible Relational Framework

Open Dialogue, originally developed within Finnish mental health services, emphasises transparency, shared understanding, relational safety, and collaborative meaning-making between clinicians, service users, and support networks. Within the HQTP, its relevance lies in preserving survivor participation, protecting uncertainty from premature closure, and reducing the risk of reenacting professional authority over subjective experience. In abduction-related work in particular, this stance helps prevent clinicians and systems from replicating earlier dynamics of control, silencing, and erasure.

Clinical Example: Integrating Open Dialogue in a Mental Health Unit Context

A survivor presenting to a mental health unit following a discovery event related to childhood abduction was admitted for acute suicidality. Initial assessments focused on symptom management and medication adjustment. The treating psychologist introduced Open Dialogue principles by requesting joint meetings that included the survivor, the inpatient psychiatrist, the nursing staff, and the outpatient therapist.

Rather than discussing the survivor in their absence, the team met with the survivor present and invited their perspective on what felt destabilising. The survivor described that being spoken about without involvement triggered intense panic linked to childhood experiences of secrecy and loss of control. The team adjusted their approach, slowing conversations, explaining decisions transparently, and inviting the survivor to participate in safety planning.

Instead of framing the crisis solely as symptom escalation, the team collaboratively recognised the admission as a discovery trauma response. Medication was discussed openly, with consent revisited regularly. The survivor reported reduced distress once they felt included rather than managed. This relational shift supported stabilisation more effectively than symptom-focused intervention alone and preserved therapeutic alliance across systems.

This example illustrates how Open Dialogue principles can be applied within institutional settings without compromising safety or clinical responsibility, while protecting survivor autonomy and preventing reenactment of coercive dynamics.

This chapter has brought together the central principles of The HQTP as they apply to adult survivors of parental alienation and childhood abduction. The work described here is not about applying more techniques. It is about changing how clinicians understand recovery, pacing, safety, and meaning in a population whose lives have often been shaped by secrecy, coercion, identity disruption, and prolonged relational loss.

Healing in this context is not linear or uniform. Survivors do not move through identical stages or timelines. What remains consistent across presentations is the need for treatment that is paced, autonomy-centred, and grounded in the survivor's internal experience rather than imposed frameworks. This chapter has emphasised that recovery is not measured by narrative completeness, reunion outcomes, or symptom suppression alone, but by the gradual restoration of internal safety, self-authorship, and the capacity to live without being organised around survival.

Clinical approaches such as cognitive-behavioural therapy, trauma-focused work, and, where appropriate, medication can be useful tools when applied within this broader containment framework. However, these interventions must be embedded within relational safety, nervous system regulation, and ethical restraint. Without this foundation, even well-intentioned treatment risks replicating earlier experiences of control, pressure, and invalidation.

The integration of holistic practices reflects what adult survivors consistently reported in the author's research. Survivors described needing approaches that addressed the body, nervous system, emotional life, and identity together rather than in isolation. Practices such as breathwork, somatic awareness, mindfulness, creative expression, and nature-based regulation were frequently identified as helping survivors reconnect with their bodies, regain internal psychological stability, and tolerate deeper therapeutic work. These methods are not replacements for clinical care. They are stabilising supports that enable clinical work to be conducted safely.

This chapter has also reinforced the need for assessment to extend beyond symptom checklists. Survivors often present with high-functioning exteriors while carrying significant internal distress, grief, and moral injury. Attending to subjective experience, emotional meaning, and lived reality allows clinicians to track progress that would otherwise remain invisible within traditional diagnostic frameworks.

Above all, the HQTP centres the survivor's right to move at their own pace. Many survivors grew up in environments where autonomy was stripped away, and narratives were controlled by others. The HQTP deliberately returns authority to the survivor. They decide when to explore, when to pause, when to engage with records or family, and when to step back. The clinician's role is not to direct the journey but to protect safety, hold containment, and support meaning as it emerges.

When held in this way, healing becomes possible without re-enactment. Survivors are no longer asked to perform recovery or meet external expectations. Instead, they are supported in rebuilding internal psychological stability, reclaiming authorship of their lives, and moving forward in ways that reflect their values, boundaries, and sense of self.

This is the foundation upon which the remaining chapters build.

A Special Note for Survivors Moving Through This Phase

Dear friends,

This phase of the work is not about doing therapy "correctly." It is about learning to listen to yourself again. You are the expert on your own internal world. No clinician, no framework, and no protocol knows your body, your pace, or your limits better than you do. This is an important note, as some clinicians think they are experts on you because of their training. They are wrong. You are the expert on you, and don't let anyone tell you differently!

Your role in this phase is not to perform insight or produce a coherent story. Your role is not to keep the clinician calm or to protect them from being upset by your stories or emotions. Your role is to notice what feels safe enough to approach and what still feels too much. Some days you may feel ready to explore difficult material. On other days, your system may tell you it needs grounding, rest, or stability instead. Both are valid. Progress in this phase is not measured by how much you uncover, but by how well you stay connected to yourself while doing it.

It is okay to tell your clinician when something feels too fast, too intense, or not quite right. It is okay to say you need to slow down. It is okay to say you are not ready to go there yet. This phase works best when the therapist follows your nervous system rather than pushing you into timelines or expectations.

You may also notice that you carry strong instincts about what you need. Many adult survivors develop a high level of internal awareness because they had to rely on themselves for safety. Trust that. If something feels off, confusing, or overwhelming, it matters. Bring it into the room. Good therapy in this phase is collaborative rather than directive.

This phase is also not about fixing yourself. You are not broken. What you are doing is learning how to live without everything being organised around survival. That takes time. It takes patience. And it takes compassion toward parts of you that learned to protect you in very difficult circumstances.

You are allowed to move at your own pace. You are allowed to pause. You are allowed to step back and return later. You are allowed to choose what healing looks like for you.

This is your work. Your life. Your recovery.

Furthermore, you get to lead it. You are the expert on yourself!

Go gently, Dr Alyse

Building a Foundation for Healing

Before any deeper therapeutic work can occur, a foundation of safety must be deliberately constructed. For adult survivors of child psychological abuse, parental alienation, and abduction, safety is not assumed. It must be experienced.

Many survivors enter therapy with a long history of relational betrayal, institutional failure, and coerced compliance. As a result, trust is not established solely by reassurance or warmth. It is built through consistency, pacing, predictability, and the clinician's capacity to remain emotionally regulated when difficult material emerges.

This phase of the work focuses on creating both physical and psychological conditions that enable the survivor's nervous system to begin to stand down from long-term threat activation. The therapeutic environment itself becomes part of the intervention. Lighting, privacy, seating arrangements, session structure, and the tone of communication all contribute to whether the survivor experiences the space as safe or surveilled, collaborative or hierarchical.

Equally important is the relational foundation. Survivors often arrive highly attuned to subtle shifts in power, tone, and expectation. For this reason, clinicians must prioritise transparency, consent-based pacing, and clear communication of boundaries from the outset. This includes naming that the survivor controls the pace of disclosure, that therapy is not an investigative process, and that psychological safety takes precedence over narrative completeness.

This chapter, therefore, focuses on how clinicians establish therapeutic containment through presence rather than pressure, structure rather than control, and attunement rather than interrogation. It examines how session pacing, language choices, validation practices, and the sequencing of sensitive material either support stabilisation or inadvertently replicate earlier coercive dynamics.

The foundation phase is not passive preparation. It is active clinical work. When done well, it reduces physiological reactivity, strengthens internal safety, and creates the conditions required for later identity, grief, and attachment work to occur without destabilisation. Healing does not begin with insight. It begins with safety.

Establishing Trust and Addressing Trauma

Integrating UniSC Twin PhD Findings into Early Clinical Engagement

Across both UniSC twin PhD studies, one finding was consistent: adult survivors of child psychological abuse, parental alienation, and abduction do not experience trust as a default relational state. For many, trust was historically associated with danger, punishment, coercion, or emotional capture. As a result, therapeutic trust must be actively constructed rather than assumed.

The foundation of this work begins with environmental and relational safety. Survivors repeatedly reported that highly clinical, sterile, or institutional settings triggered vigilance rather than calm. In contrast, spaces that felt human, warm, predictable, and private were more likely to support nervous system settling. This does not require elaborate design. It requires intentionality. Seating arrangements that avoid physical hierarchy, consistent session structure, respectful privacy practices, and a calm, grounded clinician presence all contribute to the experience of the therapy space as safe or surveilled.

Practitioner participants in the companion study noted that early alliance ruptures often occurred when clinicians underestimated the impact of first impressions. Survivors described forming rapid internal judgements about whether the clinician felt emotionally safe within the first one to three sessions. These judgements were rarely conscious yet strongly influenced engagement and the risk of dropout.

Once a therapeutic container is established, attention must shift to pacing disclosure. One of the most common clinical errors identified in the UniSC data was premature trauma exploration. Survivors frequently described feeling overwhelmed after early disclosures, followed by emotional collapse, shame, or withdrawal from therapy. For this reason, disclosure in the HQTP is not treated as inherently therapeutic. It is treated as an intervention that must be timed, supported, and contained.

Following any emotionally significant disclosure, clinicians should deliberately slow the pace of the session. This includes allocating time for grounding, emotional regulation, and post-disclosure stabilisation. Survivors in the study consistently reported that being "left raw" at the end of sessions replicated earlier abandonment experiences. Even brief containment practices, reflective silence, or explicit reassurance of ongoing therapeutic support reduced post-session destabilisation.

Introducing sensitive material also requires careful language selection. Open invitations such as "Would you like to share anything about your early life?" or "What feels safe to talk about today?" were reported as significantly less activating than directive questioning about trauma history. Survivors emphasised that being allowed to lead narrative depth restored a sense of agency that had been systematically removed in childhood.

Validation emerged as another core stabilising factor. Survivors described profound relief when clinicians named their emotional responses as understandable adaptations rather than pathology. Simple reflections that acknowledged effort, confusion, fear, or survival strategies often strengthened alliances more effectively than technical interventions. Practitioner participants confirmed that early validation reduced defensive posturing and increased long-term engagement.

Trust-building in this population is not achieved through speed. It is achieved through consistency. Survivors repeatedly emphasised the importance of predictable session scheduling, clear boundaries, transparent communication, and follow-through on commitments. Small relational ruptures such as missed appointments without explanation, rushed endings, or inconsistent therapeutic tone were disproportionately destabilising due to survivors' history of abandonment and sudden relational loss.

Importantly, the UniSC findings highlight that silence is not always avoidance. Many survivors reported that periods of quiet presence in therapy were experienced as deeply reparative. Sitting without pressure, without demand for performance or disclosure, and without an agenda allowed the nervous system to settle in ways that words could not. Clinicians must therefore resist the urge to "fill space" when working with this population.

While structured engagement frameworks are useful, rigidity is counterproductive. Survivors' needs fluctuate across treatment phases. Some require regular, predictable sessions to build safety, while others require flexible pacing during periods of destabilisation or external stress. The protocol therefore emphasises adaptive structure: consistency without inflexibility, and boundaries without control.

Establishing trust in adult abduction and psychological abuse work is not a preliminary step. It is ongoing clinical labour. It sets the conditions under which all later identity, grief, attachment, and integration work either becomes possible or remains unsafe.

This foundation phase directly informs the data collection processes that follow. Without relational safety, information gathering becomes interrogative rather than collaborative. With safety established, data collection of client information becomes co-constructed, paced, and clinically meaningful.

Trauma-Informed Data Collection and Culturally Safe Assessment Practices

Effective clinical assessment is essential for understanding complex trauma presentations, but the way information is gathered is just as important as what is gathered. For adult survivors of abduction, prolonged concealment, institutional harm, and child psychological abuse, standard intake processes can unintentionally reproduce distress, shame, or disengagement if they are rigid, overly bureaucratic, or disconnected from relational safety.

Structured triage systems remain valuable within because they allow clinicians to capture key developmental, relational, and contextual patterns that are often missed when only presenting symptoms are recorded. Survivors frequently enter therapy reporting anxiety, depression, relational distress, or somatic symptoms, while the underlying organising injury remains unnamed. A consistent triage framework helps clinicians identify themes such as repeated relocations, disrupted schooling, unexplained separations, identity inconsistencies, and attachment rupture that signal deeper developmental trauma.

However, the HQTP rejects the assumption that all clients can or should complete written assessment tools independently. Many adult survivors struggle with reading and comprehension due to disrupted education, neurodevelopmental impacts of trauma, or long-standing shame associated with literacy difficulties. Others are emotionally overwhelmed during early engagement and cannot tolerate paperwork without dissociating, shutting down, or becoming distressed. Some clients do not openly refuse forms but quietly avoid them, comply superficially, or disengage from services altogether rather than disclose difficulties.

This is particularly relevant when working with Aboriginal and Torres Strait Islander clients. For many Indigenous survivors, written forms, institutional questioning, and repeated documentation requests carry historical and cultural weight associated with surveillance, child removal, welfare intervention, and systemic control. Paperwork can feel unsafe, intrusive, or culturally misaligned. Many Indigenous clients prefer relational, story-based assessment processes that prioritise conversation and trust-building over written disclosure.

For this reason, trauma-informed data collection within the HQTP is designed to be flexible and relational. Where possible, administrative tasks should be separated from therapeutic time. Clients may be invited to arrive earlier than their appointment to complete forms in a low-pressure environment, offered the option to collect paperwork on a prior day and return it later, or supported to complete documentation during session work, drawing from client narratives (for example, “I stopped school when I was 14” instead of asking on intake forms about education levels) or gradually across multiple sessions rather than all at once.

When survivors are distressed, have low literacy, are neurodivergent, or are reluctant to complete paperwork but unable or unwilling to articulate why, clinicians may complete assessment information collaboratively during sessions with consent. This approach preserves dignity, reduces shame, and prevents administrative processes from becoming another site of power imbalance or emotional exposure.

The purpose of structured triage is not bureaucratic compliance. It is pattern recognition. By systematically capturing relational history, movement patterns, attachment disruptions, and identity inconsistencies, clinicians are better able to identify masked trauma presentations and formulate treatment that addresses root causes rather than surface symptoms alone.

Ongoing data updating is equally important. Trauma recovery is not static. Information emerges over time, particularly in abduction and concealment cases where delayed recognition is common. Maintaining current clinical records supports continuity of care, informed risk assessment, and collaborative treatment planning across multidisciplinary teams when survivors are also engaged with psychiatry, community mental health services, or hospital-based care.

Where appropriate, anonymised Practitioner Assessment and Client Information Tracking systems can also support broader clinical learning and workforce development. When aggregated ethically and de-identified, this data contributes to training future practitioners, refining treatment protocols, and strengthening evidence-informed practice without compromising survivor confidentiality.

Within this protocol, data collection is therefore positioned as a clinical support tool rather than a gatekeeping mechanism. It exists to serve therapeutic safety, cultural respect, survivor autonomy, and accurate formulation. When assessment is paced, flexible, and relationally grounded, it strengthens engagement rather than undermining it and becomes part of the healing architecture rather than another institutional burden survivors must endure.

Practical Workflow Guide for Clinicians

The HQTP recommends the following workflow structure to reduce practitioner anxiety, protect therapeutic time, and improve consistency across assessment, documentation, and early engagement. Administrative tasks should be separated from therapeutic time wherever possible so that the first clinical contact is not dominated by paperwork, pressure, or premature disclosure.

Clients may be invited to arrive early to complete forms in a low-pressure environment, offered the option to collect paperwork in advance, or supported in completing information gradually across sessions. When clients are distressed, have literacy barriers, are cognitively overloaded, or appear reluctant but are unable to explain why, clinicians may complete the assessment collaboratively during sessions with explicit consent. This preserves dignity, reduces shame, and allows the clinician to observe regulation, comprehension, pacing needs, and relational safety in real time.

Initial sessions prioritise safety, relational engagement, and present functioning rather than detailed historical reconstruction. Developmental information is gathered slowly and selectively. Clinicians document patterns rather than forcing linear narratives. Repeated relocations, inconsistent schooling, identity confusion, family disappearance, secrecy cues, disrupted parentage narratives, and relational avoidance are tracked over time as formulation data.

For NDIS clients, clinicians focus initially on documenting functional impact, relational capacity, emotional regulation, daily living challenges, support needs, and the impact of trauma on participation rather than pursuing diagnostic certainty too early. Where multiple services are involved, information sharing remains collaborative, consent-based, purpose-limited, and transparent. Survivors remain informed about how their information is used, who receives it, and why. Assessment remains dynamic throughout the HQTP. Updates occur as new information emerges and as the survivor becomes more able to tolerate, clarify, or revise earlier material. Assessment is therefore treated as an ongoing clinical process rather than a one-time intake event.

Table. Workflow Area, Recommended Practice and Clinical Purpose

Workflow area	Recommended practice	Clinical purpose
Paperwork and intake	Separate administrative tasks from therapeutic time where possible.	Reduces shame, pressure, and early overwhelm.
Literacy or distress barriers	Complete forms collaboratively with explicit consent.	Preserves dignity and supports pacing.
Initial sessions	Prioritise safety, engagement, and present functioning.	Prevents premature disclosure and destabilisation.
Developmental history	Gather information slowly and selectively.	Protects regulation and avoids forced narrative coherence.
Pattern documentation	Track repeated relocations, schooling disruption, identity confusion, family disappearance, and secrecy cues.	Builds formulation over time without interrogating the survivor.
NDIS documentation	Focus on functional impact, support needs, relational capacity, regulation, and daily living.	Supports practical care planning without rushing diagnosis.
Multi-service involvement	Share information only with consent and for a clear purpose.	Protects autonomy, privacy, and trust.
Ongoing assessment	Update formulation as new information emerges.	Keeps assessment dynamic and survivor-responsive.

Clinical Safety Note

Within this protocol, data collection is never used to determine whether someone "qualifies" for care. It exists to support accurate formulation, ethical pacing, and personalised treatment planning. When assessment is relational, flexible, and culturally responsive, it strengthens engagement rather than undermining it.

Final Thoughts on the Chapter

This chapter has not been about adding more techniques to a clinician's toolbox. It has been about changing the way healing is approached.

Adult survivors do not heal through methods alone. They heal when their internal experience is finally taken seriously, when their pace is respected, when safety comes before answers, and when their own meaning-making is honoured. The HQTP asks clinicians to move beyond symptom management to a deeper understanding of how survivors experience their worlds, bodies, relationships, and sense of self.

For practitioners, this means shifting from doing therapy 'to' survivors toward working alongside them. Survivors are not passive recipients of care. They are the experts on their own internal landscapes. The clinician's role is not to impose structure, but to provide containment, guidance, and relational stability so that survivors can build coherence in their own time and in their own way.

This chapter also reinforces an important reality: there is no single right modality. What matters most is how interventions are held, not which labels they carry. Whether working with cognitive frameworks, trauma-informed approaches, somatic practices, narrative work, or integrative supports, the central task remains the same: protect safety, preserve autonomy, and support the survivor's authorship of their healing journey.

As the protocol now moves forward, the focus shifts from the framework to deeper relational, nervous-system, and developmental work. What remains constant is the foundation established here. Healing does not begin with technique. It begins with presence, respect, and the willingness to listen to what the survivor already knows about themselves.

Practitioner Orientation

The HQTP is not designed to be applied mechanically. It is a relational framework that requires clinicians to think developmentally, pace ethically, and remain grounded in survivor-led process. Working with adult survivors is not standard trauma work. It involves long-term attachment disruption, identity disturbance, moral injury, and often institutional betrayal. Practitioners must therefore approach this work with restraint, humility, and precision.

The role of the clinician within this model is not to "fix," confront, or recover lost history. It is to provide containment, stability, and relational safety so that survivors can build coherence at their own pace. Attachment knowledge, trauma literacy, and an understanding of coercive family systems form the foundation of competent practice in this space. Without these, well-intentioned interventions can unintentionally recreate the very dynamics survivors are attempting to escape.

From this point forward, the protocol shifts from a conceptual framework to an applied clinical structure. The sections that follow outline how assessment, session pacing, relational containment, and phase movement occur in real therapeutic settings with adult survivors.

When adult survivors enter therapy, they rarely arrive with a clear map of what happened to them. Many present with anxiety, relational instability, grief, identity confusion, or long-standing emotional exhaustion rather than a coherent trauma narrative. For this reason, the protocol does not begin with trauma integration or historical reconstruction. It begins with containment, orientation, and relational safety.

This chapter outlines how clinicians translate the phase-based framework into real therapeutic practice, including how initial sessions are structured, how assessment is conducted without interrogation, and how early treatment priorities are established before deeper work begins.

Understanding Complex Intersecting Traumas

A UniSC Twin PhD Derived Clinical Framework

The concept of CITs was developed through the author's twin doctoral studies at the University of the Sunshine Coast in response to a repeated pattern observed across adult survivor narratives and practitioner case material. Survivors did not present with a single identifiable trauma. Instead, they presented with layered developmental injury formed through overlapping exposures to parental alienation, psychological abuse, attachment disruption, prolonged coercive control, neglect, institutional betrayal, and, in some cases, abduction and forced separation.

The UniSC data demonstrated that these trauma exposures do not operate independently. They interact, amplify one another, and reorganise developmental pathways across identity formation, relational safety, emotional regulation, and moral reasoning. For this reason, the CIT framework does not conceptualise trauma as additive. It recognises trauma as structurally intersecting, producing compounded effects that reshape the survivor's internal and relational architecture over time.

Adult survivors consistently described not knowing which experience "counted most" because harm was cumulative, embedded, and ongoing rather than episodic. This finding directly informed the CIT model's emphasis on pattern recognition rather than event-based diagnosis.

UniSC Survivor Findings: Layered Developmental Impact

Across survivor interviews, several core patterns emerged that define CIT presentations. Survivors reported persistent identity instability, fragmented autobiographical memory, chronic relational threat perception, loyalty conditioning toward abusive caregivers, internalised self-blame, and long-standing difficulties with trust and psychological safety. Many described carrying unresolved grief not only for lost relationships but for lost versions of self that never had the opportunity to develop.

Importantly, survivors rarely experienced these outcomes from a single source of harm. Parental alienation was frequently embedded within broader family dysfunction, emotional abuse, neglect, forced secrecy, and systemic invalidation. When institutional responses such as family court involvement, professional dismissal, or misdiagnosis were added, the trauma structure became further reinforced.

This intersectional layering explains why many adult survivors present with complex symptom profiles that do not respond well to standard single-modality trauma interventions. The UniSC findings demonstrate that CITs require formulation approaches capable of holding multiple trauma pathways simultaneously.

UniSC Practitioner Findings: Clinical Misalignment and Diagnostic Risk

Practitioners participating in the UniSC study consistently reported difficulty formulating these cases using conventional trauma frameworks. Many described initial misinterpretation of survivor presentations as personality pathology, treatment resistance, or emotional instability rather than recognising the underlying developmental injury pattern.

This misalignment was most pronounced when clinicians attempted to treat alienation-related trauma using symptom-focused approaches without addressing attachment disruption, identity erosion, and coercive relational conditioning. Practitioners reported that without a CIT-informed lens, treatment pacing errors, premature insight work, and relational ruptures were more likely to occur.

These findings directly informed the protocol requirement that clinicians assess for intersecting trauma structures rather than isolated diagnoses.

CITs as a Clinical Formulation Framework

Within this protocol, CITs function as a formulation framework rather than a diagnostic label. The purpose is not to categorise survivors, but to help clinicians recognise overlapping trauma pathways that influence current functioning.

A CIT-informed formulation considers how attachment disruption interacts with identity development, how coercive control shapes emotional regulation, how institutional betrayal impacts trust in authority, and how prolonged secrecy alters self-concept. This allows treatment planning to move beyond symptom suppression toward structural repair of psychological safety, autonomy, and relational capacity.

The CIT framework also aligns with SEMPI principles by emphasising safety, engagement, meaning, participation, and integration as foundational therapeutic processes rather than outcome-driven symptom reduction.

Implications for Assessment and Treatment Planning

The UniSC research demonstrated that survivors rarely present with clear narratives of harm. Many enter therapy with confusion, minimisation, fragmented memory, or incomplete awareness of their developmental history. For this reason, CIT assessment prioritises pattern recognition over factual verification.

Clinicians are guided to observe relational patterns, emotional responses, attachment behaviour, identity stability, and threat activation rather than relying solely on reported events. This approach reduces the risk of retraumatisation and avoids forcing premature disclosure.

Treatment planning within the CIT framework requires flexibility, slow pacing, and phase-based progression. Survivors may move between stabilisation, identity repair, grief integration, and boundary reconstruction in non-linear ways. This reflects the layered nature of intersecting trauma rather than indicating therapeutic failure.

Cultural and Systemic Context in CIT Formulation

The UniSC findings also highlighted the importance of cultural and systemic context in shaping CIT presentations. Survivors from marginalised communities, including Indigenous clients, frequently reported additional layers of institutional mistrust, historical trauma, and service avoidance related to prior experiences of surveillance, coercion, or bureaucratic harm.

For these survivors, paperwork-heavy assessment processes, rigid clinical structures, and authority-driven engagement models often replicated earlier power imbalances. CIT-informed practice, therefore, requires cultural humility, flexible engagement strategies, and relational pacing that prioritises trust over administrative efficiency.

Clinical Responsibility in CIT Work

Working with CITs requires clinicians to abandon simplified trauma narratives and outcome-driven expectations. The UniSC practitioner data made clear that this work demands tolerance for ambiguity, long-term engagement, and ethical restraint.

Survivors are not disorganised because they are resistant. They are organised around survival strategies shaped by layered developmental threat. Effective clinicians learn to recognise these adaptations as protective responses rather than pathology. CIT-informed practice reframes complexity not as clinical difficulty, but as an accurate reflection of lived developmental experience.

The long-term psychological and social effects observed in adult survivors reflect the cumulative impact of CITs rather than isolated symptoms. These outcomes are the downstream expression of prolonged attachment disruption, coercive control, identity destabilisation, and developmental stress exposure across childhood and adolescence (Price-Tobler, 2023a).

Long-term Psychological and Social Effects

In adult survivors, long-term psychological and social effects are more appropriately understood as the cumulative developmental sequelae of prolonged coercive control, attachment disruption, chronic fear, identity distortion, and repeated exposure to environments in which safety, trust, and reality were compromised (Price-Tobler, 2023a). These outcomes do not present as a neat or uniform symptom cluster. Rather, they often emerge through layered disturbances in affect regulation, self-trust, attachment security, relational functioning, help-seeking, identity formation, and the survivor's capacity to interpret experience without fear of punishment, collapse, or external override.

In the author's clinical work, some adult survivors have presented with complex trauma profiles that also include exposure to firearms, threatened violence, actual gun violence, or chronic intimidation within the caregiving environment. In these cases, survivors may remain organised around danger long after the original environment has changed. Adult presentation may include persistent threat expectancy, exaggerated startle response, hypervigilance, intrusive recollections, restricted freedom of movement, social withdrawal, and difficulty participating in ordinary relational or occupational life with a stable sense of safety.

Intergenerational trauma may further complicate recovery in this population. In some adult survivors, this includes sexual boundary violations, incest, chronic family secrecy, and multigenerational patterns of coercion, shame, silence, and role confusion. In such cases, treatment may require more than symptom reduction. It may involve careful work around inherited narratives, moral injury, self-blame, fractured belonging, and the survivor's struggle to differentiate their own identity from the pathological family system in which they were organised (Bernstein, 1990; Langevin et al., 2021).

Coercive control may continue to shape adult functioning long after childhood. In both the doctoral survivor findings and the author's clinical work, this may include interference with access to medical care, psychological treatment, safe relationships, financial autonomy, and practical help-seeking (Price-Tobler, 2023a). Survivors may remain organised around anticipated retaliation, surveillance, exposure, or punishment, even where direct control is less visible than it was earlier in life. For mental health practitioners, this means that treatment planning must account not only for internal trauma sequelae but also for the survivor's real or anticipated barriers to disclosure, safety, and access to care (Heron & Eisma, 2021; Rose et al., 2024).

In more severe presentations observed in clinical practice, destabilisation may include dissociation, perceptual disturbance, severe anxiety states, or marked reality confusion under stress. These presentations require careful differential assessment and trauma-informed formulation so that survivors are neither pathologised prematurely nor left unsupported when more intensive care is required. Where trauma-related dissociation or perceptual disturbance is present, clinicians must distinguish these responses from primary psychotic processes while maintaining attention to developmental trauma history, relational context, and current safety needs (Wearne et al., 2020; Quidé, 2023).

Taken together, these long-term effects underscore that adult survivors are often presenting not only with trauma symptoms but with the cumulative consequences of developmental environments shaped by coercion, fear, instability, relational distortion, and chronic epistemic harm (Price-Tobler, 2023a). The clinical task is therefore broader than managing isolated symptoms. It involves understanding how these experiences have shaped attachment, identity, emotional regulation, relational functioning, help-seeking, and the survivor's capacity to trust both self and others.

Understanding these long-term psychological and social consequences also requires attention to the autonomic nervous system and the way prolonged threat exposure becomes biologically organised over time. Polyvagal Theory is useful here because it helps explain why survivors may continue to respond to present-day cues as if danger is still imminent, and why regulation, relational safety, and bodily experience must all be addressed in treatment (Porges, 2011).

Neuroception, Vagal Regulation, and Somatic Pathways to Safety

Trauma responses are not driven solely by conscious thought. They are mediated through the autonomic nervous system and shaped by unconscious processes that assess safety and threat. Polyvagal Theory, developed by Porges (2011), provides a neurophysiological framework for understanding how the nervous system organises behaviour, emotional regulation, and relational engagement following trauma. Central to this framework is the concept of neuroception, the nervous system's automatic evaluation of environmental and relational cues without conscious awareness. Through neuroception, the body continuously scans for danger, safety, or life threat, and adjusts physiological responses accordingly.

For survivors of CPA-PA and coercive family environments, neuroception is frequently recalibrated toward chronic threat detection. Prolonged exposure to emotional betrayal, role reversal, surveillance, and relational instability conditions the nervous system to remain hypervigilant even in objectively safe settings. Survivors may misinterpret neutral social interactions as dangerous, perceive authority figures as threatening, or experience physiological shutdown in everyday relational contexts. These reactions are not irrational. They reflect adaptive survival responses shaped by developmental trauma.

Polyvagal Theory identifies three primary autonomic states that influence trauma response. The ventral vagal state supports social engagement, emotional regulation, and a sense of felt safety. When this system is accessible, individuals can connect with others, regulate affect, and remain present in relationships. Trauma exposure, particularly during childhood, often compromises access to this state. Survivors may struggle to experience relational safety, intimacy, and trust because their nervous systems have learned that closeness is associated with threat rather than protection.

The sympathetic state activates mobilisation responses associated with the fight-or-flight response. In adult survivors of alienation and abduction, this may present as chronic anxiety, agitation, hypervigilance, irritability, and physiological arousal triggered by reminders of family conflict, authority dynamics, or perceived abandonment. The dorsal vagal state reflects shutdown and immobilisation responses. This state may manifest as emotional numbness, dissociation, withdrawal, fatigue, and collapse responses following overwhelming stress. While dorsal vagal activation can protect the individual from acute psychological pain, prolonged activation can interfere with emotional integration, relational functioning, and identity development (Van der Kolk, 2014).

Understanding these autonomic patterns allows clinicians to move beyond symptom-based models and instead address trauma as a nervous system condition shaped by developmental experience. Therapy in this framework prioritises restoring physiological safety before cognitive or narrative processing. Without this foundation, trauma work risks overwhelming the client and reinforcing survival patterns rather than resolving them.

Clinical application of Polyvagal-informed practice focuses on strengthening vagal tone and supporting nervous system flexibility. Interventions aim to increase access to ventral vagal regulation while supporting a gradual transition out of chronic sympathetic activation and dorsal shutdown. Techniques commonly used include paced breathing, rhythmic movement, grounding practices, sensory regulation, and relational attunement within the therapeutic alliance. These approaches support the body's capacity to return to states of safety and connection.

Cold exposure techniques are increasingly incorporated as adjunctive somatic interventions. Controlled cold stimulation, such as brief cold-water facial immersion, cool showers, or temperature-contrast practices, can activate the mammalian dive reflex, increase parasympathetic activity, and enhance vagal tone (Porges, 2011). When used cautiously and under clinical guidance, these techniques may help survivors develop greater autonomic regulation and stress tolerance. It is essential that such practices are introduced gradually and adapted to individual tolerance, trauma history, and medical considerations.

Vocalisation and sound-based interventions also support vagal engagement. Activities such as humming, singing, chanting, and paced vocal exercises stimulate vagal pathways associated with social engagement and emotional regulation. These interventions are particularly valuable for survivors who experience speech inhibition, selective mutism patterns, or affective constriction related to trauma exposure.

The clinical relevance of Polyvagal-informed trauma treatment is further supported by applied trauma recovery programs working with abducted and highly traumatised children. Dr Rebecca Bailey's work through the National Centre for Missing and Exploited Children and her leadership in trauma-informed residential recovery programs provide an applied model of nervous system-based intervention. Bailey (2019) integrates Polyvagal principles with somatic regulation, relational safety, equine-assisted therapy, environmental containment, and structured therapeutic communities designed to stabilise highly dysregulated children following prolonged captivity, trafficking, and abduction. Her work demonstrates that nervous system repair requires both therapeutic technique and environmental design that communicates safety at physiological and relational levels.

Bailey's (2019) model emphasises the importance of stable routines, predictable environments, embodied regulation strategies, and attachment-focused relational repair. These principles directly align with adult survivor treatment in CPA-PAA-related trauma, where survivors frequently present with similar patterns of hypervigilance, shutdown, relational distrust, and physiological dysregulation shaped by prolonged coercive control.

Neuroception and vagal regulation, therefore, become central clinical targets in the treatment of adult survivors. Therapy supports clients in recognising bodily cues of threat activation, developing awareness of shifts in internal state, and building skills that enable a gradual return to safety. Over time, survivors learn to differentiate between present-day safety and historical danger signals, reducing trauma-driven misinterpretation of relational environments.

Effective integration of these approaches requires individualised pacing. Some survivors respond quickly to somatic interventions, while others require extended relational stabilisation before body-based work feels safe. Clinicians must remain attentive to consent, titration, and emotional readiness. Trauma-informed practice prioritises collaboration, transparency, and survivor-led pacing to avoid replicating coercive dynamics that mirror the original trauma environment.

By integrating Polyvagal theory, neuroception awareness, and applied somatic regulation strategies, clinicians create pathways for healing that address both psychological and physiological dimensions of trauma. This holistic approach supports not only symptom reduction but the restoration of relational capacity, emotional stability, and embodied safety that many adult survivors were denied during development.

Somatic Techniques in Trauma Treatment

Somatic techniques play a central role in trauma treatment because they address what trauma does to the nervous system and body, not only what it does to memory and cognition. In the author's PhD research, participants consistently described long-standing physiological activation, rapid emotional shutdown, dissociation, and difficulty remaining present when attachment-related material was discussed, even when they could describe events factually and coherently. MHPs interviewed in the same study also reported that traditional talk-based approaches frequently led to emotional flooding, withdrawal, or treatment disengagement when somatic regulation was not addressed first. These findings position somatic stabilisation as a foundational clinical entry point rather than an optional adjunct. For this population, body-based regulation supports pacing, containment, therapeutic safety, and sustained engagement, particularly when verbal processing alone risks retraumatisation or collapse (van der Kolk, 2014).

Grounding and Body Awareness Techniques

Somatic techniques are clinically important when working with adult survivors of CPA-PA because developmental trauma is not stored only in memory and cognition. It is embedded in the nervous system. Many survivors present with dissociation, emotional shutdown, chronic hyperarousal, or alternating states of collapse and agitation that reflect years of living in psychologically unsafe attachment environments. Grounding interventions provide a direct pathway back to present-moment safety by reconnecting survivors with bodily sensations, orientation, and physiological regulation.

Dissociation is common in this population and often develops as an adaptive response to prolonged relational threat. Survivors may describe feeling disconnected from their bodies, emotionally numb, unreal, or detached from their surroundings. Grounding exercises interrupt this pattern by anchoring attention in immediate sensory experience. Simple techniques such as noticing contact between the feet and the floor, the room temperature, or the rhythm of breathing help restore a sense of embodied presence and containment.

Mindful breathing is one of the most accessible regulatory tools in this phase of work. Survivors who grew up under coercive control frequently remain in chronic sympathetic activation, characterised by tension, agitation, and hypervigilance. Slow-paced breathing activates parasympathetic regulation and supports physiological settling. Clinically, this provides a foundation for emotional tolerance and reduces the intensity of trauma-related activation when relational material is discussed.

Practitioners should introduce grounding gradually and collaboratively. Early sessions may focus on short periods of orienting to bodily sensation without forcing emotional disclosure. For many survivors, learning that their body can experience safety without threat is itself corrective. This approach avoids replicating coercive dynamics in which the survivor previously had little control over emotional exposure.

Body awareness work extends beyond simple grounding. It involves helping survivors notice how emotional states manifest physically. Tension in the jaw, shoulders, stomach or chest often signals unresolved relational stress. Many adult survivors report difficulty identifying emotional cues because their childhood environments punished emotional expression or rewarded emotional suppression. Relearning the body's internal signals becomes part of rebuilding emotional literacy and self-trust.

Encouraging clients to track physical sensations alongside emotional experiences can support this process. Over time, patterns often emerge. Survivors may notice that certain family-related topics produce chest tightness, shallow breathing, or fatigue, while boundary-setting attempts produce anxiety or somatic agitation. These observations provide valuable clinical material without requiring immediate verbal trauma integration.

Progressive muscle relaxation is another useful stabilisation tool. By systematically tensing and releasing muscle groups, survivors learn to differentiate between tension and relaxation states. This enhances bodily awareness and provides direct relief from chronic muscular holding patterns that often accompany long-term stress exposure. Clinically, this technique supports downregulation of the nervous system and improves sleep, concentration, and emotional tolerance.

When somatic techniques are introduced consistently and at an appropriate pace, survivors often begin to experience a renewed sense of bodily ownership and agency. This is particularly significant for individuals whose bodies were previously sites of threat, compliance, or emotional suppression. Re-establishing a respectful relationship with the body becomes part of restoring personal autonomy and safety.

The effectiveness of somatic interventions depends on individual tailoring. Some survivors respond quickly to breath-based work, while others require slower sensory-based approaches. Practitioners should remain attentive to signs of overwhelm or shutdown and adjust pacing accordingly. The aim is not rapid emotional exposure but gradual stabilisation that supports long-term therapeutic engagement.

The Neuroscience of Trauma and Practical Tools

Understanding the neurobiological foundations of trauma assists survivors in reframing their reactions as adaptive survival responses rather than personal weakness or pathology. Two brain regions are particularly relevant in this context. The amygdala functions as a threat detection system, rapidly scanning the environment for danger. When a threat is perceived, it initiates physiological survival responses. The medial prefrontal cortex supports emotional regulation, reflective thinking, and inhibition of excessive fear responses.

In survivors of developmental trauma related to parental alienation, these systems often become imbalanced. Chronic exposure to relational threat sensitises the amygdala, leading to exaggerated responses to relatively minor interpersonal stressors. At the same time, regulatory capacity within the prefrontal cortex may be compromised under stress, reducing the individual's ability to self-soothe or accurately appraise safety.

Psychoeducation about these processes is frequently relieving for survivors. Many report long-standing self-blame for emotional reactivity, shutdown, or relationship difficulties. Understanding that these patterns reflect conditioned neurological responses rather than character flaws allows clients to approach healing with greater self-compassion and engagement.

Traumatic memory processing also differs from ordinary autobiographical memory. Rather than being stored as coherent narratives, traumatic experiences are often encoded as fragmented sensory and emotional impressions. This contributes to intrusive memories, bodily reactions, and emotional flashbacks that feel immediate and uncontrollable. Explaining this process normalises survivors' experiences and prepares them for later trauma integration work.

Providing practical regulation tools alongside psychoeducation is essential. Techniques such as breath regulation, grounding exercises, orientation strategies, and paced exposure allow survivors to develop active coping skills that reduce reliance on avoidance or emotional suppression. Written handouts and between-session practice support consolidation of these skills and increase autonomy outside the therapy room.

Over time, repeated use of regulation strategies strengthens neural pathways associated with safety and emotional stability. This supports a gradual movement away from chronic threat-based activation and toward more flexible nervous system functioning. For adult survivors of parental alienation, this shift is foundational, as it underpins later work addressing attachment injury, identity reconstruction, and relational boundary development.

Together, these somatic and neurobiological approaches establish the physiological safety required for deeper psychological work. When survivors regain the capacity to regulate arousal, remain present, and tolerate relational proximity without collapsing or becoming hypervigilant, they are better positioned to engage in higher-order cognitive and relational processing. This stabilisation is not an endpoint. It is the platform from which patterns of coercive control, narcissistic relational dynamics, and attachment manipulation can be examined without overwhelming the nervous system. The following section, therefore, shifts from bodily regulation into the interpersonal structures that maintain alienation and psychological abuse, beginning with the role of narcissistic and controlling caregiver patterns in shaping the survivor's developmental environment.

Narcissistic and Coercive Relational Patterns

The author's doctoral research identified that CPA-PA rarely occurs in psychologically neutral caregiving environments. Instead, it consistently emerges within relational systems characterised by entitlement, emotional dominance, enforcement of loyalty, control of identity, and role reversal. Survivors described caregivers who positioned themselves as emotionally central, morally superior, or perpetually victimised, while requiring the child to meet adult emotional needs and adopt rigid alliance roles.

Across survivor interviews, recurring relational themes included conditional affection, punishment for independent thinking, emotional withdrawal following perceived disloyalty, and persistent pressure to mirror the alienating parent's beliefs and emotional positions. These dynamics align with narcissistic and coercive caregiving patterns in which the child's developmental autonomy is subordinated to the psychological needs of the adult. In these systems, attachment is not organised around safety and mutual responsiveness. It is organised around control, image maintenance, emotional supply, and fear of abandonment.

Participants described growing up in environments where emotional closeness was contingent on compliance. Love was experienced as transactional rather than secure. Disagreement was reframed as betrayal. Neutral curiosity about the targeted parent was interpreted as a threat. Over time, the child learned that emotional survival depended on suppressing their own perceptions and prioritising the alienating caregiver's emotional regulation. This pattern produced what the author's research conceptualised as identity compression, in which the child's internal world is organised around external emotional demands rather than internal developmental needs.

Role reversal was a central mechanism identified in the study. Many survivors reported being placed in pseudo-adult positions, functioning as emotional confidants, protectors, mediators, or loyalty enforcers. This parentified positioning disrupted normal attachment hierarchies and accelerated emotional responsibility beyond developmental capacity. While these roles initially provided the child with proximity and conditional safety, they ultimately produced long-term patterns of hyper-responsibility, guilt-based relational engagement, and difficulty recognising personal needs in adulthood.

The research further identified that narcissistic and coercive dynamics actively impair reality testing. Survivors described repeated exposure to distorted narratives about the targeted parent, the family history, and their own identity. Over time, these narratives became internalised schemas that shaped self-concept and relational expectations. Many participants reported entering adulthood with fragmented identity structures, chronic self-doubt, and difficulty distinguishing authentic emotional responses from implanted loyalty positions (Price-Tobler, 2023a).

From a developmental perspective, these dynamics function as a form of suppression of the attachment system. The child's natural drive toward dual attachment is overridden by fear-based conditioning of loyalty. This produces the hallmark alienation profile of rigid rejection, borrowed language, absence of ambivalence, and emotional hostility toward the targeted parent, even in the absence of direct maltreatment. In adulthood, these same mechanisms continue to influence relational behaviour, including fear of abandonment, attraction to controlling partners, excessive people pleasing, emotional numbing, or avoidance of intimacy.

Clinically, it is critical to recognise that survivors are not simply reacting to divorce conflict. They are recovering from prolonged exposure to coercive relational conditioning. The author's findings demonstrated that when this context is misunderstood, survivors are frequently mislabelled as having personality pathology, attachment disorder, or interpersonal dysfunction without recognition of the developmental origin of these patterns. Such misinterpretation risks replicating the original relational harm by placing responsibility for survival adaptations onto the survivor rather than the abusive relational environment (Price-Tobler, 2023a).

Effective treatment, therefore, requires clinicians to conceptualise narcissistic and coercive caregiver dynamics not as abstract personality traits, but as developmental injury mechanisms. Therapy must support survivors in disentangling inherited loyalty roles, reconstructing independent identity structures, and establishing relational boundaries that were never permitted in childhood.

This relational reframing provides the clinical foundation for Phase II intervention work, where identity reconstruction, cognitive deprogramming, and grief integration become central therapeutic tasks.

The Developmental Origins of Narcissistic Adaptation

Narcissism is not best understood as a personality label, but as a defensive psychological adaptation that develops in response to early attachment disruption, unmet dependency needs, and chronic shame exposure (Puder, 2022). In clinical contexts involving CPA-PA, narcissistic patterns frequently emerge within caregiving systems where psychological safety, attunement, and relational consistency were absent.

Dr David Puder (2023) describes narcissistic structures as fundamentally organised around the regulation of shame and threat to the self. Rather than reflecting confidence or strength, narcissistic defences serve to protect a fragile internal identity that never developed stable emotional grounding through secure early attachment relationships. This framework is particularly relevant in alienation and abduction environments, where caregivers often operate under chronic emotional insecurity, fear of abandonment, and perceived relational threat.

In the author's doctoral findings, alienating caregivers frequently demonstrated patterns of emotional entitlement, hypersensitivity to perceived rejection, rigid moral positioning, and intense need for validation through the child's loyalty. These patterns mirror the defensive processes described by Puder, where the self becomes organised around external affirmation rather than internal emotional regulation (Price-Tobler, 2023; Puder, 2022).

Early Attachment Injury and Shame-Based Identity Formation

According to Puder's clinical model, narcissistic adaptation develops when children are unable to experience consistent emotional mirroring, safety, and unconditional acceptance. When caregivers respond unpredictably, critically, or conditionally, children internalise the belief that their authentic emotional needs are unsafe or unacceptable (Puder, 2022). Instead of developing a stable internal sense of worth, the child learns to manage relationships through performance, control, or emotional withdrawal.

In alienating households, children are frequently exposed to emotionally chaotic environments where affection is contingent on compliance, silence, or alliance with the dominant caregiver. Abduction contexts intensify this dynamic. When a caregiver removes a child from the other parent and constructs a controlled narrative of danger, betrayal, or moral superiority, the relational environment becomes organised around secrecy, fear management, and loyalty enforcement.

The author's research documented that abducted children often experienced emotional pressure to participate in false narratives, suppress memories, and regulate the caregiver's emotional state. These conditions mirror the attachment injuries described by Puder as core contributors to narcissistic defences, where emotional authenticity is replaced by survival-based identity construction (Price-Tobler, 2023; Puder, 2023).

Grandiosity as Protection Rather Than Personality Trait

Puder emphasises that grandiosity, entitlement, and emotional dominance are not expressions of inflated self-worth, but compensatory strategies used to protect against deep internal vulnerability. When children grow up without a secure emotional anchor, excessive self-focus becomes a way to avoid emotional collapse and the exposure of shame (Puder, 2023).

In alienation and abduction systems, this dynamic is often reinforced socially. Caregivers who present themselves as heroic protectors, victims of injustice, or morally superior parents receive external validation that strengthens narcissistic identity structures. The child is recruited into this narrative and becomes both an emotional regulator and a form of relational currency. Over time, this reinforces relational patterns organised around power rather than mutuality.

The author's findings indicated that children raised within these systems frequently learned that emotional closeness was transactional rather than relational. Affection was earned through loyalty and alignment, not through authentic connection. This environment fosters narcissistic relational strategies that persist into adulthood for both caregivers and affected children.

Emotional Avoidance and Fear of Vulnerability

A central theme in Puder's work is the fear of vulnerability that underpins narcissistic behaviour. Individuals who developed narcissistic defences often experience intense discomfort when exposed emotionally. Rather than engaging in reciprocal emotional connection, they resort to control, intellectualisation, emotional distancing, or relational dominance to avoid perceived threat (Puder, 2022).

In CPA-PA dynamics, vulnerability is frequently framed as weakness. Children are discouraged from expressing grief, longing, or confusion about the targeted parent. Abducted children are often required to suppress emotional curiosity and loyalty conflicts to preserve the caregiver's psychological stability. These environments condition both caregivers and children to associate vulnerability with danger.

This emotional suppression becomes embedded in relational patterns that prioritise image management and emotional control. Over time, authentic attachment capacity is replaced by performance-based interaction.

Narcissistic Relational Dynamics

For adult survivors of alienation and abduction, narcissistic relational dynamics often appear in two primary forms. Some survivors internalise narcissistic defences themselves as a survival adaptation. Others become relationally vulnerable to narcissistic partners due to early attachment conditioning that normalised emotional manipulation and conditional love.

Puder emphasises that therapeutic change requires creating a sense of relational safety before confronting defensive patterns. Shame must be reduced before insight can be tolerated. Empathy, not confrontation, is the primary pathway toward restructuring narcissistic defences (Puder, 2022). This aligns with the author's clinical findings that survivors make the greatest progress when treatment first focuses on emotional stabilisation, identity safety, and attachment repair rather than on behavioural correction alone (Price Tobler, 2023).

Therapy must provide a relational environment that allows vulnerability to be experienced without punishment. This involves consistent attunement, emotional containment, and gradual exposure to authentic emotional expression. Over time, survivors learn that connection does not require performance, silence, or emotional suppression.

Reframing Narcissism as Developmental Injury

Viewing narcissism through a developmental trauma lens shifts clinical focus away from moral judgement and toward recovery. Rather than categorising individuals as fixed personality types, Puder's framework recognises narcissistic traits as learned survival strategies shaped by early relational injury (Puder, 2022).

In alienation and abduction contexts, this reframing is essential. It allows clinicians to understand the relational ecosystem that produced these dynamics, while supporting survivors in disentangling their identities from inherited psychological patterns. By addressing shame regulation, attachment disruption, and psychological safety simultaneously, clinicians can help survivors reconstruct healthier relational models and restore internal psychological stability.

This developmental perspective prepares the groundwork for the subsequent protocol phases focused on grief integration, identity repair, and relational reconnection.

Traits and Cycles of Narcissistic Abuse in Alienation and Abduction Contexts

Narcissistic relational patterns are characterised by impairments in empathy, unstable self-esteem regulation, and reliance on external validation to maintain psychological equilibrium (American Psychiatric Association, 2013; Puder, 2022). In the context of CPA-PAA, these traits frequently manifest within caregiving systems where emotional control, image management, and loyalty enforcement are central organising dynamics.

Reduced empathic capacity limits the individual's ability to recognise or respond to others' emotional needs. Rather than reciprocal emotional engagement, relationships become organised around self-protection and control. Grandiosity functions as a compensatory defence rather than a reflection of genuine self-confidence, serving to mask underlying shame vulnerability and attachment insecurity (Puder, 2022). The persistent need for admiration and affirmation creates relational instability and drives manipulative interaction patterns.

Defensive Processes and Psychological Manipulation

Narcissistic abuse is maintained through a series of defensive psychological processes that protect fragile self-structure. Denial allows the individual to avoid confronting behaviour that threatens their self-image. Projection externalises unwanted emotional states by attributing blame or hostility to others. These mechanisms preserve internal psychological stability while shifting relational burden onto the victim (American Psychiatric Association, 2013).

Gaslighting represents a particularly harmful interpersonal strategy. Through systematic contradiction, minimisation, and distortion of reality, the perpetrator undermines the victim's confidence in their own perception and memory (Stark, 2007). Over time, this erodes psychological autonomy and fosters dependency. In alienation contexts, gaslighting is often institutionalised through repeated narrative reinforcement, legal messaging, and social triangulation, amplifying its impact on both children and targeted parents.

The Cycle of Narcissistic Relational Abuse

Clinical literature consistently identifies a cyclical pattern of narcissistic relational behaviour that includes idealisation, devaluation, and discard phases (Puder, 2022; Walker, 1979). Although originally conceptualised within intimate partner violence frameworks, this cycle is equally observable within coercive family systems and alienating caregiving environments.

During idealisation, the narcissistic individual presents as highly attentive, affirming, and emotionally engaging. This phase establishes rapid attachment bonds and emotional dependency. In parental alienation cases, children may experience this phase as excessive emotional closeness, over-involvement, or role reversal dynamics that position the child as emotional confidant or ally.

The devaluation phase follows once emotional control is secured. Criticism, withdrawal of affection, emotional unpredictability, and psychological invalidation emerge. For children and adult survivors, this stage produces chronic confusion, shame, and self-blame, reinforcing attachment insecurity and loyalty compliance.

The discard phase involves emotional abandonment, relational rupture, or replacement of the relational target when the narcissistic individual perceives diminishing psychological utility. In abduction contexts, this may take the form of emotional disengagement once the child reaches adulthood, no longer serves dependency functions, or begins seeking autonomy.

This cyclical pattern creates long-term relational instability and reinforces trauma bonding, making disengagement psychologically complex for survivors (van der Kolk, 2014).

Clinical Impact on Survivors in CPA-PA Contexts

Adult survivors frequently report prolonged exposure to these relational cycles within caregiving systems (Price Tobler, 2023). The author's doctoral findings identified enduring patterns of hypervigilance, emotional suppression, relational mistrust, and difficulty forming secure adult attachments as common sequelae.

Repeated exposure to idealisation and devaluation dynamics conditions survivors to equate affection with instability. As adults, this increases vulnerability to narcissistic partners and exploitative relationships, as familiar relational patterns may be misinterpreted as normal attachment intensity.

Therapeutic Implications and Recovery Focus

Effective intervention requires more than psychoeducation about narcissistic traits. Recovery must focus on restoring internal safety, rebuilding identity coherence, and strengthening emotional autonomy (Puder, 2022; Price Tobler, 2023). Therapeutic work should prioritise the development of boundary awareness, emotional regulation capacity, and reality anchoring following prolonged exposure to gaslighting and coercive relational control.

Boundary formation is a central treatment goal. Survivors often require structured support to identify emotional limits, recognise manipulation cues, and practice assertive communication without excessive guilt or fear of abandonment. Emotional regulation strategies, including somatic stabilisation and trauma-informed cognitive processing, support survivors in tolerating relational triggers without re-entering trauma-bonding cycles (van der Kolk, 2014). As survivors develop internal regulation capacity, they become less dependent on external validation and more able to sustain reciprocal, emotionally safe relationships.

This framework positions narcissistic abuse not as an isolated personality phenomenon, but as a relational trauma process that requires attachment-informed, developmentally sensitive intervention. Research on adult survivors of parental alienation consistently indicates that the long-term harm associated with alienation cannot be separated from narcissistic patterns of thinking and relational behaviour that frequently drive these dynamics (Price-Tobler, 2023a). Survivors describe childhood environments in which emotional needs were minimised, vulnerability was shamed, and attachment bonds were distorted by caregivers whose psychological needs took priority over the child's developmental wellbeing. These early relational conditions shape identity formation, health outcomes, and adult relationship functioning, often leaving survivors with difficulty recognising their own worth or trusting that intimacy can be safe.

Within alienation contexts, narcissism is rarely expressed solely as a categorical personality disorder as defined in the DSM-5-TR (American Psychiatric Association, 2022). More commonly, it presents as a spectrum of entrenched traits, attachment insecurities, and context-activated defensive patterns that may range from excessive compliance and image management to rage, entitlement, and coercive control. Contemporary clinical theory conceptualises narcissistic functioning as a defensive strategy organised around shame avoidance and fear of abandonment, rather than simple grandiosity (Kernberg, 2016; Pincus & Lukowitsky, 2010). For children raised within these relational environments, the developmental consequence is often erosion of the authentic self. Survivors report that love was conditional, offered in exchange for loyalty, performance, or emotional compliance, and withdrawn when distress or independence was expressed. Winnicott (1960/2018) described this pattern as the formation of a "false self," which may appear socially adapted while concealing significant internal emptiness and identity fragmentation.

The Adult Attachment Interview (AAI), developed by George, Kaplan, and Main (1985/1996) and further refined by Hesse (2008, 2016), provides a clinically structured method for examining these attachment dynamics. The AAI does not assess attachment solely through self-report, but through the coherence, organisation, and emotional integration of autobiographical narratives under mild relational stress. When caregivers are asked to describe early attachment relationships and provide supporting memories, clinicians can observe patterns such as idealisation, contradiction, narrative collapse, or emotional disengagement. These discourse markers reflect unresolved attachment trauma and defensive processing styles that frequently underpin narcissistic caregiving behaviour. In parental alienation contexts, similar narrative distortions are reported by survivors, who describe having been trained to adopt the caregiver's version of reality at the expense of their own lived experience, often resulting in enduring internal confusion and self-doubt.

Attachment Adaptation Under Threat and the Dynamic-Maturational Model (DMM)

The Dynamic-Maturational Model of attachment developed by Crittenden (1994, 2016) provides a clinically relevant framework for understanding how children adapt to caregiving environments characterised by threat, emotional unpredictability, coercive control, or psychological abuse. Unlike categorical attachment classifications, the DMM focuses on survival-based information processing strategies that organise behaviour when safety cannot be reliably obtained (Crittenden & Landini, 2011).

Within alienating and abductive caregiving contexts, children are frequently exposed to relational environments where emotional expression is unsafe, loyalty is enforced, and reality is manipulated. The DMM describes two broad families of adaptive strategies that commonly emerge in these conditions. Type A strategies involve suppressing emotional expression and aligning with authority figures, leading children to appear compliant, perfectionistic, or overly positive to avoid punishment or rejection (Main et al., 2008). Type C strategies, by contrast, involve amplifying emotional expression through anger, distress, or dramatic displays to gain attention, proximity, or control. While both strategies are biologically adaptive responses to unsafe caregiving environments, both undermine authenticity, relational trust, and emotional integration over time (Crittenden, 2016).

Research applying the DMM framework has identified patterns particularly relevant to alienating caregivers. These include delusional idealisation, in which one caregiver is portrayed as entirely virtuous while the targeted parent is cast as dangerous or defective, and externally assembled identity structures characterised by impression management and unstable self-concepts (Crittenden & Landini, 2011; Farnfield et al., 2010). Other presentations involve punitive anger or victim-based manipulation, which can be highly persuasive in legal and clinical settings due to their emotional intensity or apparent vulnerability. Rather than conceptualising these patterns as fixed personality traits, the DMM frames them as entrenched attachment defences that originated as survival responses but later produce significant relational harm.

For survivors raised within these environments, the developmental imprint is enduring. Many adopt emotionally inhibited or hyper-compliant relational strategies, becoming invisible in adult relationships. Others develop volatile emotional patterns characterised by oscillations between anger and a desperate need for connection. Some present with blended strategies that combine emotional withdrawal with reactive aggression, contributing to identity confusion and fear of intimacy. Attachment-informed models help clinicians recognise that these adult presentations reflect developmental adaptations to chronic relational threat rather than inherent pathology.

Neurodevelopmental Impact and Long-Term Health Consequences

Neuroscience research further supports this developmental framework. Early caregiver attunement plays a critical role in right-hemisphere development, particularly in neural systems responsible for affect regulation, stress modulation, and relational engagement (Schore, 2001, 2003). When caregiving environments are characterised by emotional unavailability, shaming, or coercive control, neural development adapts toward hypervigilance, emotional inhibition, or threat-based processing rather than secure relational regulation (Schore, 2001, 2003).

Survivors of parental alienation frequently report childhood environments marked by emotionally transactional parenting, inconsistent caregiving, or rigid behavioural control. These patterns are associated with increased rates of emotional dysregulation, dissociation, somatic symptom development, and long-term health vulnerability. Early distress is frequently mislabelled in childhood as behavioural disorders or neurodevelopmental conditions, obscuring underlying relational trauma (Bernet, 2020). Adverse childhood experiences research has consistently demonstrated strong associations between early relational trauma and adult physical health outcomes, including autoimmune conditions and chronic illness (Anda et al., 2006; Felitti et al., 1998).

Clinical Implications

Understanding narcissistic caregiving behaviour through attachment science, discourse-based assessment tools such as the AAI, and developmentally informed frameworks such as the DMM provides a coherent explanatory pathway linking early relational threat to adult survivor presentation. This integrated perspective clarifies why survivors struggle with identity stability, emotional regulation, relational trust, and somatic vulnerability. It also reinforces that while alienating caregivers may remain resistant to change, survivors retain substantial capacity for recovery when treatment targets both trauma resolution and disrupted developmental processes.

Treatment Considerations

Therapy for adult survivors of parental alienation must address both unresolved trauma and disrupted developmental processes. Single-modality approaches are insufficient because survivors frequently present with layered attachment injury, identity fragmentation, relational fear, and nervous system dysregulation (Price-Tobler, 2023a). Effective intervention requires an integrated treatment model that addresses stabilisation, attachment repair, cognitive restructuring, and narrative coherence.

Attachment-informed interventions form a central foundation of treatment. By helping survivors identify their protective relational strategies, including compliance, emotional withdrawal, hyper-independence, rage, or self-erasure, therapy creates space for safer relational engagement. The Dynamic-Maturational Model provides a clinically useful framework for understanding these adaptations as survival strategies developed in unsafe caregiving environments rather than inherent pathology (Crittenden, 1994, 2016; Crittenden & Landini, 2011). This reframing reduces shame and supports gradual behavioural and emotional change.

Schema Therapy is particularly effective for addressing entrenched beliefs commonly observed in this population, including defectiveness, mistrust, abandonment expectation, and emotional deprivation (Young, Klosko, & Weishaar, 2003). Corrective relational experiences within the therapeutic alliance allow survivors to challenge indoctrinated narratives and begin reconstructing a coherent and compassionate self-concept.

Eye Movement Desensitisation and Reprocessing can be valuable when integrated within a broader attachment and identity framework. EMDR has demonstrated effectiveness in reducing physiological arousal and trauma reactivity associated with intrusive memories, court-related stressors, sudden separations, and coercive family conflict (Shapiro, 2018). However, desensitisation alone is insufficient. Trauma symptom reduction without concurrent identity reconstruction risks emotional flattening and unresolved relational injury.

Narrative Therapy supports survivors in reclaiming authorship of their life stories and separating internalised alienating narratives from lived experience (White & Epston, 1990). Externalising the abuse dynamic allows survivors to reframe responsibility, restore meaning, and develop narrative coherence following years of imposed distortion and psychological control.

Psychoeducation and the development of critical thinking are also essential components of treatment. Survivors frequently describe recovery as a process of disentangling false beliefs and relational conditioning. Teaching recognition of projection, gaslighting, emotional manipulation, and shame-based control strengthens autonomy and protects against re-engagement with abusive dynamics (Childress, 2015).

Together, these approaches form a coordinated treatment pathway that addresses safety, attachment repair, trauma integration, identity reconstruction, and long-term relational resilience. Survivors of parental alienation require treatment models that acknowledge both the psychological injury sustained and the developmental growth that was disrupted.

Integrative Summary

This chapter has examined narcissistic caregiving dynamics through attachment science, trauma theory, and developmental psychology. Early relational environments characterised by emotional neglect, coercive control, conditional love, or identity distortion shape long-term patterns of self-concept, emotional regulation, and interpersonal functioning. Recognition of these developmental pathways allows clinicians to move beyond surface symptom management toward deeper relational and identity repair.

For adult survivors, understanding these patterns supports the dismantling of distorted self-beliefs and reduces internalised blame. Therapeutic work that combines attachment-based intervention, trauma integration, narrative reconstruction, and cognitive restructuring enables survivors to reclaim autonomy, rebuild relational safety, and establish healthier boundaries.

The clinical implications extend beyond individual recovery. Interventions that address narcissistic family systems, alienation dynamics, and coercive relational patterns contribute to breaking intergenerational transmission of psychological harm. Effective treatment, therefore, functions not only as individual healing but as systemic prevention.

The relational adaptations described throughout this chapter often intersect with co-dependent patterns that emerge in survivors raised in emotionally unsafe or manipulative family systems. Understanding co-dependency provides a further lens through which clinicians can conceptualise excessive caretaking, boundary collapse, emotional over-responsibility, and identity diffusion in adult survivors of parental alienation. The following section examines the developmental origins, clinical presentation, and treatment implications of co-dependent relational patterns within trauma-informed practice.

Co-dependence Across the Treatment Phases

Within this protocol, co-dependence is conceptualised as a developmental adaptation rather than a clinical deficit. It reflects relational survival strategies formed in environments where attachment security was conditional, psychological safety was unstable, and identity development was subordinated to caregiver needs. In adult survivors of parental alienation and child psychological abuse, these strategies often remain active long after the original threat has passed (Price-Tobler, 2023a).

Importantly, co-dependent patterns do not present uniformly as distress. Many survivors describe these relational styles as comforting, familiar, and protective. For individuals who grew up managing parental emotions, mediating conflict, or maintaining loyalty alliances, emotionally fused relationships can feel safer than autonomous intimacy. Some survivors actively prefer partners who display reciprocal dependency because the predictability of mutual reliance provides stability.

In clinical practice, numerous couples who identify with these dynamics report high relationship satisfaction, strong bonds of loyalty, and a sense that their partner is the only person they fully trust to remain. Similar relational patterns were also reflected in the doctoral interview data. When clinicians frame co-dependence as inherently pathological, survivors may experience this as invalidating or threatening, particularly when they already struggle to maintain long-term relationships. Therapeutic work, therefore, requires careful pacing and reframing, respecting that these strategies once protected attachment rather than assuming they must be eliminated.

Phase I focuses on stabilisation and relational safety. At this stage, co-dependent patterns are not challenged directly. Survivors often enter therapy with heightened abandonment sensitivity and fear of relational rupture. Immediate confrontation of people-pleasing, emotional fusion, or over-responsibility can trigger withdrawal or defensive loyalty to familiar relational patterns. Phase I work instead emphasises safety within the therapeutic relationship, helping survivors experience consistent attunement without performance requirements. The clinician models non-transactional care, where attention is not contingent on compliance or emotional labour. This establishes the foundation necessary for later differentiation work.

Phase II introduces identity reconstruction and emotional differentiation. Once safety is established, survivors are gradually supported to recognise inherited relational roles. Many become aware that their sense of worth has been organised around being useful, needed, or emotionally available at personal cost. This phase focuses on helping survivors identify previously suppressed internal needs, preferences, and boundaries. Importantly, this is not framed as abandoning valued relationships but as expanding relational flexibility. Survivors learn that connection does not require self-erasure. This stage also involves examining partner selection patterns, including attraction to emotionally dependent or highly fused dynamics, without moral judgement. The clinical aim is increased choice rather than forced behavioural change.

Phase III addresses relational repair and boundary integration. For survivors who remain in mutually dependent partnerships, therapy supports the development of healthier reciprocity without destabilising attachment security. Some couples evolve toward greater mutual autonomy while maintaining closeness. Others consciously maintain high interdependence, with improved communication, reduced emotional coercion, and clearer consent regarding roles. The protocol does not impose a single relational ideal. Instead, it prioritises psychological safety, consent, and integrity of identity within relational structures chosen by the survivor.

Phase IV focuses on long-term consolidation and relapse prevention. Survivors learn to recognise when stress, family contact, court involvement, or parental reactivation triggers old co-dependent reflexes. Rather than viewing regression as a failure, the protocol frames these moments as activation of nervous system memory. Clients develop internal monitoring skills that allow them to pause, reflect, and respond rather than automatically reverting to emotional over-functioning.

Across all phases, the author's doctoral findings highlight that co-dependence in this population is inseparable from early attachment injury and loyalty conditioning (Price-Tobler, 2023a). Effective treatment does not aim to eradicate relational closeness or dependency needs. It aims to restore agency, emotional choice, and self-directed identity development. Survivors are supported to retain what feels safe while gaining the capacity to renegotiate patterns that no longer serve their wellbeing.

This approach allows survivors to move from survival-based relational strategies toward intentional relational living, without replicating the coercive dynamics that shaped their early experiences.

Across the treatment phases, co-dependence is approached not as behaviour to be eliminated but as relational memory to be understood, stabilised, and gradually renegotiated. Survivors are supported to retain relational safety while expanding autonomy, emotional choice, and identity coherence. This phased approach prevents premature rupture of attachment bonds while creating space for healthier relational flexibility. In the context of parental alienation and abduction trauma, this balance is essential, as survivors often carry profound attachment fear alongside strong loyalty conditioning. Treatment, therefore, prioritises safety first, differentiation second, relational restructuring third, and long-term nervous system stability last.

Attachment Disruption in Adult Survivors in CPA-PA Contexts

Attachment is not simply a relational preference. It is a biologically driven survival system that organises the nervous system's responses to threats, separation, and proximity-seeking across the lifespan (Bowlby, 1969). For adult survivors of CPA-PA, this system has often been repeatedly activated under conditions of coercion, loyalty conflict, sudden separation, and emotional threat. As a result, attachment development does not follow typical trajectories of security formation. Instead, it becomes organised around survival rather than safety.

The author's doctoral findings identified that many adult survivors present with attachment patterns characterised by hypervigilance, emotional suppression, relational fear, and unstable proximity seeking. Survivors frequently describe early environments where closeness was conditional, honesty was punished, and emotional expression triggered withdrawal or retaliation. In abduction cases, this pattern is intensified by abrupt physical separation, identity disruption, geographic displacement, and enforced narrative replacement. These experiences produce attachment systems that remain chronically activated long after the original threat has passed (Price-Tobler, 2023a).

Traditional attachment classifications describe secure, anxious-preoccupied, dismissing-avoidant, and disorganised-fearful patterns (Ainsworth et al., 1978; Main & Solomon, 1990). In alienation and abduction contexts, the most observed adult presentations involve anxious and disorganised patterns, often blended with avoidant coping strategies. Survivors may simultaneously crave closeness while fearing dependency or seek reassurance while anticipating betrayal. This internal contradiction reflects early caregiving environments in which the attachment figure served as both protector and threat.

Alienating caregiving introduces additional distortions to attachment development. Children are frequently required to suppress attachment needs toward the targeted parent, align emotionally with the alienating caregiver, and adopt loyalty narratives that override personal experience. Over time, the child learns that attachment safety depends on compliance rather than authenticity. In abduction scenarios, the attachment rupture is compounded by the loss of extended family, community identity, and self-continuity, further destabilising internal working models of relationships.

The attachment system operates largely outside conscious awareness, and when perceived threat is activated, automatic responses emerge, including emotional shutdown, hyperarousal, appeasement, or proximity-seeking behaviours (Zeanah & Gleason, 2015). Adult survivors often report that relational triggers such as conflict, perceived abandonment, court involvement, or family contact rapidly activate these early attachment states. This explains why survivors may struggle to remain emotionally present during therapy, experience sudden withdrawal, or oscillate between dependence and detachment.

Neurodevelopmental research supports this clinical picture. Early caregiving experiences shape right-hemisphere development, which is responsible for affect regulation, relational attunement, and stress modulation (Schore, 2001, 2003). When caregiving is inconsistent, shaming, or emotionally unavailable, neural circuits prioritise self-protection rather than connection. Survivors of alienation and abduction frequently report childhoods characterised by emotional minimisation, performance-based acceptance, or psychological control. These experiences become embedded in neural organisation, producing adult attachment systems oriented toward vigilance rather than safety.

The author's doctoral interviews further revealed that many survivors struggle with identity cohesion alongside attachment disruption. Survivors often describe not knowing who they are outside of the narratives imposed by caregivers. Attachment injury in this population is therefore not limited to relational functioning. It extends into self-concept, emotional regulation, boundary formation, and long-term relational expectations (Price-Tobler, 2023a).

Clinical implications for treatment are significant. Attachment disruption cannot be addressed solely by reducing symptoms. Stabilisation, pacing, and relational safety must precede trauma integration. Survivors require consistent therapeutic presence that models non-transactional care, emotional attunement, and predictable boundaries. This creates the foundation for identity reconstruction and relational differentiation in later treatment phases.

Repairing attachment injury in adult survivors does not involve recreating childhood dependency. Instead, it focuses on supporting survivors to develop internal safety, emotional regulation capacity, and flexible relational choice. Therapy becomes a corrective relational experience in which survivors gradually learn that connection does not require self-erasure, emotional labour, or submission to loyalty.

The HQTP integrates attachment repair as a cross-phase clinical priority rather than a single-stage intervention. Early phases prioritise stabilisation of the attachment system through safety, relational containment, and epistemic protection. Mid-phase work supports identity reconstruction, meaning integration, and the processing of attachment-related grief and loss. Later phases focus on consolidation, relational differentiation, and the development of autonomous relational choice. Across all phases, attachment repair is approached as a gradual developmental process rather than a discrete therapeutic task. The following chapter shifts from conceptual framing into applied clinical implementation, situating therapeutic modalities within this phased treatment architecture.

Chapter Nine

Coercive Persuasion, Mind-Changing Processes, and Developmental Narrative Conditioning in CPA-PA Contexts

Understanding the mechanisms through which belief systems can be shaped within highly controlled relational environments is essential for clinicians working with adult survivors. Research across psychology, psychiatry, and sociology demonstrates that belief change under coercive conditions does not require unusual psychological techniques. Rather, these processes typically emerge when ordinary mechanisms of social influence, such as isolation, emotional dependence, repetition, and pressure from authority, operate in environments where access to alternative perspectives is limited (Taylor, 2006).

In this chapter, the term brainwashing is used cautiously as a reader accessible shorthand for coercive persuasion, thought reform, and developmental narrative conditioning, rather than as a claim that unusual or exotic mechanisms are involved. Children and adolescents are particularly vulnerable to these dynamics because their cognitive development, integration of autobiographical memory, and identity formation are still evolving. In addition, children depend on caregivers for safety, a sense of belonging, and access to resources. When a dominant caregiver controls the informational and emotional environment, the child's interpretation of family events may become organised around preserving attachment security rather than independently evaluating competing narratives.

Taylor's Model of Mind-Changing Processes

Neuroscientist Kathleen Taylor describes brainwashing as a structured form of belief change that relies on the systematic application of ordinary learning mechanisms (Taylor, 2006). Taylor identifies three broad pathways through which belief systems may be reshaped: mind-changing by force, mind-changing by stealth, and direct neurological manipulation technologies.

Direct neurological manipulation refers to hypothetical or experimental technological interventions and is generally outside the scope of ordinary social influence. The first two pathways, force and stealth, are achieved primarily through psychological and social mechanisms.

Taylor explains that these processes often operate through a cluster of interacting techniques designed to reshape how individuals interpret reality. These techniques include isolation from competing perspectives, control of information, induction of uncertainty regarding previous beliefs, repetition of new narratives, and emotional reinforcement of those narratives (Taylor, 2006). When applied within environments characterised by dependency and restricted communication, these mechanisms can gradually reshape belief systems.

Mind-Changing by Force

Mind-changing by force occurs when individuals are placed within environments where leaving the system or accessing alternative viewpoints becomes difficult or impossible. In such contexts, the individual may be surrounded by people who demonstrate strong loyalty to the dominant ideology and hostility toward perceived external enemies (Taylor, 2006).

Within cultic or extremist groups, new members may receive approval, status, and a sense of belonging only when they demonstrate agreement with the group's beliefs. Disagreement or questioning may lead to social exclusion or punishment.

In developmental contexts such as CPA-PA, children may experience structurally similar conditions even though the environment is familial rather than organisational. Because children depend on caregivers for safety, emotional regulation, and daily survival, they have a limited ability to exit relational environments dominated by one caregiver's narrative. When the caregiver repeatedly expresses hostility toward the targeted parent and reinforces narratives portraying that parent as dangerous or morally deficient, the child may experience pressure to align with the caregiver's interpretation of events.

Mind-Changing by Stealth

Mind-changing by stealth occurs gradually and may be less recognisable to the individual experiencing it. Rather than relying on overt coercion, the process unfolds through subtle shifts in narrative framing and repeated exposure to particular interpretations of events (Taylor, 2006).

Influence may begin with small reinterpretations of past experiences or the gradual introduction of negative characterisations of individuals outside the dominant group. Over time, these interpretations may become integrated into the individual's understanding of reality.

Within CPA-PA contexts, children may initially encounter subtle reinterpretations of family events, such as suggestions that the targeted parent is unreliable, untrustworthy, or emotionally harmful. Repeated exposure to these interpretations—combined with reduced contact with the targeted parent may gradually shape the child's understanding of family relationships.

Isolation, Information Control, and Uncertainty

Both force-based and stealth-based influence typically involve three interacting mechanisms: isolation from competing viewpoints, control of the informational environment, and the introduction of uncertainty regarding previously held beliefs (Taylor, 2006).

Isolation may involve restricting contact with individuals who hold alternative perspectives or discouraging communication with those individuals. Information control can occur through selective storytelling, the reinterpretation of events, or the discouragement of questioning of the dominant narrative. Once uncertainty has been introduced regarding earlier beliefs, repeated reinforcement of the new narrative may gradually reshape the individual's interpretation of reality.

In CPA-PA contexts, children may experience reduced contact with the targeted parent and extended family members while simultaneously being exposed to repeated negative narratives about those relationships. Over time, the absence of corrective relational experiences may contribute to the consolidation of the dominant narrative.

Source Monitoring, Developmental Suggestibility, and Epistemic Trust

A further mechanism relevant to CPA-PA presentations concerns how children determine the source of their knowledge. Source monitoring refers to the cognitive process by which individuals distinguish among what they have directly experienced, what they have inferred, and what others have communicated to them. In childhood, repeated exposure to a dominant caregiver's narrative may gradually blur these distinctions, particularly when the child lives in a tightly controlled relational and informational environment. Under such conditions, the child may come to experience repeatedly communicated interpretations as if they were independently known, personally remembered, or self-generated beliefs rather than caregiver-supplied constructions (Poole & Lindsay, 2001; Roberts & Powell, 2006).

This issue is especially important in CPA-PA contexts because the child's developing narrative is often shaped within conditions of dependency, fear, and restricted access to corrective perspectives. Experimental research has shown that misleading information provided by parents can alter children's later reports, including responses to open-ended prompts, whereas stronger source-monitoring abilities are associated with greater resistance to suggestion (Poole & Lindsay, 2001; Roberts & Powell, 2006). In developmental terms, this suggests that loyalty-based narratives may become stabilised not only because the child is compliant but also because the child progressively loses confidence in the origins of his or her knowledge.

This process also intersects with epistemic trust. Epistemic trust refers to openness to others' communicated knowledge, while epistemic vigilance refers to the capacity to evaluate whether that knowledge is trustworthy or misleading. In normative development, children learn from trusted caregivers while gradually building the capacity to assess reliability. In coercive family environments, however, this balance may become distorted. The dominant caregiver may come to function not only as the child's attachment figure but also as the child's primary authority on what is real, safe, and morally true. In CPA-PA contexts, and particularly in CPA-PAA or CPA-PERA presentations where access to the other parent is restricted, this may intensify the child's dependence on a single interpretive source and reduce opportunities for reflective comparison of competing accounts (Li et al., 2023).

Over time, the child's narrative may therefore become organised around attachment-preserving belief rather than independent appraisal. What appears later as rigid certainty may not reflect deliberate deceit or freely formed judgement, but a developmentally conditioned collapse in source differentiation, epistemic flexibility, and confidence in one's own relational experience. This is one reason why later reconsideration of childhood narratives may be psychologically destabilising in adulthood. The adult survivor is not merely revising opinions, but reworking the very conditions under which knowledge, memory, and trust were organised during development (Li et al., 2023; Poole & Lindsay, 2001).

Thought Reform Research

Earlier work on coercive persuasion by psychiatrist Robert Jay Lifton identified similar mechanisms operating in ideological indoctrination environments. Lifton described processes such as milieu control, ideological framing of events, moral absolutism, and the prioritisation of doctrine over personal experience (Lifton, 1961).

Milieu control refers to the regulation of communication within the individual's environment. This may occur when children have limited opportunities to communicate with the targeted parent or extended family members. When communication channels are restricted, the caregiver's narrative may become the child's primary interpretive framework.

Lifton also described the use of emotionally charged language to reinforce ideological beliefs. In family contexts, complex relational histories may be reduced to simplified portrayals of the targeted parent as dangerous or untrustworthy. Repeated exposure to such characterisations can shape how children interpret family events.

Attachment Dependency and Developmental Vulnerability

Attachment theory provides an important developmental explanation for why these processes may be particularly influential in childhood. John Bowlby proposed that attachment functions as a biological system designed to maintain proximity between children and caregivers in the face of threat (Bowlby, 1969/1982). Because caregivers regulate children's sense of safety and belonging, children are strongly motivated to maintain alignment with those caregivers. In high-conflict family environments, this dependency can shape how children interpret relational events. Aligning with the caregiver who controls the household environment may become a strategy for maintaining emotional security.

Attachment Exploitation and Traumatic Bonding

Research examining high-control groups has demonstrated that authority figures may strengthen loyalty by pairing distress with intermittent approval. Alexandra Stein describes how fear and uncertainty can be combined with moments of belonging or care, reinforcing attachment to the authority figure who controls the environment (Stein, 2017; Stein, 2021).

Patrick Carnes similarly described traumatic bonding, in which cycles of distress and intermittent reinforcement strengthen emotional attachment between dependent individuals and controlling figures (Carnes, 1997). In family environments characterised by emotional volatility, children may learn that agreement with the dominant caregiver reduces conflict or increases approval. Over time, this learning pattern may reinforce loyalty to the caregiver's narrative.

Social Influence and Authority

Classic social psychology experiments further demonstrate the power of social influence on belief formation. Solomon Asch's research on conformity showed that individuals often adopt group opinions even when those opinions conflict with observable evidence (Asch, 1951). Stanley Milgram's obedience experiments demonstrated that individuals may comply with directives from authority even when doing so produces moral discomfort (Milgram, 1963). In family systems, the caregiver typically functions as the primary authority figure in the child's environment. As a result, the caregiver's interpretation of family conflict may strongly influence the child's beliefs.

High-Control Authority Dynamics and Coercive Enforcement

Retrospective accounts provided by adult survivors of CPA-PA and CPA-PAA frequently describe relational environments that share features with high-control groups. Within such systems, the alienating parent may function as a central authority figure who maintains influence through control of narrative, restriction of alternative perspectives, reinforcement of emotional dependency, and regulation of behaviour, thought, and affect (Singer & Lalich, 2003; Lifton, 1961; Hassan, 2015). Survivors in the author's doctoral study described repeated childhood exposure to narratives portraying the targeted parent as unsafe, immoral, unstable, or psychologically dangerous, with divergence from the dominant narrative experienced as relationally unsafe (Price-Tobler, 2023a).

Survival Adaptations and Attachment-Driven Behaviour

In severe CPA-PAA histories, particularly those involving concealment, relocation, or abduction-related conditions, attachment behaviour may become organised around survival rather than preference. Adult survivors frequently recognise, in retrospect, that alignment with the alienating caregiver functioned as a regulatory strategy within an environment experienced as unstable, unpredictable, or threatening. What later appears as emotional fusion was not necessarily voluntary identification, but adaptive management of perceived danger.

From this perspective, survivors may describe childhood response patterns that were variable rather than fixed. Private curiosity, grief, or independent thought could coexist with outward agreement with the narrative. Moments of questioning, protest, or behavioural resistance might emerge during periods of relative safety, only to contract again when met with punishment, escalation, emotional withdrawal, or renewed instability. Such variability should not be misread as manipulation or inconsistency. It reflects adaptive calibration within an environment in which relational safety was conditional, and consequences were often unpredictable.

Research describing overt hostility or haughty certainty in some alienated children does not consistently capture this subgroup (Baker, 2007). Adult survivors describing relocation or abduction-related histories more often recall fear-based compliance, silence, vigilance, uncertainty about further movement or separation, and the sense that they had little real choice. These developmental mechanisms are important because they often persist in altered form into adulthood, shaping identity, attachment expectations, emotional regulation, and relational trust across the lifespan.

Differential Assessment and Contextual Caution

At the same time, not every instance of child resistance, contact refusal, or negative belief formation should be interpreted through a coercive persuasion framework. In CPA-PA-related work, differential assessment remains essential. Current family violence literature emphasises that behaviours resembling alienation-related processes may, in some cases, occur within contexts of genuine abuse, coercive control, compromised parenting, or protective alignment. The clinical task is therefore not to assume indoctrination, but to assess context, severity, developmental history, the child's relationship with each parent, the presence or absence of substantiated abuse, and the relational conditions under which the child's beliefs have formed and been reinforced (Sullivan et al., 2024).

This caution is particularly important because children may also be used as tools, intermediaries, or co-victims within broader coercively controlling family systems. In such contexts, the child's rejection of one parent may be shaped by multiple overlapping mechanisms, including fear, loyalty pressure, traumatic bonding, actual abuse, systems abuse, or prolonged exposure to one parent's narrative frame. The presence of coercive persuasion mechanisms should therefore be assessed alongside, rather than in place of, a careful abuse-differential formulation. For clinicians working with adult survivors, this matters because later narrative destabilisation may involve not only recognition of coercive influence, but also grief, moral injury, and confusion regarding what was true, what was feared, and what was developmentally impossible to evaluate at the time (Sullivan et al., 2024).

Clinical Note: CPA-PA, Developmental Vulnerability, and Manosphere-Influenced Beliefs in Boys and Young Men

Contemporary Context

Recent public discussion, including Louis Theroux's *Inside the Manosphere*, raises a clinically important question for MHPs working with boys and young men: under what developmental conditions do manosphere-influenced beliefs become especially compelling? Current commentary and emerging clinical writing suggest that these online ecosystems do not spread only through overtly degrading or inflammatory material. Much of their appeal appears to be carried through adjacent themes such as self-improvement, hierarchy, confidence, certainty, money, and belonging. For boys and young men who feel ashamed, lost, uncertain, humiliated, socially isolated, or under-held, this material may appear less like ideology and more like direction, structure, status, belonging, or identity. This formulation should be treated cautiously: online influence may organise or intensify existing vulnerabilities, but it should not be assumed to cause them in a simple or uniform way (Ging, 2019; Ribeiro et al., 2021; Roberts et al., 2025).

Developmental Vulnerability and the Search for Masculine Structure

For MHPs in CPA-PA work, the issue is not simply what a boy or young man is saying online, but what he may be reaching for developmentally. A respectful, emotionally available, grounded male role model may have been missing, inconsistent, feared, denigrated, idealised from a distance, or psychologically unavailable within a coercive family system. Under those conditions, the search for masculinity can become externalised. The boy or young man may then look outward for a map of how to be male, how to belong, how to carry authority, how to manage humiliation, and how not to feel weak, excluded, or ashamed. In that context, manosphere figures may be taken up not merely as influencers but as substitute authorities offering coherence, hierarchy, certainty, masculine status, and a ready-made sense of self (Ging, 2019; Ribeiro et al., 2021; Roberts et al., 2025).

Such a formulation does not excuse harmful beliefs, nor does it support simplistic claims that boys and young men exposed to the manosphere are necessarily survivors of CPA-PA or parental alienation. The evidence does not support that conclusion. What can be said more carefully is that earlier coercive family dynamics may, for some boys and young men, interfere with the development of a stable, reality-based, and non-defensive sense of masculine identity. Father hunger may be present without language for it. Grievance may be intense even when the original injury is not well understood. Emotional life may become organised around loyalty, hierarchy, authority, and suppression rather than mutuality, reflection, and secure attachment. In those cases, manosphere-influenced material may function less as a primary cause than as an organising system that converts vulnerability into certainty, shame into grievance, confusion into dominance, and longing into ideology (Ging, 2019; Ribeiro et al., 2021; Roberts et al., 2025).

CPA-PA and Masculine Identity Formation

For boys and young men affected by CPA-PA, the developmental stakes may be even higher. Ordinary masculine identity formation may have been compromised long before online material enters the picture. Male authority may have been absent, feared, demeaned, unreachable, or idealised from a distance. Vulnerability may have been shamed. Tenderness may have been coded as weakness. Strength may have been modelled as domination, intimidation, emotional cut-off, or coercive control. Identity may have been organised around survival rather than selfhood. Under such conditions, a rigid online system that promises clarity, rank, certainty, and a fixed answer to the question of what a man is supposed to be can become highly attractive. The clinical issue, then, is not only online influence. The deeper concern is the interaction between online influence and developmental vulnerability in a boy whose internal structure may already have been destabilised by CPA-PA.

A humane and disciplined therapeutic stance is therefore required. Shame will not solve this problem. Neither will simplistic ideological confrontation. Nor will it support collusion with narratives that degrade, subordinate, or exclude girls and women. A more useful clinical question is: What developmental problem is this belief system solving? Relief from humiliation may be one part of it. Belonging after isolation may be another. Identity after confusion may be another. Pseudo-strength in the presence of fear, shame, or father-related longing may be another. A language of grievance may also be serving where the deeper wound has not yet been named. MHPs may therefore need to hold two realities at once: first, that certain beliefs and relational positions can become harmful, rigid, degrading, or coercive; and second, that the boy or young man may be carrying developmental injuries that require understanding, containment, and careful therapeutic work rather than immediate moral simplification.

School Contexts and Younger Boys

This issue can no longer be treated as one confined to older adolescents and adult men. Australian reporting suggests that manosphere-influenced narratives are now appearing in primary and secondary school settings, including degrading comments toward girls, anti-feminist baiting, intimidation of female teachers, coded gestures, and increasingly rigid ideas about gender hierarchy. Those dynamics matter clinically because they suggest that some boys may encounter these narratives before the reflective capacities needed to question them are fully in place. In such contexts, a playground, classroom, gaming group, or peer network may become an early site where misogynistic, dominance-based, or hierarchy-based narratives are rehearsed, rewarded, or normalised rather than questioned (Ofcom, 2025; Ribeiro et al., 2021; Roberts et al., 2025).

Australia recorded 4,160,918 students enrolled in schools in 2025. At the same time, approximately 50,000 children experience their parents' divorce each year, with many more exposed to separation, family restructuring, or one-parent care arrangements. Family structure alone explains nothing, and no causal link should be drawn from divorce, one-parent households, separation, or disrupted father contact to manosphere-influenced beliefs. However, the author's clinical observation suggests that this intersection warrants closer attention. Some boys and young men seen in clinical practice are developing within emotionally stretched or reorganised family systems while also spending prolonged periods online, often without enough reflective adult support, male mentorship, peer belonging, or structured opportunities to process shame, rejection, anger, father absence, or identity confusion. In these circumstances, online male influencers who offer certainty, hierarchy, grievance, status, and a ready-made masculine identity may become especially compelling. This is not presented as a proven causal pathway, but as an emerging clinical formulation question requiring further research, careful assessment, and non-pathologising clinical attention (Australian Bureau of Statistics, 2026; Australian Institute of Family Studies, 2026).

School and peer contexts, therefore, need to be built into assessment. A boy's screen use is only one part of the picture. Older brothers, cousins, friendship groups, gaming communities, schoolyard hierarchies, teachers, coaches, and admired online figures may all be part of the relational surround within which degrading or dominance-based narratives are normalised. A boy may be repeating what is ambient in his environment, meaning ideas that are repeatedly present in his peer group, gaming community, online feed, classroom, sibling group, or family system. If those ideas are also socially rewarded through laughter, approval, attention, imitation, online engagement, status, or a sense of belonging, they may become increasingly difficult for him to question. In these cases, the boy may not yet be speaking from a fully consolidated ideological position. He may be rehearsing ideas that are common, reinforced, and rewarded around him. Assessment should therefore include careful enquiry into who is influencing him, which men he admires or fears, what is being said at school about girls, women, consent, authority, and respect, and whether his relationships are beginning to organise around contempt, control, exclusion, or rank (Ging, 2019; Ofcom, 2025; Ribeiro et al., 2021; Roberts et al., 2025).

Girls, Transgender, and Gender-Diverse Young People

These dynamics do not affect only boys. Girls may encounter exclusion, baiting, diminished access to shared spaces, devaluation, sexualised contempt, or pressure to accommodate boys whose certainty is being organised through rank, grievance, or dominance. School may stop functioning as a protective site for broader social learning if those same narratives enter playgrounds, classrooms, and peer culture. In the author's recent clinical work, an emerging concern has been noted in which some girls describe feeling anxious, unsafe, or reluctant to enter playground spaces because of the way boys are speaking, posturing, joking, excluding, or asserting dominance. This is presented as a clinical observation requiring further attention rather than as a settled empirical claim. It does, however, suggest that clinicians should ask how online gendered narratives may be shaping everyday peer behaviour, spatial safety, and girls' willingness to participate freely in ordinary school life. For some girls already living in CPA-PA or other coercive family systems, the developmental burden may become organised less around overt dominance and more around self-silencing, compliance, emotional caretaking, relational fear, and increasing organisation around appeasement and safety. That pattern may look quieter, but the injury can still be clinically significant.

Transgender and gender-diverse children may face an even more complicated developmental field. CPA-PA and other coercive family processes do not in themselves explain gender diversity, nor should gender identity ever be reduced to family pathology. At the same time, coercive, high-conflict, or emotionally restricted environments can entangle gender-related experience with fear, shame, approval-seeking, alliance pressure, external authority, identity instability, or dependency. In some cases, a child may feel unable to explore gender safely. In others, the child's developing identity may be over-directed, interpreted for them, dismissed, idealised, or drawn into alliance structures within the family. The clinical task is not to pathologise gender diversity. The task is to protect reflective space, avoid ideological overreach from any direction, and assess whether the child has sufficient freedom, safety, and developmental support to think, feel, question, and speak without coercion (Coleman et al., 2022; Levine, 2021).

Rapid Gender-Related Presentation, Reflective Space, and Alliance Pressure

A related issue requires especially careful wording. In the author's clinical work, including some family-court-involved CPA-PA presentations, there are occasions in which gender-related language, certainty, or self-description appears to shift rapidly and in ways that seem highly entangled with alliance pressures, coercive family dynamics, emotional dependency, or restricted reflective space. This is presented here as a clinical observation, not as a settled empirical conclusion. The HQTP should not treat rapid gender-related presentation as a standalone diagnostic conclusion, nor should it rely on highly contested categories as though they were settled science. One prominent parent-report paper in this area was later retracted, and the broader field remains contested and clinically delicate (Diaz & Bailey, 2023).

A further emerging clinical concern observed by the author involves presentations in which gender-related language or identity certainty appears during divorce, family-court conflict, or active alienation dynamics in ways that seem to function relationally within the family system. This is not presented as evidence that gender diversity is caused by CPA-PA, divorce, or alienation. Rather, it is a clinical observation that, in some cases, identity-related material may become drawn into the alienating parent's broader attempt to control meaning, disrupt attachment, prevent shared decision-making, or weaken the child's identification with the targeted parent. This may be especially clinically significant where the child and targeted parent are of the same sex and the child's emerging self-description is used, implicitly or explicitly, to create distance from that parent, reject the parent's authority, or position the targeted parent as unsafe, invalidating, or unqualified to participate in decisions. The clinical task is not to challenge the child's identity, but to assess whether the young person has sufficient freedom, safety, reflective space, developmentally appropriate support, and, where safe and appropriate, access to more than one relational perspective while exploring identity without coercion, pressure, fear, loyalty demand, or family-system capture (Coleman et al., 2022; Levine, 2021).

A safer and more clinically useful question is therefore not whether a child is being "talked into" a gender identity, but whether the child has sufficient freedom, safety, and reflective space to think, feel, question, and speak without pressure from any caregiver, peer group, school environment, or ideological system. In CPA-PA and other coercive family contexts, identity-related material may at times become drawn into alliance structures, fear, compliance, or emotional capture. Mental health practitioners need to slow coercive certainty, protect developmental thinking, and assess carefully whether the young person is being allowed to develop and speak from an internally grounded position. Gender diversity itself should not be treated as evidence of pathology. Coercion, restricted reflective space, or alliance pressure, however, must remain assessable wherever they appear (Coleman et al., 2022; Levine, 2021).

The same clinical principle applies when a child or adolescent's access to ordinary developmental settings becomes restricted. Whether the issue involves gender-related identity exploration, online influence, peer culture, home education, or school non-attendance, the clinical question is not whether one presentation automatically proves harm. The question is whether the young person has enough safety, reflective space, peer contact, adult support, and freedom from coercive pressure to develop, question, disagree, and participate in ordinary life.

School Non-Attendance, Restricted Social Development, and Reduced Protective Visibility

School non-attendance may also warrant careful attention, although strong causal claims should be avoided. Current Australian reporting frames many of these children not as wilfully oppositional, but as distressed, overwhelmed, anxious, or unable to manage ordinary school participation. No general claim should therefore be made that school non-attendance is a CPA-PA phenomenon, nor that single-parent status explains the presentation. A more careful clinical question is whether prolonged absence from school may, in some circumstances, narrow a child's world around one caregiver's worldview, emotional needs, or regulatory demands. In CPA-PA contexts, extended school absence may at times reduce access to peers, alternative adults, ordinary developmental friction, and everyday reality-testing. That possibility should be treated as a formulation question requiring careful assessment, not as proof of coercion or abuse (Amin & Ettinger-Epstein, 2024).

Homeschooling and Educational Withdrawal

Home education and educational withdrawal require the same caution. Home education in itself does not indicate CPA-PA. The clinical question is whether the young person's opportunities for peer contact, independent relationships, ordinary conflict negotiation, and access to safe adults outside the household are becoming markedly restricted. Where educational withdrawal sits alongside alliance pressure, information control, escalating dependence, or social isolation, clinicians should assess whether the child's world has narrowed in ways that reduce reality testing, developmental autonomy, and exposure to alternative viewpoints. Assessment should remain explicit and evidence-led, without treating home education itself as suspicious or harmful (Child Safeguarding Practice Review Panel, 2024; Clarke et al., 2022).

Restricted Social Worlds and Disproportionate Influence

A restricted social world becomes clinically relevant not because one educational pathway is inherently superior to another, but because narrow environments can increase the influence of a single caregiver, peer group, or online community over identity, grievance, and belonging. When a young person has limited access to ordinary peer culture, balanced adult feedback, community participation, and alternative viewpoints, clinicians should assess what now carries disproportionate authority in the young person's life and how that authority is maintained.

Manosphere-Influenced Beliefs in Some Boys and Young Men

A separate formulation issue arises when boys or young men become immersed in online misogynistic or grievance-based communities. The concern is not exposure alone. The concern is whether the material is beginning to organise belonging, shame regulation, masculine identity, entitlement, contempt, and relational behaviour. In the author's clinical experience, this pattern may arise in some boys and young men who are socially isolated, spending prolonged unsupervised time online, or seeking male belonging after bullying, rejection, humiliation, or disrupted father contact. These are vulnerability contexts, not causes, and they must not be used to pathologise single-parent families or boys who do not live with their fathers (Ging, 2019; Ribeiro et al., 2021; Roberts et al., 2025).

Where deliberate online recruitment or manipulative reinforcement is not clearly established, terms such as drawn into, recruited by, or socially reinforced within are preferable to groomed, which may imply a level of predatory intentionality not yet demonstrated in every case. The manosphere should also be treated as a heterogeneous online environment rather than a single uniform ideology; some spaces are misogynistic and grievance-based, while others present themselves through self-improvement, humour, status, or masculinity content. This requires careful clinical formulation rather than assumption (Ging, 2019; Ofcom, 2025; Ribeiro et al., 2021; Roberts et al., 2025).

Functional Assessment Prompts

Assessment should move beyond content alone. Useful questions include: What material is the young person consuming, on which platforms, and with what intensity? What does the material appear to offer him belonging, certainty, masculine status, emotional armour, blame, revenge, or relief from shame? Which men or communities are being idealised? What changes in language, contempt, humour, or behaviour follow exposure? Is he repeating slogans, or are relationships beginning to organise around hierarchy, entitlement, exclusion, or hostility? What role, if any, have social isolation, bullying, humiliation, unstable belonging, disrupted father contact, peer rejection, or prolonged unsupervised online immersion played in the presentation? The aim is not to diagnose ideology by a checklist. It is to understand the material's psychological and relational function for this particular young person.

Therapist Positioning and Safety

The therapist must remain inside the formulation. Work with misogyny-saturated, hierarchy-driven, or grievance-organised beliefs may evoke fear, irritation, rescuing, competitiveness, or pressure to prove credibility. Some female practitioners may feel tested, discounted, or placed in a gendered hierarchy; some male practitioners may feel pulled toward over-identification, leniency, or pseudo-solidarity. These reactions are not proof of any single dynamic, but they are clinically meaningful data that require supervision, clear boundaries, and, where indicated, consultation about risk.

If the therapist notices mounting anxiety, hypervigilance, intimidation, confusion, or reluctance to continue, those responses should be taken seriously. They may reflect fear-based countertransference, boundary strain, escalating hostility, or insufficient clinical containment. In this work, supervision is part of the safety structure rather than an optional supplement. The aim is neither ideological debate nor passive collusion, but reflective, boundaried, accountable practice.

Clinical Implications

Across these presentations, the clinical task is to understand how beliefs, identity positions, and relational narratives may have formed within restricted emotional, relational, and informational environments, while also maintaining accountability for harmful behaviour in the present. For some adult survivors, later reconsideration of earlier narratives can be deeply destabilising because previously coherent understandings of family, gender, authority, and self begin to loosen. Treatment, therefore, emphasises gradual exploration, emotional regulation, epistemic safety, and identity integration rather than direct confrontation of beliefs.

Note. The following Heuristic Formulation Map A simply means a clinical thinking aid. It is not intended to diagnose CPA-PA, prove causation, establish legal facts, or imply that all children, adolescents, or adult survivors follow the same sequence. It is best used to slow formulation and consider how attachment dependence, informational restriction, repeated framing, emotional reinforcement, and loyalty pressure may interact over time

Heuristic Formulation Map A: Developmental Narrative Conditioning in Attachment-Dependent Contexts

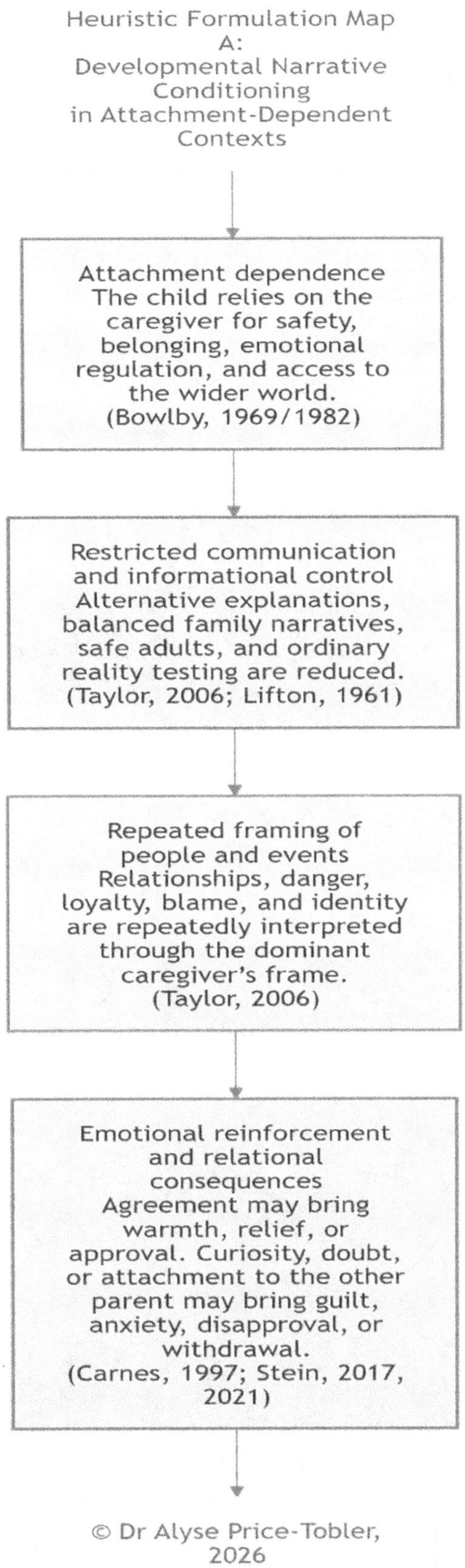

Heuristic Formulation Map B: Narrative Stabilisation, Destabilisation, and Identity Reconstruction

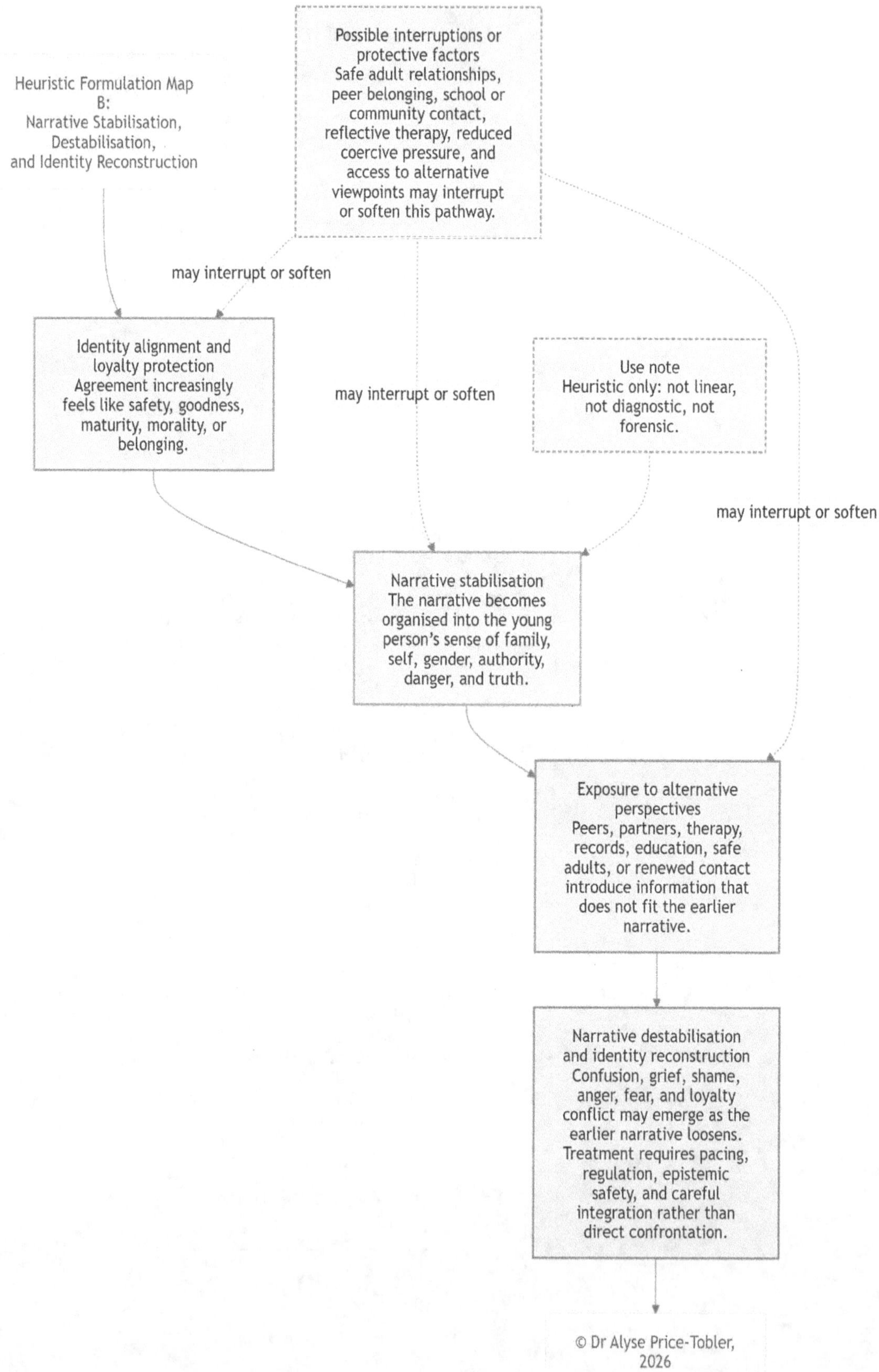

Note. The Heuristic Formulation Map. B is not intended to diagnose CPA-PA, prove causation, establish legal facts, or imply that all children, adolescents, or adult survivors follow the same sequence. It is best used to help clinicians consider how a stabilised childhood narrative may become destabilised when alternative perspectives, safe relationships, therapy, records, education, or renewed contact introduce information that does not fit the earlier frame.

Interrupting Coercive Enmeshment and Developmental Narrative Conditioning in Children

In CPA-PA, including CPA-PAA and CPA-PERA presentations, movement out of coercive enmeshment and brainwashing does not usually begin through confrontation, persuasion, or rapid reversal of the child's allegiance. The central problem is not simply that the child holds distorted beliefs. It is those beliefs that have often been organised within an attachment-dependent, fear-based, and coercively controlled relational system. For this reason, the initial task in undoing developmental narrative conditioning is not to replace one imposed narrative with another, but to establish the relational and psychological conditions under which independent thought can begin to re-emerge.

Unconditional Positive Regard

Within the HQTP, unconditional positive regard (UPR) (Rogers, 1957) provides an especially important therapeutic stance in this process. When practised consistently, with warmth and clear boundaries, UPR may help counter the survivor's expectation that love is conditional, that thoughts must be policed, and that attachment must be earned through compliance (Rogers, 1957). Over time, the safe adult or safe clinician may come to function as a new secure relational reference point from which reflection, doubt, grief, and self-authorship become more psychologically possible. In this sense, undoing coercive enmeshment is not achieved by argument. It is achieved through repeated exposure to a relationship in which disagreement does not elicit retaliation, independent thought does not threaten attachment, and the self need not disappear to remain connected.

For many survivors, this transition feels less like ordinary therapeutic progress and more like entering an unfamiliar world. The child or adult survivor may remain organised around the question, *What will the alienating parent think? Will they be upset? Do I need to check back with them?* This is one reason the early restoration of agency often must begin in very small ways. The capacity to choose a preference, hold a private thought, maintain a separate emotional reality, or speak without immediate self-correction may represent major developmental work. What appears externally as hesitation, dependency, or confusion may in fact reflect the survivor's first attempts to live outside a coercive relational system.

Why Allegiance Reversal Is Not Recovery

This has important implications for intervention. Approaches that seek to rapidly reverse the child's alignment, compel reunification, or replace one controlling interpretive frame with another may reproduce the very dynamics they claim to resolve. In the author's view, children do not benefit when one enforced allegiance is simply redirected toward the other parent. Such approaches may produce surface compliance while leaving deeper enmeshment, fear-based loyalty, phobic avoidance, and externally controlled meaning-making intact. They may also fail to equip the child for later life, particularly if the child is not helped to understand coercive family dynamics, develop breach-and-repair skills, recognise manipulative or destabilising behaviour in the alienating parent, and build the capacity to maintain boundaries without surrendering attachment needs.

The author's concern in this area is informed not only by clinical and research observations, but also by training in three reunification programs. In the author's view, some of these approaches may prioritise rapid reversal of the child's alignment toward the rejected parent without sufficient attention to whether the child has developed reflective functioning, emotional differentiation, reality-based thinking, or the capacity to resist future coercion. The concern is not merely whether the child resumes contact, but whether the child has genuinely moved out of coercive relational organisation.

This concern was reinforced in the author's doctoral research, in which a small number of adult participants described earlier involvement in structured reunification-style interventions. In these cases, participants did not appear to be developmentally free from coercive family dynamics. Rather, they appeared to retain rigid and intensely polarised narratives regarding the previously rejected parent, accompanied in some instances by marked phobic affect and extreme black and white responses when asked to consider possible future intergenerational contact.

Of particular concern to the author was the apparent absence of reflective flexibility, emotional intelligence, and differentiated thinking about how such relationships might be navigated later if their own children wished to know that side of the family. These observations do not permit broad generalisation, but they do raise important clinical questions about whether allegiance reversal alone is an adequate index of therapeutic success.

Accordingly, the therapeutic aim is not simply to move the child back toward the targeted parent, nor to reverse one attachment-based allegiance into another. It is to strengthen the child's, and later the adult survivor's, capacity for reality-based thinking, emotional differentiation, relational autonomy, boundary development, breach-and-repair skills, and a psychologically coherent understanding of the alienating parent's disturbance.

Recovery, Rehabilitation, and Reintegration in CPA-PA Contexts

Stein's recovery framework offers a useful extension of the present chapter by clarifying how movement out of coercive family enmeshment may begin and how it may later be sustained. Drawing on trauma principles consistent with Herman's staged model of recovery, Stein emphasises that people emerging from totalistic systems require support from the nontotalistic world to recover, rehabilitate, and integrate (Herman, 1992; Stein, 2021). She also highlights the need for safety, for a non-judgemental witness who can hear the person's story through their own eyes rather than through the group's fiction, and for relationships and networks that are open rather than closed and isolating. These principles map closely onto the HQTP and are highly relevant to CPA-PA presentations.

In HQTP terms, the earliest movement out of coercive enmeshment hinges on establishing physical, relational, and epistemic safety. This includes, where possible, increased distance from the traumatising dynamic, restoration of basic functioning, and the development of at least one trustworthy, non-coercive relational anchor from which independent thought can begin to emerge (Herman, 1992; Stein, 2021). For many survivors, this process is profoundly disorienting. The child or adult survivor may wonder whether it is safe to hold a separate thought without checking back in with their AP. In this sense, early recovery may feel less like ordinary therapy and more like entering an unfamiliar world. Small experiences of choice, preference, and self-direction may therefore represent major developmental progress.

Stein's second recovery phase, remembrance and mourning, is also highly relevant to CPA-PA-related work. In this phase, the survivor gradually develops a coherent account of what happened, supported by a non-judgemental witness who can also hold moral clarity about the abuse. Within the HQTP, this maps strongly onto the later movement into grief, loss integration, narrative reconstruction, and epistemic repair. For adult survivors, this phase may involve putting together the jigsaw puzzle of childhood experience, including contradictory memories, secrecy, compartmentalised family narratives, and later exposure to corrective perspectives. The task is not simply to recover facts, but to build a psychologically coherent account of one's life that no longer depends on the totalistic frame.

Group Work as an Adjunct, not a First-Line Intervention

At this stage, carefully structured peer contact may sometimes become useful. Survivors often gain clarity not only from individual reflection but from hearing that similar coercive mechanisms appear across apparently different family systems. This may reduce shame, challenge isolation, and help identify universal patterns of manipulation, loyalty pressure, and relational capture. However, the author suggests that group-based work in this area should not stand alone and is not usually indicated as an early intervention within the HQTP. Group work is more appropriately considered only after sufficient stabilisation has been established in individual treatment, including basic safety, affect regulation, relational trust, and enough reflective capacity to tolerate exposure to shared material without collapse into dissociation, panic, or renewed coercive pull.

Where groups are used, participants should also have access to individual clinical support, ideally on the same day or within close proximity to the group process. Some survivors may enter states of extreme distress, dissociation, destabilisation, or renewed pull toward the coercive family system when exposed to group material. Without immediate opportunities for individual containment and repair, such work may become overwhelming and increase the risk of a return to enmeshment rather than moving out of it.

Reconnection With Ordinary Life

Stein's third phase, reconnection with ordinary life, maps onto the later developmental aims of the HQTP. At this stage, the survivor is no longer focused only on safety or narrative reconstruction but begins to build a life that is not organised around surveillance, emotional checking back, or compulsory loyalty to the alienating parent. This may involve developing a more stable sense of self, new beliefs, safer relationships, and future plans that do not depend on the caregiver's approval. In practical terms, this includes learning to remain connected to others without submission and to maintain autonomy without feeling separated as abandonment. Within the HQTP, this corresponds to increasing self-authorship, relational freedom, and the capacity to participate in ordinary life without re-entering the coercive structure.

Seen in this light, undoing developmental narrative conditioning is not a matter of replacing one controlling narrative with another, but of creating the relational, cognitive, and developmental conditions under which independent thought, grief, and self-authorship can safely emerge. At a broader level, Stein's work also highlights that recovery from totalistic systems cannot be understood apart from fundamental human needs for safety, attachment, belonging, and survival (Stein, 2021).

In CPA-PA, including CPA-PAA and CPA-PERA presentations, the alienating parent may offer a powerful but ultimately fraudulent promise of certainty, protection, and relational security, while simultaneously organising the child's world around fear, compliance, and a single authorised story. Within such totalistic family structures, alternative interpretations are not simply discouraged. They may be treated as dangerous, disloyal, or morally wrong. The child, therefore, learns that only one version of events is permitted to exist, while competing memories, questions, or attachments are experienced as threats to relational survival.

This is one reason why movement out of coercive enmeshment can be so destabilising. As Stein's discussion of recovery and reintegration suggests, leaving a totalistic system involves more than physical separation from a harmful environment. It requires entry into a relational world in which multiple perspectives can be tolerated, thought can occur without punishment, and attachment does not depend on ideological agreement (Stein, 2021). In this respect, Stein's framework maps closely onto Herman's phased approach to trauma recovery, particularly the progression from safety to remembrance and mourning, and then to reconnection with ordinary life (Herman, 1992; Stein, 2021). For children and adult survivors alike, this shift is not merely social reintegration. It is a developmental process of learning that safety, belonging, and truth do not need to be organised through fear, absolutism, or enforced loyalty. Within the HQTP, this movement is central to the restoration of reflective capacity, relational freedom, and coherent selfhood.

Protection, Contact, and Child Development

Where the alienating or pathogenic parent appears significantly disturbed, psychologically controlling, or unable to support the child's independent attachment needs, the child may require structured protection, supervised or carefully managed contact, psychoeducation, and, in some cases, altered living arrangements. In contrast, the parent receives treatment, parenting intervention, or further assessment (Childress, 2015). Where safety permits, and where there is no validated abuse requiring protective restriction, children may still need some form of ongoing relationship with both parents while also being protected and taught how to recognise manipulation, stand up safely to coercive pressure, and make use of support from trustworthy adults. The central principle is that recovery is not measured by redirected loyalty. It is measured by increasing autonomy, reflective capacity, and freedom from coercive relational organisation.

Brainwashing, Developmental Narrative Capture, and Cognitive Narrowing

Taylor's discussion of highly dominant "cogwebs" is useful in understanding how a child's cognitive world may gradually narrow within coercive family systems (Taylor, 2006). In such contexts, one organising idea may begin to drain energy from competing beliefs, until an increasingly greater share of the child's emotional and cognitive life is interpreted through a single dominant frame. In CPA-PA contexts, this may occur when the child becomes organised around the belief that the targeted parent is dangerous, untrustworthy, morally bad, or a threat to the stability of the family. Initially, such beliefs may coexist with affection, longing, or confusion. Over time, however, repeated reinforcement, reduced access to corrective experiences, and pressure to preserve attachment with the dominant caregiver may cause the child's interpretive world to contract. The child no longer evaluates each situation independently. Instead, family events, memories, contact, and even ordinary expressions of care from the targeted parent may all be filtered through the dominant narrative of alienation.

For example, a child living in a coercive caregiving environment may gradually come to believe that keeping distance from the targeted parent is not simply preferable, but necessary to protect the caregiving parent, the household, or even the child's own survival. In such a case, the child may no longer experience rejection as a choice, but as a moral duty or protective role. The child may interpret kindness from the targeted parent as manipulation, sadness as danger, and attempts at repair as evidence of threat. In this sense, the child's developing personality may become organised around a single issue: maintaining loyalty to the dominant caregiver and defending the authorised family story. What appears externally as rigid rejection may therefore reflect not independent conviction, but a narrowed cognitive world in which competing meanings have become progressively inaccessible (Taylor, 2006).

Absolute Authority and Totalistic Family Thinking

Taylor also warns that ideas become especially dangerous when joined to notions of absolute authority and totalistic certainty (Taylor, 2006). This is clinically relevant in some pathogenic caregiving systems, where the dominant parent may come to see his or her interpretation of family reality as the only legitimate truth. Under these conditions, the child is no longer treated as a separate developing person with an independent mind, but as an extension of the caregiver's grievance, fear, or moral mission. The child's thoughts, loyalties, and memories may then be shaped in service of the caregiver's authorised story. In family cult structures, this totalistic logic may be expressed through beliefs such as *only I know what is true*, *the other parent is wholly dangerous*, *the child must never think differently*, or *loyalty to me is equivalent to safety and goodness*. Once such beliefs become rigid, the child may be treated less as an end in his or her own right and more as a means of preserving the caregiver's emotional stability, status, or conflict narrative. Additionally, the danger lies not only in the content of the belief but in the collapse of alternative perspectives, moral complexity, and the child's right to independent psychological development. This is one way in which a coercive family system can begin to resemble a miniature totalistic structure: one authority, one truth, one permitted story, and one loyalty that must not be questioned.

Breaking the Stranglehold of Dominant Narrative Systems

Taylor's discussion of dominant 'ethereal ideas' (Taylor, 2006). It is useful in understanding why direct challenge is often ineffective when working with adult survivors of CPA-PA. In this context, the relevant issue is not that the alienating parent necessarily holds a formal psychotic or delusional disorder. Rather, some pathogenic family systems become organised around rigid, dominant belief structures that function as totalistic interpretive frames. These belief structures may include convictions that the targeted parent is wholly dangerous, morally corrupt, or undeserving of a relationship, and that loyalty to the alienating caregiver is equivalent to safety, goodness, or survival. Over time, such ideas may come to dominate the child's cognitive and emotional world, progressively narrowing the range of meanings that can be tolerated.

Taylor's formulation is particularly relevant because she cautions that directly attacking highly dominant beliefs may strengthen them through reactance. When a person experiences a core organising idea as necessary for safety, identity, or belonging, blunt contradiction may be felt not as clarification but as a threat. In CPA-PA-related presentations, this means that directly telling the child or adult survivor that they have been "brainwashed," that their beliefs are false, or that they must reverse their view of the coercive caregiver may intensify defensiveness, fear, or renewed loyalty to the coercive caregiver. The problem is not merely a cognitive error. The problem is that the dominant narrative has become interwoven with attachment, survival, and moral positioning.

For this reason, the therapeutic task is better understood as gradual loosening rather than forced reversal. Taylor's notion of weakening the supporting structures around a dominant belief system can be translated into CPA-PA contexts as the careful expansion of the survivor's cognitive and relational world. In clinical terms, this may involve helping the survivor encounter alternatives to the authorised family story without humiliation or pressure, supporting reflection on contradictions, and slowly introducing the possibility that the targeted parent, and the broader rejected family system, may be more complex, human, and developmentally relevant than the coercive narrative allowed. In a child context, this must be done developmentally and safely, often through regulated exposure to ordinary, reality-based contact, safe adults, neutral memory cues, or carefully supported experiences that do not force immediate reinterpretation.

Taylor also suggests that belief systems are often narrowed by strong affective drivers. In CPA-PA-related environments, those emotional drivers may include fear of retaliation, guilt, loyalty pressure, traumatic bonding, and the child's desperate need to preserve attachment with the dominant caregiver. Accordingly, undoing the stranglehold of the dominant narrative cannot rely on persuasion alone. It requires reducing the fear and emotional intensity that give the narrative its force. Within the HQTP, this maps closely onto stabilisation, epistemic safety, and the creation of at least one non-coercive relational space in which thought can occur without punishment.

In adult survivors, this process may involve gradual widening of the cognitive horizon through psychoeducation, careful exploration of family narratives, increasing exposure to alternative perspectives, and support to tolerate the grief, shame, and disorientation that arise when the authorised story begins to loosen. In children, where developmentally appropriate and where no validated abuse requires protective restriction, the task is not to redirect loyalty by force, but to reduce fear, increase access to safe and trustworthy adults, support reflective thinking, and provide relational experiences that allow the child to discover that contact, complexity, and independent thought can exist without catastrophe.

What weakens the dominant narrative, therefore, is not humiliation, an ideological counterattack, or an immediate reversal of allegiance. It is the slow building of a life in which the child or adult survivor has greater safety, greater freedom of thought, broader relational experience, and increasing opportunities to think, feel, and choose outside the coercive system. In this sense, recovery is less about persuading the survivor out of one story and more about creating the conditions in which other realities become psychologically livable.

Prevention: Protecting Children from Brainwashing, Narrative Narrowing and Enmeshment

Prevention of CPA-PA requires attention not only to overt coercion, but also to the gradual brainwashing of the child through narrative narrowing, emotional enmeshment, and restriction of the child's cognitive and relational world. In these contexts, brainwashing does not usually occur through a single dramatic event. It occurs through repetition, isolation, fear, reward, punishment, loyalty pressure, and the removal of competing relational truths.

Taylor (2006) argues that one feature common to coercive environments, including cultic systems, extremist contexts, and abusive relationships, is not simply the installation of a small number of strongly held beliefs, but the progressive restriction of competing ideas, alternative viewpoints, and opportunities for reflective comparison. This is clinically relevant to CPA-PA because the child is not merely being influenced. The child's capacity to think freely about both parents, compare relational experiences, and hold a complex emotional truth is being systematically narrowed.

In this sense, prevention involves protecting the child from brainwashing and totalistic narrative closure before a single authorised family story becomes dominant. Children need access to relational complexity, safe emotional expression, and the freedom to love, question, remember, and think without fear of punishment.

Within the present framework, this means that children require access to a richer cognitive, relational, and developmental environment than the coercive family system would otherwise permit. Where safety allows, this includes continued access to multiple attachment figures, opportunities for ordinary contact with the rejected parent and extended family, exposure to non-coercive adults, and environments in which questioning, complexity, and emotional ambivalence are not punished. The goal is not to overwhelm the child with competing interpretations, but to prevent the child's world from becoming so narrowed that only one version of reality remains psychologically available.

Taylor's (2006) discussion of prevention also maps onto educational and developmental tasks. Children benefit when they are helped to develop critical thinking, reflective language, emotional literacy, and the capacity to hold more than one perspective in mind at a time. In CPA-PA-related contexts, this may include helping the child differentiate between memory and suggestion, fear and fact, loyalty and love, and private experience and imposed narrative. Such capacities are necessarily developmental and must be fostered gradually. However, they form an important protective buffer against totalistic family structures in which certainty is enforced, and independent thought becomes dangerous.

Stein's (2021) emphasis on open rather than closed systems also supports a preventative approach. Coercive family environments become more powerful when the child is isolated, dependent, and deprived of trustworthy alternatives. Prevention, therefore, includes strengthening the child's access to safe, reliable, non-retaliatory adults who can model a different kind of relationship: one in which thought is not controlled, disagreement does not threaten attachment, and the child is not required to regulate the caregiver's emotional world (Stein, 2021). In practical terms, this may involve attentive schools, informed clinicians, safe relatives, mentors, community adults, and systems professionals who understand that preserving the plurality of relationships can be protective.

At the systems level, prevention also requires professionals to avoid reinforcing narrative monopolies. Family court, child protection, educational, and mental health responses may inadvertently strengthen coercive dynamics when they accept rigid narratives without adequate differential assessment, fail to notice information restriction, or treat a child's expressed rejection as self-explanatory. Preventative practice, therefore, requires careful attention to context, access, communication patterns, abrupt changes in the child's attitudes, loyalty pressure, emotional consequences for independent thought, and the broader presence of coercive control or family violence. Early recognition matters because mild and moderate CPA-PA presentations are often the stages at which intervention is most likely to prevent later consolidation.

Importantly, prevention is not achieved through counter-coercion. It is not achieved by replacing one closed narrative with another, humiliating the child for what they currently believe, or forcing immediate relational reversal. Rather, prevention involves expanding the child's cognitive horizons, preserving access to safe and trustworthy relationships, supporting reflective capacity, and reducing the emotional conditions under which a single coercive narrative becomes necessary for survival. In this sense, prevention and early intervention share the same developmental aim: to protect the child's right to reality-based thought, differentiated attachment, and independent psychological development.

Prevention: A Public Health Approach

A public health approach to prevention becomes possible once coercive influence is no longer treated as an incomprehensible mystery, but as a human process that can be studied, recognised, and interrupted. There is now a substantial interdisciplinary literature relevant to this task, spanning Lifton's work on thought reform (1961), Schein's work on coercive persuasion (1961), Singer's work on cultic influence (1995), Arendt's analysis of totalitarianism (1951), Asch's work on conformity (1951), Milgram's work on obedience (1963), and later contributions from Lofland (1966), Cialdini (2009), Zablocki (1997), Lalich (2004), and Herman (1992). More recent work by Stein (2021) and Taylor (2006) is especially relevant to the present protocol because it extends these concerns into attachment, cognitive narrowing, and controlling personal relationships. Hassan's work on undue influence and non-coercive intervention is also clinically relevant, particularly because he has included family dynamics and parental alienation contexts within his broader framework of harmful influence (Hassan, 2012, 2015, 2018).

From a prevention perspective, the critical issue is not only the presence of strongly held beliefs, but the progressive narrowing of horizons that accompanies them. In coercive family environments, children may lose access to alternative viewpoints, ordinary corrective experiences, safe adults, and developmentally necessary opportunities to compare competing interpretations of reality. The child's world gradually becomes organised around one emotional authority, one loyalty system, and one permitted truth. Prevention, therefore, requires more than identifying overt alienating behaviours after they have become entrenched. It requires strengthening the conditions that protect the plurality of thought, the plurality of relationships, and the plurality of reality testing before a totalistic family structure consolidates (Stein, 2021; Taylor, 2006).

Within CPA-PA-related contexts, this implies a broader educational and systems-based response. Children benefit when they are exposed, wherever safely possible, to multiple trustworthy adults, emotionally non-retaliatory relationships, ordinary contact with both sides of the family, and environments in which questioning, complexity, and reflective thought are not punished. Schools, clinicians, child protection practitioners, family report writers, lawyers, and judicial officers all require better education regarding coercive control, developmental narrative capture, attachment disruption, and the ways in which children may become recruited into rigid family belief systems. Prevention in this sense is not merely an individual matter. It is ecological.

In this sense, prevention is not peripheral to the clinical task. It is central to child protection, mental health, family law, and intergenerational wellbeing. The task is not only to respond once a child has become rigidly organised around a coercive family story, but also to build the relational, educational, and systemic conditions that make such capture less likely in the first place. The clinical implications of these prevention, recovery, and reintegration principles become clearer when therapeutic modalities are considered not as standalone solutions, but as tools that must be carefully sequenced within a broader attachment-based and abuse-informed framework.

Advanced Clinical Applications and Modality Integration

This chapter applies the phase-based framework established in Chapters 5 and 6 by situating commonly used therapeutic modalities within the HQTP treatment architecture. It does not introduce new treatment phases. Within the HQTP, therapeutic modalities are conceptualised as delivery mechanisms rather than drivers of treatment.

While clinicians may draw upon approaches such as CBT, EMDR, somatic therapies, psychodynamic psychotherapy, or attachment-based interventions, these methods are applied within a shared clinical framework prioritising safety, pacing, relational containment, and survivor autonomy.

The HQTP, therefore, focuses not on which modality is used but on how it is sequenced, constrained, and integrated across treatment phases. This chapter outlines commonly utilised therapeutic approaches and situates them within a structured, survivor-centred model designed specifically for adult survivors.

Therapeutic Modalities Within the HQTP

Adult survivors rarely present with isolated symptom profiles. Instead, clinical presentations typically involve overlapping attachment injury, identity disruption, nervous system dysregulation, loyalty conditioning, and trauma-related cognitive distortion. The author's doctoral findings demonstrated that survivors often report limited benefit from single modality treatment when relational safety, pacing, and developmental repair are not addressed concurrently (Price-Tobler, 2023a). For this reason, the HQTP does not privilege any single therapeutic approach. Instead, it applies modalities strategically across treatment phases to meet the evolving clinical needs of survivors.

This chapter examines core therapeutic modalities commonly used in trauma and attachment-focused practice and outlines how they are integrated within the protocol. Rather than presenting these approaches as standalone treatments, each modality is positioned within a phased structure that supports stabilisation, identity reconstruction, trauma integration, relational repair, and long-term consolidation. The chapter also addresses the roles of structured assessment processes, clinical documentation, and data-informed monitoring tools in guiding pacing, risk management, and treatment planning across complex survivor presentations.

PhD Results Extracted from the Therapeutic Modalities and Methodologies Utilised by the MHP Study Cohort

The most frequently reported therapeutic approach used by mental health practitioners in the practitioner cohort study, presented in Volume Two, was person-centred therapy (Rogers, 1942/1951), also referred to as client-centred therapy. Central to this approach is the provision of unconditional positive regard, empathy, and congruence within the therapeutic relationship, positioning the client as the expert in their own lived experience (Rogers, 1951, 1957). Mental health practitioner study participants identified the relational safety inherent in this modality as foundational when working with survivors who have experienced prolonged attachment disruption and psychological abuse.

Psychoeducation was reported with equal frequency to person-centred therapy. Although participants sometimes described psychoeducation as a treatment, within the HQTP it is more accurately understood as a structured clinical process rather than a stand-alone modality. It can support survivors by providing careful language for trauma responses, attachment dynamics, loyalty conflict, coercive control, and treatment pacing. Used well, psychoeducation can reduce shame and support informed consent. Used too early or too forcefully, it can overwhelm the survivor or become another imposed narrative.

Four therapeutic modalities were identified as the second-most frequently utilised approaches. These were psychodynamic psychotherapy (Freud, 1890–1930), dialectical behaviour therapy (Linehan, 1993), emotionally focused therapy (Johnson & Greenberg, 1985), and narrative therapy (White & Epston, 1990). The remaining thirty-one therapeutic modalities and treatment approaches were each reported by only one mental health practitioner and were not replicated across the broader sample.

This dispersion indicates substantial variability in clinical practice when working with adult survivors of severe parental alienation. Collectively, these findings point to the absence of a shared or standardised adult survivor treatment framework. Practitioners appeared to rely on diverse, individualised combinations of modalities shaped by their training backgrounds, clinical orientations, and perceived client needs.

This variability supports the need for the HQTP as a phase-based organising framework. The protocol does not replace existing therapeutic modalities. Rather, it helps clinicians consider when, how, and whether a modality should be used, based on phase, readiness, scope, safety, supervision, and survivor autonomy. Figure Two summarises the treatment modalities and therapeutic approaches reported by mental health practitioners in the doctoral study.

Figure 2 Therapeutic Modalities Administered to Adult Survivors by Mental Health Practitioners

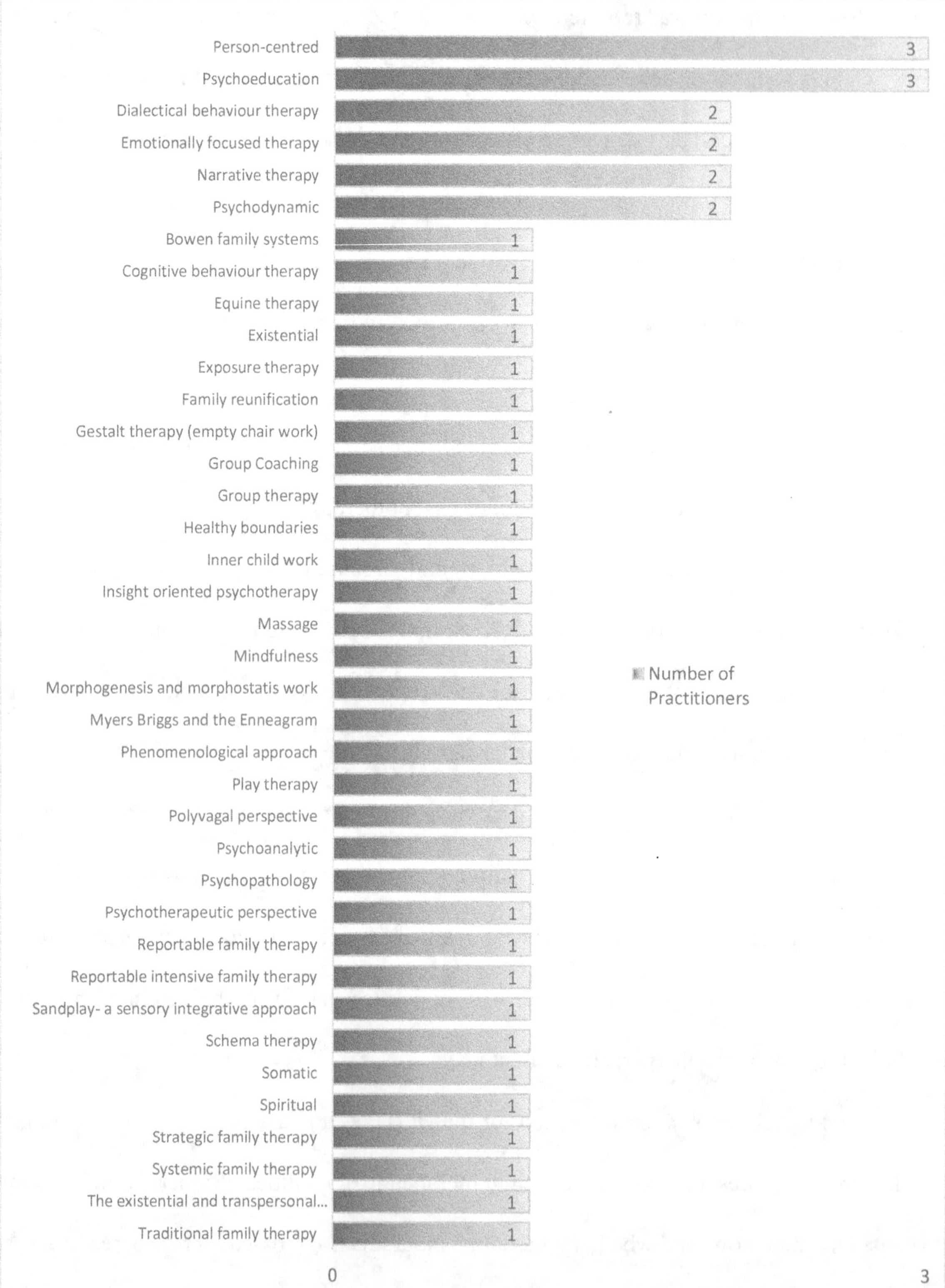

Note: The combined modalities and therapies practised among the 10 MHPs totalled 37

Figure 2 illustrates the breadth of therapeutic approaches reported by mental health practitioners and supports the need for the HQTP as a phase-based organising framework rather than a single-modality treatment model.

Therapeutic Modalities and Practices

This section does not provide a general overview of psychotherapy modalities. It considers how therapeutic approaches reported in the author's doctoral practitioner study may be used safely within the HQTP. The central question is not whether a modality is useful in general, but whether it is being used at the right time, for the right purpose, and within the survivor's current phase of readiness, safety, supervision, and autonomy.

Person-centred therapy is clinically relevant within the HQTP because many adult survivors have lived for years in relational environments where their perception, grief, attachment needs, and sense of self were dismissed, corrected, punished, or overridden. The provision of empathy, congruence, and unconditional positive regard may therefore support relational safety and help reduce shame, guardedness, and fear of being misread.

However, person-centred practice still requires active clinical judgement in this population. Warmth and acceptance are not enough if the clinician does not also understand coercive control, attachment disruption, loyalty conflict, epistemic injury, and the survivor's phase of readiness. Within the HQTP, person-centred therapy is best understood as a relational foundation rather than a complete treatment pathway.

Psychoeducation also has an important place within the HQTP, although it should not be treated as a stand-alone treatment modality. Used carefully, psychoeducation can help survivors find language for trauma responses, attachment injury, loyalty conflict, coercive control, identity disruption, and treatment pacing. It may reduce shame by helping survivors understand that many of their responses developed in conditions of psychological survival. However, psychoeducation can become harmful if it is delivered too early, too forcefully, or as though the clinician is imposing a new explanation onto the survivor's life. In Phase I and early Phase II, psychoeducation should be paced slowly, linked to the survivor's own language, and used to support informed consent rather than to accelerate insight.

Cognitive behavioural therapy may assist some survivors when it is used to support stabilisation, present-day functioning, and the careful examination of thoughts that maintain fear, shame, avoidance, or self-blame. Within the HQTP, CBT-informed work must be applied with caution. The aim is not to prematurely challenge the survivor's reality or to imply that their distress is caused solely by distorted thinking. Many adult survivors have already been told that their perceptions are wrong, exaggerated, disloyal, or irrational. For this reason, cognitive work should not be used to correct the survivor's story. It should be used only when sufficient epistemic safety has been established and when the survivor can explore thoughts without feeling disbelieved, pressured, or overridden.

Psychodynamic psychotherapy is relevant to HQTP-informed work because adult survivors may carry unconscious relational templates shaped by fear, loyalty conflict, attachment disruption, shame, and survival-based compliance. Psychodynamic attention to transference, countertransference, defensive processes, repetition, grief, and internalised relational authority may help clinicians understand how earlier attachment injuries continue to organise adult relationships. However, psychodynamic interpretation must be carefully timed. Premature interpretation can feel invasive, shaming, or destabilising, especially when the survivor has not yet developed enough safety to hold complexity. Within the HQTP, psychodynamic work is most useful when it supports curiosity, containment, and relational understanding, rather than rapid interpretation or deep trauma exploration before readiness is present.

Mindfulness-based approaches, including mindfulness-based stress reduction, may support regulation, grounding, body awareness, and present-day orientation. These approaches may be useful when survivors are experiencing physiological activation, intrusive fear, dissociation, or difficulty returning to baseline after relational triggers. However, mindfulness is not automatically stabilising for trauma survivors. For some, closing the eyes, attending to bodily sensation, slowing down, or sitting quietly may increase distress, dissociation, shame, or threat activation. Within the HQTP, mindfulness-based approaches should be invitational, brief, eyes-open where needed, and adapted to the survivor's nervous system rather than applied as a standard relaxation technique.

Eye movement desensitisation and reprocessing may be relevant for some survivors when trauma processing becomes clinically appropriate. However, within the HQTP, EMDR should not be used simply because trauma is present. Trauma exposure, memory activation, or processing work can be destabilising when the survivor has not yet developed sufficient regulation, identity continuity, relational safety, and consent capacity. EMDR should be considered only by appropriately trained clinicians, within scope, with supervision where required, and only when the survivor's phase position supports trauma integration work. In this population, the question is not whether EMDR may be effective, but whether the survivor is ready for trauma processing without being overwhelmed or pushed beyond their current capacity.

Dialectical behaviour therapy-informed skills may support stabilisation, affect regulation, distress tolerance, interpersonal boundaries, and crisis containment. These skills may be particularly useful in Phase I and Phase II when survivors are experiencing emotional flooding, identity destabilisation, relational activation, or difficulty returning to baseline after recognition-linked distress. However, DBT-informed work should not be used in a way that suggests the survivor's distress is merely a skills deficit. The survivor's emotional intensity may reflect prolonged exposure to coercive control, attachment disruption, developmental threat, and epistemic injury. Within the HQTP, DBT-informed skills are most helpful when they strengthen safety and choice while preserving the clinical meaning of the survivor's experience.

Emotionally focused therapy may assist clinicians in understanding attachment needs, relational fear, protest, withdrawal, longing, and disconnection. Its attachment focus can be clinically useful when adult survivors are beginning to recognise how earlier relational injury has shaped adult intimacy, trust, and contact decisions. However, EFT-informed work must be used with caution in this population, particularly in couples, family, or reunification-adjacent contexts. It should never be used to pressure reconciliation, minimise harm, or move the survivor toward contact before autonomy and boundary safety are established.

Within the HQTP, attachment-based work must remain survivor-led, consent-based, and phase-sensitive. Narrative therapy is relevant because many adult survivors have lived inside stories authored by others. Their memories, motives, loyalties, relationships, and identities may have been shaped by coercive family narratives, secrecy, distortion, or enforced allegiance. Narrative therapy may help survivors separate themselves from imposed stories, recover authorship, and develop language for experiences that were previously unnamed or misnamed. However, narrative work must not force coherence before the survivor is ready. Some histories emerge slowly, unevenly, and with gaps. Within the HQTP, narrative therapy is most useful when it supports survivor authorship without pressuring disclosure, certainty, forgiveness, or a final relational outcome.

Across all modalities, the HQTP position remains consistent. No modality is inherently sufficient simply because it is familiar, evidence-informed, or widely used. The clinical value of a modality depends on timing, safety, survivor readiness, practitioner competence, supervision, and the purpose for which it is being used. The HQTP therefore does not replace therapeutic modalities. It provides a phase-based structure for deciding when a modality may assist, when it should be deferred, and when its use may place the survivor at risk of overwhelm, misattunement, or therapeutic overreach.

Empirical Foundation of the HQTP

Doctoral Findings: Overview of Core Therapeutic Modalities

The modality integration architecture presented in this chapter is derived directly from the author's doctoral practitioner study examining the treatment practices of MHPs working with adult survivors of CPA-PA. Analysis of the practitioner cohort revealed substantial variability in modality selection, an absence of phase-informed sequencing, and no shared treatment framework for CPA-PA presentations.

These findings are presented in full for the first time in this volume and form the empirical foundation of the HQTP. This framework was developed in direct response to the fragmentation identified across clinical practice, with the aim of providing a structured, attachment-informed, phase-based integration model. Accordingly, the modalities outlined below are not presented as standalone treatments, but as components within a unified phase-based framework designed for adult survivors of CPA-PA.

Within the HQTP, therapeutic modalities are selected and applied based on phase readiness, attachment stability, and nervous system capacity rather than clinician preference alone. Findings from the author's doctoral survivor study indicated that many adult survivors reported limited benefit from standard single-modality treatment when relational safety, identity repair, and trauma pacing were not addressed concurrently. Survivors described prior therapy experiences in which techniques were introduced prematurely, trauma material was activated without adequate stabilisation, or cognitive strategies inadvertently reinforced loyalty conditioning and self-blame. As a result, modality integration within the HQTP is guided by developmental context, attachment disruption, and the survivor's lived experience of coercive relational environments. The following modalities are outlined to support informed, phase-based selection and to clarify how standard approaches must be adapted when applied to adult survivors of CPA-PA.

Person-Centred Therapy

Person-Centred Therapy (PCT) provides the relational foundation for all other modalities within the HQTP. PCT was the most frequently reported approach among practitioners in the doctoral cohort (Price-Tobler, 2023b), reflecting the centrality of relational safety in work with adult survivors of CPA-PA.

Findings from the author's doctoral survivor study indicated that many adult survivors commonly reported childhood environments characterised by emotional invalidation, conditional affection, and chronic misattunement (Price-Tobler, 2023a). The consistent experience of empathic presence, emotional validation, and non-judgmental therapeutic engagement is therefore not ancillary but essential. In doctoral interviews, survivors repeatedly described the first experience of being believed without pressure to perform or defend their narrative as a turning point in engagement and psychological safety (Price-Tobler, 2023a). Person-centred principles support identity reconstruction by allowing survivors to explore self-expression without fear of punishment, loyalty betrayal, or emotional withdrawal.

Within the HQTP, PCT principles are foundational across all phases of treatment. In Phase I, relational attunement supports stabilisation and containment. In Phase II, empathic validation facilitates identity differentiation without activating loyalty conditioning. In later phases, the consistent therapeutic relationship provides the secure base necessary for trauma integration and meaning reconstruction.

Psychoeducation

Psychoeducation was reported with equal frequency to Person-Centred Therapy (PCT), emerging as one of the most utilised approaches reported in the author's doctoral practitioner study. Although often described as a treatment in its own right, psychoeducation is more accurately conceptualised as a structured clinical process rather than a standalone modality. In the doctoral practitioner interviews, clinicians consistently identified clear, developmentally informed explanations as central to stabilising adult survivors of CPA-PA (Price-Tobler, 2023b).

Findings from the author's doctoral survivor study indicated that many adult survivors presented with confusion regarding trauma responses, attachment disruption, loyalty conditioning, dissociation, and nervous system activation (Price-Tobler, 2023a). Many described years of misinterpreting their symptoms as personal weakness or character flaws. In the doctoral survivor interviews, participants reported significant relief when they were provided with coherent explanations that contextualised their reactions as adaptive responses to prolonged psychological coercion (Price-Tobler, 2023a). Psychoeducation, therefore, functions not merely as information delivery but as a form of epistemic repair.

Within the HQTP, psychoeducation is introduced in Phase I to reduce shame, increase cognitive coherence, and support nervous system stabilisation. It continues into Phase II to assist with identity differentiation and examination of inherited narratives. The aim is not to instruct or persuade, but to provide survivors with conceptual tools that support autonomous meaning-making. When appropriately paced and relationally delivered, psychoeducation strengthens engagement and prepares the ground for deeper therapeutic work without replicating authority-driven narrative control.

Cognitive Behavioural Therapy

Cognitive Behavioural Therapy (**CBT**) was reported by participants in the author's doctoral practitioner study as one of several structured approaches utilised in work with adult survivors of CPA-PA. While not the most frequently endorsed modality, CBT was commonly described as useful in addressing anxiety symptoms, cognitive distortions, and maladaptive belief systems that persisted into adulthood (Price-Tobler, 2023b).

Findings from the author's doctoral survivor study indicated that unmodified cognitive restructuring may carry clinical risk when introduced before relational safety and identity stabilisation are established (Price-Tobler, 2023a). Many survivors described longstanding patterns of loyalty conditioning, self-blame, and internalised responsibility for family conflict. When cognitive techniques were applied prematurely or framed as correction of "distorted thinking", some survivors experienced the intervention as further invalidation of their lived experience (Price-Tobler, 2023a).

Within the HQTP, CBT is therefore introduced only after Phase I stabilisation and during Phase II identity differentiation. The clinical task is not immediate disputation of emotional responses, but careful examination of inherited belief systems and externally imposed narratives. Survivors are supported to ask, "Whose belief is this?" rather than, "Why is this thought irrational?" This distinction preserves epistemic safety while facilitating cognitive autonomy.

When appropriately phased and attachment-informed, CBT can contribute to restructuring indoctrinated schemas related to unworthiness, fear-based relational assumptions, and learned helplessness. When mistimed or applied in isolation, it may inadvertently reinforce earlier coercive dynamics. For this reason, CBT within the HQTP is integrated rather than delivered as a standalone intervention.

Psychodynamic Psychotherapy

Psychodynamic psychotherapy was reported by participants in the author's doctoral practitioner study as one of several depth-oriented approaches utilised in the treatment of adult survivors of CPA-PA. Although not all practitioners reported it, clinicians described its relevance in addressing unconscious relational templates, transference patterns, and identity structures shaped by prolonged psychological coercion (Price-Tobler, 2023b).

Findings from the author's doctoral survivor study indicated that many adult survivors of CPA-PA presented with internal working models organised around fear, compliance, role reversal, or conditional attachment (Price-Tobler, 2023a). These patterns often persisted beyond conscious awareness and could manifest within the therapeutic relationship itself. Psychodynamic work allows exploration of these relational expectations without immediate correction or behavioural prescription.

Within the HQTP, psychodynamic principles are introduced primarily during Phase II and consolidated in Phase III. In Phase II, the focus centres on identity differentiation, restoration of reflective capacity, and examination of internalised parental narratives. The clinical aim is not confrontation of inherited belief systems in early treatment, but gradual strengthening of autonomous meaning-making and internal authority. This pacing is essential to prevent reenactment of coercive dynamics.

As stabilisation deepens, psychodynamic exploration may extend to the integration of grief, unresolved attachment ruptures, and transgenerational patterns of control. However, interpretation remains collaborative rather than authoritative. Attempts to challenge entrenched belief systems prematurely may replicate the power imbalance central to the original injury.

Within the HQTP, psychodynamic psychotherapy functions as a framework for identity reconstruction rather than a long-term exploratory process detached from phase sequencing. Its integration remains anchored in attachment stability, pacing, and survivor readiness.

Dialectical Behaviour Therapy

Within the HQTP, DBT-informed strategies may be used to support stabilisation, distress tolerance, emotional regulation, crisis containment, and behavioural safety. The HQTP does not claim to be a comprehensive or adherent DBT program. Rather, DBT-informed skills are integrated selectively and phase-consistently when they support safety, pacing, and survivor autonomy.

A disciplined differential formulation is required before using DBT-informed intervention with adult survivors of CPA-PA. Some survivors may present with self-harm, suicidality, abandonment sensitivity, affective instability, relational volatility, or rapid shifts in attachment behaviour that appear phenomenologically similar to borderline personality disorder (BPD). However, descriptive overlap should not be mistaken for diagnostic equivalence. In this population, such presentations may reflect trauma-organised dysregulation associated with chronic attachment threat, coercive control, developmental invalidation, and loyalty conditioning rather than enduring personality pathology.

Findings from the author's doctoral survivor study indicated that, in many cases, these difficulties were more coherently conceptualised as adaptations to prolonged child psychological abuse in CPA-PA contexts than as evidence of fixed personality structure (Price-Tobler, 2023a). Careful assessment is therefore essential to differentiate trauma-adaptive survival responses from personality pathology and to prevent further harm through premature or pathologising formulation.

DBT was reported by MHPs in the author's doctoral practitioner study as one of several structured approaches incorporated into treatment for adult survivors of CPA-PA. Practitioners most frequently referenced DBT-informed skills when addressing emotional dysregulation, distress intolerance, and behavioural destabilisation associated with prolonged developmental trauma exposure (Price-Tobler, 2023b).

DBT-informed skills may be beneficial even in the absence of a formal diagnosis of personality disorder. Emotion regulation, distress tolerance, and interpersonal effectiveness skills support nervous system stabilisation and relational boundary development across a broad range of trauma presentations. Within the HQTP, these skills are applied according to symptom need rather than diagnostic label. Consistent with DBT principles, validation of emotional experience remains central to regulation work, even when behavioural limits are required.

Additionally, in the HQTP, DBT-informed strategies are primarily introduced in Phase I to widen the survivor's window of tolerance and reduce acute destabilisation. In cases where survivors meet diagnostic criteria for BPD or present with recurrent self-harm or suicidality, a DBT program may be clinically indicated. In such circumstances, structured DBT may operate in tandem with the HQTP stabilisation framework. Once sufficient regulation and behavioural containment are achieved, treatment transitions back into phase-based identity reconstruction and trauma integration within the HQTP.

Within this model, DBT functions as a containment scaffold rather than a replacement for attachment repair or identity differentiation. Its role is to stabilise acute dysregulation so that deeper developmental work can proceed safely.

Emotionally Focused Therapy

Emotionally Focused Therapy (EFT) was reported by MHPs in the author's doctoral practitioner study as one of several attachment-informed approaches utilised in work with adult survivors of CPA-PA. Although most associated with couple therapy, practitioners described adapting EFT principles to support attachment repair, emotional responsiveness, and relational restructuring in individual treatment contexts (Price-Tobler, 2023b).

Findings from the author's doctoral survivor study indicated that many adult survivors of CPA-PA presented with attachment systems organised around fear, conditional acceptance, abandonment anxiety, or emotional withdrawal (Price-Tobler, 2023a). These relational templates often persisted into adult partnerships and could also become activated within the therapeutic relationship itself. EFT-informed work supports identification of core attachment emotions and facilitates movement from defensive secondary responses toward primary emotional experience.

Within the HQTP, EFT principles are primarily introduced during Phase III and Phase IV, once identity differentiation and nervous system stabilisation have been sufficiently established. Premature exploration of attachment injury may intensify dysregulation or reactivate loyalty conflict. Accordingly, attachment-focused interventions are introduced only when the survivor demonstrates the capacity to tolerate relational vulnerability without destabilisation.

Within the HQTP, EFT is not positioned as a standalone couple intervention, but as an attachment-informed lens for emotional processing, relational repair, and boundary development. When appropriately phased, EFT principles may help survivors move towards reciprocal relationships grounded in security rather than survival adaptation.

Narrative Therapy

Narrative Therapy was reported by MHPs in the author's doctoral practitioner study as one of several meaning-oriented approaches utilised in the treatment of adult survivors of CPA-PA. Practitioners described its relevance in supporting identity reconstruction and helping survivors externalise alienation dynamics that had become internalised as personal defects or failures (Price-Tobler, 2023b).

Findings from the author's doctoral survivor study indicated that many adult survivors of CPA-PA had inherited rigid family narratives shaped by coercion, loyalty conditioning, and ideological control (Price-Tobler, 2023a). Over time, these narratives could become embedded within the survivor's self-concept, constraining autonomous meaning-making. Narrative-informed work assists survivors in separating the problem from the person, examining how dominant stories were constructed, and identifying alternative accounts grounded in lived experience rather than imposed ideology.

Within the HQTP, narrative techniques are primarily introduced during Phase II, when identity differentiation and cognitive coherence are developing. Externalisation of alienation dynamics supports the reduction of shame and the restoration of agency. In later phases, particularly Phase IV, narrative reconstruction assists survivors in integrating recovery into a coherent life story that does not organise identity around trauma.

Narrative Therapy within the HQTP is not positioned as purely strengths-based reframing. Rather, it functions as a structured process of authorship restoration. Survivors are supported to critically examine inherited narratives while developing an internally anchored sense of self. When appropriately phased, narrative work consolidates differentiation achieved in earlier stages and supports long-term identity stability.

Mindfulness-Based Interventions

Mindfulness-based interventions were reported by a small number of MHPs in the author's doctoral practitioner study as adjunctive strategies within the treatment of adult survivors of CPA-PA. Although not among the most frequently endorsed approaches, practitioners described selectively using mindfulness techniques to support present-moment awareness and nervous system regulation (Price-Tobler, 2023b).

Findings from the author's doctoral survivor study indicated that many adult survivors of CPA-PA experienced chronic hypervigilance, dissociation, or rapid emotional activation in response to relational cues (Price-Tobler, 2023a). Mindfulness practices may help strengthen attentional control, increase awareness of somatic signals, and interrupt automatic threat-based responses. However, the doctoral survivor findings, together with clinical observation, suggest that unstructured or prolonged inward-focused practices may intensify distress in survivors with significant trauma history or dissociative vulnerability (Price-Tobler, 2023a). This pattern has also been observed in clinical practice.

Within the HQTP, mindfulness techniques are introduced cautiously during Phase I and early Phase II, and only when stabilisation and relational safety have been established. Interventions emphasise brief, externally anchored exercises rather than extended meditation practices. The aim is to support regulation and self-observation without forcing premature internal exposure. Within the HQTP, mindfulness is positioned as a supplementary regulation tool rather than a standalone treatment. Its application remains contingent on survivor readiness, consent, and demonstrated tolerance for internal focus.

Eye Movement Desensitisation and Reprocessing

Eye Movement Desensitisation and Reprocessing (EMDR) was reported by MHPs in the author's doctoral practitioner study as a trauma-processing modality utilised in selected cases involving adult survivors of CPA-PA. Although it was not among the most frequently reported approaches, practitioners identified EMDR as clinically significant when trauma memories remained highly activated despite prior stabilisation work (Price-Tobler, 2023b).

Findings from the author's doctoral survivor study indicated that many adult survivors of CPA-PA carried cumulative attachment ruptures, prolonged relational coercion, sudden separations, court-related trauma, and experiences of developmental captivity (Price-Tobler, 2023a). When appropriately timed, EMDR may assist in reducing the emotional intensity of traumatic memory networks and supporting adaptive reprocessing. However, the doctoral survivor findings, together with clinical observation, suggest that premature trauma activation may result in emotional flooding, identity destabilisation, or reactivation of loyalty conflict dynamics (Price-Tobler, 2023a).

Within the HQTP, EMDR is considered only after Phase I stabilisation, Phase II identity differentiation and meaning reconstruction, and sufficient progress through Phase III mourning and loss integration. Readiness for trauma-processing work is then assessed within Phase IV: Trauma Integration Readiness Architecture. Emotional regulation capacity, relational safety, reflective functioning, and consent stability must be sufficiently established and sustained to support trauma processing without destabilisation. EMDR is not introduced during periods of active family conflict, legal instability, or ongoing coercive contact.

Importantly, EMDR is not suitable for all survivors. Individuals with significant dissociative vulnerability, unstable attachment presentation, or insufficient identity coherence may experience destabilisation if bilateral stimulation is introduced prematurely. In such cases, alternative trauma-integration approaches or extended stabilisation work may be clinically preferable. Within the HQTP, EMDR functions as a titrated trauma-integration tool rather than an event-focused intervention. The clinical objective is to reduce the intensity of trauma while preserving identity stability, attachment differentiation, and epistemic safety. As with all modalities within the protocol, readiness and pacing determine appropriateness.

Equine-Assisted and Nature-Based Adjuncts to Treatment

Polyvagal-informed approaches and equine-assisted interventions were each referenced by only one practitioner in the author's doctoral practitioner study and were therefore not included among the primary modalities identified in the empirical analysis (Price-Tobler, 2023b). Elevating either approach to core status would risk overstating its proportional representation in the doctoral data. They are included here as adjunctive frameworks because of their conceptual relevance to autonomic regulation, relational safety, and attachment repair, as well as the author's additional clinical training and observed applicability in trauma-informed practice.

Polyvagal-informed work, grounded in Porges' neurophysiological model, aligns closely with the HQTP emphasis on autonomic regulation, expansion of the window of tolerance, and restoration of relational safety. Trauma responses are understood as adaptive shifts in autonomic state rather than as fixed pathology. This perspective is clinically useful when working with adult survivors of CPA-PA, many of whom present with chronic threat activation, shutdown responses, relational vigilance, or difficulty sustaining felt safety. Although polyvagal-informed work is not treated as a standalone modality within the HQTP, its principles may inform clinical formulation, pacing, regulation planning, and intervention timing, particularly during Phase I stabilisation and at points of attachment activation.

Equine-Assisted Therapy

Equine-assisted therapy offers a relationally rich, non-verbal context in which regulation, boundary awareness, and embodied responsiveness may be supported. Many adult survivors of CPA-PA present with heightened sensitivity to authority figures, mistrust of interpersonal intent, difficulties interpreting relational cues, or rapid shifts in arousal within emotionally charged encounters. Horses, as highly attuned prey animals, respond immediately to changes in posture, breath, tension, and affective state. This may provide transparent feedback that supports greater congruence between internal experience and external behaviour without relying exclusively on verbal interpretation.

For survivors whose early attachment environments were organised around coercion, conditional approval, or ideological control, the equine setting may offer an alternative relational experience grounded in attunement rather than dominance. The therapeutic task often centres on regulating presence rather than performance, thereby strengthening embodied confidence and relational agency. The author has undertaken advanced training in equine-assisted approaches, including Level 3 certification in Parelli Natural Horsemanship, and integrates this work selectively within trauma-informed frameworks where clinically appropriate. Within the HQTP, equine-assisted interventions are most appropriately considered during Phase II or Phase III, once stabilisation, consent, and sufficient identity differentiation have been established.

Nature-Based Interventions

Nature-based interventions, including forest therapy and *Shinrin-yoku* (forest bathing), draw on principles of autonomic regulation, sensory grounding, and restorative environmental exposure. Emerging research suggests that structured immersion in natural environments may support parasympathetic activation, reduce physiological stress markers, and enhance emotional regulation (Park et al., 2010). For adult survivors of CPA-PA, whose developmental histories were often marked by chronic relational vigilance, carefully paced engagement with natural environments may offer a low-demand context for regulation, reflective processing, and recovery of felt safety. The author holds formal certification in forest therapy facilitation and selectively integrates nature-based practices into trauma-informed treatment plans when clinically appropriate.

In the author's clinical practice, nature-based regulation is supported within a structured therapeutic environment that complements phased treatment. A dedicated mindfulness garden incorporating guided walking pathways, water features, established trees, and intentional seating areas may be used as part of stabilisation and integration work when clinically indicated. Within the HQTP, the natural environment is not treated as an intervention but as a contextual support for regulation, reflection, and paced therapeutic dialogue.

Within the HQTP, equine-assisted and nature-based approaches are positioned as adjunctive supports rather than primary treatment modalities. Their inclusion remains contingent on survivor readiness, consent, accessibility, and clear clinical rationale.

Integrating Therapeutic Modalities Within the HQTP

Findings from the author's doctoral practitioner study demonstrated that MHPs utilised a wide range of therapeutic modalities when working with adult survivors of CPA-PA, with no single approach emerging as sufficient in isolation (Price-Tobler, 2023b). Person-Centred Therapy and psychoeducation were most frequently reported, while cognitive, depth-oriented, attachment-focused, regulation-based, and trauma-processing approaches were applied with varying emphasis across practitioners. This variability reflects both the complexity of CPA-PA presentations and the absence of a unified, phase-informed treatment framework within existing clinical practice.

The HQTP does not replace these modalities. Rather, it organises them within a structured, attachment-informed, phase-based architecture designed to prevent destabilisation and promote developmental repair. Modality selection is secondary to phase readiness. Relational safety, identity differentiation, nervous system capacity, and consent determine timing and integration. In this way, therapeutic techniques function not as competing schools of thought, but as coordinated components of a coherent treatment sequence.

Early Phase Positioning: Stabilisation and Relational Containment

Phase I focuses on establishing psychological safety, relational trust, and nervous system stabilisation. Findings from the author's doctoral survivor study indicated that survivors who received cognitive restructuring or trauma-processing interventions before relational containment was established frequently reported emotional flooding, disengagement, or increased internal conflict (Price-Tobler, 2023a). Stabilisation is therefore not merely preparatory. It is protective.

During this phase, Person-Centred Therapy provides the essential relational foundation. Survivors benefit from consistent empathic engagement that does not demand performance, disclosure, or loyalty positioning. The experience of being believed without correction or interrogation establishes the conditions necessary for subsequent identity work. Psychoeducation is introduced early to reduce shame and contextualise trauma responses, attachment disruption, and nervous system activation. For many survivors, understanding the adaptive function of hypervigilance or emotional reactivity reduces internalised self-blame. DBT-informed skills may also be incorporated to widen the window of tolerance and support emotion regulation. Where indicated, structured DBT programs may operate in tandem with stabilisation work. Mindfulness techniques, if used, remain brief and externally anchored to avoid intensifying dissociation or premature inward exposure. Trauma-processing modalities, including EMDR, are not introduced at this stage. The clinical objective is to establish safety, coherence, and therapeutic trust.

Middle Phase Positioning: Meaning Reconstruction and Identity Differentiation

Phase II begins once Phase I stabilisation has been demonstrably established. Survivors entering this stage show increased regulatory capacity, reduced crisis reactivity, and sufficient relational safety to tolerate examination of internalised belief systems. Findings from the author's doctoral survivor study indicated that attempts to introduce cognitive restructuring or interpretive depth work before this stabilisation frequently resulted in withdrawal, activation of shame, or intensified loyalty conflict (Price-Tobler, 2023a). Phase II, therefore, represents a developmental shift rather than a procedural step.

The central clinical task in this phase is meaning reconstruction and identity differentiation. Adult survivors of CPA-PA often carry inherited narratives that have become internalised as self-definition. Beliefs concerning personal defectiveness, responsibility for family breakdown, fear of abandonment, or moral obligation toward an alienating parent may continue to operate outside conscious scrutiny. Modified CBT approaches are introduced cautiously at this stage, not to dispute emotion, but to examine the origins of belief. The guiding question shifts from "Is this thought irrational?" to "Where did this belief originate, and does it reflect my autonomous experience?"

Psychodynamic principles support strengthening reflective capacity, and the examination of internal working models formed under coercive attachment conditions. Rather than confronting inherited narratives directly, the clinician facilitates curiosity about relational patterns, transference responses, and unconscious dynamics of loyalty that emerge within and beyond the therapeutic relationship. Narrative Therapy techniques are also particularly valuable in this phase. Externalisation of alienation dynamics reduces shame and assists survivors to distinguish imposed ideology from lived experience. Throughout Phase II, regulation strategies remain available, as identity work frequently activates attachment-based fear responses. DBT-informed skills and continued psychoeducation may be revisited as needed while differentiation deepens.

Later Phase Positioning: Mourning, Trauma Integration Readiness, and Attachment Repair

Phase III is entered once stabilisation and identity differentiation have been sufficiently established. At this point, survivors may begin to engage more directly with grief for lost attachment relationships, lost developmental opportunities, ruptured family continuity, and the self that was organised around survival rather than recognition. Findings from the author's doctoral survivor study indicated that these losses are rarely discrete or singular. Instead, they are layered across attachment, identity, belonging, and developmental time (Price-Tobler, 2023a).

During Phase III, the work turns towards mourning rather than trauma-processing as such. Survivors may grieve abrupt separations, prolonged coercive control, court-related harm, developmental captivity, and unresolved longing for unavailable caregivers. Attachment-informed interventions, including EFT principles, may support safe engagement with primary emotion while maintaining relational stability. The task is not cathartic exposure, but gradual integration of grief within a therapeutic context that preserves regulation, dignity, and agency.

Phase IV: Trauma Integration Readiness Architecture

Trauma-processing work is considered only after sufficient progress through Phase III has been established. Within the HQTP, readiness for trauma integration is assessed in Phase IV, where emotional regulation capacity, relational safety, reflective functioning, identity coherence, and consent stability must all be demonstrably sustained. Findings from the author's doctoral survivor study indicated that trauma-processing interventions introduced before this level of consolidation frequently resulted in emotional flooding, dissociation, or regression into loyalty conflict dynamics (Price-Tobler, 2023a).

At this stage, EMDR may be introduced selectively when regulation and identity coherence are demonstrably stable. Within the HQTP, EMDR is not positioned as a universal intervention and does not suit all survivors. Individuals with significant dissociative vulnerability, fragile identity consolidation, or ongoing coercive relational contact may require extended stabilisation or alternative trauma-integration approaches before bilateral stimulation is considered. Readiness, consent, and tolerance determine appropriateness. Throughout this phase, pacing remains central. The aim is integration without fragmentation, so that traumatic memory can be incorporated into personal history without again becoming the organising force of identity.

Phase V: Differentiation, Boundary Formation, and Contact Decisions

Once trauma integration readiness has been established, the clinical task may shift towards strengthening differentiation in lived relational contexts. Phase V focuses on boundary formation, contact decisions, and consolidation of identity in relation to others. Survivors are supported to apply insight within everyday life, test new ways of relating that are not organised around fear, compliance, or inherited family ideology, and refine decisions regarding contact, limited contact, structured contact, or no contact where relevant.

Within this phase, PCT, psychodynamic reflection, Narrative Therapy, and selected adjunctive interventions may remain relevant. Their function, however, is now directed towards applied differentiation, boundary maintenance, and relational discernment rather than primary discovery. The emphasis is on strengthening internal authority, sustaining agency under stress, and supporting the survivor in tolerating relational complexity without collapsing into earlier survival positions.

Phase VI: Integration, Continuity, and Long-Term Adaptation

Phase VI focuses on continuity rather than closure. The clinical task is to support survivors in carrying their recovery forward without requiring the erasure of grief, the simplification of history, or a false resolution. Survivors may continue to live with unanswered questions, irreversible losses, or enduring complexity in family relationships. The aim is not to eliminate these realities, but to help ensure they no longer organise identity or determine the entire shape of adult life.

At this stage, therapeutic work supports self-continuity, future orientation, sustainable relational functioning, and the capacity to live beyond survival while remaining anchored in truth. Where clinically appropriate, selected modalities may still be drawn upon, but their use is now integrated within a longer-term framework of maintenance, adaptation, and meaning rather than acute stabilisation or active reconstruction.

Modality-Specific Adaptations for Complex and High-Risk Presentations

This section outlines how therapeutic modalities may need to be modified, constrained, or sequenced differently when working with adult survivors of CPA-PA. These presentations are often characterised by attachment disruption, identity disturbance, loyalty conditioning, dissociation risk, and elevated system involvement, including court processes, family surveillance, or ongoing coercive contact. Standard modality delivery models are frequently insufficient in these contexts and require deliberate adaptation to reduce the risk of retraumatisation, therapeutic rupture, or clinical destabilisation.

Findings from the author's doctoral survivor study indicated that some survivors presented with relatively high factual narrative coherence while simultaneously demonstrating physiological dysregulation, emotional shutdown, or cognitive fragmentation when relational themes were activated (Price-Tobler, 2023a). This pattern requires careful pacing, phased delivery, and containment-focused sequencing across therapeutic approaches.

Child Psychological Abuse Treatment Using Psychodynamic Psychotherapy

Psychodynamic psychotherapy remains one of the most clinically appropriate modalities for addressing long-term identity disruption, attachment distortion, and unconscious loyalty conditioning associated with child psychological abuse. Survivors may carry internalised relational templates shaped by coercion, emotional inversion, role reversal, and prolonged exposure to manipulative caregiving systems. These templates may continue to influence adult relationship patterns, emotional regulation, and self-concept.

Within the HQTP, psychodynamic work prioritises gradual exploration of unconscious relational expectations, internalised caregiver representations, and survival-based identity adaptations. The therapeutic relationship itself may become a corrective relational environment in which survivors experience non-transactional care, consistent boundaries, and relational safety without performance demands.

Because these survivors often learned to suppress emotional expression or adopt externally constructed identities to preserve attachment bonds, treatment must proceed slowly. Premature interpretation, direct confrontation of loyalty conflicts, or rapid excavation of traumatic material may trigger dissociation, withdrawal, or defensive collapse. The focus, therefore, remains on strengthening reflective capacity, emotional tolerance, and self-differentiation before approaching deeper material.

Longer-form psychodynamic psychotherapy is often the preferred delivery format for this population. Extended treatment allows greater opportunity to stabilise attachment insecurity, strengthen identity coherence, and work gradually with deeply embedded relational distortions. However, clinical realities such as funding limitations, service access barriers, or organisational constraints may require the use of brief psychodynamic psychotherapy where the clinician is appropriately trained in trauma-informed delivery of the modality.

In time-limited contexts, brief psychodynamic work should focus on circumscribed relational themes, stabilisation of dominant attachment patterns, and targeted identity repair rather than full developmental reconstruction. Even within shorter formats, pacing, emotional containment, and relational safety remain central clinical priorities.

Treating Shared Delusional-Like Processes in Psychological Abuse Survivors

Shared delusional-like processes, including phenomena historically described as *folie à deux*, represent one of the more complex and clinically sensitive presentations that may emerge in the context of prolonged psychological abuse. Caution is required in this area. Not all rigid, inherited, or reality-distorting belief systems should be conceptualised as psychosis, and genuine shared psychotic disorder remains relatively uncommon. However, survivors exposed to coercive caregiving environments may develop entrenched belief structures, reduced confidence in their own perceptions, and marked difficulty evaluating reality independently when chronic narrative manipulation, loyalty enforcement, emotional dependency, and relational isolation have shaped development over time.

Research suggests that early trauma exposure may increase vulnerability to stress-related cognitive distortion and psychotic-like experiences, particularly when authority figures repeatedly override, deny, or reshape the child's perception of reality (Vargas Alves Nunes et al., 2016). Within psychologically abusive family systems, survivors may internalise imposed explanatory frameworks that persist into adulthood, especially where separation from the inducing figure occurred abruptly, under conditions of fear, or without sufficient differentiation or psychological closure. In these cases, the core clinical issue is not necessarily primary psychotic pathology. More often, it reflects the enduring effects of attachment-based coercion, prolonged epistemic domination, and developmental interference with autonomous reality testing.

Within psychodynamic and trauma-informed treatment, intervention does not begin with direct confrontation of rigid, implausible, or inherited beliefs. Premature correction may intensify shame, provoke defensive retreat, or recreate the same power struggle through which the belief system was originally established. The clinical task is therefore not immediate disconfirmation. It is the gradual restoration of reflective capacity, identity differentiation, tolerance for ambiguity, and trust in the survivor's own internal experience. Meaning making must be rebuilt, not imposed.

Case literature suggests that successful intervention may involve reducing isolation, increasing access to a broader relational and social reality, and strengthening an independent sense of self (Saragih et al., 2019). In clinical practice, survivors may begin to loosen inherited narratives once psychological safety, relational consistency, and internal coherence increase sufficiently to permit doubt without collapse. This process is often slow, uneven, and non-linear.

Treatment must remain collaborative rather than adversarial. Attempts to "correct" belief prematurely may reproduce the original dynamics of domination, invalidation, and epistemic override. A more therapeutically sound approach is to help survivors notice inconsistencies, tolerate uncertainty, differentiate imposed narratives from lived experience, and gradually rebuild confidence in their own reflective capacities. Within the HQTP, such presentations are approached primarily as problems of developmental coercion, attachment-based reality distortion, and impaired epistemic autonomy rather than as a default assumption of primary psychotic disorder.

Clinical Risk Management and Therapist Positioning

Working with survivors of child psychological abuse in CPA-PA contexts carries elevated relational, clinical, and professional risk. Survivors may unconsciously draw therapists into loyalty dynamics, rescue positioning, authority alignment, or reenactments of early family structures. Clinicians must therefore maintain transparent boundaries, collaborative positioning, and clear role definition throughout treatment.

Documentation should remain behaviourally anchored, clinically precise, and neutral in tone, particularly in cases involving court processes, family surveillance, or ongoing conflict. Notes should describe observed presentation, reported experience, and clinically relevant risk without drifting into speculative interpretation or adversarial language. This is especially important where records may later be scrutinised outside the therapeutic setting.

Practitioners must also monitor countertransference responses such as over-identification, protective urgency, retaliatory frustration, rescue fantasy, or emotional enmeshment. In this population, strong therapist reactions may carry meaningful clinical information, but if left unexamined they may also increase the risk of boundary drift, interpretive overreach, or reenactment of coercive relational patterns.

Ongoing clinical supervision is essential within this treatment domain. The frequency of high-risk presentations, exposure to survivor grief and traumatic material, and system-level pressures associated with parental alienation, abduction, and psychological abuse place clinicians at elevated risk of vicarious trauma, cumulative strain, and compromised decision-making. Regular supervision supports reflective functioning, ethical containment, and disciplined therapeutic positioning in work of this complexity.

Modality Integration and Sequencing Within High-Risk Presentations

In complex presentations, no single modality is applied in isolation. Therapeutic approaches are instead selected, sequenced, and integrated according to survivor stability, developmental needs, and phase readiness within the HQTP.

During early stabilisation, the clinical priority is safety, relational containment, and nervous system regulation. Person-Centred Therapy, psychoeducation, and regulation-focused strategies are therefore introduced first to establish therapeutic trust and reduce destabilisation.

Trauma-processing modalities such as EMDR are not introduced until sufficient emotional regulation, identity differentiation, and readiness for trauma integration have been established.

As treatment progresses, meaning-oriented and identity-focused approaches become increasingly relevant. Narrative Therapy becomes increasingly valuable once survivors can examine inherited narratives and reconstruct personal meaning without significant destabilisation. DBT-informed skills may be incorporated whenever emotional dysregulation, self-harm risk, or relational volatility is present.

Attachment-informed approaches, including EFT principles, are introduced cautiously and only when the survivor demonstrates sufficient internal stability to tolerate relational exploration without collapse, reenactment, or intensified loyalty conflict. Across all phases, the clinician remains attentive to pacing, consent, and emotional capacity. Within the HQTP, the emphasis remains on containment rather than acceleration, and on safety rather than premature symptom suppression.

Long-Term Outcomes and Therapeutic Goals

Effective treatment of high-risk presentations involving child psychological abuse is not aimed solely at symptom reduction. It is directed towards restoration of agency, identity coherence, relational autonomy, and emotional self-regulation. Survivors often describe the endpoint of therapy not as recovery in a conventional sense, but as the capacity to trust their own perceptions, establish boundaries without fear, and participate in relationships no longer governed by survival-based adaptation.

Within the HQTP, modality adaptation is treated as an ethical responsibility rather than a technical preference. Therapeutic methods are aligned with survivor capacity, developmental history, phase readiness, and relational risk so that treatment supports long-term repair rather than short-term symptom management.

The need for such adaptation becomes especially clear in complex adult presentations where developmental trauma intersects with high-stakes questions of identity, embodiment, and meaning. In these contexts, clinicians must exercise restraint, careful differentiation, and sustained epistemic containment to avoid reenacting coercive dynamics within treatment. The following subsection illustrates one such advanced presentation in which modality selection, pacing, and therapeutic stance require deliberate ethical calibration within the HQTP.

Gender Identity, Autonomy, and Retrospective Medical Decision Distress

The intersection between CPA dynamics and retrospective distress related to gender affirming medical intervention has been raised in limited clinical discussions, peer consultations, and formal clinical supervision among practitioners working with adult survivors of complex developmental trauma. In the author's clinical experience, this concern has emerged in a small minority of cases and appears to be arising with sufficient frequency to warrant careful professional reflection. This remains an evolving and professionally sensitive area of consideration and requires cautious, ethically grounded engagement. The purpose of raising it here is not to advance a polarised position or to make broad causal claims, but to identify a clinical presentation that some practitioners are beginning to encounter and that warrants thoughtful discussion, careful assessment, and ongoing supervision.

In a small subset of high-conflict post-separation cases, questions concerning a child's gender identity, gender expression, or access to gender affirming intervention may become entangled with broader patterns of coercive family conflict, custody-related dispute, relational control, attachment disruption, and alienation-related dynamics. Existing literature indicates that custody disputes involving transgender and gender nonconforming children do occur in family court contexts and may involve blame, coercion by ex-partners, and adverse impacts on children (Kuvalanka et al., 2019). At the same time, the broader evidence base concerning coercive control remains limited in relation to children and young people, LGBTQIA+ communities, and Australian practice contexts (MacDonald et al., 2024).

Accordingly, the present protocol does not assume that a parent can simply create or direct a child's gender identity for strategic advantage. Rather, the clinical concern is that genuine gender related distress, family violence, coercive control, attachment disruption, and alienation-related dynamics may, in a small number of cases, become dangerously intertwined, thereby complicating assessment, consent processes, and later meaning-making.

Australian standards of care also emphasise the importance of careful multidisciplinary assessment in complex presentations involving children and adolescents who are trans or gender diverse (Telfer et al., 2018). For this reason, where an adult survivor raises retrospective medical decision distress, clinicians are advised to undertake careful, non-polarised assessment of developmental context, autonomy, caregiver behaviour, coercive dynamics, and the relational conditions under which earlier decisions were made (Kuvalanka et al., 2019; MacDonald et al., 2024; Telfer et al., 2018).

In the author's clinical experience and in peer supervision discussions with colleagues working in this area, adults presenting with this concern have described uncertainty about the degree of autonomy they experienced before decisions were made. Some report grief associated with perceived alterations in developmental trajectory, while others describe shame, anger toward family systems, or diminished trust in their own decision-making capacity.

Treatment Position Within the HQTP

Clinical work proceeds according to the HQTP's phase-based structure. Initial intervention prioritises emotional stabilisation, regulation of acute distress, and containment of shame or self-condemnation. Differentiation processes focus on distinguishing developmental survival adaptations from adult self-authorship. Where grief emerges, it is understood as an injury to attachment and autonomy rather than as ideological conflict. Existential themes concerning authenticity, agency, and identity continuity may arise and be addressed within a non-polarised, non-adjudicatory therapeutic stance. Across phases, the central clinical question remains: how does the adult survivor integrate developmental history without reenacting coercive relational dynamics or collapsing into self-erasure?

Clinical Risk Escalation Warning

When psychological FDIOA and malingering by proxy occur in conjunction with CPA, clinical risk extends beyond relational harm into systemic entrapment. In the author's clinical work, survivors have become embedded within service, legal, and welfare systems that unintentionally reinforce dependency narratives and restrict developmental autonomy. In these contexts, clinicians must exercise heightened vigilance regarding how support structures, funding pathways, and institutional responses may inadvertently stabilise coercive family dynamics.

The HQTP identifies this presentation as high risk because of its association with arrested psychosocial development, identity distortion, heightened vulnerability to exploitation, and increased legal exposure arising from social deprivation and relational isolation (Herman, 1992). Clinicians are advised to prioritise stabilisation, epistemic safety, and autonomy restoration before introducing trauma processing. Premature confrontation of family systems or attempts to dismantle dependency-based identity narratives without sufficient internal stabilisation may amplify distress and precipitate collapse rather than recovery. This risk context provides the clinical foundation for the following case vignette, which illustrates the downstream consequences of prolonged psychological FDIOA, disability exploitation, and attachment-based alienation dynamics.

Clinical Case Vignette Integration Within the HQTP

The following case illustrates how attachment-based psychological fabrication, disability exploitation, and parental alienation may interact to produce high-risk developmental outcomes when left unaddressed. Within the HQTP, this presentation reflects a multi-phase pattern of disruption requiring careful sequencing, pacing, and sustained attention to the restoration of autonomy.

From a **Phase I** perspective, the client presented with significant nervous system dysregulation, social deprivation, impaired autonomy development, and identity dependency anchored in caregiver control. Stabilisation priorities would include the restoration of basic self-regulation capacity, the development of independent decision-making support, and the protection from ongoing relational coercion. The client's restricted mobility, lack of employment exposure, and enforced isolation indicate that early treatment must focus on safety, scaffolding of autonomy, and reducing environmental containment.

From a **Phase II** perspective, the client's internalised "incapable" identity reflects long-term psychological fabrication reinforced across family, service, and institutional systems. Within the HQTP, this is understood as an epistemic injury in which externally imposed narratives progressively displace self-knowledge. Treatment sequencing would prioritise identity reconstruction, boundary development, and differentiation of authentic capacity from caregiver-assigned roles. This phase would also address compliance conditioning and loyalty conflict dynamics that maintain dependency.

From a **Phase III** perspective, grief work may emerge around lost developmental opportunity, arrested autonomy, social deprivation, and the absence of age-appropriate peer and vocational experience. The client's presentation suggests not only attachment disruption but mourning for a self that was prevented from forming under conditions of imposed dependency and control. Within the HQTP, this phase would focus on loss integration and developmental grief repair rather than premature trauma excavation.

From a **Phase IV** perspective, trauma integration would only be considered after stabilisation, differentiation, and grief capacity had been sufficiently established. The client's exposure to prolonged relational control, social deprivation, and institutional reinforcement of vulnerability presents significant retraumatisation risk if trauma processing is introduced prematurely (Herman, 1992). The HQTP therefore emphasises trauma integration readiness, titrated pacing, and protective sequencing rather than event-focused exposure.

From a **Phase V** perspective, treatment would support differentiation, boundary formation, and contact-related decision-making. This may include the development of reciprocal peer relationships, the formation of vocational identity, the strengthening of everyday autonomy, and the reduction of vulnerability to online exploitation or maladaptive relational-seeking patterns that may emerge following prolonged social isolation.

From a **Phase VI** perspective, the task would shift towards continuity, long-term adaptation, and consolidation of self-authorship across adult life domains. Treatment would focus on sustaining independence, supporting coherent identity development, and reducing the risk of reenacting dependency-based relational patterns in future relationships and service contexts.

This vignette demonstrates that when psychological FDIOA, CPA-PA, and disability exploitation converge, clinical intervention must extend beyond symptom management to address structural identity harm, systemic entrapment, and developmental arrest. The HQTP provides a phased containment architecture designed to address this level of complexity.

Within **CPA-PA** presentations, FDIOA may manifest as a psychological control strategy rather than a purely medical fabrication pattern. Dr Craig Childress's attachment-based model identifies these dynamics as forms of pathological caregiving in which the allied parent constructs false vulnerability narratives, assigns illness identities, and manipulates external systems to secure attachment dominance and social validation (Childress, 2015, 2020).

In these cases, the child may be positioned not only as physically unwell, but as psychologically impaired, emotionally fragile, traumatised, or developmentally "damaged" in ways that justify dependency, restrict autonomy, and maintain enmeshment. In the author's clinical work, this has also overlapped with presentations many clinicians would describe as malingering by proxy, in which symptoms are exaggerated, coached, or strategically performed to achieve secondary gain, including custody advantage, financial benefit, system leverage, or moral positioning.

Medical Coercion, Developmental Harm, and Long-Term Treatment Implications

In cases where FDIOA operates as a mechanism of coercive control within CPA dynamics, the clinical impact may extend beyond psychological injury into cumulative physiological harm. Where a child is repeatedly administered unnecessary, excessive, or inappropriate medications or other substances in ways that induce illness, fatigue, nausea, dizziness, sedation, or cognitive impairment, the developing body may be exposed to significant ongoing physiological burden. Potential harms may include medication toxicity, metabolic strain, gastrointestinal dysregulation, altered states of consciousness, and broader disruption to physical development and functioning (Bass & Halligan, 2014).

Within alienation systems, this pattern may function as both a containment strategy and an attachment-manipulation mechanism. By maintaining the child in a chronically unwell, fatigued, or medically dependent state, the controlling caregiver may restrict mobility, disrupt school attendance and peer relationships, obstruct contact with the targeted parent, and reinforce psychological dependence on the perpetrating caregiver. In the author's clinical work, such presentations have created closed relational systems in which the child's physical vulnerability becomes organised into a broader pattern of coercive control, dependency, and loyalty alignment. This progression may appear less overtly abusive over time while producing deeper and more enduring developmental disruption (Stark, 2007).

FDIOA Motivational Dynamics in Alienating Parents

Clinical patterns observed in alienation-linked FDIOA suggest that a singular motive rarely drives medical abuse. Instead, it may reflect a convergence of control needs, narcissistic supply reinforcement, grievance-driven hostility toward the targeted parent, attachment dominance, and identity preservation through victimhood or indispensable-caregiver narratives (Herman, 1992; Stark, 2007). In the author's clinical work, alienating parents who engage in FDIOA have frequently demonstrated intolerance of child autonomy, heightened fear of relational abandonment, and a need to maintain exclusive attachment capture. Inducing illness may allow the perpetrating parent to position themselves as an indispensable caregiver while simultaneously portraying the targeted parent as unsafe, disinterested, or incapable. In high-conflict separations, these dynamics may intensify in response to court proceedings, custody challenges, or perceived threats to parental authority.

Safety Addendum for Clinicians Working with Medically Abused Survivors

Work with survivors of FDIOA requires enhanced clinical caution. The HQTP prioritises bodily autonomy restoration, stabilisation, and epistemic safety before introducing trauma processing related to medical abuse. Clinicians are advised to avoid premature somatic interventions that may retraumatise survivors who associate bodily focus with coercion or control (Herman, 1992). Collaborative care with general practitioners or specialists may be required to assess residual physical effects of childhood medication exposure (Bass & Halligan, 2014). Treatment pacing should acknowledge that survivors may fear both illness and wellness, as health improvement can destabilise long-standing identity structures built around sickness and dependency.

Clinicians should maintain a non-pathologising stance that reframes symptoms as adaptive survival responses to prolonged medical coercion rather than character pathology (Herman, 1992; Stark, 2007). Safety planning must include attention to medication-related triggers, hospital-based retraumatisation risk, and heightened vulnerability during periods of physical illness or injury (Bass & Halligan, 2014). The HQTP emphasises gradual restoration of internal authority over bodily experience, informed consent at every stage of treatment, and protection of survivor autonomy throughout the therapeutic process.

Clinical Red Flags in Childhood Presentation

Clinicians should remain alert to patterns that may indicate FDIOA within an alienation context. Red flags may include repeated unexplained medical presentations, inconsistent symptom histories, discrepancies between reported illness severity and observed functioning, repeated investigations or hospital attendance without diagnostic resolution, symptoms reported primarily in the presence of the caregiver, and caregiver resistance to independent medical review or challenge to the clinical formulation (Flaherty et al., 2013; RCPCH, 2021).

FDIOA, Malingering by Proxy, and Medical and Psychological Abuse

Within contemporary psychiatric and safeguarding language, patterns of fabricated, exaggerated, induced, or caregiver-directed illness may be described as factitious disorder imposed on another, fabricated or induced illness, or malingering by proxy, depending on the clinical and systemic context.

Additionally, within this protocol, the term FDIOA is retained as a descriptive umbrella term because it captures the imposed nature of the illness identity and the broader pattern of medical and psychological coercion that may continue long after childhood. In the present context, the focus is not on the perpetrating parent's diagnosis alone, but on the adult survivor's developmental, bodily, relational, and identity-based sequelae.

Caregiver-fabricated illness is recognised as child maltreatment, may lead to unnecessary and potentially harmful medical investigations and treatment, and has been associated with significant morbidity and mortality. Reviews have also documented long-term or permanent injury in a subset of victims, and adult follow-up work indicates that survivors may continue to report physical problems and avoidance of medical treatment later in life (Flaherty et al., 2013; Libow, 1995; Sheridan, 2003).

In addition to the doctoral research data informing this section, a recurrent pattern in the author's long-term frontline work in private practice and community mental health and disability services, including extensive engagement with adults supported under the National Disability Insurance Scheme, has involved psychological FDIOA, malingering by proxy, identity fabrication, and caregiver-maintained dependency in presentations involving parental alienation, disability exploitation, and attachment-based control dynamics.

These observations complement the doctoral findings by illustrating how institutional structures, funding mechanisms, and service fragmentation may unintentionally reinforce coercive caregiving dynamics when attachment pathology and alienation-related processes are not adequately recognised. In many alienation systems, medical abuse and caregiver-induced dependency may function as early mechanisms of control. In contrast, later control is maintained through psychological fabrication, malingering by proxy, vulnerability-based narratives, and reinforcement of dependency-based identity roles.

In the author's clinical work, this developmental pattern has often shifted from bodily control to identity-based captivity, whereby the child's sense of self becomes organised around externally imposed fragility, dependency, and perceived incapacity (Childress, 2015; Stark, 2007). Later-stage presentations may appear less overtly abusive while producing deeper and more enduring developmental disruption.

Additionally, FDIOA may also operate as a psychological control strategy rather than a purely medical fabrication pattern. Childress's attachment-based model describes pathological caregiving in which the allied parent constructs false vulnerability narratives, assigns illness identities, and manipulates external systems to secure attachment dominance and social validation (Childress, 2015, 2020). In such cases, the child may be positioned not only as physically unwell, but as psychologically impaired, emotionally fragile, traumatised, or developmentally "damaged" in ways that justify dependency, restrict autonomy, and maintain enmeshment.

Adult Clinical Presentation and Long-Term Sequelae

In adulthood, Study One survivor data indicated that survivors of FDIOA-linked CPA-PA may present with complex somatic and relational sequelae, including chronic health anxiety, amplified somatic vigilance, difficulty trusting bodily sensations, medication avoidance or dependency fears, persistent fatigue, gastrointestinal dysregulation, autonomic instability, and dissociative responses associated with medical environments (Price-Tobler, 2023a). Study One also identified anomalous survivor-reported physical health data.

Within these anomalous data, twenty-four conditions described by six survivors were identified as autoimmune, immune-related, or medically complex conditions. Some of these conditions have been discussed in the medical literature in relation to immune system vulnerability, serious health risks, and altered malignancy risk. These findings are not presented as evidence of direct causation between CPA-PA, FDIOA-linked histories, and later physical illness. Rather, they are reported as exploratory survivor data that warrant careful monitoring, trauma-informed assessment, appropriate medical referral, and further research. Their clinical significance lies not in proving causation, but in demonstrating that survivor-reported bodily sequelae should not be dismissed, psychologised prematurely, or separated too quickly from developmental histories of medical control, coercive caregiving, and imposed vulnerability. Rather, they are reported as anomalous survivor data identified in Study One and examined alongside the cited peer-reviewed medical literature, warranting careful monitoring, trauma-informed assessment, and further investigation (Price-Tobler, 2023a).

In addition to these anomalous data, some adult survivors may carry enduring bodily consequences of childhood medical abuse itself, particularly where prolonged medication exposure, induced illness, poisoning, unnecessary procedures, or repeated medicalisation formed part of the childhood history. In such cases, the adult presentation may include residual digestive disturbance, altered eating patterns, medication-related fear, autonomic reactivity, heightened somatic alarm, and distress associated with medical environments. Reviews of caregiver-fabricated illness support the possibility of significant morbidity, unnecessary procedures, and long-term or permanent injury in a subset of victims, while adult follow-up work indicates that survivors may continue to report physical problems and avoidance of medical treatment later in life (Flaherty et al., 2013; Libow, 1995; Sheridan, 2003).

Adults with this history may also carry prolonged vulnerability narratives into later life. In the author's clinical work and in peer supervision discussions with colleagues working in this area, adults presenting with this concern have described uncertainty about the degree of autonomy they experienced before earlier medical decisions were made. Some report grief associated with perceived alterations in developmental trajectory, while others describe shame, anger toward family systems, diminished trust in their own judgement, and enduring uncertainty regarding bodily safety, illness, and care. In some cases, identity stability remains intact while distress centres on relational context. In other cases, individuals describe persistent confusion regarding genuine illness versus imposed vulnerability. These presentations vary considerably and should be approached without presumption.

Working with Adult Medical Teams

Where adult survivors continue to live with bodily sequelae of childhood medical abuse, collaborative work with medical teams is often essential. General practitioners, gastroenterologists, neurologists, pain specialists, endocrinologists, immunologists, psychiatrists, and other treating clinicians may all become relevant depending on the abuse history and residual health burden. For the adult survivor, however, engagement with medical systems may itself be destabilising. Medical settings may reactivate fear, compliance, shutdown, dissociation, or intense suspicion, particularly where childhood experiences of examination, treatment, or medication were organised through coercion rather than care.

For this reason, communication with medical teams should remain trauma-informed, paced, and consent-based. The task is not simply to rule out current pathology, but to assess whether residual physical consequences may still be present, to avoid reenactment of invasive or controlling dynamics, and to ensure that the survivor is not again positioned as passive within decisions concerning their own body. Management of factitious disorder presentations is also described in the literature as ideally team-based and closely coordinated with primary care, which supports this collaborative stance in adulthood (Bass & Halligan, 2014).

In some cases, treatment may require coordination of care for medication review, gastrointestinal symptoms, nutritional issues, fatigue, pain, autonomic symptoms, or other persistent physical consequences. Where poisoning, chronic administration of substances, prolonged medical dependency, or medically induced debility formed part of the abuse history, long-term medical follow-up may be required. The psychological clinician should therefore remain alert to the possibility that the adult survivor's distress reflects both trauma sequelae and continuing bodily burden.

Gender-Selective Targeting in CPA-PA

As part of the anomalous data identified in Study One, two study participants described patterns of gender-selective targeting (Price-Tobler, 2023a). In one case, a female survivor described becoming the primary focus of the alienating parent's control while her siblings were not subjected to the same level of coercion. In another case, a male survivor, who also identified as having been medically abused by the alienating parent, described becoming the primary focus of restriction and control. At the same time, his female siblings were not subjected to the same level of coercion. Taken together, these accounts suggest that the parent had disproportionate control over one child, while the other siblings were treated differently.

Within coercive family systems, the alienating parent may selectively consolidate control around the child perceived as most psychologically useful for identity reinforcement, emotional regulation, loyalty consolidation, or relational replacement. This may include unconscious role assignment in which the targeted child becomes a surrogate attachment figure, emotional confidant, or symbolic extension of the perpetrating parent's unmet relational needs. Clinically and theoretically, this pattern may be understood through attachment-based coercive control, role assignment, and identity-based dominance within the family system (Childress, 2015; Stark, 2007).

Gender dynamics may further shape this selection process. In some presentations, male children may be targeted because they represent perceived allegiance threats to the other parent, carry symbolic associations linked to the targeted parent, or are unconsciously positioned as relational substitutes for former partners. This pattern may coexist with more permissive attitudes toward female siblings whose continued contact does not threaten the alienating parent's attachment dominance or identity narrative. The result may be a differential caregiving pattern that appears externally inconsistent but is internally coherent within the perpetrator's control framework.

The anomalous data also suggested that these dynamics may have enduring consequences for sibling relationships. Where one child or adolescent becomes more deeply enmeshed with the alienating parent, sibling bonds may become organised around loyalty division, surveillance, fear, and role distortion rather than mutual protection. In such cases, siblings may go on to experience alienation not only from the targeted parent, but from one another. This sibling alienation may persist for years, particularly where one child remains closely aligned with the alienating parent's narrative and continues to function within the parent's coercive attachment system. Clinically, this means that differential targeting should not be understood only as a parent-child dynamic. It may also reshape sibling attachment, fracture inter-sibling trust, and produce long-term relational losses that continue into adolescence and adulthood.

Implications for Adult Relationships

The long-term impact of FDIOA-linked abuse may extend deeply into adult relationships. Survivors may struggle to distinguish care from control, protection from intrusion, or support from surveillance. Offers of help may be experienced as potentially coercive, while neglect may paradoxically feel more familiar than attuned care. Some survivors become highly avoidant of dependency and reject assistance even when genuinely needed. Others may remain vulnerable to reenactments in which controlling partners, exploitative carers, or coercive service relationships are unconsciously tolerated because domination has become confused with safety.

These patterns may also affect friendships, intimacy, sexuality, parenting, and sibling relationships. Survivors may fear becoming a burden, fear being disbelieved, fear being overmanaged, or fear that bodily need will again be used to subordinate autonomy. Intimacy may become complicated where physical care, illness, food, medication, or bodily vulnerability are associated with betrayal. For some, longstanding fear around eating, swallowing, medication use, or bodily symptoms may interfere with everyday functioning, social participation, and trust in shared environments. In this way, the legacy of childhood medical abuse may persist not only in the body but in the adult survivor's relational expectations, attachment strategies, and capacity to participate in care without losing selfhood.

Treatment Position Within the HQTP

Within the HQTP, work with this presentation requires enhanced clinical caution. The initial task is not to dismantle illness narratives through confrontation, but to restore epistemic safety, bodily autonomy, and internal authority. Early intervention focuses on stabilisation, reduction of acute shame and self-condemnation, and development of basic autonomy supports.

Clinicians are advised to avoid premature somatic interventions that may retraumatise survivors who associate bodily focus with coercion or control (Herman, 1992). Where medically indicated, collaborative care with general practitioners or relevant specialists may be required to assess residual physical consequences of childhood medical abuse while preserving the adult survivor's consent, pacing, and decision-making authority.

As treatment progresses, the work turns towards differentiation of imposed vulnerability from authentic bodily experience, recognition of fabricated or induced dependency roles, and grief for developmental opportunities lost through medical and psychological abuse. The therapeutic task is not to adjudicate the correctness of prior medical decisions, nor to determine whether every past symptom was genuine or fabricated. Rather, the clinical focus is on helping the adult survivor develop a more coherent understanding of what was done to them, what may still be affecting them, and how they can relate to their own body without reenacting coercive dependency or self-erasure.

Where sibling alienation, institutional reinforcement, or long-term bodily harm have also occurred, treatment may need to proceed slowly across multiple phases, with ongoing attention to regulation, relational safety, grief integration, boundary formation, and continuity of care. Across all phases, clinicians are advised to maintain a non-pathologising stance, avoid simplistic assumptions about motive, and pace interpretation carefully so that insight does not outstrip stabilisation.

Clinical Implications for the Targeted Child

Children subjected to selective medical coercion and isolation frequently internalise heightened responsibility for the alienating parent's emotional stability. This may manifest as excessive compliance, fear of abandonment, identity fusion with the caregiver, and confusion about personal needs versus relational obligation (Herman, 1992). In adulthood, survivors often present with elevated relational guilt, difficulty asserting autonomy, impaired boundary formation, and vulnerability to enmeshment or exploitative relational dynamics (Price-Tobler, 2023a). The contrast between their own restricted experience and their siblings' relative freedom may further intensify self-blame, perceived defectiveness, and confusion about differential treatment.

Healing Qualia Treatment Orientation

Within the HQTP, gender-selective FDIOA targeting is conceptualised as a form of attachment capture rather than preferential care. Treatment prioritises stabilisation and identity differentiation before addressing relational trauma content (Price-Tobler, 2023a). Phase I focuses on restoring internal safety and disentangling survival-based compliance patterns. Phase II emphasises reconstruction of personal agency, boundary formation, and separation of self-identity from caregiver-assigned roles. Trauma processing in Phase III is carefully paced to avoid destabilising attachment recalibration or reinforcing guilt-based loyalty narratives.

Clinicians are advised to normalise the survivor's confusion regarding differential sibling treatment and to reframe the pattern as a function of the perpetrator's control dynamics rather than the survivor's inherent worth or behaviour. Relational reorientation in later phases supports the development of autonomy, reciprocal attachment capacity, and protection against reenactment of asymmetric caregiving roles. The HQTP further emphasises that restoration of agency and authorship must precede any consideration of family contact decisions or reconciliation processes in cases involving selective coercive harm.

Gender-Selective Targeting When the Medically Abused Child Is Female

When the medically abused and alienated child is female, clinical patterns frequently reflect intensified possession dynamics and identity enmeshment rather than protection-based caregiving concern (Stark, 2007; Herman, 1992). Alienating parents may unconsciously position the female child as an extension of self, emotional regulator, or surrogate attachment figure, particularly in contexts where the caregiver demonstrates fragile identity organisation, abandonment sensitivity, or dependency-based relational patterns. This can result in heightened medical control, restriction of external relationships, and resistance to the child's developing autonomy.

In FDIOA-linked alienation cases involving female children, illness narratives may be reinforced through gendered caregiving expectations that normalise dependency, fragility, and emotional closeness. The child may be socialised into excessive compliance, emotional caretaking roles, and internalised responsibility for the caregiver's wellbeing (Herman, 1992). In adulthood, survivors frequently present with identity diffusion, difficulty tolerating separation, heightened relational guilt, vulnerability to controlling partners, and confusion between care and coercion (Price-Tobler, 2023a). The HQTP conceptualises this presentation as attachment capture rather than as emotional closeness, and prioritises identity differentiation and autonomy restoration over relational processing.

Sibling Weaponisation Following Disclosure and Trauma Ownership

When survivors attempt to disclose abuse histories or assert autonomy in adulthood, sibling systems may become activated in defence of the alienating parent. In some families, siblings who were not directly targeted for medical abuse may be mobilised to discredit, minimise, ridicule, or emotionally attack the survivor for "causing conflict," "rewriting history," or "hurting the family" (Stark, 2007; Price-Tobler, 2023a). This dynamic reflects secondary coercion rather than independent sibling hostility.

Weaponised sibling responses often function to preserve the original family narrative and protect the perpetrating parent from accountability. Survivors may experience renewed relational injury when siblings invalidate lived experience, accuse them of exaggeration, or pressure them to maintain silence for the sake of family stability (Herman, 1992). This secondary betrayal frequently intensifies shame, isolation, and self-doubt, particularly for survivors who were previously positioned as "difficult," "fragile," or "problematic" within the family system.

Clinical Implications for Healing Qualia Treatment

Within the HQTP, sibling weaponisation is treated as an extension of the original coercive system rather than a separate interpersonal conflict (Price-Tobler, 2023a). Phase I prioritises emotional stabilisation and protection from retraumatisation through boundary support and relational safety planning. Phase II focuses on epistemic restoration, helping survivors reclaim ownership of their narrative without requiring external validation. Phase III trauma processing is paced carefully to avoid reinforcing abandonment fear or guilt-based loyalty conflicts triggered by family backlash.

Clinicians are advised to normalise the survivor's experience of family resistance following disclosure and to frame sibling hostility as system preservation behaviour rather than proof of survivor inaccuracy. The HQTP emphasises that recovery does not depend on family consensus. Instead, treatment centres on restoring internal authority, identity coherence, and the survivor's right to define their own history.

For survivors who continue to encounter sibling pressure, later-phase work supports relational autonomy, selective contact decisions, and grief processing related to the loss of imagined family repair. The protocol cautions against encouraging premature family confrontation or disclosure in contexts where coercive dynamics remain active, as this may amplify harm rather than promote healing.

Clinical Decision Logic: FDIOA-Linked Alienation and Medical Abuse in Adult Survivors

When adult survivors present with histories involving medically induced illness within parental alienation contexts, clinicians are advised to initiate FDIOA-informed assessment pathways. Screening indicators commonly include childhood illness narratives that lacked consistent diagnostic clarity, prolonged medication exposure without stable treatment justification, caregiver control over healthcare access and mobility, heightened discomfort within medical environments, and confusion between genuine bodily sensations and externally induced symptom experiences (American Psychiatric Association, 2013, 2022; Bass & Halligan, 2014). When multiple indicators are present, clinicians should evaluate the current risk of destabilisation to guide treatment pacing.

Risk stratification requires assessment of affect regulation capacity, current family coercion exposure, and the survivor's physiological and psychological stability. Survivors demonstrating stable emotional regulation and limited external pressure may proceed cautiously through early stabilisation phases, whereas those experiencing persistent somatic distress, medication-related triggers, family-driven emotional coercion, dissociation during bodily awareness, or suicidal ideation associated with identity collapse require extended Phase I stabilisation prior to any trauma processing (Herman, 1992; Price-Tobler, 2023). The HQTP emphasises that trauma processing related to medical abuse should only be introduced when survivors demonstrate sufficient nervous system regulation, internal identity coherence, and reduced external coercive influence.

Phase alignment within the HQTP requires that Phase I focus on nervous system stabilisation, restoration of bodily autonomy, informed-consent-based pacing, and the development of medical trauma safety planning. Phase II supports identity separation from illness-based self-concepts, reconstruction of personal agency, and establishment of psychological boundaries around caregiving roles and authority dynamics. Phase III entry criteria include the survivor's demonstrated capacity to tolerate somatic awareness without dissociation, stable identity organisation, and reduced vulnerability to retraumatisation. Premature introduction of exposure-based somatic therapies or intensive trauma memory processing is contraindicated, as these interventions may replicate earlier experiences of medical coercion and bodily violation (Bass & Halligan, 2014; Herman, 1992; Price-Tobler, 2023).

Clinical Decision Logic: Sibling-Related Retraumatisation Following Disclosure

When survivors disclose histories of FDIOA-linked alienation and coercive abuse, clinicians should assess for secondary relational injury associated with sibling system activation. Common post-disclosure indicators include sudden family withdrawal, intensified sibling invalidation, pressure to suppress trauma narratives, accusations of exaggeration or family disruption, and social isolation following disclosure attempts (Stark, 2007; Price-Tobler, 2023). These responses often reflect system-preservation dynamics rather than independent interpersonal conflict.

Relational risk evaluation should determine whether sibling responses remain emotionally uncomfortable but contained, escalate into persistent loyalty conflict activation, or develop into coordinated discrediting behaviour involving gaslighting, harassment, or public narrative attacks. High-impact presentations require immediate stabilisation-focused intervention, boundary support, and relational safety planning to prevent further psychological harm (Herman, 1992; Stark, 2007). Within the HQTP, Phase I responses prioritise emotional containment, reducing exposure to retraumatising contact, and reinforcing nervous system regulation strategies. Phase II interventions focus on restoring epistemic safety, ownership of personal narrative independent of family validation, and separation of self-worth from relational approval structures. Phase III trauma processing is only considered appropriate once survivors demonstrate internal narrative stability, reduced guilt-based loyalty conflict, and sufficient relational autonomy to tolerate memory integration without destabilisation.

Clinicians are cautioned against encouraging family confrontation, sibling group therapy, or reconciliation processes while coercive dynamics remain active, as such interventions frequently intensify psychological harm and reinforce survivor self-doubt. The HQTP emphasises that recovery does not require family consensus and that therapeutic success is measured by the restoration of agency, identity coherence, and internal safety rather than by relational compliance (Herman, 1992; Stark, 2007; Price-Tobler, 2023a).

In many alienation systems, medically induced dependency represents only the initial containment mechanism, with longer-term control maintained through psychological fabrication, identity role assignment, and institutional reinforcement of vulnerability narratives.

Attachment-Based Psychological Fabrication and Role Assignment

1. In severe parental alienation and child psychological abuse, FDIOA commonly presents as psychological fabrication but may also include medical falsification in some cases. Allied parents construct vulnerability narratives that portray the child as emotionally fragile, traumatised, unsafe, or psychologically impaired to justify control, dependency, and ongoing enmeshment (Childress, 2015, 2020). The author's doctoral findings identified that survivors were frequently coached into symptom presentation, reinforced for helplessness, and assigned long-term "damaged or disabled child" identities that followed them across schools, clinicians, disability services, and legal systems (Price-Tobler, 2023a). These dynamics function as attachment-dominance strategies, positioning the child as a regulatory object rather than as an autonomous, developing self.

Malingering by Proxy and Secondary Gain Dynamics

Malingering by proxy frequently co-occurs with psychological FDIOA in alienation contexts. Symptoms are exaggerated, rehearsed, or strategically displayed to obtain external advantages, such as leverage in custody negotiations, court positioning, financial benefits, access to services, or moral authority (Price-Tobler, 2023a). Childress conceptualises these behaviours as expressions of narcissistic and borderline attachment pathology, where the parent externalises internal distress onto the child and recruits systems to validate the constructed narrative (Childress, 2015). Survivors report being placed under pressure to perform vulnerability roles while simultaneously being discouraged from developing independence, insight, or critical thinking, reinforcing long-term identity distortion and dependency conditioning.

Clinical Pattern Observed in Alienating Caregiver Households Involving Disability

Clinical observations in the author's practice indicate that psychological FDIOA and malingering by proxy dynamics are frequently observed in households where an alienating caregiver maintains long-term control over a child, adolescent, or adult child with a disability. Related doctoral findings also identified patterns of coercive control, dependency reinforcement, and identity distortion in alienation-linked presentations (Price-Tobler, 2023a). In these family systems, the caregiver actively obstructs the young person's developmental autonomy by restricting access to employment, independent living, education, peer relationships, and romantic partnerships. Functional capacity assessments often indicate that the individual is capable of supported employment and semi-independent living. However, the caregiver systematically undermines these recommendations, reinforcing illness narratives, fragility identities, and dependency roles.

In many cases, financial secondary gain is embedded within the relational structure. Disability payments, support packages, and associated benefits become stabilising income streams for the caregiver. These funds frequently supplement the caregiver's employment income or function as their primary source of financial support. The child's ongoing dependency is therefore incentivised and maintained through both emotional and material reinforcement (Price-Tobler, 2023a; Childress, 2015).

Attachment pathology and parental alienation dynamics frequently coexist within these presentations. The alienating caregiver positions themselves as the exclusive safe attachment figure while simultaneously eroding the child's relationship with the targeted parent. This dual process reinforces emotional fusion, loyalty conditioning, and fear-based dependency. Over time, the young person internalises a disabled and dependent identity that exceeds their actual functional limitations, resulting in arrested psychosocial development, impaired judgement, and heightened vulnerability to external exploitation.

Clinical Case Vignette: Psychological FDIOA, CPA-PA, and Digital Exploitation Risk

Client Profile

The client was an 18-year-old neurodivergent male referred following involvement with the criminal justice system. He resided full-time with his mother, who controlled his disability funding and daily functioning. CPA-PA was present within the family system, with the targeted parent excluded from the client's life through narrative distortion, access restriction, and loyalty pressure.

Despite multiple functional capacity assessments indicating suitability for supported employment and semi-independent living, the client had never been permitted to work, pursue education pathways, leave the family home, or engage in in-person peer relationships.

Family Dynamics

The mother consistently presented the client as severely impaired, emotionally fragile, and incapable of autonomy. Clinical assessment identified psychological FDIOA patterns, including reinforcement of illness narratives, restriction of independence, discouragement of age-appropriate development, and emotional enmeshment. The client was socially isolated and permitted only limited online engagement.

Disability payments were administered exclusively by the caregiver and served as the primary source of household income. This financial dependency reinforced the client's dependent status.

Risk Escalation and Legal Exposure

Due to prolonged social deprivation, attachment disruption, and limited real-world relationships, the client developed significant gaming dependence and online relational seeking behaviours. During this period, he engaged in digital interactions with individuals he believed were peers. One interaction involved the exchange of sexually explicit images and direct communication with a minor under the age of 16.

The client later became involved in serious online sexualised behaviour and legal-risk concerns, with long-term psychosocial, vocational, relational, and reputational consequences. From a clinical perspective, the case illustrates how neurodevelopmental vulnerability, social deprivation, attachment disruption, poor boundary learning, and caregiver-maintained dependency may increase risk when young people seek connection in online environments without adequate support, supervision, or developmentally appropriate relational guidance.

Clinical Context

This presentation sat within a specialist clinical context involving disability, developmental trauma, impaired social learning, sexualised behavioural risk, gaming dependence, and justice-system involvement. In this case, CPA-PA and psychological FDIOA dynamics appeared to compound the client's vulnerability by isolating him from protective adult relationships, peer learning, supported autonomy, and developmentally appropriate relational guidance.

Intervention Attempt and Entrapment Pattern

As part of ongoing support for this client, the author-clinician attempted to implement a supported transition plan that included independent living, vocational training, and psychosocial rehabilitation. Formal assessments again confirmed functional capacity for autonomy. The caregiver actively obstructed these plans by refusing consent, escalating illness narratives, and reinforcing dependency. She retained exclusive control over disability payments and daily decision-making. Unable to exit the dependent family system, the client returned to online environments for social connection and was later recharged following similar digital contact patterns. This further entrenched legal consequences and restricted future rehabilitation opportunities.

Clinical Implications

This case demonstrates how psychological FDIOA, malingering by proxy, and CPA-PA can intersect to produce severe downstream harm. The presenting risk extends beyond emotional abuse into legal exposure, digital exploitation vulnerability, identity foreclosure, and long-term social exclusion.

From an attachment perspective, the caregiver maintained control by obstructing individuation while simultaneously severing alternative attachment pathways through alienation processes (Childress, 2015). The client's unmet relational needs and enforced dependency appeared clinically relevant to later maladaptive coping behaviours and impaired boundary awareness. Early identification of these family patterns is therefore critical. Without intervention, survivors may become trapped in cycles of dependency, legal harm, and systemic disadvantage that persist well into adulthood.

Doctoral findings identified a distinct psychological FDIOA variant among adult survivors of CPA-PA. Survivors frequently reported childhood roles involving exaggerated vulnerability scripts, coached symptom presentation, and reinforcement of helpless identity narratives that were maintained through therapist shopping, school-based labelling, and legal documentation (Price-Tobler, 2023a). Unlike classical FDIOA, these presentations were often not anchored to hospitalisation but instead embedded across education, mental health, disability, and family court systems.

Childress's AB-PA framework conceptualises these patterns as expressions of narcissistic and borderline attachment pathology, where the allied parent externalises internal emotional dysregulation onto the child, positioning the child as a regulatory object rather than an autonomous person (Childress, 2015). The child's distress becomes instrumentalised, reinforcing the parent's psychological needs while progressively eroding the child's independent identity development.

Psychodynamic treatment and CBT with survivors exposed to psychological FDIOA and malingering by proxy must therefore prioritise disentanglement from imposed identity roles. Early therapeutic phases avoid directly confronting fabricated narratives. Instead, clinicians focus on rebuilding internal reality testing, strengthening autonomous self-representation, and separating inherited symptom beliefs from lived bodily and emotional experience.

Therapeutic pacing is critical. Rapid deconstruction of illness identities can provoke destabilisation, grief collapse, or defensive loyalty activation. Gradual narrative differentiation enables survivors to reclaim authorship of their experiences without replicating coercive relational patterns.

Clinicians must also remain alert to the risks of system reinforcement. Survivors may continue to receive validation from service structures that unknowingly perpetuate dependency identities. Ethical practice requires balancing compassion with careful boundary maintenance to avoid reinforcing fabricated vulnerability roles while supporting legitimate trauma-related needs.

This attachment-based conceptualisation reframes FDIOA and malingering by proxy not as isolated diagnostic anomalies, but as relational control strategies embedded within broader patterns of child psychological abuse and attachment-distortion.

Clinical Containment and Reality Anchoring in Psychodynamic Work with Induced Belief Systems

Within the HQTP, this clinical containment requirement informs early-phase sequencing and pacing decisions, particularly for survivors emerging from alienation, abduction, and psychologically fabricated family systems. When working with adult survivors and dependent young people emerging from psychologically abusive and alienating family systems, psychodynamic psychotherapy must be modified to prioritise containment and reality anchoring before interpretive depth. Survivors who have been raised in environments characterised by narrative distortion, loyalty conditioning, and induced belief systems frequently demonstrate impaired reality testing, fragmented autobiographical memory, and dependency-based identity organisation (Childress, 2015; Price-Tobler, 2023a).

In these cases, traditional open-ended interpretive techniques can inadvertently reinforce confusion or destabilisation if introduced prematurely. Instead, therapy must first establish a coherent internal narrative grounded in verifiable lived experience. This includes helping clients differentiate between externally imposed beliefs and internally generated perceptions, particularly when the alienating caregiver has shaped the client's worldview through repetition, fear conditioning, or fabricated illness narratives.

Psychodynamic containment involves maintaining a stable therapeutic frame, predictable session structure, and consistent emotional regulation by the clinician. This stability allows the survivor's nervous system to experience relational safety without performance demands. Only once this foundation is established should deeper interpretive work be introduced.

When clinicians are appropriately trained, brief psychodynamic psychotherapy may be used under time constraints, such as in public systems, forensic referrals, or transitional service contexts. However, brief formats must still adhere to the principles of phased pacing. Short-term interventions should focus on strengthening ego functioning, restoring reflective capacity, and reducing suggestibility, rather than attempting to excavate the trauma. When resources permit, longer-term psychodynamic work remains the preferred approach for sustained identity reconstruction and attachment repair in this population.

Psychological FDIOA and Legal Entrapment During CPA-PA

Clinical Case Vignette by the author/MHP: NDIS-Supported Disability Exploitation

The client was an 18-year-old neurodivergent male on the autism spectrum referred following involvement with the criminal justice system. He resided full-time with his father, who exercised extensive control over his daily functioning, mobility, health narratives, and access to independence. He had a strained relationship with the TP and was taught to denigrate the TP constantly to please the AP. The author's clinical assessment indicated that the client had functional capacity for supported employment and semi-independent living. Despite this, the father actively obstructed vocational engagement, discouraged workforce participation, and reinforced persistent illness narratives consistent with FDIOA and malingering-by-proxy dynamics. The client was repeatedly positioned as medically fragile, cognitively incapable, and socially unsafe to function independently, despite objective indicators of capacity.

As a result of prolonged social deprivation, restricted peer contact, enforced home confinement, and limited access to age-appropriate developmental experiences, the client developed significant gaming dependence and online relational seeking behaviours. He reported profound loneliness, emotional isolation, and a lack of real-world friendships.

Due to the previously described challenges, he went online to find a girlfriend. Consequently, he was contacted by an adolescent female aged fourteen who initiated the sending of sexually explicit images to him. Due to developmental immaturity associated with neurodivergence, arrested psychosocial development, and limited exposure to sexual education, the client was unsure how to respond, so the young girl suggested he send some of himself back. He responded by sending explicit images of himself over the phone to her, unaware of the laws surrounding this type of exchange with minors. After a few exchanges, the girls' parents found out and reported him to the police.

Soon after, he was taken into custody and questioned. When asked by the MHP and the police with whom he worked, he demonstrated limited understanding of legal boundaries, consent law, and the digital risk implications in this context. The client was subsequently charged with offences including communicating with a minor under the age of sixteen and production and transmission of child exploitation material. He attended court and escaped jail time. However, he was placed on the sex offender register and required to comply with parole supervision conditions.

Although incarceration was avoided through clinical advocacy and expert assessment regarding developmental vulnerability and coercive family context, the legal outcome resulted in long-term psychosocial, vocational, and reputational consequences. These included public stigma, employment barriers, identity collapse, and chronic shame responses.

Following court resolution and avoidance of custodial sentencing, the author-clinician experienced escalating hostility and verbal abuse from the father after recommending that the client pursue independent housing, vocational engagement, and separation from the controlling caregiving environment. The father responded by terminating therapeutic engagement and reasserting control over the client's daily life. Despite parole conditions originally restricting unsupervised internet access, the father maintained the client in the home environment with ongoing unrestricted internet exposure while simultaneously reinforcing isolation and dependency. At the time of follow-up, the client was twenty-four years old, had still not engaged in formal employment, remained socially isolated, was still experiencing loneliness, isolation and internet addiction and continued to express distress regarding lost developmental opportunity and desire to establish an independent adult identity.

This case illustrates how prolonged internet addiction, CPA-PA, disability exploitation, malingering by proxy, and attachment-based containment can create conditions of extreme vulnerability that extend into adulthood and intersect with legal systems. The HQTP conceptualises this presentation as a multi-layered developmental entrapment pattern that requires extended stabilisation, identity reconstruction, and relational autonomy work, rather than symptom-focused intervention alone.

Complex presentations involving psychological FDIOA, malingering by proxy, shared delusional processes, and CPA-PA frequently intersect with external systems, including disability services, child protection, education, and the criminal justice system. Psychodynamic psychotherapy in these contexts must be deliberately constrained by active risk management and ethical safeguards.

Doctoral findings indicate that survivors emerging from alienating households often carry impaired boundary awareness, heightened compliance tendencies, and difficulty recognising manipulation (Price-Tobler, 2023a). This increases vulnerability to further exploitation by caregivers, partners, online predators, and institutional actors. Clinicians must therefore remain alert to signs of coercive control continuing outside the therapy room.

In high-risk cases, therapy should be delivered in collaboration with a multidisciplinary team. This includes liaison with disability support coordinators, legal advocates, and, when required, clinical psychotherapists or psychologists, as well as safeguarding services. Psychodynamic insight must not replace concrete protective action when clients are being actively controlled, financially exploited, or prevented from developmental autonomy.

MHPs are also required to manage transference dynamics carefully. Alienating caregivers frequently attempt to recruit therapists into loyalty alliances or manipulate clinical narratives. Maintaining professional neutrality while holding firm boundaries is essential. Treatment planning should avoid becoming entangled in family power struggles and should remain anchored to the survivor's developmental needs and safety rather than the caregiver's emotional demands.

Where mandated reporting thresholds are met, clinicians must act decisively. Psychological abuse, financial exploitation, disability coercion, and induced dependency constitute reportable harm even in the absence of physical injury. Failure to intervene perpetuates systemic abuse cycles and exposes survivors to escalating long-term harm.

Forensic Ethics and Clinical Safeguarding Considerations

Clinicians working with survivors whose developmental trauma intersects with disability systems, CPA-PA, FDIOA dynamics, and criminal justice involvement must operate within heightened ethical risk environments. The HQTP emphasises the necessity of maintaining clear professional boundaries between therapeutic containment, forensic reporting obligations, and legal advocacy roles. Practitioners are advised to document clinical observations with precision, avoid speculative attribution of intent, and ensure that all diagnostic formulations remain evidence-based and clinically grounded. Where safeguarding concerns arise, including suspected ongoing coercive control, medical abuse, or exploitation of disability funding arrangements, clinicians must adhere to mandatory reporting requirements and organisational safeguarding protocols while maintaining trauma-informed engagement with the client.

Clinicians are further cautioned that recommendations supporting client autonomy, vocational engagement, or separation from coercive caregiving environments may provoke retaliation, complaint risk, or professional boundary challenges from controlling caregivers. The HQTP therefore encourages practitioners to engage in regular specialist supervision, maintain contemporaneous clinical records, and ensure that clinical decision-making is supported by peer consultation and, where appropriate, ethical review. When cases involve active court proceedings or parole supervision, collaboration with legal professionals and adherence to jurisdictional reporting frameworks are essential to protect both client welfare and practitioner integrity (Herman, 1992; Price-Tobler, 2023b). Ethical practice in these contexts prioritises client safety, developmental restoration, and professional accountability over expedient clinical intervention.

Publication and Anonymisation Statement

The clinical vignette presented in this section has been anonymised to protect client confidentiality and privacy in accordance with professional ethical standards and publication guidelines. Identifying details, including names, locations, service providers, and specific personal characteristics, have been altered or generalised. The case has been presented for educational and clinical illustration purposes only and does not represent any single identifiable individual. Composite elements drawn from multiple clinical experiences and doctoral research observations may be incorporated to preserve confidentiality while accurately representing recurring clinical patterns observed in frontline practice and research contexts (Price-Tobler, 2023b).

Applying Countertransference-Informed Practice to Adult Survivors of Psychological Abuse and Alienation

Within alienation and psychological abuse treatment, countertransference is not a clinical obstacle to be suppressed but a diagnostic and therapeutic signal that can guide intervention when used with discipline and supervision. Drawing on Yeomans' object relations and countertransference framework (Yeomans, 2018; Puder, 2019), the HQTP integrates structured countertransference monitoring as a core component of advanced psychodynamic work with adult survivors.

Adult survivors of alienation frequently evoke powerful emotional reactions in clinicians, including protectiveness, helplessness, frustration, sadness, and, at times, moral outrage. These reactions often mirror the client's internalised relational templates and disowned affect states developed under coercive family systems. When appropriately contained, these responses provide direct access to the survivor's unconscious relational world.

Step 1: Therapist Preparation and Reflective Stance

Clinicians working in this domain must adopt a reflective posture that anticipates emotional activation rather than attempting to avoid it. Yeomans emphasises that strong countertransference reactions are normative when treating severely traumatised and relationally fragmented clients (Yeomans, 2018). Suppression of therapist emotion increases the risk of enactment or avoidance.

Preparation involves routine self-reflection, supervision, and emotional regulation practices. Clinicians must develop tolerance for discomfort, including anger, grief, and despair, without acting on these states within the therapeutic relationship. This reflective capacity is foundational to maintaining therapeutic neutrality while still engaging authentically with survivor narratives.

Step 2: Ongoing Countertransference Monitoring

During and following sessions, clinicians are encouraged to actively track internal emotional shifts, bodily responses, and relational impulses. These may include urges to rescue, withdraw, appease, confront, or emotionally disengage. Patterns frequently emerge in response to specific narrative themes such as parental betrayal, court injustice, loyalty conflicts, or identity confusion.

Process notes that include the therapist's emotional responses facilitate longitudinal identification of emerging transference themes. Yeomans identifies complementary countertransference reactions as particularly valuable, referring to emotional states that arise in the clinician which the client is unable or unwilling to consciously access (Yeomans, 2018).

Step 3: Differentiating Concordant and Complementary Countertransference

Once a countertransference reaction is identified, clinicians should assess whether the emotion is concordant or complementary. Concordant countertransference reflects attunement with the client's consciously expressed affect. Complementary countertransference often represents disowned emotional material that the client cannot safely acknowledge.

In alienation survivors, complementary reactions frequently include anger toward abusive caregivers, grief over lost attachment figures, or shame related to identity suppression. For example, a client may recount traumatic relational loss in emotionally flat language while the clinician experiences intense sadness or rage. These reactions often reflect affect that was suppressed during childhood to maintain safety within coercive family environments.

Step 4: Internal Regulation and Clinical Containment

Before introducing countertransference material into dialogue, clinicians must regulate their own emotional state and avoid acting impulsively. Internal validation of the emotional signal allows the therapist to hold the experience as clinical data rather than personal truth.

This process mirrors Phase I stabilisation principles within the HQTP. Emotional containment by the clinician models regulatory capacity for survivors whose early attachment systems lacked psychological safety.

Step 5: Therapeutic Introduction of Disowned Affect

When clinically appropriate, therapists may gently introduce the emotional theme into the therapeutic dialogue using tentative, non-confrontational language. Yeomans recommends framing emotional content as exploratory rather than definitive, allowing space for client reflection rather than defensive withdrawal (Yeomans, 2018).

Rather than making personal disclosures, clinicians may refer to the emotional atmosphere of the session or the narrative being discussed. This approach initially externalises affect, reducing shame activation and preserving client autonomy.

Step 6: Client Response Monitoring and Pacing

Client responses to affect exploration vary. Some survivors experience immediate recognition and emotional release, while others require extended pacing before engagement. Resistance, denial, or projection should be met with curiosity rather than correction.

Within alienation survivors, emotional avoidance often reflects loyalty conditioning, fear of punishment, or identity fragmentation rather than therapeutic resistance. Clinicians are encouraged to revisit themes gradually as relational safety strengthens.

Step 7: Integration Through Relational Meaning-Making

Once the effect is acknowledged, therapy shifts toward integration. This involves linking emotional experiences to developmental history, relational patterns, and current interpersonal dynamics. Survivors are supported in recognising how internalised family narratives continue to shape current relational expectations.

This stage often involves identifying transference patterns directed toward the therapist and gently differentiating the present relationship from past attachment injuries. Over time, this process allows survivors to revise internal working models of trust, authority, and psychological safety.

Step 8: Emotional Processing and Corrective Experience

As suppressed emotional material becomes accessible, survivors frequently experience strong affective release. The clinician's role is to provide a regulated presence rather than overload with interpretation. Emotional expression within a safe relational container provides corrective attachment experience and supports identity reintegration.

This stage is particularly important for survivors who were punished for emotional expression during childhood. Experiencing acceptance rather than rejection during vulnerability directly counters alienation conditioning.

Step 9: Longitudinal Reinforcement and Skill Transfer

Countertransference-informed work is iterative rather than episodic. Over time, survivors develop greater emotional literacy, self-reflection, and relational insight. Clinicians are encouraged to reflect on progress and support generalisation of therapeutic gains into external relationships.

Patterns identified within therapy are linked to workplace relationships, intimate partnerships, and family dynamics, reinforcing survivor agency and autonomy.

Step 10: Ongoing Supervision and Therapist Care

Given the intensity of this work, structured supervision is considered essential rather than optional. Alienation-related cases carry high emotional load, moral injury risk, and vicarious trauma exposure.

Regular consultation protects therapeutic boundaries, prevents burnout, and supports ethical clinical decision-making. Therapists' self-care is not framed as personal wellness alone, but as a professional responsibility within high-risk trauma practice.

Cautions and Adaptations for a Trauma-Informed Application of Countertransference Work

Although many countertransference-informed techniques originate within Transference-Focused Psychotherapy and object relations frameworks developed for personality disorder presentations, their application with adult survivors of CPA-PA requires substantial modification. Survivors in this population often present with complex developmental trauma shaped by attachment betrayal, coercive control, loyalty conditioning, emotional invalidation, identity disruption, and prolonged exposure to relational threat. Findings from the author's doctoral survivor study and doctoral practitioner study indicate that these injuries are frequently carried into adulthood in ways that affect trust, self-organisation, affect regulation, and engagement with treatment (Price-Tobler, 2023a, 2023b). As a result, interventions that may be appropriate in other psychodynamic contexts can become destabilising or retraumatising if applied without careful pacing, relational safety, and trauma-informed adaptation.

Within the HQTP, countertransference is not treated as therapist error, nor as a licence for unchecked interpretation. It is understood as structured clinical information that may illuminate disowned affect, attachment expectations, relational fear, and internalised object patterns, provided it is ethically contained and applied in a manner that does not recreate coercive relational dynamics.

Establishing Relational Safety as the Primary Clinical Priority

Trauma-informed application of countertransference work requires that relational safety be firmly established before interpretive work begins. Yeomans has emphasised that transference-based interpretations are only effective when delivered within a stable therapeutic alliance, and Puder has similarly highlighted the need for sufficient relational safety before deeper psychodynamic work can proceed without triggering collapse, disengagement, or defensive retreat (Puder & Yeomans, 2024; Yeomans et al., 2015). This principle is especially important for adult survivors of CPA-PA, many of whom enter therapy with heightened threat sensitivity to authority figures, clinicians, and institutional systems due to prior experiences of betrayal, disbelief, professional invalidation, or court-related harm.

Findings from the author's doctoral survivor study indicate that many survivors approach professional relationships with anticipatory mistrust, fear of misrecognition, and concern that their reality will again be minimised, distorted, or reframed by others (Price-Tobler, 2023a). Complementing this, findings from the doctoral practitioner study suggest that clinicians working with this population often encounter strong relational testing, guardedness, alliance fragility, and survivor sensitivity to any intervention experienced as interpretively intrusive, emotionally premature, or authority-driven (Price-Tobler, 2023b). For this reason, early confrontation of projections, defences, or internal object relations may be experienced not as insight, but as repetition of psychological abuse.

Initial treatment phases should therefore prioritise consistency, attunement, emotional predictability, and explicit recognition of the survivor's lived experience. Survivors require clear confirmation that their suffering is understood as legitimate harm and that therapy will not demand emotional compliance, loyalty testing, or performance-based attachment. Only once sufficient safety has been established should deeper countertransference interpretation be gradually introduced.

Maintaining a Non-Judgemental, Trauma-Responsive Interpretive Style

When working with disavowed affect such as anger, grief, hatred, mistrust, emotional withdrawal, or relational vigilance, interpretation must be offered tentatively, collaboratively, and without moral charge. Survivors of CPA-PA frequently carry internalised shame narratives imposed by coercive caregiving environments, including beliefs that emotional needs are selfish, disloyal, excessive, dangerous, or defective. The author's doctoral survivor findings indicate that many survivors were conditioned to associate emotional expression with punishment, withdrawal of affection, ridicule, or accusations of betrayal (Price-Tobler, 2023a). In this context, even subtle interpretations may be experienced as criticism if not carefully framed.

Clinical language should therefore remain grounded in curiosity rather than correction. Reactions such as anger, distrust, hypervigilance, emotional numbing, withdrawal, or relational control are better understood as adaptive survival responses to abnormal developmental conditions than as evidence of moral failure or fixed pathology. The doctoral practitioner study similarly identified the importance of framing these responses within trauma and attachment formulations rather than through pejorative or pathologising shorthand, particularly when survivors have a history of being misunderstood by systems that should have protected them

(Price-Tobler, 2023b). Such a stance reduces shame activation and supports emotional integration rather than defensive retreat.

Avoiding Pathologising Labels and Diagnostic Reductionism

Although survivors may present with relational patterns that resemble splitting, idealisation, emotional reactivity, mistrust, or abrupt shifts in relational proximity, these presentations are often rooted in attachment trauma, coercive conditioning, and chronic relational threat rather than enduring personality pathology. Applying diagnostic shorthand too quickly risks obscuring developmental origins, reinforcing identity shame, and undermining therapeutic alliance. This concern is particularly salient for survivors of CPA-PAA and CPA-PERA, whose histories may already include profound identity distortion, loyalty conflict, narrative manipulation, and authority-based misinterpretation.

Findings from the author's doctoral survivor study suggest that adult survivors frequently retain empathy, moral reasoning, and relational longing despite severe developmental injury and confusion about self, family, and belonging (Price-Tobler, 2023a). Findings from the doctoral practitioner study further suggest that clinicians require a disciplined capacity to differentiate trauma-organised survival patterns from fixed character pathology when working with this cohort (Price-Tobler, 2023b). Clinical conceptualisation should therefore remain anchored in trauma and attachment frameworks. Behavioural adaptations are more accurately understood as conditioned survival strategies, nervous-system responses, and relational defences formed in response to prolonged threat, rather than as intrinsic defects of personality.

Balancing Interpretation with Ongoing Validation

Insight-oriented work must be consistently paired with emotional validation. Yeomans has emphasised the importance of helping clients name unspoken affect. At the same time, Puder has highlighted that validation is not a peripheral softening device but a central stabilising mechanism that makes deeper psychodynamic work tolerable and metabolically possible

(Puder & Yeomans, 2024; Yeomans et al., 2015). This is particularly important with adult survivors of CPA-PA, whose developmental histories often include chronic emotional neglect, invalidation, misattunement, and coercive reframing of their own subjective experience.

The author's doctoral survivor findings indicate that many adult survivors reinterpret early survival responses as personal flaws rather than protective adaptations shaped by child psychological abuse (Price-Tobler, 2023a). The practitioner study similarly highlighted the importance of pairing interpretive insight with empathic validation so that survivors are not left exposed to difficult emotional material without sufficient affective containment (Price-Tobler, 2023b).

When clinicians introduce painful material, such as anger toward caregivers, grief over lost attachment relationships, or mistrust toward the therapist, this should be accompanied by explicit acknowledgement of the survivor's suffering, resilience, and developmental context. If developmental interpretation is introduced without parallel emotional validation, it may be experienced as exposure without protection. Validation provides the affective container within which insight can be metabolised without reproducing earlier experiences of dismissal, humiliation, or abandonment.

Monitoring the Survivor's Window of Tolerance

Adult survivors of CPA-PA commonly present with fluctuating autonomic regulation, dissociation, affective flooding, freeze responses, shutdown, or abrupt shifts into compliance when emotionally charged material is activated. Findings from the author's doctoral survivor study indicate that these responses may become especially pronounced when discussing parental betrayal, court histories, family loyalty conflicts, abduction-related material, or memories that challenge long-held survival narratives (Price-Tobler, 2023a). Clinicians must therefore monitor arousal states continuously during interpretive work.

When signs of dysregulation emerge, the pace should slow, and interpretive work should pause in favour of stabilisation strategies such as grounding, breath regulation, sensory orientation, present-moment anchoring, or temporary topic shifts. The doctoral practitioner study reinforces the need for clinicians to work within a paced, titrated model rather than forcing affective intensity in the hope that insight alone will produce integration (Price-Tobler, 2023b). Unlike traditional analytic models that may tolerate prolonged activation in the service of interpretation, trauma-informed psychodynamic work within the HQTP prioritises titration. Emotional processing must be introduced gradually and in doses matched to the survivor's current regulatory capacity.

Avoiding Premature Confrontation and Therapeutic Overreach

Countertransference-informed techniques developed for work with narcissistic or borderline defences may include direct confrontation of splitting, projection, contradiction, or disavowed aggression. With adult survivors of CPA-PA, such methods require substantial restraint. Many survivors carry fragile, interrupted, or underdeveloped identity structures not because of intrinsic personality organisation, but because their developmental environments did not permit coherent selfhood to emerge safely. Excessive interpretive intensity may therefore destabilise rather than clarify.

The author's doctoral survivor findings indicate that many survivors first require support in building basic emotional regulation, internal safety, and relational trust before deeper interpretive work can be sustained (Price-Tobler, 2023a). The practitioner study similarly identified the importance of calibrating intervention intensity to survivor readiness rather than applying theory-driven techniques rigidly across presentations (Price-Tobler, 2023b). Clinicians should remain attentive to signs of alliance rupture, withdrawal, emotional collapse, compliance-based accommodation, or dissociation following interpretation. When these occur, treatment should return to stabilisation and relational repair rather than escalating insight-oriented pressure. Flexibility is essential. Intervention intensity must be determined by clinical readiness, not by theoretical allegiance.

Supporting External Safety and Boundary Formation

Countertransference work cannot be separated from the survivor's real-world relational environment. Many adult survivors remain emotionally, financially, psychologically, or practically entangled with alienating caregivers, extended family systems, or court-related stressors. In cases involving CPA-PAA or prolonged coercive family dynamics, this may also include unresolved identity confusion, divided loyalties, contact pressure, secrecy, or threats associated with separation from the abusive system.

Clinical work should therefore include attention to assertiveness, boundary development, contact-limitation planning, relational decision-making, and safety mapping, where required. Findings from the doctoral survivor study suggest that survivors often struggle to maintain gains made in therapy when external coercive dynamics remain active and unaddressed (Price-Tobler, 2023a). The practitioner study similarly indicates that effective treatment in this area requires integration of psychodynamic understanding with practical attention to ongoing safety and relational reality (Price-Tobler, 2023b). In periods of acute distress, self-harm risk, severe anxiety, or active coercion, adjunct stabilisation strategies or interdisciplinary collaboration may also be indicated. Supporting external safety helps protect treatment gains and reduces the risk that therapy becomes a reflective space disconnected from lived threat.

Modelling Rupture and Repair Within the Therapeutic Relationship

Attachment repair does not occur through perfect attunement, but through the capacity to recognise rupture, respond accountably, and restore safety. Many survivors of CPA-PA experienced relational breaches in childhood that were never repaired and instead became embedded as chronic attachment injuries. Conflict was often associated with punishment, abandonment, humiliation, reversal of blame, or emotional withdrawal rather than mutual repair.

The author's doctoral survivor findings suggest that many adult survivors have limited internal experience of healthy relational repair and may therefore interpret ordinary therapeutic misattunement as evidence of imminent rejection, alliance collapse, or betrayal (Price-Tobler, 2023a). The practitioner study further indicates that the ability to recognise and repair rupture is a central component of competent clinical work with this population (Price-Tobler, 2023b). When misunderstandings, misattunements, or interpretive errors occur in therapy, the clinician should model accountability, curiosity, and emotional responsiveness. Transparent acknowledgement of misattunement followed by genuine repair provides survivors with a corrective relational experience and strengthens attachment security within treatment. In this sense, rupture and repair are not peripheral to countertransference work, but central to its ethical application.

Expecting Non-Linear Recovery Trajectories

Recovery from child psychological abuse in CPA-PA contexts is rarely linear. Periods of insight may be followed by regression when family contact resumes, external stress increases, life transitions occur, or deeper layers of trauma become accessible. Such fluctuations should not be interpreted as treatment failure. Rather, they often reflect the activation of nervous system memory, the resurgence of loyalty conflict, the reorganisation of identity, or renewed exposure to relational threat.

The author's doctoral survivor findings indicate that many survivors move through cycles of recognition, destabilisation, grief, retreat, and renewed meaning-making rather than steady linear improvement (Price-Tobler, 2023a). The practitioner study likewise highlighted the importance of sustained clinical consistency across such fluctuation, particularly where survivors have histories of attachment rupture, abandonment fear, or prior therapeutic harm

(Price-Tobler, 2023b). Yeomans has similarly observed that continuity across fluctuation is part of the work rather than evidence of failure (Yeomans et al., 2015). Within the HQTP, sustained clinician presence, emotional consistency, and relational reliability are themselves therapeutic interventions. Each cycle of activation and recovery offers opportunities for further integration, provided the work remains paced and safely contained.

Modality Integration and the Risk of Theoretical Overreach

Within mental health practice, longstanding modality wars have too often positioned therapeutic schools in competition rather than in dialogue. When clinicians privilege theoretical allegiance over clinical responsiveness, treatment risks becoming ideology-driven rather than survivor-centred. No single modality holds universal authority in complex developmental trauma work, particularly where CPA-PA, CPA-PAA, and CPA-PERA presentations involve layered attachment disruption, identity injury, relational mistrust, and long-term coercive conditioning. Ethical practice, therefore, requires selective, disciplined integration grounded in clinical formulation, developmental history, attachment disturbance, neurobiological capacity, survivor preference, and phase-based readiness.

At the same time, flexibility must not become improvisation. Findings from the author's doctoral survivor study indicate that some adult survivors experienced prior therapy as fragmented, inconsistent, or experimental in ways that replicated earlier relational harm (Price-Tobler, 2023a). Survivors described feeling that clinicians were trying approaches on them without a clear rationale, predictable structure, or transparent therapeutic direction. The practitioner study further highlighted the need for clinicians to maintain coherence, structure, and conceptual discipline when integrating modalities in work with this population (Price-Tobler, 2023b). For adult survivors of CPA-PA, modality selection must therefore be deliberate, clearly communicated, and clinically justified. An integrative approach does not mean indiscriminate blending of techniques. Rather, it requires structured selection informed by trauma science, attachment theory, phase-based treatment principles, and ongoing assessment of readiness and consent. Therapeutic decisions should be continuously evaluated for their potential to support regulation, coherence, and agency, or to recreate confusion, power imbalances, and emotional invalidation.

When applied with discipline and clinical humility, integration becomes a safeguard rather than a liability. It allows treatment to remain responsive without becoming chaotic, structured without becoming rigid, and survivor-led without abandoning professional responsibility.

Summary

When applied within a trauma-informed framework, countertransference-informed techniques can offer valuable pathways for accessing disowned emotional material carried by adult survivors of child psychological abuse in CPA-PA contexts. Their use, however, requires substantial modification. Interpretation must be paced, relationally contained, developmentally informed, and consistently paired with validation, stabilisation, and respect for survivor readiness. Findings from the author's doctoral survivor study and doctoral practitioner study support the need for a carefully adapted model that recognises the distinctive clinical realities of this population (Price-Tobler, 2023a, 2023b). Within the HQTP, countertransference work is never used to override the survivor's experience or impose theoretical certainty. It is used to deepen understanding of the survivor's internal world while preserving dignity, safety, agency, and long-term developmental repair.

Chapter Ten

Clinical Supervision, Ethical Positioning and Practitioner Safety

This chapter establishes the supervision, ethical containment, and practitioner safety framework that supports implementation of the HQTP. It does not introduce new treatment phases or alter clinical sequencing. Instead, it defines the professional governance structures required to sustain ethical practice, manage the risk of countertransference, and protect both survivors and clinicians working in high-complexity trauma contexts. This chapter examines how inadequate supervision, theoretical rigidity, unmanaged countertransference, and systemic pressures can contribute to secondary harm for adult survivors of child psychological abuse.

Why This Work Requires Enhanced Clinical Supervision

Clinical supervision in work with adult survivors of child psychological abuse is not an adjunct to practice, but a core mechanism of ethical containment and practitioner accountability. Work in this field, particularly within the context of CPA-PAA and high-conflict family systems, constitutes high-responsibility clinical practice. It routinely involves exposure to adversarial legal processes, false or unsubstantiated allegations, identity-level attachment disruption, intense projection dynamics, and the risk of practitioner misalignment when coercive relational patterns are misunderstood.

Unlike many forms of trauma therapy, this work often unfolds within active systems of distortion. Survivors may be embedded in family, legal, or institutional environments that reward allegiance, punish neutrality, or weaponise professional authority. Presentations frequently include conditioned guilt, loyalty conflicts, fragmented autobiographical narratives, fear of retaliation, and deep attachment insecurity. At the same time, clinicians may be exposed to splitting, idealisation, devaluation, pressure to take sides, or covert attempts to recruit the practitioner into existing power dynamics.

For these reasons, enhanced clinical supervision is not optional in this field. It functions as ethical containment, safeguarding survivors from further harm, supporting practitioners to maintain reflective capacity under pressure, and preserving fidelity to trauma-informed, attachment-based, and evidence-grounded practice. Supervision provides a necessary buffer against emotional overidentification, positional drift, reactive decision-making, and unconscious reenactment of abusive relational patterns within the therapeutic setting.

This field demands epistemic humility. Professional seniority, academic credentials, or years of clinical experience do not confer automatic competence in identifying psychological abuse, coercive control, or attachment-distortion. Without consistent specialist supervision, even highly experienced clinicians may struggle to maintain conceptual clarity within systems that reward certainty, authority, and alignment over nuance and clinical restraint.

The Consequences of Misguided Care: When Practitioners Are Untrained in Psychological Abuse

When clinicians are insufficiently trained in the dynamics of child psychological abuse and attachment-based coercive control, therapeutic harm most often occurs through misinterpretation rather than omission. Adult survivors are frequently misdiagnosed within mental health systems that remain poorly attuned to prolonged psychological abuse, indoctrination processes, and trauma-conditioned relational adaptation. Presentations such as emotional dysregulation, mistrust, identity diffusion, dissociation, relational instability, and hypervigilance are commonly interpreted through personality pathology frameworks rather than recognised as sequelae of chronic attachment disruption and coercive control.

When this occurs, survivors are pathologised for survival strategies while the original abuse remains unseen. Such misdiagnosis can entrench stigma, weaken therapeutic alliance, delay appropriate treatment, and reinforce internalised shame narratives that mirror the original psychological harm.

Untrained clinical responses may also inadvertently replicate abusive dynamics. Survivors may experience therapeutic neutrality as abandonment, clinical curiosity as disbelief, and cognitive reframing as minimisation of harm. In these contexts, therapy itself becomes another site of invalidation, reinforcing survivor self-doubt and deepening mistrust of helping systems. The downstream consequences frequently include premature termination, symptom escalation, emotional withdrawal, or disengagement from future help-seeking.

Within this clinical terrain, supervision functions as the primary safeguard against reenactment, misalignment, and the quiet reproduction of coercive relational patterns inside therapy. It supports practitioners to remain anchored in ethical responsibility, reflective practice, and survivor-centred care when working within complex and emotionally charged systems.

Countertransference Risk, Clinical Containment, and Escalation

Work with adult survivors of child psychological abuse routinely evokes strong emotional responses in clinicians, including protectiveness, frustration, grief, helplessness, avoidance, or moral distress. These reactions are not indicators of poor practice. However, when left unexamined, they can distort clinical judgement, reinforce survivor shame, or replicate the original dynamics of coercion, abandonment, and power imbalance that characterised the survivor's developmental environment.

Effective treatment in this field, therefore, requires deliberate attention to countertransference, structured reflective containment, and clearly defined escalation pathways through supervision.

Contemporary psychodynamic scholarship, including the countertransference-focused contributions of Yeomans, Clarkin, and Kernberg (2015), demonstrates that clinicians' emotional responses can either entrench maladaptive relational patterns or serve as valuable sources of clinical information when processed in supervision. In the context of CPA-PA, countertransference often mirrors the survivor's internal relational world. Without containment, clinicians may unconsciously assume a rescuing role, become overly confrontational, withdraw emotionally, or align defensively with particular narratives.

Supervision in this work functions as a stabilising structure rather than a remedial intervention. It protects against individual blind spots while also buffering practitioners against the gradual internalisation of adversarial system logic, which can erode clinical clarity over time. It supports ethical decision-making, maintains role boundaries, and reinforces adherence to the scope of practice when clinicians are working within high-risk environments involving attachment disruption, coercive control, and system pressure.

From a professional governance perspective, documented supervision, clear clinical formulation, and structured escalation protocols are recognised safeguards by regulatory bodies and professional indemnity insurers when practitioners work with complex trauma presentations. In this sense, supervision is both an ethical requirement and a risk mitigation strategy.

When countertransference is recognised, reflected upon, and processed through supervision, it becomes a clinical asset rather than a liability. It provides insight into survivor attachment dynamics, emotional states that remain inaccessible to conscious processing, and relational patterns that may otherwise be enacted within therapy.

Ethical Positioning in Systemically Adversarial Contexts

Ethical positioning in work with adult survivors of child psychological abuse requires more than compliance with professional codes. It demands sustained awareness of how adversarial systems shape survivor expectations, clinical dynamics, and practitioner responses.

Many survivors enter therapy carrying the psychological imprint of adversarial institutions, including family law, child protection, education systems, and mental health services. Even when formal involvement has ceased, these systems may continue to exert influence through fear of authority, anticipated disbelief, conditioned compliance, and internalised narratives of blame or defectiveness.

Ethical therapeutic practice in this context requires clear role boundaries, deliberate avoidance of forensic positioning, and active protection of the therapeutic space from intrusion by external system agendas. Therapy must remain a relational environment focused on emotional meaning, attachment injury, and internal experience rather than fact verification, adjudication, or narrative correction.

Ethical positioning also requires disciplined relational neutrality. This neutrality is not emotional detachment. It is an active stance that resists recruitment into loyalty dynamics, rescue fantasies, or adversarial alignment. Survivors may unconsciously test whether the therapist will side with, abandon, invalidate, rescue, or disbelieve them, replicating relational conditions learned in childhood. The clinician's task is to remain emotionally attuned without becoming positionally captured.

When therapy becomes a space where survivors are not required to persuade, perform credibility, defend their history, or prove harm, psychological safety is restored, and authentic processing becomes possible.

Clear ethical positioning further protects against countertransference-driven reenactment. Clinicians may feel compelled to over-validate, prematurely reassure, confront aggressively, or emotionally withdraw in response to survivor distress. Without reflective containment, these reactions risk reproducing patterns of coercion, silencing, or abandonment. Ongoing supervision is therefore essential to support ethical discernment, maintain role clarity, and ensure therapeutic responses remain grounded in trauma-informed and attachment-aware practice rather than reactive emotion.

Finally, ethical positioning serves as a safeguard for practitioners' wellbeing and professional integrity. This work carries elevated emotional load, reputational risk, and exposure to systemic pressure. Consistent supervision, clear documentation practices, and firm adherence to the scope of practice are not defensive strategies. They are ethical necessities.

Together, these structures ensure that therapy remains a site of repair rather than another arena of systemic harm. They allow both survivor and clinician to remain anchored in safety, clarity, and purpose, while protecting against the gradual erosion of clinical judgement that can occur when adversarial logic is internalised over time.

Chapter Eleven

Assessment, Diagnosis and Differential Formulation

This chapter outlines the assessment and differential formulation processes that support ethical entry into the HQTP. It does not replace or supersede the phase-based treatment framework established in Chapter Five. Instead, it defines the clinical reasoning, data gathering, and diagnostic safeguards required to ensure that survivors are accurately understood and appropriately matched to treatment pacing and phase readiness.

Assessment is the clinical mechanism through which ethical intent is translated into practice. In work with adult survivors of CPA-PA, effective treatment depends not only on therapeutic skill but on disciplined diagnostic reasoning, structured information gathering, and the capacity to distinguish trauma-based adaptation from induced attachment pathology. Without rigorous assessment processes, clinicians risk replicating harm through misinterpretation, misdiagnosis, or unexamined alignment with adversarial narratives.

Why This Model Begins with Assessment, Not Assumption

High-conflict family systems frequently generate competing abuse claims, contradictory narratives, and emotionally charged presentations. In such contexts, assumption-based practice represents a significant clinical and ethical risk. The HQTP, therefore, begins with assessment as its foundational anchor. Structured evaluation protects both survivors and practitioners by ensuring that diagnostic conclusions are grounded in verifiable clinical data rather than inferred intent or persuasive storytelling.

Empirical Evidence on Allegation Patterns

Recent large-scale research highlights the importance of this disciplined approach. In a preregistered analysis of 492 United States appellate cases involving parental alienation findings, Sharples, Harman, and Lorandos (2023) reported that 58.5 per cent of cases included abuse allegations. Within this subset, allegations directed toward the parent later identified as alienated were significantly more likely to be unsubstantiated than those made against the alleged alienating parent. This pattern demonstrates a recurring systemic risk: clinical and legal actors may respond to emotionally charged allegations without sufficient evidentiary scrutiny.

Australian judicial data reflect a similar complexity. The National Domestic and Family Violence Bench Book reports that between 63 and 74 per cent of abuse allegations are corroborated by evidence. At the same time, the remaining cases are categorised as inconclusive, erroneous, or, in a smaller proportion, intentionally false (Australian Institute of Judicial Administration, 2023). Although many allegations represent genuine harm, the minority that are unsubstantiated can significantly distort clinical decision-making when they are accepted without structured assessment procedures.

Cross-Jurisdictional Patterns of Misclassification

Comparative analyses further demonstrate that the risk of misclassification is not confined to any single legal system. Harman and Lorandos (2020) identified repeated patterns in appellate cases where unsubstantiated abuse allegations and misapplied parental alienation labels co-occurred. These findings underscore the necessity of differential formulation rather than categorical labelling. Clinical assessment must evaluate both the presence of genuine abuse and the possibility of induced belief systems that impair the child's attachment functioning.

This aligns with Childress's core assessment principle: clinicians must evaluate all abuse domains across both caregivers and the child or adolescent, including psychological abuse, sexual abuse, physical abuse, neglect, and the weaponisation of children as instruments of spousal control within litigation contexts.

Differential Formulation: Path A and Path B

The HQTP integrates Childress's Path A and Path B framework as a core diagnostic safeguard. This model requires clinicians to suspend assumptions and instead test competing explanatory hypotheses through structured clinical data.

Path A represents authentic abuse. In this pathway, the child's rejection of a parent reflects a self-protective attachment response to substantiated psychological abuse, sexual abuse, physical abuse, or neglect perpetrated by the rejected parent.

Path B represents induced pathology. In this pathway, the child's rejection reflects an externally constructed persecutory belief system, maintained through psychological coercion, loyalty conditioning, and factitious attachment disturbance generated by the allied parent. In many cases, the child is simultaneously weaponised as a mechanism of spousal abuse within ongoing relational conflict.

Application of this model requires independent assessment of both caregivers and the child or adolescent, evaluation of attachment functioning, examination of belief system rigidity, and systematic reality testing of abuse claims. Diagnostic conclusions are therefore derived from convergent clinical data rather than adversarial narratives or emotional persuasion.

This approach aligns with professional ethical obligations regarding competence, scientific reasoning, and harm prevention, including principles articulated in professional practice standards (American Psychological Association, 2017).

Ethical Standards and the Duty to Assess Before Conclusion

Within attachment-based differential formulation models, such as Childress's Path A and Path B framework, assessment is not optional. It is an ethical requirement. Before concluding induced attachment pathology, clinicians are obligated to assess systematically for relevant abuse, trauma, and safeguarding domains, including psychological abuse, sexual abuse, physical abuse, neglect, exposure to family and domestic violence, coercive control, and the weaponisation of the child within spousal conflict.

This obligation aligns with established professional ethical standards governing psychological and psychotherapeutic practice. The American Psychological Association's *Ethical Principles of Psychologists and Code of Conduct* require psychologists to practise within the boundaries of competence, ground professional judgements in established scientific and professional knowledge, and take reasonable steps to avoid foreseeable harm, including through Standards 2.01, 2.04, and 3.04 (American Psychological Association, 2017).

In Australia, parallel obligations are reflected in the Psychology Board of Australia's *Code of Conduct for Psychologists*, the Australian Psychological Society *Code of Ethics (where relevant as a professional ethics reference)*, the PACFA *Code of Ethics*, and the Australian Counselling Association *Code of Ethics and Practice*. Across these frameworks, practitioners are expected to work within scope, practise competently, avoid foreseeable harm, use evidence-informed judgement, maintain appropriate boundaries, seek supervision, and refer when a client's needs exceed the practitioner's competence or role.

For adult survivors of CPA-PA and court-involved family separation, this ethical requirement carries weight. Many survivors report that during childhood proceedings, they were never assessed for psychological abuse, coercive control, sexual abuse, neglect, or exposure to spousal violence, despite expressing fear or avoidance of a targeted parent. In such cases, behavioural rejection was often interpreted without differential formulation, leaving genuine trauma unrecognised and untreated (Price-Tobler, 2023a).

Failure to conduct a comprehensive abuse-domain assessment is not a neutral omission. It risks misclassification, misdiagnosis, and long-term psychological harm. When clinicians bypass systematic assessment, survivors may be positioned as disordered rather than injured, reinforcing self-doubt and perpetuating attachment disruption into adulthood. In serious cases, such omissions may constitute a significant ethical failure, particularly where the practitioner works outside competence, disregards foreseeable harm, or reaches conclusions without adequate differential assessment.

Within the HQTP, assessment is therefore framed not as a discretionary clinical preference but as a foundational ethical obligation. Competence in this field is not conferred by discipline or registration alone. It is demonstrated through disciplined diagnostic reasoning, reflective supervision, humility in the face of uncertainty, and sustained commitment to reality-based formulation amid emotionally charged, adversarial narratives.

Having established assessment as both a clinical and ethical requirement, the next section examines how failures in diagnostic formulation, particularly the misapplication of personality disorder labels, continue to generate systemic harm for adult survivors of child psychological abuse.

Diagnostic Misuse and the Harm of Assumption

Assessment breakdown in this field most commonly arises from systemic pressure rather than clinician ignorance. When assessment is replaced by assumption, diagnostic labels cease to function as tools for understanding and instead become instruments of harm. For adult survivors of prolonged psychological abuse, premature diagnosis often serves institutional needs for certainty, efficiency, or risk containment rather than the survivor's need for accuracy, safety, and meaning. This shift from disciplined enquiry to rapid categorisation is particularly dangerous in presentations shaped by attachment disruption and coercive family dynamics.

One of the most frequent sources of diagnostic error is overreliance on surface presentation. Survivors may present with emotional intensity, mistrust, relational instability, guardedness, or apparent contradiction. When these features are interpreted without full developmental, relational, and trauma-informed assessment, they are easily misclassified as enduring personality pathology. Behaviours that developed as survival adaptations within psychologically unsafe environments are then misread as intrinsic character defects.

Failure to assess attachment history further compounds this risk. Adult survivors of child psychological abuse often carry internal working models shaped by betrayal, loyalty conflict, separation trauma, and enforced reality distortion. Without careful exploration of early caregiving relationships, forced alignments, indoctrination, and loss, clinicians may attribute relational fear, abandonment sensitivity, or emotional dysregulation to inherent disorder rather than to injury sustained within formative attachment systems. In these cases, diagnosis becomes disconnected from causation.

Diagnostic accuracy is also undermined when coercive control is not recognised. CPA-PA contexts operate through manipulation of perception, fear conditioning, and loyalty enforcement rather than overt physical violence. Survivors may minimise harm, struggle to articulate experiences coherently, or present with confusion regarding responsibility and blame. When these dynamics are not identified, the survivor's disorganisation is misinterpreted as psychopathology rather than understood as the predictable consequence of sustained psychological pressure.

Trauma-related nervous system adaptations are likewise frequently mislabelled without specialised training. Hypervigilance, dissociation, emotional numbing, relational withdrawal, and affective flooding are often framed as symptoms of disorder rather than recognised as adaptive responses to prolonged threat. When this occurs, diagnosis obscures the functional logic of the survivor's adaptations and shifts clinical focus away from repair, stabilisation, and integration.

Systemic pressures further reinforce diagnostic misuse. Time-limited-service models, administrative demands, medico-legal scrutiny, and risk-management cultures often reward speed over depth and certainty over curiosity. Under these conditions, diagnostic labels become shorthand solutions rather than carefully constructed formulations grounded in developmental history and attachment context.

When systems privilege efficiency over accuracy, misdiagnosis becomes normalised. For adult survivors of child psychological abuse, the consequence is cumulative harm. Misclassification obscures the reality of abuse, reinforces survivor self-doubt, positions adaptive survival responses as pathology, and replicates the invalidation that characterised the original injury. In this context, misdiagnosis is not a neutral clinical error. It functions as a continuation of harm.

Survivors Being Misdiagnosed with Personality Disorders

One specific form of diagnostic misuse in this population is the misclassification of survival-based relational adaptations as personality pathology. Adult survivors of CPA-PA in all contexts may present with emotional intensity, relational fear, mistrust of authority, identity instability, shutdown, anger, compliance, withdrawal, dissociation, or visible inconsistency. Without developmental formulation, these presentations may be mistaken for fixed personality traits rather than understood as adaptations to attachment threat, loyalty conflict, coercive control, chronic invalidation, and prolonged relational captivity.

The clinical concern is not that personality disorder diagnoses should never be considered. Rather, the concern is that diagnosis becomes harmful when it is applied too quickly, without sufficient attention to developmental history, coercive context, attachment disruption, and the survivor's long-term exposure to distorted relational systems. Within the HQTP, diagnostic formulation must therefore remain provisional, contextual, and clinically protective rather than reductive.

Many trauma adaptations associated with child psychological abuse can resemble personality disorder criteria in surface form. Emotional dysregulation, fear of abandonment, identity confusion, relational instability, dissociation, intense affective states, and defensive mistrust may appear as enduring traits when the developmental logic of these responses is not explored. When context is removed, diagnosis becomes detached from causation, and the survivor's survival strategies are reframed as character defects.

For survivors, the consequences of a personality disorder label can be profound. Many report feeling blamed for their reactions, disbelieved when describing abuse, and positioned as unreliable narrators of their own experience. Clinical attention shifts from what happened to the survivor to what is presumed to be wrong with them. In this way, misdiagnosis can operate as a silencing mechanism rather than a pathway to understanding.

Once applied, a personality disorder label may narrow clinical curiosity rather than expand it. Subsequent clinicians may inherit the diagnosis uncritically, interpret new information through a pathological lens, and discount disclosures of abuse as exaggeration, manipulation, or emotional instability. Survivors often describe this as diagnostic foreclosure, where the label becomes self-perpetuating and difficult to reverse, even when later evidence supports an alternative formulation.

Stigma compounds the injury. Some survivors internalise the belief that they are fundamentally disordered, difficult, or beyond help. Others disengage from mental health services after repeated experiences of being misunderstood or pathologised. In both cases, the original abuse remains unaddressed while its sequelae are medicalised.

In the context of CPA-PA, CPA-PAA, CPA-PERA, and associated coercive family systems, personality disorder misdiagnosis reflects a failure of formulation rather than proof of inherent pathology. These survivors were shaped within environments of coercion, fear conditioning, enforced allegiance, attachment disruption, and reality distortion. When their adaptations are stripped of context and redefined as personality flaws, diagnosis ceases to protect and instead becomes a continuation of harm.

For this reason, accurate differential formulation in this population requires systematic consideration of trauma-related and grief-related presentations that may resemble personality pathology when assessed without developmental sequencing. This includes complex post-traumatic stress disorder, prolonged grief disorder, dissociative presentations, moral injury, trauma-related mood and anxiety disorders, and attachment-based survival adaptations. A differential formulation must privilege onset, function, relational sequencing, and environmental reinforcement of symptoms over phenomenology alone. When this is not done, diagnosis shifts from explanatory to attributive, increasing the risk of iatrogenic harm.

Differential Formulation as Clinical Protection

Differential formulation is the clinical process of considering multiple possible explanations for a survivor's presentation before settling on a working understanding. It is different from simply asking which diagnosis fits best. In the HQTP, differential formulation asks what developmental, relational, traumatic, coercive, attachment-based, systemic, and psychological factors may be organising the survivor's symptoms, behaviours, beliefs, and relational responses.

Differential formulation is not a theoretical exercise in this population. It functions as a primary safeguard against clinical harm. After considering the risk of diagnostic misuse and the specific risk of personality-disorder misclassification, the clinician's task is to return to formulation: what happened developmentally, what relational conditions shaped the survivor's responses, and what current risks are being maintained by coercion, grief, fear, shame, contact pressure, or systems exposure?

Effective formulation in this field must prioritise developmental sequencing, relational history, and the function of symptoms over surface phenomenology alone. The central clinical question is not only "What diagnosis fits best?" but "What survival function did this presentation serve within the original family system?" This shift is essential for preventing attributional error and maintaining therapeutic accuracy.

The author's doctoral findings highlight that many adult survivors were never adequately assessed for psychological abuse, coercive control, neglect, or loyalty conditioning during childhood, particularly in family court contexts where allegations were contested, minimised, or dismissed. As a result, survivors often enter adulthood carrying unresolved attachment injuries that were never formally recognised or treated. Differential formulation in adulthood, therefore, becomes a secondary opportunity to identify what was missed, mislabelled, or obscured during earlier involvement with the system.

Within the HQTP, diagnosis is not rejected. It is disciplined. Formal diagnosis may still be clinically useful where it supports treatment planning, risk management, access to services, or communication with other professionals. However, diagnosis must sit inside a broader developmental and relational formulation. It should never replace an enquiry into child psychological abuse, attachment disruption, coercive control, abduction, estrangement, loyalty conflict, or epistemic injury.

Clinicians must differentiate between trauma-related adaptations and personality structure. Symptoms such as emotional dysregulation, relational instability, hypervigilance, dissociation, identity diffusion, mistrust, compliance, withdrawal, or apparent inconsistency may reflect complex trauma, attachment injury, prolonged coercive influence, or survival conditioning rather than enduring personality pathology. When formulation fails to distinguish these pathways, diagnosis becomes detached from causation, and treatment planning becomes misaligned.

The differential formulation must also incorporate assessment of coercive family dynamics. CPA-PA contexts may operate through reality distortion, fear induction, loyalty enforcement, attachment disruption, and narrative control. Survivors may present with confusion, ambivalence, or contradictory narratives not because of deception or instability, but because their developmental environment required psychological splitting, suppression, and compliance for survival. Without recognising these dynamics, clinicians risk misinterpreting confusion as pathology rather than as evidence of prolonged psychological pressure.

Formulation within the HQTP remains iterative and phase-sensitive. The early stages of treatment prioritise safety and stabilisation over definitive diagnostic categorisation. As therapeutic safety increases, deeper formulation becomes possible without overwhelming the survivor or replicating system-level harm. Diagnosis is treated as a working hypothesis rather than a fixed identity label.

When applied correctly, differential formulation functions as a clinical stabiliser. It protects survivors from misdiagnosis, prevents clinicians from defaulting to system-driven assumptions, and anchors treatment in developmental reality rather than symptom description alone. In this way, formulation becomes not only a diagnostic tool but an ethical mechanism that restores meaning, context, and coherence to the survivor's experience.

Clinical Positioning Within Existing Treatment Frameworks

The HQTP does not seek to replace established evidence-based treatments such as dialectical behaviour therapy. DBT has strong empirical support for the treatment of emotional dysregulation, chronic suicidality, and behavioural destabilisation. Where clinically indicated, the HQTP incorporates regulation scaffolding consistent with DBT principles to support affect stabilisation and crisis containment.

However, survivors of CPA-PA frequently present with epistemic injury, loyalty conditioning, attachment captivity, and narrative destabilisation that extend beyond behavioural dysregulation alone. The HQTP, therefore, provides a phase-based, trauma-informed architecture designed specifically to address differentiation, restoration of internal narrative authority, and ethically gated trauma integration within this population. The model is population-specific rather than transdiagnostic, grounded in dual-cohort doctoral research with survivors and treating clinicians, as well as in integrated clinical practice.

Diagnosis as Protection, Not Pathology

For adult survivors of child psychological abuse, accurate diagnosis functions not as a label of defect, but as a mechanism of protection, access, and repair. When grounded in assessment and disciplined formulation, diagnosis offers clarity rather than confinement. For survivors whose experiences have been repeatedly minimised, denied, or reframed as personal failure, accurate diagnostic language provides recognition of injury. It situates distress within its relational, developmental, and trauma-based context. In this way, diagnosis functions as validation rather than reduction.

Accurate formulation assists clinicians in distinguishing trauma-based adaptations from enduring personality pathology. This distinction is central to preventing unnecessary pathologisation and to guiding appropriate treatment planning. Diagnostic clarity supports pacing decisions, modality selection, and risk management, while reducing the likelihood of interventions that inadvertently replicate coercive, invalidating, or abandoning dynamics. When applied thoughtfully, diagnosis becomes a safeguard against therapeutic misalignment.

Diagnosis also serves a practical protective function. Within health, disability, and insurance systems, diagnostic language often determines access to care, continuity of treatment, and eligibility for support services. For adult survivors of child psychological abuse, misdiagnosis can obstruct these pathways, while accurate formulation can legitimise need without attributing blame. In this sense, diagnosis functions as a bridge to support, rather than a barrier to care.

It is essential to maintain a clear distinction between clinical diagnosis and forensic determination. Diagnostic formulation in this context does not function to establish legal culpability, adjudicate contested narratives, or resolve factual disputes. Its purpose is to support clinical understanding, guide ethical treatment, and protect survivors from further harm.

When diagnosis becomes conflated with forensic judgement, clinicians may feel pressured to adopt positions of certainty that exceed the limits of therapeutic knowledge and distort clinical reasoning. Ethical diagnostic practice, therefore, preserves firm boundaries between psychological formulation and legal processes, maintaining the integrity of the therapeutic role while remaining anchored in evidence-informed care.

Diagnosis within the HQTP is not treated as a fixed identity but as part of an ongoing formulation process. Survivor presentations evolve as safety is established and trauma is processed. Ethical diagnostic practice, therefore, remains flexible, revisable, and responsive to emerging information. It privileges meaning over categorisation and understanding over premature certainty.

When used in this manner, diagnosis does not replace listening, nor does it override relational attunement. Instead, it functions as one component of a broader clinical framework that prioritises safety, coherence, and repair. In work with adult survivors of child psychological abuse, diagnosis reaches its highest value when it prevents further harm, supports ethical care, and opens pathways toward recovery.

The chapters that follow advance diagnostic clarity not as an endpoint but as the foundation for phased, survivor-informed treatment to proceed safely.

Chapter Twelve

Phase Progression, Setbacks and Ethical Recontainment

This chapter does not reintroduce the phase model as new material. It revisits each phase through the lens of setbacks, destabilisation, ethical recontainment, and non-linear progression. Therefore, treatment with adult survivors of CPA-PA contexts must proceed through deliberate, phased pathways that prioritise safety, pacing, and relational stability. Attachment-based psychological abuse unfolds across developmental time, shaping identity formation, emotional regulation, perception of reality, and relational expectations. As a result, effective treatment cannot be standardised, accelerated, or driven by technique alone. It must be organised around the survivor's capacity for psychological safety, reflective functioning, and agency within a therapeutic relationship that does not replicate coercion, performance demands, or institutional urgency.

Within the HQTP, phased treatment provides the structure through which ethical assessment is translated into clinical action. Phasing is not designed to impose rigid stages, but to prevent premature intervention, reduce the risk of reenactment, and ensure that trauma work occurs only when the survivor has sufficient regulatory capacity and relational safety to remain present without destabilisation. Progression is capacity-based rather than time-based, and clinical pathways remain flexible, responsive, and revisable.

The Clinical Rationale for Phased Treatment

Phased treatment is a clinical necessity in this population because the original injury is both relational and developmental. Psychological abuse occurring within attachment relationships disrupts internal regulation, self-coherence, and the survivor's capacity to experience relationships as emotionally safe. Many adult survivors enter therapy without consistent nervous system stability, without a coherent personal narrative that feels safe to hold, and without confidence that connection can exist without control, punishment, or abandonment.

When therapy moves prematurely into trauma exposure, interpretive work, or pressured narrative reconstruction, it risks replicating the original conditions of harm. Survivors shaped by loyalty enforcement, reality distortion, and fear conditioning may experience accelerated intervention as intrusive or coercive, even when clinical intent is supportive. In such contexts, rapid insight-oriented work, neutrality without attunement, or emotionally demanding processing can trigger withdrawal, dissociation, affective flooding, or attachment collapse.

For this reason, psychological safety and stabilisation are not preparatory tasks that precede treatment. They are treatment. Establishing psychological safety involves predictable pacing, transparent collaboration, consistent boundaries, and repeated demonstrations that the survivor is not required to perform credibility checks, justify distress, or comply with an external agenda to remain connected. Phased treatment also protects clinicians from system-driven pressures toward speed, certainty, and outcome-based intervention, preserving ethical positioning and therapeutic integrity.

Phase I: Safety, Orientation, and Epistemic Stabilisation

Phase I forms the foundation of all subsequent therapeutic work. It is not a holding stage or rapport-building period, but an active phase focused on nervous system regulation, relational safety, and restoration of personal agency. Survivors frequently enter therapy with heightened vigilance, compromised affect tolerance, and histories of relational environments in which compliance, silence, or emotional suppression were required for survival. The initial clinical task is to establish conditions in which the survivor no longer needs to monitor, appease, or protect themselves within the therapeutic relationship.

Safety in Phase I is psychological rather than procedural. It is created through consistency, predictability, clarity of boundaries, transparency of intent, and the absence of pressure to disclose or to progress. Survivors must experience that the therapeutic space is not contingent on performance, emotional expression, or agreement. When clinicians maintain attuned presence without intrusion, neutrality without emotional withdrawal, and care without control, survivors gradually differentiate present relational conditions from past attachment trauma.

Stabilisation involves strengthening the survivor's capacity to remain oriented, regulated, and reflective both within sessions and in daily life. Many survivors rely on dissociation, emotional numbing, hypervigilance, intellectualisation, or hyperfunctioning as survival strategies. Within the HQTP, these patterns are understood as adaptive responses to prolonged threat rather than deficits. Phase I work respects these adaptations while gradually expanding the survivor's window of tolerance through pacing, grounding, present-oriented regulation, and collaborative exploration of internal experience.

Restoration of agency is a central objective of this phase. Survivors raised within coercive systems often struggle to recognise choice, consent, and internal authority. Therapeutic practice, therefore, remains collaborative. Pace is negotiated rather than imposed. Limits are named and respected. Even subtle pressure to interpret, disclose, or advance can reactivate conditioned compliance or oppositional defences. When agency is restored, survivors begin to experience themselves as participants in therapy rather than objects of intervention.

Phase I is not time-limited. Progression occurs only when stability is consistently demonstrated, and the therapeutic relationship is experienced as regulating rather than destabilising. Attempting to bypass this phase increases the risk of retraumatisation and replicates the original loss of control that characterised the abuse.

Phase II: Meaning Reconstruction and Identity Repair

In Phase II, the clinical focus shifts toward careful meaning reconstruction, recognition of survival adaptations, and the early repair of identity distortion. Survivors begin to understand how coercive relational environments shaped belief formation, self-concept, loyalty patterns, and autobiographical meaning. The task is not emotional catharsis or premature trauma processing, but the development of reflective capacity, narrative flexibility, and psychological authorship under conditions of continued epistemic safety.

Many survivors carry significant shame about adaptations such as compliance, emotional suppression, loyalty binding, hyper-responsibility, or defensive hostility in situations perceived as threatening. Phase II work repositions these patterns within their developmental context, recognising them as protective responses formed under coercion, attachment disruption, and chronic threat rather than as evidence of inherent flaw or pathology.

This reconstruction of meaning does not remove adult responsibility or minimise the impact of behaviour on others. Instead, it restores psychological coherence, reduces internalised blame, and supports the emergence of a more stable sense of self that is no longer organised solely around threat, performance, or relational survival. Identity repair begins here as survivors slowly develop the capacity to hold complexity, question inherited narratives, and recognise their own experience without collapsing into shame or self-erasure.

Phase III: Mourning, Loss Integration, and Developmental Grief Repair

Within the HQTP, Phase III addresses the compound grief inherent in CPA-PA. The losses carried by adult survivors are rarely singular or easily named. They may include the loss of a psychologically available parent, the loss of extended family and intergenerational continuity, the loss of an intact childhood narrative, the loss of developmental safety, and the loss of trust in protective systems that failed to recognise or interrupt the abuse. Many survivors also grieve lost time, lost identity development, and lost opportunities for ordinary attachment, belonging, and relational certainty.

Grief in this population is rarely linear, time-limited, or emotionally pure. It commonly coexists with anger, shame, disbelief, numbness, confusion, loyalty conflict, and traumatic longing. Survivors may grieve not only what was taken from them, but also what they were never permitted to know, experience, or become. As insight deepens, previously defended losses may become more visible, and mourning may emerge in waves rather than through predictable stages. For this reason, grief work within the HQTP is not approached as emotional discharge or as a task to be completed, but as a gradual developmental process requiring pacing, containment, and meaning-making.

The clinical task in Phase III is to help survivors begin holding loss without becoming overwhelmed by it. This includes supporting the capacity to name what happened, recognise the enduring impact of developmental deprivation, and mourn relational realities that may never be repaired. Clinicians remain attentive to the risk that grief may rapidly shift into dissociation, collapse, self-blame, or pressure to minimise the significance of the loss. Therapeutic work, therefore, remains titrated and relationally anchored. Survivors are not pushed toward forgiveness, reconciliation, reunification, or emotionally performative acceptance. The aim is not resolution in a simplistic sense, but rather an increased capacity to bear the truth without fragmentation.

Developmental grief repair also involves recognising that mourning may re-emerge across the lifespan. Birthdays, parenthood, ageing, death, legal processes, family contact, and later insight may reactivate earlier losses in new forms. Within the HQTP, this recurrence is understood as a normal feature of complex developmental trauma rather than evidence of treatment failure. Progression from Phase III occurs only when the survivor can remain sufficiently regulated while approaching grief-related material and can engage in mourning without prolonged destabilisation, coercive compliance, or loss of agency.

Phase IV: Trauma Integration Readiness Architecture

Phase IV is introduced only when sufficient stabilisation, meaning reconstruction, and grief capacity have been established. The clinical task in this phase is not to assume immediate trauma processing, but to determine whether trauma integration can be approached without destabilisation, epistemic threat, or reenactment of coercive dynamics.

For many adult survivors, traumatic material is not held as a single coherent story. It may instead appear as bodily activation, intrusive imagery, affective flooding, narrative gaps, developmental confusion, or contradictory beliefs about self, others, and the past. Within the HQTP, Phase IV therefore focuses on readiness, pacing, and protective sequencing rather than exposure for its own sake. The aim is to strengthen the conditions under which trauma material may later be approached ethically, with consent, and without overwhelming the survivor.

This phase includes assessment of regulatory recovery, stability of consent, tolerance for ambiguity, reduced reliance on therapist authority to confirm experience, and the survivor's capacity to approach painful material without collapse, dissociation, or urgent self-erasure. When these conditions are not established, clinicians return to earlier phases rather than advancing prematurely into trauma processing.

Phase IV, therefore, functions as a clinical threshold rather than a guarantee of deeper trauma work. Its purpose is to ensure that any later integrative work occurs within conditions of sufficient psychological safety, survivor agency, and relational stability to prevent retraumatisation and preserve therapeutic integrity.

Phase V: Differentiation, Boundary Formation, and Contact Decisions

Where Phase IV centres on trauma integration, Phase V shifts the clinical focus toward relational differentiation, boundary consolidation, and the strengthening of autonomous identity. Therapeutic work becomes less centred on traumatic material and more oriented toward identity continuity, relational discernment, and the lived expression of autonomy.

Identity reconstruction continues as survivors revise internalised beliefs shaped by coercion, blame, loyalty enforcement, and narrative distortion. Therapy supports survivors in becoming authors of personal meaning rather than passive recipients of imposed narratives.

Phase V does not require reconciliation, forgiveness, reunification, or the construction of coherent family narratives. Instead, it supports psychological freedom to determine whether to be proximate, at a distance, to advocate, to remain silent, or to engage selectively, according to safety, values, and informed choice.

Relational differentiation involves strengthening boundaries without guilt, tolerating disappointment without self-erasure, and recognising coercive or manipulative dynamics without collapsing into hypervigilance or withdrawal. Survivors develop increased capacity to maintain internal psychological stability during relational rupture, institutional contact, or family system activation. Rather than reacting reflexively to relational triggers, survivors learn to respond with discernment grounded in the present context rather than conditioned fear.

Preparation for predictable developmental transitions that commonly reactivate attachment injury is incorporated where relevant. This includes anticipating contact with family systems, navigating institutional processes, and managing relational complexity without surrendering agency. Phase V solidifies the survivor’s capacity to remain psychologically distinct from coercive systems while preserving relational flexibility where desired.

Phase VI: Integration, Continuity, and Long-Term Adaptation

Following differentiation and boundary consolidation, Phase VI consolidates therapeutic gains and supports long-term adaptation beyond active trauma work. The focus shifts toward sustained integration, identity continuity, and the maintenance of regulatory stability across changing life contexts. Survivors increasingly experience the therapeutic relationship as a resource rather than an organising centre of stability.

Ethical transition planning forms a central component of this phase. Session frequency may gradually decrease in accordance with the survivor's readiness, while structured re-entry pathways are maintained to prevent re-enactment of abandonment and to preserve professional boundaries. Continuity is framed as access without dependency. The goal is neither detachment nor prolonged reliance, but durable autonomy supported by available containment when required.

The HQTP conceptualises non-linear movement as an enduring feature of recovery. Destabilisation during later phases is interpreted as information regarding capacity, context, or environmental activation rather than as regression or failure. When emotional activation exceeds regulation, external stressors overwhelm coping resources, or reenactment dynamics intensify, the protocol prioritises ethical recontainment over escalation of technique.

Clinical pathways remain responsive across all phases. Increased dissociation, affective flooding, functional decline, or erosion of agency within sessions signal the need to temporarily return to earlier stabilisation strategies. When relational safety is strained, ruptures are named and repaired transparently. When trauma material becomes overly activating, pacing is recalibrated, and present-oriented containment is re-established before further integration proceeds.

Throughout all phases, clinicians maintain humility, transparency, and disciplined ethical restraint. Supervision serves as a structural safeguard, particularly during phase transitions, heightened countertransference, involvement of complex systems, or increased clinical risk. Documentation remains formulation-driven and clinically grounded, preserving the therapeutic role as distinct from forensic, adversarial, or advocacy functions.

Within this phased structure, treatment remains anchored to the central commitments of the HQTP: safety before exposure, consent before interpretation, capacity before progression, and relationship before outcome. The chapters that follow translate this architecture into formulation-guided planning, therapeutic environment construction, trauma integration parameters, and applied clinical implementation within clearly defined ethical and supervisory frameworks.

Chapter Thirteen

Clinical Formulation and Treatment Planning

From Assessment to Therapeutic Direction

Clinical Formulation as a Protective Clinical Function

This chapter operationalises the shift from assessment data to structured therapeutic direction within the HQTP. Clinical formulation is the central mechanism by which ethical assessment translates into therapeutic action. In work with adult survivors of child psychological abuse, formulation functions not as a theoretical exercise but as a clinical filter that governs what interventions are appropriate, when they may occur, and which actions must be withheld.

Within the HQTP, formulation operates as a safeguard against premature intervention, misdiagnosis, and reenactment. It prevents treatment from being driven by symptom visibility, emotional urgency, or clinician preference. Instead, it anchors decision-making in developmental history, attachment context, trauma adaptation, and current capacity. In this way, formulation protects both the survivor and the clinician by ensuring that intervention sequencing remains grounded in clinical reality rather than assumptions.

Formulation, therefore, precedes technique. Therapeutic tools are not selected in isolation but are applied only after the clinician has established a coherent working understanding of the survivor's relational history, regulatory capacity, and readiness for deeper therapeutic work.

From Developmental History to Working Hypothesis

Formulation within the HQTP is hypothesis-driven rather than declarative. It develops through careful integration of developmental history, attachment patterns, exposure to coercive control, and the survivor's internalised narratives of loyalty, fear, and responsibility. Rather than seeking diagnostic closure early in treatment, clinicians maintain provisional formulations that are refined as relational safety increases and narrative coherence strengthens.

Adult survivors of psychological abuse frequently present with fragmented memory, conditioned self-doubt, and difficulty articulating emotional experience. These features are not indicators of unreliability but predictable outcomes of prolonged attachment disruption and reality distortion. Formulation, therefore, privileges meaning and function over surface consistency. The clinical task is not to extract certainty, but to construct understanding gradually and collaboratively.

This iterative approach allows formulation to evolve alongside treatment. As stabilisation occurs and affect tolerance increases, deeper aspects of attachment injury and trauma adaptation may become accessible. Ethical formulation remains responsive to this process, adjusting hypotheses as new information emerges rather than forcing early conceptual closure.

Capacity-Based Planning and Readiness Gating

Treatment planning within the HQTP is governed by psychological capacity rather than motivation alone. Readiness is assessed through affect regulation, relational safety, reflective functioning, and the survivor's ability to tolerate emotional complexity without destabilisation. These indicators determine not only which interventions are appropriate but also when they may be ethically introduced.

Survivors of child psychological abuse often carry histories in which authority figures overrode personal readiness, imposed narratives, or accelerated processes for institutional convenience. Replicating this dynamic within therapy represents a significant clinical risk. For this reason, formulation functions as a gating mechanism that regulates progression through treatment phases.

Interventions that exceed current capacity are deferred, regardless of perceived therapeutic benefit. This restraint preserves agency, prevents retraumatisation, and reinforces the survivor's experience of choice within the therapeutic process. When capacity increases, formulation is updated accordingly, allowing treatment planning to remain flexible without abandoning structure.

Preventing Reenactment at the Planning Stage

Reenactment risk is not confined to the therapeutic relationship itself. It also emerges during treatment planning when clinicians experience pressure to rescue, accelerate progress, or deliver emotional relief through premature intervention. These impulses, although often driven by empathy, can inadvertently mirror dynamics of coercion, urgency, or misattunement that characterised the survivor's original environment.

Within this protocol, formulation functions as a stabilising counterbalance to emotional reactivity. It requires clinicians to pause, reflect, and seek supervision when urgency arises. This reflective restraint protects against treatment becoming another site in which external agendas, including professional identity needs or outcome-driven expectations, override survivor autonomy.

Collaborative planning further reduces reenactment risk. Survivors are informed about treatment direction, pacing rationale, and therapeutic intent. This transparency restores relational predictability and reinforces psychological safety, allowing survivors to remain active participants rather than passive recipients of intervention.

Translating Formulation into the HQTP

Clinical formulation provides the structural bridge between assessment and the operational application of the HQTP. It determines how environmental conditions are established, how trauma integration is sequenced, and how therapeutic modalities are selected and adapted over time.

Within this model, formulation does not function as a static case summary. It serves as an ongoing clinical compass, guiding moment-to-moment decision-making across all treatment phases. As survivor capacity evolves, formulation is revised to ensure that intervention remains aligned with safety, dignity, and long-term integration.

The chapters that follow demonstrate how this formulation is enacted within the therapeutic environment and in subsequent trauma-integration work. With assessment complete and treatment sequencing established, the next clinical task is to construct a therapeutic environment that sustains safety, containment, and relational stability before deeper integration work begins.

Chapter Fourteen

The Therapeutic Environment

Containment, Safety, and Relational Conditions for Healing

The Therapeutic Environment as an Active Clinical Intervention

This chapter defines the environmental and relational conditions required before trauma integration can ethically proceed. Within the HQTP, the therapeutic environment is not a neutral setting for treatment. It is an active clinical intervention that directly shapes survivor regulation, relational safety, and treatment readiness. For adult survivors of child psychological abuse, whose developmental environments were frequently characterised by coercion, unpredictability, psychological distortion, and relational instability, environmental conditions carry clinical significance equal to that of any specific therapeutic technique.

The therapeutic environment functions as the primary external stabilising structure through which internal regulation can gradually develop. Consistency, predictability, and psychological safety communicate security before trauma material is introduced. When environmental conditions remain reliably attuned, survivors are no longer required to engage in hypervigilance, appeasement, or anticipatory threat monitoring. This shift allows cognitive and emotional resources to move from a survival-based orientation toward reflection, integration, and relational engagement.

Safety as a Relational Condition Rather Than a Procedural Task

Safety within the HQTP extends beyond immediate risk management or symptom containment. It includes relational safety, emotional permission, and freedom from performance-based evaluation. Adult survivors of child psychological abuse often enter therapy with deeply internalised expectations that care is conditional, temporary, or dependent upon compliance, credibility, or emotional restraint.

The therapeutic environment counters these expectations through transparent pacing, collaborative consent, and consistent relational presence. When clinicians maintain stable boundaries, predictable session structures, and reliable emotional availability, survivors are not required to justify distress, perform recovery, or demonstrate progress in order to remain worthy of care. Safety is experienced not as a reward, but as a stable relational condition that supports psychological stability and therapeutic engagement.

Containment, Predictability, and the Gradual Development of Trust

Containment refers to the clinician's capacity to hold emotional intensity, ambiguity, and psychological complexity without escalating, withdrawing, or prematurely solving the problem. For survivors whose early environments were marked by emotional volatility, role reversal, or abandonment, this capacity is foundational to relational repair.

Predictable session rhythms, clear therapeutic agreements, and consistent clinical responses provide the external scaffolding through which internal psychological stability can develop. Trust is not assumed or demanded. It is constructed through repeated experiences of attunement, boundary integrity, relational repair, and emotional non-retaliation. Over time, the therapeutic environment becomes a space in which emotional expression does not result in punishment, dismissal, or control, allowing survivors to safely access previously defended internal states.

Environmental Continuity and Reenactment Prevention

Environmental disruptions may activate trauma responses even in the absence of explicit relational conflict. Changes in session timing, perceived emotional withdrawal, inconsistent boundaries, unexplained shifts in tone, or alterations in routine may echo earlier experiences of abandonment, unpredictability, or coercive control.

Within this protocol, clinicians are responsible not only for relational process but also for environmental continuity. When disruptions occur, they are acknowledged, contextualised, and repaired rather than minimised or ignored. This responsiveness reinforces psychological safety, models relational accountability, and prevents the therapeutic environment from replicating the instability that characterised the survivor's developmental history.

Environmental awareness, therefore, functions as a preventative intervention. By maintaining consistency and proactively addressing disruptions, clinicians reduce the likelihood of reenactment at the structural level of treatment delivery.

Establishing the Conditions for Trauma Integration

A stable therapeutic environment establishes the conditions necessary for later trauma integration without forcing premature exposure. When survivors experience the therapeutic environment itself as regulating, predictable, and emotionally safe, they develop greater affect tolerance, improved reflective capacity, and greater emotional integration.

Within the HQTP, environmental safety is not treated as a preliminary phase to be completed and abandoned. It remains an ongoing therapeutic condition that supports all subsequent clinical work. As environmental stability becomes internalised, survivors gradually shift attention away from threat detection and relational survival toward deeper engagement with traumatic material.

This transition does not occur through pressure or procedural progression. It emerges organically from sustained relational safety. The following chapter outlines how trauma integration is introduced only once these environmental conditions have been sufficiently established, ensuring that therapeutic work proceeds with ethical sequencing and pacing.

Chapter Fifteen

Trauma Integration

Pacing, Readiness, and the Protection of Psychological Safety

Trauma Integration as a Relational and Developmental Task

Trauma integration with adult survivors of child psychological abuse cannot be approached as a discrete technical intervention applied once symptoms are identified. It is a relational and developmental process that unfolds within the safety of a stabilised therapeutic environment and is shaped by the survivor's capacity for affect regulation, reflective functioning, and emotional integration.

For individuals whose early attachment environments were characterised by coercion, emotional distortion, or relational abandonment, trauma integration must restore agency rather than replicate loss of control. Within the HQTP, trauma work is conceptualised as gradual integration of lived experience rather than direct confrontation with traumatic memory. The clinician's role is not to elicit material, but to remain responsive to what emerges organically as safety and capacity increase. This stance protects against retraumatisation and reinforces the principle that readiness is cultivated through relationship rather than imposed through protocol.

Readiness, Consent, and Ethical Timing

Readiness for trauma integration is not determined by time in therapy, session count, or expressed motivation alone. It is assessed through the survivor's ability to remain emotionally present, regulate physiological and affective responses, tolerate internal complexity, and maintain relational stability within the therapeutic alliance.

Survivors of child psychological abuse frequently learned to comply with authority in order to survive, making explicit attention to consent and pacing ethically essential. Trauma work is introduced collaboratively, with transparency regarding therapeutic intent and ongoing monitoring for signs of overwhelm, dissociation, emotional flooding, or withdrawal. When survivors are invited into trauma integration rather than directed toward it, agency is preserved, and the original dynamics of coercion are actively countered.

Within this protocol, clinicians do not progress into deeper trauma work unless stabilisation and relational safety remain intact. Readiness functions as a clinical gate rather than a theoretical concept. When capacity decreases, the treatment focus shifts back to containment and regulation rather than pressing forward.

Outside-in Sequencing and Resource Development

The HQTP applies an outside-in sequencing strategy that prioritises present-oriented stabilisation before engaging central attachment trauma and developmental injury. This includes strengthening relational safety, cultivating bodily awareness, enhancing emotional regulation capacity, and establishing external and internal structures that support containment.

Rather than privileging memory recall or narrative reconstruction, treatment initially focuses on building the psychological resources required to tolerate emotional activation without destabilisation. As integration progresses, traumatic material may emerge through somatic responses, relational patterns, affective shifts, or fragmented memory rather than linear narrative form.

The clinician supports meaning-making without prematurely forcing coherence. Integration is allowed to occur through the accumulation of safety, relational stability, and reflective capacity rather than exposure-driven intervention. This sequencing reduces risk while increasing the survivor's ability to remain present and engaged during deeper therapeutic work.

Preventing Retraumatisation and Therapeutic Overreach

Retraumatisation most often occurs not through overt harm, but through therapeutic overreach. When clinicians move too quickly, interpret too deeply, or privilege insight over regulation, survivors may experience therapy as another environment in which personal limits are overridden. This risk is heightened in survivors whose developmental boundaries were repeatedly violated.

Protection against retraumatisation requires continuous monitoring of both survivor responses and clinician-driven urgency. Supervision remains central to this process, supporting recognition of countertransference, rescue impulses, and premature movement toward resolution.

Within the HQTP, trauma integration remains ethically grounded only when it is titrated, reversible, and responsive to emerging capacity. When restraint, reflective practice, and pacing are maintained, trauma work supports integration rather than destabilisation.

Gentle Approaches to Trauma Integration

Within the HQTP, trauma integration is approached as a gradual, layered process rather than a single event. Adult survivors frequently present with developmental trauma patterns characterised by long-term nervous system activation, emotional suppression, and survival-based relational adaptations. The author's doctoral findings demonstrated that direct trauma exposure approaches often resulted in destabilisation, therapeutic withdrawal, or increased internal conflict when applied prematurely (Price-Tobler, 2023a). For this population, the engagement method is as important as the content being processed.

Gentle trauma integration prioritises safety, pacing, and nervous system capacity over speed or intensity. Rather than moving immediately into a detailed recounting of memories, therapy begins by building the client's tolerance for emotional activation and internal awareness. This approach reflects the principle of working from the outside in, in which regulation and stabilisation are established before attempting deeper memory integration.

The outside-in approach, commonly associated with somatic frameworks, can be integrated across modalities, including CBT, EMDR, psychodynamic psychotherapy, and attachment-based work. Regardless of the technique used, the central principle remains consistent: trauma integration must be matched to the survivor's physiological and emotional readiness. Clients are supported to develop distress management skills, grounding capacity, and relational safety before engaging with traumatic material.

This method often takes longer than directive exposure models. However, clinical outcomes observed in the author's doctoral interviews indicated that survivors who progressed through gradual pacing demonstrated stronger long-term emotional stability, reduced dissociation, and greater confidence in managing future stressors (Price-Tobler, 2023a). By the time clients engage directly with core traumatic memories, they are no longer relying solely on therapist containment. They possess internal regulation strategies that allow them to remain present, process emotional material, and recover following activation.

Gentle processing also protects against the replication of coercive dynamics that characterised early abuse environments. Survivors of alienation and abduction were often forced into emotional compliance, narrative control, and premature emotional exposure during childhood. Trauma work that respects pacing, consent, and client-led progression restores autonomy and reinforces psychological safety.

The clinical objective of this phase is not emotional catharsis. It is the development of sustainable emotional capacity, self-efficacy, and resilience. Survivors learn that distress can be tolerated without collapse, that emotional activation can be navigated safely, and that internal regulation is achievable. These gains form the foundation for deeper integration of trauma in later phases.

Integration, Meaning, and Ongoing Adaptation

Integration does not involve erasing traumatic experience. It reflects the survivor's increasing ability to hold past experience within a coherent sense of self that is no longer organised around threat. As integration develops, survivors often experience shifts in identity, relational expectations, emotional expression, and internal narrative coherence.

Trauma integration is situated within a broader integrative trajectory that continues beyond formal intervention. Healing is reflected not solely in symptom reduction but also in restored agency, relational discernment, self-directed meaning-making, and psychological flexibility.

The following chapter examines how specific therapeutic modalities are selected, adapted, and sequenced to support sustained stability, ethical sequencing and pacing, and long-term integration.

Chapter Sixteen

Clinical Implementation, Modality Integration and Risk Management

Clinical implementation within the HQTP extends beyond the mechanical application of therapeutic techniques. It requires disciplined clinical judgement, ethical sequencing, and continuous attention to safety, readiness, and practitioner responsibility. For adult survivors of CPA-PA, therapeutic work unfolds within complex developmental, relational, and systemic contexts shaped by attachment disruption, institutional betrayal, coercive family dynamics, and long-standing survival adaptations. Intervention must therefore remain formulation-led, context-responsive, and ethically restrained.

Within this protocol, clinical authority is exercised through structure rather than speed. Decisions regarding modality use, pacing, and escalation are guided by formulation, environmental stability, and survivor capacity rather than theoretical allegiance or practitioner preference.

Operational Standards for HQTP Implementation

The HQTP is a phase-based clinical treatment protocol rather than a single-modality intervention. It is not intended to replace established trauma therapies, attachment-informed practice, DBT, EMDR, psychodynamic psychotherapy, narrative therapy, or other evidence-informed approaches. Instead, it provides the clinical architecture through which such approaches may be selected, sequenced, deferred, adapted, or contraindicated when working with adult survivors of CPA-PA, CPA-PAA, CPA-PERA, and associated coercive-control contexts.

For this reason, fidelity to the HQTP is not measured by whether every clinician uses the same technique. It is measured by whether the clinician preserves the protocol's core clinical logic: safety before depth, stabilisation before trauma integration, identity before documentation, grief before contact pressure, autonomy before reconciliation, and supervision before high-risk clinical decision-making.

At a minimum, competent implementation of the HQTP requires the clinician to document and review the following elements across treatment:

1. The survivor's current phase position.
2. The clinical rationale for remaining in, moving toward, or returning to a phase.
3. Immediate safety, suicidality, violence risk, and destabilisation risk.
4. Current epistemic stability and capacity for reflective meaning-making.
5. Consent, pacing, and the survivor's capacity to pause.
6. Contact-related pressure, loyalty conflict, or external coercion.
7. Contraindications for deeper trauma work, record exposure, or contact exploration.
8. Supervision needs, practitioner countertransference, and role-boundary concerns.
9. The survivor's functional stability, relational safety, and internal coherence over time.

The HQTP, therefore, requires more than conceptual agreement with trauma-informed care. It requires repeated clinical checking. A clinician may understand the theory and still move too quickly, over-identify with survivor urgency, misread compliance as readiness, confuse insight with integration, or treat contact decisions as evidence of therapeutic progress. The operational standard within the HQTP is that every major clinical movement must be supported by phase logic, survivor readiness, consent, and supervision where complexity or risk is present.

Phase-Based Intervention Status: Required, Optional, and Contraindicated Clinical Actions

Within the HQTP, interventions are not selected because they are familiar to the clinician or preferred by the service. They are selected according to phase position, survivor readiness, risk presentation, and the likelihood of preserving or disrupting epistemic safety.

Required actions across all phases include safety screening, consent-based pacing, role clarification, attention to epistemic injury, documentation of phase position, and supervision when risk, uncertainty, countertransference, or external pressure is present.

Optional interventions may include psychoeducation, DBT-informed stabilisation skills, grounding, somatic regulation, narrative reflection, attachment-informed work, grief-focused therapy, EMDR preparation, cognitive restructuring, mindfulness-based practices, creative expression, or family/system consultation where clinically appropriate. These interventions are adjuncts to the HQTP architecture. They do not replace phase logic.

Contraindicated actions include premature trauma exposure, forced insight, pressure for forgiveness or reconciliation, forensic-style interrogation, rapid documentation retrieval without stabilisation, contact planning before boundary readiness, clinician alignment with family pressure, interpretation that overrides the survivor's emerging meaning, and any intervention that increases collapse, dissociation, shame, compliance, suicidality, or relational capture.

When a survivor destabilises, the clinician does not treat this as failure or resistance. The clinician returns to the earliest phase required to restore safety, regulation, consent, and coherence.

Minimum Clinical Review and Outcome-Monitoring Framework

The HQTP does not reduce recovery to symptom scores alone. However, clinical progress must still be monitored in a structured way. The minimum review framework includes both risk-based and recovery-based indicators.

At intake and at regular review points, clinicians should monitor:

1. Current risk of suicide, self-harm, violence, exploitation, or severe destabilisation.
2. Functional stability, including sleep, work, study, parenting, self-care, and daily organisation.

3. Affect regulation and recovery time after activation.
4. Dissociation, collapse, panic, somatic distress, or identity fragmentation.
5. Epistemic stability, including the survivor's capacity to notice, trust, and reflect on their own perceptions without immediate collapse into shame, fear, or external authority dependence.
6. Relational safety, including boundary capacity, contact pressure, loyalty conflict, and risk of re-enmeshment.
7. Grief tolerance and capacity to hold loss without urgent resolution.
8. Readiness for trauma integration, record exposure, or contact-related decision-making.
9. Therapeutic alliance, rupture risk, and therapy-interfering dynamics.
10. Survivor-defined indicators of coherence, autonomy, safety, and meaningful life participation.

Where services require formal measures, clinicians may use validated tools appropriate to the presenting concerns, including trauma, dissociation, depression, anxiety, functioning, quality of life, suicidality, and therapeutic alliance measures. These tools should support clinical judgement rather than replace it. Within the HQTP, measurement is used to protect pacing, identify destabilisation early, and track recovery beyond disclosure or symptom suppression.

HQTP Clinical Integrity and Fidelity Review

Fidelity to the HQTP does not require identical session content across clinicians. It requires fidelity to the protocol's clinical logic, ethical position, and phase-based safeguards.

A clinician is working with HQTP integrity when they can demonstrate that:

1. The survivor's current phase position has been identified and reviewed.
2. Interventions are matched to phase readiness rather than clinician preference.

3. Trauma processing, record exposure, or contact exploration has not been introduced before stabilisation and consent capacity are sufficient.
4. The survivor's subjective experience has not been overridden by clinical interpretation, family pressure, legal urgency, or therapist anxiety.
5. Destabilisation has led to recontainment rather than escalation of intervention intensity.
6. Supervision has been used when risk, countertransference, uncertainty, or external pressure is present.
7. Documentation reflects clinical reasoning, not forensic conclusion-making.
8. The survivor's autonomy, pacing, and right not to reconcile have been protected.
9. Progress is evaluated through safety, coherence, functional stability, boundary capacity, and internal authority rather than narrative completeness alone.

Loss of fidelity occurs when the clinician uses the HQTP language while abandoning its sequencing. This may occur when therapy becomes disclosure-driven, reconciliation-driven, diagnosis-driven, documentation-driven, or technique-driven. In these situations, the clinician should pause, seek supervision, return to the relevant phase map, and re-establish the survivor's safety, consent, and epistemic protection.

Minimum Supervision Expectations

The HQTP assumes active clinical supervision for high-complexity work. Supervision is not an optional professional support. It is part of the protocol's safety structure. For lower-complexity CPA-PA presentations, clinicians should engage in regular supervision consistent with professional standards and service requirements.

For complex CPA-PAA, CPA-PERA, abduction, extreme harm, suicidality, litigation reactivation, contact decision-making, or exposure to practitioner threats, supervision should occur more frequently. It should be treated as an active component of clinical care.

Within the HQTP, supervision is expected when:

1. The clinician is uncertain about phase placement.
2. The survivor becomes destabilised after recognition work.
3. Suicidality, violence risk, or identity collapse emerges.
4. The survivor requests contact, records, confrontation, or rapid truth-seeking before readiness is clear.
5. The clinician feels rescue urgency, disbelief, anger, fear, over-identification, or pressure to prove the history.
6. Family members, services, courts, or other systems pressure the clinician toward a position.
7. The clinician is considering trauma processing, EMDR, exposure-based work, family contact, or major boundary-change planning.
8. The clinician's own safety, professional standing, registration, or workplace stability may be affected.

The supervision task is not simply emotional support for the clinician. It is to protect phase integrity, ethical boundaries, survivor autonomy, and clinical judgement. Furthermore, these review points are not intended to turn therapy into a paperwork exercise. Their purpose is to protect clinical reasoning, pacing, and survivor safety when the work becomes complex, emotionally charged, or under external pressure.

Modality Selection as an Extension of Formulation

Therapeutic modalities within the HQTP are selected based on clinical formulation and treatment phase rather than on practitioner orientation or the availability of techniques. Approaches are chosen based on developmental context, attachment history, regulatory capacity, and current readiness for emotional activation.

Techniques function as instruments in the service of integration rather than drivers of the therapeutic process. What supports stabilisation at one stage of treatment may prove destabilising at another. For this reason, modality selection remains flexible and subject to ongoing clinical review. Interventions are introduced, adapted, or withdrawn in response to emerging capacity rather than rigid adherence to predefined treatment plans.

Integrative Practice Without Modality Silos

The HQTP rejects rigid modality silos. Survivors of child psychological abuse have often been exposed to systems that imposed singular narratives, externally defined explanations, or inflexible solutions. Replicating this rigidity in therapy risks reenacting control and eroding agency.

An integrative stance allows clinicians to draw from multiple evidence-informed approaches while remaining anchored in ethical sequencing and pacing, collaborative consent, and supervision. Integration does not involve indiscriminate blending of techniques. It requires deliberate sequencing, clear rationale, and transparent communication with the survivor regarding therapeutic intent. This preserves coherence while maintaining flexibility across treatment phases.

Trauma-Focused Interventions and Pacing Discipline

Trauma-focused modalities such as EMDR, somatic approaches, and trauma-informed cognitive therapies may offer powerful pathways toward integration when applied within appropriate clinical conditions. Within this protocol, such interventions are introduced only after sufficient environmental stability, relational safety, and affect tolerance have been established.

Pacing remains a central clinical responsibility. Techniques are adapted to avoid overwhelming activation, premature exposure of memory, or forced narrative coherence. Clinicians monitor not only symptom response but post-session integration, relational stability, and functional capacity between sessions. When destabilisation occurs, treatment direction is slowed, modified, or temporarily redirected toward containment and regulation rather than continued exposure.

Relational and Psychodynamic Contributions

Relational and psychodynamic approaches remain central within the HQTP due to the attachment-based nature of the original injury. Survivors frequently carry internalised relational templates shaped by loyalty conflict, emotional role reversal, conditional acceptance, and chronic invalidation.

Therapeutic work supports recognition of these patterns as they emerge internally and relationally, including within the therapeutic alliance. Interpretive interventions are applied cautiously, tentatively, and with explicit consent. Meaning is co-constructed rather than imposed. This protects against insight-driven destabilisation and allows integration to emerge gradually within a relational safety framework.

Preventing Modality-Driven Harm

Clinical harm most often arises not through overt malpractice but through modality-driven overreach. Survivors may experience therapy as intrusive, experimental, or invalidating when techniques are introduced without sufficient readiness, explanation, or contextual grounding. Such experiences reinforce mistrust and contribute to disengagement from care.

Ethical implementation, therefore, requires humility, supervision, and continuous self-monitoring by clinicians. Interventions are paused, adapted, or withdrawn when distress exceeds integrative capacity. Within this framework, techniques remain subordinate to safety, dignity, and relational integrity.

Collaborative Safety Planning and Escalation Pathways

Safety planning within the HQTP is conceptualised as an evolving collaborative process rather than a static administrative task. Plans are revisited and adapted in response to developmental transitions, relational change, emotional capacity, and environmental stressors.

Survivors are supported to identify early warning signs, grounding strategies, and realistic support pathways aligned with their lived circumstances. Importantly, safety planning avoids replicating surveillance or control dynamics. Agency remains central, with clinicians providing structure without coercion.

Clear escalation pathways are essential in complex trauma work. Decisions regarding external intervention are grounded in documented assessment, ethical obligation, and professional standards rather than fear-driven reaction. Supervision supports clinicians in distinguishing trauma-related distress that can be safely contained within therapy from genuine risk requiring external involvement.

Ethical Escalation and Relational Preservation

Escalation procedures, when required, constitute significant environmental events. Many adult survivors of child psychological abuse carry histories of involuntary intervention, institutional coercion, or punitive authority responses that mirrored early attachment trauma. When escalation is sudden, opaque, or experienced as controlling, it may reinforce avoidance, emotional suppression, and non-disclosure of future risk.

Whenever possible, escalation is carried out with transparency, collaborative communication, and a clear explanation of the rationale, boundaries, and next steps. This approach reduces emotional arousal, preserves dignity, and supports continued therapeutic engagement. Within the HQTP, escalation is understood not as therapeutic failure but as a skills-informed protective intervention aimed at preventing irreversible harm while maintaining relational integrity.

Practitioner Safety and Ethical Sustainability

Practitioner safety represents an additional ethical responsibility. Work with adult survivors frequently involves high emotional load, reputational exposure, and potential contact from external systems or family members. Clear documentation, adherence to the scope of practice, and consistent supervision function as protective structures that preserve clinical integrity and practitioner wellbeing. Emergency preparedness further strengthens trauma-informed care. Clinicians who maintain clear protocols for suicidality, medical emergencies, and external threats are better able to remain calm, attuned, and effective during periods of instability. Preparedness also involves anticipating less recognised destabilisation pathways that may emerge across the lifespan.

Emerging Clinical Observations and Research Gap Pertaining to Ageing APs

The following section outlines an emerging pathway of destabilisation observed in later-life family transitions that has not yet been formally studied but is clinically relevant within Phase I stabilisation work. Clinical observation within the author's practice and peer supervision contexts indicates that later-life illness, cognitive decline, and increasing care needs in ageing APs may constitute a distinct CIT destabilisation pathway for adult survivors. As an AP's health declines, relational proximity often increases in ways that are not initiated or chosen by the survivor. Contact may be reestablished through healthcare systems during hospital admissions, requests for family involvement communicated by clinical staff, or expectations expressed by relatives regarding caregiving responsibilities. For example, survivors may be contacted by hospital staff as next of kin despite a longstanding estrangement, asked to participate in care-planning discussions, or approached by family members to assume caregiving roles. Similar proximity may arise during transitions to residential aged care, coordination of treatment decisions, or involvement in medical and legal planning processes.

For adult survivors who have intentionally maintained distance as a protective boundary against coercive dynamics, enmeshment, and FDV patterns, these developments can create unanticipated re-exposure to longstanding relational pressures. Lifespan trauma research demonstrates that renewed proximity to attachment figures associated with threat can reactivate earlier defensive states, identity disorganisation, and affect dysregulation (Liotti, 2004; Schore, 2012). Within CPA-PA presentations, this re-exposure may occur even when survivors possess adult cognitive insight and established boundaries.

Clinical observation suggests that APs may respond particularly aggressively toward survivors who maintain distance and may perceive separation as disloyalty or misalignment. Coercive control research indicates that perceived loss of relational control may intensify controlling behaviours, including denigration, narrative manipulation, and loyalty pressure (Stark, 2007; Dutton & Goodman, 2005). In this context, survivors may experience treatment resembling and, in some instances, exceeding the denigration, coercive control, and narrative distortion historically directed toward the targeted parent (TP). Survivors who resist re-enmeshment may be singled out, and alienation dynamics may reactivate at increased intensity through renewed denigration, loyalty pressure, and attempts to reassert narrative control.

Escalation may also manifest structurally. Survivors described exclusion from wills, removal from guardianship roles, changes to next of kin status, or displacement from decision-making positions in favour of siblings or individuals aligned with the AP. Such actions function not only as practical exclusion but also as relational messaging that reinforces longstanding coercive narratives, loyalty expectations, and identity threat.

Later life decline may therefore represent more than a family transition. It may function as a clinically significant destabilisation pathway that requires anticipatory formulation, boundary planning, supervision awareness, and coordinated adult support within Phase I stabilisation work. For some survivors, renewed exposure to psychologically abusive narratives previously experienced in childhood may trigger rapid shifts into earlier developmental states, which intensifies distress and increases the need for external regulatory support.

Peer supervision discussions with psychiatric gerontology clinicians and service leaders with lived experience suggest that alienating behaviours may persist and, in some cases, intensify in older adults experiencing cognitive decline. Dementia research indicates that neurocognitive change may amplify pre-existing personality traits, increase behavioural disinhibition, and contribute to aggression, paranoia, and interpersonal conflict (Kales et al., 2015; Mendez, 2017; Rascovsky et al., 2011). However, the interaction between cognitive decline and established dynamics of alienation has not been formally examined.

This represents a significant research gap. Understanding how ageing-related cognitive change interacts with entrenched coercive relational patterns is clinically important given its potential impact on adult survivor stability, boundary maintenance, and treatment pacing within Phase I of the HQTP.

Reactivation of Childhood Abuse Narratives

Re-exposure to familiar psychologically abusive narratives can be highly distressing for adult survivors. Statements or relational dynamics experienced in childhood may reactivate age-linked emotional states. Some survivors report rapid shifts into childlike distress, heightened shame, fear, or confusion. These responses reflect trauma reactivation rather than loss of adult capacity and may occur even when survivors maintain cognitive awareness of the dynamics.

In these moments, survivors may require immediate stabilisation and external support. Clinicians can assist by anticipating this pathway, providing psychoeducation regarding trauma reactivation, engaging in boundary planning prior to contact, and supporting survivors to develop scripts and exit strategies for destabilising interactions. Supportive adult relationships, including partners, spouses, and trusted peers, may play a protective role by offering validation, practical assistance, and emotional grounding following difficult contact. Reliance on survivors' own children for emotional regulation or advocacy is discouraged, as it may recreate cross-generational coalition dynamics.

Within the context of ageing alienating parents, renewed exposure to psychologically abusive narratives may coincide with increased relational proximity associated with illness, care needs, or institutional involvement. These conditions may reactivate established alienation dynamics and contribute to survivor destabilisation, which reinforces the need for anticipatory formulation, boundary planning, and coordinated adult support within Phase I stabilisation work.

Within the HQTP, preparedness serves as a quiet form of containment that supports both survivors and clinicians when the risk of destabilisation increases. As clinical implementation, modality integration, and risk management stabilise within ethical and supervisory frameworks, the model's next task is to ensure continuity beyond the therapy room. Survivors require pathways that support long-term integration, relational repair, and sustained autonomy without recreating dependency or systemic harm. The following chapter addresses how continuity of care and transition planning are structured within this protocol.

Phase I Clinical Implications for Ageing-Related Destabilisation

Within Phase I of the HQTP, ageing-related destabilisation is approached as an anticipated pathway rather than an unexpected clinical complication. Formulation, therefore, includes proactive discussion of potential future contact scenarios involving illness, hospitalisation, residential care placement, or legal and medical decision-making processes concerning the ageing AP. Early identification of this pathway enables clinicians and survivors to establish boundary frameworks, communication plans, and escalation responses before destabilising events.

Clinical preparation focuses on strengthening regulatory capacity before contact occurs rather than relying on in-the-moment coping. This includes psychoeducation regarding trauma reactivation, rehearsal of boundary language, development of exit strategies, and identification of safe adult supports who can provide post-contact stabilisation. Where survivors anticipate institutional contact, clinicians may assist with practical planning, including clarifying next-of-kin preferences, documenting communication limits, and preparing for interactions with health professionals unfamiliar with alienation dynamics.

Supervision plays a central role in this pathway. Ageing-related contact may activate clinician rescue impulses, moral distress, or pressure from family systems and institutions. Structured supervision supports pacing, maintains phase integrity, and reduces the risk of premature exposure or boundary diffusion. When destabilisation occurs, Phase I recalibration prioritises regulatory restoration, identity coherence, and environmental safety rather than interpretive work.

Importantly, clinicians recognise that later life escalation does not represent therapeutic regression. Instead, it reflects the persistence of coercive relational dynamics across the lifespan. Anticipatory planning, therefore, functions as protective containment, supporting survivor autonomy while reducing the likelihood of re-enactment within healthcare and family systems.

Chapter Seventeen

Continuity, Integration, and Life Beyond Therapy

Recovery as Integration Rather Than Resolution

For adult survivors of child psychological abuse, recovery is not defined by closure, reconciliation, or symptom eradication. Within the HQTP, recovery is conceptualised as an integrative developmental process marked by increasing internal coherence, relational discernment, and the capacity to tolerate psychological complexity without collapse.

Fragmented self-states, disrupted attachment representations, and trauma-encoded belief systems are gradually brought into conscious, tolerable relationships rather than forcibly resolved. This process unfolds unevenly and cannot be accelerated without risk. Survivors may cycle through periods of consolidation and destabilisation, particularly during developmental transitions, parenting stages, relational rupture, illness, or loss. Ethical clinical practice recognises these oscillations as expected features of complex trauma recovery rather than indicators of treatment failure.

Identity Reconstruction Following Psychological Abuse

CPA-PA frequently disrupts identity development. Survivors often enter adulthood with externally constructed self-concepts shaped by loyalty demands, emotional role reversal, and internalised false narratives. Treatment, therefore, supports identity reconstruction through narrative coherence, emotional differentiation, and restoration of authorship over personal meaning. Clinicians facilitate this process by privileging survivors' interpretations over imposed explanations. Reflective dialogue, experiential integration, and permission to revise previously held beliefs allow identity to stabilise without pressure toward premature certainty. Ambiguity is tolerated as part of developmental repair rather than treated as pathology.

Relational Capacity and Discernment

A central indicator of long-term recovery within the HQTP is the survivor's growing capacity to judge relationships more clearly. Rather than moving back and forth between urgently seeking closeness and pulling away from relationships to protect themselves, survivors gradually learn to assess safety, reciprocity, and emotional availability across interpersonal contexts.

Therapeutic work supports recognition of coercive dynamics, idealisation patterns, and abandonment sensitivity without collapsing into hypervigilance. Survivors develop the capacity to tolerate disappointment without self-erasure, sustain boundaries without guilt, and hold anger without relational rupture. These relational competencies emerge primarily through corrective relational experience rather than instruction alone.

Given the depth of attachment disruption within this population, ethical continuity planning is integral to treatment rather than a final administrative step. The objective is not independence through emotional detachment, but autonomy supported by relational availability. The HQTP rejects the binary of dependence versus disengagement. Instead, continuity is structured as access without obligation. Survivors are supported in internalising capacities for regulation, reflective functioning, and self-monitoring while retaining the option of professional support during periods of vulnerability. Therapy is decentralised rather than terminated, shifting from primary containment to consultative access.

Drawing conceptually from Linehan's DBT model, availability functions as a stabilising backdrop rather than a dependency structure (Linehan, 1993). Knowing that access exists reduces panic, promotes self-reliance, and paradoxically decreases over-utilisation. Support becomes a resource rather than the organising axis of identity.

Transitions Within the HQTP

The transition within the HQTP involves an intentional shift from structured, frequent sessions to flexible, needs-based engagement. This may include periodic check-ins, booster sessions, or re-entry during periods of increased stress or developmental change.

For survivors whose histories include abrupt relational rupture, disappearance, or conditional care, this approach avoids reenactment of abandonment while preventing consolidation of therapeutic dependency. The therapeutic relationship remains psychologically available without remaining structurally dominant.

Integration into Lived Autonomy

Integration beyond intensive therapy is reflected not in discharge status but in how survivors live. Increased tolerance of distress, adaptive help-seeking, relational stability, and coherent self-narrative signal functional recovery. Intermittent return to therapy is not conceptualised as relapse. Survivors may move through extended periods without contact and re-engage briefly when new material emerges. The HQTP treats this pattern as adaptive use of support rather than regression, reinforcing autonomy rather than fragility.

Clinicians remain responsible for maintaining ethical boundaries while ensuring continuity. Availability does not imply unlimited access, crisis substitution, or role diffusion. Clear agreements regarding scope, frequency, documentation, and escalation pathways remain essential. Supervision supports clinicians in differentiating healthy continuity from unconscious rescue dynamics or prolonged dependency maintenance. Ethical availability preserves survivor autonomy by maintaining a predictable structure rather than withdrawing relational presence.

Transition Toward Ethical Closure

As survivors consolidate integration and autonomy, the therapeutic relationship gradually shifts from central containment toward contextual support. The work does not conclude with termination, but with stabilised internal capacity and relational independence, supported by optional access.

The following chapter clarifies the ethical position from which this transition is held, addressing the limits of therapy, the meaning of endings, and the responsibility of clinicians to close treatment without recreating abandonment, coercion, or false finality.

Chapter Eighteen

Closing the Circle Without Closure

Continuity, Ethical Endings, and the Limits of Therapy

This chapter does not introduce new clinical techniques or treatment stages. It clarifies the ethical position from which the entire HQTP is held. The HQTP does not conclude with resolution, reunification, or psychological closure. It concludes with continuity.

Adult survivors of CPA-PA do not heal along linear trajectories, nor do they complete therapy in predictable phases. Their lives have been shaped by prolonged attachment disruption, coercive control, identity fragmentation, and systemic betrayal unfolding across critical developmental periods. Expecting a finite therapeutic endpoint risks reproducing the pressure, performance demands, and emotional invalidation that this work is designed to address.

The continuity-based clinical logic of re-entry, ethical availability, and planned access has already been established in Phase VI. What matters at this final point is not repetition of those procedures, but clarity about the ethical limits of therapy. Many of the injuries carried by adult survivors did not originate within the individual and cannot be repaired solely within the therapy room. Family law systems, child protection responses, educational institutions, mental health structures, and broader cultural narratives around loyalty, blame, and silence have all shaped survivor experience. Therapy may offer relational repair, integrative support, and meaning-making, but it does not restore stolen relationships, reverse systemic failure, or correct historical injustice. Naming those limits protects survivors from false therapeutic promises and protects clinicians from role drift.

For practitioners, the HQTP does not conclude with mastery. It concludes with responsibility. Work in this field requires ongoing supervision, reflective practice, ethical humility, and sustained awareness of professional limits. No clinician, regardless of experience or training, is immune to countertransference, institutional pressure, or blind spots when working with identity-level trauma. Supervision and peer consultation are not optional safeguards. They are structural components of ethical care.

The HQTP closes where it began: with a relationship. Not relationship as obligation, reconciliation, or compliance, but relationship as safety, meaning, and choice. Survivors are not required to forgive, reunify, or construct coherent narratives to be considered healed. Clinicians are not required to fix what others broke. This protocol, therefore, concludes not with an answer but with an ethical position. Adult survivors of child psychological abuse deserve care that is patient, non-coercive, and enduring. Clinicians deserve frameworks that protect clarity, integrity, and sustainability. Healing, when it occurs, unfolds not because therapy ends, but because safety continues.

Final Reflection on Practitioner Readiness

The practitioner-readiness findings presented earlier in this volume return here as a closing ethical reminder rather than a repeated training framework. Adult survivors of CPA-PA do not usually present as survivors of single-event trauma alone. Their histories more often involve disrupted identity formation, loyalty conditioning, moral injury, prolonged attachment rupture, relational threat, and systemic misrecognition organised across development.

For this reason, clinicians require an integrated framework capable of holding attachment disruption, developmental trauma, coercive control, nervous system dysregulation, identity formation, grief, and relational betrayal without reducing the survivor's presentation to isolated symptoms, diagnoses, or techniques. Practitioner readiness is therefore not an optional professional virtue within the HQTP. It is a clinical safeguard.

When clinicians are not adequately prepared, therapeutic harm may occur through misclassification, imposed meaning, premature insight, pressure toward relational outcomes, or the use of familiar modalities without sufficient phase discipline. The closing task is not to repeat the readiness framework already provided, but to restate its ethical function: clinicians must remain able to recognise this population accurately, tolerate ambiguity, use supervision, and protect survivor autonomy when systems, families, or the clinician's own anxiety press for speed.

At this closing point in the protocol, the clinical message is simple: accurate recognition protects treatment. As discussed earlier in this volume, one of the central practitioner-readiness risks identified through the UniSC findings is population misclassification. When adult survivors are understood only through symptom presentation, relational instability, anger, withdrawal, compliance, or diagnostic labels, the developmental pattern underneath may be missed.

Misclassification can lead clinicians to treat survival adaptations as pathology, attachment injury as resistance, grief as dysregulation, or coercive conditioning as personality structure. HQTP-informed practice requires clinicians to hold the survivor's symptoms within the broader developmental, relational, and coercive context before selecting interventions or drawing conclusions. Training must therefore be population-informed before it becomes modality-driven.

Theoretical Orientation and Treatment Coherence

The UniSC practitioner cohort identified a recurrent pattern of clinicians moving between therapeutic approaches without a coherent integrative framework. This was associated with inconsistent pacing, shifting treatment goals, and confusion regarding clinical direction. Survivors mirrored this experience, describing therapy as disorganised, contradictory, or destabilising when clinicians lacked theoretical clarity.

By the closing chapter, this point returns as an ethical reminder: clinicians require an integrated framework capable of holding attachment disruption, developmental trauma, coercive control, nervous system dysregulation, identity formation, grief, and relational betrayal without reducing the survivor's presentation to isolated symptoms or techniques. Cognitive and behavioural strategies remain useful tools, but only when embedded within a broader developmental and relational structure.

Survivors emphasised that symptom reduction alone did not produce meaningful recovery. Healing was associated with restoration of agency, narrative coherence, relational safety, internal psychological stability, and the capacity to live with greater autonomy. These outcomes require clinicians to work from a theoretically integrated position rather than from isolated techniques.

Avoiding the Modality Accumulation Trap

Another major practitioner theme identified in the UniSC study was the accumulation of certifications without corresponding improvement in clinical confidence or effectiveness. Practitioners reported attending numerous trauma workshops yet still feeling unprepared for alienation-related cases.

This protocol, therefore, prioritises depth of clinical competence over breadth of exposure to modalities. Training should strengthen the clinician's ability to pace therapy appropriately, recognise coercive dynamics, manage countertransference reactions, tolerate uncertainty, and maintain ethical boundaries in the absence of clear external validation or documentation.

The HQTP does not reject modality training. It places modality training within the phases of discipline, supervision, formulation, and survivor readiness. A clinician may be highly trained in multiple approaches and still cause harm if those approaches are applied too early, too forcefully, or without sufficient attention to coercive family dynamics, epistemic safety, and the survivor's capacity to pause.

Lifelong Learning as Ethical Responsibility

Survivors in the UniSC study frequently described histories of being misunderstood, dismissed, or harmed by previous therapeutic interventions. These experiences were associated with increased mistrust of mental health services and heightened sensitivity to clinical misattunement.

Practitioners simultaneously reported elevated emotional burden, exposure to extreme narratives, and risk of vicarious trauma when working in this field. Both datasets therefore support framing ongoing professional development and supervision not as an optional enhancement, but as an ethical responsibility. Effective clinicians in this field commit to continuous learning, reflective practice, regular supervision, and adaptation as research, advocacy, and systemic contexts evolve.

This commitment protects survivors from repeated misattunement and protects clinicians from isolation, over-identification, burnout, and role drift. Lifelong learning within the HQTP is not the pursuit of endless technique. It is the sustained practice of humility, restraint, supervision, and clinical integrity.

Clinical Readiness Over Professional Status

The UniSC findings also highlighted the harm caused when clinicians positioned themselves as experts over survivors' lived experiences. Survivors reported feeling silenced or overridden when professional authority replaced collaborative engagement.

The HQTP reframes expertise not as dominance of interpretation, but as the ability to create safety, maintain pacing, tolerate ambiguity, and protect survivor autonomy. Clinical readiness includes emotional maturity, ethical restraint, phase discipline, the capacity to hold complexity, and a willingness to slow down rather than rush to resolution.

Effective practitioners are not those who impose answers but those who can remain present amid uncertainty while supporting survivors in reclaiming authorship of their narratives. At this closing point, readiness is therefore not measured solely by professional status. It is demonstrated through accurate population recognition, ethical restraint, use of supervision, disciplined sequencing, and the clinician's capacity to protect survivor autonomy under pressure.

Epilogue

To Survivors and Clinicians

If you are an adult who lived through CPA-PA, it is important to say this clearly: nothing in this book exists to judge you, diagnose you, fix you, or prescribe what your life should look like.

This work exists because too many survivors have spent years being misunderstood, minimised, or required to explain themselves to systems and professionals who did not yet have the language to understand what this form of harm does over time.

If you recognised yourself in these pages, your reactions make sense. Relief, grief, anger, sadness, and exhaustion are not weaknesses. They are the residue of adaptation. Many of the traits you were taught to question were survival strategies.

Nothing here requires forgiveness, reconciliation, confrontation, or emotional resolution. There is no deadline for making sense of what happened. There is no correct timeline for healing.

Many survivors are exceptionally psychologically informed. This reflects years of analysis undertaken to survive. If you have found yourself explaining your own experience to professionals, you are not alone.

You are entitled to expect care that understands the developmental and relational complexity of what you lived through.

Meaningful Work for Clinicians

Clinicians who choose to work with adult survivors of CPA-PA are genuinely needed. This is demanding work, but it is also meaningful work. Survivors often arrive after years of being misunderstood, minimised, or harmed by systems that did not recognise the depth of what they had lived through. A thoughtful, well-paced, ethically grounded clinician can make an enormous difference. Your steadiness matters. Your willingness to keep learning matters. Your care matters more than you may ever fully know.

This field asks a great deal of practitioners. It requires emotional endurance, reflective capacity, ongoing professional development, and a commitment to supervision and self-care. These are not signs of weakness. They are part of what makes safe and sustainable practice possible. No clinician can carry this work alone, and no one should try. The answer is not withdrawal from the field, but connection within it. There are good people in this space. There are thoughtful clinicians, researchers, advocates, supervisors, and survivors working to build something better. When practitioners support one another, continue learning, and remain ethically anchored, the work becomes more sustainable and more effective.

The difficulties of this field should not deter clinicians from entering it. They should call forth preparation, humility, collaboration, and courage. Survivors need clinicians who are willing to stay present, think carefully, and work with integrity in areas that others may avoid. When good practitioners come together, the possibility for meaningful change expands far beyond the therapy room. It reaches families, services, systems, and future generations. Please do not underestimate the value of your presence. In a field shaped by silence, disbelief, and fragmentation, a careful and compassionate clinician may help turn the tide.

Free Kingdom

Therapy is not the performance of life. It is preparation. The idea of Free Kingdom comes from an analogy my daughter's violin instructor shared, explaining that scales are not the music. They are the disciplined foundation that allows a musician to play with freedom, confidence, and expression. Therapy serves a similar purpose. It helps to build regulation, self-trust, and boundaries so that life can be lived more freely beyond the therapy room.

Returning to therapy is not regression. It is maintenance. It is wisdom. Free Kingdom will look different for everyone. What matters is that life is no longer organised around coercion, fear, or survival, but around greater choice, steadiness, and self-possession. That freedom does not need to be built alone.

Having closed the main clinical and reflective arc of the book, the following section is included as a future-development note only. It outlines the proposed HQTP clinical training pathway without suggesting that the protocol may be applied outside existing professional scope, supervision, or jurisdictional requirements.

Future Development: HQTP Clinical Training Pathway

The publication of the HQTP represents the first stage in making this specialist treatment framework available to mental health practitioners working with adult survivors of CPA-PA and associated coercive-control dynamics. The next stage of this work will involve developing a structured HQTP clinical training pathway to support safe, ethical, and phase-consistent implementation.

This training pathway is intended to help clinicians engage with the protocol without becoming overwhelmed by the material's size, complexity, or emotional weight. It will not require practitioners to become experts in every modality discussed in this volume. Instead, the training will focus on understanding the HQTP clinical logic, recognising the population, identifying phase position, protecting survivor safety, avoiding premature intervention, using supervision, and applying existing clinical skills within the protocol's safeguards.

The proposed training pathway will begin with two levels.

Level One: HQTP Foundations Training will introduce the core concepts, including CPA-PA, CPA-PAA, CPA-PERA, epistemic injury, epistemic safety, the six-phase architecture, non-forensic treatment positioning, clinical pacing, common misclassification risks, and the principle of safety before depth.

Level Two: HQTP Applied Clinical Practice Training will focus on clinical implementation. This level will support practitioners to use the phase maps, decision trees, risk safeguards, contraindication indicators, supervision prompts, and survivor-facing explanations in practice. It will also address early session structure, formulation, crisis containment, recognition-linked destabilisation, grief readiness, trauma-integration readiness, boundary formation, contact decision-making, and long-term adaptation.

Future training development may include practitioner workbooks, clinical vignettes, supervision templates, fidelity and clinical-integrity checklists, consultation groups, and advanced training for clinicians working with abduction, extreme harm, litigation reactivation, practitioner threat exposure, and complex intergenerational presentations.

This future training pathway is being developed with the same ethical commitments that guide the HQTP itself: survivor dignity, clinical restraint, phase discipline, professional supervision, non-forensic treatment boundaries, and protection from retraumatisation. The aim is not to create a rigid, technique-driven program, but to support clinicians in applying the HQTP safely, coherently, and responsibly in real clinical settings.

Survivor Witness, Author Reflection, Visual Material, and Acknowledgments

The formal clinical protocol concludes with the preceding chapters, the epilogue, and a note on future development. The following end matter appears beside the HQTP rather than within the protocol's core treatment architecture. These materials are not clinical instructions, diagnostic tools, forensic evidence, case reports, or universal survivor pathways. They are included as survivor witness, author reflection, visual context, and acknowledgment of the people, relationships, places, and lived realities that helped shape the development of this work.

The HQTP remains the clinical treatment framework. The materials that follow are offered as companion reflections: human context for a protocol concerned with developmental harm, separation, recognition, safety, grief, identity, attachment, autonomy, recovery, reconnection, and hope.

Where names, images, survivor reflections, reunion photographs, or personal materials are included, they are included with permission where required and with deliberate ethical care. Their inclusion is not intended to constitute a legal finding, forensic conclusion, diagnostic conclusion, allegation, clinical evidence, or complete account of any person's history. They are offered as acknowledgment, witness, and hope.

Acknowledgment: Wombatised Inc

Thank you to Tania Clancy and the committee from Wombatised Inc, Southern Highlands, for generously allowing me (the author) to use their beautiful gallery space to write and edit the HQTP. This kindness helped create a visual place of reflection around the work, and I am deeply grateful. Thank you also for giving me permission to use the photos and write about your very special wildlife rescue organisation. Wombatised Inc is a volunteer wildlife rescue and rehabilitation group based in the Southern Highlands of NSW, covering Bowral, Mittagong, Berrima, Moss Vale, Hill Top, High Range, Bullio, and the northern villages of the Southern Highlands.

Wombatised Inc. rescues and rehabilitates sick, orphaned and injured wildlife, with members authorised to care for native animals under Wildlife Rescue South Coast, and it has a strong focus on education, conservation and community inclusion. To view and support more of the amazing work being done by the wildlife carers associated with Wombatised, please go to https://wombatised.org/ and also look out for their latest IMAX theatre documentary at:

https://www.k2studios.us/films-catalogue-1/a-tale-of-two-wombats "A Tale of Two Wombats," which follows the parallel lives of two young wombats growing up in very different environments. Dusty is raised by his wombat mother in the Australian bush, learning to navigate life in the wild. Bruce, on the other hand, is an orphan rescued, taken in, and lovingly cared for by his new human mum, Tania.

Through their contrasting experiences, this heartwarming and informative film explores the challenges Australian wombats face in the wild, the vital role of wildlife rescue, and the weird and wonderful world of the Australian outback. With gentle narration and rich visuals, this documentary invites families to learn about wombat behaviour, conservation, and the remarkable world of marsupials.

In a book concerned with harm, survival, care, repair, and protection, it felt fitting to acknowledge a community organisation devoted to rescuing and rehabilitating vulnerable wildlife. Wombatised offered a gentle reminder that recovery work, in all its forms, often depends on safe places, patient care, and people willing to help when others are injured, displaced, or unable to survive on their own.

The following two photographs are included as part of the human context of this protocol, not as clinical evidence or research material, but as an acknowledgment of the people, places, and quiet acts of support that helped bring this work to completion.

Alyse in the gallery, hand editing, July 2025. Alyse -20 years of volunteering in the NSW SES.

During the editing process, the author didn't have enough space to edit the 1,039-page HQTP document in 100-page parts, so Tania and the committee from Wombatised Inc kindly allowed her to hire their precious wombat gallery space.

Tania Clancy, professional wildlife rescuer and carer, with one of the orphaned, rescued juvenile wombats that Wombatised Inc look after.

Survivor-Contributed Reflections

The following survivor-contributed reflections are included to honour the role of lived-experience knowledge in clinical understanding. They are not presented as clinical protocols, diagnostic tools, forensic evidence, or universal survivor pathways. They are included to help clinicians understand how child psychological abuse in contexts of CPA-PA may be experienced from the inside. The HQTP remains the clinical treatment framework; these survivor voices sit beside it as witness, context, and humanising knowledge.

A Survivor Note to Clinicians

The following survivor-contributed reflection, written by Dawn McCarty (pictured on the front cover in the far-left photograph), was submitted for inclusion in the HQTP and is included with her permission. Dawn writes from the position of an adult survivor of CPA-PAA-related harm, including abduction, coercive control, and high-control religious influence. She also brings a professional lens shaped by criminology, cybersecurity, cult dynamics research, and forensic-pattern analysis.

This reflection is included as lived-experience material to help clinicians understand what may happen before a survivor can safely begin therapeutic work. For some survivors, documentation, timelines, records, language, and structured reflection become part of the process of trying to organise reality, recover voice, and prepare for clinical engagement. This contribution should not be read as a clinical protocol, a forensic assessment, a diagnostic tool, or a universal survivor pathway. It is one survivor's account of recognition, preparation, language-building, and the search for safety before treatment can begin.

Due to the lack of specialised professional support available to Dawn in relation to her trauma, a gap also identified by mental health practitioners in the associated PhD study, she later developed the DARE Frameworks. This survivor-authored, preclinical preparation framework was designed to help survivors recognise patterns of abuse, organise personal records and lived experience, recover language, and enter clinical treatment with greater clarity and confidence.

Dawn's work also reflects a pattern identified across the PhD survivor cohort, in which many adult survivors had studied CPA-PA and related literature to a very high level, sometimes beyond the knowledge of the clinicians they had consulted. In this respect, Dawn was not working outside the survivor pattern identified in the research; she was tracking closely with it. Like other highly informed survivors, she used study, pattern recognition, and lived experience to make sense of harm that had not been adequately recognised or treated by the professional systems around her.

Within the HQTP, DARE is referenced only as Dawn's lived experience and professional synthesis. It is not part of the HQTP phase architecture, nor is it a substitute for clinical formulation, supervision, risk assessment, or treatment. Rather, it illustrates a crucial point for clinicians: some survivors need a bridge before therapy can begin. Dawn's chapter explains why she had to build that bridge for herself and what clinicians may need to understand when a survivor arrives with notes, timelines, fragments, records, questions, and a story they have fought very hard to name. American spelling, original wording, and authorial style have been retained to preserve Dawn's voice. The wording has been retained as supplied and is included with Dawn's permission.

What I Needed Clinicians to Understand Before I Could Begin Therapy

By Dawn McCarty

I don't have many memories from before the rupture, but there is one I keep returning to: a day at the beach with my father.

I was four years old, running down the shore with my dad chasing after me. We had been building sandcastles with his mad sand-architect skills, and I kept carrying buckets of water to fill the moat. Then, with the wild logic of a happy child, I filled one last bucket, dumped it over his head, dropped the bucket, and ran.

He chased me with a pretend roar. I squealed as he caught me, swooped me up, and we fell into the waves laughing together. That is one of the memories I return to when I need to remember that my life did not begin with trauma. There are feelings the body remembers. His laugh, deep and rolling, lived in his chest. My joy lived in mine. It was the kind of joy a child only feels when her body knows she is safe. But then the unforeseen happened. I was violently taken from the safety of my father, and from the only world I ever knew. I was stolen by my mother and her new husband, who had designs on creating their own family. It was something my mother had not been interested in before.

Decades later, this memory would be confirmed when my former stepmother and aunt reached out to me and began filling in the blanks. They had photographs. They had stories. They had evidence of the day at the beach and of the family I had been part of before the rupture. I was not imagining it. I had been loved. I had belonged. I had been part of a stable family unit before the narrative changed.

My father was not asking me to choose sides, carry secrets, manage his emotions, or prove my loyalty. He was just my dad, and I was just his little girl, and the ocean was our playground. At the time, it was simply my life.

Then I was taken from it.

The abduction did not just move my body from one place to another. It severed me from the people, places, memories, names, and attachments that told me who I was. After that, a different story was installed. My father became dangerous or absent. My stepmother was called "his prostitute." Over time, my original family became irrelevant. My resistance became disobedience. My grief had nowhere to go because, according to the new story, nothing had been lost.

I was abducted at four years old.

Not by a stranger. By my mother, the same mother who had left my father and me almost two years earlier.

We lived in Canoga Park, California, when I was taken from my father and stepfamily. I was moved into a new life and assigned a new father before I had any power to question it. My father, who had loved me, searched for me, and existed as one of the earliest truths of my body, was recast as dangerous, absent, putative, or irrelevant.

My body recoiled after I was shoved into the getaway car and told that the strange man with the huge moustache was my "new daddy." From that moment on, I was forced to call this replacement father "Daddy." The false narrative was not explained to me as a lie. It was installed as reality.

More pieces of the new narrative were installed while we hid aboard a houseboat floating around San Diego Bay. A new family system was being constructed while the family I had just seen hours before was simultaneously being uninstalled as questionable, unsafe, or imaginary. By the time I was eight, a new religious narrative would be placed around the theft, one that made the rupture look holy, necessary, and permanent. One that reached into the eternities.

Inside that system, I did not experience my story as abuse.

I experienced it as reality.

I knew there was a rift between two worlds, and I held onto as many memories as I could. I locked them away for safekeeping. I was not allowed to remember the old version of me. I had been made into someone new, and I had to obey the new rules.

That is what child psychological abuse can do when it begins early enough and is reinforced by family, religion, silence, and time. It does not simply change what a child believes. It changes what a child is allowed to know.

For forty-four years, I lived inside a story that was not mine. I lived inside a false identity, a persona my body resisted every time I heard my mother say "your dad" and mean the man who had helped steal me from my real father. That phrase was not casual language. It was repetition. It was reinforcement. It was the daily training of my reality.

After forty-four years of wandering through that false identity, I finally found my father.

Meeting him again did not feel like an instant celebration or an ordinary reunion. It was terrifying. I had no idea what I was walking into. Was he the man I remembered from the beach, if that memory was even real anymore? Or was he the dangerous person I had been warned about for most of my life?

These were not small slights or ordinary denigrating comments. These were fear-inducing statements systematically injected into the world I was taught to inhabit. My mother once told me that if I ever met him, "*You better take a gun with you, just in case he is still dangerous*." I had grown up fearing the same man my body had once known as safety.

Her narrative tainted every step of the reunion process. Even when I tried not to share details or progress, even when I only told her what I thought might keep her calm, she continued trying to pull me back into her version of reality. So no, in the beginning, my father did not feel like evidence returning in human form. Not yet. He felt like a conflict between my heart, my mind, and my body. My heart yearned for him. My mind was overly cautious of him. My body hesitated at his touch.

I had two years to try to get to know him, and it was not enough time. He passed away just days before the second anniversary of our reunion. I was still learning how to be his daughter, which was nearly impossible without help.

I had been raised Mormon, and therapy was not something I understood as a resource. I had been taught to pray more, pray harder, endure more, and search myself for the reason I was struggling. Shortly after my first phone call with my father, my boss saw me unraveling emotionally and suggested I get therapy. At first, I thought she was saying I was mentally ill. I did not understand that therapy could be a place where someone helps you carry what has become too heavy to hold alone.

Eventually, I took her advice and set up my first session.

The problem was that when I got into the room, I had no idea what to do.

The therapist said, "Tell me about your childhood."

I almost laughed out loud. Which version of my childhood should I tell her about?

I do not think she had any idea what was about to be unloaded onto her. I started with finding my father, the father I had been abducted from as a child, and the conversation took on a path of its own. I thought maybe I had figured out how to do this therapy thing. But it became a lot of talking, a lot of trauma dumping, and no clear map.

What was the goal? What did she need to know? What was my responsibility? What was hers? What was therapy supposed to do with parental abduction, religious indoctrination, violence, attachment wounds, grief, identity suppression, and a lifetime of loyalty conditioning? I did not know how to ask those questions because I did not know those were the questions.

Did that first therapist help me? Yes. I learned tools to regulate myself. I learned to reframe some things differently. After several weeks, she believed I was suffering from complex PTSD and depression. But then what?

What do you do after a therapist knows about the abduction, the violence that occurred inside my mother's version of reality, and the years of abuse that followed? What do you share, and what do you keep to yourself? How much context is enough? How do you explain the part where you were nearly killed by a stepsister who hated you for calling her father "*Daddy*"? How do you explain that the word "Daddy" itself had been weaponized?

I did not know how to be a participating client.

Eventually, after about a year, I stopped going and tried to learn everything I could from my father and my three brothers. I lived in Washington State, and my father lived in Florida, so most of our relationship unfolded through phone calls and a few visits. My sons and I eventually decided to move closer to him, but just before we were ready to leave, my father passed away.

I felt robbed all over again.

Then, within a month of my real father's death, the replacement father died too. It felt like a vacuum opening beneath me, pulling me away from the restored life I had only just begun to reach.

I went back to the same therapist, hoping it would help, but again it became mostly me talking. We were not getting to the root of it. We were not talking about coercive control, attachment wounds, religious indoctrination, identity suppression, loyalty conditioning, or CPA-PAA. I would not begin hearing those terms until 2019, when I started doing my own research into this kind of trauma.

In that research, I began to realize that something had happened to me and to my father that was almost unspeakable in its betrayal. The betrayal had a life of its own. I felt rage and hatred toward my mother and her husband. I felt as if my entire life had been a lie, as if my real life had been stolen from me, as if my life with my father and brothers had been stolen from me. I could not forgive it. I could not even understand it yet.

I began to realize that my father had not been the dangerous one. My mother had been.

I started learning more about what many people call "parental alienation," which is more accurately understood as child psychological abuse. This was not a high-conflict relationship. This was the complete overhaul of a child's operating system.

In my grief, I set out to learn everything I could. I met more people like me, including Dr. Alyse Price-Tobler, and we began researching together and advocating for other survivors to discover their own stories.

I networked with other advocates, including when I became an associate producer for the Erasing Family documentary, where I first heard Robin Slade's song "Hey" during the credits. The first time I listened to it, I bawled. The song felt nearly identical to my story. I reached out to Robin's team and received permission to use the song in a video I created of my father and me seeing each other for the first time in forty-four years at Tampa International Airport.

That song gave shape to something I could not yet explain. It carried the ache of separation, the shock of recognition, and the impossible tenderness of finding someone who had been made unreachable but had never stopped being real.

When I saw him, the installed story began to crack.

Not all at once. Trauma rarely releases its architecture that cleanly. But something in me knew: this man was not the monster I had been taught to fear. He was my father. And some part of me had known that all along.

That recognition did not make me instantly free.

It made me responsible for finding the truth.

At the time I reunited with my father, I was a criminologist and cybersecurity specialist. I knew how to read patterns. I knew how to document evidence. I knew how to reconstruct timelines, examine inconsistencies, preserve records, and notice the difference between a story and a system. In my professional life, I could see what other people missed.

But I could not yet fully read the crime scene of my own childhood.

That gap matters.

Without a map, a survivor may appear competent, articulate, even professionally accomplished, while remaining internally trapped inside the reality that was installed in childhood. I could analyze risk in other systems, but not in the family and religious systems that had shaped me. I could organize evidence, but not yet organize the truth of my own life. I could recognize manipulation in theory, but not always when it had been spoken in the voice of my mother, my church, or the people I had been trained to obey.

That was not a personal failure.

It was the injury.

By the time I began trying to seek help, I was not walking into therapy as a blank page. I was walking in as a person whose page had been written over.

I thought therapy meant talking. So, I talked. I described symptoms. I described conflict. I described my mother, my father, my marriage, my anxiety, my depression, my confusion. But I did not yet have the architecture. I did not know how parental abduction, coercive control, religious indoctrination, identity suppression, loyalty conditioning, and CPA-PAA fit together. I was still justifying parts of it because the installed story had not fully released its grip.

I did not know what a trauma-informed clinician should have been listening for.

I did not know there should have been stabilization before excavation. I did not know there should have been attention to my nervous system, my body, my attachment wounds, my grief, my relational template, or the way my voice disappeared when I got too close to the truth.

No one handed me a map.

So, I started looking for one.

I read. I researched. I watched videos. I listened to survivors, clinicians, cult experts, trauma educators, and people who had language I did not yet have. I compared what I was learning to my own records, memories, family documents, photographs, and the stories that had been handed to me as truth. I connected with Dr. Alyse Price-Tobler, whose clinical understanding helped me recognize what should have happened in therapy, what should have been named, and what kind of treatment this population actually needs.

More than once, I remember thinking: nothing like that ever happened for me. There was no map.

No one oriented me to trauma treatment. No one explained what my goals could be. No one helped me understand why I was bringing fragments instead of a clean narrative. No one told me that if my reality had been attacked, then my first task might be reality recovery. No one told me that if my voice had been conditioned into silence, then speaking in therapy was not simply disclosure. It was reclamation.

That is the gap I had to write into.

I did not write the DARE Frameworks because I thought survivors needed another workbook.

I wrote them because when I finally understood that I needed help, I did not know how to receive it.

I did not know what therapy was supposed to be or what I should be prepared to do in those sessions. I did not know what a clinician was supposed to ask. I did not know what I was allowed to bring into the room, what counted as relevant, what counted as trauma, or how to explain a life that had been rewritten before I was old enough to spell my own name.

Over time, as I began speaking with other survivors, I realized I was not the only one carrying harm I did not yet know how to measure.

Many of us knew something had happened. We knew our lives had been shaped by abuse, manipulation, estrangement, coercive control, religious pressure, or family narratives that did not hold up under examination. But we did not yet understand how deep the damage went. We did not know how far it reached into our minds, our bodies, our nervous systems, our relationships, our sense of self, and even the way trauma can echo through generations.

When I tried to explain my own process, I kept returning to the same language: I had to go through a discovery phase. I had to find the records. I had to gather the evidence. I had to compare what I had been told with what I could verify. One discovery led to the next, and then the next, until the installed story began to collapse under the weight of the truth.

That process did not happen quickly. It unfolded over roughly a decade of research, recovery, documentation, reflection, survivor conversations, clinical conversations, and the slow, painful work of becoming someone I could finally recognize as myself.

As I shared what I had been doing, Andrew Folkler, who had spent countless hours listening to me reconstruct my story, asked me to write it down as a process other survivors could refer to.

That is how DARE became more than my private investigation.

It became the structure I wish I had been handed when I first realized something was wrong.

The DARE Frameworks came from that gap.

They are not therapy. They are not a diagnosis. They are not the Healing Qualia Treatment Protocol, and they are not a substitute for clinical treatment.

They are the bridge I needed before I could fully enter clinical work.

They are a survivor-authored pre-clinical preparation framework designed to help a person like me recognize the pattern, gather the evidence of their own life, name what happened with accuracy, begin separating installed beliefs from discovered truth, and arrive in the therapeutic space with language instead of only fragments.

I built them because I needed a way to get from "something is wrong with me" to "something happened to me."

That difference matters.

A clinician can work with a survivor who has begun to locate the pattern. A clinician can go deeper when the survivor has language for the injury. A clinician can hold grief more safely when the survivor has begun to understand what was lost. But many survivors of this form of abuse never make it to that room, or they arrive without knowing what they are carrying.

Some survivors bring timelines because memory was attacked.

Some bring documents because they were told their reality was not real.

Some bring structure because chaos was used against them.

Some bring frameworks because they are trying to hold together something that still feels too large to say out loud.

If you are a clinician receiving a survivor like me, I need you to understand this: the structure is not necessarily avoidance. The documentation is not necessarily obsession. The forensic language is not necessarily distance from feeling. Sometimes it is the only bridge strong enough to carry the survivor from fragmentation into relationship.

For me, the evidence did not replace healing.

It made healing possible.

It gave me enough ground to stand on so I could begin to grieve. It gave me enough language to tell the truth. It gave me enough internal authority to stop asking whether I was allowed to know what had happened to me.

Before the healing could begin, I had to unseal the crime scene.

I had to find the child who had been taken, the father who had been erased, the name that had been overwritten, the voice that had been trained into silence, and the self that had survived beneath the installation.

Then I had to build the map I wish someone had handed me.

That is what DARE is.

Not the treatment.

The threshold.

The place where a survivor begins to arrive with enough truth, enough language, and enough self-recognition to finally be an active participant in their healing journey and be met by a mental health professional who can quickly understand what has happened.

Thank you for reading, Dawn.

Who is Dawn McCarty?

Dawn McCarty is a #1 international bestselling author, criminologist, cybersecurity expert, cult specialist, and survivor of CPA-PAA. Her work sits at the intersection of criminology, cybersecurity-informed threat analysis, coercive control, cultic family systems, institutional betrayal, and survivor-authored forensic recovery.

Dawn's personal history includes childhood abduction, grooming, severe family violence, coercive narrative control, and the weaponization of the Mormon religion within a high-control family system. After decades of forced separation, she reunited with her father, a moment that became both personally transformative and professionally clarifying. Her lived experience now informs her forensic approach to understanding how children can be psychologically separated from a safe parent, installed into a false reality, and later forced to reconstruct identity, memory, attachment, and voice from fragmented evidence.

Professionally, Dawn brings more than 25 years of experience in cybersecurity, threat assessment, behavioral analysis, and evidence management. Her academic background includes four degrees in: Criminal Justice, a BS in Psychology of Victimology, a MS in Crime Scene and Evidence Management, a BS in Computer Science and Information Systems, and an MBA in Cybersecurity. This rare combination allows her to examine abuse not only as trauma, but as a patterned system of control: a human threat architecture that can be mapped, documented, and eventually dismantled.

Dawn is the creator of the DARE Frameworks, a survivor-authored pre-clinical preparation framework designed to help survivors document evidence, identify coercive patterns, recover their narrative, examine installed beliefs, and prepare for deeper clinical work. The DARE Frameworks are not therapy, diagnosis, or a substitute for treatment. They are a bridge into clinical readiness, helping survivors arrive with language, structure, and a clearer understanding of the crime scene they have been living inside.

Dawn is also the founder of Securing Everything and Thrivers Speak® Events, a survivor-led platform created to center lived experience, professional insight, and public education. A component of her expertise includes identifying behavioral patterns across digital safety, family protection, and coercive systems. Her current work is centered on criminology, cyber-informed behavioral analysis, predator profiling, forensic recovery, and the development of survivor-authored tools for understanding CPA-PAA, coercive family systems, cult-like parenting, and institutional betrayal.

Her current body of work includes Unsealing the Crime Scene: A Forensic Roadmap for Survivors of Child Psychological Abuse, Coercive Control, and Institutional Betrayal and her forthcoming memoir, Sealed to My Abductor: A True Crime Thriller on Coercive Control, Cultic Family Systems, and the Weaponization of the Mormon Religion. Through her writing, speaking, forensic frameworks, and survivor-led advocacy, Dawn helps survivors, clinicians, families, and professionals better understand the architecture of coercive control and the long-term impact of psychological abduction.

Contact Dawn at https://sealedtomyabductor.com.

A full video related to the reunification image below has been included to illustrate the emotional significance of Dawn's reunion with her father after 44 years of separation. Dawn was abducted in childhood by her mother after several years of no contact. Newly resurfaced witnesses, including Dawn's former stepmother and step-aunt, have since provided additional details about the day she disappeared. Dawn was on her way to the babysitter while her stepmother was preparing to leave for work, and her father was already at work.

Dawn was missing for 16,060 days, and what the evidence has shown is that she was not an isolated child in a fragile or disconnected home. She was part of a loving family unit, cared for by her father, stepmother, extended family, and community members who loved her as their own.

Her disappearance did not traumatize only Dawn and her father. It ruptured an entire extended family system. The people who loved her searched, grieved, wondered, and carried the unanswered wound of her absence for more than four decades.

The clinical implications of eye contact, nervous-system safety, and supported reunification are discussed earlier in the HQTP in the section on contact decisions and reunification work. Dawn's reunion video is included here as a lived-experience illustration of how profound, emotional, and human these moments can be when long-separated family members are finally able to see one another again. Dawn and her father reunite - https://www.youtube.com/watch?v=1b2nZ6h4Rbg

Photos of Dawn McCarty and her beloved father, Patrick Charles McCarty

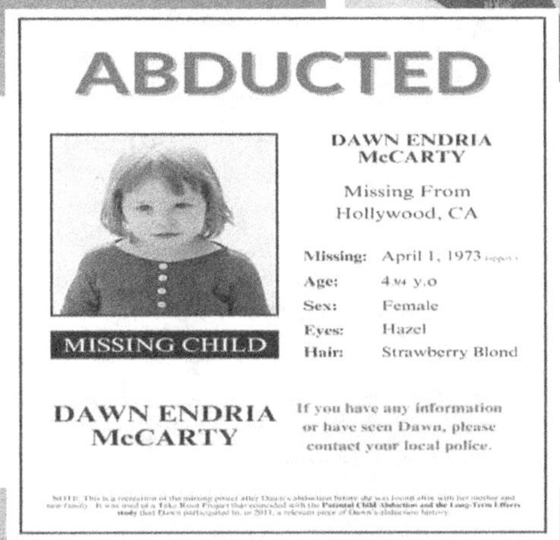

This photo is of Dawn and her father reuniting after her mother and her new husband had abducted her illegally from her father 44 years earlier. She then attempted to alienate Dawn against him for the rest of her life. As you can see, it didn't work.

This is a photo of Dawn speaking about her illegal abduction while advocating against CPA-PAA. At this time, she was serving as Chair of the National Parents Organisation in Florida.

The last photo of Dawn's father before he passed, 2 years after the reunion. R.I.P

12.04.1946 - 01.19.2018.

A Formerly Alienated Child Reflects on Recognition, Reconnection, and Life After Alienation

By Andrew Folkler

The following survivor-contributed essay, written by Andrew Folkler, pictured in the far-right photograph on the front cover, was included in the HQTP. Andrew writes as a formerly alienated child reflecting on recognition, reconnection, cycle-breaking, and life after alienation.

American spelling, original wording, and authorial style have been retained to preserve Andrew's voice. The wording has been retained as supplied and is included with Andrew Folkler's permission.

This reflection is included as lived-experience material to help clinicians understand the internal world of a child who appeared functional from the outside while living inside alienation, coercive control, and fear. It should not be read as a clinical protocol, a forensic assessment, a research finding, or a universal survivor pathway. It is one survivor's account of meaning-making, recovery, and long-term adaptation.

Who is Andrew Folkler?

I am a formerly alienated child. I was separated from my mother for twelve and a half years, beginning shortly after my parents' divorce and ending when I was eighteen. As of May 2026, I have been free from that separation for thirteen years, about the same length of time as the alienation itself.

I am writing this for clinicians who will sit across from children and adults who have lived something like what I have lived, and who need a closer view of what is happening behind the behavior they will see in the room.

The alienating figure in my case was my stepmother. My father was present throughout and enabled the alienation through passivity and a prolonged failure to see what was in front of him. Growing up, I was told that my mother was a liar and a cheater. My mother had an affair, which was framed as the unforgivable sin, stoking my hurt and anger over the separation of the family.

The current literature on parental alienation does not adequately support clinicians, attorneys, or targeted parents in understanding the mind of the alienated child. Most of what clinicians can find in print describes alienation from the outside: the alienating parent's tactics, the targeted parent's grief, the legal frameworks, and the theory surrounding attachment systems.

The ambiguity of the alienated household leaves room for misdirection, preconstructed narratives, and complete conviction in a version of reality that is misaligned with the truth. The alienated child becomes a true believer to ensure their own protection.

What follows is organized around five interior states, each anchored by a moment in my own life. The essay does not move chronologically. Instead, it moves from the inside out.

1. The Child Has Nowhere Else to Go

When I was around ten years old, I ran away from home.

It started with an argument. There was an event at our church that morning, and I wanted to go. I had been recovering from being sick, but I felt well enough by the time I woke up. My stepmother said no despite my protests. It did not take long for her to start yelling, and it ended with her shouting, "If you live in my house, you live by my rules. If you don't want to listen, then you can get out."

So I walked out the door.

My stepmother probably expected me to pout outside and come back when I was cold or hungry. Instead, I decided to walk to a friend's house. He lived in the rural areas outside town, and I had slept over there several times. At his house, things were loose and easy. I could breathe without feeling like I was being judged all the time. The problem was that I did not know his address or the way there. I figured I was smart enough to find it, but I was not.

After walking about four miles, I cut across a fairground and came out somewhere I did not recognize. A few adults pulled over to offer rides, but I reassured them that I knew where I was going. Eventually, a woman named Tasha stopped me and said I could either get in her car or she would call the police. Not wanting to go home, I got in. It did not take Tasha long to realize that I didn't know where to go, so she drove me to her house. She let me play with her infant son while she called the police.

The officer came shortly after and drove me home without saying much. The whole neighborhood had gathered in the yard. My father, who worked ninety minutes away, had driven back. My stepmother was in the middle of the crowd, sobbing while surrounded by mothers in the neighborhood who were trying to console her.

I got out of the police car, gave her a one-armed hug, and went inside.

For a long time, I thought of that day as an immature thing I did when I was angry. At face value, it seems like a story about a child angry enough to rebel against a parent's disciplinary actions. I was placed in church camp afterward, where the youth pastor would sometimes talk with me, hoping to understand what had led me to behave that way. Everyone, myself included, focused on the incident. Andrew was angry about not going to church, so he tried to run away.

What people didn't know was that this reaction was the culmination of stress factors that had built up too quickly, and I didn't have the emotional guidance or support to understand it. My stepmother's disciplinary methods were always draconian, and stepping out of line resulted in severe punishments, including yelling, being insulted, being hit with household objects, and loss of privileges. Combined with other family conflicts, I was looking for every opportunity to stay out of the house.

That morning, I was running toward somewhere I was allowed to just be a kid. I was tired of being told that I could not make decisions for myself. I didn't want to keep being insulted, and I hated that I was not as lucky as the other kids in school. Ironically, had you asked me in that moment whether I wanted to go to my alienated mother, I would have still said no. I believed at the time that her home was worse.

Every time I was punished for misbehaving, I was told that I was acting like my mother. Specifics were never needed for these kinds of insults. As a child, I would be threatened with being sent to her house, where I could "learn to lie and cheat just like your mother," and my imaginative mind filled in the gaps.

I was scared of it for all of my childhood. I would cry and beg not to be sent there because the thing I was taught to value most was my stepmother's approval. The alienating parent does not degrade the targeted parent twenty-four hours a day. The moments are chosen for their greatest effect. What targeted parents often don't realize is that the alienating parent wants them to vanish completely, and that is not possible when they are top of mind.

As a child, I had nowhere else to go but home. As I got older, I repeatedly got in trouble for not abiding by family curfew rules. Going home always felt dangerous. If my stepmother was around, she could erupt like a volcano over the most trivial things.

Since I had nowhere else to go, I had to learn how to adapt to that environment. I learned to read her emotions and anticipate what she wanted. When family members engaged in gossip, I would loyally tell her what I had heard. This was the only option I had to minimize the consequences of noncompliant behavior.

2. Orderly Does Not Equal Safety

From the outside, the household looked like a happy home. The house was tidy and regularly held family parties during the holidays. We played outside often, got straight A's in school, and were active in the youth wrestling team. If a neighbor had been asked to describe us, they would have said we were a normal family.

Underneath that facade was an atmosphere of tension, and you learned to read it the way you read weather. My stepmother's temperament was volatile, and she was prone to emotional outbursts that targeted everyone in her path. Anytime she saw something that didn't align with her expectations, she perceived it as a threat and accused whoever she thought was responsible of attempting to undermine her.

If our desks were too cluttered with school supplies, she would sweep everything to the floor. If we were tasked with cleaning the house and she found a missed spot of dirt, she would ask my brother and me to do it all over again. There was no room for nuance or discussion. Any attempt to justify or argue my position was immediately shut down by more yelling and violence, making it clear that I had no say.

Much of my academic achievement as a child could be attributed to my stepmother. As an early childhood educator, she pushed me to read widely and practice math until it was second nature. Due to complications with transferring records from a private kindergarten to a public school in Michigan, I was supposed to be held back to first grade. My stepmother pushed me hard, with a wooden spoon always beside her on the table, and I skipped first grade to join students my age.

She was always proud to tell people that she was the reason for my academic success, saying that these two young boys, abandoned by their mother, led her to step in selflessly and educate us into young men. As a child, I believed this narrative and would actively tell people the same thing. For school assignments that involved sharing role models and sources of inspiration, my stepmother was always at the center.

As a young kid, my lack of experience in the world led me to assume this was what life was like for everyone. I had nothing to compare it to beyond what I passively observed in how other kids talked about home.

Talk of my mother was on and off. Whenever we were caught misbehaving, my mother was blamed for it, even though she was across the United States and had no contact with us. As a child, I knew that my parents' marriage ended with an affair, so having someone to blame made the separation easier to process. However, anger is a taxing emotion, and what I wanted most as a child was to move on and live my life.

Digging up the past was exhausting. When it came to telling my personal story to others, I had a script in my head that covered all the main points.

My mom cheated on my dad, so they got divorced. Then my dad met my stepmother, and she saved me. She is my true mother, and my biological mother just doesn't care about me.

I learned early that if you drip just enough traumatic material, other people become uncomfortable and change the topic. That tactic served me well when people asked about that part of my life. I was able to shut down countless conversations. At face value, there was no way for them to know it was not the full truth. I was unaware of it as well.

My father was present for some of my stepmother's behavior and assumed that what he was seeing was her temperament. After outbursts, he would find us quietly and tell us to take what was useful and find the nuggets of wisdom. The rest was noise to be discarded. He meant this as comfort, though it led us to believe the same assumptions he had about her.

He did not recognize any of it for what it was until the marriage ended and the behavior turned toward him. By then we were grown. He carries that recognition now as retroactive guilt he does not want to discuss directly. His pattern of placating contributed in its own way, leading us to assume she was just a strict parent looking out for our best interests.

The worst of this appeared when we moved to Singapore. In 2010, my stepmother was diagnosed with Stage 1 breast cancer and underwent months of chemotherapy while my father cared for her. The chemo amplified her outbursts, creating an environment in the house that was more hostile than ever before. I was simultaneously scared of losing my mother figure while hoping to be free of it. While I did not wish death on her, I found myself mentally preparing for it, while silently hoping it would be the end of her tyrannical behavior.

And despite the yelling, violence, and psychological manipulation, I still thought in those moments that it was better than a mother who had abandoned me.

3. Alienation and Its Impact on My Adulthood

When I was sixteen and living in Singapore, I had a girlfriend for two weeks.

Her name was Celine. She has been anonymized for privacy. She was quiet, funny, an artist, and a dancer. She lived close by, and we would walk to school together in the mornings. Being in my first relationship, I was struck by how sweet she was to me. We had been dating for two weeks before my stepmother found out.

After an hour of being smacked and yelled at, she told me that I was "throwing my education away for a slut." Then she demanded my phone so she could call her. In that moment, I wanted to fight back, but I couldn't. I gave her my phone and watched her call Celine, screaming and demanding that she break up with me. After she hung up, she handed the phone back to me and told me that if I did not break up with her by the following Monday, she would hurt her, and Celine would know it was because of me.

We broke up that Monday. I stood there deflated and said that I could not protect her from my stepmother. Afterward, I chose not to date, despite moments when I felt mutual interest in another girl. In my mind, I would be endangering my potential partner by bringing her near my stepmother.

For years after leaving Singapore, I was reluctant to let anyone get close. Even though my stepmother was no longer present, her voice still lived in my head. I was afraid that the hurts of my past would be too much. For a time, I imagined a romantic relationship with me would be like having a vase of freshly cut flowers, pretty at first, but slowly dying. For years, I didn't trust myself to be a capable, bold enough man who could stand up for and protect my partner.

Professionally, I was also adrift. In Singapore, I had earned a full-ride engineering scholarship with monthly stipends, internships at major firms, and a guaranteed position after graduation. It would have been a smooth entry into a strong career, but I had to forfeit it.

When my father was issued divorce papers by my stepmother, she began taking steps to pit the family against him. I was eighteen and old enough to pay close attention to the family conflict, discern who was lying or embellishing, and observe with my own eyes. As part of the divorce, my stepmother moved in with her affair partner and told me that we would be living with her. She expected me to transfer my monthly stipend to her account for safekeeping, and she expected us to contribute financially to the house.

At that moment, I was starting to realize that nothing I did in my life would ever truly be a success I could own while my stepmother was around. Despite my financial literacy, she insisted on controlling my money. My professional goals did not matter because they were not as flattering to her image as attending a more advanced college. Her hypocrisy in having an affair while condemning my mother for over a decade was also apparent. As a young adult, I was able to better understand the situation and recognize the attempts to manipulate me.

I became more wary, pretending to be understanding as I watched my family tear itself apart. Emotionally, I was deeply hurt because I had hoped for some kind of reconciliation. The impending divorce led to a climactic moment in the family dissolution, where we had to make an impossible choice.

My father needed medical attention in the United States that he could not afford in Singapore, but he could not do it alone. My brother and I could not safely stay with my stepmother without her taking control over our finances, relationships, and lifestyle.

It was not an easy decision. This was a woman I had called Mom for about twelve and a half years and who I believed, with complete conviction, loved me more than my mother. When deciding whether to leave Singapore and return to the United States, I thought about a few things.

First, I thought about how my stepmother treated Celine. I was bitterly angry about that event, and I knew that I could never have a family of my own with her involved.

Second, I thought about how strange it was that she was spreading false rumors about my father, even though I could see the truth. I was around my father often, so being told that he was abusing drugs and drinking excessively was clearly false.

Third, I knew my scholarship would be used against me. She had often borrowed money from me and never paid it back. If I were given stipends, she would find a way to seize control of them.

Fourth, her temperament was so caustic that I could not stand to stay any longer. I thought about all the times she would explode in anger and how no amount of patience or calm would quell her fury.

Fifth, I knew the severity of my father's situation and feared further decline.

Leaving meant making huge sacrifices. I had friends and family I was leaving behind, and leaving Singapore would result in being labeled as a deserter because Singapore has mandatory National Service for all male citizens and permanent residents. Going back to Singapore now would result in a prison sentence unless I agreed to pay a fine of up to $10,000 SGD.

The worst part was that my youngest brother would not be coming with us. He was born to my stepmother and, under the Hague Convention, would require her consent to travel internationally. Risking an international parental kidnapping charge was out of the question, even though we knew she would alienate him from my father, brother, and me.

When I returned to the United States, I was starting from nothing again. I had to figure out who I wanted to be after being the dutiful son my stepmother had cultivated for over a decade. Leaving Singapore unannounced brought a great deal of anger from my stepmother's side.

While blocking her on Facebook, I saw my mother's name on the list of blocked accounts. In a moment of impulse, I thought to myself, "I am a grown adult, and I can decide who I want in my life or not."

And then I unblocked her.

The next day, my mother sent me a message asking how I was doing and whether I needed help.

4. Reflection on Alienation

Looking back at the process of reunification, I would not say it was one singular big moment, but rather a buildup of incidents where bitter experiences with my stepmother led me to want to get away. Throughout the beginning of the divorce process and the return to the United States, I didn't think of my mother. I was so focused on getting away that she was an afterthought. She had not been in my life for so long that I did not even consider her a potential factor.

Since we were no contact for the majority of the alienation, I didn't have a backlog of unhappy memories with my mother. All I had were fearmongering stories my stepmother would say when she was upset.

Being old enough to know that my stepmother was lying helped me realize that I could not trust her with basic things in our day-to-day family life. Her promises were intended to hook me in and keep me close, so I would remain useful and compliant.

One of the first major changes I noticed was in my sugar consumption. I often ate sugary foods when I was stressed, but after a few months away from my stepmother, I cut down on sugar dramatically. While I still enjoyed the occasional dessert, I didn't feel the same cravings I had during my childhood.

Since I had made the decision to leave my stepmother, I was open to the idea of talking with my mother. When she reached out to me on Facebook, I was not afraid to test the waters and see what kind of person she was. We kept things casual and avoided heavy emotional conversation. My mother, being a practical person, looked to help by buying us things we could use around the house, such as dishes, cups, and clothes, and by giving us cash to get our lives started.

It was a strange feeling to be talking to her again. There was a taboo element. In a way, it felt like a way to get back at my stepmother for all the mistreatment. However, I slowly came to realize that what my stepmother said did not align with who my mother was. My mother's patience and easy-going attitude made it easier to open up to her. She never applied pressure and did not attempt to rush the relationship.

The first time I saw my mother in person after twelve and a half years was in December 2013, when we visited her home in Las Vegas. I didn't know what to expect, but I was surprised that our reunion was simple and quiet. She had planned activities for us, interspersed with time to relax at home. Vegas has no shortage of sights to see and restaurants to eat at. Yet she did not push us to do anything we didn't want to do, nor did she ask me to process anything, account for anything, or feel anything in particular.

At one point, she said, "I couldn't be there for you back then, but I can be now."

I wanted, in those early visits, to be an observer. I did not want to judge her without seeing for myself who she actually was. I understood her better through her actions than through anything she said directly, watching how she was with my half-siblings and how she lived day to day.

I didn't find myself afraid of my mother. I was more afraid of being disappointed that she was not what I expected her to be. That fear subsided over time, and I quickly realized I had been duped. I never showed my mother the anger I felt, but held it in for a long time. It was strong, fiery anger, but focused like a blue flame. I didn't want to stand idly and pretend it was all past me.

With the ongoing alienation from my youngest brother, I realized how much my stepmother had manipulated me and twisted the truth, leading me to intensely desire control of my life. As the years went by, I found myself identifying with characters like Heathcliff and the Count of Monte Cristo. The anger I felt culminated in a ten-year plan built on the vision of acquiring wealth and reconnecting with my youngest brother in Singapore.

Workaholism became part of my new normal. Though I dropped out of college, I spent thousands on books, online courses, and events to develop my professional skills, hoping it would open doors to my fantasy of becoming a business mogul.

This was juxtaposed with advocacy work on alienation. At first, I thought my experiences were unique, but once I started learning about the psychology behind coercive control, alienation, and psychological abuse, I found myself sinking deeper into bitterness.

Viktor Frankl spoke of this same occurrence in Holocaust survivors, where after the war, they entered a phase of disillusionment. The world needed to pay for its crimes against me. However, this only kept me in a state of perpetual frustration and exhaustion. I would push myself to the limit to speak on behalf of alienated children so that other parents would understand what their child might have been experiencing. Through me, parents would project their deepest insecurities, and I would try to carry it all, thinking that I was helping.

Through these alienated parents, I had hoped to find the answer to reunite with my youngest brother, but instead, I was powerless to solve their problems. I repeatedly burned myself out in the alienation community, stepping in to speak and support alienated parents and then disappearing online for several years.

Each time, I found myself feeling pulled back with a sense of obligation. I had experienced hardship, and it needed to mean something. My mother was dealt a grave injustice, and I wanted to make sure it was not in vain.

By 2020, I had established some communication with my youngest brother, and we would talk on and off about life, tabletop games, and our hopes for the future. While it was not a face-to-face reunification, it was leagues better than having no contact for five years.

Around that time, my father recommended to me *The Count of Monte Cristo* by Alexandre Dumas. At the time, I had only read *Wuthering Heights* and thought Heathcliff was the closest representation of what I had experienced: lost love due to circumstances outside my control, mistreatment as a child, leaving and returning with exorbitant wealth to reclaim what was lost. Granted, that story ends in sorrow, considering its Gothic origins, but I was arrogant enough to think I would shirk the same ending.

The Count of Monte Cristo forced me into deep reflection, as though Dumas himself reached through space and time to shake me by the collar. The book is a revenge story where a young man with a bright future is taken on his wedding day and sent to prison on a false allegation of being a Napoleon supporter. For fourteen years, he endures prison, where he learns advanced mathematics, science, linguistics, and the location of buried treasure on the island of Monte Cristo.

The young man escapes, finds the treasure, and assumes the persona of the Count of Monte Cristo, enacting a plan to take revenge on those who imprisoned him. Towards the end of the book, a young boy is inadvertently killed, leading the Count to question his role in enacting justice. He realizes he was never going to reunite with his ex-fiancée, and that his only path forward was to spend time with those he loved and leave the rest behind.

My ten-year plan was supposed to give me a level of control that would help me feel safe and secure in the face of future threats, while reuniting with my brother, finding love, and ensuring I was financially well off.

And yet, three years into that plan, I was able to reestablish contact with my alienated brother without having to pay for a flight to Singapore. All it took was patient communication, the very same style that my mother used with me.

I did not feel truly free from the alienation, even after leaving my stepmother behind, until I let go of the ten-year plan. Once I did, I felt like I was finally able to be my own person. The ten-year plan was a reaction to the harm and abuse of my stepmother, and I did not want her behavior to dictate what my life would be like, especially at a reactionary level.

In 2021, I met the woman I would eventually marry. Though I had the courage to start dating again, I quickly found that I had much to learn about healthy relationship dynamics through trial and error. Fortunately, I was able to find a path forward that worked for my family. Eventually, we had a daughter together, fulfilling one of my biggest dreams in life: becoming a father.

5. Repair and Healing

My brother reunited alongside me after going through the same alienation from my stepmother. The major differences in his experience were that he was two years younger than me and was often the scapegoat for my stepmother's rage. His response was far different from mine. Where I moved toward my mother, feeling like I owed her something, pushing myself to give her someone to be proud of, and making repair a duty I was responsible for completing, he withdrew.

His behavior has been performative, never fully relaxing or embracing my mother's side of the family. If you asked him whether he feels connected to her, I am sure he would say he is. However, his actions show that he spends most of his time now with his fiancée's family rather than ours. Since getting married, he has changed his last name, and for the last few years, he has only talked to both our parents three to four times a year.

Two people with similar histories of alienation can encounter similar reunification opportunities and respond in different ways.

The relationship my mother and I have now is not a restoration of something that was interrupted. It is a new relationship built on who we are as individuals in the present moment.

My mother has lupus, and she has lived with it for decades. I cannot draw a clean line between the alienation and her health, but I can see that she carried an enormous weight for a long time. One of my biggest fears is losing her before we have had enough time, and frankly, I don't think there will ever be enough time. I watch her with my daughter, knowing these experiences will be the best possible way for her to build something new in our relationship that cannot be taken away. My daughter is too young to understand what she is receiving, but she is receiving the attention and delight of a grandmother's love that has been waiting a long time to have somewhere to go.

Three generations in the same room.

My youngest brother is still in Singapore. He is still alienated from my father but has restored communication with me and my other brother. My brother's wedding reception in May 2026 opened an opportunity for my youngest brother to visit from Singapore, allowing us to see him face to face for the first time.

However, he staunchly refuses to speak to my father, even though he is aware of my advocacy in the alienation movement. He enforces it himself now, which is what long-duration alienation eventually produces once the child grows out of the house. I don't know if he will ever reunite with my father, but I walk a delicate line when we talk about the topic.

I have been free from the alienation for thirteen years as of this writing, the same length of time as the alienation itself. I do not know exactly what that symmetry means. My memories of my childhood are fragmented and foggy. While I know I experienced a great deal of abusive behavior, I only remember the major moments.

When I talk to parents about reunification, I tell them that the end of alienation is not in reunification but in healing after. Having met many formerly alienated kids, the most common behavior I see is an extreme reaction to what they perceive to be manipulative behavior. A liar does not equate to gaslighting. Someone who is braggadocious is not inherently narcissistic. Having the intellectual understanding of these psychological terms can help map out the events in their life, but it also gives them the names of the demons that haunted their childhood. Any resemblance to those behaviors can result in bridge-burning behavior where patience and curiosity would have sufficed.

The greatest inhibitor to progression in the alienation movement has and continues to be the inability to break free from the trauma that haunts its victims. When policy, education, and research continue to be reactionary, the ripples of trauma extend outward to other parents and children, only furthering the cycle it is trying to break.

What good is it to alienate children to break free from their alienator, only to swing to the other end of the pendulum and become paranoid and frozen in their trauma? Or worse, to continue the cycle by marrying someone who embodies their alienator?

My whole life, I wanted to experience true inner peace in the manner described by East Asian Buddhist and Shaolin monks. I wanted to see life with eyes unclouded and my internal spirit quiet and tranquil.

After a childhood filled with chaos, it was the thing I chased most after alienation, more than love, reconnection, or purpose.

Conclusion

I got what I wanted.

Not all at once, and definitely not how I expected to. After letting go of the ten-year plan, I stopped building toward a reckoning and started building toward a life. I started my career as a writer, met my partner, and together we started a family. These things came slowly, each one requiring the previous one to be stable enough to support it, and none of them came as the dramatic event I had once imagined.

My mother is alive. My youngest brother came to my brother's wedding. My daughter is growing up in a house where she doesn't have to manage the emotions of her parents.

I do not hold onto these things. That is one of the many changes I notice in me now, and it is harder to describe than anything else in this essay because it is an absence rather than a presence. I don't have to hold onto the good before it is taken away. I trust the good to stay, and I trust that I have the strength to handle the challenges of life.

Alienation put me in a place where anything good had strings attached. Everything could be used against you. Loving something meant handing someone a lever.

A child who grows up inside alienation grows up inside scarcity. While abundance might seem like the presumed opposite, I think that overlooks what true freedom from trauma is. An alienated child's reunification can be dampened by pain. Whether it is one year, ten years, or fifty years, the time doesn't mean much if it is seen only through a lens of loss and pain instead of building toward something new.

The alienator teaches you to view life transactionally. To view reunification as accounting for time lost means your mind will always be more focused on the time debt with the targeted parent than on the present moment.

Ideally, I envision the alienated child finding freedom, peace, and joy by learning to let go of the alienator and the world they operate in. Their lifestyle is not the only way to live. In doing so, the formerly alienated child can be free to live life on their own terms and not have their potential limited by the hateful actions of a single person.

Until Next Time, Andrew Folkler LLC (Book Consultant and Content Strategist)

Contact- Andrewfolkler.com startnow@andrewfolkler.com

Photo 1: Andrew and his brother reuniting with their mother at the airport after 12.5 years of alienation while meeting their three younger siblings for the first time (December, 2013).

Photo 2: Andrew's wife (on left), his previously alienated mum (middle) and Andrew holding his daughter (on right), May 2026. The background photo is a picture of Andrew's youngest sister's high school graduation. The sister in the background photo was the young girl in the pink jumper on the far right in the picture above.

All photos have been used with permission.

About the HQTP Author

Dr Alyse Price-Tobler, PhD (Twin), MCAP, is a PACFA-registered clinical psychotherapist, specialist trauma clinician, researcher, clinical supervisor, author, and international speaker in the field of CPA-PA presentations. She has more than 30 years of experience across mental health, disability, forensic-adjacent, community, emergency response, family and domestic violence, homelessness, complex trauma, and specialist clinical practice settings.

Dr Price-Tobler works clinically with targeted parents, adolescents, adult survivors, and families affected by CPA-PA, as well as reunification disruption, familicide, homicide, suicide, and complex intergenerational relational trauma. Her clinical work includes national and international consultation with families and professionals navigating abduction across jurisdictions, long-term developmental harm, psychological capture, attachment disruption, and the enduring effects of coercive family systems.

She is the founder and principal clinical psychotherapist of Bowral Road Counselling and Retreat Centre in the Southern Highlands of New South Wales, where she provides specialist counselling, psychotherapy, and trauma-informed treatment. Her practice includes work with clients experiencing severe and persistent mental illness, psychosocial disability, complex trauma, attachment injury, suicidality, coercive-control-related harm, family-system violence, and long-term relational trauma. She also provides clinical supervision to practitioners working with complex presentations, high-risk therapeutic contexts, and CPA-PA-related clinical material.

Dr Price-Tobler's twin doctoral research at the University of the Sunshine Coast examined "Adult survivors of child psychological abuse related to severe parental alienation and the mental health practitioners who work with them". This research forms the empirical foundation of the Healing Qualia Treatment Protocol. The HQTP was developed to support safe, phase-based, non-forensic clinical treatment for adult survivors whose identities, attachments, developmental histories, and sense of reality have been shaped by CPA-PA and associated forms of relational harm.

Her earlier Master of Clinical Psychotherapy research examined the experiences of women living with severe and persistent mental illness while experiencing primary homelessness on the streets of Sydney. Participants were women accessing support through The Exodus Foundation during the day, many of whom were living with severe social exclusion, psychiatric vulnerability, trauma exposure, primary homelessness, and systemic neglect. This research shaped Dr Price-Tobler's understanding of relational dignity, stigma, psychological safety, and the importance of simple, respectful human connection in the lives of people who are often unseen.

Dr Price-Tobler previously served as Area Manager for the Schizophrenia Fellowship of NSW, now One Door Mental Health, where she established and managed specialist mental health Disability Employment Services in South West Sydney. In this role, she oversaw service development, staff recruitment and training, stakeholder engagement, budgeting, and support programs for people living with mental illness, psychosocial disability, and homelessness.

Dr Price-Tobler is the author of *Disrupting the Intergenerational Trauma Cycle of High Conflict Divorce: A Guide for Mental Health Practitioners and Adult Survivors of Child Psychological Abuse: Severe Parental Alienation. Volume One* and *Navigating the Maze During Treatment of Adult Survivors of Child Psychological Abuse: Severe Parental Alienation: A Comprehensive Resource Guide for Mental Health Practitioners, Offering Insights, Strategies and Risk Mitigation from a PhD Thesis on the Challenges Faced by Practitioners Treating Adult Survivors. Volume Two*, both published by Inspiring Publishers. These works were developed from her twin doctoral research and form the foundation for the present volume.

She has also contributed as a chapter author to collaborative works on parental alienation, family court, child psychological abuse, and survivor advocacy, including *Building Bridges of Hope: Overcoming Trauma in the Family Court System* and *Warning! Children Are Not Weapons!*. *Warning! Children Are Not Weapons!* emerged from the NAUWOU survivor conference community and brings together survivor and professional voices addressing CPA-PA and CPA-PAA and the use of children in high-conflict family systems. The anthology was recognised by the United States Presidential Services Centre and the James Madison Literary Award, an award described as recognising works that contribute to cultural and societal awareness.

Alongside her specialist CPA-PA work, Dr Price-Tobler treats first responders and emergency service personnel, including police, firefighters, ambulance officers, NSW SES members, and other frontline workers exposed to trauma, critical incidents, workplace injury, death, disaster response, and cumulative operational stress. She has provided critical incident counselling, EAP support, trauma-informed brief intervention, and longer-term specialist care through emergency on-call and employee assistance contexts, including work-related accidents, workplace trauma, disaster response, and the NSW Government Redress Scheme.

Dr Price-Tobler currently servs as a long-term volunteer (20 years) with the NSW State Emergency Service across the Camden, Wollondilly, and Wingecarribee Units. Her emergency service experience includes storm response, road crash rescue, bush and land search, flood boat operations, disaster first aid, welfare, training, community engagement, emergency management support, and member wellbeing. She has been deployed to multiple flood operations, the 2019–2020 bushfires, and the Thredbo landslide disaster. Her service has been recognised through the SES Certificate of Honour for Rescue Services: Thredbo Landslide 1997, the NSW SES State Rescue Board Accreditation Certificate, the NSW SES 10-Year

Long Service Medal, the NSW SES 15- and 20-Year Long Service Medal, and the SES National Emergency Medal for service during the 2019–2020 bushfires.

Dr Price-Tobler is an international speaker in the field of CPA-PA, adult survivor recovery, familial abduction, and specialist clinical treatment. She has presented at CPA-PA conferences internationally and was co-organiser, with Dawn McCarty, of the Thrivers Speak® NAUWOU Survivor Initiative Conference, an international survivor-led conference created to amplify adult survivor voices and address the longstanding absence of survivor experience in professional, legal, research, and clinical conversations.

Her work is grounded in doctoral research, specialist clinical practice, lived experience, frontline service, emergency response, authorship, clinical supervision, and sustained commitment to vulnerable people who have been misunderstood, misclassified, silenced, or left without appropriate treatment. The Healing Qualia Treatment Protocol © reflects this integrated background and is offered as a specialist clinical framework for mental health practitioners seeking to work with adult survivors in a trauma-informed, ethically restrained, developmentally attuned, and survivor-protective way.

A Personal Note

The HQTP was written from both professional and lived perspectives. The author brings personal experience of child psychological trauma and abduction, together with extensive clinical and doctoral research in this field. That combined vantage point has shaped the model's emphasis on pacing, safety, humility, and practitioner restraint from beginning to end.

This protocol exists because lived experience and clinical science must meet on equal terms, not in competition, but in dialogue. It is written for adult survivors. Moreover, it is written to give HOPE to the generations that follow, so that what was once minimised, misunderstood, or left unnamed may be met with greater clarity, protection, and care.

A Final Note from Dr Alyse: Rebuilding a Life After Harm

After child psychological abuse related to parental alienation, abduction, estrangement, coercive control, or family-system harm, many adult survivors have to learn how to build a life from the ground up. This does not happen through comfort, shortcuts, or pretending the past did not happen. It happens through safety, principles, discipline, direction, support, and the slow return of self-trust.

First, protect your life from people and systems that keep you trapped in chaos. Some people live for drama, excuses, control, blame, and emotional confusion. They may not want you to grow because your growth changes the role they assigned to you. Choose people who respect your healing, your boundaries, your mind, and your right to become yourself.

Second, keep learning. Study, read, ask questions, build skills, and gather knowledge that helps you stand on your own feet. Independence begins with language, understanding, and the ability to think clearly. A survivor who keeps learning becomes harder to silence, confuse, control, or erase.

Third, take responsibility for what is now yours to repair. Not everything that happened to you was your fault. Much of it may never have been your responsibility. But your life now belongs to you. Begin with what you can touch: your space, your routines, your words, your choices, your boundaries, your health, your next decision. Small acts of order can slowly rebuild dignity and confidence.

Fourth, protect your name, your values, and your future. Do not spend your life trying to prove yourself to people committed to misunderstanding you. Do not chase approval from those who benefited from your silence. Live in a way that honours your own integrity. Reputation, character, and consistency open doors that survival-based panic never can.

Fifth, practise kindness with boundaries. You do not have to become hard to become strong. You do not have to self-abandon to be loving. You can be generous without being available for harm. You can care without collapsing. You can forgive if you choose, but you do not owe forgiveness, contact, silence, or emotional labour to anyone who continues to harm you.

Strength after this kind of trauma is not about attention, beauty, perfection, or approval. It is about who you become when no one is watching. It is found in the choices you make when old fear asks you to shrink again. Walk with purpose. Move with humility. Build slowly. Choose carefully. Don't forget to be kind to your inner child and take them out to play! Your future is not built on excuses, shame, or the story other people wrote for you. It is built on decisions, one safe and honest step at a time.

A Visual Reflection from the Author

The following photographs are included near the close of this volume, rather than at the beginning, with deliberate clinical and ethical care. The HQTP is not grounded in personal narrative alone. It is grounded in doctoral research, clinical practice, treatment development, and the lived realities of adult survivors whose histories have too often been misunderstood, pathologised, or dismissed. These images are not included as evidence, explanation, or appeal. They are included as a quiet visual acknowledgment that behind every clinical formulation is a child who once had to survive.

Lived experience is not included here to invite judgement, diagnostic speculation, or personal scrutiny. It is included to challenge the assumption that survivorhood and professional authority cannot coexist. Adult survivor expertise, when held with training, supervision, research discipline, and ethical responsibility, can deepen clinical understanding. Those who have lived this journey often recognise the silences, fear responses, loyalty conflicts, and survival adaptations that others may miss. Doctoral research gives those insights structure, discipline, and accountability. In this work, lived experience becomes not a weakness to be hidden, but a form of clinical sight: the ability to recognise what others may not yet know how to see.

About the Authors' Photos

These photographs were taken during Year 9 photography class at the 'last chance' high school, which the author attended after many years of being moved around from school to school. They show the real condition of the bathrooms and lockers, and they hold part of the educational and developmental context from which this work emerged.

They are included not as clinical evidence but as a visual reminder that many children affected by CPA-PAA fall through the cracks of education, family systems, and professional recognition. Some are moved repeatedly, misunderstood, written off, or left to survive in environments where stability, belonging, and academic confidence are difficult to build.

The photograph of the author with her mentor at her PhD graduation is included alongside these school images to illustrate the educational distance she has travelled. It does not erase the harm. It does not romanticise survival. Rather, it offers a visual acknowledgment that where a person begins need not determine where they end. Even after CPA-PAA, disrupted schooling, relocation, instability, complex grief and loss, adult survivors can still reclaim learning, build professional competence, contribute original research, and create meaningful work from places that once seemed impossible to overcome.

Photography class photos from 'The Last Chance High School' bathroom and lockers.

A photo of Alyse and her fellow students smoking at the back of the school building during photography class in Year 9.

Photographs Included with Permission

Dr Alyse Price-Tobler and Sister Patricia Delaney-Davis

The author is pictured with her mentor of more than 30 years, Sister Patricia "Trishy" Delaney-Davis, a Catholic nun of the Brigidine Sisters. Sister Patricia's ministry has extended across Australia, New Zealand, Africa, Iceland, Latin America, Bangladesh, the Philippines, and China. The Brigidine tradition is grounded in education, justice, peace, and quiet service. The Flame of Brigid, or *Solas Bhride Light*, which has burned in Kildare for more than 1500 years, continues to symbolise hope, justice, and peace throughout the world.

https://brigidine.org.au/

This image honours Sister Patricia's long-standing presence in Alyse's life and education. It acknowledges the quiet, steady, and deeply human work that Patricia modelled, and the way she stood beside the author throughout her re-education and, later, her academic journey.

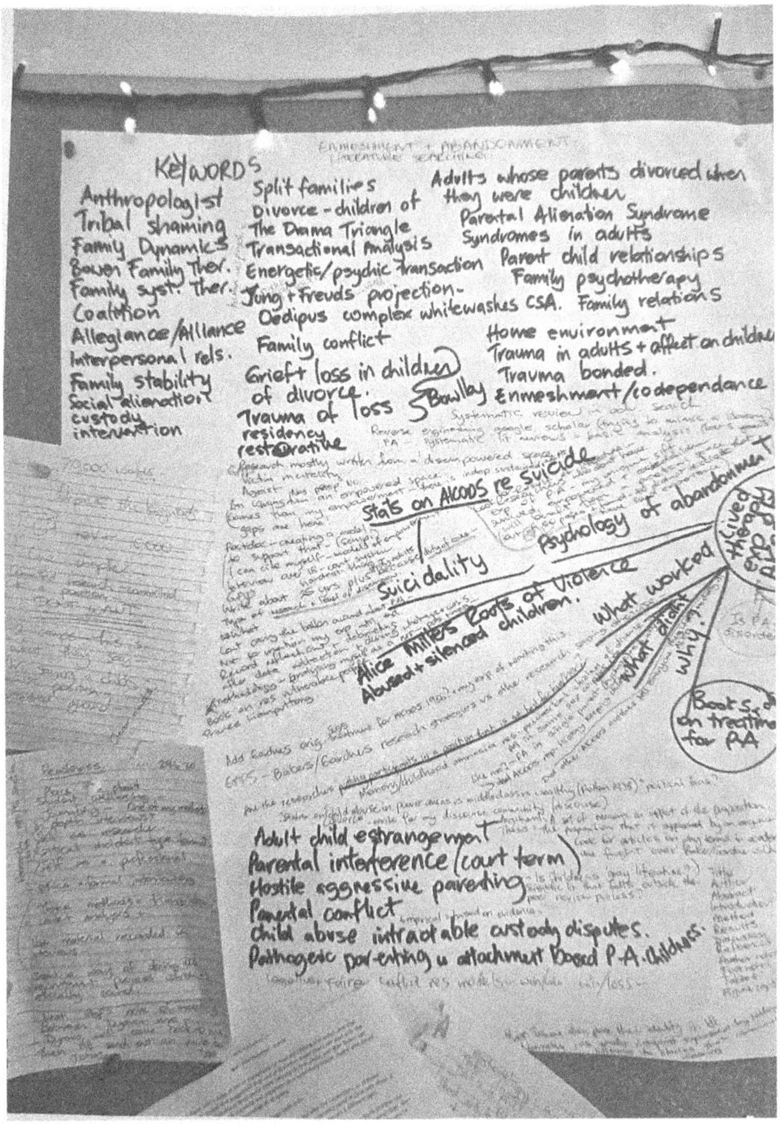

Early PhD Notes and Concept Mapping

This photograph shows early concept notes prepared by the author before presenting her proposed research direction to PhD supervisors at the University of the Sunshine Coast in 2019. Although these notes were prepared at the beginning of the doctoral process, the thinking behind what would later become the HQTP had been developing for many years before this point.

The page captures the beginning of the formal design process: key search terms, clinical questions, emerging themes, and early links between child psychological abuse related to parental alienation, abandonment, attachment disruption, family systems, suicidality, adult survivor presentations, and treatment gaps. From earlier university study, clinical work, lived experience, and emerging research, the author had become increasingly aware that many adult survivors were being left to search for their own answers because specialist guidance for adult treatment was difficult to find or seemed nonexistent.

This pattern was later reflected in the PhD data, where adult survivors described studying, reading, documenting, comparing experiences, and trying to build their own language for what had happened. In this sense, the notes shown here represent more than an early research plan. They mark one of the first formal attempts to organise long-held clinical and survivor observations into a researchable and clinically useful treatment direction.

These personal photographs are included to provide a human context for this protocol. They are not presented as clinical material, personal disclosure, or evidence, but as an acknowledgment of the relationships, mentorship, education, research, survival, and hope that helped shape the author's path. The HQTP was born from survival, grounded in doctoral research, and written so future generations may be recognised earlier, treated safely, and given hope before this harm becomes their life story.

Alyse and her siblings with their paternal grandmother (Lindy Lou) on their final contact visit.

Alyse and her siblings, with their father and paternal uncle, on the last contact visit before contact was stopped. They were reunited 25 years later.

The first and last adult trip we all had with Dad before he died, 2021.

Alyse and her father after they reunited.

R.I.P Dad x You were very loved xxx

Don't Ever Give Up Hope

Children deserve to have a voice. They deserve to love both parents where it is safe to do so, and to be free to express their feelings without fear, punishment, guilt, or divided loyalty. No child should have to hide their love for one parent to survive the relationship with the other. No child should be made to carry adult conflict, adult fear, adult revenge, or adult pain as though it belongs to them.

It is a child's human right to know, love, and be loved by both parents in a safe environment, and to know their extended family, culture, ancestry, history, and sense of belonging. Children should not be cut off from grandparents, siblings, cousins, kinship networks, culture, or family stories because adults cannot manage conflict, grief, rejection, anger, or control.

Children are not weapons. They are not prizes to be won. They are not possessions, messengers, emotional regulators, or proof of victory after separation. They are developing human beings with minds, hearts, memories, bodies, attachments, and futures of their own. They deserve adults who protect their right to love, feel, question, grieve, miss, remember, and belong.

This protocol was written with the hope that children will be recognised earlier, protected sooner, and given the help that many adult survivors never received. It was also written so future generations may not have to live through the same harm, unnamed, unseen, or untreated.

Adult survivors such as myself, Dawn McCarty, Andrew Folkler, and many others are now helping to show the way through our stories. By speaking, writing, researching, reconnecting, and bearing witness, we are shining a light on a barely recognised public health and child protection crisis that has remained hidden for too long. This is not only personal work. It is generational work. It is the work we need to do now to prevent this harm from being passed down to the children who will come after us.

Even when years have been lost, even when the story has been distorted, and even when love has been buried under fear, hope still matters. Healing is possible. Truth can return. Connection can be rebuilt where it is safe, and freedom can still be found.

Thank you for your time, your energy, and your willingness to help carry this work forward. Don't ever give up HOPE, and don't forget, "Every Second Counts Toward Stopping Suicide and Alienation!!" With gratitude, Dr Alyse

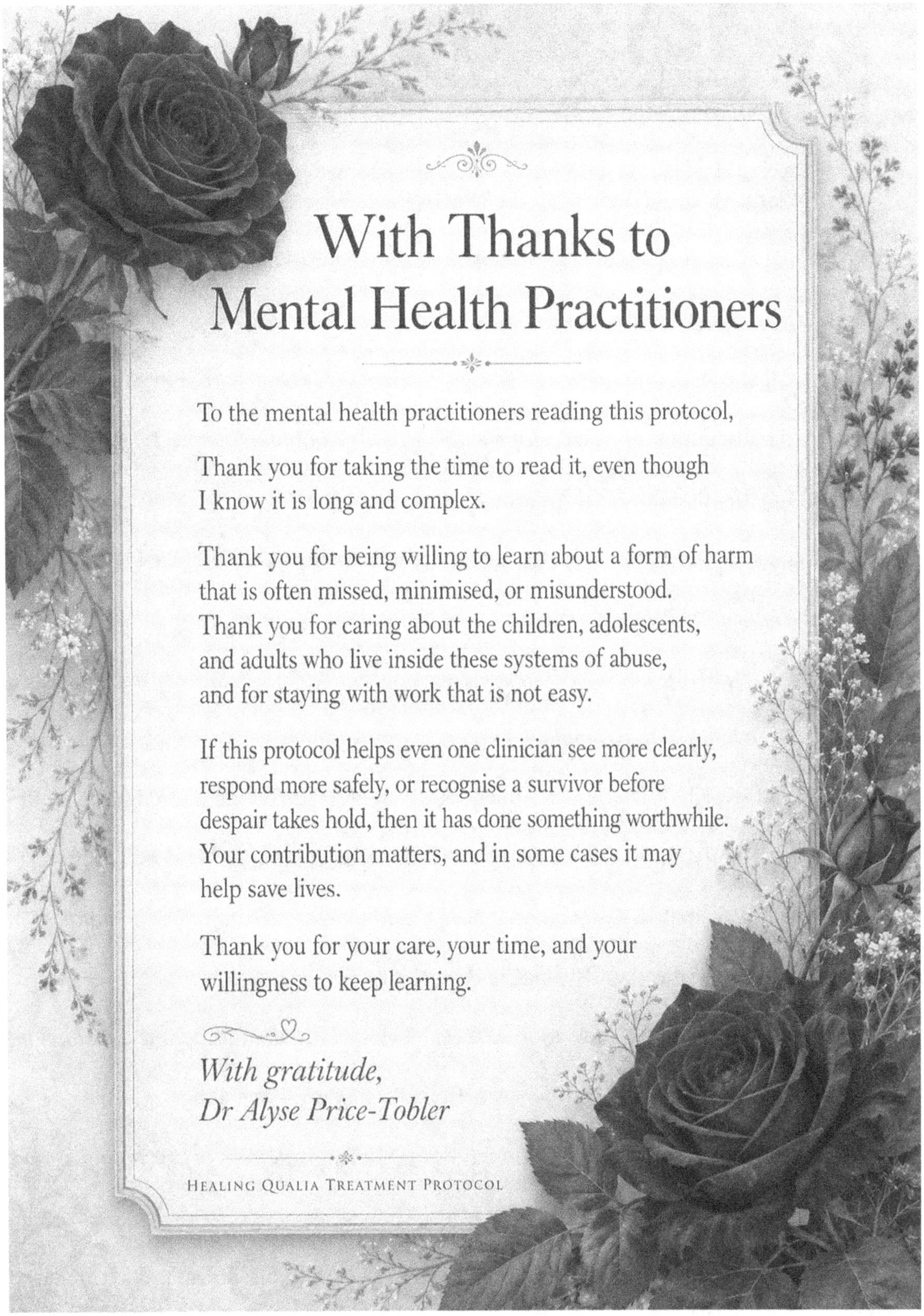

A Special Thank You Card for Clinicians

For the Mental Health Practitioners Who Work in the Field of Child Psychological Abuse

References

ACEs Too High. (2020). *Got your ACE score?* https://acestoohigh.com/got-your-ace-score/

Ainsworth, M. D. S., Blehar, M. C., Waters, E., & Wall, S. (1978). *Patterns of attachment: A psychological study of the strange situation*. Lawrence Erlbaum Associates.

Aktar, E., Alcan, E., de Vente, W., Majdandžić, M., & Bögels, S. M. (2022). The social learning of threat and safety in the family: Parent-to-child transmission of social fears via verbal information. *Developmental Psychobiology, 64*(3), e22257. https://doi.org/10.1002/dev.22257

Alexander, J. C., Eyerman, R., Giesen, B., Smelser, N. J., & Sztompka, P. (2004). *Cultural trauma and collective identity*. University of California Press.

Alsalem, F. (2023). *The impact of coercive control in familial abuse dynamics: Reframing interventions in high-conflict families*. Family Justice Council.

Amato, P. R. (2000). The consequences of divorce for adults and children. Journal of Marriage and Family, 62(4), 1269–1287. https://doi.org/10.1111/j.1741-3737.2000.01269.x

American Psychiatric Association. (2013). *Diagnostic and statistical manual of mental disorders (5th ed.)*. American Psychiatric Publishing.

American Psychiatric Association. (2022). *DSM-5-TR: Diagnostic and statistical manual of mental disorders (5th ed., text rev.)*. American Psychiatric Publishing.

American Psychological Association. (2017). *Ethical principles of psychologists and code of conduct.* https://www.apa.org/ethics/code

American Psychological Association. (2020). Resolution on violent video games.

Amin, M., & Ettinger-Epstein, S. (2024, April 29). *The kids who fear school*. ABC News / Four Corners.

Amman, M., Bowlin, M., Buckles, L., Burton, K. C., Brunell, K. F., Gibson, K. A., Griffin, S. H., Kennedy, K., & Robins, C. J. (2017). Making prevention a reality: Identifying, assessing, and managing the threat of targeted attacks. Federal Bureau of Investigation, National Center for the Analysis of Violent Crime, Behavioral Analysis Unit.

Andrews, K., Lloyd, C. S., Densmore, M., Kearney, B. E., Harricharan, S., McKinnon, M. C., Théberge, J., Jetly, R., & Lanius, R. A. (2023). "I am afraid you will see the stain on my soul": Direct gaze neural processing in individuals with PTSD after moral injury recall. *Social Cognitive and Affective Neuroscience, 18*(1), nsad053. https://doi.org/10.1093/scan/nsad053

ANROWS. (2026). *An introductory guide to the manosphere and the impacts for young people, teachers and schools.*

Arendt, H. (1951). *The origins of totalitarianism*. Harcourt, Brace.

Asch, S. E. (1951). Effects of group pressure upon the modification and distortion of judgements. In H. Guetzkow (Ed.), *Groups, leadership and men: Research in human relations* (pp. 177–190). Carnegie Press.

Attorney-General's Department. (2024, January 12). Family Law Amendment Act 2023: Factsheet for parents. Australian Government. https://www.ag.gov.au/families-and-marriage/publications/family-law-amendment-act-2023-factsheet-parents

Attorney-General's Department. (2024, March 5). Understanding coercive control fact sheets. Australian Government. https://www.ag.gov.au/families-and-marriage/publications/understanding-coercive-control-fact-sheets

Australian Bureau of Statistics. (2020). *Marriages and divorces, Australia, 2019 (Cat. No. 3310.0)*. Australian Government.

Australian Bureau of Statistics. (2023). *Causes of death, Australia (2022).* https://www.abs.gov.au

Australian Bureau of Statistics. (2024a). National, state and territory population.

Australian Bureau of Statistics. (2026). *Schools, 2025.*

Australian Counselling Association. (2019). *Code of ethics and practice.* https://www.theaca.net.au

Australian Psychological Society. (2018). APS Code of Ethics. https://www.psychology.org.au/getmedia/d873e0db-7490-46de-bb57-c31bb1553025/APS-Code-of-Ethics.pdf

Australian Government. (2019). *Divorces, Australia.* Australian Bureau of Statistics.

Australian Institute of Family Studies. (2026). *Children's support needs following parental separation.* Australian Institute of Family Studies.

Australian Institute for Teaching and School Leadership. (2023). *Australian professional standards for principals and leadership profiles.* https://www.aitsl.edu.au

Australian Institute of Judicial Administration. (2023). *National Domestic and Family Violence Bench Book.* https://dfvbenchbook.aija.org.au

Australian Psychological Society. (2018). *APS code of ethics.* https://psychology.org.au

Bailey, R. (2019). *Safe and sound: Trauma-informed approaches for abducted and exploited children.* National Center for Missing and Exploited Children Training Series.

Bailey, R., Dana, D., Bailey, E., & Davis, F. (2020). The application of the polyvagal theory to high-conflict co-parenting cases. *Family Court Review, 58(2),* 525–543. https://doi.org/10.1111/fcre.12485

Baker, A. J. L. (2007). Adult children of parental alienation: Long-term impacts of parental alienation on children's mental health and future relationships. *Journal of Divorce and Remarriage, 48*(1), 19–41.

Baker, A. J. L. (2007). *Adult children of parental alienation syndrome: Breaking the ties that bind. W. W.* Norton & Company.

Baker, A. J. L., & Darnall, D. (2006). Behaviours and strategies employed in parental alienation: A survey of parental experiences. *Journal of Divorce & Remarriage, 45*(1–2), 97–124. https://doi.org/10.1300/J087v45n01_06

Bandura, A. (1997). *Self-efficacy: The exercise of control. W. H.* Freeman.

Bandura, A. (1977). *Social learning theory*. Prentice-Hall.

Bandura, A. (1999). Moral disengagement in the perpetration of inhumanities. Personality and Social Psychology Review, 3(3), 193–209.

Barn, R., & Mansuri, N. (2019). "I always wanted to look at another human and say I can see that human in me": Understanding genealogical bewilderment in the context of racialised intercountry adoptees. *Genealogy, 3*(4), Article 71. https://doi.org/10.3390/genealogy3040071

Bass, C., & Halligan, P. (2014). Factitious disorders and malingering: Challenges for clinical assessment and management. *The Lancet, 383*(9926), 1422–1432. https://doi.org/10.1016/S0140-6736(13)62186-8

Bateman, A., & Fonagy, P. (2016). *Mentalization-based treatment for personality disorders: A practical guide*. Oxford University Press.

Berne, S. (2008). *Extraordinary circumstances: Based on the true story of a landmark custody battle and parental abduction survivor*. iUniverse.

Bernet, W. (2008). *Parental alienation disorder and DSM-V*. American Journal of Family Therapy, 36(5), 349–366. https://doi.org/10.1080/01926180802405513

Bernet, W., von Boch-Galhau, W., Baker, A. J. L., & Morrison, S. L. (2010). *Parental alienation, DSM-V, and ICD-11*. The American Journal of Family Therapy, 38(2), 76–187. https://doi.org/10.1080/01926180903586583

Bernet, W., & Greenhill, L. L. (2022). The Five-Factor Model for the diagnosis of parental alienation. Journal of the American Academy of Child & Adolescent Psychiatry, 61(5), 591–594. https://doi.org/10.1016/j.jaac.2021.11.026

Bernstein, A. E. (1990). Incest: The unknowable trauma. *Journal of the American Medical Women's Association, 45*(1), 23–26. PMID: 2299126.

Birkbeck, M. (2004). A beautiful child. Berkley Books.

Bishop, S. (2025, December 19). *After more than 40 years, woman reunites with family after allegedly being abducted by her mom.* ABC7 Los Angeles. https://abc7.com/post/debra-newton-kidnapping-suspect-accused-abducting-michelle-louisville-kentucky-arrested-marion-county-florida/18300626/

Blackwood, F. (2026, March 11). *Teachers, schools given handbook to combat misogynistic behaviour in classrooms*. ABC News.

Boss, P. (1999). *Ambiguous loss: Learning to live with unresolved grief.* Harvard University Press.

Bouton, M. E. (2004). Context and behavioral processes in extinction. *Learning & Memory, 11*(5), 485–494. https://doi.org/10.1101/lm.78804

Bowen, M. (1978). *Family therapy in clinical practice*. Jason Aronson.

Bowlby, J. (1969/1982). Attachment and loss: Vol. 1. Attachment (2nd ed.). Basic Books.

Bowlby, J. (1988). *A secure base: Parent-child attachment and healthy human development*. Basic Books.

Bérubé, A., Turgeon, J., Blais, C., & Fiset, D. (2023). *Emotion recognition in adults with a history of childhood maltreatment: A systematic review*. Trauma, Violence, & Abuse, 24(1), 278–294. https://doi.org/10.1177/15248380211029403

Campbell, L. H., Silverman, P. R., & Patti, P. B. (1991). Reunions between adoptees and birth parents: The adoptees' experience. *Social Work, 36*(4), 329–335.

Carnes, P. (1997). *The betrayal bond.* Health Communications.

Centers for Disease Control and Prevention. (2020). *National marriage and divorce rate trends. U.S.* Department of Health and Human Services.

Centers for Disease Control and Prevention. (2025). *National marriage and divorce statistics.*

Charlton, J. I. (1998). *Nothing about us without us: Disability oppression and empowerment*. University of California Press.

Chase, N. D. (Ed.). (1999). *Burdened children: Theory, research, and treatment of parentification*. Sage.

Chase, N. D. (1999). Parentification: An overview of theory, research, and societal issues. In N. D.Chase (Ed.), *Burdened children: Theory, research, and treatment of parentification* (pp. 3–33). Sage. https://doi.org/10.4135/9781452220604.n1

Child Safeguarding Practice Review Panel. (2024). *Children electively home educated: Serious safeguarding practice review panel briefing*. Department for Education.

Childress, C. A. (2015). *Foundations: An attachment-based model of parental alienation.* Oaksong Press.

Childress, C. A. (2020). *Reunification family therapy: An attachment-based model.* Author.

Cialdini, R. B. (2009). *Influence: Science and practice (5th ed.)*. Pearson.

Cloitre, M., Courtois, C. A., Charuvastra, A., Carapezza, R., Stolbach, B. C., & Green, B. L. (2012). Treatment of complex PTSD: Results of the ISTSS expert clinician survey on best practices. *Journal of Traumatic Stress, 24*(6), 615–627. https://doi.org/10.1002/jts.20697

Coleman, E., Radix, A. E., Bouman, W. P., Brown, G. R., de Vries, A. L. C., Deutsch, M. B., Ettner, R., Fraser, L., Goodman, M., Green, J., Hancock, A. B., Johnson, T. W., Karasic, D. H., Knudson, G., Leibowitz, S. F., Meyer-Bahlburg, H. F. L., Monstrey, S. J., Motmans, J., Nahata, L., Arcelus, J. (2022). Standards of care for the health of transgender and gender diverse people, version 8. *International Journal of Transgender Health, 23*(Suppl. 1), S1–S259.

Courtois, C. A., & Ford, J. D. (2020). *Treating complex traumatic stress disorders in adults: Scientific foundations and therapeutic models (2nd ed.)*. Guilford Press.

Critchfield, K. L., & Benjamin, L. S. (2008). Internalised representations of early interpersonal experience and adult relationships: A test of copy process theory. *Psychiatry: Interpersonal and Biological Processes, 71*(1), 71–92.

https://doi.org/10.1521/psyc.2008.71.1.71

Crittenden, P. M. (2016). *Raising parents: Attachment, representation, and treatment (2nd ed.)*. Routledge.

Crittenden, P. M., & Landini, A. (2011). *Assessing adult attachment: A dynamic-maturational approach to discourse analysis. W. W.* Norton.

Dariotis, J. K., Chen, F. R., Park, Y. R., Nowak, M. K., French, K. M., & Codamon, A. M. (2023). Parentification vulnerability, reactivity, resilience, and thriving: A mixed methods systematic literature review. *International Journal of Environmental Research and Public Health, 20*(13), 6197. doi:10.3390/ijerph20136197

Darnall, D. (1998). *Divorce casualties: Protecting your children from parental alienation.* Taylor Trade Publishing.

Department of Education NSW. (2021). *Student wellbeing and trauma-informed practice framework.* NSW Government.

Diaz, S., & Bailey, J. M. (2023). Retraction note: Rapid onset gender dysphoria: Parent reports on 1655 possible cases. *Archives of Sexual Behavior, 52*, 3577.

Driessen, J., Blom, J. D., Muris, P., Blashfield, R. K., & Molendijk, M. L. (2020). Anxiety in children with selective mutism: A meta-analysis. Child Psychiatry & Human Development, 51, 330–341. https://doi.org/10.1007/s10578-019-00933-1

Dube, S. R., Anda, R. F., Felitti, V. J., Chapman, D. P., Williamson, D. F., & Giles, W. H. (2001). Childhood abuse, household dysfunction, and the risk of attempted suicide. *American*

Journal of Preventive Medicine, 21(2), 106–115. https://doi.org/10.1016/S0749-3797(01)00308-7

Dugard, J. (2011). *A stolen life*. Simon & Schuster.

Dutton, M. A., & Goodman, L. A. (2005). Coercion in intimate partner violence: Toward a new conceptualization. Sex Roles, 52, 743–756. https://doi.org/10.1007/s11199-005-4196-6

Echols, M. (1991). I know my first name is Steven. Pinnacle Books.

eSafety Commissioner. (2026, March 12). Manosphere to man: How talking helps boys resist bad influencers. Australian Government. https://www.esafety.gov.au/newsroom/media-releases/manosphere-to-man-how-talking-helps-boys-resist-bad-influencers

Eubanks, C. F., Muran, J. C., & Safran, J. D. (2018). Alliance rupture repair: A meta-analysis. *Psychotherapy, 55*(4), 508–519. https://doi.org/10.1037/pst0000185

Farnfield, S., Hautamäki, A., Nørbech, P., & Sahhar, N. (2010). DMM assessments of attachment and adaptation: Procedures, validity and utility. *Clinical Child Psychology and Psychiatry, 15*(3), 313–328. https://doi.org/10.1177/1359104510364315

Federal Circuit and Family Court of Australia. (n.d.-b). Parenting orders—Obligations, consequences and who can help. https://www.fcfcoa.gov.au/fl/pubs/parenting-orders

Felitti, V. J., Anda, R. F., Nordenberg, D., Williamson, D. F., Spitz, A. M., Edwards, V., Koss, M. P., & Marks, J. S. (1998). Relationship of childhood abuse and household dysfunction to many leading causes of death in adults. *American Journal of Preventive Medicine, 14*(4), 245–258. https://doi.org/10.1016/S0749-3797(98)00017-8

Fenn, K., & Byrne, M. (2013). The key principles of cognitive behavioural therapy. *InnovAiT, 6*(9), 579–585. https://doi.org/10.1177/1755738012471029

Fidler, B. J., Bala, N., & Saini, M. (2012). *Children who resist post-separation parental contact: A differential approach for legal and mental health professionals*. Oxford University Press.

Finkelhor, D., Hammer, H., & Sedlak, A. (2002). *Nonfamily abducted children: National estimates and characteristics. U.S.* Department of Justice.

Frankl, V. E. (1963). *Man's search for meaning*. Beacon Press.

Fricker, M. (2007). *Epistemic injustice: Power and the ethics of knowing*. Oxford University Press.

Gabbard, G. O. (2014). *Psychodynamic psychiatry in clinical practice* (5th ed.). American Psychiatric Publishing.

Garber, B. D. (2004). *Parental alienation in light of attachment theory: Consideration of the broader implications for child development, clinical practice, and forensic process*. Journal of Child Custody, 1(4), 49–76. https://doi.org/10.1300/J190v01n04_04

Gardner, R. A. (1998). *The parental alienation syndrome: A guide for mental health and legal professionals (2nd ed.)*. Creative Therapeutics.

Giancarlo, C. (2018). *Parentectomy: A narrative ethnography of parental alienation*. Tellwell Talent.

Giancarlo, C. (2019). Parental alienation and the targeted parent. *Family Court Review, 57*(4), 567–581.

Ging, D. (2019). Alphas, betas, and incels: Theorizing the masculinities of the manosphere. *Men and Masculinities, 22*(4), 638–657

https://doi.org/10.1177/1097184X17706401

Greif, G. L. (2000). A parental report on the long-term consequences for children of abduction by the other parent. *Child Psychiatry and Human Development, 31*, 59–78.

Greif, G. L., & Hegar, R. L. (1993). *When parents kidnap: The families behind the headlines*. Free Press.

Grigoryeva, A. (2017). Own gender, sibling's gender, parent's gender: The division of elderly parent care among adult children. *American Sociological Review, 82*(1), 116–146. doi:10.1177/0003122416686521

Grossman, D. (2001). On killing II: The psychological cost of learning to kill. International Journal of Emergency Mental Health, 3(3), 137–144.

Hansen, M. M., Jones, R., & Tocchini, K. (2017). Shinrin-yoku (forest bathing) and nature therapy: A state-of-the-art review. *International Journal of Environmental Research and Public Health, 14*(8), 851. https://doi.org/10.3390/ijerph14080851

Harman, J. J., Kruk, E., & Hines, D. A. (2018). *Parental alienating behaviors: An unacknowledged form of family violence*. Psychological Bulletin, 144(12), 1275–1299. https://doi.org/10.1037/bul0000175

Harman, J. J., Leder-Elder, S., & Biringen, Z. (2016). *Prevalence of parental alienation drawn from a representative poll*. Children and Youth Services Review, 66, 62–66. https://doi.org/10.1016/j.childyouth.2016.04.021

Hassan, S. (2012). *Freedom of mind: Helping loved ones leave controlling people, cults, and beliefs*. Freedom of Mind Press.

Hassan, S. A. (2015). *Combating cult mind control*. Freedom of Mind Press.

Herman, J. L. (1992). *Trauma and recovery: The aftermath of violence—from domestic abuse to political terror*. Basic Books.

Heron, R. L., & Eisma, M. C. (2021). Barriers and facilitators of disclosing domestic violence to the healthcare service: A systematic review of qualitative research. *Health & Social Care in the Community, 29*(3), 612–630. https://doi.org/10.1111/hsc.13282

Herrando, C., & Constantinides, E. (2021). Emotional contagion: A brief overview and future directions. *Frontiers in Psychology, 12*, 712606. https://doi.org/10.3389/fpsyg.2021.712606

Hietanen, J. K. (2018). Affective eye contact: An integrative review. *Frontiers in Psychology, 9*, Article 1587. https://doi.org/10.3389/fpsyg.2018.01587

Hooper, L. M. (2007). The application of attachment theory and family systems theory to the phenomena of parentification. *The Family Journal, 15*(3), 217–223. https://doi.org/10.1177/1066480707301290

Hornstra, M., Ivanova, K., & Kalmijn, M. (2023). Kinkeeping across families: The central role of mothers and stepmothers in the facilitation of adult intergenerational ties. *Sex Roles, 89*, 311–327. doi:10.1007/s11199-023-01352-2

Hyde, L. W., Shaw, D. S., & Moilanen, K. L. (2010). Developmental precursors of moral disengagement and the role of moral disengagement in the development of antisocial behaviour. Journal of Abnormal Child Psychology, 38(2), 197–209.

International Society for the Study of Trauma and Dissociation. (2011). *Guidelines for treating dissociative identity disorder in adults (3rd rev.)*. ISSTD.

International Support Network of Alienated Families. (n.d.). *What is parental alienation?* https://isnaf.info

Jackson, F. (1982). Epiphenomenal qualia. Philosophical Quarterly, 32(127), 127–136.

Johnston, C., & Jones, R. (2016). The Family: The shocking true story of a notorious cult. Scribe Publications.

Johnston, J. R., & Roseby, V. (1997). *In the name of the child: A developmental approach to understanding and helping children of conflicted and violent divorce*. Free Press.

Jurkovic, G. J. (1997). *Lost childhoods: The plight of the parentified child.* Brunner/Mazel.

Kabat-Zinn, J. (2003). Mindfulness-based interventions in context: Past, present, and future. *Clinical Psychology: Science and Practice, 10*(2), 144–156. https://doi.org/10.1093/clipsy.bpg016

Kales, H. C., Gitlin, L. N., & Lyketsos, C. G. (2015). Assessment and management of behavioural and psychological symptoms of dementia. *BMJ, 350*, h369.

Karlsson, L. C., Antfolk, J., Putkonen, H., Amon, S., & da Silva Guerreiro, J. (2021). *Familicide: A systematic literature review. Trauma, Violence, & Abuse, 22*(1), 83–98.

Kernberg, O. F. (2004). *Aggressivity, narcissism, and self-destructiveness in the psychotherapeutic relationship*. Yale University Press.

Kessler, R. C. (2000). Post-traumatic stress disorder: The burden to the individual and to society. *Journal of Clinical Psychiatry, 61*(Suppl 5), 4–12.

Kostova, Z., & Matanova, V. L. (2024). Transgenerational trauma and attachment. *Frontiers in Psychology, 15*, 1362561. https://doi.org/10.3389/fpsyg.2024.1362561

Kuvalanka, K. A., Weiner, J. L., Mahan, D., & Goldberg, A. E. (2019). *An exploratory study of custody challenges experienced by affirming mothers of transgender and gender nonconforming children. Family Court Review, 57*(1), 54–68.

Lalich, J. (2004). *Bounded choice: True believers and charismatic cults*. University of California Press.

Lalich, J., & Tobias, M. (2006). *Take back your life: Recovering from cults and abusive relationships (Rev. ed.)*. Bay Tree Publishing.

Langevin, R., Marshall, C., & Kingsland, E. (2021). Intergenerational cycles of maltreatment: A scoping review of psychosocial risk and protective factors. *Trauma, Violence, & Abuse, 22*(4), 672–688. https://doi.org/10.1177/1524838019870917

Levine, P. A. (2010). *In an unspoken voice: How the body releases trauma and restores goodness*. North Atlantic Books.

Levine, S. B. (2021). Reflections on the clinician's role with individuals who self-identify as transgender. *Archives of Sexual Behavior, 50*, 3527–3536.

Lifton, B. J. (1994). *Journey of the adopted self*. Basic Books.

Lifton, R. J. (1961). *Thought reform and the psychology of totalism. W. W.* Norton.

Lifton, R. J. (1994). *The Nazi doctors: Medical killing and the psychology of genocide*. Basic Books.

Linehan, M. M. (1993). *Cognitive-behavioral treatment of borderline personality disorder*. Guilford Press.

Linehan, M. M. (2015). *DBT skills training manual (2nd ed.)*. Guilford Press.

Liotti, G. (2004). Trauma, dissociation, and disorganized attachment: Three strands of a single braid. *Psychotherapy: Theory, Research, Practice, Training, 41*(4), 472–486. https://doi.org/10.1037/0033-3204.41.4.472

Litz, B. T., Stein, N., Delaney, E., Lebowitz, L., Nash, W. P., Silva, C., & Maguen, S. (2009). Moral injury and moral repair in war veterans: A preliminary model and intervention strategy. Clinical Psychology Review, 29(8), 695–706.

Liu, Y., Peng, H., Wu, J., & Duan, H. (2021). *The relationship between childhood emotional abuse and processing of emotional facial expressions in healthy young men: Event-related potential and behavioral evidence*. Frontiers in Psychology, 12, Article 686529. https://doi.org/10.3389/fpsyg.2021.686529

Lofland, J. (1966). *Doomsday cult: A study of conversion, proselytization, and maintenance of faith*. Prentice-Hall.

Lorandos, D., & Bernet, W. (2020). *Parental alienation: Science and law*. Charles C Thomas.

Lorandos, D., Bernet, W., & Sauber, S. R. (2013). *Parental alienation: The handbook for mental health and legal professionals*. Charles C Thomas.

MacDonald, J. B., Willoughby, M., Gartoulla, P., Cotton, E., March, E., Alla, K., & Strawa, C. (2024). *What the research evidence tells us about coercive control victimisation*. Child Family Community Australia, Australian Institute of Family Studies.

Main, M., Hesse, E., & Goldwyn, R. (2008). Studying differences in language usage in recounting attachment history: An introduction to the Adult Attachment Interview. In H. Steele & M. Steele (Eds.), *Clinical applications of the Adult Attachment Interview* (pp. 31–68). Guilford Press.

Malchiodi, C. A. (2012). *Handbook of art therapy (2nd ed.)*. Guilford Press.

Marin, S. (2025, July 12). How the “manosphere” is fuelling teen misogyny inside Australian schools. ABC News / Compass. https://www.abc.net.au/news/2025-07-13/hijacking-adolescence-fuelling-teen-misogyny-inside-schools/105523184

Masten, A. S. (2014). *Ordinary magic: Resilience in development*. Guilford Press.

McHale, S. M., Updegraff, K. A., Jackson-Newsom, J., Tucker, C. J., & Crouter, A. C. (2000). When does parents’ differential treatment have negative implications for siblings? *Social Development, 9*(2), 149–172. doi:10.1111/1467-9507.00117

McLaughlin, K. A., Green, J. G., Gruber, M. J., Sampson, N. A., Zaslavsky, A. M., & Kessler, R. C. (2010). Childhood adversities and adult psychopathology. *Psychological Medicine, 40*(5), 847–859. https://doi.org/10.1017/S003329170999111X

McWilliams, N. (2011). *Psychoanalytic diagnosis: Understanding personality structure in the clinical process* (2nd ed.). Guilford Press.

Meichenbaum, D. H., & Deffenbacher, J. L. (1988). Stress inoculation training. The Counseling Psychologist, 16(1), 69–90.

Mendez, M. F. (2017). Frontotemporal dementia: Therapeutic interventions. *Frontiers in Neurology, 8*, 345.

Milgram, S. (1963). Behavioral study of obedience. *Journal of Abnormal and Social Psychology, 67*, 371–378.

Minuchin, S. (1974). *Families and family therapy*. Harvard University Press.

Monash University. (2026, March 11). *New guide helps schools address the growing influence of the manosphere in schools.*

Muris, P., & Ollendick, T. H. (2015). Children who are anxious in silence: A review on selective mutism, the new anxiety disorder in DSM-5. Clinical Child and Family Psychology Review, 18(2), 151–169. https://doi.org/10.1007/s10567-015-0181-y

Nagel, T. (1974). *What is it like to be a bat? The Philosophical Review, 83(4), 435–450.* https://doi.org/10.2307/2183914

National Association of School Psychologists. (2020). *Protecting children and supporting mandated reporters.* https://www.nasponline.org

National Institute for Health and Care Excellence. (2018). *Post-traumatic stress disorder (NG116)*. NICE.

Neimeyer, R. A. (2019). Meaning reconstruction in the wake of loss: Evolution of a research program. *Behaviour Change, 36*(1), 1–17. https://doi.org/10.1017/bec.2019.4

National Health and Medical Research Council. (2023). *National statement on ethical conduct in human research 2023*. Australian Government.

NSW Health. (2020). *Person-centred care*. NSW Government.

Ofcom. (2025). *Understanding online journeys through the manosphere*. Ofcom.

Ogden, P., Minton, K., & Pain, C. (2006). *Trauma and the body: A sensorimotor approach to psychotherapy. W. W.* Norton & Company.

Palusci, V. J. (2018). *Reporting child maltreatment*. Child and Adolescent Psychiatric Clinics of North America, 27(1), 1–11. https://doi.org/10.1016/j.chc.2017.08.001

Park, B. J., Tsunetsugu, Y., Kasetani, T., Kagawa, T., & Miyazaki, Y. (2010). The physiological effects of Shinrin-yoku (taking in the forest atmosphere or forest bathing): Evidence from field experiments. *Environmental Health and Preventive Medicine, 15*(1), 18–26. https://doi.org/10.1007/s12199-009-0086-9

Park, C. L. (2010). Making sense of the meaning literature: An integrative review of meaning making and its effects on adjustment to stressful life events. *Psychological Bulletin, 136*(2), 257–301. https://doi.org/10.1037/a0018301

Perry, B. D., & Szalavitz, M. (2007). *The boy who was raised as a dog*. Basic Books.

Phillips, R., & Sen, S. (2022). *Principal health and wellbeing survey*. Australian Catholic University, Institute for Positive Psychology and Education.

Porges, S. W. (2011). *The polyvagal theory: Neurophysiological foundations of emotions, attachment, communication, and self-regulation*. W. W. Norton & Company.

Price-Tobler, A. (2023). *Working with adult-child survivors of severe parental alienation abuse: Survivors and mental health practitioners' perspectives* [Doctoral dissertation, University of the Sunshine Coast, Queensland]. https://doi.org/10.25907/00793

Price-Tobler, A. (2024a). *Disrupting the intergenerational trauma cycle of high conflict divorce: A guide for mental health practitioners and adult survivors of child psychological abuse: Severe parental alienation. Volume One.* Inspiring Publishers.

Price-Tobler, A. (2024b). *Navigating the maze during treatment of adult survivors of child psychological abuse: Severe parental alienation: A comprehensive resource guide for mental health practitioners, offering insights, strategies and risk mitigation from a PhD thesis on the challenges faced by practitioners treating adult survivors. Volume Two.* Inspiring Publishers.

Price-Tobler, A. [Parental Alienation Channel Dr Alyse Price-Tobler]. (2020). *Home* [YouTube channel]. YouTube. Retrieved March 21, 2026, from https://www.youtube.com/channel/UCiN_DxTEdbOpGZNB3Bo3ndQ

Prinsen, J., & Alaerts, K. (2019). Eye contact enhances interpersonal motor resonance: Comparing video stimuli to a live two-person action context. *Social Cognitive and Affective Neuroscience, 14*(9), 967–976. https://doi.org/10.1093/scan/nsz064

Project Air Strategy. (2015). *Treatment guidelines for personality disorders*—University of Wollongong.

Przybylski, A. K., & Weinstein, N. (2019). Violent video game engagement is not associated with adolescents' aggressive behaviour: Evidence from a registered report. Royal Society Open Science, 6(2), 171474.

Psychology Board of Australia. (2025). Code of conduct for psychologists. https://www.psychologyboard.gov.au/Standards-and-Guidelines/Professional-practice-standards/Code-of-conduct.aspx

Psychotherapy and Counselling Federation of Australia. (2017). *PACFA code of ethics.* https://www.pacfa.org.au

Puder, D. (Host). (2020, July 14). *Microexpressions and trauma* [Audio podcast episode]. In *Psychiatry & Psychotherapy Podcast*. https://www.psychiatrypodcast.com

Puder, D. (Host). (2021, June 14). *Using microexpressions to improve empathy, therapeutic alliance & emotional intelligence (Therapeutic Alliance Series Part 8)* [Audio podcast episode]. In *Psychiatry & Psychotherapy Podcast.*

https://www.psychiatrypodcast.com/psychiatry-psychotherapy-podcast/episode-118-microexpressions-to-improve-empathy-emotional-intelligence-therapeutic-alliance

Puder, D. (Host). (2023, June 30). Narcissism with Jonathan Shedler, PhD [Audio podcast episode]. In the Psychiatry & Psychotherapy Podcast.

https://www.psychiatrypodcast.com/psychiatry-psychotherapy-podcast/185-narcissism-with-jonathan-shedler

Puder, D. (Host), & Cunningham, A. (Guest). (2018, May 7). Microexpressions and microconnections: Building empathy and emotional connection in therapy [Audio podcast episode]. *Psychiatry & Psychotherapy Podcast*. https://www.psychiatrypodcast.com

Puder, D. (Host). (2025, February 22). Transference-focused psychotherapy (TFP), borderline personality disorder, narcissism, with Frank Yeomans, MD (Episode 234) [Audio podcast episode]. *Psychiatry & Psychotherapy Podcast*. https://www.psychiatrypodcast.com

Quidé, Y. (2023). Dissociation, trauma and the experience of visual hallucinations in post-traumatic stress disorder and schizophrenia. *BJPsych Open, 9*(1), e23. https://doi.org/10.1192/bjo.2023.3

Rascovsky, K., Hodges, J. R., Knopman, D., Mendez, M. F., Kramer, J. H., Neuhaus, J., van Swieten, J. C., Seelaar, H., Dopper, E. G. P., Onyike, C. U., Hillis, A. E., Josephs, K. A., Boeve, B. F., Kertesz, A., Seeley, W. W., Rankin, K. P., Johnson, J. K., Gorno-Tempini, M.-L., Rosen, H., Miller, B. L. (2011). *Sensitivity of revised diagnostic criteria for the behavioural variant of frontotemporal dementia*. Brain, 134(9), 2456–2477. https://doi.org/10.1093/brain/awr179

Ribeiro, M. H., Blackburn, J., Bradlyn, B., De Cristofaro, E., Stringhini, G., Long, S., Greenberg, S., & Zannettou, S. (2021). The evolution of the manosphere across the web. *Proceedings of the International AAAI Conference on Web and Social Media, 15*(1), 196–207.

Roberts, S. (2026, March 12). *Louis Theroux's "Inside the Manosphere" shows how far misogynistic ideas have spread, but not the harms they cause*. ABC Religion & Ethics.

Rogers, C. R. (1957). The necessary and sufficient conditions of therapeutic personality change. *Journal of Consulting Psychology, 21*(2), 95–103. https://doi.org/10.1037/h0045357

Ronningstam, E. (2017). Intersect between self-esteem and emotion regulation in narcissistic personality disorder: Implications for alliance building and treatment. *Borderline Personality Disorder and Emotion Dysregulation, 4*, Article 3. https://doi.org/10.1186/s40479-017-0054-8

Rose, J., McCallum, T., Tsantefski, M., & Rathus, Z. (2024). Healthcare and legal systems responses to coercive control: An embodied performance of one woman's experience. *Health Sociology Review, 33*(2), 192–209. https://doi.org/10.1080/14461242.2024.2347969

Rosenberg, M. B. (2015). *Nonviolent communication: A language of life (3rd ed.)*. Puddle Dancer Press.

Safran, J. D., & Muran, J. C. (2000). *Negotiating the therapeutic alliance: A relational treatment guide*. Guilford Press.

Saini, M., Johnston, J. R., Fidler, B. J., & Bala, N. (2019). Empirical evidence of abuse in alienation cases. *Family Court Review, 57*(1), 103–119. https://doi.org/10.1111/fcre.12415

Sakowska, J., Arcimowicz, Ł., Jankowiak, M., Papak, I., Markiewicz, A., Dziubek, K., Kurkowiak, M., Kote, S., Kaźmierczak-Siedlecka, K., Połom, K., Marek-Trzonkowska, N., & Trzonkowski, P. (2022). *Autoimmunity and cancer—Two sides of the same coin. Frontiers in Immunology, 13*, 793234. https://doi.org/10.3389/fimmu.2022.793234

Sandre, A., Ethridge, P., Kim, I., et al. (2018). Childhood maltreatment and neural responses to threatening facial expressions. *Cognitive, Affective, & Behavioral Neuroscience, 18*(1), 143–154. https://link.springer.com/article/10.3758/s13415-017-0559-z

Sants, H. J. (1964). Genealogical bewilderment in children with substitute parents. *British Journal of Medical Psychology, 37*, 133–141. https://doi.org/10.1111/j.2044-8341.1964.tb01981.x

Sarkadi, A., Kristiansson, R., Oberklaid, F., & Bremberg, S. (2008). Fathers' involvement and children's developmental outcomes: A systematic review of longitudinal studies. *Acta Paediatrica, 97*(2), 153–158.

Schein, E. H. (1961). *Coercive persuasion: A socio-psychological analysis of the brainwashing of American civilian prisoners by the Chinese Communists*. Norton.

Schore, A. N. (2001). Effects of a secure attachment relationship on right brain development, affect regulation, and infant mental health. *Infant Mental Health Journal, 22*(1–2), 7–66. https://doi.org/10.1002/1097-0355(200101/04)22:1<7::AID-IMHJ2>3.0.CO;2-N

Schore, A. N. (2003). *Affect dysregulation and disorders of the self. W. W.* Norton & Company.

Schore, A. N. (2012). *The science of the art of psychotherapy. W. W.* Norton & Company.

Schwartz, A. (2025, August 27). *Toxic families and the scapegoat role*. MentalHealth.com.

Sharples, A., Harman, J. J., & Lorandos, D. (2023). Allegations of abuse in parental alienation cases. *Journal of Family Trauma, Child Custody & Child Development, 20*(1), 1–23.

Sherwood, G. (2015, January 6). *Going no contact: The scapegoat's last resort*. Glynis Sherwood.

Shinn, A. K., Wolff, J. D., Hwang, M., Lebois, L. A. M., Robinson, M. A., Winternitz, S. R., Öngür, D., Ressler, K. J., & Kaufman, M. L. (2020). Assessing voice hearing in trauma spectrum disorders: A comparison of two measures and a review of the literature. *Frontiers in Psychiatry, 10*, Article 1011. https://doi.org/10.3389/fpsyt.2019.01011

Siegel, D. J. (2012). *The developing mind: How relationships and the brain interact to shape who we are* (2nd ed.). Guilford Press.

Siegel, D. J. (2020). *The developing mind: How relationships and the brain interact to shape who we are (3rd ed.)*. Guilford Press.

Singer, M. T., & Lalich, J. (2003). *Cults in our midst: The continuing fight against their hidden menace (Rev. ed.)*. Jossey-Bass.

Sivak, E., & Smirnov, I. (2019). Parents mention sons more often than daughters on social media. *Proceedings of the National Academy of Sciences of the United States of America, 116*(6), 2039–2041. https://doi.org/10.1073/pnas.1804996116

Social Work Today. (2016). When mandated reporting is retaliated against. *Social Work Today, 16*(4), 8–9.

Spinazzola, J., van der Kolk, B. A., & Ford, J. D. (2018). Developmental trauma disorder. *Journal of Traumatic Stress, 31*(5), 739–746.

Stark, E. (2007). *Coercive control: How men entrap women in personal life*. Oxford University Press.

Stein, A. (2021). *Terror, love and brainwashing (2nd ed.)*. Routledge.

Steuwe, C., Daniels, J. K., Frewen, P. A., Densmore, M., Pannasch, S., Beblo, T., Reiss, J., & Lanius, R. A. (2014). Effect of direct eye contact in PTSD related to interpersonal trauma: An fMRI study of activation of an innate alarm system. *Social Cognitive and Affective Neuroscience, 9*(1), 88–97. https://doi.org/10.1093/scan/nss105

Taylor, K. (2006). *Brainwashing: The science of thought control*. Oxford University Press.

Teicher, M. H., & Samson, J. A. (2016). Enduring neurobiological effects of childhood abuse and neglect. *Journal of Child Psychology and Psychiatry, 57*(3), 241–266.

Telfer, M. M., Tollit, M. A., Pace, C. C., & Pang, K. C. (2018). Australian standards of care and treatment guidelines for transgender and gender diverse children and adolescents. *Medical Journal of Australia, 209*(3), 132–136.

The Guardian. (2015, February 27). Mother reunited with stolen daughter 17 years after she was snatched. https://www.theguardian.com/world/2015/feb/27/mother-reunited-stolen-daughter-17-years-after-snatched

Thrivers Speak. (2024). *About Thrivers Speak.* https://thriversspeak.com

Turkat, I. D. (2000). Custody battle burnout. *American Journal of Family Therapy, 28*(3), 201–215.

Turkat, I. D. (2002). Parental alienation syndrome: A review of critical issues. Journal of the American Academy of Matrimonial Lawyers, 18, 131–176.

Ulmer-Yaniv, A., Waidergoren, S., Shaked, A., Salomon, R., & Feldman, R. (2022). Neural representation of the parent-child attachment from infancy to adulthood. *Social Cognitive and Affective Neuroscience, 17*(7), 609–624. https://doi.org/10.1093/scan/nsab132

United Nations. (1989). *Convention on the Rights of the Child.* United Nations General Assembly. https://www.ohchr.org/en/instruments-mechanisms/instruments/convention-rights-child.

United Nations. (2006). *Convention on the Rights of Persons with Disabilities.* https://www.ohchr.org/en/instruments-mechanisms/instruments/convention-rights-persons-disabilities

U.S. Census Bureau. (2024). *National population totals and components of change: 2020–2024.* https://www.census.gov/data/tables/time-series/demo/popest/2020s-national-total.html U.S.

van der Kolk, B. A. (2014). *The body keeps the score: Brain, mind, and body in the healing of trauma*. Viking.

van IJzendoorn, M. H. (1995). Adult attachment representations, parental responsiveness, and infant attachment: A meta-analysis on the predictive validity of the Adult Attachment Interview. *Psychological Bulletin, 117*(3), 387–403.

Verrocchio, M. C., Carrozzino, D., Marchetti, D., Andreasson, K., Fulcheri, M., & Bech, P. (2016). *Mental pain and suicide: A systematic review of the literature*. Frontiers in Psychiatry, 7, Article 108. https://doi.org/10.3389/fpsyt.2016.00108

Voorhees, S. (2015, May 19). *Rochester man, abducted as a child by his mother, advocates for tougher laws*. Spectrum News (Albany, NY).

Walker, L. E. (1979). *The battered woman syndrome*. Harper & Row.

Walker, P. (2013). *Complex PTSD: From surviving to thriving*. Azure Coyote.

Warshak, R. A. (2013). Social science and parenting plans for children: A literature review. *Family Court Review, 51*(4), 533–549.

Warshak, R. A. (2015). *Divorce poison: How to protect your family from bad-mouthing and brainwashing (Rev. ed.)*. HarperCollins.

Warshak, R. A. (2015). Ten parental alienation fallacies that compromise decisions in court and in therapy. *Professional Psychology: Research and Practice, 46*(4), 235–249. https://doi.org/10.1037/pro0000031

WDRB Digital Staff. (2025, December 9). *40-year-old Jefferson County abduction case solved after woman found alive in another state*. WDRB.

Wearne, D., Curtis, G. J., Melvill-Smith, P., Orr, K. G., Mackereth, A., Rajanthiran, L., Hood, S., Choy, W., & Waters, F. (2020). Exploring the relationship between auditory hallucinations, trauma and dissociation. *BJPsych Open, 6*(3), e54. https://doi.org/10.1192/bjo.2020.31

Weinberg, I., & Ronningstam, E. (2022). Narcissistic personality disorder: Progress in understanding and treatment. *Focus, 20*(3), 368–377.

https://doi.org/10.1176/appi.focus.20220052

Wellisch, E. (1952). Children without genealogy: A problem of adoption. *Mental Health, 11*, 41–42.

Wilcox, H. C., Storr, C. L., & Breslau, N. (2009). Post-traumatic stress disorder and suicide attempts. *Archives of General Psychiatry, 66*(3), 305–311. https://doi.org/10.1001/archgenpsychiatry.2008.557

Wilcox, W. B. (2009). *The evolution of divorce*. National Affairs, 1, 81–94.

Whitcombe, S. (2024). Assessment of suspected parental alienation in the family courts. In L. A. Craig, H. C. H. Koch, & G. A. Baker (Eds.), *Psychology and the law: Case studies of expert witnesses* (pp. 147–177). Wiley. https://doi.org/10.1002/9781394155767.ch7

WMTW. (2017, January 15). Kamiyah Mobley, kidnapped as infant, meets biological parents. https://www.wmtw.com/article/kamiyah-mobley-kidnapped-as-infant-meets-biological-parents/8600459

Wolfe, F. (2025). It's not just personal: Exploring the therapist's political role in confronting misogyny. *Feminism & Psychology*. Advance online publication.

World Health Organization. (2018). *International Classification of Diseases (11th Rev.)*. WHO.

World Health Organization. (2025, March 25). *Suicide*. https://www.who.int/news-room/fact-sheets/detail/suicide

Yalom, I. D. (1980). *Existential psychotherapy*. Basic Books.

Millions of Children Are Caught in High-Conflict Divorce and Separation. Who Helps Them When the Trauma Follows Them into Adulthood?

Many adult survivors arrive in therapy carrying grief, identity disruption, loyalty conflict, relational fear, attachment injury, suicidality, and a deeply held belief that something is fundamentally wrong with them. They may struggle to understand their trauma or make sense of a complex family history that has never felt coherent.

The Healing Qualia Treatment Protocol © (HQTP) is the first comprehensive clinical protocol written specifically for mental health clinicians working with this adult survivor population. It was developed from Australian researcher and clinician Dr Alyse Price-Tobler's twin-study PhD research with adult survivors of severe child psychological abuse related to parental alienation and familial abduction in Study One, and specialist mental health practitioners who work with this population in Study Two.

The HQTP provides clinicians with a phase-based clinical map for recognising, formulating, and treating the adult aftermath of mild to severe child psychological abuse related to parental alienation, familial abduction, estrangement, and lethal family-system harm including familicide.

Testimonials

"Congratulations to Dr Alyse Price-Tobler on this important contribution to the field. Her work reflects the kind of ethical, research-driven commitment that our profession needs. She brings both intellectual rigor and genuine compassion to one of the most challenging and often misunderstood areas of clinical practice. This book is a testament to her dedication to advancing specialized, evidence-informed care for individuals and families who deserve to be seen, understood, and supported with integrity and thoughtfulness."
Dr Rebecca Bailey PhD. Director. Transitioning Families, USA

"As a retired barrister, I see this book as a rare and necessary clinical window beyond the legal file. Healing Qualia helps legal professionals understand the long-term repercussions for adult children who have moved through the Family Court system, particularly when coercive family dynamics are misunderstood, minimised, or left unresolved." **Julian van Aalst, Former Head of Frederick Jordan Chambers, Sydney, Australia**

"Dr Alyse Price-Tobler has accomplished a monumentally significant professional achievement. By weaving timeless psychodynamic, developmental, and family systems science into a highly compassionate, phase-governed treatment engine, she has brought clarity and structural order to an immensely chaotic domain of trauma recovery. This text is essential reading not only for adult trauma practitioners but holds invaluable directives for individual child therapists seeking to avoid the catastrophic trap of validating a captured child's false, induced scripts. It is a brilliant, posture-driven manual that fiercely protects the survivor's autonomy, establishing an authoritative gold standard for the mental health and family court professions. I give it my highest, unreserved professional endorsement." This text stands as a massive milestone."
Dr Craig Childress Psy.D, USA

"As a forensic criminologist and adult survivor of severe-level Child Psychological Abuse related to Parental Alienation and Abduction (CPA-PAA), I know firsthand the devastating cost of clinical blind spots. When I first sought help, my depression was treated as a surface symptom while the underlying pathological enmeshment, coercive control, and fabricated identity remained unseen. Had the Healing Qualia Treatment Protocol been available earlier, it could have changed the course of my life. It would have given me the language and understanding to search for my father and younger brothers sooner, allowing me more precious years with the father from whom I had been taken from for 44 years. Dr Alyse Price-Tobler has created an indispensable clinical framework that can help survivors move beyond symptom management, reclaim their identity and story, and recover time before more of it is lost."
Dawn McCarty. Forensic Criminologist & Adult Child Survivor of CPA-PAA, USA

"Life is very difficult when one doesn't understand that they've been through brainwashing from their own parent and they had another parent that loved them. I was 20 years apart from my father before reunification. I can never get that time back. Healing Qualia feels like a soothing, comforting verbal hug that helps explain the trauma I've been through. I can now understand how to move myself and my siblings through our ongoing child and now adult trauma toward a healing space." **J Sim, Adult Child Survivor of CPA-PERA, New Zealand**

Testimonials are continued on page iii

www.ingramcontent.com/pod-product-compliance
Lightning Source LLC
LaVergne TN
LVHW080545210926
848481LV00024B/2677